XOANA AND THE ORIGINS OF GREEK SCULPTURE

American Philological Association
American Classical Studies

The Harmonics of Nicomachus and the Pythagorean Tradition	Flora R. Levin
The Etymology and the Usage of ΠΕΙΡΑΡ *in Early Greek Poetry*	Ann L. T. Bergren
Two Studies in Roman Nomenclature	D. R. Shackleton Bailey
The Latin Particle Quidem	J. Solodow
On the Hymn to Zeus in Aeschylus' Agamemnon	Peter M. Smith
The Andromache of Euripides	Paul David Kovacs
A Commentary on the Vita Hadriani in the Historia Augusta	Herbert W. Benario
Creation and Salvation in Ancient Orphism	Larry J. Alderink
Eros Sophistes: Ancient Novelists at Play	Graham Anderson
Ancient Philosophy and Grammar: The Syntax of Apollonius Dyscolus	David Blank
Autonomia*: Its Genesis and Early History*	Martin Ostwald
Language and Metre: Resolution, Porson's Bridge, and Their Prosodic Basis	A. M. Devine
Descent from Heaven: Images of Dew in Greek Poetry and Religion	Deborah Boedeker
Iamblichus and the Theory of the Vehicle of the Soul	John F. Finamore
Epicurus on the Swerve and Voluntary Action	Walter G. Englert
Seneca's Anapaests	John G. Fitch
Xoana *and the Origins of Greek Sculpture*	A. A. Donohue

A.A. Donohue

Xoana and the Origins of Greek Sculpture

Scholars Press
Atlanta, Georgia

XOANA AND THE ORIGINS OF GREEK SCULPTURE

A.A. Donohue

Library of Congress Cataloging-in-Publication Data

Donohue, A.A.
Xoana and the Origins of Greek Sculpture

(American classical studies ; no. 15)
1. Xoana. 2. Greece--Antiquities. 3. Greece--Religious life and customs. I. Title. II. Series.
DF129.D66 1987 938 86-6511

ISBN 1-55540-154-6
ISBN 0-89130-955-1 (pbk)

TABLE OF CONTENTS

PREFACE

Xoana are probably the most elusive monuments of Greek art. Unlike other forms of Greek sculpture, they are known almost entirely from literary sources, and cannot therefore be collected and studied directly. Yet they are perennially fascinating: the ancient literary testimony suggests that they were cult images of the highest antiquity which, if they could be found, would illuminate the very origins of Greek sculpture, the process by which the religious urge to represent the gods led to the most remarkable artistic development of ancient Greek civilization. The success of archaeology in recovering the material culture of preclassical Greece raises the possibility that now, at last, there might exist enough monumental evidence to permit a systematic archaeological treatment of *xoana*. This was the hope with which I began this study; the results, however, were entirely unexpected.

At the start, archaeology and art history had temporarily to take second place to collecting the literary references that are the fundamental evidence for *xoana*. This was not as simple a task as it initially seemed, because the philological questions of meaning and usage proved surprisingly complex. It became clear that the definition of *xoanon* changed so much in the course of antiquity that the collection of literary *xoana* in no way constitutes or corresponds to a unified archaeological category of sculpture. The term *xoanon* does not consistently denote one specific kind of image, but instead reflects the development of Greek thought about statuary. It thus proved impossible to assemble a catalogue of *xoana* along archaeological lines (geographical, for example, or typological). What is said about individual *xoana* is less significant than who said it and why.

The attempt to understand the context of the testimonia about *xoana* then necessitated a wider consideration of the ancient traditions about the origins of statuary and of idolatry. These traditions belong to several identifiable lines of theory and speculation and provide an explanation of the various usages of *xoanon*. The collection of literary *xoana* turned out to offer evidence not so much for the history of art as for its historiography.

At the same time it became clear that a considerable amount of modern theory concerning the beginnings of Greek sculpture depends directly on ancient literary testimony that is too tendentious to be reliable. It is possible to trace the influence of this testimony on art-historical scholarship beginning with Winckelmann; even in more recent times, when a considerable amount of material evidence for the formative periods has become available, the ancient written sources have continued to guide the interpretation of the archaeological remains. This literary testimony, which furnishes a plausible theory of the origin of Greek sculpture in primitive wooden *xoana*, receives no support from either the historical picture of Greece that has emerged from excavation or the monuments surviving from the preclassical periods.

At this point it was necessary to admit that the topic as I had conceived it had disappeared entirely. The conclusions at hand were discouragingly negative. Instead of a neat marriage of literary and archaeological evidence, mutually enhancing and collectively illuminating, there had emerged only an array of sources that were no sources and of "*xoana*" that amounted to nothing. Yet there is a positive gain that outweighs the negatives. The better understanding of the nature and limitations of the ancient literary sources allows a more independent historical and art-historical evaluation of the monumental evidence for early Greek statuary. The traditions themselves, rather than deserving simply to be discarded, take their place in the history of Greek theory and allow us to look consciously into the Greek past with the Greek mind's eye.

I began working on *xoana* in 1977, and the research was substantially complete in 1980. The appearance shortly thereafter of J. Papadopoulos' *Xoana e sphyrelata* provided a welcome check on my collection of testimonia, which had been hunted and gathered by skimming texts, trusting indices, tracking footnotes, and maintaining a box for contributions from sympathetic colleagues. Only in the latest stages of preparation of the study did a sizeable number of files of the Thesaurus Linguae Graecae become available. Despite the fact that clearly no such study should again be attempted without reliance on the TLG, I do not regret my palaeolithic methods of collection. I doubt, for instance, that the crucial importance of context for the meaning of *xoanon* would have become so clear without hours of puzzling over the seemingly inconsequential squabblings of iconoclastic polemicists. There is in addition a particular advantage to the slow road for one who approaches unfamiliar areas of study: one's limitations become more obvious more quickly, and one is less tempted to cavalier conclusions. The question of *xoana* cuts across so many specialized fields of classical studies that the the diverse material bearing on it cannot, I think, be evenly controlled by any single worker.

I hope that the help I have received from colleagues in many fields is only the first step in a cooperative effort to investigate further the subjects treated here; it will be a long time before the final word on *xoana* is said.

It is a pleasure to thank the institutions and individuals that have helped the progress of this work. I am grateful to the Dr. M. Aylwin Cotton Foundation and the J. Paul Getty Trust for generous grants towards its publication. The study was first submitted as a dissertation to the Institute of Fine Arts of New York University, and I owe much to those there who helped see the project to completion. The librarians and staffs of the American School of Classical Studies at Athens and of Bryn Mawr College have assisted me so helpfully and tolerantly that no expression of appreciation could be adequate. I owe special thanks to the College for my past year there as Research Affiliate, during which I completed work on the manuscript. For many useful references and stimulating discussions, and for much meticulous criticism and practical help, I thank colleagues from many institutions: P.F. Benbow, J. Binder, D. Birge, B. Bohen, A.B. Brownlee, D. Burgess, D.M. Clay, C.N. Edmonson, M. deJ. Ellis, S. Glass, R. Hamilton, J.L. Hanson, E.B. Harrison, T.N. Howe, H.R. Immerwahr, S. Lachs, T.C. Loening, W.G. Moon, L.F. Nixon, İ. Özgen, G.F. Pinney, and B.S. Ridgway. D. Goldstein improved many of the translations of testimonia. Access to the data banks of the Thesaurus Linguae Graecae was kindly provided by W.E. Smith of the University of Pennsylvania and J. Rusten of Harvard University. I thank T.F. Brunner, Director of the Thesaurus Linguae Graecae, for permission to include in Appendix I texts from the TLG data banks. The book was typeset at the Publications Office of the American School of Classical Studies at Athens using the Ibycus system; I am grateful to Sarah George Figueira for her expert advice and help in production. The encouragement and support of J.R. McCredie and J.J. Pollitt made the appearance of this study possible, and my gratitude to them is great.

The successful parts of this work reflect the generous interest of all these people. The mistakes and flaws are of course my own fault and responsibility.

May, 1986

Published with the assistance of the
J. Paul Getty Trust

ABBREVIATIONS

Abbreviations of classical sources are for the most part those given in the ninth edition of LSJ and the second edition of the *OCD*; fuller forms have sometimes been used for the sake of clarity.

AA: *Archäologischer Anzeiger.*
AAA: Ἀρχαιολογικὰ ἀνάλεκτα ἐξ Ἀθηνῶν (*Athens Annals of Archaeology*).
AE: Ἀρχαιολογικὴ Ἐφημερίς.
AJA: *The American Journal of Archaeology.*
AJP: *The American Journal of Philology.*
AK: *Antike Kunst.*
AM: *Mitteilungen des Deutschen Archäologischen Instituts, Athenische Abteilung.*
ANRW: H. Temporini ed. *Aufstieg und Niedergang der römischen Welt*. Berlin, 1972–.
APh: *L'année philologique.*
AR: *Archaeological Reports.*
ARV²: J.D. Beazley. *Attic Red-figure Vase-painters*. 2nd ed. Oxford, 1963.
ARW: *Archiv für Religionswissenschaft.*
ASAtene: *Annuario della R. Scuola Archeologica di Atene.*
Adam, *Technique:* S. Adam. *The Technique of Greek Sculpture in the Archaic and Classical Periods. BSA* Supplementary Volume 3, 1966.
Adler: A. Adler ed. *Suidae Lexicon*. Lexicographi Graeci I. 5 vols. Leipzig, 1928–1938.
Agora: *The Athenian Agora*. Results of the Excavations Conducted by the American School of Classical Studies at Athens. Princeton, 1953–.
AnnInst: *Annali dell'Instituto di Correspondenza Archeologica.*
AntCl: *L'antiquité classique.*
ArchPap: *Archiv für Papyrusforschung.*
Arnim, *SVF:* H. von Arnim ed. *Stoicorum Veterum Fragmenta*. 4 vols. Leipzig, 1903–1924.
BABesch: *Bulletin van de Vereeniging tot Bevordering der Kennis van de Antike Beschaving.*
BCH: *Bulletin de correspondance hellénique.*
BICS: *Bulletin of the Institute of Classical Studies of the University of London.*
BMC: *A Catalogue of Greek Coins in the British Museum.*
BMusInscr: *Ancient Greek Inscriptions in the British Museum*. Oxford, 1874–1916.
BSA: *The Annual of the British School at Athens.*

BSAAlex: *Bulletin de la Société archéologique d'Alexandrie.*

Baldry, *Unity:* H.C. Baldry. *The Unity of Mankind in Greek Thought.* Cambridge, 1965.

Banier, *Mythology:* A. Banier. *The Mythology and Fables of the Ancients Explain'd from History.* Anon. trans. London, 1739–1740. Repr. in S. Orgel ed. *The Renaissance and the Gods.* New York and London, 1976.

Bennett, "Study": F.M. Bennett. "A Study of the Word ΞΟΑΝΟΝ." *AJA* 21 (1917) 8–21.

Bennett, "Statues": ———. "Primitive Wooden Statues Which Pausanias Saw in Greece." *CW* 10 (1917) 82–86.

Benveniste, "Kolossos": E. Benveniste. "Le sens du mot κολοσσός et les noms grecs de la statue." *RPh* 6 (1932) 118–135.

Boardman, *Archaic:* J. Boardman. *Greek Sculpture. The Archaic Period. A Handbook.* New York and Toronto, 1978.

Boisacq, *Dictionnaire:* E. Boisacq. *Dictionnaire étymologique de la langue grecque.* 2nd ed. Heidelberg and Paris, 1923.

Breccia, *Iscrizioni:* E. Breccia ed. *Iscrizioni greche e latine. Nos. 1–568.* Service des Antiquités de l'Égypte. *Catalogue général des antiquités égyptiennes du Musée d'Alexandrie.* Cairo, 1911.

Bruneau, *Cultes:* P. Bruneau. *Recherches sur les cultes de Délos à l'époque hellénistique et à l'époque imperiale.* Paris, 1970.

Buck, *Grammar:* C.D. Buck. *Comparative Grammar of Greek and Latin.* Chicago, 1933.

Buck, *Synonyms:* ———. *A Dictionary of Selected Synonyms in the Principal Indo-European Languages.* Chicago, 1949.

BullEpig: *Bulletin épigraphique.* In *REG.*

Burkert, *Structure:* W. Burkert. *Structure and History in Greek Mythology and Ritual.* Sather Classical Lectures 47. Berkeley, Los Angeles, and London, 1979.

Burton, *Diodorus:* A. Burton. *Diodorus Siculus. Book I. A Commentary.* Leiden, 1972.

CAH: *The Cambridge Ancient History.* Cambridge, 1923–1939.

CAH[2]: ———. 2nd ed. Cambridge, 1961–1971.

CAH[3]: ———. 3rd ed. Cambridge, 1970– .

CIG: A. Boekh ed. *Corpus Inscriptionum Graecarum.* Berlin, 1828–1877.

CP: *Classical Philology.*

CPCP: *University of California Publications in Classical Philology.*

CQ: *Classical Quarterly.*

CR: *Classical Review.*

CRIPEL: *Cahiers de recherches de l'Institut de Papyrologie et d'Egyptologie de Lille.* Lille, 1973– .

CSCA: *California Studies in Classical Antiquity.*

CVA: *Corpus Vasorum Antiquorum.*

CW: *Classical Weekly*; becomes *Classical World.*

Casson, *Technique:* S. Casson. *The Technique of Early Greek Sculpture.* Oxford, 1933.

Chantraine, *Dictionnaire:* P. Chantraine. *Dictionnaire étymologique de la langue grecque. Histoire des mots.* Paris, 1968– .

Chantraine, *Etudes:* ———. *Etudes sur le vocabulaire grec.* Paris, 1956.

Chantraine, *Noms:* ———. *La formation des noms en grec ancien.* Paris, 1933.

Charlesworth, "Pseudepigrapha Research": J.H. Charlesworth, "A History of Pseudepigrapha Research: The Re-emerging Importance of Pseudepigrapha." *ANRW* II.19.1 (Berlin and New York, 1979) 54–88.

Collins, "Sibylline Oracles": J.J. Collins. "Sibylline Oracles (Second Century B.C.–Seventh Century A.D.)." *OTP* I, 317–472.

Cook, *Zeus:* A.B. Cook. *Zeus. A Study in Ancient Religion.* 3 vols. Cambridge, 1914–1940.

DOP: *Dumbarton Oaks Papers.*

DOS: *Dumbarton Oaks Studies.*

Daremberg-Saglio: C. Daremberg, E. Saglio, and E. Pottier. *Dictionnaire des antiquités grecques et romaines.* 3rd ed. 5 vols. Paris, 1881–1919.

Daly, *Contributions:* L.W. Daly. *Contributions to a History of Alphabetization in Antiquity and the Middle Ages.* Brussels, 1967.

Del.: *Ἀρχαιολογικὸν Δελτίον.*

Délos: *Exploration archéologique de Délos.*

Délos 11: A. Plassart. *Les sanctuaires et les cultes du Mont Cynthe.* Paris, 1928.

Délos 20: F. Robert. *Trois sanctuaires sur le rivage occidental.* Paris, 1952.

Diller, *Tradition Geographers:* A. Diller. *The Tradition of the Minor Greek Geographers.* Lancaster, 1952.

Diller, *Tradition Strabo:* ———. *The Textual Tradition of Strabo's Geography.* Amsterdam, 1975.

Dinsmoor, *Architecture*[3]: W.B. Dinsmoor. *The Architecture of Ancient Greece.* 3rd ed. London, New York, Toronto, and Sydney, 1950.

EAA: *Enciclopedia dell'arte antica.* Rome, 1958–1973.

Evans, *PM:* A.J. Evans. *The Palace of Minos at Knossos.* 5 vols. London, 1921–1936.

FGrH: F. Jacoby ed. *Die Fragmente der griechischen Historiker.* Berlin and Leiden, 1923–1958.

FHG: C. Müller ed. *Fragmenta Historicorum Graecorum.* 5 vols. Paris, 1841–1870.

Farnell, *Cults:* L.R. Farnell. *The Cults of the Greek States.* 5 vols. Oxford, 1896–1909.

Farnell, "Origins": ———. "The Origins and Earliest Developments of Greek Sculpture." *Archaeological Review* 2 (1889) 167–184.

Frazer, *Apollodorus:* J.G. Frazer tr. *Apollodorus. The Library.* 2 vols. LCL, 1921.

Frazer, *Pausanias:* ——— tr. and comm. *Pausanias's Description of Greece.* 2nd ed. 6 vols. London, 1913.

Frisk, *Wörterbuch:* H. Frisk. *Griechisches etymologisches Wörterbuch.* Heidelberg, 1954– .

GCS: Die griechischen christlichen Schriftsteller der ersten Jahrhunderte. Berlin, 1897– .

GRBS: Greek, Roman and Byzantine Studies.

Gardner, "Processes": E.A. Gardner. "The Processes of Greek Sculpture, as shown by some unfinished statues in Athens." *JHS* 11 (1890) 129–142.

Geffcken, *Oracula Sibyllina:* J. Geffcken ed. *Die Oracula Sibyllina.* GCS 8; Leipzig, 1902; repr. 1967.

Gifford, *Eusebius:* E.H. Gifford ed. *Eusebii Pamphili evangelicae praeparationis libri XV.* 4 vols. Oxford, 1903.

Goldman, "Herm": H. Goldman, "The Origin of the Greek Herm." *AJA* 46 (1942) 58–68.

Gow and Page, *Anthology:* A.S.F. Gow and D.L. Page eds. *The Greek Anthology. Hellenistic Epigrams.* 2 vols. Cambridge, 1965.

Gow and Scholfield, *Nicander:* A.S.F. Gow and A.F. Scholfield eds. *Nicander. The Poems and Poetical Fragments.* Cambridge, 1953.

Grant, *Authors:* M. Grant. *Greek and Latin Authors 800 B.C.–A.D. 1000.* New York, 1980.

Griffiths, *Temple Treasures:* A.H. Griffiths. *Temple Treasures. A Study Based on the Works of Cicero and the Fasti of Ovid.* Diss. University of Pennsylvania. Philadelphia, 1943.

Groningen, *Grip of the Past:* B.A. van Groningen. *In the Grip of the Past. Essay on an Aspect of Greek Thought.* Philosophia antiqua 6. Leiden, 1953.

Gross, "*Xoanon*": W.H. Gross. "*Xoanon.*" *RE* II.9B (1967) 2140–2149.

Guthrie, *History:* W.K.C. Guthrie. *A History of Greek Philosophy.* 6 vols. Cambridge, 1962–1981.

Guthrie, *In the Beginning:* ———. *In the Beginning. Some Greek views on the origins of life and the early state of man.* Ithaca, 1957, 1965.

HSCP: Harvard Studies in Classical Philology.

HTR: Harvard Theological Review.

HUCA: Hebrew Union College Annual.

Harrison, *Epilegomena:* J.E. Harrison. *Epilegomena to the Study of Greek Religion* [1921] and *Themis. A Study of the Social Origins of Greek Religion.* New Hyde Park, 1962.

Hastings Encyclopaedia: J. Hastings ed. *Encyclopaedia of Religion and Ethics.* 13 vols. New York, 1908–1927.

Head, *Historia Numorum:* B.V. Head. *Historia Numorum.* Oxford, 1887, 1911.

Herrmann, "Entstehung": H.-V. Herrmann. "Zum Problem der Entstehung der griechischen Grossplastik." In *Wandlungen. Studien zur antiken und neueren Kunst. Ernst Homann-Wedeking gewidmet.* Waldsassen-Bayern, 1975, 35–48.

Hood, *Arts:* S. Hood. *The Arts in Prehistoric Greece.* The Pelican History of Art, 1978.

Hunger, *Literatur:* H. Hunger. *Die hochsprachliche profane Literatur der Byzantiner.* 2 vols. Handbuch der Altertumswissenschaft XII.5.1, 2. Munich, 1979.

ICr: *Inscriptiones creticae.*

ID: *Inscriptions de Délos.*

IEJ: *Israel Exploration Journal.*

IG: *Inscriptiones graecae.*

*IG*²: *Inscriptiones graecae*, editio minor.

*IG*³: *Inscriptiones graecae*, editio tertia.

IGRR: R. Cagnat ed. *Inscriptiones graecae ad res romanas pertinentes.* 4 vols. Paris, 1906–1927.

IgSK: Inschriften griechischer Stadte aus Kleinasien.

Imhoof-Blumer and Gardner, *NCP:* F. Imhoof-Blumer and P. Gardner. *Ancient Coins Illustrating Lost Masterpieces of Greek Art. A Numismatic Commentary on Pausanias.* New ed. by A.N. Oikonomides. Chicago, 1964.

IstMitt: *Mitteilungen des Deutschen Archäologischen Instituts, Abteilung Istanbul.*

JdI: *Jahrbuch des Deutschen Archäologischen Instituts.*

JEA: *The Journal of Egyptian Archaeology.*

JHS: *The Journal of Hellenic Studies.*

JOAI: *Jahreshefte des österreichischen archäologischen Instituts.*

JRS: *The Journal of Roman Studies.*

JWAG: *The Journal of the Walters Art Gallery.*

JWCI: *Journal of the Warburg and Courtauld Institutes.*

JWarb: *Journal of the Warburg Institute.*

Jacoby, F.: See *FGrH.*

Jex-Blake and Sellers, *Pliny:* K. Jex-Blake and E. Sellers. *The Elder Pliny's Chapters on the History of Art.* London, 1896.

KP: *Der kleine Pauly. Lexicon der Antike*. 5 vols. Stuttgart, 1964–1975.

Kaibel: G. Kaibel ed. *Epigrammata graeca ex lapidibus conlecta*. Berlin, 1878.

Kern, *Inschriften:* O. Kern. *Die Inschriften von Magnesia am Maeander*. Berlin, 1900.

Kock: T. Kock ed. *Comicorum atticorum fragmenta*. 3 vols. Leipzig, 1880–1888.

Kyrieleis, "Holzfunde": H. Kyrieleis. "Archaische Holzfunde aus Samos." *AM* 95 (1980) 87–147.

LCL: Loeb Classical Library. London and Cambridge, Mass., 1912–.

LIMC: *Lexicon Iconographicum Mythologiae Classicae*. Zurich and Munich, 1981– .

LSJ^{9}: H.G. Liddell and R. Scott, rev. H. Stuart Jones and R. McKenzie. *A Greek-English Lexicon with Supplement*. 9th ed. Oxford, 1968.

Lacroix, *Reproductions:* L. Lacroix. *Les reproductions de statues sur les monnaies grecques*. Bibliothèque de la Faculté de Philosophie et Lettres de l'Université de Liège, fasc. CXVI. Liège, 1949.

Landtman, "Origin": G. Landtman. "The Origin of Images as Objects of Cult." *ARW* 24 (1926) 196–208.

Leaf, *Strabo:* W. Leaf. *Strabo on the Troad*. Cambridge, 1923.

Linders, *Studies:* T. Linders. *Studies in the Treasure Records of Artemis Brauronia Found in Athens*. Acta Instituti Atheniensis Regni Sueciae, Series in 4°, XIX. Stockholm, 1972.

Linfert, *Kunstzentren:* A. Linfert. *Kunstzentren hellenistischer Zeit. Studien an weiblichen Gewandfiguren*. Wiesbaden, 1976.

Lorimer, *Homer:* H.L. Lorimer. *Homer and the Monuments*. London, 1950.

Lodge: G.H. Lodge tr. *J.J. Winckelmann. The History of Ancient Art*. 2 vols. Boston, 1872.

MAMA: W.M. Calder ed. *Monumenta Asiae Minoris antiqua*. 8 vols. London, 1928–1962.

MDAIK: *Mitteilungen des Deutschen Archäologischen Instituts. Abteilung Kairo*.

MMS: *Metropolitan Museum Studies*.

MacBain, *Prodigy:* B. MacBain. *Prodigy and Expiation: a study in religion and politics in Republican Rome*. Collection Latomus 177. Brussels, 1982.

Marcadé, *Musée Délos:* J. Marcadé. *Au musée de Délos. Etude sur la sculpture hellénistique en ronde bosse découverte dans l'île*. Paris, 1969.

MemLinc: *Memorie. Atti della Accademia nazionale dei Lincei, Classe di scienze morali, storiche e filologiche*.

Mihailov, *Inscriptiones:* G. Mihailov ed. *Inscriptiones graecae in Bulgaria repertae.* 4 vols. Sofia, 1956–1966.

MonAnt: *Monumenti antichi.*

Momigliano, *Alien Wisdom:* A. Momigliano. *Alien Wisdom.* Cambridge, 1975.

Moore, "Baetylia": G.F. Moore. "Baetylia." *AJA* 7 (1903) 198–208.

Moretti, *Inscriptiones:* L. Moretti ed. *Inscriptiones graecae urbis Romae.* 3 vols. Rome, 1968–1979.

Müller, "Kultbild": V. Müller. "Kultbild." *RE* Suppl. V (1931) 472–511.

NTA: R. McL. Wilson ed. English edition of W. Schneemelcher ed., E. Hennecke, *New Testament Apocrypha.* 2 vols. Philadelphia, 1963–1964.

Nauck[2]: A. Nauck ed. *Tragicorum graecorum fragmenta.* 2nd ed. Leipzig, 1926. Repr. with *Supplementum* by B. Snell. Hildesheim, 1964.

Nikiprowetzky, *Sibylle:* V. Nikiprowetzky. *La troisième Sibylle.* Etudes juives 9. Paris and The Hague, 1970.

Nilsson, *GgR:* M.P. Nilsson. *Geschichte der griechischen Religion.* 2 vols. Handbuch der Altertumswissenschaft V.2.1–2. Munich, 1941–1950.

Nock, *Essays:* Z. Stewart ed. *Arthur Darby Nock. Essays on Religion and the Ancient World.* 2 vols. Cambridge, Mass., 1972.

Nomisma: H. von Fritze and H. Gaebler eds. *Nomisma. Untersuchungen auf dem Gebiete der antiken Münzbunder.* Berlin, 1907–1923.

OCD[2]: N.G.L. Hammond and H. Scullard eds. *The Oxford Classical Dictionary.* 2nd ed. Oxford, 1970.

ODCC[2]: F.L. Cross and E.A. Livingstone eds. *The Oxford Dictionary of the Christian Church.* 2nd ed. Oxford and New York, 1974; repr. 1983.

OTP: J.H. Charlesworth ed. *The Old Testament Pseudepigrapha.* 2 vols. Garden City, 1983–1985.

Orlandos, *Matériaux:* A. Orlandos. *Les matériaux de construction et la technique architecturale des anciens Grecs.* 2 vols. Paris, 1966–1968.

OxJArch: *The Oxford Journal of Archaeology.*

PECS: R. Stillwell ed. *The Princeton Encyclopedia of Classical Sites.* Princeton, 1976.

PGM: K. Preisendanz ed. *Papyri graecae magicae. Die griechischen Zauberpapyri.* 2 vols. Leipzig and Berlin, 1928–1931.

POxy: B.P. Grenfell, A.S. Hunt *et al.* eds. *Oxyrhynchus* Papyri. London, 1898– .

PRIMI I: A. Vogliano ed. *Papiri della Regia Università di Milano* I. Milan, 1937.

PSI: Pubblicazioni della Società italiana per la ricerca dei papiri greci e latini in Egitto. *Papryi greci e latini.* Florence, 1912–1957.

Pack^{2}: R.A. Pack. *The Greek and Latin Literary Texts from Greco-Roman Egypt*. 2nd ed. Ann Arbor, 1965.

Page, *Further Greek Epigrams:* D. Page ed. *Further Greek Epigrams.* Rev. R.D. Dawe and J. Diggle. Cambridge, 1981.

Page, *Rufinus:* ——— ed. *The Epigrams of Rufinus.* Cambridge, 1978.

Page, *Sappho and Alcaeus:* ———. *Sappho and Alcaeus.* Oxford, 1955.

Papadopoulos, *Xoana:* J. Papadopoulos. *Xoana e sphyrelata. Testimonianza delle fonti scritte*. Studia archaeologica 24. Rome, 1980.

Papathomopoulos, *Antoninus:* M. Papathomopoulos ed., tr. *Antoninus Liberalis. Les métamorphoses*. Paris, 1968.

Pearson, *Fragments:* A.C. Pearson ed. *The Fragments of Sophocles*. 3 vols. Cambridge, 1917.

Pekáry, "Statuen": T. Pekáry. "Statuen in kleinasiatischen Inschriften." In *Studies Dörner*, 727–744.

Perdrizet, "Nikopolis": P. Perdrizet. "Οὐπλ. Νικόπολις πρὸς Μέστῳ." In *Corolla Numismatica*. Numismatic Essays in Honour of Barclay V. Head. London, New York, and Toronto, 1906, 217–223.

Pfeiffer, *Callimachus:* R. Pfeiffer ed. *Callimachus*. 2 vols. Oxford, 1949–1953.

Pfeiffer, *History:* ———. *History of Classical Scholarship from 1300 to 1850*. 2 vols. Oxford, 1976.

Picard, *Man.:* C. Picard. *Manuel d'archéologie grecque: la sculpture*. 4 vols. Paris, 1935–1966.

Plassart, A.: See *Délos* 11.

Pokorny, *Wörterbuch:* J. Pokorny. *Indogermanisches etymologisches Wörterbuch*. 2 vols. Bern, 1959–1969.

Pollitt, *Ancient View:* J.J. Pollitt. *The Ancient View of Greek Art*. New Haven, 1974.

Poulsen, "Typenbildung": F. Poulsen. "Zur Typenbildung in der archaischen Plastik." *JdI* 21 (1906) 177–221.

Price, *Rituals:* S.R.F. Price. *Rituals and Power. The Roman Imperial Cult in Asia Minor*. Cambridge, 1984.

Proc. Boiotia 1: *Proceedings of the First International Conference on Boiotian Antiquities*, Montreal, 1972. *Teiresias* Suppl. 1, 1972.

Proc. Boiotia 2: J.M. Fossey and A. Schachter eds. *Proceedings of the Second International Conference on Boiotian Antiquities*, Montreal, 1973. *Teiresias* Suppl. 2, 1979.

RA: *Revue archéologique*.

RE: *Paulys Realencyclopädie der classischen Altertumswissenschaft*. Rev. G. Wissowa. Stuttgart, 1893– .

REA: *Revue des études anciennes*.

REG: *Revue des études grecques*.

RGVV: Religionsgeschichtliche Versuche und Vorarbeiten.

RHR: *Revue de l'histoire des religions.*

RPh: *Revue de philologie.*

RVAp: A.D. Trendall and A. Cambitoglou. *The Red-figured Vases of Apulia*. Oxford, 1978– .

Radt, *TGF* IV: S. Radt ed. *Tragicorum graecorum fragmenta* IV. *Sophocles*. Göttingen, 1977.

RendAccLinc: *Rendiconti della R. Accademia dei Lincei.*

RhM: *Rheinisches Museum für Philologie.*

Richter, *Korai*: G.M.A. Richter. *Korai*. London, 1968.

Ridgway, *Archaic*: B.S. Ridgway, *The Archaic Style in Greek Sculpture*. Princeton, 1977.

Ridgway, *Fifth Century*: ———. *Fifth Century Styles in Greek Sculpture*. Princeton, 1981.

Robertson, *History*: C.M. Robertson. *A History of Greek Art*. 2 vols. Cambridge, 1975.

Rose, "Images": H.J. Rose. "Concerning Images." In *idem*, *Some Problems of Classical Religion*. Eitrem Lectures, 1955. Oslo, 1958, 34–50.

Rouse, *GVO*: W.H.D. Rouse. *Greek Votive Offerings*. Cambridge, 1902.

Rumpf, "Bupalos": A. Rumpf. "Zum Bupalos und Athenis." *AA* 1936, 52–64.

SEG: *Supplementum epigraphicum graecum.*

*SIG*³: W. Dittenberger ed. *Sylloge inscriptionum graecarum*. 3rd ed. Leipzig, 1915–1924.

SMEA: *Studi micenei ed egeo-anatolici.*

SVF: See Arnim, *SVF*.

Sammelbuch: F. Preisigke *et al.* eds. *Sammelbuch griechischer Urkunden aus Agypten*. 1913– .

Sandys, *History* I: J.E. Sandys. *A History of Classical Scholarship from the Sixth Century B.C. to the End of the Middle Ages*. Cambridge, 1903.

Schachter, *Cults*: A. Schachter. *Cults of Boiotia* 1. *Acheloos to Hera*. *BICS* Supplement 38.1. London, 1981.

Schoedel, *Athenagoras*: W.R. Schoedel ed., tr. *Athenagoras. Legatio and De resurrectione*. Oxford, 1972.

Serta Turyniana: J.L. Heller ed. *Serta Turyniana. Studies in Greek Literature and Palaeography in honor of Alexander Turyn*. Urbana, Chicago, and London, 1974.

Sokolowski, *LSAM*: F. Sokolowski. *Lois sacrées de l'Asie Mineure*. Paris, 1955.

Sokolowski, *LSCG*: ———. *Lois sacrées des cités grecques*. Paris, 1969.

Stern, *Authors*: M. Stern. *Greek and Latin Authors on Jews and Judaism* I. *From Herodotus to Plutarch*. Jerusalem, 1974.

Studies Dörner: S. Şahin *et al.* eds. *Studien zur Religion und Kultur Kleinasiens. Festschrift Karl Dörner.* 2 vols. Leiden, 1978.

Studies Schachermeyr: K.H. Kinzl ed. *Greece and the Eastern Mediterranean in Ancient History and Prehistory. Studies Presented to Fritz Schachermeyr on the Occasion of his Eightieth Birthday.* Berlin and New York, 1977.

TAPA: *Transactions of the American Philological Association.*

TDNT: G. Kittel *et al.* eds. *Theological Dictionary of the New Testament.* Grand Rapids, 10 vols. 1964–1976.

TGF: *Tragicorum graecorum fragmenta.*

Tcherikover, *Civilization:* V. Tcherikover. *Hellenistic Civilization and the Jews.* Philadelphia, 1959.

Tcherikover, "Ideology": ———. "The Ideology of the Letter of Aristeas." *HTR* 51 (1958) 59–85.

Treadgold, *Bibliotheca:* W.T. Treadgold. *The Nature of the Bibliotheca of Photius. DOS* 18. Washington, D.C., 1980.

Trendall and Webster, *Illustrations:* A.D. Trendall and T.B.L. Webster. *Illustrations of Greek Drama.* London, 1971.

Trypanis, *Callimachus:* C.A. Trypanis ed., tr. *Callimachus. Aetia. Iambi. Lyric Poems. . . .* LCL, 1958, 1975.

van der Valk, "*Bibliotheca*": M. van der Valk. "On Apollodori *Bibliotheca.*" *REG* 71 (1958) 100–168.

Ventris and Chadwick, *Documents*[2]: M. Ventris and J. Chadwick. *Documents in Mycenaean Greek.* 2nd ed. Cambridge, 1973.

Vico Symposium: G. Tagliacozzo and H.V. White eds. *Giambattista Vico. An International Symposium.* Baltimore, 1969.

Wallach, "Palestinian Polemic": L. Wallach. "A Palestinian Polemic Against Idolatry. A Study in Rabbinic Literary Forms." *HUCA* 19 (1945–1946) 389–404. Repr. in H.A. Fischel ed. *Essays in Greco-Roman and Related Talmudic Literature.* New York, 1977, 111–126.

Walton, *Diodorus* XI: F.R. Walton tr. *Diodorus of Sicily* XI. LCL, 1957.

Walton, *Diodorus* XII: ——— tr. *Diodorus of Sicily* XII. LCL, 1967.

Webster, "Theories": T.B.L. Webster. "Greek Theories of Art and Literature down to 400 B.C." *CQ* 33 (1939) 166–167.

Wilson, *Scholars:* N.G. Wilson. *Scholars of Byzantium.* Baltimore, 1983.

Winckelmann: J.J. Winckelmann. *Geschichte der Kunst des Altertums.* Vollständige Ausgabe. Vienna, 1934.

Yalouris, "Bassai": N. Yalouris. "Problems Relating to the Temple of Apollo Epikourios at Bassai." In J.N. Coldstream and M.A.R. Colledge eds. *Greece and Italy in the Classical World.* Acta of the XI International Congress of Classical Archaeology. London, 1979, 89–104.

ZPE: *Zeitschrift für Papyrologie und Epigraphik.*

INTRODUCTION

Ξόανον literally means "something scraped." It occurs in literary texts, inscriptions, and papyri as a term for statues, but it is neither common nor consistently applied. Pausanias uses the word more frequently and more precisely than other writers; for him, a *xoanon* is a wooden statue, or the wooden part of a statue made of several materials, almost invariably of a god. He calls many *xoana* "ancient," and furthermore believes that in early times all statues were *xoana*.[1] Pausanias' usage is the basis of the modern understanding of the term. The *xoana* of archaeology are, simply speaking, ancient wooden images of gods, with the further connotation of a specific type or style of statue. Greek sculpture that looks "early," that is primitive, crude, or stiff and "wooden" in appearance, and pieces that are or approach being aniconic, are frequently called or related to *xoana*.[2]

The case of *xoana* is extreme even in the field of ancient art, one that is often concerned with the reconstruction of monuments that no longer exist: for it is generally agreed that the wooden *xoana* have all perished. It is therefore necessary to rely almost entirely on literary sources to learn about them. A considerable number of references to *xoana* does in fact exist, and while most are not very detailed and simply record the existence of such-and-such a *xoanon* in such-and-such a place, some are more informative. From these texts scholars have drawn a number of conclusions about *xoana*, points of which have been illuminated and supplemented by archaeological material.

Much of the difficulty in dealing with *xoana* arises because the term is an ancient word that has been taken into modern scholarly vocabulary without a clear idea of what it meant in antiquity.[3] The inconsistency of modern usage that has often been noted results in large part from the lack of any comprehensive study of literary *xoana*. The most detailed treatments are also the most limited in scope. For example, Bennett provides the most thorough discussion of the definition of *xoanon*, but only for Pausanias.[4] Conversely, attempts to place *xoana* in wider perspectives, such as Müller's remarks about them in his survey of "cult images," and Picard's

[1] For *xoanon* in Pausanias: *infra* pp. 140–147. Pausanias' definition of *xoanon* has been clearly established by Frazer, *Pausanias* II, 69–70 *ad* 3.3.5, followed by Bennett, "Study" and "Statues." See also Rumpf, "Bupalos." Casson, *Technique* 66 and n. 3, notes that Pausanias is a purist in his use of *xoanon*. For Pausanias' *xoana* as wooden: *infra* p. 2 n. 8. For their antiquity: *infra* p. 3 n. 9 and p. 4 n. 14.

[2] General treatments of *xoana*: Gross, "*Xoanon*" and *KP* V (1975) 1435 *s.v. Xoanon*; E. Paribeni, *EAA* VII, 1236–1237 *s.v. Xoanon*.

[3] For inconsistencies in the modern use of *xoanon*: Bennett, "Study" 8–11; Lacroix, *Reproductions* 30 n. 2.

[4] Bennett, "Study" and "Statues."

about their place in the early history of Greek statuary, are highly selective.[5] The most recent study of *xoana* is that of Papadopoulos, who arranges the testimonia in a geographical catalogue. Although she includes a summary of the ancient usage of *xoanon*, her work is expressly intended to serve as a sourcebook for further study, and is not a detailed treatment.[6]

Another source of difficulty is the wide relevance of *xoana*. Because they are of interest to both the historian of Greek art and the historian of Greek religion, approaches to *xoana* are often piecemeal, addressing specific interests rather than the subject as a whole. It is therefore useful to survey the general view that emerges from the various specialized treatments. The following paragraphs attempt to present, briefly, the major lines of opinion about the word *xoanon* and the statues to which it refers. It should be noted that the oral tradition of the classroom has played an important part in shaping current thoughts about *xoana*. Ideas and convictions that emerge in discussions often do not reflect the published scholarship closely, and because they elude documentation their influence is difficult to evaluate.

° ° °

Modern etymological studies confirm the derivation offered by ancient sources of *xoanon* from ξέω (*xe-o*), the verb "to scrape."[7] Although there are references to *xoana* in a variety of materials, the application of the word by authors such as Pausanias and Plutarch to wooden statues suggests that it directly reflects the process of hewing images from wood.[8] The

[5] Müller, "Kultbild" 490, shows that *xoanon* is not only used for "cult images"; Picard, *Man.* I, 87 n. 1.

[6] Papadopoulos, *Xoana*; VII for the author's purpose. A review with extensive discussion of the meaning of *xoanon* is given by W.H. Gross, *Gnomon* 54 (1982) 570–573.

[7] An example of such an ancient etymology is the entry *s.v.* of Orion of Thebes, *Etymologicon* 112.9 **[185]**: *Xoanon*: derived from *xeo*, *xeanon*, and by the change of *e* to *o*, *xoanon*. Modern discussions: *e.g.*, Chantraine, *Dictionnaire s.v.* ξόανον, v. ξέω. For the etymology of *xoanon*: *infra* pp. 9–12.

[8] For references to *xoana* in materials other than wood: Gardner, "Processes" 133–134; Gross, rev. Papadopoulos (*supra* p. 2 n. 6) 572. For Pausanias' *xoana* as wooden statues: Frazer, *Pausanias* II, 69–70 *ad* 3.3.5; Bennett, "Study" 14, B I for passages in which *xoana* are contrasted with statues of stone and metal; 14, B II for acrolithic *xoana*, where again a contrast between materials demonstrates the connection of *xoana* with wood. Pausanias' list of woods from which *xoana* are made (8.17.2) **[258]** is suggestive, but does not conclusively restrict the meaning of the word.

Page, *Further Greek Epigrams* 376–377, accepts Hesychius' definition of *xoana* **[144]** as being carved κυρίως ἐκ ξύλων, and dismisses the ἢ λίθων as "an afterthought, applicable only to relatively late usage." He criticizes LSJ[9] for the obscurity of its definition "then, generally, *image, statue*," asserting that all the citations given refer to wooden images. Page finds no non-wooden *xoana* in literature before Rufinus, *AnthPal* 5.36 **[328]**, and lists several references to wooden or possibly wooden statues.

technique lives on, as it were, in the name of the statues that have themselves vanished.

Both the nature of the process and the ancient references—again, mostly in Pausanias—to "ancient" *xoana* suggest further that the making of wooden statues is an extremely old practice.[9] It is frequently assumed in the field of Greek archaeology that wooden statuary preceded sculpture in stone, and the association of a wooden image with a cult is often taken to indicate the high antiquity of that cult.[10] This idea has more support than the ancient testimony alone. Common sense suggests that wood was more easily available and easier to work than stone, which would have required comparatively advanced technology to quarry and carve.[11] Archaeological evidence points to the abrupt appearance of large sculpture in stone around the middle of the seventh century B.C., and many scholars have maintained that the earliest stone statuary bears traces of wood-working techniques.[12] A similar theory explains features of the stone Doric order as petrified versions of wooden prototypes.[13] Both architecture and sculpture, then, would seem to have begun their development in wood, and this progression suggests a consistent pattern of technological advance. *Xoana* are likely, therefore, to represent not simply individual statues made in wood, but also an entire stage in the development of Greek sculpture. The Greeks themselves also held such a view. Plutarch expressly states that the making of *xoana* is an

[9] For "ancient" *xoana* in Pausanias: Bennett, "Study" 15–16, B XVI.

[10] A recent example: J.E. and F.E. Winter, "The Date of the Temples near Kourno in Lakonia," *AJA* 87 (1983) 5: "The elaborately socketed block seen by Le Bas and still on the site was perhaps the base for a wooden cult image. Such an image would suggest an old and primitive cult." For this base see also *infra* p. 65 n. 153.

[11] For the primacy of wood as a material for sculpture because of its ease of acquisition and working: A. de Ridder and W. Deonna, *L'art en Grèce* (Paris, 1924) 346; H.B. Walters, *The Art of the Greeks* (New York, 1922) 59. For the development and influence of this argument: *infra* pp. 208–218.

[12] For the appearance of large-scale stone statuary in the seventh century B.C.: most forthright statement by G.M.A. Richter, *The Sculpture and Sculptors of the Greeks*[3] (New Haven and London, 1950) 51 and n. 1; J. Boardman, *Pre-Classical* (Harmondsworth, 1967) 95–98; Ridgway, *Archaic* 17–42, summary 37 (for probable translation of Daedalic style into soft limestone statuary c. 650 B.C.). For suggestions that traces of carpentry technique appear in early work in stone: Casson, *Technique* 83–84 (challenged by Adam, *Technique* 3–5); Boardman, *Archaic* 18 for the contrast between marble and "the readily accessible limestone (*poros*) or sandstone which required nothing more complicated than a carpenter's tools and might even betray the woodworker's technique"; Herrmann, "Entstehung" 40–41 for a formal continuity between wooden and stone sculpture in sharp, precise carving (*cf.* Kyrieleis, "Holzfunde" 102–103); Ridgway, *Archaic* 23–25 for the appearance of columnar profiles and for piecing in Cretan stone statues as a possible reflection of wood-carving practice, and 21–22 for suggestion that "features typical of wood carving can be detected in some of the Daedalic terracottas." See *infra* pp. 212–214.

[13] An influential statement of the theory is by Dinsmoor, *Architecture*[3] 55–58, esp. 57.

ancient and early practice, and gives examples of famous early wooden statues; Pausanias asserts his belief that in the past all statues were *xoana*—that is, made of wood.[14] Tradition and archaeological evidence stand together here, and there seems every reason to believe that the word *xoanon* is a contemporary witness to an early stage in the history of Greek sculpture.

Most scholars accept the high antiquity of the word *xoanon*, but there is some disagreement about its significance. Among etymologists, for example, Chantraine believes it to have been part of a religious vocabulary, while Benveniste denies that it was ever a religious term.[15] Historians of sculpture are similarly divided. Picard does not believe that *xoanon* had specifically religious associations; Marcadé, however, in discussing the Hellenistic sculpture from Delos, asserts that even in those late times the word had a fixed, religious meaning.[16] Although Müller has demonstrated that *xoanon* in the ancient testimonia does not always refer to "cult images," there is strong evidence connecting *xoana* with religion.[17]

In the first place, the great majority of references to *xoana* is in fact to images of gods. This is especially true in the case of Pausanias, whose list of individual *xoana* is the longest of any writer's, and it is also true generally, among authors whose usage of *xoanon* does not otherwise share Pausanias' purism.[18] Furthermore, the ancient authors who discuss the images of the gods as a whole use *xoanon* to refer to them. Ammonius, for example, includes *xoana* among ἱερά (*hiera*), "sacred things," and Pollux lists *xoana* among words denoting things ἃ θεραπεύομεν, "to which we give service."[19] These illustrations have been stripped of their contexts to serve as reference-book entries, but *xoanon* is also found with the same meaning in fuller texts. Philo Judaeus, for example, heaps abuse on the images of the gods with a constant litany of contempt for "*agalmata* and *xoana* and *aphidrumata*."[20] Christian writers such as Clement of Alexandria and Eusebius, who are also concerned with idolatry, use *xoanon* as a standard term for the images of the gods that are worshipped.[21] The connection of *xoana* with religion would seem secure.

[14] Plut. *ap*. Eus. *PE* 3.8.1 [**108**]; Paus. 2.19.3 [**213**]; *cf*. 3.17.5 [**235**].
[15] Chantraine, *Noms* 198–199 §153; Benveniste, "Kolossos" 130–131.
[16] Picard, *Man*. I, 87 n. 1; Marcadé, *Musée Délos* 91–92.
[17] Müller, "Kultbild" 490.
[18] See lists in Bennett, "Study" 12–16, Table A, and Papadopoulos, *Xoana* 103–113.
[19] Ammonius *s.v.* ἱερά [**6**]; Pollux, *On*. I.7 [**322**].
[20] For Philo Judaeus: *infra* pp. 100–102.
[21] For Clement of Alexandria: *infra* pp. 127–133; for Eusebius: *infra* pp. 133–137, 160–161.

The evidence tying wooden *xoana* to religion also provides explicit testimony about their origin and early form. A key passage in Clement's *Protrepticus* [44] outlines the earliest development of *xoana*:

> In ancient times, then, the Scythians used to worship the dagger, the Arabians their stone, the Persians their river. Other peoples still more ancient erected conspicuous wooden poles and set up pillars of stones, to which they gave the name *xoana* [scraped objects] because the rough surface of the material had been scraped off. Certainly the *agalma* of Artemis in Icarus was an unwrought stock and that of Cithaeronian Hera in Thespiae was a felled tree-trunk. That of Samian Hera, as Aëthlius says, was at first a *sanis* but afterwards, when Procles was ruler, it was made into human form. When the *xoana* began to be represented as men, they acquired the additional name *brete*, from *brotoi* [mortals]. In Rome, of old time, according to Varro the prose-writer, the *xoanon* of Ares was a spear, since craftsmen had not yet entered upon the fair-seeming but mischievous art of sculpture. But the moment art flourished, error increased.[22]

Clement's discussion need not be accepted in every detail. For example, the word *bretas* is now understood to be a non-Greek, non-Indo-European word that was taken into the Greek vocabulary.[23] Nonetheless, Clement does offer a coherent and plausible version of an important development in Greek art and religion that can be supported by other evidence: the evolution of aniconic monuments into iconic images.

There is abundant testimony for the existence of aniconic worship among the Greeks. By aniconic worship is meant here the veneration of objects that represent but do not purport to show the appearance of deities. The list of stones, pillars, pyramids, and other objects that were worshipped in ancient Greece is long.[24] In comparison to the making of images that portray the gods, aniconism seems like an intrinsically less advanced kind of worship, and it is not surprising that scholars have pursued anthropological parallels with modern-day primitive cultures.[25] For the history of Greek art and religion, however, more relevant evidence comes easily to hand: Greek tradition itself recognizes aniconic practice as an ancient form of worship and places it in historical context. Plutarch, for instance, makes this comment about a grid-like symbol of Castor and Pollux: "The Spartans call the ancient *aphidrumata* of the Dioscuri '*dokana*'."[26] Pausanias says that "In a

[22] Clem.Al. *Protr.* 4.40 P.–41 P. [44].

[23] Benveniste, "Kolossos" 118–135, *passim*; Chantraine, *Etudes* 9. See *infra* p. 25 n. 62.

[24] For Greek aniconic worship: *infra* pp. 219–229.

[25] *E.g.*, Landtman, "Origin" 196–208.

[26] Plut. *De frat. amor.* 1 [318]; *infra* p. 186 n. 27. Ἀφίδρυμα literally means "something set up" and is often translated as "image," which is not possible here; "monument" is closer. See *infra* p. 82 n. 199.

still older age, among all the Greeks, too, rough stones received the honors of the gods, instead of *agalmata*."[27] Callimachus compares the "well-carved" images of the gods with the unworked monuments of the past.[28]

Scholars have visualized the evolution of aniconic into iconic representations in different ways. Farnell, for example, outlines a steady improvement in the rendering of the human form, almost as if one could see a figure slowly taking shape within a block.[29] Perdrizet explains that *xoana* were worked and smoothed tree trunks topped by heads or masks and draped; thus they achieved the transition from aniconic to figural representations.[30] Ridgway draws attention to another pre-Greek word, *κολοσσός* (*kolossos*), which seems originally to have meant a column-like image, and postulates a development from "presumably ill-shaped" wooden statues to anthropomorphic figures whose lower parts were still essentially columnar.[31] All these versions of the transformation find illustrations in archaeological material. Farnell sees in the blocky, to his eyes scarcely recognizable, forms of the dedication of Nikandre the first steps toward anthropomorphic rendering; Perdrizet adduces the vase-paintings showing draped pillars topped by masks of Dionysus; Ridgway cites representations of the Apollo Amyklaios and other columnar figures.

Clement's discussion of *xoana* ends with a reference to the introduction of the art of sculpture. This remark leads back to the question of the technical aspects of *xoana*. Primitive, columnar form need not have been determined solely by the iconographic tradition of aniconic monuments; the inherent qualities of wood may also have contributed to the forms of the statues made from it.[32] Ridgway has recently discussed the possible influence of purely technical considerations on early wooden statuary, and her discussion shows how the interplay between iconography and technique might have given rise to a group of statuary less than fully accomplished in the rendering of the human form.[33]

Taken together, then, the ancient sources seem to offer an outline of the development of *xoana* that finds support in archaeological evidence. The picture of *xoana* that emerges is one of wooden "cult statues" that were primitive in style as well as type. They resembled the logs and planks from which they were formed partly because they were aniconic in origin, and partly because they reflected the artistic limitations of their makers. Religious conservatism accounts not only for the actual preservation into quite

[27] Paus. 7.22.4 [**251**]; *infra* pp. 184, 195, 224.
[28] Call. *ap*. Eus. *PE* 3.8.1 [**108**]; *infra* pp. 195–196.
[29] Farnell, "Origins"; *infra* p. 192.
[30] Perdrizet, "Nikopolis" 226–227.
[31] Ridgway, *Archaic* 23–24, 37.
[32] See *supra* p. 3 n. 12.
[33] Ridgway, *Archaic* 23–25.

late times of so many *xoana*, but also for the retention of their primitive form by later statuary. Marcadé asserts that even in Hellenistic times wooden statues were made in imitation of the ancient *xoana* that continued to be venerated, following the type and technique of these "primitive images."[34] In historical terms, *xoana* would appear to have had their start in religious practice and to stand at the beginning of all Greek sculpture.

° ° °

This short summary has attempted to present the view of *xoana* that can be gained from published scholarship.[35] One fact, self-evident but nonetheless worth emphasizing, is clear: the literary testimonia are the fundamental evidence for *xoana*. Not only do the written sources provide all the definite statements that can be made about specific *xoana*, but further, they guide the interpretation of other evidence that seems relevant to the reconstruction of the group.

It is characteristic of both archaeological and philological studies of *xoana* that the literary evidence is approached as if it were the text of a catalogue that so far can be illustrated only with comparative material. That is to say, it is taken for granted that the ancient testimony can be readily translated into archaeological information. The sources that have the most obvious archaeological relevance are given the greatest weight, and every effort is made to reconcile divergent testimony in order to arrive at a comprehensive and coherent archaeological view. This approach is especially clear in the most recent treatment of the testimony for *xoana*. Papadopoulos divides the *xoana* that do not refer to specific images from those that do, and arranges the latter by cult and by location, producing a map of their geographical distribution.[36] Her work reflects the conviction that *xoana* form a group amenable to such cataloguing. The same is true of the attempts to refine the definition of *xoana*. For example, Gardner, in discussing the techniques of sculpture, draws attention to *xoana* in materials other than wood.[37] The examples are culled from several sources; stone *xoana* of Strabo balance the wooden ones of Pausanias, and the archaeological definition of *xoana* is adjusted accordingly.

In short, the desire to establish archaeological reliability has determined the way the ancient references to *xoana* are studied. The testimonia

[34] Marcadé, *Musée Délos* 89–90.

[35] The informal view of *xoana* tends to be simpler, distilling from the fuller treatments the essence of "primitive wooden cult statue." Frequently the aniconic aspect is not fully recognized, the primitive form being attributed exclusively to early artistic incompetence.

[36] Papadopoulos, *Xoana* 15–25 ("Fonti letterarie generiche e mitiche"), 27–63 ("Fonti letterarie con riferimento topografico"), 101–102 (maps), 103–113 (list by deity), 115 (list by type of wood), 117–123 (list by author).

[37] Gardner, "Processes" 133–134.

are viewed as primarily archaeological documentation, with little attention paid to the background and context of the individual sources. The differences in the meaning of the word from author to author tend to be seen as deviations from a standard *xoanon*.[38] Even Gross' emphasis on the variety of meanings found in the sources offers no real alternative scheme in which to place the testimonia.[39] Yet the passages already cited from Plutarch, Pausanias, and Clement show that *xoana* do not come without strings. In these authors, *xoana* are firmly tied to well-developed historical conceptions, to beliefs about the role of these images in the development of Greek religion and art—precisely the kind of ideas that are likely to have influenced the facts that the writers choose to report. It must be recognized that the testimonia for *xoana* are, in a sense, pre-digested, and that without a clear idea of their historical and intellectual context, the information that they preserve is open to misinterpretation.

The following chapters attempt to put the primary evidence for *xoana* in context. The first deals with the meaning of the word in the ancient sources, discussing the testimonia as far as possible in chronological order. The second treats the ancient testimony concerning the origin of Greek sculpture, analyzing the concept of the "*xoanon*," the primitive wooden "cult statue," as it is put forward by the ancient sources and developed by modern scholars, and examining its relationship to archaeological evidence. For both chapters the reader is referred to Appendix I, where the texts and translations of the passages discussed are given; the numbers assigned to these testimonia appear in boldface.

[38] A sensible statement on the perils of continuing to "insist on discovering terms that refer uniquely to particular types of objects" when approaching the terminology for statues is given by Price, *Rituals* 176. Price correctly emphasizes that *xoanon* refers not "just to archaic wooden statues," but to a wide variety of statues.

[39] Gross, rev. Papadopoulos (*supra* p. 2 n. 6) 572, and *supra* p. 1 n. 2.

CHAPTER I

THE WORD *XOANON*

Liddell and Scott's *Lexicon* defines *xoanon* as "*image carved* of wood," and "then, generally, *image*, *statue*, esp. of a god."[1] Although this definition is true for many *xoana*, it does not hold good for all. It does not take into account the changes in the meaning of the word over time and according to context, and so presents too simplified a view. This chapter treats the meaning of *xoanon* in detail, focusing first on its etymology, then on its use in the ancient sources. The appearances of the word in literary texts and in inscriptions are presented, as far as possible, chronologically, in order to show the development of its usage.

1. The Etymology of *Xoanon*

The etymology of *xoanon* is not entirely clear, and there is even disagreement over whether the word is a noun or a substantive adjective.[2] Latte has suggested that *xoanon* comes from the adjective *ξοανός*, the existence of which he conjectures on the basis of an emendation of a gloss in Hesychius (A.D. V) [**145**]. Instead of the punctuation and accentuation *ξοάνων· προθύρων ἐξεσμένων* (*xoana*: carved front doors; all genitive plurals), he would read *ξοανῶν προθύρων· ἐξεσμένων* (*xoan*-ed front doors: carved). His argument begins with the assumption that the phrase *rasilem forem* in Catullus 61.161 (168) is modelled on that of an earlier, Greek, author, because in the Italy of Catullus' time there were no doorposts that could be called *rasilis*.[3] This assumption is not wholly understandable. Latte's reference to Lycurgus' law prohibiting the use of any tool but an axe (Beil) for working doorposts (Türpfosten) (Plut. *Lyc.* 13.5) implies that he believes it to be a question of wooden elements. Yet *rasilis* is used of both stone and wood, and there is ample evidence for doorways of these materials in the architecture of first-century B.C. Rome and its surrounding

[1] LSJ[9] *s.v.* *ξόανον*.

[2] General discussions: Chantraine, *Dictionnaire s.v.* *ξόανον v.* *ξέω*; Frisk, *Wörterbuch s.v.* *ξόανον v.* *ξέω*; Pokorny, *Wörterbuch* 585–586.

[3] K. Latte, "Zur griechischen Wortforschung," *Glotta* 32 (1953) 35–36; 35 for Voss' comparison of the gloss and the line from Catullus; p. 35: "Es ist zunächst unbedingt sicher, dass Catull von einem älteren Vorbild abhängt, denn in dem Italien seiner Zeit waren geglättete Türpfosten nichts. . . . "

areas.[4] It has also been noted that wear from daily use might be meant.[5] The antiquarian argument by itself is not strong enough to support Latte's assignment of the phrase to Sappho, on whose *Epithalamia* Catullus certainly depended, although to what extent it is difficult to determine. If the phrase *xoanōn prothurōn* is in fact a phrase, it could fit into a dactylic scheme.[6] No help in identifying the author of the lemma is forthcoming from the preserved text of Hesychius, because the names of his sources, promised in the preface, have been deleted by abridgement, leaving only the lexical material.[7] Arguments can be advanced for either version of the gloss, and various scholars have expressed a preference for one or the other.[8] It is not impossible that *xoana* here are carved doors, since in Sophocles they are musical instruments.[9] Yet there is no reason to reject the adjective *xoanos*; at least one example of it survives, in an inscription from Perta in Asia Minor.[10] This is a Christian, and so a late text, but the earliest extant appearances of *xoanon* also point to its being less a noun of fixed meaning than a substantive that could be applied to a variety of objects.

Ancient etymological research derived *xoanon* and some similar words directly from verbs: ξέω-ξόανον, πλέκω-πλόκανον, and ἔχω-ὄχανον appear as standard examples. In modern etymological research, there is more certainty about the suffix of *xoanon* than about its stem. Within *-anon* is the *-no-* that characterizes an important group of Greek adjectives and nouns. This *-no-* is frequently combined with a preceding vowel to form

[4] Plutarch in fact refers to the axe (πέλεκυς) in connection with the roof, and the saw (πρίων) with doors. See M.E. Blake, *Ancient Roman Construction in Italy from the Prehistoric Period to Augustus* (Washington, D.C., 1947) 68–69 for wooden door elements; 69 for testimonia for wood in luxury architecture; 55 for the common use of white marble for doorframes at this time; 21–22 for occasional limestone doorjambs. Vitruvius offers no comments on this point: 2.9–10, on woods as building materials, concentrates on their qualities but does not mention their preparation; 4.6, 5.6, and 6.3, on doorways, are concerned with placement and proportions alone. For the smooothing of fine woodwork with skate- or shark-skin and the use of wax or oil of cedar or juniper during finishing: J. Liversidge in D. Strong and D. Brown, *Roman Crafts* (New York, 1976) 162. An elaborate wooden doorway is preserved in the Casa del Tramezzo, Herculaneum: *EAA* IV, 533 fig. 626. I know of no study that specifically addresses Latte's point. No relevant information comes from D.A. Walsh, "Doors in the Greek and Roman World," *Archaeology* 36 (1983) 44–50. For Greek doors: A. Büsing-Kolbe, "Frühe griechische Türen," *JdI* 93 (1978) 66–174.

[5] C.J. Fordyce, *Catullus* (Oxford, 1961, 1965) 250 *ad* line 161; also for *rasilis* applied to a variety of materials.

[6] For Sappho's meters for *epithalamia*: Page, *Sappho and Alcaeus* 123.

[7] For Hesychius: *Infra* p. 169 n. 419.

[8] Frisk, *Wörterbuch s.v.* ξέω, retains the traditional reading of the gloss, taking *xoanon* as a noun ("nicht mit Latte"); Chantraine, *Dictionnaire s.v.* ξέω, takes Latte's reading to indicate the existence of ξοανός, whence ξοάνιον and ξοανηφόροι.

[9] Sophocles fr. 238 Radt, Pearson **[36]**; *Infra* p. 16 and n. 32.

[10] *MAMA* VIII, 49 no. 275 **[396]**; *infra* p. 152 n. 366. See also *infra* p. 32 n. 78.

complex suffixes; *-ano-* is notable among these.[11] The substantives of this group often denote things that have been acted upon in some way. Chantraine remarks especially on the occurrence of verbal roots among these words, and emphasizes that the substantives frequently appear as names of both objects and instruments: for example, *πλόκανον*, plaited work, and *ὄχανον*, a shield-handle. The one *-ano-* suffix can thus denote either an instrument or a product.[12]

The derivation of the *xo-* stem is not entirely clear. The *o* will have resulted from the systematic change of vowels that marks the different forms of nouns and verbs as they are developed from a single root. This vowel gradation is a characteristic process of Indo-European word formation.[13] While the "original" vowel of *xoanon* would not have been *o*, opinions differ with regard to the ultimate root. Two verbs, *ξέω* and *ξύω*, have been suggested. Both words basically mean "scrape," but the lexicon definitions for *xuo* lean more toward "scratching," while the sense of *xeo* seems to be more "shaving" or "carving" or "polishing."[14] Various Indo-European roots have been postulated for these words, for example, *qs-es-, *qs-eu-, and *ksu.[15] (The verb *ξαίνω* may also be noted as a close relation; it seems to be connected especially with the working of wool.[16]) Elaborate forms such as *qs-ou̯-n̥no-m have also been postulated.[17]

Recent discussions of *xoanon* have tended to simplify a somewhat complex etymological scheme. Chantraine emphasizes the closeness of *xeo*, *xuo*, and *xaino*, and derives *xoanon* specifically from *xeo*.[18] It is clear in any

[11] Chantraine, *Noms* 196–197 §152; Buck, *Grammar* 322 §464. Chantraine, *Noms* 200, §154, notes that this Indo-European *-ano-* can wrongly be confused with the terminal *-ano-* of some words that seem to be pre-hellenic, among which names of plants and objects are conspicuous.

[12] Buck, *Grammar* 322 §464 notes that the *-no-* types of adjectives in Sanskrit "serve mostly as passive participles." Chantraine, *Noms* 197–199 §153. *Πλόκανον* comes from *πλέκω*, *ὄχανον* from *ἔχω*; for these pairs, the definition of *ochanon*, and more examples: Eustathius *ad* H. *Il.* 1.572 **[129]** (*infra* p. 168). See also Frisk, *Wörterbuch s.v. ξέω*. Benveniste, "Kolossos" 130–131, sees *xoanon* as removed from the two groups of *-ano-* words (names of instruments and "adjectives of aptitude").

[13] For a basic introduction to vowel gradation in Greek, with helpful examples of the different grades of vocalization: L.R. Palmer, *The Greek Language* (Atlantic Highlands, New Jersey, 1980) 215–220. The simplest illustration in English is "sing, sang, sung, song."

[14] LSJ[9] *s.v. ξέω, ξόανον*; Buck, *Synonyms* §6.91, 6.93. For *ξε-* and *ξυ-* words in the working of wood, stone, and clay: Orlandos, *Matériaux* I, 42 n. 1; Daremberg-Saglio V, 333–334.

[15] For these conjectures: Boisacq, *Dictionnaire s.v. ξαίνω, ξέω, ξόανον, ξύω* for parallel forms *qs-en-, *qs-es-, and *qs-eu-, as well as *qes-; Chantraine, *Dictionnaire s.v. ξαίνω, ξέω, ξύω*; Pokorny, *Wörterbuch* 585 *s.v. ξέω*; Buck, *Synonyms* §6.93.

[16] Boisacq, *Dictionnaire s.v. ξαίνω*; Chantraine, *Dictionnaire s.v. ξαίνω*.

[17] Boisacq, *Dictionnaire s.v ξόανον* for *qs-ou̯-n̥no-m; cf. Ventris and Chadwick, *Documents*[2] 338 §237 for *qso^{u}n̥^{n}om; Pokorny, *Wörterbuch* 585 for *ks-ou̯-$_{e}$nom.

[18] Chantraine, *Dictionnaire s.v. ξέω*.

case that the Greek words for scraping, cutting, and similar activities are closely and confusingly related; the etymology of *xoanon* is not in itself a wholly satisfactory guide to its usage.

It is important to note that there appears to be no relationship between the words for "scrape" and the similar word for "wood," *ξύλον*. The Indo-European root of this word may be *ksulo; several words in various languages, for instance, the Russian *šúlo* and the Lithuanian *šulas* ("post"), seem to confirm this derivation. Chantraine remarks that while a popular etymology at best might link *xulon* with *xuo*, a real connection is not plausible. It seems to be usual among Indo-European languages for the word for "wood" to be related to that for "tree," but this is not true of Greek. While it is therefore tempting to look for some connection between the word for "wood" and words for activities that seem appropriate to wood as a raw material—carving, scraping, and so forth—there seems to be no such link.[19] Ancient etymologists, however, derived *ξύλον* from *ξύω*, a connection which may have had some bearing on special usages of *xoanon* in late classical times.[20]

The fundamental meaning of *xoanon*, then, appears to be "something that has been scraped," or perhaps "carved." The exact nature of the process remains obscure, and it should be remembered that the English words for such techniques are themselves so highly colored that a precise correlation may be misleading. The important point is that, etymologically, *xoanon* is associated with a process alone and has no inevitable connection with any specific material.[21]

[19] Chantraine, *Dictionnaire s.v. ξύλον*; Buck, *Synonyms* §1.43; *TDNT* s.v. *ξύλον*. Harrison, *Epilegomena* 165 n. 1, mentions Myres' observation that Greek has no word for "tree" in general, *dendron* being a fruit tree. For *dendron*: O. Szemerényi, rev. Benveniste, *Le vocabulaire des institutions indo-européennes*, *JHS* 92 (1972) 215. See also *infra* p. 163 n. 405. *Cf.* LSJ[9] *s.v.* *δρῦς*, "originally, *tree*." See P. Friedrich, "Proto-Indo-European Trees," in G. Cardona *et al.*, eds., *Indo-European and Indo-Europeans* (Philadelphia, 1970) 11–34.

[20] *EtMag* 611.19 *s.v.* *Ξύλον*: Παρὰ τὸ ξύω . . . (*Xulon*: Derived from *xuo*).

[21] As noted by Gardner, "Processes" 133–134, who draws attention to the association of *xeo* with stone.

2. *Xoanon* to the End of the Fifth Century B.C.

As has been noted in the Introduction, there is a consensus that *xoanon* is a very old word, contemporary with the early images to which it is thought to refer. The grounds for this supposition are both philological and historical. Chantraine has drawn attention to the occurrence of the substantive suffix *-ano-* in some very old words, the Ionian-Attic *xoanon* among them, and also to the religious meaning of some of these words; such religious associations also tend to evoke the idea of high antiquity.[22] The question of the age of *xoanon* is related to the existence of pre-Greek words for statues such as *bretas* and *kolossos* (which will be discussed later). Chantraine sees these words as being replaced by the Greek *xoanon*.[23] His theory relies on the work of Benveniste, who finds in *xoanon* the oldest name for "statue" by far, a contemporary of the ancient *bretas*.[24]

The belief in the extreme antiquity of *xoanon*, while in good accord with the general concept of the primitive origin of Greek statuary, finds little support in the preserved occurrences of the word. The first secure appearance of *xoanon* is in Sophocles. Although the word is connected with three earlier authors, none of these associations can be upheld.

Xoanon occurs in Proclus' summary of Arctinus' *Iliou Persis* [**325**]. The (perhaps) eighth-century B.C. poem survives only in epitome, and about the episode of the rape of Cassandra Proclus says this: "Ajax, the son of Ilis, tearing Cassandra away by force, dragged down the *xoanon* of Athena." This passage, like the rest of the fifth-century A.D. epitome of the cyclic poems, is a bare outline of the narrative having no pretensions to preserving the vocabulary of the original texts. The *xoanon*, then, cannot be considered an example of the word from the eighth century B.C.[25]

The earliest author with whom *xoanon* has regularly been connected is Acusilaus of Argos, in a fragment preserved in Apollodorus [**21**].[26] The

[22] Chantraine, *Noms* 198–199 §153.

[23] Chantraine, *Etudes* 9.

[24] Benveniste, "Kolossos" 130–131. "C'est de beaucoup, avec son diminutif *ξοάνιον*, le nom le plus ancien de la statue, le témoin de la même époque où *βρέτας* nous reportait."

[25] Proclus, *Chrestomathia* 261–263 [**325**]; A. Severyns ed., tr., *Recherches sur la Chrestomathie de Proclus* IV (Paris, 1963). To my knowledge this passage has never been used as evidence for *xoanon* in Arctinus; *e.g.*, Papadopoulos, *Xoana* 23, 122, and 117 (*ex silentio*), assigns this *xoanon* to Proclus.

[26] Acusilaus, *FGrH* 2 F 28 [**21**]. The authorship of the mythological handbook which is known now as the *Bibliotheca* is not certain. There did exist a work of this name by Apollodorus, an Athenian grammarian of the second century B.C., but the text in question here is usually believed to be a product of the first or second century A.D. Some scholars call the author of this work Pseudo-Apollodorus, but for the purposes of this study it is not necessary to draw attention repeatedly to the uncertainty. For the *Bibliotheca*: Frazer, *Apollodorus* I, ix–xliii; A. Diller, "The Text History of the *Bibliotheca* of Pseudo-Apollodorus," *TAPA* 66 (1935) 296–313; van der Valk, "*Bibliotheca*." Today there does not seem to be great interest

beginning of Book 2 of the *Bibliotheca* contains a summary of early Argive history in which the madness of the daughters of Proetus is a prominent episode. Two different explanations of their madness are offered:

αὗται δὲ ὡς ἐτελειώθησαν, ἐμάνησαν, ὡς μὲν Ἡσίοδός φησιν, ὅτι τὰς Διονύσου τελετὰς οὐ κατεδέχοντο, ὡς δὲ Ἀκουσίλαος λέγει, διότι τὸ τῆς Ἥρας ξόανον ἐξηυτέλισαν.

"When these [daughters] were grown up, they went mad, according to Hesiod, because they would not accept the *teletai* [rites] of Dionysus, but as Acusilaus says, because they disparaged the *xoanon* of Hera." (2.2.2) Acusilaus, an Argive mythographer, is thought to have lived in the early fifth century B.C.[27] If the fragment in the *Bibliotheca* is a direct quotation, it would be the earliest known appearance of the word *xoanon*.

Acusilaus' works are represented by comparatively few fragments, even fewer of which certainly preserve his own text. The absence of *xoanon* from the other fragments cannot, therefore, be taken to show that he did not use the word. There is reason to think, however, that the fragment in the *Bibliotheca* is a summary of, and not an extract from, his writings.

The context of the fragment suggests that Acusilaus is only one of several sources of which no more than the gist has been given. His explanation of the madness (ὡς δὲ Ἀκουσίλαος λέγει) occurs in a passage that records the opinions of several authors on a number of different subjects. Beginning with 2.2.1, the reader is informed in fast succession that "some say" that Proetus went to the court not of Iobates, but of Ampianax (ὡς δέ τινές φασι), that Homer calls someone one name but "the tragic poets" call her another (ὡς μὲν Ὅμηρος . . . ὡς δὲ οἱ τραγικοί), that Hesiod says one thing, Acusilaus something different. The repeated *men* . . . *de*'s suggest strongly that this entire passage gives the results of Apollodorus' comparison of several authorities. The information presented is unembellished and to the point, and notable variations between versions are mentioned crisply.

The passage that immediately follows the reference to Acusilaus is very different. It is a highly detailed and colorful account of the healing of the daughters by the seer Melampus. This single episode of the story takes up approximately the length of text in which the entire annotated genealogy from Lynceus to the Proetides had been distilled from at least five sources. The luxury of the Melampus narrative emphasizes the ruthless

---

in the question of the authorship of the *Bibliotheca*; the works cited here offer an exhaustive discussion of the subject first raised by C. Robert, *De Apollodori Bibliotheca* (Berlin, 1873), which I have been unable to consult. For F 28: A. Kordt, *De Acusilao* (Basel, 1903) 34–35 Fr. 22.

[27] Josephus, *Ap.* 1.13 puts him shortly before the Persian attack on Athens: *FGrH* 2 T 3. Frazer, *Apollodorus* I, xx gives no reason for calling Acusilaus "the early Boeotian genealogist." For Apollodorus' reliance on Acusilaus: van der Valk, "*Bibliotheca*" 131–134.

summary of the preceding passage. It seems likely that such a summary would preserve the sense and content of a source, but not necessarily its vocabulary. While *xoanon* would be a natural word for a late Hellenistic or later writer to use, as will be shown, that is not proof one way or the other in the case of the Acusilaus fragment. It is possible to say only that there is an extremely good chance that the citation does not preserve the actual words of Acusilaus, and that it therefore should not be used as evidence for the appearance of the word in the early fifth century.[28]

Xoanon appears in another passage of the *Bibliotheca* that may go back to a fifth-century source. The section in question is the account of the origin of the Palladion in 3.12.3 [**22**], a passage that has been condemned by some editors as a later interpolation. The point in its favor made by van der Valk, however, deserves consideration: the last line of the passage, *καὶ περὶ μὲν τοῦ παλλαδίου ταῦτα λέγεται* (and concerning the Palladion this is said) certainly might be taken to indicate that the section is part of the text—a real digression, that is to say, rather than a marginal addition.[29] The story would then take its place in the account the *Bibliotheca* gives of the early history of Troy, which is generally thought to go back to the *Troica* of Hellanicus of Lesbos, a contemporary of Herodotus.[30] The attribution depends on similarities between the text of the *Bibliotheca* and the series of Homeric scholia in which Hellanicus is named as the authority.

The scholarship of these questions of source is complex, and it is difficult to move beyond probabilities. The Palladion passage does, however, stand clearly apart from the surrounding text not merely because of the last line, but also because its first line announces it as a digression and because it is entirely in indirect discourse, unlike what precedes and follows. It can also be pointed out that the *men* of the last line lacks a satisfactory *de* anywhere.[31] The whole passage thus seems surely to have been taken from somewhere else and roughly cut to fit into the history. Whoever was

[28] Webster, "Theories" 166, says that *xoanon*, like *eikon*, does not appear before the fifth century B.C.; but his references (n. 16) are Acusilaus and Sophocles' *Xoanephoroi*, for which see *infra*.

[29] Van der Valk, "*Bibliotheca*" 142–143.

[30] Porphyry, *ap.* Eus. *PE* 10.3.466 b, asserts that Hellanicus' *Barbarian Customs* borrows heavily from Herodotus. Van der Valk, "*Bibliotheca*" 134, notes that Hellanicus is not mentioned in the *Bibliotheca*. L. Pearson, *Early Ionian Historians* (Oxford, 1939) 181, mentions the agreement in details of Trojan genealogy between Apollodorus and Hellanicus, but wonders whether Hellanicus' arrangement could have been as disorderly as that in the *Bibliotheca*.

[31] I am grateful to T.C. Loening for drawing my attention to the widowed *men*. If the phrase *μετ' Ἄτης καὶ* (along with Ate) is indeed an interpolation, it suggests that a story that did not belong to the rest of the history of early Troy was especially adapted to make reference to the hill of Ate (*Ἄτης λόφον*) mentioned in the immediately preceding text.

responsible for grafting this section onto the text, the obvious marking off and textual discontinuity suggest that the passage might not be uniform with the rest of the account, which seems to follow Hellanicus closely. There is, however, no obvious clue to its source. Again, the date of the *Bibliotheca* itself is the earliest demonstrable date for this *xoanon*.

Xoanon, then, is not yet securely attested in the work of any author before the middle of the fifth century B.C. at the earliest. Its first certain appearance is in Sophocles. *Xoana* are found twice in the fragments of this author, neither time without difficulties.

The first of the two occurrences is surprising. Athenaeus 14.637 a **[36]** preserves two lines of Sophocles' *Thamyras*:

πηκταὶ δὲ λύραι καὶ μαγάδιδες
τά τ' ἐν Ἕλλησι ξόαν' ἡδυμελῆ.

In Gulick's sentimental translation these lines run "well-built lyres and *magadides* and all the instruments of polished wood wherewith the Greeks make sweet melody." Gulick has rendered the sense of the passage well, and his version underlines the unique usage of *xoanon*. This seems to be the only example of the word applied to musical instruments. At the same time, it is also the first truly secure appearance of the word. It is thought that the *Thamyras* is an early play, largely because of the tradition that Sophocles himself played the lyre during its performance. In addition, the exotic elements—foreign vocabulary and the subject itself—have been taken to betray the influence of Aeschylus and so to indicate that the play belongs to Sophocles' first, Aeschylean period. On these slight grounds the piece has been dated to shortly after the *Triptolemus* of 468 B.C.[32]

The second appearance of *xoanon* in a Sophoclean context is in what may be the title of a lost play, the Ξοανηφόροι, *Xoanon-bearers*. It occurs in the scholia to line 304 of Aeschylus' *Seven Against Thebes* **[4–5]**: "It is also said in the *Xoanephoroi* of Sophocles that the gods carry out from Troy on their shoulders their own *xoana*, seeing that the city is being captured."[33]

[32] S. fr. 238 Radt, Pearson; 217 Nauck² **[36]**. Pearson's suggestion (*Fragments* I, *ad loc.*) that the intention is "to give a generic description of stringed instruments" is convincing (*cf.* Chantraine, *Dictionnaire s.v.* ξέω: "nom d'un instrument de musique"). He repeats the reference of F. Ellendt, *Lexicon Sophocleum* (Berlin, 1872) *s.v.* ξόανον, to Hesychius' *xoana*. For the date of the *Thamyras*: K. Reinhardt, *Sophokles* (Frankfurt am Main, 1947) 235; T.B.L. Webster, *An Introduction to Sophocles*² (Oxford, 1969) 3, 144, 174–175; Trendall and Webster, *Illustrations* 69–70. It is not necessary to believe that Sophocles himself played Thamyras: Pearson, *Fragments* I, 178–179. For the earliest known representation of Thamyras and the Muses, dated c. 470–460 B.C.: J. Marcadé, "Une représentation précoce de Thamyras et les Muses dans la céramique attique à figures rouges," *RA* 1982, 223–229.

[33] Sch. A. *Sept.* 304 (291 Wecklein) **[5]** = S. fr. 452 Radt, Pearson (see *Fragments* I *ad loc.* for the comparison to Thuc. 1.9 and the suggestion that ἐπὶ τῶν ξοανηφόρων may be meant); 414 Nauck². The line numbers of W. Dindorf, ed., *Aeschyli tragoediae superstites* (Oxford,

Welcker objects vigorously to interpreting *xoanephoroi* as the title of a play, largely on the grounds that a chorus of gods is unthinkable. He argues that the "title" is no more than the result of carelessness in treating a reference to a scene concerning such an episode.[34] There is little doubt that at some time the gods of Troy were believed to have deserted the doomed city. The image appears again in scholia to an earlier line of the *Seven*, Eteocles' bitter reflection that the gods abandon cities, not save them (Sch. A. *Sept.* 217) [1–3], and there is testimony about comparable episodes in historic contexts.[35] The similarity between the scholia convinced Welcker that what is in question is the reporting of such an apparition rather than its enactment on stage. The confusion, and hence the title, seem to have originated in the commentary.

There are indeed considerable difficulties in accepting the *xoanephoroi* as the title of a play such as the scholia describe. While such a title might not necessarily mean that the chorus consisted of gods carrying their own images, they must nonetheless have figured prominently in the dramatic action. It is hard to imagine the collective appearance on stage of characters who are accustomed to dominate plays singlehandedly. In Greek art, the gods do appear en masse in mythological scenes in which each has some narrative or symbolic role. For example, the scenes of the marriage of Peleus and Thetis and the return of Hephaestus on the sixth-century B.C. François vase teem with divinities, but these are renderings of assemblies in the supernatural world, and are not at all comparable to the portrayal of refugees from human catastrophe. The gods of the Parthenon east frieze are shown together, presumably as honored spectators of a human ceremony, but again, this is a formal and dignified assembly. A collection of fleeing gods burdened with their own images irresistibly suggests comedy, but comedy does not seem to be what the scholiast has in mind. I know of

---

1841–1851) are followed by D. Page, ed., *Aeschyli septem quae supersunt tragoediae* (Oxford, 1972), and by O.L. Smith, ed., *Scholia graeca in Aeschylum quae exstant omnia* II.2. *Scholia in Septem Adversus Thebas* (Leipzig, 1982); those of N. Wecklein, *Aeschyli Fabulae* I (Berlin, 1885) are followed by A.W. Verrall, ed., *The "Seven Against Thebes" of Aeschylus* (London, 1887). Verrall (xxxiii–xxxv) gives a short, helpful introduction to the scholia of the *Seven*; see now, however, Smith's new edition, which has replaced "the uncritical Dindorf edition" (O.L. Smith, "The So-called 'Sch. Rec.' in Editions of the Scholia of Aeschylus," *Philologus* 126 [1982] 139).

[34] F.G. Welcker, *Die griechische Tragödien mit Rücksicht auf den epischen Cyclus geordnet* (Bonn, 1839) I, 65–67. For discussions: Pearson, *Fragments* II, 104–105; Radt, *TGF* IV, 374.

[35] Sch. A. *Sept.* 217 (203 Wecklein) [2, 3]: Welcker, *Tragödien* (*supra* p. 17 n. 34) 66; Pearson, *Fragments* II, 105, with some references to other divine abandonments. Rose, "Images" 40–41, asserts that the difficulties in accepting *xoanephoroi* as a title in no way undermine the accuracy of the scholia with respect to the relationship of the gods to their images.

no representation in Greek art of a god carrying his own image, and although this is very far from a conclusive argument, there is a good possibility that the scholiast's explanation is idiosyncratic. Welcker's misgivings seem justified, and if his suggestion about the origin of the ostensible title is correct, there is a good chance that the word *xoanephoroi* should be entirely dissociated from Sophocles.[36]

If, however, the word *xoanephoroi* is correctly associated with Sophocles, it is necessary to ask whether the "*xoan-*" in the compound meant to Sophocles what it meant to the scholiast. A simple way to separate the title from the scholiast's explanation would be to have human beings carrying images of the gods: the story of Aeneas' escape from Troy might be adduced, for example, as well as artistic representations removed from the Trojan cycle, such as the stele of Polyxena of the late fifth century B.C.[37] Welcker's analysis of the scholia dealing with the Ilioupersis might, however, be taken even further. Sophocles' presumed text may have had nothing to do with the report of it given in the scholium. *Xoanon*, as will be seen, is commonly used in late Hellenistic and later times for statues of gods, and with that meaning it is perfectly standard in late commentaries. Certainly whoever wrote the scholium had this definition in mind. It is also in Hellenistic times that the testimony for divine desertions begins to be more explicit and colorful. A comparison can be made between Herodotus' account (8.41) of the evacuation of Athens before the Persian invasion, in which the Athenians infer from the fact that the Acropolis snake had left its monthly honey-cake uneaten that Athena had abandoned the city, and Curtius' version of Alexander's siege of Tyre (4.3.21–22) **[56]**, in which the *simulacrum* of Apollo is chained to the altar of Hercules in the hope that the hero would be strong enough to stop the god from leaving the city.[38] The scholiast's explanation of *xoanephoroi* is in harmony with both the late usage of *xoanon* and the vivid and sensational late conceptions of divine abandonments, but seems less at home in the fifth century B.C. Sophocles'

[36] François vase, Florence 4209: *ABV* 76.1; conveniently illustrated in P.E. Arias and M. Hirmer (tr. and rev. B. Shefton), *A History of 1000 Years of Greek Vase Painting* (New York, 1963) figs. 40–46; c. 570 B.C. Parthenon east frieze: F. Brommer, *Der Parthenonfries* (Mainz, 1979) pl. 165. For assemblies of gods: H. Knell, *Die Darstellung der Götterversammlung in der attischen Kunst des VI. und V. Jahrhunderts v. Chr.* (Freiburg, 1965). On coins of the Kibyra–Ephesus alliance in the time of Alexander Severus (A.D. 222–235), the Artemis of each city holds the image of the other as they stand on either side of an altar: *LIMC* II.1 (1984) 679 no. 742 (L. Kahil).

[37] I owe the suggestion that an episode such as Aeneas' escape might be meant to E.B. Harrison; B.S. Ridgway has reminded me of the example of Polyxena's stele. For the stele: Ridgway, *Fifth Century* 148–149 and pl. 108. For gods shown near images of themselves, see *infra* p. 56 n. 132.

[38] For Curtius Rufus 4.3.21–22 **[56]**: *infra* pp. 73–74.

own vocabulary reinforces this impression; he does not elsewhere use *xoanon* for statues; his images of gods are *agalmata*.[39] Furthermore, in the fragment of the *Thamyras* he uses *xoana* for musical instruments. The possibility exists that if *xoanephoroi* is in fact Sophocles' word, the interpretation of it as "statue-bearers" is entirely the scholiast's. It is not impossible that a commentator combined various information in order to explain a word that was the sole vestige of a lost play.

The certifiably Sophoclean *xoana*—that is, musical instruments—are good candidates for being carried. Literary and archaeological evidence attests the importance of music in the education of a Greek gentleman; this aspect of noble cultivation seems to be shown, for example, in a scene by the Triptolemos Painter in a procession of young men carrying lyres.[40] One might well see in these youths *xoanephoroi*—bearers of *xoana* like those mentioned in the fragment from the *Thamyras*.

Because the scholia to the *Seven* are the only evidence for the word, it may never be possible to know exactly what *xoanephoroi* means. Nevertheless it is important to recognize that if it has any textual relevance to Sophocles at all, it may refer not to statues of gods, but instead to *xoana* as they appear in the fragment from the *Thamyras*. The *xoan-* of the fragment raises another point: should the bearers be understood as carriers each of one *xoanon* (as, for instance, Liddell and Scott render "image-bearers"), or is it a question of a less specific, perhaps more collective *xoana*?

The next author to use *xoanon* is Euripides. In three of his plays the word makes a total of four appearances which, taken together, tend to pull it away from the orbit of standard Greek terminology for statues.

Xoanon appears once in the *Iphigeneia Among the Taurians*, the play which, not surprisingly, contains more references to statues than any other. Its plot hinges on Orestes' theft of the image of the Taurian Artemis during the course of his escape with his sister. The statue is mentioned twenty-seven times, fourteen as *agalma*, twelve as *bretas*.[41] Only once in the text is

[39] Ellendt, *Lexicon* (*supra* p. 16 n. 32) *s.v.*, notes *agalma* for *statua divorum* at *OT* 1379 (*cf.* "ornament" at *Ant.* 704); *hedos* at *OT* 886 is usually translated "image of a god." *Xoanon* is not favored as a restoration for P.Oxy. 3151 fr. 2.9–10: ˘']νον: *POxy* 44 (1976) 8.

[40] I am grateful to G.F. Pinney for discussing this scholium with me and suggesting that Sophocles' own definition of *xoana* might also hold good for the scholiast's *xoanephoroi*. To her are due also the references to *ARV*² 365.62 + 63: E.R. Knauer, "Fragments of a Cup by the Triptolemos Painter," *GRBS* 17 (1976) 209–216, pl. 5 figs. 1–2; 214 n. 18 for the playing of the lyre as an important educational activity. She has further suggested that a connection with the Ilioupersis would be possible if the *xoanephoroi* collectively bore a single *xoanon*; Euripides uses *xoanon* to refer to the Wooden Horse **[91]** (see *infra*).

[41] *Agalma*: 997, 1000, 1176, 1448; θεᾶς, 87, 1014, 1038, 1158, 1480; σεμνὸν θεᾶς, 1316; ξεστόν, 112; διοπετές, 978; τό τ' οὐρανοῦ πέσημα, τῆς Διὸς κόρης, 1385; ἱερόν, 1441. *Bretas*:

it called a *xoanon*, in the outcry from the Taurian shore to the escaping Greeks: "By what *logos* do you, stealing *xoana* and priestesses from the land, carry them [away]?" (. . . *τίνι λόγῳ πορθμεύετε / κλέπτοντες ἐκ γῆς ξόανα καὶ θυηπόλους;*) (*IT* 1358–1359) [**90**]. The composer of the hypothesis, in contrast, considers *xoanon* the proper term for the image, beginning his summary of the plot [**89**] with the word that evidently came first to his mind: "In accordance with an oracle, Orestes, coming with Pylades to the Taurians of Scythia, determined to steal away the *xoanon* of Artemis that is honored among them." The hypothesis is of a type that can be dated to the first century B.C., and its wording is therefore likely to reflect usage much later than Euripides.[42]

The reference to *xoana* in line 1359 is not without difficulties. Both fourteenth-century manuscripts on which the text of the play completely depends read there two singulars, *xoanon* and *thuepolon*.[43] These have been emended to plurals for the sake of the meter, a change on grounds of which I am not competent to judge the validity, but one that has the approval of subsequent editors.[44] Although the plural forms in themselves have met no resistance, a satisfactory explanation of their meaning has yet to be proposed: one suggestion is that they add a degree of humor; another, that they make the charge of theft "seem more serious."[45]

1040, 1044, 1453, 1481; *θεᾶς*, 980, 1179, 1477; *τῆς θεοῦ*, 1165, 1199; *οὐράνιον θεᾶς*, 986; *σεμνόν*, 1291, 1489. For Loutsa, near Brauron, and the shrine of Artemis Tauropolos: *AR* 1977–78, 15; *Del.* 27 (1972) *Chron.* 151–152; tests yield three phases from the fifth to the second century B.C. See also M.B. Hollinshead, "Against Iphigeneia's Adyton in Three Mainland Temples," *AJA* 89 (1985) 435–438 for Loutsa.

[42] For tragic hypotheses: G. Zuntz, *The Political Plays of Euripides* (Manchester, 1955) 129–152; 134–139 for a first-century B.C. date for the summary-type, to which belongs that of the *IT*. See also E.G. Turner, "Euripidean Hypotheses in a New Papyrus," *Proceedings of the IX International Congress of Papyrology* (Oslo, 1961) 7–8. *Cf.* the ready use of *xoanon* for the Taurian image in Apollodorus 6.26–27 [**24**]: *infra* p. 119.

[43] For the manuscripts of the *IT*: M. Platenauer, ed., *Euripides. Iphigenia in Tauris* (Oxford, 1938, 1967) xxi.

[44] D. Sansone, ed., *Euripides. Iphigenia in Tauris* (Leipzig, 1981), credits Reiske with the change to *xoana*, Musgrave with *thuepolous*. Most previous editors give Musgrave alone. (*Cf.* F.A. Paley, *Euripides with An English Commentary* III [London, 1880] *ad* 1358: *xoana* Seidler and Elmley, *thuepolous* Matthiae.) For Musgrave: I. Barnes, ed., *Euripidis Tragoediae fragmenta epistolae* III. *Musgravii Notas* (Leipzig, 1788) *ad loc.*

[45] Humor: Platenauer, *Iphigenia* (*supra* p. 20 n. 43) *ad loc.*; seriousness of charge: W.N. Bates, ed., *Euripides. Iphigenia in Tauris* (New York, 1904) *ad loc.* I. Flagg, ed., *Euripides. Iphigenia among the Taurians* (Boston and London, 1891) *ad loc.*, bids the reader notice "the contemptuous effect of the generalizing plural." He has too a note on kidnapping and adds, "It would be interesting to know how large a demand there was for *ξόανα*."

The question of number is of considerable interest, because the meaning of *xoanon* in the fifth century may in some degree be related to it. The plural *xoana* of Sophocles' *Thamyras* [**36**] suggest not the simple equation of *xoanon* with a musical instrument, but rather, as Pearson says, a "generic description."[46] The use of the plural recalls Latte's suggestion that *xoanon* is a substantive.[47] If *xoanon* preserves its adjectival nature to the extent that it has not yet become an independent entity, so to speak, denoting (whether by intrinsic meaning or by convention) only one object, but instead can readily be applied to a variety of things that share a common feature, then the use of the plural might in some way enhance its descriptive meaning. One might compare, for example, some collective modern terms for families of musical instruments, such as "brasses," "woodwinds," or "strings."

The other three appearances of *xoanon* in Euripides clearly demonstrate the variety of its application. *Xoana* occurs in line 1403 of the *Ion* [**88**], when Creusa, abandoning sanctuary, has "leaped, having left the *xoana* of the altar" (Ion: Θεομανὴς γὰρ ἥλατο / βωμοῦ λιποῦσα ξόανα. . . .). It is possible that carved ornaments of some kind are meant, perhaps on the order of the elaborate figural decoration of the altar of Poseidon at Soloeis described by Scylax.[48] While the passage might seem to imply that Creusa's safety lies in the *xoana*, and so link them, for instance, with the *brete* and *agalmata* at which the chorus of Aeschylus' *Seven Against Thebes* takes refuge, it is certain that in Greek religion the altar itself can give sanctuary.[49] It is therefore not necessary to suppose that the *xoana* of the *Ion* are independent statues, although one *xoanon*, which seems to be a statue, is mentioned in connection with a *bomos* in an inscription from Asia Minor of the imperial period [**383**]. What remains unclear is why Euripides speaks of plural *bomou xoana*.[50]

[46] Pearson, *Fragments* I *ad* fr. 238.

[47] For Latte's suggestion: *supra* pp. 9–10 and n. 3.

[48] A.S. Owen, ed., Euripides, *Ion* (Oxford, 1939, 1957) *ad* 1403 considers the *xoana* to be "carved figures with which the altar was decorated." A well-known passage from a geographical work of about the fourth century B.C. preserved under the name of the earlier (VI B.C.) writer Scylax describes an elaborate altar of Poseidon [**329**]. For an explicit representation of figural decoration on an altar: H. Prückner, *Die lokrischen Tonreliefs* (Mainz, 1968) 17 fig. 1.

[49] J.P. Gould, "Hiketeia," *JHS* 93 (1973) 74–103, esp. 77–78 for sources for and discussion of "Supplication by contact with an altar of a god or other sacred ground."

[50] For the discovery of a bronze statuette *in situ* on the provisional altar of a post-Persian installation at Kalapodi in Boeotia: R.C.S. Felsch, "Apollon und Artemis oder Artemis und Apollon? Bericht von den Grabungen im neu entdeckten Heiligtum bei Kalapodi," AA 1980, 89–99; figs. 71–75 for the kouros (ht. 10.6 cm.) affixed to the top of the altar, an *ad hoc* and

Xoanon and *xoana* both appear in the *Trojan Women*. In line 525 [**91**], *xoanon* refers to the Trojan Horse, which had been called *bretas* in line 12. The Horse is far from the ordinary conception of a "cult statue," but it was deposited at the gates of Troy ostensibly as a votive offering of some kind; in line 525 it is the *hieron xoanon* that the Trojans begin to lead up to Athena. In this passage, then, *xoanon* again has connections with religion. The Horse is called χρυσεοφάλαρον, "decked with gold *phalara*." *Phalara* might mean bosses or discs, or perhaps the cheek-pieces of a bridle, as attested in both late authors and sources of the fifth century B.C. The latter meaning would be especially fitting for the Horse. Either way, the word indicates that this *xoanon* was a splendid construction, outfitted or ornamented with precious materials.[51]

Gold is also featured in line 1074 of the *Trojan Women* [**93**], where the meaning of *xoana* is not clear. The context is a lament for the ruined Troy. One of the disasters bemoaned is that, along with the all-night festivals and other religious activities and objects, the χρυσέων τε ξοάνων τύποι have ceased to exist. This phrase resists translation. The meaning of *tupos* is uncertain; no appearance of the word in any source is without controversy. In this passage, the association of the word with architectural models and the like seems much less likely than with relief-work, and the phrase might be construed as "reliefs of golden carved-work," or something similar.[52]

---

unpolished arrangement perhaps suggesting a votive rather than an image for worship in the sense of a "cult image."

E.B. Harrison has reminded me that statues are shown beside or behind altars of supplication in vase-paintings of dramas, and that such nearby statues might be meant here rather than carvings on an altar.

[51] LSJ[9] *s.v.* φάλαρον. The *xoanon* of the scholium *ad loc.* [**92**] merely repeats the word from the text.

[52] G. Roux, "Le sens de ΤΥΠΟΣ," *REA* 63 (1961) 5–14, argues that *tupos* means "relief" rather than "model." (For the *tupoi* of Timotheos at Epidaurus: G. Roux, "Sur quelques termes d'architecture: 1) ΞΥΛΩΜΑ 2) ΤΑΡΣΟΙ 3) ΤΥΛΩΣΙΣ 4) ΤΥΠΟΙ," *BCH* 80 [1956] 518–521.) Roux's disscussion of the *Troades* passage ("*Tupos*" 6–7) points out the difficulties of these lines; Parmentier's rendering, "Statues carved in wood and gold," may approach the underlying sense. Roux's suggestion that votive tablets are meant ("les tablettes à l'emblème des statues d'or") is not finally convincing; it seems too narrow, and he seems too to rely on the standard lexicon definition of *xoanon*. Nor is LSJ[9] *s.v.* τύπος V, with the suggestion of "periphrasis for χρύσεα ξόανα," completely satisfying. Note, for this passage, LSJ[9] *s.v.* χρύσεος I.4 for χρύσεον, "a gold plaque," *SIG* I, 122.7, from Selinus, fifth century B.C. For a review of the controversy over the meaning of *tupos*: Pollitt, *Ancient View* 272–293. Add now: [S.] fr. 1126 Radt, Pearson [**48**]; D.H. *Isoc.* 3; Poll. *On.* I.7 [**322**] (τυπώματα); Eus. *PE* 5.2.182 a; 5.9.195 d (= Porph.); 5.14.202 c (= Porph.); 5.15.204 a; and Moretti, *Inscriptiones* I, 76.1, 146.B.3; III, 1216.2, 1268.4, 1411.6. For *tupos* in Greek Christian exegesis: K.E. McVey, "The Domed Church as Microcosm," *DOP* 37 (1983) 97 and n. 18.

Despite the difficulty of translating the phrase, three aspects of these *xoana* stand out clearly: the use of the plural, the association with religious ceremonies and objects, and the connection with gold, which points to expensive and elaborate work. The mention in lines 1075–1076 of the Phrygian *selanai* adds an exotic touch to the catalogue of vanished glories.

Conclusions

The meaning and usage of *xoanon* up to the end of the fifth century B.C. differ substantially from what might be expected on the basis of the current interpretation of the word. The idea that *xoanon* is an old word, coeval with the primitive wooden cult statues it denotes, is not supported by its meaning in its earliest appearances. One of the more surprising aspects of its usage is that *xoanon* does not occur in places where it might be expected; it is not attested at all before the middle third of the fifth century, and it does not hold a secure position in Greek terminology for statuary.

Neither *xoanon* nor any word like it is yet attested in Linear B.[53] It does not appear in any of the Homeric or Hesiodic texts. The significance of the negative evidence from early poetry, however, should not be overstated, since in general the poets do not seem to have been much interested in statues or representations as such. To some extent this remains true in later times, as for instance when honorary statues are decreed in terms of "a bronze [name] will be set up," or when sculptors are credited with making not a statue of something, but instead the something itself. The idea of an image as an object does not seem important.[54] A good example of this habit of thought in the description of the Trojan embassy to the temple of Athena in *Iliad* 6.262–312. The women approach Athena and lay the robe on her knees. No word for statue is used throughout the passage, and in the end it is the goddess herself who shakes her head in rejection. There are, however, good reasons to suspect that this passage bears traces of later Athenian revision, specifically in the matter of the placement of the garment on the

[53] The closest word in the tablets is the adjective so-we-ne-ja in a furniture inventory from Pylos. This adjective comes from so-we-no, a word that occurs on other tablets. So-we-no refers to an element of decoration, but its meaning is not certain. It is perhaps related to *σωλήν-σωλῆνος*, "gutter," "groove," "pipe," or "shellfish"; no connection with *xoanon* seems possible: Ventris and Chadwick, *Documents*² §237 (pp. 337–338, 499–500; 338: "Hardly *ξόανον*") Ta 709 + 712, line 2. The discussion is repeated from M. Ventris, "Mycenaean Furniture on the Pylos Tablets," *Eranos* 53 (1955) 116. In Ta 721 (*Documents*² §245) 2 and 3, the so-we-no's are part of the inlaid ornament of footstools. L.R. Palmer, "A Mycenaean Tomb Inventory," *Minos* 5 (1957) 65, suggests a connection of so-we-no with *ἑλενοί*, for a vine motif.

[54] For Homer: Webster, "Theories" 177.

knees of the goddess, which is suspiciously close to the ceremony of the Panathenaia. If so, it is possible that Homer mentioned no statues at all.[55]

Xoanon seems to be absent from the life and literature of Archaic Greece. No *xoanon* appears in the corpus of dedicatory inscriptions collected by Lazzarini. Some poets of the seventh and sixth centuries B.C. carry on the earlier apathy toward images; at least, no statues appear in the extant texts of Archilochus, Alcman, Sappho, Theognis, or Anacreon. When statues are mentioned at this time, however, *xoanon* does not occur: the words used are ἄγαλμα and ἀνδριάς.[56] *Agalma* has been restored in a papyrus that seems to preserve part of Stesichorus' *Iliou Persis*. The episode is, as might be expected, the rape of Cassandra, and the restored *agalma* is further restored as *hagnon* ("pure," "chaste," "undefiled," or "holy").[57] Alcaeus also calls Cassandra's Athena an *agalma*.[58] In the fifth century, Pindar uses *andrias* and *agalma*.[59] If Latte's suggestion that the phrase *xoanon prothurōn* comes from Sappho is correct—and his theory cannot be proved or disproved on the basis of current evidence—she would then have used the adjective *xoanos* to refer to carved doors, but not to statues.[60]

That *xoanon* is not securely based in fifth-century Greek terminology for statues is shown both by its absence from contexts where it would be

[55] For the *Supplicatio* in its present form as an Athenian revision of the sixth century: Lorimer, *Homer* 442–449.

[56] M.L. Lazzarini, *Le formule delle dediche votive nella Grecia arcaica* (*MemLinc* 19; Rome, 1976). For recent references and comments on Greek terminology for statues: Pekáry, "Statuen" 727–744.

[57] P.Oxy. 2619 fr. 1 (=1 + 47); text reconstituted from Barrett's join in D. Page, ed., *Supplementum Lyricis Graecis* (Oxford, 1974) 25–26, S 88. The papyrus is dated A.D. II or III. The fragment mentions Trojans hurrying up to the acropolis, to the temple. The lines concerning the image are heavily restored (fr. 1, col. ii, lines 10–11):

ἁγνὸν ἄ[γαλ]μα [..].. αὐτεῖ καται-
[cχ]ύνωμε[ν ἀ]εικ[ελί]ως

The pure *agalma* . . . here we
dishonor shamefully.

[58] P.Oxy. 2303 (*POxy* 21 [1951] 84–87; A.D. I) fr. 1 (a): E. Lobel and D. Page, eds., *Poetarum Lesbiorum Fragmenta* (Oxford, 1955) 233 no. 298, fr. Q 1; Page, *Sappho and Alcaeus* 283–285, fr. Q 1. Page restores line 7 [σέμνωι] . . . ἀγάλματι, "the holy image." W. Barner, *Neuere Alkaios-Papyri aus Oxyrhynchos* (Hildesheim, 1967) 188, 192–193 *ad loc.*, supplies αλλ[ως]. For material related to Alc. fr. 298: H. Lloyd-Jones, rev. *POxy* 29, *CR* 15 (1965) 72, on a supplement from a Cologne papyrus, and for a join of frr. 84 and 108 of P.Oxy. 2506 (A.D. II) that yields "Kassandra" and "*agalma*"; the text seems to treat a series of individual biographical subjects (see also J.A. Davison, rev. *POxy* 29, *JHS* 85 [1965] 197).

[59] *Andrias*: *Pyth.* 5.40; *cf.* ἀνδριαντοποιός (maker of *andriantes*, who seems also to make *agalmata*), *Nem.* 5.1. *Cf.* the μονόδροπον φύτον: *Pyth.* 5.42.

[60] *Supra* p. 9 n. 3.

expected and by its meaning when it does occur. The word scarcely appears in Attic tragedy, where images of various kinds are mentioned fairly often. Aeschylus does not use it at all. In the passage in the *Seven Against Thebes* in which the chorus clings suppliant to the city gods, the statues are called *agalmata* (*Sept.* 258–265), and once in the *Eumenides* the *theōn agalmata* (statues of the gods) are mentioned in a general way (*Eum.* 55). Aeschylus' more usual word for statues of gods, however, is *bretas*, whether he refers to such images in general or to specific ones.[61]

It is often said that *bretas* is the tragic or poetic equivalent of *xoanon*.[62] Certainly it is true that *bretas* and *agalma* are the words most frequently used in drama. Although for Euripides as well as Aeschylus an *agalma*

[61] In A. *Sept.* 239–241, the terrified chorus has fled for refuge to the acropolis with the *archaia brete* (211–212). These old *brete* are the *agalmata* of lines 258 and 265. *Cf.* Rose, "Images" 40, on cult statues: "We know the technical name for such a statue; it is *βρέτας*. . . . An ordinary statue, not necessarily an object of cult, is an *ἄγαλμα*. . . . " The chorus of the *Sept.* is much given to flinging itself before images (*brete daimonōn*, 95), and is criticized for it (*brete polissuchōn theōn*, 185). A. *Eum.* 55, the *theōn agalmata* before which the trappings of the Furies are unfit to appear, is the only occurrence of the word in that play; throughout it, the image of Athena is called *bretas*: *Eum.* 80, 242, 259, 409, 439, 446, and 1024. In *Pers.* 809 the Persian destruction of sanctuaries and images in general includes *brete*. In *Suppl.* 429, 463, and 885, the *brete* are looked to for help by the suppliants, who at one point threaten to hang themselves publicly from them, making a new and grisly sort of votive. See F.T. van Straten, "Did the Greeks kneel before their gods?" *BABesch* 49 (1974) 162 for A. *Sept.* 92 *etc.*, *ποτιπέσω* before *brete*, and other examples of kneeling at images. *Agalma* in Aeschylus most frequently means "ornament."

[62] *Bretas* is a non-Indo-European word of unknown origin. Attempts have been made to include it in the "prehellenic Indo-Europoean" language "Pelasgian," esp. by A.J. van Windekens, *Le Pélasgique* (Louvain, 1952) 83–84, but the suggestion has been refuted: see D.A. Hester, "'Pelasgian'," *Lingua* 13 (1964/65) 371. Its suggested connection with German *Brett*, "board," Sanskrit *bardhaka*, "shaving, carving," and Indo-European *bheredh-, "cut," is not valid. No certain attribution to any non-Indo-European language has been made: Chantraine, *Dictionnaire s.v.* *ξέω*, sees *xoanon* as equivalent to the "vieux mot *βρέτας*," which he suggests may be Dorian; see Benveniste, "Kolossos" 128–129 for the pre-Greek origin of the word. Aristophanes (*Eq.* 31, 32 + Sch.; *Lys.* 262), Euripides (see *infra*), and Aeschylus all use *bretas* for images of gods. For Sophocles: *POxy* 44 (1976) no. 3151 fr. 2.8, perhaps from the Αἴας Λοκρός, for the Trojan statue of Athena. H.J. Rose, *A Commentary on the Surviving Plays of Aeschylus* I (Amsterdam, 1958) 171 *ad Sept.* 98–99, on the meaning of *bretas* as "cult statue," questions the habit of commentators in assuming that it is a purely tragic word meaning a wooden image; *cf.* his comment on "cult statues" in "Images" (40) quoted *supra* p. 25 n. 61. Aeschylus' usage shows that even this distinction is not completely accurate. A. Henrichs, "Greek Maenadism from Olympias to Messalina," *HSCP* 82 (1978) 139 n. 55, offers a useful discussion of *bretas*; in calling it a "rare and mostly poetic term for any divine image," however, care should be taken in distinguishing prehellenistic from later usage: see the unusual dedication of a *bretas* in the second century A.D.: *IG*² VII, 118.7, *ζάθεον βρέτας τόδ'*; Palaeochori, Megara.

means some kind of ornament, either real or figurative, more frequently than it does a statue, Euripides also uses the word for statues in general and for individual images of gods. The dying Hippolytus, for example, will never again tend the *agalmata* of Artemis; the *agalma* of Thetis is seen to stare at the wicked Hermione. *Bretas* in Euripides usually means a visible image of a god—what is usually called a "cult image"—but there are exceptions. He uses the word once for the Trojan Horse, and three times gives reports that a βρέτας Διὸς τροπαίου has been raised immediately after a victory in battle.[63] Sophocles' few extant references to statues do not include *brete*; his images are *agalmata*. Thus, while in the fifth century *bretas* does (so far) appear restricted to poetry, to find in it a generally "tragic" equivalent of *xoanon* begs all questions and obscures the usage of both words, in poetry as well as prose. It is worth pointing out that Herodotus' prose is as free of *xoana* as of *brete*.

The absence of *xoanon* from the vocabulary of Herodotus is indeed striking. Herodotus is interested in statues and mentions many of them, using a variety of terms. *Agalma* is his usual word for statue. Three others may also be considered general words for statues; another seems to be reserved for reliefs of various kinds; and one more occurs only three times, once to mean a ghost.[64] It does not appear possible to distinguish

[63] *Agalma* in Euripides: a delight: *Supp.* 632, *IT* 273 (*cf.* S. *Ant.* 1115 *et al.*); a real piece of finery: *Or.* 1434, *El.* 871, 873, *Tr.* 1212, 1220 (of funeral finery); a picture: *Hel.* 262; cloud-image of Helen: *Hel.* 705, 1219 (for *agalma* in the *Helen*, see C. Segal, "The Two Worlds of Euripides' '*Helen*'," *TAPA* 102 [1971] 569 and n. 51); statues in an agora: *El.* 388; images of the gods: *Hipp.* 116 (Aphrodite), 1399 (Artemis), *Andr.* 115 (approached by suppliant), 246 (Thetis, watches Hermione). These are representative examples.

Bretas in Euripides: *Alc.* 974 (the harsh goddess *Ananke*, "Necessity," has no *brete*, no altars, no sacrifices—no visible trappings at all); *Tr.* 12 (the Trojan Horse; a variant reading is βάρος); *Heracl.* 936–937, *Ph.* 1250, 1473 (perhaps some kind of *ad hoc* trophies).

[64] J.E. Powell, *A Lexicon to Herodotus* (Cambridge, 1938; second ed. Hildesheim, 1960), gives at least six words that Herodotus uses for statues and images. *Agalma* appears 66 times, by far the most frequent of all the words. *Eikon* and *andrias* both occur thirteen times, *kolossos* twelve. Τύπος occurs ten times, and seems to be restricted to relief work of various kinds, including reliefs carved from living rock, and mummy cases. For *tupos*, see *supra* p. 22 n. 52. *Eidolon* appears only three times and does not fit completely comfortably among the other words. Once it means the ghost of Periander's wife Melissa (5.92), once a gold statue said to be the portrait of a baker dedicated at Delphi (1.51), and once the image carried in a procession in honor of a Spartan king killed in battle (6.58). The emphasis thus seems to be on the likeness of the image to the person it represents. *Cf.* A. fr. 276 (H. Lloyd-Jones in the Appendix to *Aeschylus* II [LCL, 1971]) lines 6–7: an *eidolon* is τὸ Δαιδάλου μίμημα· φωνῆς δεῖ μόνον (a likeness by Daedalus; it wants only speech); that is to say, it is a splendid work (in lines 11–12 it is paraded as καλλίγραπτον), something Daedalus could have made, even though it is the portrait of a satyr and thus so ugly that it would repel even the creature's own

significantly between the four general words, *agalma*, *eikon*, *andrias*, and *kolossos*, since Herodotus uses all them all except *kolossos* for images of men and gods both, and uses all four to refer to images of a variety of materials and sizes and formats. Statues that he explicitly reports as being made of wood, for example, are called *agalma*, *eikon*, and *kolossos*. As several scholars have noted, *kolossos* at this time does not mean a statue of great size, but its exact definition has not been firmly established.[65]

The connection of *xoanon* with the standard terminology for statues in the fifth century, then, does not seem close. The cry of the Taurian herdsmen (E. *IT* 1359) proves that it could be used of an image, but this is the only time in all extant tragedy that it has this meaning; it does not appear at all in prose. The explanation that *bretas* is the more suitable tragic equivalent of *xoanon* does not work; *bretas* and *agalma*, a word for which no poetic coloring can be argued, appear to be equivalent when *agalma* is

---

mother. Lloyd-Jones (543) suggests that here portraiture is considered to be something new; but the point may simply be that these are theatrical masks, which could not be considered to be portraits except in the fantastic stage-world of a satyr-play. See now G. Ferrari, "Eye-Cup," *RA* 1986.1, 19–20. *Cf.* *μορμολυκεῖον*: *EtMag* 590.52 *s.v.*; W. Miller, *Daedalus and* Thespis I (New York, 1929) 131 n. 7. For *eikon* as a word for images of both human beings and gods, and among the terms connoting some kind of "animation": Benveniste, "Kolossos" 132–133. The number of occurrences of Herodotus' words may be somewhat misleading, since in long discussions he repeats words several times; *e.g.*, six of the appearances of *kolossos* are in two short sections (2.130–131; 2.143).

[65] Wooden statues in Herodotus: *agalma*, 5.85; *eikon*, 2.182; *kolossos*, 2.130, 2.143. For *kolossos*: recent discussion and references in Ridgway, *Archaic* 23–24 and 40, note for p. 23. She cites among others G. Roux, "Qu'est-ce qu'un *κολοσσός*?" *REA* 62 (1960) 5–40, who argues that the word means a statue with its legs placed tightly together, thus resembling a pillar in shape, like primitive, hieratic cult images (for which Roux, 16–17). Roux asserts (10) that Herodotus uses the word only in Book 2 for Egyptian pieces ("Il est exact, que le mot apparaît chez Hérodote seulement dans le livre II, et appliqué aux seules statues de l'Égypte—mais non à toutes.") However, Herodotus 4.152 notes three bronze *kolossoi*, kneeling figures that support a large bronze vessel: *καὶ ἀνέθηκαν ἐς τὸ Ἥραιον, ὑποστήσαντες αὐτῷ τρεῖς χαλκέους κολοσσοὺς ἑπταπήχεας τοῖσι γούνασι ἐρηρεισμένους* . . . (and they [the Samians, who made it] dedicated it in the Heraion, placing under it three bronze *kolossoi*, seven cubits tall, supported on their knees [*i.e.*, kneeling]). Neither Roux's typological definition (followed also by J. Servais, "Le 'colosse' des Cypsélides," *AntCl* 34 [1965] 144–174) nor Benveniste's meaning, emphasizing the aspect of the *kolossos* as the "double" of a living person ("Kolossos" 119–120) seems to be completely satisfactory; Herodotus, after all, has stone *kolossoi* that are architectural members (2.149; 2.153). See also J. Ducat, "Fonctions de la statue dans la Grèce archaïque: *Kouros* et *kolossos*," *BCH* 100 (1976) 246–251.

P. Karakatsanis, *Studien zu archaischen Kolossalwerken* (Europäischen Hochschulschriften ser. XXXVIII, vol. 9; Frankfurt am Main, Bern, and New York, 1986) appeared too late for me to take into account the discussions of the meaning of *kolossos* and of the origins of monumental sculpture.

used to mean a statue. There is much room for improvement in the understanding of Greek terminology for statues, but the meaning of *xoanon* can perhaps be clarified by working in another direction.

Xoanon, when it does appear, is applied to a variety of objects. Sophocles uses *xoana* to evoke (rather than denote) musical instruments. Euripides calls the Trojan Horse a *xoanon*, and uses *xoana* in the *Ion* and the *Trojan Women* for decorative work of which the nature is unclear. The plural form *xoana*, especially, seems best explained by considering the word a substantive adjective of which the meaning is closely tied to the quality of the hypothetical "*xoanos*," and not yet restricted to denoting one kind of object, as it is later. It also seems possible that the plural form may carry connotations of its own.

The quality in question seems, in its turn, closely tied to the process described by the parent verb *xeo*. Etymologically, neither *xeo* nor *xoanon* is restricted to any particular material. *Xeo* seems to refer not simply to a process of rough hewing, but also to smoothing and polishing—far higher stages of working. In Homer, *xeo* is associated with luxurious work, as in the description of Priam's *περικαλλὲς δόμος*, a "very beautiful" structure with fifty *thalamoi* of *xestoios* stone.[66] *Xeo* is thus connected with fine work, intricate of process and accomplished of workmanship, and *xoanon* seems to carry on this association.[67] Certainly a high level of luxurious craftsmanship appears to stand behind all the fifth-century *xoana* of which any idea can be had from the texts. Euripides' Trojan Horse is decked with gold, assembled so as to be large enough to conceal warriors; this is cunning workmanship in every sense.[68] The *tupoi* also incorporate gold. If archaeological comparisons are of any use, the *xoana* of the altar of the *Ion* could

[66] *Il.* 6.242–244: *ʼαλλʼ ὅτε δὴ Πριάμοιο δόμον περικαλλέʼ ἵκανεν,/ ξεστῇς αἰθούσῃσι τετυγμένον—αὐτὰρ ἐν αὐτῷ / πεντήκοντʼ ἔνεσαν θάλαμοι ξεστοῖο λίθοιο* . . . (But when he was now come to the very beautiful palace of Priam, adorned with polished colonnades—and in it were fifty chambers of polished stone; tr. adapted from A.T. Murray [LCL, 1928]). Note also the formulaic action *παρὰ δὲ ξεστὴν ἐτάνυσσε τράπεζαν* (she drew before him a polished table) of *Od.* 1.138; 7.174. See also Gross, "*Xoanon*" 2140, and H. Plommer, "'Shadowy Megara'," *JHS* 97 (1977) 81.

[67] This point is made strongly by Poulsen, "Typenbildung" 189–190, who sees in *xoanon* a term of praise, and by Picard, *Man.* I, 87 n. 1: "The word derives from Indo-European *ξέω*, to scrape, to polish, and accordingly applies to works of an already perfected art, to *ἔργα εὔξοα* (well-carved works), in contradistinction to the *ἄξοος σανίς* (uncarved plank). It is above all technical. . . . " Price, *Rituals* 176, notes that the "common characteristic" of *xoanon* is "its polished surface."

[68] For the Trojan Horse in art: J. Allen, "A *Tabula Iliaca* from Gandhara," *JHS* 66 (1946) 21–23; B.A. Sparkes, "The Trojan Horse in Classical Art," *Greece and Rome* 18 (1971) 54–70;

also have been elaborate, and Sophocles' musical *xoana* might have resembled the intricately carved ivory instruments preserved from Ionian sites.[69] These *xoana* all suggest intricate workmanship involving a variety of materials, including precious ones. The Taurian Artemis should be imagined in this context.[70]

One aspect of this lavish and highly accomplished craftsmanship is especially suggestive. The *xoana* of the fifth century are often connected with exotic places, specifically the East. Sophocles' *xoana* appear together with *magadides*, Persian instruments with a Persian name, in the context of a play which itself is characterized by exoticism. Both the subject of the *Thamyras* and the exotic vocabulary in it have been used to date its composition.[71] The *tupoi* of the *Trojan Women* are lamented along with Phrygian *selanai* in the context of the Trojan destruction. The Taurian Artemis is the barbarian image *par excellence*. The exotic connections explicit in the texts are reinforced by the possible archaeological parallels. The intricate ivory lyres from East Greece give vivid testimony to preclassical Eastern luxury production. The sixth-century B.C. chryselephantine statues discovered at Delphi display in statuary the kind of workmanship that *xoana* seem to suggest; these too are Ionian works.[72]

60–61 for the two bronze Horses of the late fifth century, Strongylion's on the Athenian Acropolis, and the Argive dedication at Delphi for the battle of Thyrea (Frazer, *Pausanias* V, 265 *ad* 10.9.12 for the connection with the raid of 414 B.C. mentioned by Thuc. 6.95, rather than the sixth-century episode). There seems to have been interest in the motif of the Horse in the later fifth century.

[69] For carved ivory parts of musical instruments, see, *e.g.*, the ivory youth from Samos, an elaborately carved and once inlaid arm of a lyre, and an ivory female figure, also from a lyre (Berlin 1964.36), in Boardman, *Archaic* 17, figs. 54, 53; both are dated to the late seventh century B.C., and the Berlin piece has stylistic similarities to Ephesian work.

[70] It is not known whether Euripides had an actual image in mind for his *Iphigeneia*, for instance, the one at Brauron that Pausanias mentions. Vase-paintings that are thought to show scenes from the play are not consistent in the rendering of the image, an indication that the painters were not tied to a standard representation: Trendall and Webster, *Illustrations* 91–94; the statue is not even always shown in an archaizing style. See Lacroix, *Reproductions* 132–135 for the numismatic evidence for this image, which "relates more to the domain of mythology than that of art history" (132); 135 for the tendency of artists of Taurian Chersonese to show the Taurian Artemis in a form similar to that given to the Palladion.

[71] *Supra* p. 16 and n. 32.

[72] Chryselephantine statues, Delphi Museum: P. Amandry, "Rapport préliminaire sur les statues chryséléphantines de Delphes," *BCH* 63 (1939) 86–119, pls. 19–42; E. Vanderpool, "Delphi," *Archaeology* 2 (1949) 66–68; B. Petrakos, *Delphi* (Clio Editions, 1977) 45–46, figs. 26, 27, 30, 33; Boardman, *Archaic* 77, fig. 127; U. Sinn, "Ein Elfenbeinkopf aus dem Heraion von Samos," *AM* 97 (1982) 35–55.

It is tempting to wonder whether *xoanon* and *xoana* might connote such lavish Eastern workmanship. This suggestion would be especially appealing in the case of the Taurian Artemis, an image which may have exemplified exotic Eastern splendor. Certainly luxury and exoticism feature prominently in fifth-century Greek ideas of the East, and it does not seem impossible that *xoanon* is related to such notions.[73]

Two aspects of the usage of *xoanon* need explanation—the modest but definite efflorescence of the word at the end of the fifth century, and the change in its meaning between the time of Sophocles and the fourth century, when it is applied without question to images of gods, a usage that appears only once in Euripides. The appearances of *xoanon* are in fact concentrated in Euripides, and can be accurately dated at the end of the fifth century: the *Trojan Women* was produced in 415, the *Iphigeneia* shortly before the *Helen* of 412, and the *Ion* shortly after.[74] Certainly *xoanon* in the sense of statues is a latecomer to the fifth century. One might wonder whether some specific event lies behind both the increase in the use of the word and the shift in its meaning.

Something that comes immediately to mind is the proliferation of major temple-statue projects in the later part of the fifth century, of which Pheidias' Athena Parthenos and Olympian Zeus are the most famous. Ridgway has recently stressed the singularity of this new genre of huge images in precious materials, together with the existence of chryselephantine statues in the Archaic Greek East. She points out too the propagandistic nature of the Parthenos project and the role of the great statues as an expression of the rivalry between *poleis* that is so strong a feature of Greek political life.[75] There is a good chance, moreover, that these grandiose Greek temple statues also reflect the Greek preoccupation with the East—specifically Persia—that seems to underlie the vast display projects of Pericles' refitting of the Athenian Acropolis. It should be noted that since Archaic times the East—as well as Egypt—had done its share to provide mainland Greece with models of huge enterprises. The vast Olympieum

[73] For the old Greek association of luxury with the Orient: C.G. Starr, "Greeks and Persians in the Fourth Century B.C.," *Iranica Antiqua* 11 (1975) 58–59; see also D.F. Graf, "Medism: the Origin and Significance of the Term," *JHS* 104 (1984) 15–30, *passim*. One thinks of modern adventure stories about exotic idols of the Far East—mysterious images that often incorporate jewels of immense size and value, and not infrequently inflict curses on those who defile them. It is tempting to see Orestes' theft of the Taurian Artemis as the forerunner of such tales.

[74] Chronology of Euripides: *OCD*² *s.v.* Euripides; T.B.L. Webster, *The Tragedies of Euripides* (London, 1967) 2–5 for chronological table and summary of metrical vs. attested dates.

[75] Ridgway, *Fifth Century* 10–11, 161.

begun by the Pisistratids, for example, is recognized as a mainland Greek answer to the temples of the East. Dinsmoor has emphasized the connection between this colossal undertaking and the regime that initiated it, remarking that "work was stopped upon the dissolution of the tyranny, not to be resumed until an Oriental despot more than three centuries later adopted the project. . . ."[76] The picture becomes more complex, however, when it is recognized that Athenian attitudes (at least) toward Oriental despotism were mixed. M.C. Root has recently argued that, in the decoration of its frieze, the Parthenon itself emulates the Persian palace at Persepolis. She sees the project as the democratic answer to Eastern imperial magnificence, a propagandistic enterprise of which both scope and content respond to the fifth century Athenian conception of empire as defined—to a great extent for the good—by Persia.[77] The Persian emperors served as *exempla* of wise and virtuous rulers and not simply as models of unjust tyrants, and were the administrators of a system of government that seemed in many ways admirable. The huge and elaborate images of the Greek gods that begin to appear in the later fifth century might also be part of this imperial enterprise. The models for the Greek answers to Persian imperial grandeur need not always have been actual examples of Persian art, either those seen in the Persian homeland or those, like the tent of Xerxes, that were captured and displayed in Greece, but might instead have been East Greek objects that also exemplified the luxury of the East. Such sumptuous work, it should be remembered, is often small in scale, like the ivory lyres; even the chryselephantine statues from Delphi are no larger than life-size. The immense size of the later fifth-century works might well have been an attempt to match an idea of oriental grandeur—the huge Parthenon requiring a huge image, a statue that would bring Greek practice up to imperial scale and quality.

It is worth speculating whether *xoanon*, connected with exotic luxury, might have been transferred to the context of divine images because of the technique of the late fifth-century images. Certainly at this time *xoanon* is associated not with subject but with process—with the artistic technique of objects, that is to say, and not with their identity. Intricate and luxurious work, with an Eastern cast of opulence, begins the career of *xoanon*; it might logically have migrated to the circle of intricate and luxurious divine statuary on a grand scale. This secondary association with images of gods would also account for the presence of *xoanon* in religious contexts, which

[76] Dinsmoor, *Architecture*³ 91.

[77] M.C. Root, "The Parthenon Frieze and the Apadana Reliefs at Persepolis: Reassessing a Programmatic Relationship," *AJA* 89 (1985) 103–120. I am grateful to Margaret Root for discussing points of her arguments with me.

is not attested in Sophocles. The Eastern connection is a possible explanation for the shift, which seems to have begun before the end of the fifth century. When *xoanon* appears next, in Xenophon's *Anabasis* of the 370s, it is applied to a copy of the statue of Artemis—of Ephesus.[78]

[78] There are two *xoana* that may be mentioned as possible examples of the word in the late fifth century, but neither is at all secure. *Xoanon* has not been attested in Aristophanes, but an emendation that has received favorable comment would replace the *παραξόνια* of *Ran.* 819 with *παραξόανα*. The emendation was proposed by van Herwerden; for his comments, with references and discussion by V. Coulon, see the latter's "Notes critiques et exégetiques sur divers passages controversés d'Aristophane," *REG* 66 (1953) 47–48. The emendation was also suggested by Wilamowitz; for the significance of this proposed example of *ξοανός*, see Latte, "Wortforschung" (*supra* p. 9 n. 3) 36. Kock preferred to see *xeo* rather than *ἄξων* as the stem of *paraxonia*. W.B. Stanford, ed., *Aristophanes. The Frogs* (London, 1958) *ad* lines 818–821, suggests *παραξονίων*.

Xoanon appears in Apollodorus 3.14.6 [23]. Jacoby (*FGrH* III B Suppl. 397–398 *ad* 328 F 94) wishes to see the late fourth-century B.C. Athenian Philochorus as the source of this information, since he (F 8, F 9) makes Erichthonius the founder of the Panathenaia. But *cf.* p. 275 *ad* F 8–10: "F 8/9 do not absolutely prove that Ph. followed the earlier tradition of the *Atthides* which regarded Erichthonios, the (foster)son of the goddess, as the founder of the Panathenaia. . . ." It does not seem impossible that some late fifth-century work was Apollodorus' (ultimate) source. In any case, the arguments against attributing the word *xoanon* to the source rather than the compiler hold good.

3. *Xoanon* in the Fourth Century B.C.

There is little secure evidence for *xoanon* in the fourth century. The word is attested certainly in the work of only two authors. Four other examples are plagued by the familiar difficulty of determining the origin of vocabulary in summaries of lost texts.

The *xoanon* of Xenophon (*Anabasis* 5.3.12) **[369]** has already been mentioned in the context of the fifth-century meaning of the word. It refers to the cypress-wood replica of the statue of Artemis of Ephesus that Xenophon placed in his own sanctuary of Artemis at Scillus. The word thus appears to have emerged in the fourth century carrying the comparatively new meaning denoting images of gods while retaining a hint of the old connotations of eastern splendor. The passage in question was probably written sometime in the 370s, perhaps around 377, or perhaps as late as 370.[79] Whatever the case, it can be said that by 370 *xoanon* seems firmly established as a term for statues of gods; from this point it begins a new series of changes of meanings within this definition. It cannot, however, be said positively on the basis of this passage that the association of *xoanon* with wooden images in particular, as attested later in authors like Pausanias, has already begun. The word is sufficiently explained by the comparisons with fifth-century examples, and caution is needed in suggesting additional connotations.

The second fourth-century author with whom *xoanon* can be surely associated is Theopompus. The word appears in Ammonius' *Lexicon*, a compilation based ultimately on a work of the first or second century A.D.[80] The entry is one of the few attributions of *xoanon* to a lost text that inspires confidence, since the *Lexicon* concerns itself exclusively with vocabulary. Under ἱερά (241 Nickau) **[6]** is given a list of objects considered to be "sacred things." Ammonius says that *xoana* are mentioned by Theopompus in the twenty-sixth book. This means the twenty-sixth book of the *Philippica*, which seems to have treated the pillaging of Delphi by Philo in 347/6 B.C.

[79] The date of the sections of the *Anabasis* after 5.3.6 is not certain. *OCD*² *s.v.* Xenophon prefers c. 377. C.L. Brownson, tr., *Xenophon Hellenica . . . Anabasis, Books I–III* (LCL, 1921) 235, suggests that 5.3.7–13 was "probably composed as late as 370 B.C."

[80] K. Nickau, ed., *Ammonii qui dicitur liber ad adfinum vocabulorum differentia* (Leipzig, 1966) XI–LXXII. Ammonius, a figure of the late fourth century A.D., gives an abridged version of a lexicon of the grammarian Herennius Philo of Byblos (Philo Byblius, A.D. I–II). Because other Byzantine lexica that preserve materials from the earlier work seem to be parallel to, rather than derivative from, Ammonius, it is possible that Ammonius depends on an epitome of Herennius. For Ammonius: Sandys, *History* I, 142, 355, 370. Some idea of the complexity of the questions surrounding the work can be quickly gained from comments on Nickau's edition: P. Chantraine, *RPh* 42 (1968) 164–165; M.G. Bonanno, *Gnomon* 42 (1970) 752–756.

Theopompus may have used the word as Xenophon did, but there is no way to be certain on the basis of the slender evidence of the citation. Ammonius or his source may have included *xoana* among *hiera* on the basis of his own understanding of the word, which may have differed from Theopompus'. It is possible, for instance, that by *xoana* Theopompus might have meant votive statues, a meaning that begins to be attested in the third century; the *anathemata* in a sanctuary would have belonged to the realm of the sacred rather than the secular. The date of the *Philippica* has not been established. It could not have been finished before 377 B.C., and is thought to have been begun in the late 350s or early 340s.[81]

Seven other *xoana* appear in uncertain quotations of fourth-century authors—Aristotle, three historians, and a philosopher. A section of the epitome of Aristotle's *Politeia* by Heraclides Lembus, a writer of the mid-second century B.C., mentions a *xoanon* of Artemis [**138**]. The episode is the Molossian desecration of the Cephallenian shrine of Artemis; the image casts off a golden crown made to replace the one removed by the invaders. Because the story has close links with Callimachus' accounts of the image of the Leucadian Artemis, a discussion of this *xoanon* is best undertaken together with an examination of the related passage in the *Aetia*. For now, it can be said that although Heraclides seems to have been a slavish condenser, the history of his text does not inspire the greatest confidence. There appears to have been room for considerable alteration until late in the manuscript transmission, and without the actual text of Aristotle, the presence of the word in the *Politeia* cannot be guaranteed.[82]

Xoanon may or may not have been used by three historians of the fourth to third centuries. A long scholium to Euripides' *Hippolytus* 73 [**87**] lists explanations of the "plaited crown" or "wreath" offered to Artemis. *Xoanon* appears three times, once in the introductory gloss, and twice in the body of the discussion. The scholiast explains that some previous commentators favored an allegorical interpretation, seeing a hymn offered to the goddess rather than a crown to her statue. He cites Philochorus twice,

[81] For Theopompus of Chios: *FGrH* 115. For the date of the *Philippica*: W.R. Connor, *Theopompus and Fifth-Century Athens* (Washington, D.C., 1968) 4–5; 96 for F 159. For the plundering of Delphi, *cf.* D.S. 16.56.

[82] Heraclides Lembus, *Excerpta politiarum* 45 [**138**]. M.R. Dilts, ed., tr., *Heraclidis Lembi Excerpta Politiarum* (Greek, Roman and Byzantine Monographs 5; Durham, 1971). Substantially the same text is given by F.G. Schneidewin, ed., *Heraclidis Politiarum quae extant* (Göttingen, 1847) XVII, who brackets the last sentence. I owe this reference to D. Birge. For the connection of this text with *Dieg.* Call. *Aet.* fr. 31 B and the emendation of *θυσίαν* to *θυείαν*: *infra* pp. 50–52. For the *xoana* in Joannes Philoponus' commentary on *De anima* 1.3, 406 b 11 [**153**]: *infra* pp. 165–166. For the *xoanon* in D.L. 1.6 [**64**], a passage close to references (1.8) to works of Aristotle: *infra* p. 155. See Dilts 8 for Heraclides' carelessness.

the first time in a long passage mentioning Artemis in Agrai and interpreting Hippolytus' speech; *xoanon* is not mentioned here. The second citation is shorter: "But Philochorus says that he offers a plaited wreath to the *xoanon*, but a hymn to the goddess." The sentence sounds much more like a summary than a quotation. Jacoby suggests that Philochorus is named while other commentators are not because the scholiast agreed with him. This explanation is plausible, but does not establish the reliability of the text with respect to Philochorus' actual words. Because the shorter citation is so obviously a summary it seems certain that the *xoanon* there is the scholiast's own word. The gloss that begins the whole scholium is also the scholiast's contribution. Both the gloss and the second citation of Philochorus seem to depend on and to be derived from the first, longer citation of that author, which does not mention *xoanon*. Thus the two *xoana* appear to stem from the scholiast's own paraphrases and explanations. In general, it seems doubtful that much of Philochorus himself survives in the scholium. *Xoanon* appears a third time, in an alternative explanation (ἄλλως) in which the scholiast, in his own voice, continues to worry the question of the *plekton*. That *xoanon* is part of his own vocabulary is clear, and it becomes easier to see how, in the preceding passages, the scholiast might have imposed the word on Philochorus, so to speak, rather than deriving it from him.[83]

Clement of Alexandria cites the *Argolica* of Demetrius on the subject of a *xoanon* of Hera at Tiryns (*Protr.* 4.41 P.) **[44]**: Δημήτριος γὰρ ἐν δευτέρῳ τῶν Ἀργολικῶν τοῦ ἐν Τίρυνθι τῆς Ἥρας ξοάνου καὶ τὴν ὕλην ὄγχνην καὶ τὸν ποιητὴν Ἄργον ἀναγράφει. (Demetrius in his second book of *Argolic History*, speaking of the *xoanon* of Hera in Tiryns, records both its material, pear-tree wood, and its maker, Argus.) Jacoby identifies Clement's Demetrius not with Demetrius of Troezen, but instead with Damon of Argos, who also wrote an *Argolica*. Whoever the source, he appears to have

[83] Sch. E. *Hipp.* 73 [87]: W. Dindorf, ed., *Scholia Graeca in Euripidis Tragoedias* I (Oxford, 1863) 84–86 *ad loc.*; *FGrH* 328 F 188. Jacoby's text is much emended. He accepts Schwartz's τῷ μελιλώτῳ (a kind of clover) for τῷ μὲν λόγῳ, thus dissociating Philochorus from the paraphrase of Hippolytus' speech. He believes that both citations to Philochorus are true, but that the first is out of place, and that the two need not have come from the same work. The first he assigns tentatively to an excursus in the *Atthis* on Agrai, the second, to a special study of such literary questions. This may go too far in trying to wring accuracy from the scholium, and does not take into sufficient account the nature of the note. It may be preferable to leave the text alone and have the scholiast's version of what Philochorus said about Artemis of Agrai, together with the paraphrase of the speech (which very likely may not in fact belong to Philochorus in vocabulary or sense), be the source for the second citation. This leaves the reader with less of Philochorus, but perhaps a better idea of the text of the note itself, which is repetitive and confused in the extreme. For Philochorus, who lived in the second half of the fourth and first half of the third century B.C.: *FGrH* 328.

provided the information that the image was made by Argus and made from pear-wood. The word *xoanon* itself, however, as in the case of other specific *xoana* mentioned by Clement, may not be that source's own term. Because Clement seems to give a summary rather than a quotation, this *xoanon* cannot be assumed to preserve a fourth-century usage, and its meaning should be established by examining its content in Clement. It should be noted that references to this image of Hera present special difficulties, since the traditions surrounding the Hera of Argos are complex, and outright propaganda, as well as a variety of tendentious conceptions of the legendary past, colors the several versions of the founding of the cult and the transfer of the image from Tiryns to Argos. The same questions of propaganda and biased antiquarianism surround another *xoanon* that is associated with a historian. Clement, again in *Protrepticus* 4.41 P. [**44**], mentions the *xoanon* of the Samian Hera, attributing his information to the *Samiaca* of Olympichus. As always in Clement's citations, the vocabulary is likely to be his own, and there is no assurance that *xoanon* was used by Olympichus, who may belong either to the fourth or the third century B.C.[84]

The last *xoanon* with any claim to being associated with a fourth-century author appears in Strabo 13.1.48 [**345**]. After describing the *xoanon* of Apollo Smintheus in Chryse, Strabo relates several of the stories told about the mice connected with the sanctuary. Among these is one told by Heraclides of Pontus, who "says that the mice which swarm around the *hieron* are regarded as holy, and that this is why the *xoanon* is represented standing on a mouse." In this summary of the various stories, Strabo has simply continued using his own term for the statue. Whether his source is Heraclides at first hand or at several removes, *xoanon* cannot be guaranteed to have belonged to that writer.[85]

Conclusions

The evidence for *xoanon* in the fourth century, then, is sparse. Only two authors can confidently be said to have used it: Xenophon and Theopompus.[86] Neither testimonium adds much precise information about the

[84] Demetrius, *Argolica* Book 2 [**44**]: *FHG* IV, 383; *FGrH* 304 F 1. For the traditions about the Argive image of Hera: *infra* p. 196 n. 53.

Olympichus [**44**]: *FHG* IV, 466; *FGrH* 537 F 1. Only a *terminus ante quem* of c. 200 B.C. exists for his date; Jacoby prefers the third to the fourth century.

[85] For Heraclides of Pontus (c. 390–c. 310 B.C.): Guthrie, *History* V, 483–490. For Strabo 13.1.48 [**345**]: *infra* p. 80 and n. 194.

[86] The *xoanon* of Philemon, a comic poet of the fourth or third century B.C., *ap.* Ath. 13.606 a [**35**], is an emendation by Bentley that contradicts all manuscripts and seems unnecessary: Philemon fr. 139 Kock. LSJ[9] *s.v.* ζῷον II remarks that it occurs mostly in the plural,

meaning of *xoanon*. Ammonius, attributing the word to Theopompus, includes it in a list of "sacred things," but there is a chance that this entry reflects the meaning familiar to the compiler, rather than the usage it had in Theopompus' now lost text. On the other hand, by the fourth century B.C. *xoanon* had probably become established in religious vocabulary, as its appearance in Xenophon suggests.[87] *Xoanon* in Xenophon can be understood in terms of the late fifth-century usage of the word, in which the connotations of intricate and exotic workmanship become associated with statues of gods. The *xoanon* that copies the Ephesian Artemis still sits comfortably in the context of high-quality craftsmanship, and even retains the association with Eastern work. It cannot be asserted that because Xenophon's *xoanon* of Artemis was made of wood the word at this time has become linked specifically with wooden statuary, as it is in some later authors. The connotations of *xoanon* seem to lean toward the religious rather than the secular, but the word does not seem to be restricted with respect to the form or material of the pieces to which it is applied. This flexibility in its meaning, which is largely only inferred for the fourth century, is demonstrated by its appearances in the third.

---

but the singular form seems acceptable here. For thoughts on the implications of *zoion* as applied to arts: R.L. Gordon, "The Real and the Imaginary: Production and Religion in the Graeco-Roman World," *Art History* 2 (1979) 9–10.

[87] Caution is needed in assessing the religious vocabulary of the fourth century. For example, Anaxandrides, a fourth-century comic poet, uses *bretas* for "blockhead": *AnecBekker* I.85.19 (fr. 11 Kock). *Cf. AnecBekker* I.223.4 for *bretas* defined as a Cyrenaean term for "blockhead." *Cf.* *ξύλινος νοῦς*, "stupid": Page, *Further Greek Epigrams* 18; and modern Greek *xoanon* as a blockhead, dolt, or klutz.

4. *Xoanon* in the Third Century B.C.

Xoanon begins to appear more frequently in the third century B.C., and in more reliable contexts. The word is also first attested epigraphically in this century.

A stone support for an offering table found on Delos bears a metrical dedicatory inscription that identifies its findspot as the sanctuary of Asclepius [**386**]. The text appeals to Asclepius to show his appreciation of the piety of Nikon, son of Damonoos, "who once gave this splendid *xoanon* and dedicated a token of your priesthood (*ξόανον τόδε τὸ κλυτὸν ὅς ποτε ὄπασσεν καὶ σφετέρας θῆκεν σᾶμα ἱεραπολίας*)." The fragments of the table were found in and just outside a small building near the temple of Asclepius. *Xoanon* seems not to refer to the table itself, which may be the *sama*. In view of the association of the word with images, established in the late fifth century B.C., and the meaning it has in third-century literary texts, the *xoanon* is almost certainly a statue of some kind. Presumably table and statue were installed in close proximity, but the text is not conclusive on this point. Nor does it yield much information about the appearance of the *xoanon*. Since the piece is called *kluton*, "splendid," it must have made a good showing among the surrounding dedications. In this way it continues the fifth-century association of the word with luxurious craftsmanship. Nikon is also known epigraphically as the proposer of two resolutions, and thus his monument can be dated to the first twenty years of the third century. The inscription demonstrates the use of *xoanon* in a non-literary text, and its application to a splendid dedication in a sanctuary.[88]

Xoanon appears securely in the work of three epigrammatists of the third century: Anyte of Tegea, Moero of Byzantium, and Leonidas of Tarentum. These authors all use *xoanon* for images of divinities, but with markedly different associations.

The *xoanon* of Anyte (*AnthPal* 9.144) [**20**] is an image of Cypris (Aphrodite) that is *liparon*. It is not clear whether *liparos* is meant literally, "shining with oil," or figuratively. If the former, it suggests that a statue which could be oiled—perhaps a wooden one—is meant.[89] *Liparos* does,

[88] Delos Inv. A 4202 [**386**]: *BCH* 50 (1926) 571; *Délos* 11, 125–126, n. 1; the identification as a throne is rejected, and the fragments are drawn and identified as a table in *Délos* 20, 105–107; *BullEpig* 1952, no. 142; Bruneau, *Cultes* 359; Marcadé, *Musée Délos* 91–92. For offering tables: D.H. Gill, "The Classical Greek Cult Table," summary of Diss. Harvard University, *HSCP* 70 (1965) 265–269; and "Trapezomata: A Neglected Aspect of Greek Sacrifice," *HTR* 67 (1974) 117–137. Gill's dissertation does not seem to discuss the table from Delos; I thank T.N. Howe for checking it for me.

[89] For Anyte of Tegea: D. Geoghean, *Anyte. The Epigrams* (Rome, 1979); Gow and Page, *Anthology* II, 89–91; 90 for a date c. 300 B.C.; 99 for *AnthPal* 9.144 [**20**], where *xoanon* "should properly mean a wooden statue and there is no reason to doubt that meaning here."

however, appear in other contexts as an epithet that is highly evocative, but not literal.[90] While it is possible that Anyte's *liparon xoanon* belongs with the statues oiled for symbolic or practical reasons, in the context of the poem, in which the sea trembles at beholding the image, a figurative meaning seems preferable.[91] A comparison can perhaps be drawn between this *liparos* image of Cypris and Callimachus' Muses, who stand "wearing fineries and shimmering tunics," ointment flowing always from their hair, and with "anointed hands" (*Aet.* I fr. 7.11–14) [**41**]. These lines seem to refer to statues on Paros; the Greek tendency not to distinguish between image and subject appears to be at work here, and may also be in Anyte's epigram.[92] *Liparos* should not automatically be taken to prove that Anyte's *xoanon* is wooden; it should rather be understood as a figurative epithet that links the image to rich and splendid workmanship, as *klutos* did the *xoanon* of Nikon.

Moero of Byzantium mentions *xoana* that similarly belong to the realm of fine craft (*AnthPal* 6.189) [**171**].[93] Cleonymus sets up *xoana* for the

---

Thus a literal meaning of *liparos* is implied. *Cf.* Theophr. *Char.* 16.5, "shining with oil," of oiled stones.

[90] *Cf.* Pindar's *liparos* cities, esp. Athens (fr. 92 Turyn, 76 Schroeder), of which Aristophanes says the epithet is more fitting for a sardine (*Ach.* 639–640); W.M. Calder, III, "Ulrich von Wilamowitz-Moellendorff's First Visit to the Akropolis," in L. Bonfante and H. von Heintze, eds., *In Memoriam Otto J. Brendel* (Mainz, 1976) 234, seems to relish the almost tangible greasiness of Pindar's epithet. For arguments against a literal meaning of *liparos* in these epithets: L. van Hook, "On the meaning of ΛΙΠΑΡΟΣ," in *Classical Studies Presented to Edward Capps* (Princeton, 1936) 343–346.

[91] For notes on oil and statues: Gow and Page, *Anthology* II, 99 *ad* XV; Pfeiffer, *Callimachus* I, 14–15 *ad Aet.* I fr. 7.12. *N.B.* the use of oils for the conservation of wooden statues (*e.g.*, Paus. 9.41.7; Vitruv. 2.9.13; and perhaps Artemid. *On.* 2.33). There seems too to be some degree of imitation of human practices. For the application of oils to the body and their connection with vitality: R.B. Onians, *The Origins of European Thought* (Cambridge, 1951) 188–192, 210–211. Although it should be remembered that oil had practical use in human maintenance (soap is first mentioned as a washing agent for the human body only in the second century A.D., by Galen; see R.J. Forbes, *Studies in Ancient Technology* III [Leiden, 1955] 181), the evidence for symbolic associations is strong. Ethnographic testimony exists for the anointing of statues with oil and grease, and in these examples there is a clear combination of practical and symbolic aspects: *e.g.*, the Punjabi practice of covering the household image of the goddess Durga every day with ghee: *The Times Literary Supplement* (London) 4032 (4 July 1980) 752 (modern practice); and the Teutonic custom of rubbing images with fat: *Hastings Encyclopaedia* X, 504 b §7.

[92] *Cf.* Linear B references to oil or unguent for robes: Pylos Fr. 1225; E.L. Bennett, Jr., *The Olive Oil Tablets of Pylos* (Salamanca, 1958) 55–56; Ventris and Chadwick, *Documents*² 482 *ad* 310; Bennett 44 (anointing, perhaps perfuming?).

[93] For Moero of Byzantium: Gow and Page, *Anthology* II, 413–414; 415 for *AnthPal* 6.189 [**171**] and doubt concerning the reading "Hamadryads." *Cf.* the *kalon xoanon* of *AnthPal* 16.249 [**15**], and the *perisson* (remarkable) *xoanon* of 9.601 [**13**].

Nymphs (ὃς τάδε καλά / εἵσαθ' ὑπαὶ πιτύων ὕμμι, Θεαί, ξόανα); they are placed under the pines, presumably outdoors in the open air, but they are *kala* nonetheless. The meaning of *kalos* here should not perhaps be pressed too vigorously in the direction of *klutos*; by itself it is far from conclusive. What argues for its association with the accomplished craftsmanship of other *xoana* is comparison with the epithet given to another group of *xoana*, also dedicated to the Nymphs, by Leonidas of Tarentum.[94] Leonidas (*AnthPal* 9.326) [**156**] has the wayfarer Aristocles dedicate his drinking cup to the Nymphs after being refreshed at what seems to be a sanctuary or spring. Aristocles apostrophizes the establishment enthusiastically, hailing the Νυμφέων ποιμενικὰ ξόανα, "rustic *xoana* of the Nymphs." This phrase is the first association of *xoanon* with anything but sophisticated craftsmanship; it marks a complete break with all that is *klutos*. There can be no clearer contrast between the accomplished and the rustic than what is demonstrated by the various *xoana* of the third century. A *xoanon* can now belong to either sphere. The word seems to have shed its connotations and come to mean an image that needs to be specially qualified before it can be visualized. Only the association with divinities and dedications, which seems to have been fixed only in the fourth century, is intact.

Probably the most interesting appearance of *xoanon* in the third century is in the fourth book of the *Argonautica* of Apollonius Rhodius [**27**].[95] The heroes are in mortal danger, for after a flood-tide has carried the Argo far up onto the desolate shore of Syrtis, near Libya, the receding waters have left the ship stranded amid a thin wash of foam. The helmsman Ancaeus assesses the hopelessness of the situation so cogently that the rest of the crew promptly surrender to despair. Apollonius describes them as they wander apathetically along the shore; it is as if they feel themselves already dead, for the poet compares them to men in a city awaiting some catastrophe who are like ἄψυχα εἴδωλα, "specters without souls." The simile is powerful and repays attention. Doom will overtake the city—whether by war, plague, or famine—but the phantom-like men simply wait passively. Despondency, not alarm, is the order of the day, apparently because the portents guarantee inevitable destruction: darkness at noon, bellowings from temples, and *xoana* sweating blood of their own accord.

Fränkel's discussion of the passage concentrates on showing how the simile in fact serves to underline the differences between the doomed groups; for example, divine fanfare heralds the destruction of the city,

[94] For Leonidas of Tarentum: Gow and Page, *Anthology* II, 307–309; 313–315 for *AnthPal* 9.326 [**156**], where the *poimenika* images are "presumably rough wooden figures carved by [herdsmen]."

[95] A.R. *Arg.* 4.1277–1289 [**27**]: H. Fraenkel, ed., *Apollonii Rhodii Argonautica* (Oxford, 1970).

while the famous heroes must die in utter oblivion.[96] The only real similarity between the victims is their apathy. *Apsycha eidola* seems to refer to components that are separated at death; the *psyche* has fled, and only an *eidolon* is left. The Greek terminology regarding such matters is complex, but it is probably safe to assume that the audience is meant to imagine rather sad, listless shades that preserve the outward appearance of the living, but are deprived of all animation, of all force of body or mind.[97] It is deep apathy indeed that can maintain itself in the midst of the uncanny sights and sounds of the city.

Fränkel notes that the simile is unusual and finds only a distant predecessor in a few lines from the *Iliad* (10.5–10) in which troubled Agamemnon cries out in his sleep in much the same way that Zeus produces sudden lightning. The comparison between the passages is indeed unsatisfying, and the sources of Apollonius' simile remain to be found.

Apollonius mentions three portents: *xoana* sweat blood of their own accord (*αὐτόματα*); bellowings (*μυκαί*) issue from *sekoi*; and night falls at noon. Portents from the world of nature have a long classical history, and the inclusion of an eclipse is not diagnostic.[98] Uncanny behavior of statues and odd events in sacred buildings find some comparisons in the fifth century and earlier.[99] Herodotus, for example, dismisses the story of the kneeling *agalmata* of Auxesia and Damia (5.82–86). In Euripides' *Iphigeneia in Tauris*, lines 1165–1167, Iphigeneia's story that the *bretas* of Artemis moved is a ruse to fool the not overbright barbarian king so that the Greek party can make its escape. The wording of the passage can be noted: Thoas asks whether the *bretas* moved *automaton*, of its own accord, or if the earth shook; Iphigeneia replies emphatically that it moved *automaton*, and adds craftily that its eyes closed, too. Surely, some purification is needed![100] It is possible that Apollonius' use of *automatos* reflects the Euripidean passage, but the word is certainly fully explicable within Apollonius' own usage.[101] It has already been seen that *xoanon* in the *Iphigeneia* holds a marginal

[96] H. Fränkel, *Noten zu dem Argonautika des Apollonius* (Munich, 1968) 591–592 *ad* 1280–1289.

[97] *Apsychos* is a *hapax* in the poem. In the other occurrence of *eidolon* in the *Argonautica*, 3.1004, the word is applied to the constellations (*οὐρανίοισιν εἰδώλοισιν*).

[98] For portents from the natural world: MacBain, *Prodigy passim*.

[99] The nodding of (the statue of) Athena in *Iliad* 6 may be noted in this connection, but the text emphasizes the will of the goddess, not the uncanny nature of the sign; no statue is even mentioned (*supra* pp. 23–24).

[100] ΙΦ.: *βρέτας τὸ τῆς θεοῦ πάλιν ἕδρας ἀπεστράφη*. ΘΟΑΣ: *αὐτόματον, ἤ νιν σεισμὸς ἔστρεψε χθονός*; ΙΦ.: *αὐτόματον· ὄψιν δ' ὀμμάτων ξυνήρμοσεν* (Iph.: The *bretas* of the goddess turned back from its place. Thoas: By itself, or did a shaking of the earth turn it? Iph.: By itself; and it closed its eyes).

[101] *Cf.* especially A.R. *Arg.* 1.871 and 4.41.

position at best. In sum, other sources should be sought for Apollonius' *xoana*.

The incidence of uncanny events connected with statues begins to increase in the fourth century B.C., as does the interest they provoke in both believers and sceptics. In the fourth century too begins a tradition of debunking such marvels: according to Theophrastus, Theopompus' Περὶ θαυμασία included an explanation for uncanny emissions from statues, and Cicero and Plutarch [**316**, **317**] later offered rational explanations for the phenomenon of statues that appeared to sweat blood.[102] It may be that such tales, which Plutarch says are told by "not a few" earlier writers [**316**], lie behind Apollonius' portents. It is possible, however, that a more specific group of omens can be associated with the passage: these are the omens concerning Alexander the Great.

Alexander's effect on statues seems to have been pronounced. Plutarch reports (*Alex.* 14.8–9 [**313**]) that the *xoanon* of Orpheus at Leibethra sweated when Alexander set off to the East. A version of the story is preserved in the late romance of Alexander in which the *agalma*/*xoanon* of Orpheus at Bebrycia sweated when the king looked at it [**150**, **151**]. Sweating statues appear again in connection with Alexander's destruction of Thebes in 335 B.C. Diodorus recounts at some length (17.10) [**60**] the dire portents that appeared before the event. Among other sinister signs are the following: when Alexander arrived in the city, the *andriantes* in the agora began to sweat profusely; the marsh at Onchestus emitted "a sound like a bellow" (μυκήματι παραπλήσιον φωνήν); and at the fountain Dirce there ran a ripple in the water that looked like blood (αἱματοειδῆ).[103]

The accounts of Alexander's exploits seem to have become more sensational as time passed, culminating in the improbable anecdotes of the *Historia Alexandri Magni*. It is nevertheless possible that Apollonius knew of such omens in some form. The three elements of uncanny statues, of blood, and of eerie bellowings appear in Apollonius' simile. The situation of Thebes in general, too, resembles but reverses that of the city in the simile. Diodorus' remarks introducing the omens are of interest: the rest of the Greeks pity the Thebans, but make no move to help them because the disaster they face is quite inevitable, and anyway self-inflicted. The Thebans maintain their courage, but find themselves at something of a loss over the sayings of the *manteis* and the *semeia* of the gods. To those who take an interest in portents, however, the signs are obviously bad. It is difficult to

[102] Theopompus, Περὶ θαυμασία, *ap.* Thphr. *Hist. Plant.* 5.9.8; Cic. *De div.* 2.27.58; Plut. *Cam.* 6 [**316**]; *Cor.* 38 [**317**].

[103] *Cf.* Luc. *SyrD* 10 [**160**] for sweating, oracular *xoana* and a cry (βοή) often heard from the *neos*.

decide which city is more depressing: Apollonius', filled with informed but hopeless shadows, or Thebes, where fools stand fast amid clear portents that they do not understand.

If Apollonius did have in mind the portents associated with Alexander, and especially those connected with the destruction of Thebes, accounts of them may suggest what Apollonius meant by *xoana*. According to the sources that are preserved, the portents involved a variety of statues. Two accounts emphasize images of Orpheus; their nature is not clarified by either of the late sources, because the word *xoanon* in both texts refers only generally to statues, as will be seen. Orpheus is, however, a mythological personage rather than a god. Diodorus specifically mentions the *andriantes* in the agora; these would seem to be images of human beings, or perhaps mythological personages, and again not statues of gods. If Apollonius had in mind portents involving a variety of statues, not simply those of gods or those in temples, his use of *xoanon* would fit well among the dedicated *xoana* attested in the third century. The connection of the simile to accounts of Alexander's portents is tenuous, however, and by no means answers the question of Apollonius' usage of *xoanon*. The sense of the passage, however, and the evidence for contemporary usage of the word suggest that his definition may have been fairly broad.

There are two additional points to keep in mind with respect to Apollonius' *xoana*: Alexandrian scholarship, and the location of Alexandria. The kind of academic and literary activity characteristic of Apollonius' circle virtually guarantees his having chosen his words for some definite reason—and certainly a reason more pressing than metrical convenience. *Xoanon* is an odd word to introduce into an epic; Homer does not use it, and it is unlikely to have appeared anywhere in the epic corpus. Apollonius would certainly have had his own ideas about its meaning, perhaps influenced by the kind of etymological researches that will be discussed later. It is also possible that his idea of *xoanon* in Greek literary tradition was influenced by its usage in his own time and milieu. Until this point, it has been possible to treat the evidence for *xoanon* as if it were essentially homogeneous; but in Hellenistic times, the testimonia begin to show signs of regional differences. There is some reason to think that the usage of *xoanon* in Egyptian or Egyptian-influenced contexts may reflect attitudes and practices different from those of mainland Greece and the areas within its immediate cultural sphere. Apollonius' apparently rather expansive understanding of *xoanon* may be the first hint of changes in the meaning of the word that have important implications in later times.

The last reasonably certain appearance of *xoanon* in the third century is in what Josephus says is a quotation *kata lexin*, *verbatim*, from the work of Manetho, an Egyptian who wrote in Greek during that century (*Ap.*

1.244; 1.249) [**155**]. Josephus' *Contra Apionem* is a systematic refutation of slanders against the Jews, one of which is Manetho's account of them as a horde of diseased Egyptian outcasts who invaded the kingdom of Amenophis. Josephus proves every detail of the story, beginning with the pharaoh himself, to be fictitious. The passage in question follows the imaginary Amenophis as he readies Egypt for the invasion of the outcasts. Among other precautions, he orders the priests to hide the *xoana* of the gods (*Ap.* 1.244). After he and his army retreat to Ethiopia, the invaders commit every kind of outrage, including (finding and) damaging the *xoana* (*Ap.* 1.249). Since Josephus assures his readers (*Ap.* 1.237) that he repeats Manetho word for word, it seems that these passages are secure evidence for *xoanon* used in the third century for images of gods, presumably temple images, that must be hidden from danger and that it is sacrilege to injure. Nevertheless it seems curious to find in the third century a meaning that does not become established until sometime in the second, and is in fact closer to Josephus' own usage than to any attested in the third century or earlier. The explanation of the appearance of the word may lie in the fact that Manetho is an Egyptian author who may have struggled with a Greek terminology unsuited to expressing Egyptian conceptions or categories of images. Josephus' assurance that the quotation is *kata lexin* does not, however, exclude the possibility of textual changes before his time; Josephus himself knew several versions of Manetho.[104]

Several *xoana* have dubious or unreliable associations with authors of the third century B.C. One is a figwood *xoanon* in the countryside, a herm, perhaps, or a figure of Priapus. It appears in an epigram from the *Anthology* (9.437) [**364**] of which the ascription to Theocritus is exceedingly doubtful. This *xoanon* is *artiglyphes*, probably "newly carved" and, so, likely a rustic production. It has bark but no ears, and whether it has the three legs granted by the codices or loses them all to the qualms of editors, it is a willing laborer for Aphrodite. Whatever the date of the poem, it continues the bucolic associations of *xoanon* first encountered in Leonidas.[105]

[104] For the difficulties in determining Manetho's identity and date, and a summary of the major work by Laqueur (*RE* 14.1 [1928] 1060–1101 *s.v.* Manethon) on the degrees of authenticity of the fragments: W.G. Waddell, tr., *Manetho* (LCL, 1940) vii–xx. *Infra* p. 105 n. 248 for Josephus and his sources.

[105] Theocritus *Ep.* 4 = *AnthPal* 9.437 [**364**]. A.S.F. Gow, ed., *Theocritus* (Cambridge, 1950) II, 347 *ad Id.* 17.136, calls *Ep.* 4 "of very doubtful authenticity"—a strong statement, especially in view of the generally low reputation of the epigrams attributed to Theocritus (II, 527). Gow notes that *artiglyphes* is a *hapax*. He prefers (II, 530) Jahn's ἀσκελές to the τρισκελές of the codices, believing that Priapus figures, like herms, are legless, and that the notion of the phallus counting as an extra leg is "grotesque" (Gow and Page, *Anthology* II, 536). Monuments noted in H. Herter, *De Priapo* (RGVV 23; Giessen, 1932) show that this immigrant from the Hellespont in the age of Alexander can have a complete body, unlike the semi-figural herm. *Triskeles* should be a joke, although the point of the *alla* would be lost.

Xoanon appears in doubtful connection with two more poets of the third century, Callimachus and Euphorion. For both it is a question of lost or fragmentary works, and the word can be securely attributed to neither.

The reference to a *xoanon* in Euphorion is the most straightforward of all the passages. Apollonius Rhodius describes at some length the manufacture and dedication by the Argonauts of an image of Rhea on Mount Dindymon (1.1117 ff.) [**25**]. The statue that Argos smooths out of a vine-stump (ἔξεσε δ' Ἄργος) is called *hieron bretas* (1.1119). The scholium to the passage [**26**] defines *bretas* and goes on to say that Euphorion, on the basis of this passage, says that the *xoanon* of the Mother of the Gods is made of vine wood because the grape-vine is sacred to Rhea (*βρέτας δὲ τὸ βροτῷ ἐοικός. καὶ Εὐφορίων δὲ ἐκ τούτου κινηθεὶς τὸ ξόανον τῆς μητρὸς τῶν θεῶν φησιν ἀμπέλινον εἶναι, διὰ τὸ τὴν ἄμπελον ἴσως ἱερὰν εἶναι τῆς* Ῥέας).[106] As in the case of similar bald extracts of facts from lost works, it is impossible to determine whether the scholiast has taken *xoanon* from the text of Euphorion or has chosen it himself. There are, however, several reasons for thinking that the word is the scholiast's own contribution.

The definition of *bretas* that begins the scholium gives the contrived etymology with *brotos*, "mortal," that appears over and over in ancient etymologica. In many cases this explanation of *bretas* occurs together with definitions of *xoanon*.[107] It is possible that the scholiast was influenced by such definitions to the extent that after glossing *bretas* he continued his note using a word that is frequently given as a synonym or near-synonym. On the other hand, *xoanon* might simply have been the word that came first to his mind when he began to summarize what Euphorion said about the statue of Rhea. *Xoanon* does not begin to be a standard term for statues of gods until sometime in the second century B.C., when its appearances increase in frequency. It is also a term that is clearly at home in scholia with precisely this meaning, reflecting this later popularity. The scholium to Apollonius should not, therefore, be taken as proof that *xoanon* appeared in the text of Euphorion.

Still less does the scholium provide conclusive evidence for the typological connotations of the word in the third century B.C. Because in later

[106] Sch. A.R. 1.1117–1119 [**26**]. For Wendel's *τὴνἄμπελον* read *τὴν ἄμπελον*, as in Wellauer and Keil. For the scholia on the *Argonautica* and editions of them: G.W. Mooney, ed., *The Argonautica of Apollonius Rhodius* (Dublin, 1912) 56–60; C. Wendel, ed., *Scholia in Apollonium Rhodium vetera* (Berlin, 1935) X–XXVI. For Euphorion: A. Meineke, *Analecta Alexandrina* (Berlin, 1843; repr. Hildesheim, 1964) 150–151, CXLVI, with references to the Ephesian Artemis and notes on some statue terminology. The date of Euphorion is not certain. The *OCD*[2] *s.v.* (2) notes that c. 275 B.C. has been challenged as too high a date for his birth.

[107] *Bretas*, being a non-Greek and apparently non-Indo-European word, cannot be so explained; nonetheless, the connection with *brotos* was standard: *infra* pp. 169–171. For *bretas*: *supra* p. 25 n. 62 and p. 37 n. 87.

authors like Plutarch and Pausanias the association of *xoanon* with wooden statues is securely established, there is a temptation to find in the scholium proof of such a meaning in Euphorion; similarly, one meaning given by Clement to *xoanon*—a crudely carved wooden pole (*Protr.* 4.40 P. [**44**])—would fit well with the image of Rhea, which Apollonius says was carved on the spot from a stump. The meanings attested in later times, however, cannot be directly assigned to Euphorion; it is only through the scholiast that Euphorion's *xoanon* is known, and there is every chance that the commentator's own conception of *xoanon* influenced his choice of a term for the image of Rhea. If it is assumed that the material of the image determined the choice of word, it is the scholiast and not Euphorion who seems to be responsible; for the scholium suggests that it was the iconographical significance of the grape-vine that interested Euphorion, and not the woody nature of the stump.

The scholium to Apollonius, then, is a poor witness for *xoanon* in the third century B.C. By itself it cannot guarantee that the word appeared in Euphorion. Nor can it, even granting the possibility that Euphorion used *xoanon*, contribute sure information about its meaning: there are no specific connotations that cannot be explained as the scholiast's own conceptions. Assuming that, as the note asserts, Euphorion was influenced by Apollonius' description of the making of the *bretas*, it is possible at most to place the hypothetical *xoanon* somewhere in the context of *xoana* as the group was extended by Leonidas of Tarentum to include rustic, as well as elaborate and fine, works. More than this is not certain; and so the meaning of Euphorion's *xoanon* is as obscure as its existence is questionable.

The association of *xoanon* with Callimachus raises questions that are considerably more complex. The word appears in connection with two fragmentary *Aetia*, one concerned with the Samian Hera, the other, with the Artemis of Leucas.

Four lines by Callimachus mentioning the early monuments of the Hera of Samos and the Athena of Lindos are preserved in a text of the fourth century A.D. In the *Praeparatio evangelica* (3.7.98 d–3.8.99 d) [**108**], Eusebius gives—he says *verbatim*—a section of work of Plutarch, perhaps to be identified as the treatise *De Daedalibus Plataeensibus*. Plutarch, in turn, quotes the fragment of Callimachus. The passage as a whole is an important document for the history of both the word *xoanon* and Greek ideas about the origin of statuary. Each of the three authors presents a distinctive view of the manufacture and form of early images, and the differences between their conceptions emerge clearly from the juxtaposition. A discussion of the entire passage is best postponed until the contributions of Plutarch and Eusebius can be seen in their contexts.[108]

[108] *Infra* pp. 133–137.

Garbled forms of *xoanon* occur in the first line of the Callimachean fragment as given by the codices, and the word can be confidently restored in an ancient commentary on the poem. If it could be shown that *xoanon* belongs in this work of Callimachus, the fragment would provide valuable evidence for the meaning of the word. The preserved lines contrast the image of Hera that was made by Scelmis with the monument of earlier times, which, "according to the old custom, [was] a plank not carved by chisels; for thus did they then set up the gods; and thus at Lindos Danaus placed the simple *hedos* of Athena." A *xoanon* in this context would be the crude, wooden, plank-like forerunner of sculpture often envisioned in archaeological scholarship. The passage, however, is not without difficulties.

The beginning of the first line of the fragment makes no sense in the form preserved in the codices.[109] The first words, *οὔπω Σκέλμιον ἔργον*—"not yet the work of Scelmis"—are clear, but they are followed by *εἰσοξόανα*, *εἰς ξόανα*, or *εἰς ξόανον*. None is intelligible. None can be anything but a corruption, and the first version seems to be a yet more garbled descendant of the second and third. The explanation for these corruptions probably lies in the text surrounding the fragment; both Plutarch and Eusebius mention *xoana*, and their discussions might well have inspired the attempt to insert a *xoanon*-like word. The accepted emendation suggested by Bentley, *ἐΰξοον*, "well-carved," is suitable in both form and sense, and is recognizable as the armature of the garbled supplements. Thus the fragment should begin, "not yet the well-carved work of Scelmis," and it is this well-carved work that is contrasted with the earlier uncarved monuments. There is no *xoanon*.[110]

Xoanon, does, however, seem to be rightly restored in a papyrus that preserves a commentary on this *Aetion* [**42**]. Although only the terminal *-νον* survives, it is almost beyond question that the passage recounts the history of the *xoanon* of Samian Hera.[111] The commentary belongs to the *Diegeseis*, which are summaries and descriptions of Callimachus' poems. The account it gives of the Samian image suggests a *xoanon* very close to the primitive wooden objects postulated as the earliest sculpture: the monument was at first little more than a wooden plank, because the art of sculpture did not yet exist; only later did it assume the form of a statue. This

[109] Call. *Aet.* IV fr. 100 *ap.* Eus. *PE* 3.8.1 [**108**]: Pfeiffer, *Callimachus* II, 104–105 for the text. The scholium to Paus. 7.4.4 on Smilis notes that ὁ δὲ Καλλίμαχος Σκέλμιν ἀντὶ Σμίλιδος φησι. Some editors (*e.g.*, Gifford) emend accordingly.

[110] Callimachus does call the earlier monument of Hera a *sanis*, "plank." This is also the word applied to the Hera by Clement (*Protr.* 4.40 P. [**44**]) in a passage based on the fifth-century B.C. writer Aëthlius.

[111] *Diegesis* to Call. *Aet.* IV fr. 100 [**42**], line 23; *το ξοα* is restored. Pfeiffer, *Callimachus* I, 104–105.

explanation places *xoanon* squarely at the point of transition from unworked object to art, at the very beginning of sculpture, and points the way to a more specific meaning of *xoanon* than is attested in any earlier source. It is not certain, however, that this evolutionary conception can actually be assigned to Callimachus, or even to his century.

The *Diegeseis*, as has been mentioned, summarize and describe the poems of Callimachus. Three sets of these commentaries exist, all known from papyri. The *Milan Diegesis*, from which the Samian *xoanon* comes, is a papyrus of the late first or early second century A.D.[112] It gives the name διηγήσεις, and is the best preserved of the three. It appears, however, actually to be a shorter and simpler version of a commentary perhaps represented by P.Oxy. 2263 and the "Florentine Scholia."[113] These are papyri of the late second or the third century A.D., but the date of the Milan papyrus, c. A.D. 100, gives the *terminus ante quem* for the kind of extended commentary which they preserve.[114]

The date of the commentary on which the three extant *Diegeseis* all seem to depend is uncertain. A papyrus of the second half of the second century B.C. preserves part of the *Aetia*, together with a commentary; this is the earliest known commentary on Callimachus, and appears to have been made shortly after his death.[115] The extant *Diegeseis*, however, are likely to depend on later scholarship.

As will be shown later in more detail, the *Diegesis* on the Samian *xoanon* goes considerably beyond being a simple summary, and seems to include explanatory material not directly attributable to Callimachus' poem.[116] It is immediately obvious, for example, that the precise historical detail is intrusive. There is a good chance that the word *xoanon* originated in the source of the commentary, or even in the commentary itself. Because the *Milan Diegesis* is itself an abridgment of a fuller commentary, and because it incorporates material that is unlikely to have come from Callimachus' poem, the restored *xoanon* cannot be proved to be earlier than the papyrus itself. *Xoanon* applied to the Samian Hera in the context of the earliest forms of sculpture would accord with the meanings of the word familiar in the first century A.D. The presence of the word in the *Diegesis*

[112] *PRIMI* I, 66 no. 18; Pfeiffer, *Callimachus* II, xii–xiii no. 8; Pack² no. 211.

[113] P.Oxy. 2263 fr. I, ii, 3–30 [378]: *POxy* 20 (1952) 126–127; Pfeiffer, *Callimachus* II, xviii–xix, no. 26; Pack² no. 205. "Florentine Scholia": *PSI* 11.1219, 9.1094; Pfeiffer, *Callimachus* II, xviii, no. 24; Pack² nos. 196, 219.

[114] Pfeiffer, *Callimachus* II, xxviii; *POxy* 20 (1952) 125. Brief remarks on the importance of the *Diegeseis* are made by Trypanis, *Callimachus* xiv.

[115] For this papyrus: C. Meillier, "Callimaque," *CRIPEL* IV (1976) 257–360, which I have not been able to consult; résumé in *APh* 47 (1976) 71 no. 890.

[116] *Infra* pp. 195–196.

does not prove that it also appeared in Callimachus' text at all, and still less that it carried the associations which, as will be seen, are attested only later.

Xoanon occurs twice in the *Diegesis* to another of Callimachus' *Aetia*. P.Oxy. 2263 [378] preserves a substantial part of the commentary on a poem concerning the Leucadian Artemis (*Aet.* I fr. 31 b–c). Only one line of the poem itself survives, and it, unfortunately, does not mention the statue. The *Diegesis*, however, is well enough preserved to give the outline of the story and in this account the statue is twice called a *xoanon*.[117]

The *Diegesis*—and presumably also the *Aetion*—undertakes to explain why the *xoanon* of Artemis on Leucas has a mortar (θυ<ε>ίαν) on its head. The Epirotes plundered the Leucadian sanctuary of Artemis, and, having appropriated the golden crown which the goddess wore, replaced it with a mortar, mocking her. The Leucadians in turn replaced the offending mortar (still reeking, it would seem, of the Epirotes' garlic) with a new crown, but it fell off, even after they nailed it to the *xoanon*. The commentary breaks off with yet another attempt to restore the crown; but however many times the Leucadians may have tried, the outcome is clear: the goddess chose to retain the mortar.

The *Diegesis* gives little specific information about the *xoanon* itself—only that it wore a golden crown (and later a mortar) that could be removed, and that the Leucadians nailed the crown to the statue. These facts do not even permit the material of the statue to be determined. Since the crown, and not the entire statue, was taken, the rest of the image is not likely to have been of precious material; but whether the crown was easily removed, or needed to be forcibly detached, is not clear. The Leucadians' attempt to nail (προσηλόω) the new crown to the statue would seem to indicate that the image was of wood, but even that modest conclusion is not inevitable. The verb can mean "to fix to," which would allow for a variety of techniques, such as riveting, for example, which would be appropriate for a metal image. Because the verb seems usually to mean "nailing," however—as in crucifixion—a fairly energetic process is probably being imagined. It is conceivable that even a stone or a bronze image would have been hammered, if the level of Leucadian frustration was sufficiently high.[118] Nor is the failure of the attempt telling: the crown fell off not because the material of the statue was resistant to any predictable degree, but because the goddess willed it; this is the whole point of the story.

[117] For P.Oxy. 2263 [378]: *supra* p. 48 n. 113.

[118] LSJ^9 *s.v.* προσηλόω. There is a long tradition of metal attachments to stone sculpture in Greece, but as a rule the metal parts were kept in place by means of holes drilled in the stone and not by being directly nailed in; surely nailing would invite breakage. For metal attachments: Adam, *Technique* 47, 53, and *passim*.

It may be recalled that in antiquity the Leucadians had a reputation for being "mean-spirited": [Arist.] *Physiognomena* 808 a 29.

Information about the *xoanon* may be looked for outside the *Diegesis*. Coins of Leucas dating after 168 B.C. show on the obverse what has been identified as a statue of Artemis. The figure is unremarkable in type; its headdress is not entirely clear, but seems to include a crescent. The prow featured on the reverse, however, suggests a deity connected with navigation, and numismatic opinion favors identification of the goddess as Aphrodite Aeneas.[119] Yet even if the coins do show an image of Artemis, and it is the Artemis of the sanctuary, there is a chance that the statue of the story does not, in the end, lend itself to such archaeological illustration.

The *Diegesis* is extremely similar to an entry in Heraclides Lembus' *Epitome* of Aristotle's *Politeia* (*Politiarum* 45) [**138**]. This passage from the second-century B.C. author has already been mentioned among the dubious occurrences of *xoanon* in the fourth century B.C. The difficulties it presents may now be discussed in more detail.

The excerpt appears with the heading Μολοττῶν. It concerns the Molossian sack of the *hieron* of Artemis on Cephallenia. The invaders carried off the golden crown of the *xoanon* and "made a sacrifice in return for it" (θυσίαν ἐτίθεσαν ἀντ' αὐτοῦ). The Cephallenians replaced the crown, but the goddess threw it aside, and it was found on the ground.

What seems to be a scribal error obscures the resemblance between this entry and the *Diegesis* on the Leucadian Artemis. Surely θυσίαν is the θυείαν, "mortar," of the *Diegesis*, and so the Molossians, "having torn away the golden crown of the *xoanon*, put a mortar in its place." Huxley has noted how the "easy correction" of θυσίαν to θυείαν would thus allow a version of the story to be traced back to Aristotle.[120] There are significant differences between the two accounts. The *Diegesis* has the Epirotes invading Leucas; Heraclides, the Molossians plundering Cephallenia. It is conceivable that "Epirotes" and "Molossi" are interchangeable names, since the Molossi dominated a powerful confederation of Epirote tribes from about 370 to 232 B.C.[121] Leucas and Cephallenia, in contrast, are neighboring but different islands. Unless the *Diegesis* has completely abandoned his text, Callimachus certainly placed the story on Leucas. It would seem clear that two versions of the story existed by the third century.

[119] Coins of Leucas: P. Gardner, *BMC Thessaly to Aetolia* (London, 1883) 179–180, pl. 28.15, 16. For Aphrodite Aeneas, as suggested by Curtius and accepted by Head, *Historia Numorum* 330–331: Lacroix, *Reproductions* 138–140. *Cf.* Pfeiffer, *Callimachus* II, 111.

[120] For Heracl. Lemb. *Excerpta politiarum* 45 [**138**]: *supra* p. 34 and n. 82; G. Huxley, "Two Notes on Hellenistic Poems," *GRBS* 13 (1972) 309–311. I thank D. Burgess for bringing this article to my attention. P.Oxy. 2263.21 [**378**] has τηνθυϊαν; both θυίαν and θυείαν are attested in Hellenistic times.

[121] N.G.L. Hammond, *Epirus* (Oxford, 1967) 508–594 for Molossian expansion and dominance.

In terms of real history, Callimachus' Leucas is perhaps more likely than Heraclides' Cephallenia, as it is much closer to the limit of Molossian influence. There is little precise information about the relationship of either island to the Epirote tribes; it is not even certain, for instance, that Pyrrhus received Leucas as well as Corcyra in the dowry of Agathocles' daughter in the 290s.[122] Neither island is noted for its worship of Artemis, but Leucas, with its coins of the later second century B.C. showing a statue of Artemis, seems to have a stronger claim than Cephallenia, which boasts only one inscription, now destroyed, bearing her name.[123]

The substitution of *θυσίαν* for *θυείαν* also raises questions. The manuscripts of Heraclides unanimously give *θυσίαν*. The easiest explanation of the change is an error in copying at some point in the manuscript transmission. It has always been noticed that the statement that the Molossi made a sacrifice in return for the crown makes little sense. The suggestion that *θυσίαν* should be replaced by *καυσίαν*, a Macedonian cap, was rejected by Sintenis and Schneidewin on the grounds that *ἄλλον* showed that the Molossi had placed nothing on the statue.[124] Since, however, *ἄλλον στέφανον* is understood in any event, this objection does not rule out either *καυσίαν* or *θυείαν*. It is difficult to tell when the change to *θυσίαν* took place. In the skeletal account given by Heraclides, the mention of a mortar makes little obvious sense; anyone not already familiar with the story might well have attempted to "correct" the text. It is possible that Heraclides himself worked from a much-abridged account and made the change; or he may simply have copied from an already emended version. (In that case, Sintenis and Schneidewin might be correct about the significance of *ἄλλον*.) The question of Heraclides' source thus arises.

It should be noted that the story of the statue as given by Heraclides is not the kind of subject found in either the *Politeia* of Aristotle, which is the work epitomized, or in his *Nomima Barbarica*, four entries of which are also included by Heraclides, and which might also conceivably have included a Molossian entry. What the account does resemble, in both the subject and the telling, are those in the *De mirabilis auscultationibus*, a collection of curious and marvelous facts and events that are wrongly ascribed to Aristotle. The Molossian entry in Heraclides reads like an account of a miracle that has been reworked for inclusion in an ethnographic catalogue.

[122] E. van Hille, in W. Dörpfeld, *Alt-Ithaka* (Munich, 1927) I, 384. Both islands had been involved in the western struggles of the Peloponnesian War, but major actions were the work of the great powers: *e.g.*, the Athenian invasion of Leucas with forces from Acarnania and the western islands (Thuc. 3.94.1–2); could this be termed "Epirote" harassment?

[123] For coins of Leucas: *supra* p. 50 n. 119. For the inscription from Cephallenia: *RE* 11.1 (1921) 209 *s.v.* Kephallenia.

[124] Schneidewin, *Heraclidis* (*supra* p. 34 n. 82) 84 *ad* XVII; *FHG* II, 217–218, *ad* XVII.

On the basis of Heraclides' text, it is not possible to be sure about the original source and form of the account, or even about its versions and their transmission. New texts may someday provide more material related to Heraclides' excerpts, and perhaps, as in the case of the *Athenaion Politeia*, may confirm his fidelity to Aristotle. Until then, however, the excerpt and its *xoanon* cannot be definitely tied to Aristotle.

In any event, the *Diegesis* suggests that Callimachus' *Aetion* had a slightly different point from that of the story preserved in Heraclides Lembus. Whereas in the *Diegesis* the origin of the mortar is the focus, the Molossian excerpt concentrates on the statue's rejection of the crown; in other words, one is an *aetion*, the other, a miracle-story. In this respect the account of the *Diegesis* stands apart from that of Heraclides, quite aside from the differences in cast and locale. While there is no clear indication, as in the case of the commentary on the Samian *xoanon*, that the *Diegesis* has added material from other sources to its summary of Callimachus, it is nonetheless possible that whatever source lies behind the excerpt of Heraclides—or even the excerpt itself, although this is less likely—also influenced the explication of the Leucadian *Aetion*. Of course, the influence might equally have gone the other way; although the extant *Diegesis* comes from a papyrus centuries later than Heraclides, and is therefore liable to contain quite late material, its foundations may go back to the third century. Rather than attempting to argue the details of influence and transmission, it is better simply to point out that commentaries can grow to some extent independently of the original texts they treat. Because there existed abundant opportunities for commentators to add material they considered helpful, taken from a great variety of sources, it cannot be assumed that even an ostensible summary like that given by the *Diegesis* preserves in a pure form the work from which it derives. The *xoana* of the Leucadian *Diegesis* can be dissociated from Callimachus simply on the grounds that the prose explication need not have maintained the original author's vocabulary.[125] The commentator is likely to have presented his summary in the terms with which he was comfortable. The interest of the Leucadian *Diegesis* lies more in the elusive connection with Heraclides, a connection that allows a look into the complexities of the Hellenistic and later secondary sources in which *xoanon* flourishes.

[125] *Agalma* and *bretas* are attested in Callimachus. *Agalma*: *Hymn* 5.39 (Argive image of Athena); *Hymn* 4.307 (image of Aphrodite on Delos); *Epigr.* 35.1. *Bretas*: *Hymn* 3.238, 248 (Artemis of Ephesus); restored in P.Oxy. 2171 fr. 2 col. ii.8 = *Iamb.* VI fr. 196.29 [377]; Pfeiffer, *Callimachus* I, 190 (Olympian Zeus of Pheidias). The word scarcely exists on the papyrus, but both spacing and sense make it a reasonable restoration: βρ[έ]τα[ς: *POxy* 18 (1941) 58–59, pl. IX. The Zeus is here *hagios*, "holy" or "pure"; for this word: E. Williger, *Hagios. Untersuchungen zur Terminologie des Heiligen* (RGVV 19.1; Giessen, 1922).

Conclusions

The evidence for *xoanon* in the third century B.C., while not plentiful, presents several interesting features. In this century the word is first attested epigraphically, and in the single inscription and in literature both, it shows a wider and more explicit range of associations than had previously been attested. That it is applied to images of gods and nymphs, some of which are dedications, shows that the meaning of *xoanon* is not restricted to what are usually called "cult statues." Apollonius' use of the word and its tentative ascription to Manetho raise the question of regional variations in definition. If Manetho did use *xoanon*, and use it to refer specifically to worshipped images, Josephus' quotation would preserve the earliest use of the term applied collectively to such statues. At the same time there appears a split in typological connotations; while one dedication is *kluton*, "splendid," another is *poimenikos*, "rustic." It should be emphasized too that, in line with earlier usage, the *xoana* can be contemporary images. The only examples of *xoanon* used in ways that have become standard in modern scholarship, for crude or ancient images, come not from demonstrably third-century sources, but instead from later commentaries and from texts that are also later in composition or revision.

5. *Xoanon* in the Second Century B.C.

Although *xoanon* begins to appear more frequently in the second century B.C., it remains a rare word. It makes great strides in inscriptions, but nonetheless only six, or perhaps seven, *xoana* take their places among the far more numerous *agalmata* and other images found in the epigraphical corpus. Literary *xoana* are even scarcer. I have so far found only five that may plausibly be assigned to the second century, and only two of these are largely free from vexing questions of source and transmission.

The three dubious second-century *xoana* appear in texts that are considerably later. The most straightforward of the three is the *xoanon* of Nike Athena mentioned by Harpocration in his *Lexicon* to ten Attic orators, a work dated to the reign of Marcus Aurelius.[126] The entry for Νίκη Ἀθηνᾶ [**137**] derives only the goddess' name from Lycurgus' *On the Priestess*; nothing at all is known of how the cult figured in the speech.[127] Harpocration attributes the rest of the information in the entry—a description of the wingless *xoanon* of Nike Athena venerated by the Athenians—to the first book of Heliodorus' *On the Acropolis*. Heliodorus was an Athenian perigete who, according to Athenaeus (6.229 e; 9.406 d), wrote fifteen books on the subject of the Athenian Acropolis. He is usually placed in the middle of the second century B.C., but there is no solid evidence for this date.[128]

Testimony about a *xoanon* of Athena Nike in Athens comes from another source: Pausanias twice refers to the image of Nike Apteros

[126] Harpocration *s.v.* Νίκη Ἀθηνᾶ [**137**]: W. Dindorf, ed., *Harpocrationis Lexicon in Decem Oratores Atticos* (Oxford, 1853) I, 214.6. For the date of Harpocration and the two versions of the *Lexicon*: M. Naoumides, "The Papyrus of the *Lexicon* of Harpocration," *TAPA* 92 (1961) 384–388.

[127] For Lycurgus' Περὶ τῆς ἱερείας: N.C. Conomis, ed., *Lycurgus. Oratio in Leocratem* (Leipzig, 1970) fr. VI.13 (40); and "Notes on the Fragments of Lycurgus," *Klio* 39 (1961) 107–120, esp. 115–116. The priestess in question seems to be she of Athena Polias, with whom Athena Nike is occasionally associated, as in *IG* II², 334 (335/4 B.C.; for the provision of offerings to several Athenas at the Panathenaia: H.W. Parke, *Festivals of the Athenians* [Ithaca, 1977] 47–49). The two Athena cults were, however, distinct, at least from about the middle of the fifth century B.C., when *IG* I³, 35 (= *IG* I², 24) provides for the selection of the first priestess of Athena Nike and the construction of a temple. For the controversy over the subject and date of this inscription: H.B. Mattingly, "The Athena Nike Temple Reconsidered," *AJA* 86 (1982) 381–385, and bibliography in IG I³, 35. Mattingly argues for a date for the inscription in the 420s.

[128] Little is preserved of Heliodorus. *FGrH* 373; Jacoby in *RE* 8 (1913) 15–18 *s.v.* Heliodoros (11). The *OCD*² *s.v.* Heliodorus (1) assigns him a tentative date of 150 B.C. He is listed among the sources of Pliny: C. Mayhoff, ed., *C. Plini Secundi Naturalis Historiae libri XXXVII* (Stuttgart, 1906; repr. 1967) I, 114–115, 118, indices to *HN* 34 and 35: *Externis. Heliodoro qui Atheniensium anathemata scripsit* (I.xxxiv).

(Wingless) as a *xoanon* (3.15.7 [**232**]; 5.26.6 [**247**]).[129] That by "Nike Apteros" he means the goddess known from inscriptions as Athena Nike is almost beyond doubt. It is reasonable to assume that the *xoanon* of Heliodorus and the *xoanon* of Pausanias are the same image. Since there are grounds for believing that Pausanias did not consult Heliodorus, the term is likely to have been his own choice, and so to have reflected his independent definition of it. As Bennett has demonstrated, this almost certainly means that Pausanias thought the image was wooden; but no further conclusions about the statue can be drawn on the basis of the word alone.[130] Pausanias says only that the *xoanon* is wingless and that this feature was imitated by Calamis. Interestingly enough, he does not mention the image at all in the context of the Nike sanctuary on the Acropolis, which he seems not, in fact, to have entered. Nor is his description of the image comparable to that given by Heliodorus; the information in it need not have been based on an examination of the statue itself. It is justifiable to wonder whether Pausanias had actually seen the statue.

The image of Athena Nike has been identified with a figure shown on a relief found on the Athenian Acropolis. An Athena with an aegis, similar to one on the Nike Temple parapet, is seated before a narrow building in which stands a "*xoanon* of Athena Nike."[131] The figure is peculiar in design

[129] Pausanias refers twice to the temple of Nike Apteros (1.22.4; 2.30.2) and twice to her *xoanon* (3.15.7; 5.26.6). Pausanias' temple of Nike Apteros, which he describes as being on the right of the Propylaea as one approaches them, is surely to be identified with the temple now visible at the west end of the Acropolis, where the cult of Athena Nike is attested from the mid-sixth century B.C. For the altar inscribed τε̃ς Ἀθε[ναίας] τε̃ς Νίκες βομός of that date found under the temple: *AE* 1937 Γ, 786 fig. 15; A.E. Raubitschek, *Dedications from the Athenian Akropolis* (Cambridge, Mass., 1949) no. 329.

[130] Frazer, *Pausanias* I, lxxxiii and n. 3, discusses the slight evidence that Pausanias did not read Heliodorus. For *xoanon* in Pausanias and Bennett's conclusions: *infra* pp. 140–147.

[131] Athens, Acropolis Museum Inv. 4734 + Inv. 2605 + Inv. 2447: O. Walter, *Beschreibung der Reliefs im kleinen Akropolismuseum in Athen* (Vienna, 1923) 46–48, no. 76; L. Beschi, "Contributi di topografia ateniense. Lo xoanon di Atena Nike e il culto delle Charites," *ASAtene* n.s. 29–30 (1967–1968) 531–536, 533 fig. 16, with bibliography; G. Neumann, *Probleme des griechischen Weihreliefs* (Tübinger Studien zur Archäologie und Kunstgeschichte 3; Tübingen, 1979) 61, pl. 37 a. Both Beschi and Neumann call the figure in the structure a *xoanon*. For recent remarks on the *xoanon* of Athena Nike: F. Muthmann, *Der Granatapfel. Symbol des Lebens in der alten Welt* (Bern, 1982) 64–66. Muthmann compares the pomegranate held by the *xoanon* (ein altes hölzernes Kultbild; 64) with that in the hand of Polycleitus' statue of Hera in the Argive Heraion, suggesting that the fruit symbolizes a peaceful concern with the local land. As an unequivocal example of the goddess as a dispenser of fertility he cites (66) another fourth-century relief discussed by Beschi (535–536, fig. 17 right) that shows Athena with a polos, a phiale, and a pomegranate. This Athena wears an aegis, however, which the figure shown in the small structure does not. It is unclear to what extent either relief can be considered to give reliable information about the image of

and style. It is visible only to the knees, the lower legs being hidden by a bench-like construction. The frontality of the image, the stiff position of its arms (now broken away, but clearly once held straight forward from bent elbows), and the polos recall the archaistic "idols" that begin to appear on reliefs of the later fifth century; the rigid pose and the polos suggest a hieratic figure. The peculiarity of the image lies not only in its being shown only to knee-level, but also in its style, which does not conform to any readily recognizable archaism. While the head and arms establish a rigid frontality, the body curves strongly, right hip raised and right shoulder lowered. The obvious shift of weight to the right leg is inconsistent with the first impression given by the frontal pose. The drapery, too, is not what would be expected from an ostensibly hieratic figure; the clothing itself, apparently a himation over a chiton, is not one of the imitations of Archaic costume worn by archaistic figures, and the long curves and pulls of the cloth emphasize the chiastic pose.[132]

The Acropolis relief has been dated to the first half of the fourth century, still fairly close to the archaistic figures mentioned above. They are the closest comparisons for the image, even though they tend to be markedly smaller than other figures with which they appear, while the figure in the naiskos is close in size to the Athena seated before it, and although their style is wholeheartedly archaistic, whereas the archaism of the figure in question is uneven. If the stylistic peculiarities of the image in the narrow building were not introduced by the maker of the relief, but belong instead to a statue which it copies, it would be difficult to say what the original would mean in terms of the history of either sanctuary or style. The precinct of Athena Nike, for so long a relatively reliable point in later fifth century art and architecture, is currently the focus of debate, its monuments and the inscriptions connected with them being reinterpreted and redated.[133] Where the curious figure on the Acropolis relief might fit

---

Athena Nike. The seated Athena on Acropolis Museum 2447 is comparable to an Athena on the Nike Temple Parapet: R. Carpenter, *The Sculpture of the Nike Temple Parapet* (Cambridge, Mass., 1929) 56–57, pl. 24.

[132] Beschi, (*supra* p. 55 n. 131) 533–534, draws attention to the definitely non-archaic structure of the figure, but maintains that the carver of the relief clearly intended to show a *xoanon*; the stylistic inconsistencies he believes to reflect the date of the relief in the first half of the fourth century. He cites the archaistic idols as examples of gods shown with images of themselves. For more examples of these idols: E.B. Harrison, *Archaic and Archaistic Sculpture* (*Agora* 11; Princeton, 1965) 53, especially for the costume. See M.D. Fullerton, *Archaistic Draped Statuary in the Round of the Classical, Hellenistic, and Roman Periods* (Diss. Bryn Mawr College, 1982) 43–59.

[133] The Nike Temple has become a focus of intense debate, and many substantive issues concerning its construction which may have bearing on the cult have yet to be settled. See Mattingly (*supra* p. 54 n. 127); B. Wesenberg, "Zur Baugeschichte des Niketempels," *JdI* 96

within any of the proposed versions of the history of the sanctuary is uncertain. It is even possible, given the epigraphical evidence for the friendly relations between the various Athenas on the Acropolis, that the relief shows Athena Nike in connection with another goddess, and that the image in the structure is not connected with the cult of Athena Nike at all.

For now, the *xoanon* mentioned by Pausanias and Harpocration cannot be confidently illustrated by archaeological material. About Pausanias', it can be said only that it was wingless, that it can be presumed to be wooden, and that it is said to have been known by Calamis. The image cannot be proved to be much older than the date of Calamis, and nothing can be said about its appearance. What is known about the *xoanon* of Pausanias does not necessarily reflect what Heliodorus might have meant by the word. It is also entirely possible that Harpocration, and not Heliodorus, chose to call the statue a *xoanon*; the entry in the *Lexicon* is a compilation and a summary, and the terminology is likely to reflect Harpocration's vocabulary.

The case of Nike Athena at first appears to offer a neat conjunction of literary and archaeological sources that could pin down the word *xoanon*: not one, but two authors apply the term to a statue that lies almost within archaeological reach. The evidence of both the texts and the archaeological material, however, is a nest of uncertainties. If the history of the Nike sanctuary is ever unravelled, it may shed light on the *xoanon* to which Pausanias alludes; but the *xoanon* of Heliodorus must wait to be confirmed by texts.

Two *xoana* appear in the *Metamorphoseon Synagoge* of Antoninus Liberalis, where they are ascribed to Nicander, who is thought to be a writer of the second century B.C., although the evidence for his date is scanty and conflicting.[134] Nothing is known of the date of Antoninus. His name suggests the era of the Antonines and Severans, the later second and earlier third centuries A.D. The *Metamorphoseon Synagoge* is preserved in only one manuscript, Codex Palatinus graecus 398 in Heidelberg, of the second half of the ninth century.[135] The forty-one stories in the collection

(1981) 28–54; W.A.P. Childs, "In Defense of an Early Date for the Frieze of the Temple on the Ilissos," *AM* 100 (1985) 207–251. I owe to B.S. Ridgway references to recent work on the subject, and also information on I. Mark's identification of the block on the bastion usually called an *eschara* as the center of the base for the "cult statue" of Athena Nike, which he believes to have been seated, about 1 m. high, and made c. 600–550 B.C.: I. Mark, "Observations on the History of the Nike Sanctuary on the Acropolis to the Mid-Fifth Century B.C.," in the résumés of the twelfth Congrès International d'Archéologie Classique (Athens, 1983) 126.

[134] For the date of Nicander: Gow and Scholfield, *Nicander* 3–8.

[135] E. Martini, ed., *Antoninus Liberalis. Μεταμορφώσεων Συναγωγή* (Mythographi Graeci II.1; Leipzig, 1896); I. Cazzaniga, ed., *Antoninus Liberalis. Metamorphoseon Synagoge* (Milan, 1962); Papathomopoulos, *Antoninus*. For the manuscript, which also contains

are preceded by two tables of contents, and most of the individual stories are attributed to one of fourteen sources by a short note in the lower margin (or upper and lower both, if two stories appear on the same page). It is not clear whether these attributions, which frequently cite the title and chapter of the sources, belong to Antoninus or to one or more later scholiasts. Nicander is the author mentioned most frequently in the notes.

One of the *xoana* does literally appear, in the story of Aspalis of Melite, which is ascribed to the second book of Nicander's *Heteroioumena* (ἱστορεῖ Νίκανδρος ἑτεροιουμένων β′) [**16**]. This unhappy little tale ends with the disappearance of the corpse of Aspalis and its miraculous replacement by a *xoanon*, which is then included in the rites performed in Aspalis' memory. *Xoanon* certainly belongs to the text of the story, and it appears too in the second table of contents, where Metamorphosis 13 is listed as Ἀσπαλὶς εἰς ξόανον μετὰ θάνατον (Aspalis, into a *xoanon* after death) [**18**].[136]

The question is whether the *xoanon* in the text is Antoninus' or his source's. If it is his source's word, how much reliance can be placed on the marginal attributions in the manuscript? These notations, which seem to have been copied from a model text and not to be the original contribution of the scribe of Pal. 398, have been vigorously discussed. Every possibility has been set forward, from their being Antoninus' own acknowledgments to their representing some later copyist's display of his own erudition by citing additional sources for the stories. In the latter case the source of the Aspalis story would be anyone except Nicander.[137] This degree of scepticism seems extreme, but perhaps it is necessary when working with an author for whom only one manuscript and little in the way of comparative material exist. In any event, *xoanon* here can be safely assigned only to

---

Parthenius' *Eroticon Pathematon* and a variety of geographical treatises: Diller, *Tradition Geographers* 3–10, but with little on the Antoninus section. For part of an alphabetized "dictionary" of metamorphoses on a papyrus dated palaeographically to late A.D. II or early A.D. III: T. Renner, "A Papyrus Dictionary of Metamorphoses," *HSCP* 82 (1978) 277–293.

[136] The story: Ant. Lib. 13.6–7 [**16**]. Table of Contents: (2) Met. 13 [**18**]. Papathomopoulos, *Antoninus* x–xi, gives no information about this second table of contents. The first is only an incomplete list of the stories relating to birds. I have been unable to consult R. Sellheim, *De Parthenii et Antonini fontium indiculorum auctoribus* (Halle, 1930). For comments on the story of Aspalis: Burkert, *Structure* 75.

[137] Gow and Scholfield, *Nicander* 205–206, although believing that the precision of the citations indicates their reliability, admit that no judgment on the fidelity of the text to its sources is really possible. Confidence in the attributions of the manuscript has been shaken by the discovery that papyrus fragments of Euphorion's *Thrax* are not at all similar to the two sections of Parthenius (13 and 26) ascribed to this work: Papathomopoulos, *Antoninus* xix. *Bretas* is attested in Nicander (*Georgica* fr. 74.68) for images of the gods, but no *xoanon* has yet appeared in the fragments.

Antoninus, and not to Nicander. The *xoanon* of the table of contents is obviously extracted from Antoninus' text.

The case of Antoninus' *Metamorphosis* 40 **[17]** is more complicated. The table of contents **[19]** gives this summary: Βριτόμαρ<μαρ>τις εἰς ξόανον Ἀφαίαν (Britomartis into the *xoanon* [called] Aphaia). The text of the story does not contain the word *xoanon*, but it is evidently corrupt, since no metamorphosis, no statue, but only a disappearance is mentioned. Clearly some restoration is needed, and editors have suggested several places in the text where the required *xoanon* could be inserted. There is no marginal notation in the manuscript of the source of this story. Schneider has given it to Nicander on the basis of its similarity to the story of Aspalis: neither records a true metamorphosis, but only a disappearance and the consequent institution of rites.[138] There are, however, no grounds strong enough to support the attribution of the lost *xoanon* to anyone but Antoninus.

Two *xoana* can be assigned with more certainty to writers of the second century B.C. The first has already been discussed: the *xoanon* of Artemis in Heraclides Lembus' epitome of Aristotle's *Politeia* **[138]**.[139] The relationship of Heraclides' text to a similar account preserved in a *Diegesis* to Callimachus' *Aetia* suggests that the connections of this *xoanon* lie not directly with Aristotle or Callimachus, but instead with a range of secondary literature—commentaries and abridgements—that is difficult to place chronologically and not easy to analyze with respect to sources. The extract by itself is not especially helpful in establishing the meaning of *xoanon*, except insofar as the word refers to the statue of a divinity. It is possible, however, that exactly this kind of general definition may be what is meant.

The other fairly certain second-century *xoana*, and indeed the last that can so far be confidently assigned to the literature of the century, attest a meaning of *xoanon* that looks forward to the significance the word has in later literature, but is not consistent with previous usage. *Xoana* are twice found in a section of the Sibylline Oracles that appears to have been composed in Egypt near the middle of the century.[140] The Oracles, hexameter poems that are in large part the work of Jewish writers, present ideas that sound strange in the context of pagan seers' pronouncements. In Book III, lines 721–723 **[173]**, the prophetess is made to speak against the worship of images:

[138] Ant. Lib. Table of Contents (2) Met. 40 **[19]**. O. Schneider, *Nicandrea* (Leipzig, 1856) 43; his attribution is given short shrift by Gow and Scholfield (*Nicander* 208 *ad* fr. 67: "on no very conclusive grounds"). The story of Britomartis is mentioned by Pausanias, 2.30.3.

[139] *Supra* pp. 50–52 **[138]**.

[140] For the Sibylline Oracles and this passage in particular: *infra* pp. 97–99.

ἡμεῖς δ' ἀθανάτοιο τρίβον πεπλανημένοι ἦμεν,
ἔργα δὲ χειροποίητα σεβάσμεθα ἄφρονι θυμῷ
εἴδωλα ξόανά τε καταφθιμένων ἀνθρώπων.

Wandering, we had gone far from the path of the immortal, we revered with senseless spirit works made by hand, *eidola* and *xoana* of men who have perished.

Xoana here seem to be the images of the gods that are the focus of Greek idolatry. This meaning is quite different from most that have been attested before, as it would appear to exclude *xoana* that are votives and include only those that are the focus of cult. Usage is not the only striking feature of the passage. The Euhemeristic slant is a novel approach to the images of the gods; the condemnation of divine images as the products of human manufacture strongly recalls the Biblical charge that the idols have feet of clay; and the argument against the physical images of the gods, rather than against their anthropomorphic conception, is unprecedented in Greek religious thought.[141] The foreignness of the conceptions may perhaps be echoed by the choice of vocabulary: although *eidolon* does become the idol in idolatry, with its Greek history of referring to specters and illusions it is not the first word one would expect from a Greek talking about the images of the gods; nor is the rare *xoanon* the second.[142] *Eidolon* here may be a pointed term, chosen to underline the illusory nature of divine representations. On the other hand, it might simply betray a lack of familiarity with non-provincial Greek usage. Some light on the appearance of the uncommon *xoanon* as the term *par excellence* for images of the gods may be shed by the occurrences of the word in contemporary inscriptions.

Six, or at most seven, *xoana* are so far attested in inscriptions of the second century B.C. Four of the texts come mainland Greece or from islands in the Greek sphere; three come from Ionia and Egypt, and in these, *xoanon* has associations quite different from any seen previously. As it happens, two of these three "odd" inscriptions are those that can be precisely dated; of the other texts, three can be assigned only generally to the earlier part of the century, one belongs close to the first century, and the last may even be of the first century.

An inscription from Magnesia on the Maeander preserving a decree concerned with ceremonies of the cult of Zeus Sosipolis [**392**] is dated with fair certainty to 197/6 B.C. by the name of the *stephanephoros*, who is also mentioned in a peace treaty between Magnesia and Miletus. Among the elaborate ceremonial directives is the provision that the *stephanephoros*, who leads the procession, carry (φερέτω) the *xoana* of all the twelve gods,

[141] For the condemnation of images on grounds based in the tradition of Jewish iconoclasm: *infra* pp. 86–89 and n. 212.

[142] For *eidolon*: *supra* p. 19 n. 41 and p. 26 n. 64; see also LSJ[9] *s.v.*

which are to be robed in the finest garments, construct a *tholos*, presumably for the *xoana*, in the agora, near the altar of the gods, and furnish three couches—also presumably for the comfort of the *xoana*.[143] If the *stephanephoros* actually carried the twelve *xoana* himself, they must have been small; it is possible, however, that he simply conducted them. There is no other clue to the nature or appearance of these *xoana*. That they wore clothes, at least for this occasion, might tend to suggest that they are ancient images involved in an ancient kind of cult activity, since the dressing of statues is often taken to be an especially early practice. The great majority of the testimony for the custom of clothing images, however, is Hellenistic and later, and the possibility that individual instances (at least) are newer institutions rather than continuations of extremely old traditions must be considered.[144] It should not be assumed that the Magnesian *xoana* are either necessarily ancient images or, following another suggestion sometimes put forward to explain draped images, statues so primitive in form that they needed clothing to complete their appearance.[145]

The decree of Ptolemy V Epiphanes that is inscribed in three scripts on the Rosetta Stone [**402**] was passed in 196 B.C. Among the honors it assigns to the king, the dedication of images is prominent. *Eikones* of "Ptolemy, the avenger of Egypt," will stand in every temple, and beside these *eikones* the principal god of each temple will hand the king an emblem of victory. Priests will "do service to" (*therapeuein*) these *eikones* three times a day, will put the sacred ornament (*hieros kosmos*) on them, and will perform the other honors customary for the other gods in Egyptian festivals. In addition, a *xoanon* and a golden *naos* will be carried in procession in the

[143] Kern, *Inschriften* 82–84 no. 98 [**392**]; Sokolowski, *LSAM* 88–92 no. 32; 90–91 for the date; Pekáry, "Statuen" 741. The "crown-" or "wreath-bearer" Aristeas son of Demetrios is mentioned in line 91 of the treaty inscription from Miletus: G. Kawerau and A. Rehm, *Milet* I.3. *Das Delphinion in Milet* (Berlin, 1914) 341–349 no. 148, dated to the autumn of 196 B.C.; 344–345 for Aristeas. Linfert, *Kunstzentren* 165, rightly notes that the actual occasion of inscription Kern 98 is unknown; it does not concern the new foundation of the Zeus cult. For the significance of this decree and of no. **393** for the chronology of the Magnesian temples: W. Hahland, "Der Fries des Dionysostempels in Teos," *JOAI* 38 (1950) 97–103.

For the preparation of the couches (στρωμναί): L.R. Taylor, "A Sellisternium on the Parthenon Frieze?" in R.P. Casey, S. Lake, and A.K. Lake, eds., *Quantulacumque. Studies Presented to Kirsopp Lake* (London, 1937) 257.

[144] A long list of testimonia for real garments given to statues appears in F. Willemsen, *Frühe griechische Kultbilder* (Diss. Düsseldorf, 1939) 36–42. For real clothing associated with statues: Linders, *Studies* 11–12; Frazer, *Pausanias* II, 574–576; and Pekáry, "Statuen" 741–743.

[145] *E.g.*, Ridgway, *Archaic* 25 n. 12: " . . . early cult statues were often adorned with real clothes." A pleasing statement of a related assumption is given by Rouse, *GVO* 275: "It seems to have been a common thing, that the most ancient and revered idol of a city, itself often hideous or without form, was deckt out on solemn occasions with magnificent robes of state."

great festivals. The editor of the text contrasts *xoanon* with *eikon*. Both receive honorific attentions: the *eikones* are to be adorned and honored; the *xoana*, presumably in the golden *naoi*, are to be carried in processions. It is likely that here *xoanon* has precise connotations, and may even be a technical term with special meaning in the context of Egyptian traditions of worship. Whether the connotations are of size, material, form, or purpose, however, cannot be ascertained from this text. Two copies of the decree have been found. One, from Elephantine **[389]**, has lost its *xoanon*, but preserves the golden *naos*.[146]

In comparison with the *xoana* of Magnesia and Egypt, which are the focus of elaborate rituals, receiving clothing and shrines, and carried in processions, the next *xoanon* in a second-century inscription seems like a poor cousin. Sometime early in the century Dionysius, a member of a Dionysian *thiasos*, spent generously in order to erect a *neos*, a *temenos*, and *xoana* for Bacchus. These gifts and his prayer for salvation for himself, his family, and his *thiasos* are recorded in a text found in the Peiraeus **[399]**. The *xoana* are called εἴκελά σοι, "like you," meaning the god, who is addressed. They would seem to be images, then, but it is not clear why there should be more than one, or what their purpose is. It is certain only that they are set up and that they are part of a fully (as implied by καὶ πάντ') and expensively equipped sanctuary.[147]

The Peiraeus *xoana* apparently belong to a different sphere from that of the Magnesian and Egyptian images. They are not part of a public cult, but are a private dedication in the context of a private organization. Whether they served as the focus of devotion, as did their fellows in the public realm, is not possible to ascertain on the basis of the inscription;

[146] *BMusInscr* IV, no. 1065, the Rosetta Stone **[402]**; *xoanon* appears in line 41. *SEG* 16, 855; *CIG* III, 4697; *Sammelbuch* 5, 8299; F.C. Grant, ed., *Hellenistic Religions. The Age of Syncretism* (Indianapolis and New York, 1953) 67–69 (translation only); E. Bevan, *A History of Egypt under the Ptolemaic Dynasty* (London, 1927) 262–268 (translation and discussion); R.S. Bagnall and P. Derow, *Greek Historical Documents: The Hellenistic Period* (Sources for Biblical Study 16; Chico, 1981) 226–230 no. 137 (translation only). Papadopoulos, *Xoana* 70 *ad* no. 2, cites Letronne's suggestion that *chrysoun* might be restored instead as a neuter plural, so that the *xoanon* as well as the *naos* would be golden; Clement's comment on golden *agalmata* of the gods is cited in support. In the copy of the decree from Elephantine **[389]** in the Louvre (*SEG* 8, 784; *Sammelbuch* 5, 8232), however, line 9, including *xoanon*, is badly damaged, but κ̣αι̣ ν̣αον χρυσουν̣ is legible. For the copy from Leontopolis: Alexandria, Graeco-Roman Museum Inv. no. 21352; *SEG* 18, 634; P.M. Fraser, "An unpublished fragment of the Memphian decree of 196 B.C.," *BSAAlex* 41 (1956) 57–62; this copy was left unfinished and does not contain the *xoanon* section. For Egyptian statues enclosed in shrines in processions: W. Barta, "Das Götterkultbild als Mittelpunkt bei Prozessionsfesten," *MDAIK* 23 (1968) 75–78.

[147] *IG* II^2, 2948 **[399]**, with references to the shrine and the Bacchic organization in the Peiraeus known from other evidence.

again, that they are plural seems inconsistent if one thinks in terms of one god–one shrine–one cult image, the idea better embodied by the Magnesian and Egyptian *xoana*.

The *xoana* of Dionysius are, on the other hand, entirely in line with the only other *xoana* known from inscriptions before the second century. The *xoanon* that Nikon dedicated to Asclepius on Delos [**386**] is a private offering, like Dionysius', and is *kluton*, "splendid," just as Dionysius implies of his gifts when he announces that it is on them that he has chosen to spend his "plentiful silver wealth." The appearance of *xoana* as expensive private dedications continues to be attested in later inscriptions, and is among the most solidly documented of the contexts of the word.

A second decree from Magnesia on the Meander [**393**] falls somewhere within the first half of the century. It concerns ceremonies in commemoration of the *kathedrusis*, the "installation" of the *xoanon* of Artemis Leucophryene in a structure called the *Parthenon*. The intensive development of this cult began around 220 B.C. after the goddess made a spectacular epiphany; a festival was established even before the construction of a temple. The date of this temple—according to Vitruvius the work of Hermogenes—is debated. The high date of before 200 B.C. would encourage the assignment of an early date to the inscription, but does not necessitate one; even if *Parthenon* refers to the cella of the temple, it is not certain that the "preparation" is to be equated with the actual construction. Nor is the evidence of prosopography conclusive, since several relations are known who share the name that moved the proposal. Conceivably the text may even belong near the middle of the century. In any event, the decree deals with an attempt to revitalize a festival that evidently enjoyed little popular support. The *xoanon* of Artemis has been plausibly identified with an image that begins to appear on city coins after c. 190 B.C. It is a slim, standing figure, shown frontally, wearing a polos and a veil. Fillets hang from its outstretched hands. The stiff, hieratic pose is probably meant to suggest an old image; the Artemis might be an old statue connected with the scanty fifth-century architectural remains under the Hellenistic temple, or even a survivor from still earlier times. More likely, however, this statue is one of the series of Ionian and Anatolian images of goddesses that proliferate in Hellenistic and Imperial times. The mannered archaism of these statues displays itself in a uniformity of hieratic pose and in elements of costume that seem to incorporate Greek and Anatolian features. Kern notes minute traces of gold-leaf in the cracks of the statue base found in the cella, and it is possible that the image which stood on the base was gilded.[148]

[148] Kern, *Inschriften* 85–88, no. 100a [**393**]; Hahland, "Fries" (*supra* p. 61 n. 143); Sokolowski, *LSAM* 92–98 no. 33; 96 for date and circumstances; Linfert, *Kunstzentren* 164–177 for

It is not possible to be sure whether specific connotations of form or age or material determined the use of *xoanon* in the second Magnesian inscription. The statue of Artemis is comparable to the Egyptian and the other Magnesian *xoana* in that it is the focus of elaborate public cult, in contrast, again, to the Peiraeus *xoana*, which are private dedications. This circumstance suggests that by the second century *xoanon* might have developed two sets of associations. The texts from Magnesia and Rosetta seem to reflect the association of the word with temple images that are the focus of religious activities.

The next epigraphical *xoanon* of the second century B.C. is considerably later. It is mentioned in the text on a statue base on Delos [**387**], in the dedicatory inscription of Charmikos, from the Attic deme of Kikynna, who, "having become priest of Zeus Kynthios and Athena Kynthia, dedicated the *xoanon*." Charmikos' priesthood began after 113/2.[149] The inscription occupies a corner of the rightmost (to the viewer) block of four that form the surviving front section of a large statue base that carried three images. A damaged inscription on the leftmost preserved block records the dedication by *Dion*— of *agalmata*, presumably of the same deities. These *agalmata* were set in the two shallow depressions preserved in the top surface of the base; only semicircles now remain of the cuttings that would have been completed by the lost line of rear blocks. Charmikos' *xoanon* was set differently. The rear surfaces of both the block carrying the dedication and its neighbor on the left were cut in such a way that when the base was complete, a bottomless, rectangular hole would have been formed to accommodate the image. Like the *agalma* on the far left, the *xoanon* seems to

---

the architectural evidence. See R. Özgan, "Zur Datierung des Artemisaltars in Magnesia am Maeander," *IstMitt* 32 (1982) 196–209, for a date for the temple and altar in the late third century. For the base: J. Kohte in C. Humann *et al.*, *Magnesia am Maeander* (Berlin, 1904) 80–90, figs. 86, 87 (reconstruction); no remains of gold are mentioned, and the similarity of the image to the Ephesia is stressed. For the remains of gold-leaf: O. Kern, "Magnetische Studien," *Hermes* 36 (1901) 507–508. For the coins: B.V. Head, *BMC Ionia* (London, 1892) 163–165 (after c. 190 B.C. to Marcus Aurelius); 174 no. 106 for the image in a temple featured on coins of the Ephesus–Magnesia alliance (reign of Caracalla); Lacroix, *Reproductions* 141; 151 for some of these Asiatic goddesses as archaistic creations to be distinguished from truly archaic pieces. For these goddesses: R. Fleischer, *Artemis von Ephesos und verwandte Kultstatuen aus Anatolien und Syrien* (Leiden, 1973), and a "Supplement" to this title, in *Studies Dörner* I, 324–358; brief treatment in *LIMC* II.1 (1984) 762–763. For an old view of such statues as ancient pieces: F. Imhoof-Blumer, "Alte Kultbilder," *Nomima* 8 (1913) 1–22. I have been unable to consult F. Dunand, "Sens et fonction de la fête dans la Grèce hellénistique. Les cérémonies en l'honneur d'Artémis Leucophryéné," *Dialogues d'histoire ancienne* 4 (1978) 201–215.

[149] Delos Inv. E 799 [**387**]; *ID* 1881; J.A. Lebègue, *Recherches sur Délos* (Paris, 1876) 160 no. XIV; *Délos* 11, 124–125; 124 fig. 86 for drawing of the whole base; Bruneau, *Cultes* 226; Marcadé, *Musée Délos* 92.

have held something in its left hand that would have rested in the small, square cutting provided for it. All the images were apparently larger than life-size, and the *agalmata* rested on large plinths.

The inscription and base together should provide a good opportunity to pin down a *xoanon* archaeologically. The four extant blocks preserve different settings for *agalmata* and a *xoanon*—depressions for the plinths of the former, and a deep hole for the latter, suggesting an entirely different system of setting. The hole therefore offers evidence that *xoanon* carries connotations of material and structure. Firm conclusions on this point, however, are difficult to draw.

Plassart asserts that the *agalmata* were probably acroliths and that the *xoanon* would have been "a divine figure, of wood, of an archaic type." He associates some colossal stone fragments of hands with the *agalmata* and relies on the definition of *xoanon* derived from Pausanias. He suggests furthermore that the base probably carried cult figures that would have been placed in an *oikos*.[150] Marcadé, however, rejects the suggestion that the *agalmata* were acroliths. The hands belong to marble arms, and the settings for the agalmata are in no way similar to those for the acroelephantine statues in the Temple of the Athenians on Delos.[151] It may yet be possible that the *xoanon* was an acrolith, since such an image might also have needed a deep hole for an armature.[152] There has been so little systematic study of the methods by which Greek statues were set, however, that it would be unwise to rely on this base for firm conclusions about the possible structural significance of the term *xoanon*. Marcadé admits that it is not in fact known how acroliths were set up, and for the moment it is better to acknowledge ignorance on the point and turn to other lines of speculation.[153]

It is interesting that the base carried two separate dedications. All three statues seem to have been dedicated to Zeus Kynthios and Athena Kynthia; if they represented these gods, the identity of one statue is in doubt.[154] Charmikos' dedication is inscribed in letters much smaller than

[150] Plassart in *Délos* 11, 123–125; remains of "acroliths": 125, fig. 87; 124 n. 1 for a foot, perhaps to be associated, but dubious.

[151] Marcadé, *Musée Délos* 92–95, esp. 93. *Cf.* also the provisions for the Athena Parthenos: G.P. Stevens, "Remarks Upon the Colossal Chryselephantine Statue of Athena in the Parthenon," *Hesperia* 24 (1955) 244–267.

[152] For an "acrolithic *xoanon*" perhaps of the second century A.D. [14] (*AnthPal* 12.40) and the technique of acrolithic sculpture: *infra* pp. 141–142.

[153] Marcadé, *Musée Délos* 93. Winter and Winter, "Kourno" (*supra* p. 3 n. 10) suggest that an "elaborately socketed block" probably carried a wooden cult statue at Kourno, "since the rounded bottom of the socket seems unsuitable for a heavy stone pier and the base too massive for a terracotta object." For statue bases: M. Jacob-Felsch, *Die Entwicklung griechischer Statuenbasen und die Aufstellung der Statuen* (Waldsassen-Bayern, 1969).

[154] The left-hand inscription, Inv. E 798, is almost entirely restored, the only nearly complete word being *agalmata*. Plassart, *Délos* 11, 125, wonders about the identity of the *xoanon*.

those of the *Dion*— text, and one wonders about the relationship of the two dedications.[155] Were the statues offered together, or is the *xoanon* a later addition or replacement or repair? The texts are probably not far separated in time, but nevertheless it seems possible that some kind of renovation might account for the difference in settings. If, as in the case of the *xoana* of Nikon and Dionysius, *xoanon* carries connotations of splendor and expense, some kind of rivalry might even be indicated. In any case, the *xoanon* of Charmikos appears to belong to the realm of private dedications, and there is no reason to presume that it or the *agalmata* were, as Plassart suggested, installed as "cult figures."

An inscription from Anaphe [**380**], once dated in the early first century B.C., but now assigned to the very late second, twice mentions a *ξοάνιον* (*xoanion*). The text is a decree concerning the arrangements for a dedication by Timotheos, son of Sosikles, who wishes to install a shrine to Aphrodite in the sanctuary of Apollo Asgelatas; it specifies the area of the sanctuary that it is to be granted for the construction. "The altar of Ktesios and the *xoanion*" are mentioned as topographical reference points.[156]

This text preserves the only extant appearance of the word *xoanion*, which is considered to be the diminutive of *xoanon*.[157] If this meaning is correct, the sanctuary of Apollo would have contained a "little *xoanon*," perhaps to be associated with Ktesios, since the altar of that god is mentioned in the same phrase. *Xoanion* might, however, have another meaning: the suffix *-ion*, as well as indicating the diminutive, can also signify place.[158] In that case, the *xoanion* might be a location or a building or structure housing a *xoanon* or *xoana*. Such a meaning would be more appropriate in the context of the various structures mentioned in the decree. If the *xoanion* is such a structure, the *xoana* in it might be dedications, but there is no way to be sure. At any rate, whatever the meaning of *xoanion*, it recalls the *xoana* provided by Dionysius as furnishings for the *temenos*.

A fragmentary inscription from Oleros, in Crete [**398**], gives the last *xoanon* that can so far be assigned to the second century B.C. The text is dated to the end of the second century or the beginning of the first on the basis of letter forms. It concerns a *naos* and *xoana* of Athena Oleria with

[155] For Dion[ysius Dionysiou Sphettios]: *Délos* 11, 117, 123; 123 for Inv. E 798.

[156] *IG* XII.3, 248 [**380**]; *SEG* 25, 909 (with bibliography). The transcription in *CIG* II, 2477 gives the incorrect reading *xoanon* for line 21 (= 16); the addenda (p. 1091) give a full text and a correct reading, in which line 13 is completed from the wholly preserved *xoanion* in line 16. Sokolowski, *LSCG* 225–226 no. 129.

[157] *E.g.*, Benveniste, "Kolossos" 130.

[158] For *-ιον* as a suffix denoting place: H.W. Smyth, rev. G.M. Messing, *Greek Grammar* (Cambridge, Mass., 1956) §851 for expression of place by *-ιον* and *-ειον*. See also P. Walters, ed. D.W. Gooding, *The Text of the Septuagint. Its Corruptions and their Emendations* (Cambridge, 1973) 54–56 for these suffixes and the formation of names of temples.

which, at the time the Pamphylians made up the body of *kosmoi*, a list of men had something to do. The activity in question has been lost. One suggestion would have the men oversee or be in charge of the *naos* and *xoana*, but that possibility seems ruled out by the necessity for a transitive use of the verb, a usage unprecedented in Cretan inscriptions. Another supplement, by which the men would have made the *naos* and *xoana*, has been criticized as inappropriate because *xoana* are "ancient images" that could not be newly "made." Guarducci's solution is to interpret the activity not as new manufacture, but instead as repair.[159] Since, however, contemporary inscriptions show that *xoana* can be new dedications, it is not necessary to assume that these are old statues. The *naos* and *xoana* might be new dedications, just as in the case of Dionysius' *temenos*. On the other hand, an inscription from Delos [**388**] of the late first century B.C. specifically mentions the salvage of *xoana* that had long been neglected, and such a restoration cannot be ruled out in the case of the text from Oleros.[160] It is worth noting that this inscription gives yet another example of plural *xoana*.

Conclusions

Inscriptions give a more vivid picture of *xoanon* in the second century B.C. than do the scanty literary testimonia. Just as in the third century the meaning of the word developed in two directions, so too do the second-century inscriptions fall into two general groups. In the inscriptions from the Peiraeus and Delos, *xoana* are dedications in sanctuaries; in those from Anaphe and Oleros, they are furnishings in sanctuaries. In the texts from Magnesia and Egypt, in contrast, *xoana* are the focus of elaborate cult activities, of public worship on a grand scale. The *xoana* that are dedications seem to be expensive things, the sponsorship of which is understandably cause for pride. In this respect the word continues to have the associations found in the third-century inscription from Delos; it appears to be acceptably, if rarely, applied to lavish private dedications. The *xoana* from Egypt and Ionia, however, have no such connections with the private sphere, but are instead involved in public cult.

It is possible that this division is merely the result of accidents of preservation, that it just so happens that no private dedications of *xoana* survive from the areas distant from mainland Greece, and that no mentions of "cult" *xoana* are preserved except in the East. In later times, Ionia does offer several examples of dedicated *xoana*, and one might argue for unattested continuity in the meaning of the word. There are reasons to suspect,

[159] *ICr* III, 132–133 no. 1 [**398**].
[160] *ID* 2548 [**388**]; *infra* pp. 69–70.

however, that the distribution of epigraphical *xoana* reflects real and important differences in meaning in the various parts of the Greek-speaking world.

It is significant that the one contemporary literary source in which *xoanon* explicitly appears as an overall term for worshipped images is a section of the Sibylline Oracles produced in Egypt by a Jewish author. The focus of the writer's condemnation of idolatry is *eidola* and *xoana*. The former is a word used only in late sources for images, and the latter is extremely rare; from the perspective of Greek usage, neither is wholly appropriate. Furthermore, the grounds for the condemnation of such images are not at home in Greek tradition, but come instead from Jewish thought and reflect a conception of idolatry more at home in the East. What seems to be likewise a special usage of *xoanon* appears in the text of the Rosetta Stone. It has already been noted that a similar application of the term may be reflected in the *xoana* attributed by Josephus to Manetho, and possibly in those of Apollonius. The Ionian and Egyptian inscriptions and the Jewish Sibylline text give the first certain indications of the meaning that attaches to *xoanon* in later times, and of the context in which that meaning develops fully: the late Hellenistic and Greco-Roman iconoclastic controversy. In the literature of that controversy *xoanon* is a standard term for the images of pagan idolatry. This meaning is at odds with those found in the general run of contemporary inscriptions, and even with some attested in contemporary literature not concerned with iconoclasm. It is possible that the division between the eastern and western inscriptions in the second century B.C. already reflects changes in the meaning of *xoanon* that are crucial to understanding the definition with which the term entered modern scholarship.

6. *Xoanon* in the First Century B.C.

The distribution of evidence for *xoanon* in the first century B.C. is the opposite of that found in the preceding century: literary texts, not inscriptions, now shed greater light on the word. The *xoana* of the epigraphical texts are few and seem neither to extend nor to narrow second-century usage, but in literature the word becomes more popular, and there are noticeable changes in its meaning and context.

Only two inscriptions containing *xoanon* can be dated to the first century B.C.; both are late, and one may even belong to the following century. The earlier is a text from Delos [388] that mentions *xoana* of the Dioscuri.[161] The inscription is carved on a door lintel found in a small sanctuary. It commemorates the restoration of the cult by Athenobios, who rescued the "*xoana* in the *prodomoi*" (ἐν προδόμοις ξόανα) from squalid oblivion, and reinstituted the procession.

This inscription is the major evidence for identifying the place in which it was found as the sanctuary of the Dioscuri. In publishing the text, Robert attempted to match the implied lapse in cult with the archaeological history of the site, and to account for the fortunes of the sanctuary in terms of Delian political history.[162] Marcadé later discussed the fragments of marble sculpture from the area—parts of an archaic kouros set on a later base, and of a Hellenistic male statue that approximates the format of a kouros—and used them as evidence for the perpetuation of primitive types in religious art.[163]

The lintel that bears the inscription, however, was not found *in situ*. For this and other reasons, Bruneau has disputed the identification of the small sanctuary as that of the Dioscuri.[164] The objections are cogent; it does not therefore seem possible to associate the *xoana* of the text with either the architectural remains of the area or the sculpture found there. Marcadé's argument for the persistence of what he considers to be old-fashioned, nonstandard types (*xoana* and acroliths) cannot find support in the equation of the *xoana* of the Dioscuri with the archaic and archaizing sculpture from the area. The *xoana* of the inscription shed no light on that sculpture; nor does the sculpture aid in determining the meaning of *xoanon*.

The only information about the *xoana* of the Dioscuri comes from the inscription itself, but little is given. The *prodomoi* cannot be securely identified; ordinarily the word refers to domestic architecture, but here it appears

[161] *ID* 2548 [388]: F. Robert, "Inscription métrique trouvée au Dioscourion délien," *BCH* 58 (1934) 184–202; *Délos* 20, 42–45; Bruneau, *Cultes* 383–386.

[162] Robert, "Inscription" (*supra* p. 69 n. 161).

[163] Robert, *Délos* 20, 31–34; Marcadé, *Musée Délos* 303–304; *cf.* 90–91.

[164] P. Bruneau and J. Ducat, *Guide de Délos*³ (Paris, 1983) 259–260 no. 123, permit the possibility of this identification of the site, but Bruneau, *Cultes* 383–386, rejects it.

to mean part or parts of a sanctuary.[165] It is not clear whether the *prodomoi* are the places where the *xoana* moldered in the past, or a new location where their restorations shine. That the *xoana* are associated with *prodomoi* rather than a temple tends to suggest that they, like the majority of *xoana* in earlier inscriptions, were dedications or similar furnishings and not temple images. The text does not state whether the *xoana* were involved in the reinstituted procession. Whatever their functions and appearance, it is certain only that the *xoana* could be neglected and rehabilitated.[166]

Another inscription mentioning a *xoanon* may belong to the end of the first century B.C. or to the early part of the following century. It is a text in elegiac couplets on a statue base from Chalcedon that mentions a *xoanon* of Zeus Ourios **[384]**.[167] Philo, son of Antipater, bids the sailor in northern waters to invoke this Zeus and to place cakes by the *xoanon*. It is not altogether clear whether this *xoanon* is the statue that Philo himself has dedicated—the ever-gracious god he has set up as a token of good sailing—or the famous image of Zeus Ourios at the Bithynian shrine at Hieron. The image at Hieron is mentioned by Cicero as one of three statues of the same type. The Ourios at Syracuse has been identified with a standing Zeus leaning on a spear that appears on silver coins minted there around 214 B.C.[168] It seems more likely, however, that Philo refers to the statue he has set up. The *xoanon* would in that case be another private gift, and not a temple

[165] LSJ[9] *s.v.* *πρόδομος* does not include this text, and cites only a domestic context for the adjective. Dinsmoor, *Architecture*[3] 394 *s.v.* Prodomus, defines the term as "corresponding to the pronaos in the case of ordinary houses." For a comparable case, see K. Jeppesen, "Further Inquiries on the Location of the Erechtheion and Its Relationship to the Temple of the Polias 1. Προστομιαῖον and Προστόμιον," *AJA* 87 (1983) 325–333, where he argues that *προστῷων*, a term attested for domestic architecture, is applied in inscriptions to a part of the Athenian temple of the Polias. Bruneau and Ducat, (*supra* p. 69 n. 164) 259, speak of the prodomos ("pluriel noble").

[166] Their restoration provides a parallel for the suggested restoration in *ICr* III, 132–133 no. 1, from Oleros **[398]**: *supra* pp. 66–67.

[167] *BMusInscr* IV, no. 1012 **[384]**: *CIG* II, 3797; *BullEpig* 1965, *ap.* no. 488; R. Merkelbach, ed., *Die Inschriften von Kalchedon* (IgSK 20; Bonn, 1980) 27–28 no. 14; Page, *Further Greek Epigrams* 375–377, no. LXX, for the uncertain date of the epigram: "it would be at home in any part of the Hellenistic period." See also Cook, *Zeus* III, 145–147.

[168] Cicero, *Verr.* 2.128–130, discusses Verres' theft of the Syracusan image, contrasting its hard fortunes with that of the statue at the mouth of the Black Sea, which had survived all manner of upheaval. For the Syracusan image: Griffiths, *Temple Treasures* 6, 52–53. For the Syracusan coins showing Zeus leaning on a spear: Head, *Historia Numorum* 186–187. The identification by G. Abeken, "Giove Imperatore ossia Urio," *AnnInst* 1839, 62–72, is mentioned with a "perhaps" by G.F. Hill, *Coins of Ancient Sicily* (Westminster, 1903) 196. Lacroix, *Reproductions* does not treat this statue. Page, *Further Greek Epigrams* 375, believes that because the temple of Zeus Ourios stood at the eastern end of the Bosporus, "the stone must therefore have been carried to Chalcedon, perhaps as ballast."

image. The base gives few clues about the appearance of the statue. A sinking in the top of the block leaves a ten-centimeter-wide rim, the left side of which preserves two holes for dowels, filled with lead; presumably this arrangement served to secure the plinth of a stone statue.[169] Whether Philo's Ourios copied the famous type cannot be ascertained; it is, however, reasonable to think that the dedication was made to be recognizable, and so the *xoanon* would have been of conventional Hellenistic figural type, as seen in the representations of the Syracusan Ourios.

The two inscriptions from Delos and Chalcedon are the extent of the epigraphical evidence known so far for *xoanon* in the first century B.C. In both texts, *xoana* seem to be part of the private rather than the public domain, and a connection with them appears to be cause for pride. These *xoana* are in line with the majority of previous epigraphical *xoana*, then, whose major characteristics—being private dedications, and being expensive—remain constant from the early third century to the turn of the millennium. The luxurious quality of the *xoana* attested in the inscriptions can be traced to the earliest appearances of the word in the later fifth century. In only three inscriptions among those dated to the centuries before Christ are *xoana* substantially different; these are the second-century texts from Magnesia and Egypt in which *xoana* are temple images and the focus of public and elaborate cult. Possibly in the third, and certainly in the second century, *xoanon* begins to appear in literature apparently as a generic term for such temple images. The context of this usage is not purely Greek, but is instead Egyptian—on the one hand, the writing of an Egyptian historian in Greek, and on the other, a tract composed by a Jewish writer in Egypt to reach a Greek-speaking audience, earnest polemic against the worship of images couched in terms that seem peculiar from the Greek point of view. The non-Greek conceptions reflected in the curious use of *xoanon*, however, apparently influenced the usage of the word in the cosmopoliltan world of late Hellenistic and early Imperial times, and by the first century A.D. the once unusual meaning of the word was well established.

It should be emphasized that even in the first century B.C., when it enjoys its greatest efflorescence to date, *xoanon* is by no means a common word. My review of Diodorus Siculus, for example, yielded only five appearances of *xoanon* out of one hundred ten references to statues of various kinds, most of them statues of gods.[170]

[169] *BMusInscr* IV *ad* no. 1012 for the base. Such holes for a plinth, unlike those provided for the attachment of the feet of bronze statues, reveal nothing about the pose of the image. Page, *Further Greek Epigrams* 376 *ad* 6, argues strongly that a wooden image is meant by *xoanon* here. (See *supra* p. 2 n. 8.)

[170] The date of Diodorus Siculus is uncertain. The latest event he mentions occurred c. 36 B.C.: C.H. Oldfather, tr., *Diodorus of Sicily* I (LCL, 1933) ix–x.

The *xoana* of Diodorus are not easy to evaluate. The major difficulty in working with the vocabulary of Diodorus is determining the extent to which he follows his sources, and there is no consensus on this point.[171] Often it is not possible to do more than note a contrast between direct and indirect discourse. The account of the *xoanon/agalma* made by Telecles and Theodorus for the Samians (1.98.5–9) **[58]**, for example, begins with *ἱστορεῖται*, "it is related," and bears little if any relation to the surrounding text. A unit so poorly integrated with its context might not have been much changed in the transplanting. It is possible that Diodorus merely adopted the *xoanon* of his source (on which, then, the *xoanon* in his own immediately preceding remark would depend); it is, however, also possible that Diodorus chose the word.

The passage describes an Egyptian method of proportion by which the two Greek artists, one working in Ephesos and the other in Samos, each produced half an *agalma*; when the two pieces were brought together, they joined perfectly. To my knowledge, neither the passage nor the method has been satisfactorily explained, and its source remains as obscure as its meaning.[172]

In content, the *xoanon* passage stands clearly apart from the rest of the account of Egypt. The solitary appearance of *xoanon* further suggests that the sources of the section may not have been one of those for the rest of Book I. This book in fact contains the majority of Diodorus' references to statues; the word most frequently used is *eikon*, and *xoanon* does not otherwise occur. It is difficult to suggest a source for the section on the *xoanon*. Burton has mentioned the possibility of Hecataeus of Abdera, a writer of the fourth century B.C., for I.96–98 as a whole; Pollitt suggests that one section of the passage may derive from Xenocrates.[173] The tone of wonder would seem to set the discussion at least one step away from an artist's treatise, but little is known of these works. The unevenness of the passage suggests that it might not be homogeneous; the detailed explanation of the Egyptian system looks as if it could have been inserted to eke out the description of the Samian *xoanon*. Such a procedure would help to account for the overall confusion in the discussion, but would also make the search for sources more difficult.

[171] For the sources of Diodorus: Burton, *Diodorus* 1–34. For Diodorus' considerable alterations to his sources, see the summary of the conclusions of Palm given by C.B. Welles, tr., *Diodorus of Sicily* VIII (LCL, 1963) 3; *cf. CAH*² VII.1, 6.

[172] The passage is quoted by Eusebius, *PE* 10.8.482 c **[124]**. For recent discussions of the passage, see: Pollitt, *Ancient View* 13–14; Ridgway, *Archaic* 29; W.M. Davis, "Egypt, Samos, and the Archaic Style in Greek Sculpture," *JEA* 67 (1981) 74–75, with bibliography.

[173] Burton, *Diodorus* 31; Pollitt, *Ancient View* 88 n. 3.

What *xoanon* means in the passage is not entirely clear. The words referring to its manufacture name no specific process, but apply instead to preparation and finishing in general. It may be that *xoanon* is deliberately applied to a statue from the deep past manufactured in the Egyptian mode, but this suggestion is not borne out by its other appearances in Diodorus. More likely, Diodorus has used it to mean no more than the image of a god, as he seems to do elsewhere. Without more information on the source or sources of the passage, it is not possible to say whether the word is Diodorus' own choice, or a borrowing from another writer whose understanding of it may have been different.[174]

Two of Diodorus' *xoana* are images connected with Alexander the Great. The sources for the history of Alexander are extremely difficult to trace; both episodes involving *xoana* are treated by other authors in versions that cannot be perfectly reconciled. It is generally thought that Diodorus relied on Cleitarchus for his account of Alexander.[175]

The first *xoanon* of Book 17 is that of Apollo of Tyre (17.41.8) [**61**]. During Alexander's siege of the city in 332/1, Apollo appeared in a dream to a Tyrian citizen and announced his intention of deserting to the enemy. This dream was only one of several exceptionally unpromising omens, and the Tyrians accordingly tried to prevent the god's defection by fastening his *xoanon* to its base with golden cords.

Diodorus gives no details about the appearance or function of the *xoanon* of Apollo. The statue is known from other sources, but the information is scanty and conflicting and reflects not so much historical and archaeological fact as it does various traditions. Curtius' account of the siege of Tyre includes the most elaborate discussion of the statue (4.3.21–22) [**56**]: the *simulacrum* is shackled to the altar of Hercules in the hope that the hero's strength will foil the god's escape. This version differs in some ways from Diodorus', and shows Curtius' conflation of sources. For instance, in Diodorus the dreamer himself is suspected of treason, and takes refuge in the *hieron* of Heracles; Curtius' more vivid emphasis on the hero might reflect a source such as that of Arrian, in whose account of Tyre Heracles is extremely important.[176] Curtius also identifies the statue of Apollo as Carthaginian booty from Syracuse, but his assertion appears to be wrong; as reported by Diodorus (13.108.4), who derives the information

[174] Cf. Burton, *Diodorus* 288 n. 3 on *xoanon*: "the word originally means a statue carved in wood, but is also used to refer indiscriminately to any statue."

[175] For the sources of D.S. 17: J.R. Hamilton, "Cleitarchus and Diodorus 17," in *Studies Schachermeyr* 126–146.

[176] Arrian, *An.* 2.16 for the ancient temple of Heracles, and Alexander's wish to sacrifice to the Tyrian Heracles; 2.18.1 [**32**] for Heracles' appearance in a dream to Alexander—a variation of the dream epiphany of the siege episode.

from Timaeus, the Carthaginians took the statue from outside Gela in 405 B.C.[177] The episode is also treated by Plutarch, who calls the statue a *kolossos* (*Alex.* 24.5–8) **[314]** and says that the god was treated like a human deserter; his image was tied and nailed to its base. This explanation puts the Tyrian action in a slightly different light, although in another place (*Quaest. Rom.* 61; *Mor.* 279 A), in a discussion of Roman *evocatio*, Plutarch alludes to the Tyrian custom of binding images to prevent their being lured away. Because even in the time of Plutarch the meaning of *kolossos* is not consistent, it is impossible to tell whether he thinks of the statue as huge.

The differences between the various accounts of Alexander's siege of Tyre mean that even though the statue of Apollo was a real image, from an archaeological point of view it might almost as well have been a made-up one, since each author who mentions it evidently has his own conception of the episode. That is to say, taken collectively the testimonia do not yield a complete and reliable description of the image, and singly they can be interpreted only within the context of the individual writers. The testimony of Plutarch and Curtius does not contribute to understanding Diodorus' conception of the *xoanon*. It is not even clear whether Diodorus interpreted the Tyrian attempt to bind the image fast in terms of the Greek belief that gods left a city before it was destroyed, or simply dismissed the Tyrians as being superstitious on a very low level.[178] Neither the appearance nor the function and significance of the image emerges clearly from Diodorus' account. It is likely that his conception of the statue was in fact not especially detailed, and that he uses *xoanon* in the most general sense of an image of a god.

Part of the difficulty in treating the various accounts of the Apollo of Tyre is that the statue itself is less interesting to reporters than the action of tying it up, and in the different versions of that theme the image itself tends to be left aside. The same is true of the second *xoanon* in Book 17, the oracular image of Ammon in the oasis of Siwa. Again, the information given by the sources is conflicting and does little to clarify Diodorus' usage of *xoanon*.

Alexander consulted the oracle in 331/0. The episode is famous chiefly because the god may or may not have acknowledged Alexander as his son, or issue, a declaration which has important bearing on the question of the king's assumption of divinity.[179] Diororus gives a fairly detailed description

[177] For the error: J.C. Rolfe, tr., *Quintus Curtius* I (LCL, 1946) 194 n. c; for the image, to which Alexander's army attributed part of their success at Tyre: J.E. Atkinson, *A Commentary on Q. Curtius Rufus' Historiae Alexandri Magni Books 3 and 4* (Amsterdam/Uithoorn, 1980) 306 *ad loc.* and 319.

[178] For this Greek belief: *supra* p. 17 and n. 35.

[179] For recent discussions see: A.B. Bosworth, "Alexander and Ammon," in *Studies Schachermeyr* 51–75; *idem.*, "History and Rhetoric in Curtius Rufus," *CP* 78 (1983) 159; P. Gou-

of the oracle (17.50.6) [**62**]. He says that the *xoanon* περιέχεται, "is surrounded" by emeralds and other gems. It is carried in a golden boat by eighty priests whose movement it somehow directs. A large female retinue follows the boat, singing.

Curtius' account (4.7.23–24) is similar to Diodorus', at least in terms of the boat and the priests and the women, and the precious stones that surround the image. Curtius, however, says that *quod pro deo colitur, non eandem effigiem habet quam vulgo diis artifices accommodaverunt; umbilico maxime similis est habitus zmaragdo et gemmis coagmentatus* (what is worshipped as the god does not have the same form that artificers have commonly given to deities; its appearance is very like that of a navel fastened in a mass of emeralds and other gems; tr. Rolfe). Strabo (17.1.43) [**353**] has an altogether different version of the episode. He does not describe the image, but compares the nods and signs by which the god communicated his will to Homer's description of Zeus nodding his dark brows. Presumably, then, Strabo assumed that the image was anthropomorphic; indeed, Zeus Ammon was regularly represented as a horned man. Strabo says that his source is Callisthenes, the companion and historian of Alexander. Evidently this tradition is considerably different from that followed by Diodorus and Curtius.[180]

Strabo's comment on Ammon is little more than a throwaway remark in a section devoted to Alexander's relations with oracles. Both Diodorus and Curtius, in contrast, seem to have used information from a source concerned with the actual workings of the oracle. Such information may not even originally have been part of the Alexander story. The description of Ammon's procedure is similar to Macrobius' account of the oracle at Ba'albek (*Sat.* 1.23.10–20) and especially to Lucian's description of the oracular Apollo at Hierapolis (*SyrD* 36).[181] It is possible that the information about Ammon's oracle at Siwa came from a source specifically concerned with the technical aspects of oracles.[182]

---

kowsky, *Essai sur les origines du mythe d'Alexandre (336–270 av. J.C.) I. Les origines politiques* (Nancy, 1978) *passim*.

[180] Plutarch (*Alex.* 26.6–27.5) does not mention an image of Ammon; in 27.3 it is a priest who greets Alexander on behalf of Ammon and gives him the answers to his questions, even the secret responses (27.5). Arrian passes over the visit to Ammon on the grounds that the sources for the visit are deficient in exactitude; his disinclination is understandable. See J.R. Hamilton, *Plutarch. Alexander. A Commentary* (Oxford, 1969) 68–73.

[181] Cook, *Zeus* I, 357, 552, 585.

[182] Such a source, providing information close to Diodorus', seems to have inspired the note in Servius, *ad* V. *Aen.* 6.68 [**333**] about *xoana*, small statues carried in litters that gave prophecies among the Egyptians and Carthaginians. See *infra* pp. 163–164. For oracular moving statues: E.R. Dodds, *The Ancient Concept of Progress* (Oxford, 1973) 194–195.

Although Didorus' and Curtius' accounts are similar, their descriptions of the image are different. Both say that it was surrounded by emeralds and other jewels, but while Curtius describes an omphalos, Diodorus is silent about the form of the god. If both drew on the same source, it is curious that Diodorus did not mention the omphalos; Curtius may have taken this detail from another source. Some modern commentators have passed over the discrepancy; some assume that Curius' more explicit version is the more accurate; some try to reconcile the difference. Atkinson has suggested that Curtius describes not the image itself, but instead the shrine that would have contained it and been carried in procession; it is an enterprising and attractive idea.[183] That an image of Ammon did exist at Siwa cannot be doubted. It may have been of the widespread horned but anthropomorphic type. However Curtius' omphalos is to be explained, his information cannot simply be applied to Diodorus' account. Different traditions are involved, and the various testimonia do not add up to a reliable composite picture of the image. If Diodorus gave much thought at all to the appearance of the oracular Ammon, it is most likely that he would have had in mind the popular anthropomorphic type, and to this general impression of an image of the god he applied the term *xoanon*.

Diodorus' last *xoana* (31.35 Walton) **[63]** are those carried off from the Nicephorium, the Pergamene *temenos* despoiled by Prusias in 156 B.C. Three words for statues appear in this passage: *andriantes*, *xoana*, and *agalma*. Presumably they have specific connotations that are meaningful in the context of the episode, although it is just possible that they serve rhetorically to underscore the range and extent of the pillage. Diodorus specifically mentions *τὰ τῶν θεῶν ξόανα*, and since these appear to be contrasted with the *andriantes*, it is likely that he refers to images of gods in general. It should be noted, however, that the only statue singled out is the one of Asclepius reputed to be by Phyromachus, and this, which is generally thought of as a temple image, is the *agalma*.[184] Since it is likely that the

[183] *E.g.*, H.W. Parke, *The Oracles of Zeus. Dodona. Olympia. Ammon* (Oxford, 1967) 199–200, 224–226, does not attempt to reconcile the report of the omphalos with the existence of the well-established type of the horned but anthropomorphic god; he notes that images are carried inside shrines, and emphasizes the coincidence of *neuma* in Diodorus and Strabo: "The brief allusions to 'nods' and 'tokens' can be taken to refer to the same method of enquiry . . . " (225). Cook, *Zeus* I, 355–359, approves Meltzer's conclusions that Curtius' description is the most accurate and that the image was a "*baítylos*"; Atkinson, *Curtius* (*supra* p. 74 n. 177) 353 *ad* 7.23. Herodotus mentions such a shrine at Papremis in Egypt (2.63): "They carry the *agalma* in a small, wooden, gold-plated *neos* on the day before the ceremony to another *hieron oikema*. The few who are left behind with the *agalma* drag a four-wheeled cart, taking the *neos* and the *agalma* inside the *neos*. . . . "

[184] Walton, *Diodorus* XI, translates *andriantes* as "votive statues." The sack is also described by Polybius, 32.15: ἐσύλησε καὶ τοὺς ἀνδριάντας καὶ τὰ λίθινα τῶν ἀγαλμάτων

majority of statues in this (or any) sanctuary were dedications, perhaps Diodorus' *xoana* are not far removed from those in epigraphical usage. On the whole, however, it is more probable that *xoanon* here is a blanket term for images of gods, a meaning that is firmly established in the word of other first-century B.C. writers. This passage is perhaps most useful in showing that, difficult as it is to evaluate a *xoanon* in isolation, *xoana* in the company of other words for statues are equally elusive, because no term is well understood.

Dionysius of Halicarnassus, whose *Roman Antiquities* was published at the end of the first century B.C., uses *xoanon* almost exclusively for statues of gods.[185] The word appears in his text more frequently than it does in that of Diodorus; of forty-one occurrences of words for statues, *xoana* account for thirteen and, even considering the repetition of the word in certain passages, for a fair number of individual pieces.[186]

All the *xoana* of Dionysius seem to be images placed in temples or shrines. The only *xoana* that are not of gods are of Aeneas (1.50.3; 1.50.4) **[65]**, but in these situations he is the object of veneration of some kind; the images are placed in a *hieron* and a *heroon*. The statue of Athena Polias brought from Troy, which was the responsibility of a Roman priestly family (6.69.1) **[68]**, the Juno of Veii who expressed her willingness to move to enemy Rome (13.3) **[72]**, and the two images of Fortuna Muliebris, also called *agalmata* and *aphidrumata* (8.55.4–56.2–4) **[70, 71]**, are all *xoana*.[187]

The connotations of *xoanon* in Dionysius are not easy to determine. Some of the images are especially venerable; certainly all have religious connections. Age and material may or may not be significant; the evidence

([Prusias] carried off both the *andriantes* and those of the *agalmata* that were of stone). F.W. Walbank, *A Historical Commentary on Polybius* III (Oxford, 1979) 537, thus assumes that these *andriantes* "will be bronze." The fragment of Diodorus comes from the *Excerpta Constantiniana De virtutibus et vitiis* (for the literary projects of the emperor Constantine VII Porphyrogenitus [A.D. 912–959]: Wilson, *Scholars* 140–145). For the statue of Asclepius, perhaps by Phyromachus, see A. Stewart, *Attika* (*JHS* Supplementary Paper 14; London, 1979) 12–16 and *passim*; Stewart calls it a "cult-statue."

[185] D.H. 1.3.4 identifies the current year as the consulship of Nero and Piso: 7 B.C. This date is taken as the start of publication. Recently for the chronology of Dionysius: K.S. Sacks, "Historiography in the Rhetorical Works of Dionysius of Halicarnassus," *Athenaeum* n.s. 61 (1983) 65–66.

[186] Other terms for statues in Dionysius: *hedos* (10); *eikon* (9); *hidruma* (3); *andrias* (2); *bretas* (2); *agalma* (1). There are also 4 Palladia, 4 *hiera* (once equated with *eikones*), and 1 *eidolon* as a statue (twice it refers to puppets, and three times to ghosts). The totals represent my own review of the text.

[187] For the Juno of Veii see also: Livy 5.21.2–3; 5.22.4–7; Plut. *Cam.* 6.1–2 **[316]**. For *evocatio*: V. Basanoff, *Evocatio. Etude d'un rituel militaire romain* (Paris, 1947); R.D. Weigel, "The Duplication of Temples of Juno Regina in Rome," *Ancient Society* 13/14 (1982/1983) 180–183. For the speaking *agalmata*, *cf.* Plut. *Cor.* 37.3–38 **[317]**.

is too scanty to be conclusive. The *xoana* of Aeneas and Aphrodite on Zacynthus (1.50.3) [**65**] are not necessarily old, although the place itself has ancient associations. The *xoanon* in Ambracia is "small, *archaion*, and said to be of Aeneas" (1.50.4) [**65**]; presumably if *xoanon* meant an ancient image it would not have been necessary to mention the age of the statue. *Xoanon* does not appear in places where it would be expected if age or sanctity were its connotations. For example, the ancient, miraculous, and extremely venerable image of gilded wood that stood in the Temple of Fortuna (4.40.7) [**67**] is an *eikon*. The reason may be that Dionysius believed it to be a statue of Servius Tullius rather than that of a divinity.[188] This example also suggests that *xoanon* has no specific connotations of material (at least, none of wood), but again there is insufficient evidence on this point.

To judge from the *xoana* that are mentioned, Dionysius applies the word to images that are the focus of religious attention. The same is true of unspecified *xoana*: in 8.39.1 [**69**], the Roman women seek refuge at the *xoana*, and in 2.18.2 [**66**], Romulus establishes *hiera*, *temene*, and *bomoi*, and arranges for the setting up of *xoana*. These are the fundamental classical installations for worship; compare, for example, Herodotus 2.4 [**139**], in which the Egyptians claim the first establishment of *bomoi*, *agalmata*, and *neoi* for the gods, and 4.108 [**141**], in which he notes *hira* "furnished in Greek fashion, with *agalmata* and *bomoi* and *neoi*." It seems clear that *xoana* mean the images of the gods that are considered to be standard equipment for religious activity.

The broad application of *xoanon* to images of gods is best illustrated by its usage in Strabo, for whom the term apparently has no typological significance at all. *Xoanon* occurs twenty-four times in the *Geography*, the composition and publication of which span the turn of the millennium.[189] When specific images are referred to, the word is invariably applied to images of gods. One possible exception is the *xoanon* of the Parthenos in Chersonese (7.4.2) [**338**]; Strabo makes a point of mentioning the *neos* of the *daimon*. Another exception is the *xoanon* of Homer in Smyrna (14.1.37) [**347**]. As in the case of the Parthenos in the *neos*, and in that of Dionysius' *xoana* of Aeneas, however, that image belongs to a shrine, the *Homereion*,

[188] For this statue see also: Pl. *NH* 8.194, 197 (image identified as Fortuna); Livy 10.23.3 (? Pudicitia); Ov. *F.* 6.569–636 (Servius Tullius); and the discussion by J.G. Frazer, ed., tr., *The Fasti of Ovid* IV (London, 1929) 294–295.

[189] For the date of composition of Strabo's *Geography*: Diller, *Tradition Strabo* 3–7. Strabo himself provides no definite information on this point. Historical references and the curious placement of some passages in the text suggest that the work was left unfinished at the time of his death, c. A.D. 24. See also H.L. Jones, tr., *The Geography of Strabo* I (LCL, 1917) xxiv–xxvi. For remarks on Strabo's use of *xoanon*: Leaf, *Strabo* 242–243.

which has a *neos* and the *xoanon*.[190] Twice Strabo speaks of *xoana*, in the plural, that are images of heroes. One passage (1.2.8) [**334**] discusses the moral benefits of tales and artistic representations—"*graphai* or *xoana* or *plasmata*"—of exploits "such as the *athloi* of Heracles or Theseus." Another passage tackles false reports of mythological events that are given out by flatterers (15.1.9) [**349**]. Cases in point are the expeditions of Dionysus and Heracles. Strabo is fond of pouncing on inconsistencies and conflicts in information, and here he adduces some antiquarian evidence: the costume of Heracles attributed to him by people claiming to be his descendants does not conform to that shown on *archaia xoana*, but is later than the *mneme* of the Trojan War, and so must be invention of later poets. The apparent precision of the historical outline behind his critical appeal to monumental evidence gives the question of Strabo's *xoana* special interest.

Strabo's *xoana* do not appear to be limited to statues in any one material or technique. He mentions an ivory *xoanon* by Colotes (8.3.4) [**339**], and twice he applies the term to Pheidias' chryselephantine Zeus in Olympia (8.3.30) [**340**].[191] In the same passage he mentions the iamb by Callimachus describing the statue, which that poet had probably called a *bretas*.[192] Strabo also calls statues by Polycleitus in the Argive Heraeum *xoana* (8.6.10) [**341**]); presumably these include the chryselephantine statue of Hera described by Pausanias (2.17.4–5) [**211**]. Another of Strabo's *xoana* is the Nemesis of Rhamnous (9.1.17) [**342**], a marble statue by Agoracritus of which sufficient fragments have been recognized to permit identification of replicas.[193]

These passages touch on two important points concerning the connotations of *xoanon*. That chryselephantine statues are *xoana* suggests that the old associations of the word with expensive and elaborate workmanship may have continued down to the first century A.D. in literature (as they certainly did in epigraphical texts), at least to the extent that the luxurious form of these statues did not exclude them from the category. In addition, the passages show that Strabo uses *xoanon* for the works of named sculptors whose place in history was accurately known.

The second point is important because Strabo calls some *xoana archaia*, a word that in the context of images with strong legendary associations and without precise information about their authorship supports the modern idea that *xoanon* refers specifically to a class of sculpture from the

[190] See G. Petzl, ed., *Die Inschriften von Smyrna* I (IgSK 23; Bonn, 1982) 79 no. 214.

[191] For the ivory *xoanon* by Colotes, see Eustath. *ad* H. *Il.* 2.306 [**132**].

[192] For Callimachus' *Iamb*: *supra* p. 52 n. 125.

[193] For the fragments of the Nemesis of Agoracritus: G.I. Despinis, Συμβολὴ στὴ μελέτη τοῦ ἔργου τοῦ 'Αγορακρίτου (Athens, 1971) 1–108. *Cf.* Eustath. *ad* H. *Il.* 2.556 [**131**].

deep past. For example, the *archaia xoana* of Heracles have already been noted **[349]**; the passage indicates that what Strabo considers to be the authentic costume of the hero belongs to an early time. In 13.1.41 **[344]**, Strabo asserts that "many of the *archaia xoana* of Athena are shown seated," in contrast to the standing image that was then visible at Troy. In 6.1.14 **[337]**, he discusses the various *xoana* that are put forward as the real Trojan Athena. On Mount Solmissus, he says (14.1.20) **[346]**, "there are several *naoi* in the place, some *archaioi* and others built in later times; and in the *archaioi* ones there are many *archaia xoana*, but in those of later times there are works of Scopas." These passages could be taken to show that Strabo conceives of *xoana* as belonging to the ancient past, the heroic age. Against this interpretation stand the references to *xoana* by fifth- and fourth-century sculptors: Pheidias **[340]**, Agoracritus **[342]**, Polycleitus **[341]**, and perhaps Scopas **[345]** (the Apollo Smintheus at Chryse).[194]

[194] For Strabo 13.1.48 **[345]**: Leaf, *Strabo* 240–245. The textual, numismatic, and architectural evidence for the shrine and the image is difficult to reconcile. Strabo reports that the mouse from which the god takes his epithet is underneath the feet of the statue, and he cites the explanation of Heraclides of Pontus (IV B.C.) that the temple mice were sacred. Strabo speaks of the *erga*, "works," of Scopas. Eustathius *ad* H. *Il.* 1.39 **[126]** (*cf.* **[127]**) depends on Strabo, but gives instead of *erga* the singular *ergon*, thus making the mouse, but not the *xoanon*, the work of Scopas. It is often thought that this *xoanon* is to be identified with the statue of Apollo shown first on the coins of Hamaxitus and later, after the relocation of the inhabitants of that city, on the coins of Alexandreia Troas.

This statue, as shown, does not answer Strabo's description, for it has no mouse beneath its foot; furthermore, it looks too archaic in style to be the work of Scopas. Suggestions have therefore been made that it is an archaizing work, or that not the statue, but only the mouse, is the creation of Scopas: P. Gardner, *The Types of Greek Coins* (Cambridge, 1883) 176–177; V. Grace, "Scopas in Chryse," *JHS* 52 (1932) 228–232. Grace points out that grammatically, too, the *erga* of Scopas are better found in the *hieron* and the *symbolon*, the temple and the mouse, than in the genitive *xoanou* (232). The statue wears a himation and a quiver, and carries a bow in the left hand and a patera in the right. It is variously shown with and without a round, garlanded base, with and without a worshipper and a tripod, frontally and from the side, and sometimes in a temple. There are also noticeable variations in the rendering of the image which may be due to the individual die-cutters, *e.g.*, the differences in the position of the arms when frontal views are attempted: W. Wroth, *BMC Troas* (London, 1894) pls. 4.6, 5.11, 12, 13. The pose is far freer in the autonomous coins than in the Roman series; an almost striding figure changes to one with feet close together (*BMC Troas* pl. 4.2; *cf.* pl. 4.5). Lacroix's objections to identifying this statue with that mentioned by Strabo are well taken (*Reproductions* 76–86, esp. 84–86). A.F. Stewart, *Skopas of Paros* (Park Ridge, New Jersey, 1977) 111, declines to discuss this image. For a late third-century B.C. date for the scanty remains of the Smintheum: J.M. Cook, *The Troad* (Oxford, 1973) 222, 228–231 and map 190; H. Weber, "Zum Apollon Smintheus-Tempel in der Troas," *IstMitt* 16 (1966) 100–114 for the suggestion that the statue, older than the temple, would have stood in a predecessor to the third-century building. The temple is dated to the second century B.C. in the pamphlet *1981 Excavations in Turkey* (Ministry of Culture and Tourism. Directorate General of Antiquities and Museums; n.p., n.d.) 40. See also the mid-second-century date suggested in P.W. Lehmann and D. Spittle, *Samothrace. The Temenos* (Bollingen Series LX.5; Princeton, 1982)

Xoanon in Strabo seems, therefore, to be a term general enough to include statues of many ages.

Just as Strabo's *xoana* are not chronologically limited, so too do there seem to be no limitations on their form. In 13.1.41 **[343–344]**, both the seated and standing images of Athena are called *xoana*; the context shows that Strabo deliberately applies the term to statues in both poses (as well as to images that were *archaia* and those that, presumably, were not).[195] Archaeological evidence confirms this lack of distinction: Strabo calls both the seated figures of Olympian Zeus and Argive Hera (8.3.30 **[340]**; 8.6.10 **[341]**) and the standing ones of Nemesis and Apollo Smintheus (9.1.17 **[342]**; 13.1.48 **[345]**) *xoana*. Of course, it is not certain that Strabo had actually seen all these statues, and archaeological fact may not always be an accurate guide to his meaning.[196]

Given Strabo's catholic use of *xoanon*, the appearance of any such statue that is not explicitly described or known from archaeological evidence cannot be inferred from the term alone. Nor does it seem, conversely, that any particular detail of age or style accounts for the application of the term to a particular image. Thus, nothing can be said about the briefly mentioned *xoanon* of Parthenos (7.4.2) **[338]**.[197] The *xoanon* of Zeus Stratios is in an *archaios* shrine (14.2.23) **[348]**, but the image itself need not be extremely old.[198] The image of Artemis at Massalia, a Phocaean

---

259 n. 253. Lehmann (258–261) suggests that Skopas created an archaizing statue, and that the mouse appeared on its sculptured base.

Fragments of what has been identified as the "cult statue" of the temple have come to light in the new excavations of the sanctuary; a part of the right leg, 1.13 m. long, has been noted: M.J. Mellink, "Archaeology in Asia Minor," *AJA* 86 (1982) 573.

For Menander Rhetor on the Apollo: *infra* pp. 155–156 and n. 379.

[195] Strabo 13.1.41 **[343]** figures in the scholia to H. *Il.* 6.92. *Cf.* Eustath. *ad* H. *Il.* 6.92 **[135]**.

[196] For this question: Leaf, *Strabo* xxviii–xxxiv decides that there is "no direct evidence of any sort to shew that Strabo knew the Troad from personal observation" (xxxiv), and believes that Strabo followed the account of Demetrios of Skepsis; he also believes that there is positive evidence of Strabo's ignorance of some parts of the Troad. The *OCD*[2] s.v. Strabo calls that author "independent but no great traveller."

[197] Strabo 7.4.2 **[338]**: No information is given about the *xoanon* of Parthenos in her sanctuary near Chersonese. See Lacroix, *Reproductions* 135 and n. 3 for the possible identification of this *xoanon* with the figure of an armed Artemis wearing a mural crown on coins of Tauric Chersonese.

[198] Strabo 14.2.23 **[348]**: For the cult of Zeus Stratios in Labraunda, see Lacroix, *Reproductions* 93–94. The statue seems to be shown on the coins of several cities. The IV B.C. Hecatomnid issues show a Zeus of ordinary, classical-looking type in three-quarter view. The coins of Augustus and Geta show a rigidly frontal, columnar image in a still, hieratic pose; this figure bears a strong resemblance to the Ephesia, and may be an "archaizing pastiche" (Lacroix, *Reproductions* 94 n. 4). For the types: A.H. Smith, "Some Recently Acquired Reliefs in the British Museum," *JHS* 36 (1916) 65–70; 66 fig. 2 for the coins. The identification with Strabo's *xoanon* is likely, but not absolutely secure.

foundation, was an *aphidruma* taken from the Ephesian *hiera* by order of the goddess herself (4.1.4) [**335**]. The Massilian statue seems to be the *xoanon* of which the design was faithfully reproduced by the colonies of that city. Like the image on coins that is associated with the Zeus Stratios, it may have been an archaizing image.[199] Neither its style nor its function as a copy, however, seems to account for its being called a *xoanon*, since neither feature characterizes every other *xoanon*.

Many of the images that Strabo calls *xoana* seem to have only one feature in common: they are images of gods that are the focus of religious attention in temples or shrines. All that is known, for example, about the *xoanon* of the Persian Omanus, who has a *hieron* and a *sekos*, is that it takes part in a procession (15.3.15) [**350**]. Strabo's discussion of the arrangement of Egyptian temples in 17.1.28 [**352**] is extremely important in this connection. He describes such a temple in some detail, and says that the *sekos* has no *xoanon*, or at least no anthropomorphic one, but only of some animal. *Xoanon* here obviously means the image that would ordinarily be found in a (Greek) temple. The passage recalls Dionysius' remark about Romulus' establishment of *hiera*, *temene*, *bomoi*, and *xoana* [**66**] and the similar passages in Herodotus [**139, 141**]. By the end of the century, it seems that *xoanon* had become identified with the images of the gods that were customary accoutrements of temples—images that today are called "cult statues," although the phrase has no real equivalent in ancient Greek. This meaning of *xoanon* does not hold good in inscriptions, but it is well established in literature as an ordinary term for images that receive religious attention. This usage can be seen, for instance, in the hypothesis composed probably in the first century B.C. for Euripides' *Iphigeneia in Tauris* [**89**] where, in contrast to Euripides' own vocabulary, it is the term for the statue of Artemis that seems to have come first to the author's mind.[200]

Strabo uses *xoanon* once more to refer to worshipped images as a category, in a context that has particular importance for the development of the term. In 16.2.35 [**351**] he summarizes the teachings of Moses against idolatry. One sentence contains the specific prohibition against the making and reverencing of images: ἀλλ' ἐᾶν δεῖν πᾶσαν ξοανοποιίαν, τέμενος δ' ἀφορίσαντας καὶ σηκὸν ἀξιόλογον τιμᾶν ἕδους χωρίς (But all making of *xoana* must be abandoned; instead, setting off a *temenos* and a worthy *sekos*, people should worship without a *hedos*). Strabo names several of his sources for Book 16, but gives none for the excursus on Moses. It has been

[199] *Aphidruma* can refer to a copy of an image, but the phrase ἀφίδρυμά τι τῶν ἱερῶν does not make the meaning of the term clear in this case. For the meanings of *aphidruma*: L. Robert, *D'Aphrodisias à la Lycaonie. Hellenica* 13 (1965) 119–125. One of the copies of the *xoanon*, made by the Romans, was a *xoanon* on the Aventine: Strabo 4.1.5 [**336**].

[200] See *supra* p. 20 n. 42.

thought that he derived his view of Moses from Posidonius, but the evidence for this supposition is scanty.[201] *Xoanopoiia* may or may not be Strabo's own choice or invention. The question of Strabo's specific source is, however, less important than the significance of the word *xoanon* in this context.

In the compound *xoanopoiia*, *xoanon* is not merely one possible name for a statue of a god, but is instead the blanket term for the entire category of worshipped images. Along with *hedos*, it represents here the most general conception of an image made for the purpose of veneration. While Dionysius and Strabo provide other examples of *xoanon* used in this sense, in none of those passages is the singularity of the usage so apparent. It must be remembered that in the majority of epigraphical texts, *xoanon* has a different meaning altogether. Furthermore, even among the authors who use *xoanon*, the word runs a dull race with its competitors, accounting for no more than a handful even of statues of gods installed in temples. It is curious in the extreme that *xoanon* has acquired a meaning that is not

[201] The source of the Moses excursus (Strabo 16.2.35) **[351]** is unknown. For a summary of the extensive discussion of the question: Stern, *Authors* I, 264–266. The comments of A.D. Nock, "Posidonius," *JRS* 49 (1939) 5–9, are of interest in this connection, and also for the wider question of late classical attitudes toward religion. For this passage specifically: Stern, *Authors* I, 305–306. W. Aly, *Strabonis Geographica* IV. *Strabo von Amaseia . . .* (Bonn, 1957) 191–208, rejects the attribution of the section to Posidonius, noting similarities between the Moses excursus and the material attributed to Hecataeus of Abdera, but admits (197, 207) that it is not possible to say more with certainty. In any case, Hecataeus would not have been the direct source. For Hecataeus: *infra* p. 94 n. 225. J.-D. Gauger, "Eine missverstandene Strabonstelle," *Historia* 28 (1979) 211–224, argues that there are no grounds for attributing the Moses excursus to Posidonius. Strabo's sections 16.2.35 and 36 are not included in the new edition of Posidonius (L. Edelstein and I.G. Kidd, eds., *Posidonius* I. *The Fragments* [Cambridge, 1972] F 279). Jacoby, *FGrH* 87 F 70, includes all 16.2.34–45, although Posidonius' name appears only in section 43. Posidonius' dates are usually given as c. 135–51/50 B.C. (*e.g.*, *OCD*[2] *s.v.* Posidonius 2). His influence is everywhere acknowledged to have been wide, but because his works are preserved only in fragments it is difficult even to grasp his basic ideas, let alone to detect his influence.

For Hecataeus and the Jews: Tcherikover, *Civilization* 360–361; Stern, *Authors* I, 20–24. Note D.S. 40.3 on Jewish history and Moses as a lawgiver, a passage based on Hecataeus; discussion and references in Walton, *Diodorus* XII 280 n. 1. For Hecataeus' excursus on the Jews: Momigliano, *Alien Wisdom* 84; he dates the book on Egypt in which the section appears c. 315 B.C. For the date of Hecataeus and for his treatment of the Jews: M. Stern and O. Murray, "Hecataeus of Abdera and Theophrastus on Jews and Egyptians," *JEA* 59 (1973) 159–168; O. Murray, "Hecataeus of Abdera and Pharaonic Kingship," *JEA* 56 (1970) 144, gives a useful summary of the forgeries of Hecataeus. Recently on the complex questions of Hecataeus and the forgeries: J.-D. Gauger, "Zitate in der jüdischen Apologetik und die Authentizität der Hekataios-Passagen bei Flavius Josephus und im Ps. Aristeas-Brief," *Journal for the Study of Judaism* 13 (1982) 6–46; R. Doran, "Pseudo-Hecataeus," in *OTP* II, 905–919.

confirmed by contemporary texts, and that its past history in no way prepares it to assume.

The explanation for the emergence of *xoanon* as a principal term in the description of Greek worship lies not in the prevailing usage of the word, but instead in its involvement with the literature of iconoclasm—a connection made explicit here by the Mosaic context. The development of this specialized definition of *xoanon* was adumbrated in the discussion of the term in the second century B.C. It is now necessary to examine the context of that development.[202]

[202] *Supra* pp. 59–60.

7. *Xoanon* in the Context of Iconoclastic Polemic: Second Century B.C.–First Century A.D.

For the purposes of this discussion, the extremely complex background of the late classical iconoclastic controversy as it regards Jewish and then Christian objections to pagan images may be briefly summarized.[203] In the second half of the second century B.C., there was a spate of what at first appears to be Jewish apologetic literature—that is, works of various kinds that attempted to explain Jewish life and laws to a gentile world that was coming into ever greater contact with the Jewish communities of the Diaspora. The aim of such apologetic literature would have been to foster a rapprochement between Mosaic and Greek traditions; persecution of the Jews under Antiochus IV Epiphanes in the second quarter of the century seems to have made such attempts imperative. The project was not easy. It was necessary to explain (or explain away) the Jewish rejection of the religious foundations of Greek civil life; no Jew, for example, would worship at the altar or the image of a Greek city god.

Recent scholarship has advanced a different view of this ostensibly apologetic literature. These works are now seen to be addressed not truly to the gentiles, but instead to the Jewish community itself, which had become deeply Hellenized in the course of the Diaspora. A principal aim of such works was the reconciliation of Jewish tradition with the demands of participation in Greek public life, where the boundaries between the civil and the religious could be hazy. The tracts attempted to show that the Jews need not assimilate themselves completely away from the observance of Mosaic law.

One of the most important Jewish centers outside Palestine was Alexandria, which was the source of much of this pseudo-apologetic literature. In Alexandria, as everywhere else in the Greek world, the language of the Jewish community was Greek; it had even become necessary to translate the Hebrew Testaments into Greek for its benefit. Thus the Septuagint was

[203] For the controversy: H. Koch, *Die altchristliche Bilderfrage nach den literarischen Quellen* (Göttingen, 1917); L.W. Barnard, *The Graeco-Roman and Oriental Background of the Iconoclastic Controversy* (Leiden, 1974) 80–103 and *passim*; and "The Theology of Images" by the same author, in A. Bryer and J. Herrin, eds., *Iconoclasm* (Papers Given at the Ninth Spring Symposium of Byzantine Studies, University of Birmingham, March 1975; Birmingham, 1977) 7–9. For lack of a better term, I use "iconoclasm" to mean the entire range of feeling against religious images, not simply their destruction as accomplished during the Byzantine era. *Cf.* the remarks of P.C. Finney, "Antecedents of Byzantine Iconoclasm: Christian Evidence Before Constantine," in J. Gutmann, ed., *The Image and the Word* (Missoula, Montana, 1977) 27: "There is a world of difference between disapproval and destruction. Strictly speaking, iconoclasm consists in the latter. . . . " On these grounds Finney doubts the existence of significant Christian iconoclasm before the fourth century A.D.

probably intended not so much for the Greek gentiles as for the Jews whose usual language of daily life, prayer, and literature was Greek.[204]

For these reasons there came to exist a large body of Jewish literature written or translated into Greek during the second and first centuries B.C. on the subject of religious practices. One of the topics was, of course, idolatry; but here there was some reserve. For while it was just possible to maintain that the Jews, for all their differences, really did worship the same god as the Greeks (or *vice versa*), the practice of image worship was another matter. Either one bowed before the images or one did not. To refuse to do so was to condemn the practice entirely and publicly; there was no middle road. To the Greeks, the Jewish objection to idolatry meant that the Jews were obstinate in a thoroughgoing rejection of the essence of Greek religious practice.[205]

It is important not to underestimate the extent of Greek idolatry. Modern scholarship tends to focus on the images that were installed in temples. Obviously these were highly important features of Greek religion; literary sources discussed in previous chapters (*e.g.*, **66**, **352**) indicate that images in temples were absolutely standard, as necessary as altars and the temples themselves for worship. While individual cults might display different practices, there is no question that temple images were considered normal and central to religious activity.[206] At the same time, however, images in other places were also the focus of religious feelings and attention.[207] Even

[204] For second-century B.C. Jewish literature written in Greek: Tcherikover, "Ideology" 60. Although his view that this ostensibly apologetic literature was in fact addressed to the Jews themselves has generally replaced the old idea that it was Jewish propaganda, it is still not impossible that some of it was aimed at the gentile world: G. Delling, "Perspektiven der Erforschung des hellenistischen Judentums," HUCA 45 (1974) 163–170; *Studia Philonica* 5 (1978) 125–126. For Greek as the language of the Diaspora, and for the Septuagint: G.H. Box, *Judaism in the Greek Period* (Oxford, 1932) 58–59 (62–64 for Jewish "propaganda"); Tcherikover, *Civilization* 347–348; E.M. Smallwood, *The Jews Under Roman Rule* (Leiden, 1976) 123 and n. 14. For the Jews and the Greek gods: Tcherikover, *Civilization* 374–375.

[205] For Jewish attitudes toward idolatry—an extraordinarily rich and complex subject—see, *e.g.*: M. Avi-Yonah, *The Jews under Roman and Byzantine Rule* (New York and Jerusalem, 1976; repr. 1984) 74–76; M. Hengel, *Judaism and Hellenism* (Philadelphia, 1974) *passim*; and S. Lieberman, *Hellenism in Jewish Palestine* (New York, 1950) 115–127.

[206] In Strabo 17.1.28 [**352**], the Egyptian *neos* that lacks an anthropomorphic *xoanon* is the exception that proves the rule.

[207] *E.g.*, attentions to roadside images: Theophr. *Char.* 16.14 (Hecates wreathed with garlic); Nic. fr. 74.68 (*brete*); to household images: Artem. 2.33; to pagan images: [Clem.] *Hom.* 10.23 [**55**]. So far I have found nothing in Greek thought corresponding to the distinction between decorative images and images intended for worship that is found in, *e.g.*, rabbinical prohibitions: E.J. Bickerman, "Sur la théologie de l'art figuratif. A propos de l'ouvrage de E.R. Goodenough," *Syria* 44 (1967) 137; E.E. Urbach, "The Rabbinical Laws of Idolatry in the Second and Third Centuries in the Light of Archaeological and Historical Facts," *IEJ* 9

more important, the images were the symbols of polytheistic divinities that had been given visible form. Both these aspects of the Greek religious system—polytheism and the visualization of divine form—were completely alien to Jewish thought. Jewish law and custom insisted that the gods of other peoples and their installations be respected, but firmly declined; the stubbornness of the Jews in their rejection of pervasive classical idolatry seemed to the Greeks to compare most unfavorably with their own readiness to welcome foreign gods into their pantheon.[208] Jewish iconoclasm thus seemed to them fundamentally anti-social.

The profoundly different attitudes that the Greeks and the Jews held toward images meant that the entire course of the iconoclastic controversy was marked by a peculiar inability of either side to confront the opposing positions squarely. Arguments frequently seem irrelevant; rebuttals often seem to miss their targets. The various issues involved in idolatry are not always separated; it is not uncommon, for example, to find the assertion that the images show what the living gods look like used to answer the charge that the statues are dead and senseless and therefore not gods. The following attempt to trace the attitudes toward images that developed in the context of the iconoclastic controversy focuses on the specific statements about the images, but it should not be forgotten that the fundamental issue was always the nature of the divine.

One of the earliest glimpses of the struggle over idolatry is preserved in the so-called *Letter of Aristeas*. The document purports to be an account written by a courtier of Ptolemy II of the making of the Septuagint. It appears, however, to be in fact a Jewish work composed in Greek, and probably in Alexandria, sometime between the middle of the third century B.C. and the late first century A.D. A date in the second century B.C. is the most likely.[209] In the course of a defense of Mosaic Law there is a brief

---

(1959) 231–232. The question of Jewish attitudes toward figural art and the degree to which official condemnation matched actual practice is not settled, and lies far outside the present subject.

[208] For Greek adoption of foreign gods: E. Bickerman, "Anonymous Gods," *JWarb* 1 (1937–1938) 187–196. *Cf.* Clem.Al. *Strom.* 7.15.89 (886 P.–887 P.), who notes that although the Greeks and Jews criticize the disagreements among the Christians and deny the truth of Christianity because of them, the Greeks themselves easily accept discrepancies and variations among pagan cults. For Jewish prohibition of disrespect for the gods and temples of others: C. Burchard, "Joseph and Aseneth," in *OTP* II, 216 n. 10 v.

[209] Tcherikover, "Ideology" 60; A. Pelletier, ed., *Lettre d'Aristée à Philocrate* (Sources chrétiennes 89; Paris, 1962) 57–58, prefers a high date, near the beginning of the second century B.C. Others prefer a date c. 100 B.C. General opinion seems to favor a date in the second half of the second century B.C. The lowest possible date is established by Josephus' paraphrase of the *Letter* (*AJ* 12.11–118); see the useful notes in R. Marcus, tr., *Josephus* VII (LCL, 1943) 8 n. b. This paraphrase omits the section on Eleazar's defense of Mosaic law. For the date of

mention of idolatry (135) **[28]**. Moses is said to have critized idolatrous peoples in the following way: "For having made *agalmata* out of stones and stocks, they say that they are *eikones* of people who discovered something useful to them for living, and they kneel to them, [although] grasping their lack of sensation."[210]

This passage is the only mention of images in the *Letter*. The few short lines touch on several points that illustrate the often peculiar confrontation between traditional Greek practices and beliefs and the heterogeneous religious practices of the wider Hellenistic world. The issue of idolatry, for example, is mixed here with the Euhemeristic belief in the origin of the gods as respected human beings, which is a theory of the third century B.C. that is clearly anachronistic in the context of Moses. The *topos*, however, appears in other iconoclastic polemic.[211] The objection to the images as being without sensation (their *anaisthesia*) is another Jewish iconoclastic *topos* that carries over into Christian polemic. It found good application in the centuries after Christ, when magical images, to which consciousness, movement, and powers of various kinds were attributed, enjoyed wide popularity; the proliferation of such magical images marks something of a departure from traditional Greek idolatry, and may reflect new influences.[212]

---

the *Letter* and its mention of Hecataeus' favorable opinion of the Jews: Stern, *Authors* I, 22 and n. 8. See also A.-M. Denis, *Introduction aux pseudépigraphiques grecs d'Ancien Testament* (Studia in Veteri Testamenti Pseudepigraphica 1; Leiden, 1970) 105–110; and R.J. Shutt, "Letter of Aristeas," in *OTP* II, 7–11, with bibliography. Shutt favors a date c. 170 B.C. Doubts about the authenticity of the *Letter* were raised early; for this question: H.B. Swete, *An Introduction to the Old Testament in Greek* (Cambridge, 1902; repr. New York, 1968) 533–534; M. Hadas, ed., tr., *Aristeas to Philocrates (Letter of Aristeas)* (New York, 1951) 5–9. Nock, "Posidonius" (*supra* p. 83 n. 201) 8 n. 41, summarizes Tcherikover's view that the *Letter* was "directed to Jews and intended to promote intelligent conformity."

[210] This passage also appears in Eusebius' long quotation of Aristeas (*PE* 8.9.371 b): *Ἀγάλματα γὰρ ποιήσαντες ἐκ λίθων, ἢ ξύλων, εἰκόνας φασὶν εἶναι τῶν ἐξευρόντων τι πρὸς τὸ ζῆν αὐτοῖς χρήσιμον, οἷς προσκυνοῦσι, παρὰ πόδας ἔχοντες τὴν ἀναισθησίαν.*

[211] Euhemeristic theory, which teaches that the gods are deified human beings, may in fact have originated with Hecataeus of Abdera: O. Murray,"Hecataeus of Abdera and Pharaonic Kingship," *JEA* 56 (1970) 151 and n. 4. For the fragments of Euhemerus: G. Vallauri, *Euemero di Messene* (Pub. Fac. Lett. e fil. Univ. Torino; Turin, 1956). For a Euhemeristic comment on a *xoanon* of Adonis: Phot. *Lex. s.v.* *οὐδὲν ἱερόν* **[307]**. Moses is a figure of the second millennium B.C. For the question of the date and historicity of Moses and the Exodus: O. Eissfeldt, in *CAH*³ II.2, 321–323. The Exodus is dated by the *CAH*³ c. 1250 B.C., thus in the reign of Rameses II (Dyn. XIX). The standard dating of the Exodus (Glueck's) has, however, recently been challenged: J.M. Miller, "Recent Archaeological Developments Relevant to Ancient Moab," in A. Hadidi, ed., *Studies in the History and Archaeology of Jordan* (Amman, 1982) 1, 171–172.

[212] For the iconoclastic *topoi* of Hellenistic Judaism: Wallach, "Palestinian Polemic" 390–391; Wallach identifies the *topoi* (powerlessness, uselessness, and lifelessness of the idols; foolishness of idolaters) and notes traces of this polemic in several works. For the basic ideas

The brevity of Aristeas' attack on the *agalmata* is noteworthy, contrasting as it does with the extended polemics of the later Christian writers. The Jewish critics of idolatry had to tread lightly, not simply because iconoclasm as a concept hit at a central Greek religious custom, but because that custom was one of the criteria by which the Greeks defined themselves and their world and set themselves apart from barbarians. For an alien people trying to exist within the Greek world it required the greatest delicacy to criticize an attitude that was of such long standing and of such great emotional, as well as historical, significance.

In the fifth century B.C. the Greeks had already recognized the political and ethnic significance of their images. Part of this recognition was due to an ethnographic interest; by the sixth century the Greeks, especially in Ionia, had begun to think systematically about the differences between cultures, and even to examine their own customs in a comparative, almost anthropological spirit.[213] Herodotus, in commenting on a city of the Budini, Gelonus, the inhabitants of which have Greek affiliations, reports that "there are among them *hira* of the Greek gods, furnished in Greek fashion,

---

of Jewish iconoclasm: R.H. Pfeiffer, "The Polemic Against Idolatry in the Old Testament," *Journal of Biblical Literature* 43 (1924) 229–240, an essentially historical treatment with a profusion of detailed references. For later periods: Urbach, "Rabbinical Laws" (*supra* p. 86 n. 207) 149–165; 229–245. To the charge of *anaisthesia* (lack of sensation), *cf.*, *e.g.*, Ps. 135.15, 17: "The idols of the nations are silver and gold, the works of men's hands. They have mouths, but they speak not; eyes have they, but they see not; they have ears, but they hear not; neither is there any breath in their mouths." (*Cf.* Clem.Al., *Protr.* 4.44 P. [45].)

Anaisthesia is often cited as a pre-Hellenistic Greek objection to idolatry, but there is reason to think that the charge was not current before Hellenistic times. The comments of pre-Hellenistic writers are often preserved in Christian tracts in which the authors have imposed strained interpretations on the pagan sources in light of their own beliefs. One example is the interpretation of Heraclitus' well-known attack on idolatry (fr. 5 Diels-Kranz). Whereas Clement (*Protr.* 4.44 P. [45]; *cf. supra*) and Origen (Cels. 1.5 [178]; 7.62 [179]; 7.65 [180]) use the fragment as ammunition to attack the *anaisthesia* of images, it is clear from the most complete form of the quotation (Aristocritus, *Theosophia* 68) that Heraclitus objects to the anthropomorphic conception of traditional Greek belief (*i.e.*, what the images show), and not to the *agalmata* as lifeless things. For the fragment and a new translation: D. Babut, "Héraclite et la religion populaire," *REA* 77 (1975) 51–62.

For magical images: *infra* p. 133 n. 321.

[213] For Xenophanes' references to Ethiopians and Thracians in his discussion of the forms of the gods (fr. 16): G.S. Kirk and J.E. Raven, *The Presocratic Philosophers* (Cambridge, 1957) 168. For the distinction between Hellenes and barbarians: Baldry, *Unity* 20–24; Guthrie, *History* I, 372–373: "The discrepancies between the religious beliefs and customs of different people began to make a deep impression in the fifth century, as appears especially in the pages of Herodotus, and from then on gave a powerful impetus to scepticism." (*Cf.* Guthrie, *History* III, 16–17.) Religion was not the only application of such ethnology: Hippocratic writers used information about Libyan customs to combat superstitions surrounding, *e.g.*, epilepsy (*De morb. sacr.* 2): Baldry, *Unity* 48–49.

with *agalmata* and *bomoi* and *neoi* of wood" (4.108) [**141**].[214] The adverb ἑλληνικῶς, "in Greek fashion," divides the world. When Herodotus has Themistocles speak of the common cause of the Greeks, the *hidrumata*, foundations, of the gods take their place among features such as blood and language that define the unity of all Hellenes (8.144).[215]

Herodotus takes a lively interest in describing the religious practices of non-Greek peoples. For him, not surprisingly, the most significant of all these is the Persian religion, and he gives a straightforward account of his understanding of it (1.131):

> I know that the Persians have these *nomoi*: it is not their *nomos* to make *agalmata* and *neoi* and *bomoi*, but they even impute foolishness to those who do this, in my opinion, because they do not believe that the gods are human in nature, as the Hellenes do.[216]

[214] Hdt. 4.108 [**141**]. The temples are wooden because the entire city of Gelonus is made of wood. R.W. Macan, *Herodotus. The Fourth, Fifth and Sixth Books* (London and New York, 1895) I, 78 *ad loc.* doubts that Herodotus saw this city himself. For this passage and *theoi Hellenioi*: I.M. Linforth, "Greek Gods and Foreign Gods in Herodotus," *CPCP* 9 (1926–1929) 20–25.

[215] Macan, *Herodotus* (*supra* p. 90 n. 214) I, 78 *ad* 4.108, notes Stein's identification of these "three essential requisites for Hellenic temple-service." For the Greek conception of Greek and non-Greek and the importance of genealogy in its formulation: Groningen, *Grip of the Past* 58–61.

[216] Hdt. 1.131:

> Πέρσας δὲ οἶδα νόμοισι τοιοισίδε χρεωμένους, ἀγάλματα μὲν καὶ νηοὺς καὶ βωμοὺς οὐκ ἐν νόμῳ ποιευμένους ἱδρύεσθαι, ἀλλὰ τοῖσι ποιεῦσι μωρίην ἐπιφέρουσι, ὡς μὲν ἐμοὶ δοκέειν, ὅτι οὐκ ἀνθρωποφυέας ἐνόμισαν τοὺς θεοὺς κατά περ οἱ Ἕλληνες εἶναι.

P.-E. Legrand, ed., *Hérodote. Histoires* I (Paris, 1932). The passage is cited by Origen, *Cels.* 1.5 [**178**] and 7.62 [**179**]. *Anthropophues* would seem to include the appearance of human form. *Anthropomorphos* seems not to occur before the fourth or third century B.C.: *infra* p. 94 n. 225. M.C. Root, *The King and Kingship in Achaemenid Art* (Acta Iranica 19; Leiden, 1979) 169–170, believes that Herodotus is in error on this point, citing the figure of Ahuramazda; although various Parsee sects have attempted to interpret this figure in the light of the strict Zoroastrian prohibition against images, she believes that the Achaemenid texts do not bear out these later explanations. For the statue of a goddess set up by Artaxerxes II in the fourth century B.C.: M. Boyce, "Iconoclasm among the Zorastrians," in J. Neusner, ed., *Christianity, Judaism and Other Greco-Roman Cults. Studies for Morton Smith at Sixty* (Studies in Judaism in Late Antiquity 12; Leiden, 1975) IV, 95–96.

The meaning of *nomos* in Hdt. 1.131 probably lies closer to "custom" than to "law." M. Ostwald, *Nomos and the Beginnings of the Athenian Democracy* (Oxford, 1969) 41, includes this passage among examples of *nomos* in religious contexts, although he points out that it has a more general sense than in the cases where it is applied to rites and regulations. It may be better, however, to place these Persian *nomoi* in the category of "mores of a particular group," among which are the many examples of "the ways of non-Greek peoples" (Ostwald 33–34). It happens that the *nomoi* in question concern the worship of the gods, but the context of the passage is an ethnographic survey of various Persian customs in which religious practices are treated first.

Herodotus here sees all the Greek religious paraphernalia as the natural concomitant of the anthropomorphic idea. His account of Egyptian religion tends to emphasize its similarities to Greek practice, and it is not surprising that he should record the information that the Egyptians, first in so many achievements, also held themselves as the first to assign *bomoi*, *agalmata*, and *neoi* to the gods (2.4) [**139**]. It has already been noted that the same elements were later said by Dionysius of Halicarnassus to have been established by Romulus [**66**]. The acknowledged foci of classical religion have a long tradition.[217]

The importance of religious structures and paraphernalia, including images, in Greek life was crystallized by historical events. As a result of the destruction of Greek sanctuaries in the Persian Wars, especially in the invasion of the Greek mainland in 480 B.C., the images of the gods became a symbol of both the cultural unity of all Greeks and Greek solidarity against the whole barbarian world.

In Aeschylus' *Persae*, performed only a few years after the invasion, the Persians come to disaster not least because of their wanton abuse of Greek holy establishments. "Coming to the land of Greece, they felt no shame in pillaging the *brete* of the gods, nor in burning the *neoi*; *bomoi* were destroyed, and the *hidrumata* of the gods, torn up by their roots, were hurled down in utter confusion" (A. *Pers.* 809–812.)[218]

It has long been realized that the impiety of the barbarian is a Greek *topos* not perfectly founded in truth. The Persians did, on occasion, respect the Greek sanctuaries they encountered.[219] That there was a considerable

[217] D.H. 2.18.2 [**66**] is repeated by Eusebius, *PE* 2.8.78 b [**103**]. *Cf.* Luc. *Prom.* 14: Prometheus bids Hermes notice that among the improvements men have made to the world ἀπανταχοῦ δὲ βωμοὺς καὶ θυσίας καὶ ναοὺς καὶ πανηγύρεις (everywhere there are altars and sacrifices and *naoi* and festivals).

[218] A. *Pers.* 809–812: οἳ γῆν μολόντες Ἑλλάδ' οὐ θεῶν βρέτη/ ᾐδοῦντο συλᾶν οὐδὲ πιμπράναι νεώς·/ βωμοὶ δ' ἄιστοι, δαιμόνων θ' ἱδρύματα/ πρόρριζα φύρδην ἐξανέστραπται βάθρων. D. Page, ed., *Aeschyli septem quae supersunt tragoediae* (Oxford, 1972). The play was performed in 472 B.C. H.D. Broadhead, ed., *The Persae of Aeschylus* (Cambridge, 1960) 201–202, suggests that *hidrumata* here most probably means structures of some kind (*e.g.*, shrines) that have been torn from their foundations, and not statues that have been torn from their bases. Broadhead also notes the similarity of this section to Hdt. 8.144.

[219] For the *topos* of Persian impiety: R.W. Macan, *Herodotus. The Seventh, Eighth, and Ninth Books* (London, 1908) I.2, 529 *ad* 8.109 (15) and 590 *ad* 8.144 (9); Broadhead, *Persae* (*supra* p. 91 n. 218) 201 *ad* 809 ff. Later examples: for the derivation of Pl. *NH* 30 from Greek anti-Persian polemic: *JRS* 70 (1980) 187–188; for Cic. *De Leg.* 2.10.26: W.W. How and J. Wells, *A Commentary on Herodotus* (Oxford, 1912) II *ad* 8.109. There are several examples of Persian piety: *e.g.*, Hdt. 6.97 (Delos; Macan, *Herodotus* [supra p. 90 n. 214] *ad* 5.102, 6.97); Hdt. 6.118 (Datis, after a vision, returns a plundered gilt *agalma* to Delos, charging the Delians to return it to Delium, which they fail to do; *cf.* Paus. 10.28.6, where Datis succeeds in returning the image to Delium); Hdt. 7.43 (Xerxes reaches Ilium and sacrifices

degree of rhetorical enhancement of the Persian destructions is clear from a comparison of Herodotus' own dispassionate accounts of these acts with his versions of the speeches delivered on the subject. He has Themistocles paint Xerxes as a lawless and impious man "who treated holy and profane things in the same way, burning and casting down the *agalmata* of the gods" (8.109). In their reply to Mardonius' envoy, the Athenians reject the idea of any rapprochement, vowing instead to fight on, relying on the gods and heroes "whose *oikoi* and *agalmata* he [Xerxes] burned, having no religious scruple at all" (8.143). The Athenians then reassure the Lacedaemonian envoys of their commitment to all the Greeks, stressing the cultural unity that binds them: "Many and great are the reasons not to do this [*sc.* make peace with the Persians], even if we wished to do so; the first and greatest being the *agalmata* of the gods and the *oikemata* that were burned and demolished, which it is our duty to avenge to the utmost, rather than come to agreement with the one who did it" (8.144).[220]

1000 oxen). A.D. Nock, *AJA* 66 (1962) 310, notes in Aristides and Libanius the converse of the iconoclastic *topos*, in which sanctuaries survive unscathed in times of trouble.

[220] In describing the sacks of Abai (8.33) and the Athenian acropolis (8.53), Herodotus says only that the Persians *τὸ ἱρὸν συλήσαντες ἐνέπρησαν*—"setting fire to the *hiron*, burnt it." For Abai, *cf.* Paus. 10.35.2. Herodotus also, in suggesting the destruction of the temple at Sardis as the reason (or pretext) for the Persian attacks on Greek temples, says simply (5.102): *καὶ Σάρδιες μὲν ἐνεπρήσθησαν, ἐν δὲ αὐτῇσι καὶ ἱρὸν ἐπιχωρίης θεοῦ Κυβήβης· τὸ σκηπτόμενοι οἱ Πέρσαι ὕστερον ἀντενεπίμπρασαν τὰ ἐν Ἕλλησι ἱρά* (And Sardis was set on fire, and in it also the *hiron* of the epichoric goddess Kubaba; alleging this as an excuse, the Persians later burnt the *hira* in Greece in return). For this passage: J.G. Pedley, *Ancient Literary Sources on Sardis* (Archaeological Exploration of Sardis, Monograph 2; Cambridge, Mass., 1972) 74 no. 272. Macan, *Herodotus* (supra p. 90 n. 214) *ad loc.*, points out that Kubaba here "is treated by Hdt. (and by the Greeks who burnt her temple) as a non-Hellenic deity" in contrast to 1.80; see also Linforth, "Gods" (*supra* p. 90 n. 214) 23–24.

P.-E. Legrand, ed., *Hérodote. Histoires* VIII (Paris, 1953): Hdt. 8.143:

Νῦν τε ἀπάγγελλε Μαρδονίῳ ὡς Ἀθηναῖοι λέγουσι, ἔστ᾽ ἂν ὁ ἥλιος τὴν αὐτὴν ὁδὸν ἴῃ τῇ περ καὶ νῦν ἔρχεται, μήκοτε ὁμολογήσειν ἡμέας Χέρξῃ· ἀλλὰ θεοῖσί τε συμμάχοισι πίσυνοί μιν ἐπέξιμεν ἀμυνόμενοι καὶ τοῖσι ἥρωσι, τῶν ἐκεῖνος οὐδεμίαν ὄπιν ἔχων ἐνέπρησε τούς τε οἴκους καὶ τὰ ἀγάλματα.

Now go tell Mardonius that the Athenians say: As long as the sun goes in the same path it does now, that we will never come to agreement with Xerxes; but we will proceed against him, relying on the allied gods and assisted by the heroes, whose *oikoi* and *agalmata* he burned, having no religious scruple at all.

Hdt. 8.144:

Πολλά τε γὰρ καὶ μεγάλα ἐστὶ τὰ διακωλύοντα ταῦτα μὴ ποιέειν μηδ᾽ ἢν ἐθέλωμεν· πρῶτα μὲν καὶ μέγιστα τῶν θεῶν τὰ ἀγάλματα καὶ τὰ οἰκήματα ἐμπεπρησμένα τε καὶ συγκεχωσμένα, τοῖσι ἡμέας ἀναγκαίως ἔχει τιμωρέειν ἐς τὰ μέγιστα μᾶλλον ἤ περ ὁμολογέειν τῷ ταῦτα ἐργασαμένῳ· αὖτις δὲ τὸ Ἑλληνικόν, ἐὸν ὅμαιμόν τε καὶ ὁμόγλωσσον, καὶ θεῶν ἱδρύματά τε κοινὰ καὶ θυσίαι ἤθεά τε ὁμότροπα, τῶν προδότας γενέσθαι Ἀθηναίους οὐκ ἂν εὖ ἔχοι.

In later times the Greeks attributed a similar lack of respect for images to the Gauls, even though they, like all Celts, did in fact worship images. This incorrect information was not merely mistaken ethnography in a neutral context; the Gauls came to prominence in the Greek world by means of invasion and destruction, and accounts of their customs were only chapters in the record of their terrifying incursions. The Greek writers, when describing the invasions of the Gauls, tended to follow closely the accounts of the earlier Persian invasions, and it is not surprising that Gaulish iconoclasm was recounted in terms similar to those used for Persian actions and attitudes.[221] It is clear that the issue of iconoclasm was deliberately given a

---

The translation continues: "then there is the fact of being Hellenes, the being the same in blood and language, and the *hidrumata* of the gods in common, and the sacrifices, and the sameness in customs, which it would not be well with the Athenians to betray."

[221] *E.g.*, D.S. 22.9.4, in a section apparently concerning the Gauls' invasion of Greece and attack on Delphi in 249 B.C.:

> ὅτι Βρέννος ὁ τῶν Γαλατῶν βασιλεὺς εἰς ναὸν ἐλθὼν ἀργυροῦν μὲν ἢ χρυσοῦν οὐδὲν εὗρεν ἀνάθημα, ἀγάλματα δὲ μόνον λίθινα καὶ ξύλινα καταλαβὼν κατεγέλασεν ὅτι θεοὺς ἀνθρωπομόρφους εἶναι δοκοῦντες ἵστασαν αὐτοὺς ξυλίνους τε καὶ λιθίνους.
>
> Brennus, the king of the Gauls, on entering a *naos* found no *anathema* of gold or silver, and when he came upon only *agalmata* of stone and wood he laughed at them, to think that men, believing the gods to be human in form, should set them up in wood and stone. (Tr. adapted from Walton, *Diodorus* XI.)

This fragment is preserved in the tenth-century A.D. *Excerpta Constantiniana*. The passage is ambiguous, in that it is not altogether clear whether Brennus' mirth is caused by the cheapness of the *agalmata* or by the notion of anthropomorphic gods. Both the content and the vocabulary are reminiscent of discussions about idolatry. (For *anthropomorphos*: *infra* p. 94 n. 225.) The scorn imputed to Brennus for Greek idolatry is incorrect insofar as the Gauls, like all Celts, were image-worshippers. This fact was certainly known in late Hellenistic times: Caesar, *DBG* 6.17: *Deum maxime Mercurium colunt. Huius sunt plurima simulacra.* (They worship the god Mercury most of all. There are many images of him.) Lucan notes later the *simulacra* in the grove outside Massilia (3.412–413): *simulacraque maesta deorum / arte carent caesisque extant informia truncis.* The images of the gods, grim and rude, were uncouth blocks formed of felled tree-trunks. (Tr. J.D. Duff, LCL, 1928.) O.C. Phillips, "Lucan's Grove," *CP* 63 (1968) 296–300, has argued that Lucan invented the incident and based the passage on literary models; for two historical desecrations of groves: S.L. Dyson, "Caepio, Tacitus, and Lucan's Sacred Grove," *CP* 65 (1970) 36–68. Caesar's testimony comes from a time when the Celts had long been under Mediterranean influence, but there is every reason to think that iconic practice is genuinely Celtic: T.G.E. Powell, *The Celts* (New York, 1958) 130–138; 132–133 for wooden images dating to the late Bronze Age.

It is possible, however, that the domestic customs of the Celts might not have been guessed by the victims of their invasions. Although the Greeks had had close contact with the Celts in Massilia from the later fifth century B.C. on, they knew little about them until Hellenistic times. For Greek and Roman attitudes toward the Celts: Momigliano, *Alien Wisdom* 50–73. Momigliano (58 ff.) places the beginning of accurate investigations of the Celts in the second century B.C., in contrast to the superficial and inaccurate accounts of earlier times. The pillage of sanctuaries might understandably be interpreted as irreverence

highly emotional context in which xenophobia and terror overwhelmed rational inquiry.

The inflexible position taken by the Jews against Greek idolatry thus created considerable difficulties for both sides. Greeks did not ordinarily welcome religious criticism from foreigners.[222] On the other hand, the Jewish criticism could not be lightly dismissed, because the Jews had an extraordinarily high reputation among the Greeks for wisdom and piety.[223] The first Greek accounts of the Jews were noticeably positive; only later did antisemitic attitudes emerge.[224] It is worth noting that Moses' condemnation of images was included in the earliest information that reached the Greek world about the Jews. Hecataeus of Abdera mentioned it in his favorable account of the lawgiver and his intriguing nation.[225] Had Moses' aversion to

---

for images, but the attribution of iconoclastic attitudes to Brennus may also be explained by the tendency of the Greek writers to model their accounts of Brennus' invasion on those of the Persian expedition: W.W. Tarn in *CAH*² VII (1928) 102; Momigliano, *Alien Wisdom* 63 for Pausanias' imitation of Herodotus. Nock, "Posidonius" (*supra* p. 83 n. 201) 6 and n. 27, mentions the "ascription to non-Greeks of a feeling against anthropomorphism" that "became something of an ethnographic commonplace." Presumably the Greeks and Romans did not care to think of themselves as wanton destroyers of the gods and sanctuaries of other peoples: see, *e.g.*, Macrob. *Sat.* 3.1–3 (sacrilege for Romans to despoil enemy temples and gods) and *cf. supra* p. 87 n. 208.

[222] The tradition that attributes instruction by the Magi to Protagoras (Philostr. *Vit. Soph.* 1.10.1) and Democritus (D.L. 9.34) is worth noting here; it is possible that some connection was seen between such instruction and the philosophers' criticism of the traditional gods. J.A. Davison, "Protagoras, Democritus, and Anaxagoras," *CQ* 47 (n.s. 3; 1953) 33–34; Guthrie, *History* III, 262–263; M. Untersteiner, tr. K. Freeman, *The Sophists* (New York, 1954) 1 and n. 10 for Schmid's suggestion of such a connection.

[223] For Greek and Roman attitudes toward the Jews: Momigliano, *Alien Wisdom* 74–122, and bibliography 157–164, 168. Varro, *ap.* Aug. *DCD* 4.31 [**40**], mentions the Jews favorably because of their worship without images.

[224] B. Wardy, "Jewish Religion in Pagan Literature during the Late Republic and Early Empire," *ANRW* II.19.1 (Berlin and New York, 1979) 635–641, discusses "The Jews in the Early Hellenistic Age," outlining the change from the earliest, positive attitudes to later antisemitism. (*Cf.* M. Pucci, "A Note on Johann Lewy (1901–1945)," *Athenaeum* 74 [1984] 645 n. 8.) Murray, "Hecataeus" (*supra* p. 83 n. 201) 144, notes that Hecataeus' remarks on the Jews are not entirely favorable.

[225] For Hecataeus: *supra* p. 83 n. 201; recently for Hecataeus on the Jews: Wardy, "Jewish Religion" (*supra* p. 94 n. 224) 637–639. For the absence of Jewish images: Hecataeus, *FGrH* 264 F 6, *ap.* D.S. 40.3.3–4: ἄγαλμα δὲ θεῶν τὸ σύνολον οὐ κατεσκεύασε διὰ τὸ μὴ νομίζειν ἀνθρωπόμορφον εἶναι τὸν θεόν, ἀλλὰ τὸν περιέχοντα τὴν γῆν οὐρανὸν μόνον εἶναι θεὸν καὶ τῶν ὅλων κύριον (they made no *agalma* at all of the gods, because they do not believe that god is anthropomorphic, but that the heaven that encircles the earth is god and the lord of all things). Walton, *Diodorus* XII, 282–283 n. 1 *ad loc.*, notes that this passage appears to contain one of the first extant uses of *anthropomorphos*; he attributes the confusion with Hecataeus of Miletus in the manuscript not to Diodorus, but to Photius (287 n. 1): D.S. 40.3.8, περὶ μὲν τῶν Ἰουδαίων Ἑκαταῖος ὁ Ἀβδηρίτης ταῦτα ἱστόρηκεν (Hecataeus of Abdera [ms. Μιλήσιος, em. Wesseling] reported these things concerning the Jews).

images remained conveniently in the realm of armchair ethnography, it would probably not have been seen as a serious threat to Greek custom. In the real Hellenistic world, however, it became an impediment to civic co-operation. Furthermore, in the Greek mind, iconoclastic attitudes were historically linked to the worst realizations of Greek xenophobic anxieties. In practice, therefore, iconoclasm was not likely to foster harmony between gentile and Jew. This circumstance might explain why the subject is so briefly touched upon in Aristeas, and why comprehensive iconoclastic polemics appear only later, in the writings of Christians, at a time when the lines of society were differently drawn.

The most ferocious condemnation of idolatry comes from texts written by Jews and openly addressed to Jews. Good examples are the passages in the *Book of Jubilees*, a work most likely composed in the second century B.C. by a member of the extremely conservative Hasidic or Essene branches of Judaism.[226] The book is essentially a retelling of narratives from *Genesis* and *Exodus* and is derived from a rich mixture of literary genres, with a heavy emphasis on the necessity of strictly following the Law. In two passages, Abram/Abraham warns against idolatry. He pleads with his father Terah to stop worshipping idols, although the people have fallen into idolatry:

> "What help or advantage do we have from these idols before which you worship and bow down?
> Because there is not any spirit in them,
> for they are mute,
> and they are the misleading of the heart.
> Do not worship them.
> Worship the God of heaven,
> who sends down rain and dew upon the earth,
> and who makes everything upon the earth,
> and created everything by his word,
> and all life is in his presence.
> Why do you worhip those who have no spirit in them?
> Because they are works of the hands,
> and you are carrying them upon your shoulders,
> and there is no help from them for you,
> except great shame for those who made them
> and the misleading of the heart for those who worship them.
> Do not worship them." (*Jub.* 12:2–5; tr. Wintermute)

He castigates the idols because they mislead the heart, because they have no spirit within them, because they are the product of human hands, and because they give no help. These criticisms appear repeatedly in Jewish iconoclastic works and in Christian polemic modelled on Jewish sources.

[226] O.S. Wintermute, "Jubilees," in *OTP* II, 35–50, esp. 43–45.

In a subsequent passage, Abraham warns his son Jacob against the gentiles, among whose objectionable practices is idolatry. Age has only sharpened his tongue:

> "Separate yourself from the gentiles,
> and do not eat with them,
> and do not perform deeds like theirs.
> And do not become associates of theirs.
> Because their deeds are defiled,
> and all of their ways are contaminated, and despicable, and abominable.
> They slaughter their sacrifices to the dead,
> and to the demons they bow down.
> And they eat in tombs.
> And all their deeds are worthless and vain.
> And they have no heart to perceive,
> and they have no eyes to see what their deeds are,
> and where they wander astray,
> saying to the tree 'you are my god,'
> and to a stone 'you are my lord, and you are my savior';
> and they have no heart." (*Jub.* 22:16–18; tr. Wintermute)

The idea that idolatry leads men astray is strongly repeated. Error here includes, somewhat picturesquely, the worship of trees and stones.

The *Book of Jubilees* was originally composed in Hebrew. It was translated into Greek, and from Greek into Latin and Ethiopic.[227] Only fragments of the Greek text survive. It is by such translations that even the most conservative Jewish ideas concerning idolatry found their way into Greek writings, and that the foundation was laid for more sophisticated ways of arguing against the lure of classical idolatry.

Since for many, direct confrontation with Greek tradition would have been imprudent, Jewish iconoclasm also found indirect channels of opposition to images. The *Letter of Aristeas* is one example of pseudepigraphic literature, which was a sensible and popular means of expressing dangerous ideas of many kinds. The iconoclasm in the *Letter*, however, is briefly and timidly expressed; a far bolder stroke of composition placed strong iconoclastic arguments in the mouths of classical personages, such as Sophocles and the Sibyl, thereby producing impeccably pagan opponents of religious images.

Iconoclastic pseudepigrapha range from spurious lines to entire compositions. One of the best-known examples of the brief but telling quotation is the fragment attributed to Sophocles **[48]** which is repeated by many Christian writers. The open praise of monotheism and condemnation of

[227] Wintermute, "Jubilees," (*supra* p. 95 n. 226) 41–43 for the textual history.

idolatry immediately mark these lines as a Jewish production.[228] The sentiments are so blatant and so un-Greek that it may have been necessary for Clement, who quotes the lines twice, to appeal to the authority of "Hecataeus the historian" to justify including the fragment among pagan texts condemning pagan practices.[229] Of special note are two *topoi* from the Jewish iconoclastic repertory that later became standard in Christian polemic: idolaters are said to have wandered in their hearts from the path of truth, and the images are criticized for being made of wood, copper, gold, or ivory.

Further iconoclastic pseudepigrapha are found among the Sibylline Oracles, a loose body of hexameter poems that purport to be the pronouncements of the prophetess, but are of varied authorship. Oracles of the pagan Sibyls are to be distinguished from the Jewish and Christian pseudepigraphic compositions.[230] Idolatry is a frequent subject in the pseudepigrapha, and *xoana* join *eidola* and *agalmata* as objects of scorn.

One passage from the third book of the Oracles has already been mentioned (III.721–723) **[173]**: "Wandering, we had gone far from the path of the immortal, we revered with senseless spirit works made by hand, *eidola* and *xoana* of men who have perished." The salient points of the passage are the idea of idolaters as wandering from the truth, the criticisms of *eidola* and *xoana* as products of human hands, and their Euhemeristic identification as images of dead men. All are points of Jewish iconoclasm that have already been encountered in works as different as the spurious fragment of Sophocles, the *Letter of Aristeas*, and the *Book of Jubilees*.

[228] [Sophocles] fr. 1025 Nauck², fr. 1126 Pearson, Radt: *FHG* II, 396, fr. 18; Clem.Al. *Protr.* 7.74.2 and *Strom.* 5.14.113.2 **[48]**; Athenag. *Leg.* 5; Eus. *PE* 13.13.680 d–681 a, quoting Clement; Theodoret. *affect.* 7.109; Ps.-Justin *Cohort ad Gen.* 18 and *De monarchia* 2; Cyril Alex. *Adv.Iulian* 32. That the lines are not authentic was demonstrated by Bentley in 1691 in his *Epistola ad Millium*, notes on various points in Malalas' *Chronicle*: R. Bentley, *Epistola ad Joannem Millium* (repr., ed. A. Dyce; G.P. Goold, intro.; Toronto, 1962) 255–258; L. Dindorf, *Corpus Scriptorum Historiae Byzantinae* VIII (Bonn, 1831) 687–689, Add. 749–750; Pfeiffer, *History* II, 150 and n. 2; Pearson, *Fragments* III, 172–174 for a good discussion of this "impudent forgery."

[229] For the date and context of this text, see H. Attridge, "Fragments of Pseudo-Greek Poets," in *OTP* II, 821–822, 825–826 (late Hellenistic or early Roman); and Doran, "Pseudo-Hecataeus" (*supra* p. 83 n. 201) 905, 912–913 for a possible explanation of Clement's need to cite Hecataeus as the source for the lines of "Sophocles." The quotation would seem to come not from Hecataeus of Abdera, but from a Pseudo-Hecataeus.

[230] Sibylline Oracles: Geffcken, *Oracula Sibyllina*; bibliography and introduction to Sibylline literature by A. Kurfess, "Christian Sibyllines," in *NTA* II, 703–709; 706 for Alexandria as the center of Jewish Sibylline composition and for Book III as "the first truly literary Sibylline book." See also Collins, "Sibylline Oracles" 317–326. For the significance of the Jewish pseudepigrapha: Charlesworth, "Pseudepigrapha Research."

Book III of the Sibylline Oracles is a patchwork of passages from various times, and scholars disagree over the extent of its fragmentation. The book as a whole appears to be a Jewish work composed in Egypt. On the basis of content and language, the section to which lines 721–723 belong can be dated near the middle of the second century B.C.[231] Egyptian provenance has already been mentioned as a factor that may have affected the usage of *xoanon* as early as the third century; the possible *xoana* of Manetho would point the way toward a later kind of usage, and in those of Apollonius can be detected new overtones that extend the term beyond its previous limits. Book III of the Sibylline Oracles has traditionally been linked to Alexandrian Judaism. Arguments have been advanced which would associate it instead with Leontopolis, but the point is perhaps not critical here for the question of terminology.[232] There is insufficient evidence to prove the influence of Egyptian or Hellenized Egyptian concepts and practices on the meaning of *xoanon*, but the possibility of such influence remains, and the question might best be approached from the Egyptian side. It may be worth noting that the pseudonymous author of the *Letter of Aristeas*, a text recognized for the excellence of its Greek and its freedom from semiticisms, chose to use *agalmata*.[233]

By whatever means, *xoanon* and *eidolon* entered the vocabulary of iconoclasm. Disparaging comments about *eidola* appear throughout Book III, and in lines 721–723 the reference to worship puts the sense of the word beyond doubt.[234] It is possible that the traditional connection of *eidolon* with phantoms and specters may have held some positive appeal for the iconoclasts; certainly Clement of Alexandria, writing in the second century A.D., exhausts a play on the firmly established iconoclastic term when he caustically observes that the pagans were correct in having called the gods *eidola* and *daimones*. *Eidolatria* may well once have gone beyond denoting the worship of images, and preserved overtones hinting at the futility of phantom gods.[235]

A second passage in Book III of the Sibylline Oracles throws a somewhat different light on the word. The lines may be dated c. 31 B.C. and

[231] For Book III of the Sibylline Oracles: Nikiprowetsky, *Sibylle*; Momigliano, *Alien Wisdom* 118–119; and Collins, "Sibylline Oracles" 354–361 for a section-by-section analysis of text and scholarship; 354–355 for the date of the stage of composition to which lines 721–723 belong as 163–145 B.C.

[232] Collins, "Sibylline Oracles" 355–356.

[233] Denis, *Introduction* (*supra* p. 87 n. 209) 108, summary of the work of Meecham.

[234] Words for images in Book III: 277, *εἰδώλοις*; 279, *εἴδωλα*; 548, *θύεις τ'εἰδώλοις*; 554, *πολλὰ θεῶν εἴδωλα*; 587–588, *χρύσεα καὶ χάλκεια καὶ ἀργύρου ἠδ' ἐλέφαντος καὶ ξυλίνων λιθίνων τε θεῶν εἴδωλα*; *εἴδωλα χειροποίητα*.

[235] Clem.Al. *Protr.* 4.49 P.: *εἴδωλα γοῦν εἰκότως αὐτοὺς καὶ δαίμονας ὑμεῖς αὐτοὶ κεκλήκατε* (You yourselves rightly called them [the gods] *eidola* and *daimones*). For *eidolon*: *supra* p. 26 n. 64.

present a typically Sibylline prophecy of awful doom (III.57–59) [**172**]:[236] "Yet, just for today, cities, build, and all adorn yourselves with *naoi* and stadia and agoras and golden *xoana*, and silver ones, and stone ones, so that you will come to the bitter day." The vision of the destruction of the cities has Biblical precedents in the comprehensive theats of YHWH to smite the land of Israel because it had fallen into idolatry.[237] The lines from the Oracles are especially interesting in that, in the spirit of the horrendous Biblical prophecies, stadia and agoras are castigated along with the more easily understandable *naoi* and *xoana*. Their fault may lie in the fact that they, too, harbor images, as is attested by plentiful evidence from archaeology and literature. It is also possible, however, that the stadia and agoras are representatives of the entire objectionable order of Hellenized civic life. It may be recalled that one of the acts of Antiochus IV that aroused untold Jewish ill-will was his encouragement of apostate Jews by allowing them to build a gymnasium where they could exercise in Greek fashion—a gentile custom deeply offensive to Jewish traditions.[238]

Lines 57–59 are far more detailed than the other passage in Book III in the description of the *xoana*. The concrete evocation of the world of human manufacture raises the question of the precise connotations of *xoanon*. If the polemic goes so far as to specify gold and silver and stone *xoana*, might the word carry some typological significance? Although none of the texts examined so far in any context has provided evidence that a *xoanon* is defined by its material, in view of the well-established modern conception of *xoana* as wooden statues, references to specific materials in connection with the word deserve attention.

Aristeas 135 refers to ἀγάλματα . . . ἐκ λίθων καὶ ξύλων [**28**], from which it might be argued that words for statues do reflect typological distinctions based on the materials of their manufacture. It is unlikely, however, that *xoanon* in the iconoclastic context that has been outlined does

[236] For the date of III.57–59: Collins, "Sibylline Oracles": 359–360.

[237] *E.g.*, Ezekiel 6:1–14; 7:1–27; esp. the threat of YHWH in 6:6 (Wherever you live, cities shall be ruined and shrines desolated; so that your altars shall be ruined and desolate, your idols shall be broken and banished, your incense braziers shall be hewn down and what you have made wiped out) and another threat at 7:19–20 (They shall fling their silver into the streets; their gold shall be as an unclean thing. Their silver and gold shall be powerless to save them on the day of YHWH's rage. . . . Their beautiful adornment in which they took pride—out of it they made images of their abominable, loathsome things; therefore I will turn it into an unclean thing for them); M. Greenberg, tr., *The Anchor Bible. Ezekiel 1–20* (Garden City, 1983), commentary *ad loc.*; 162 for the *topos* of silver and gold and the frequent connection between idols and wealth. Charlesworth, "Pseudepigrapha Research" 75, notes the prominence of apocalyptic ideas in the pseudepigrapha. For the Jewish iconoclastic *topos* of the destruction of the idols pitted against the traditional Greek *topos* of the miraculous survival of divine images: Wallach, "Palestinian Polemic" 392–393.

[238] For the policies of Antiochus IV: Wintermute, "Jubilees" (*supra* p. 95 n. 226) 45–46.

have such significance. The *agalmata* of Aristeas are made "from stones and stocks," the emphasis being clearly on the objects, not their material *per se*. The phrase signifies little more than "sticks and stones"; it becomes a *topos* in iconoclastic polemic, and its only point is the lifelessness of the materials from which the images are made.[239] A good, later, example is Clement's attack on Orpheus and Methymnion (*Protr.* 1.4 P.): *τοὺς ἀνθρώπους ἐπὶ τὰ εἴδωλα χειραγωγῆσαι πρῶτοι, ναὶ μὴν λίθοις καὶ ξύλοις, τουτέστιν ἀγάλμασι καὶ σκιαγραφίαις, ἀνοικοδομῆσαι τὴν σκαιότητα τοῦ ἔθους* (and they were the first to lead men by the hand to the *eidola*; yes, indeed, with stones and stocks, that is to say, with *agalmata* and paintings, to build up the foolishness of custom). The reference to *skiagraphiai* makes no sense in connection with stocks and stones, as *toutestin* makes especially obvious; the irrelevance underscores the purely rhetorical aim of the *topos*. This example is especially valuable because in some passages Clement does give *xoanon* a typological significance, and does consider the materials of images, but for completely different reasons, as will be seen.

The emphasis on the lifeless materials from which images are made stems directly from the preoccupations of Jewish iconoclastic rhetoric, in which the idols are repeatedly castigated as non-living objects that try to ape the living God. The silver, gold, and stone *xoana* of the Sibylline Oracles belong to this tradition.[240] They have great rhetorical, but virtually no archaeological significance. It is not in the context of iconoclastic polemic that *xoanon* acquires typological associations.[241]

The absence of typological intention in the use of *xoanon* as a general term for images is clear in the work of Philo Judaeus (c. 30 B.C.–A.D.45),

[239] In Hellenistic usage, *xulon* can mean "tree": J.H. Moulton and G. Milligan, *The Vocabulary of the Greek Testament* (London, 1929, 1952) 434 *s.v.* *ξύλον*; "stock," however, is better in this context. Examples of the *topos* of stocks and stones: Oinomaus (A.D.II; preserved only in Eusebius, *Praeparatio evangelica*) *ap.* Eus. *PE* 5.4.217 b: *ἢ οὐ τοῖς ἀνθρώποις ἐμήνιεν ὁ Ζεύς, ἀλλὰ τοῖς λίθοις καὶ τοῖς ξύλοις*; (or was Zeus enraged not against men, but only against stones and stocks?); *ap.* Eus. *PE* 7.3.301 d: *ἐπεὶ δὲ μηδὲ ξύλων καὶ λίθων αὐτόματός ποτ᾽ ἂν οἰκοδομία συσταίη* (but since a building could never be raised from stocks and stones by itself); *ap.* Eus. *PE* 7.4.302 c: *τὰ μὲν γὰρ τῶν ὄντων εἶναι ἄψυχα, οἷα λίθους καὶ ξύλα* (for some among existing things are soulless, like stones and stocks); Origen (A.D.III), *ap.* Eus. *PE* 7.20.334 d: *ἐπεὶ μηδὲ ἀνδριαντοποιὸς χωρὶς χαλκοῦ τὸ ἴδιον ἔργον ποιῆσαι δύναται, μηδὲ τέκτων χωρὶς ξύλων, μηδὲ οἰκοδόμος χωρὶς λίθων* (since a maker of *andriantes* cannot make his own work without bronze, nor a carpenter without stocks, nor a builder without stones; in reference to God's creations from *ὕλη ἀγενητός*—unoriginated matter).

[240] *Supra* p. 88 n. 212 for *anaisthesia*; *supra* p. 99 n. 237 for the special associations of gold and silver.

[241] A pagan Sibylline delivered on the occasion of a prodigy in 125 B.C. and recorded by Phlegon **[300]**, is generally agreed to preserve old material, but a reference made in it perhaps to Hadrian suggests that the text is best treated with material of the second century A.D.: see *infra* pp. 148–149.

where the word is usually embedded in a litany of arguments against idolatry.[242] Philo condemns the worship of images in repetitive terms: *ἀγάλματα καὶ ξόανα καὶ ἀφιδρύματα* seven times; *ξόανα καὶ ἀγάλματα* five. Once *ἀγάλματα καὶ ξόανα καὶ ζωγραφήματα* are mentioned as beautiful works of art, and once Philo says that Augustus, an exceptionally good ruler, was not honored by a single *ἄγαλμα*, *ξόανον*, or *γραφή*—the monuments, it would seem, of ruler cult.[243]

The essentially rhetorical intention of the repeated phrases cannot be emphasized too strongly. A common translation of *agalmata kai xoana*, "images of stone and wood," attempts to be too precise.[244] The rendering is supported neither by the meaning of *xoanon* attested in contemporary and earlier sources, nor by the significance of the word in the specific context in Philo. The sense of the iconoclastic *topos* governs the sense of the individual words, and even so mild a typological distinction as "stone and wood," which could conceivably make archaeological sense, has no relevance.

The other iconoclastic *topoi* connected in Philo with the formulaic terms for images confirm the absence of typological associations. *Lithoi* and *xula* are said to be the fundamental beings (*ουσίαι*) of the *xoana* and *agalmata* in *De vita contemplativa* 7 [**296**], but even with the concrete extension of the conceit in the evocation of the quarrymen and woodcutters hewing the images from their matrices, it is not a specific equation of the materials with the statues that emerges; the emphasis is instead on the indignity of mere matter, an emphasis made unmistakable by the sorry fate outlined for the remaining material as waterpots, footbaths, and chamberpots. Whether "stones and stocks" were actually used for such vessels is irrelevant, for it is clear that Philo's desire to insult has directed his words.[245] In *De decalogo* 66 [**287**], *agalmata* and *xoana* and other products

[242] For Philo's dates: *OCD*[2] *s.v.* Philon (4).

[243] Ἀγάλματα καὶ ξόανα καὶ ἀφιδρύματα: *De dec.* 7 [**285**], *De dec.* 51 [**286**], *De dec.* 156 [**289**], *De ob.* 109–110 [**290**], *De virt.* 221 [**295**], *De vit. Mos.* 1.298 [**297**], *De vit. Mos.* 2.205 [**298**]. Ξόανα καὶ ἀγάλματα: *De dec.* 66 [**287**], *De dec.* 76 [**288**], *Leg. Gai.* 292 [**293**], *De spec. leg.* 1.56 [**294**], *De vit. cont.* 7 [**296**]. Ἀγάλματα καὶ ξόανα καὶ ζωγραφήματα: *De Abr.* 267 [**284**]. Μὴ ἄγαλμα, μὴ ξόανον, μὴ γραφήν: *Leg. Gai.* 148 [**292**]. Ξόανα καὶ ἀγάλματα of the gods are mentioned but not castigated in *Leg. Gai.* 98 [**291**]. For *aphidruma* as meaning simply the statue of a god, and for its presence in the "formula": L. Robert, *Hellenica* 13 (1965) 121 and n. 3. For the monuments of ruler cult: Price, *Rituals*, esp. 170–206 ("Images"). Price asserts (176 n. 27) that, except for one possible exception, *xoanon* "was not used of imperial statues." Philo's remarks would seem to suggest that it may have been. See *infra* p. 111.

[244] See, *e.g.*, the renderings of F.H. Colson and G.H. Whitaker, eds., trs., *Philo* (LCL, 1929–1962) *passim*. *Cf.* the comment of Price, *Rituals*, quoted *supra* p. 8 n. 38.

[245] A non-iconoclastic forerunner of the *topos* is the anecdote in Herodotus (2.172) in which Amasis makes from a golden footbath a statue which the Egyptians worship: "he called a

of men's hands have been made from "*xula* and *lithoi*, silver and gold"—but, says Philo, by the arts of *plastike* and *zographia*, sculpture and painting, only one of which is strictly relevant to the materials named. Painters and modellers are castigated again in *De vita Mosis* 2.205 [**298**], where it is clear once more that Philo's objection to idolatry refers to a generalized vision of the world of fine arts. Passages like this and *De Abrahamo* 267 [**284**] (in which all manner of art, including *agalmata* and *xoana*, are set up everywhere as adornment) are reminiscent of the lines in the Sibylline Oracles (III.57–59) [**172**] describing the cities, glorious with buildings and *xoana*, that will come to destruction. The Biblical precedents for such imagery have been noted; the tradition emphasizes vivid rhetoric which, while it may be concrete, should not be assumed to be archaeologically precise. Nowhere can it be demonstrated that Philo uses *xoanon* in any sense more specific than the image of a god, or that the formulaically repeated terms are more than corroborative synonynms.

---

meeting and revealed the fact that the deeply revered statue was once a foot-bath, which they had washed their feet and pissed and vomited in." (Tr. A. de Sélincourt.) In this way he convinces the Egyptians that he, although once an ordinary man, is fit to be king. *Infra* p. 178 n. 6 for other examples of statues' being made of ordinary material. Such ironies were transformed into iconoclastic conceits. *Cf.* a similar image used in an argument about aesthetics by Plotinus (5.8.1): if two λίθοι ἐν ὄγκῳ, one untouched by τέχνη, the other transformed by *techne* into the *agalma* of a divinity or a man, are compared, it is seen that beauty lies not in the material (ὕλη), but in the *techne*. A good Biblical example of this *topos* in iconoclastic context is Isaiah 44:14–20:

> A man plants a cedar and the rain makes it grow, so that later on he will have cedars to cut down; or he chooses an ilex or an oak to raise a stout tree for himself in the forest. It becomes fuel for his fire; some of it he takes and warms himself, some he kindles and bakes bread on it, and some he makes into a god and prostrates himself, shaping it into an idol and bowing down before it. The one half of it he burns in the fire and on this he roasts meat, so that he may eat his roast and be satisfied; he also warms himself at it and he says, "Good! I can feel the heat, I am growing warm." Then what is left of the wood he makes into a god by carving it into shape; he bows down to it and prostrates himself and prays to it, saying, "Save me; for thou art my god." Such people neither know nor understand, their eyes made too blind to see, their minds too narrow to discern. Such a man will not use his reason, he has neither the wit nor the sense to say, "Half of it I have burnt, yes, and used its embers to bake bread; I have roasted meat on them too and eaten it; but the rest of it I turn into this abominable thing and so I am worshipping a log of wood." He feeds on ashes indeed! His own deluded mind has misled him, he cannot recollect himself so far as to say, "Why! this thing in my hand is a sham."
>
> (*New English Bible*)

For the author of this section, writing during the later years of the Babylonian Exile (549–538 B.C.): *ODCC*[2] *s.v.* Deutero-Isaiah. For a similar Talmudic story: Price, *Rituals* 176 n. 27.

Conclusions

In the second century B.C., *xoanon* begins to appear in Jewish literature written in Greek with a definition differing from that in prevailing Greek usage. *Xoana* are equated with the idols forbidden by Jewish law, and the word becomes a term in the vocabulary of iconoclasm. Although Greek religious theories such as Euhemerism are occasionally grafted onto the arguments against images, the fundamental concepts concerning images are and remain Jewish. *Xoanon* refers to the images of the gods understood as a class and castigated on specific grounds. The images are treated collectively as man-made objects that, being themselves without life, wrongly are worshipped as the living divinity; the fact that they are made from lifeless materials is the strongest argument against them. The images are colorfully visualized as being manufactured from stocks and stones and silver and gold; but vividly as they are described, they are nonetheless essentially abstract, since the physical details are traditional rhetorical *topoi* that do not add up to a coherent factual whole. Thus, in the context of Jewish iconoclastic rhetoric, *xoanon* is a formulaic term that lacks typological significance and embodies a conception of divine images that reflects not Greek practice itself, but rather a critical vision of that practice determined by wholly different convictions. By the middle of the first century A.D. *xoanon* is a standard term in iconoclastic rhetoric, and within that context it is, to a considerable extent, independent from other contemporary usage.

8. *Xoanon* in the First and Second Centuries A.D.: Common Usage

The preceding section outlined the establishment of *xoanon* in the vocabulary of Jewish iconoclasm, where it served as a term for images of gods considered as a class of man-made objects. Before examining the Christian polemic that developed from the earlier iconographic literature—and the corresponding treatises in favor of images—it is necessary to describe the background of ordinary usage against which the specialized definitions stand out.

In the first century A.D., the extant occurrences of the word are numerically dominated by Philo's iconoclastic *xoana*. There are comparatively few other appearances of *xoanon*, and they show considerable variety in the meanings assigned to the word.

The sole inscription that can confidently be assigned to this century is precisely dated to A.D. 37. It is an honorific decree from Cyzicus [**385**], a city on the southern coast of the Sea of Marmara that came under Roman domination in the later second century B.C.[246] The decree provides for the commendation of the *basileis* Rhoimetalkes, Polemon, and Kottus, and their mother Tryphaena, and provides for a ceremony for which the priests will open the *temene*, and *proskosmein* the *xoana* of the gods. The verb can mean "adorn yet more"; whether the priests are simply to adorn the *xoana*, or to add still more ornaments to those already in place, is not clear. In either case the action recalls the earlier Magnesian ceremony [**392**] in which the *xoana* of the twelve gods wore their finest clothing.[247] The *xoana* of Cyzicus thus seem to be in line with the *xoana* mentioned in earlier inscriptions from Asia Minor: images of gods that receive elaborate religious attention.

The first century A.D. may also be the date of the *xoana* in Josephus' quotation of Manetho, in spite of Josephus' assurance that he has given the text of the earlier writer *verbatim*. There are no grounds for suggesting that Josephus has been less than careful, candid, or scrupulous about the material he uses, but changes in Manetho's text before Josephus read it cannot be ruled out; Josephus did know more than one version of the work. The two passages in the *Contra Apionem* (1.244; 1.249) [**155**] tell of the futile attempts by the Egyptians to hide their *xoana* from the Jewish invaders. The use of *xoanon* for such images collectively finds its best parallels only after the second century B.C., as does the association of antisemitic ideas and the issue of iconoclasm. If Manetho did use *xoanon*, he was before his time in terms of the meaning of the word in Greek literature, and the passages would provide a useful clue to the changes in its sense. It is also possible,

[246] Decree from Cyzicus [**385**]: *SIG*³ II, 798; *IGRR* IV, 145; E.M. Smallwood, *Documents Illustrating the Principates of Gaius, Claudius and Nero* (Cambridge, 1967) 120–121 no. 401. For the Roman domination of Cyzicus from 133 B.C.: *PECS s.v.* Kyzikos.

[247] LSJ⁹ *s.v.* προσκοσμέω. For Magnesian inscription Kern 98 [**392**]: *supra* p. 61 n. 143.

however, that the *xoana* belong in the context of Josephus' own age and situation, where they fit comfortably. One of the difficulties in dealing with the usage of Josephus is his reliance on assistants in the composition of Greek. In the *Contra Apionem* he admits (1.50) to such help in the preparation of the *Jewish War* some twenty-five years earlier; while Josephus' own style has been detected in the *Jewish Antiquities* and the *Life*, features of the *Contra Apionem* point to his having again resorted to outside help. The Greek text of the *Jewish War* seems to represent a thorough recasting of the first, Aramaic version, and its vocabulary should reflect the common usage of the good Atticizing Greek in which it is written. *Xoanon* appears once in the work, in Josephus' speech urging the Jews not to fight the Romans but instead to trust to the protection of God (5.375 ff.). He contrasts examples of Jewish triumphs by the will of God and without the use of arms to occasions in which resistance led to defeat. He cites some Biblical stories in somewhat modified form, among them the theft and recovery of the Ark: "Did not Palestine and Dagon the *xoanon* bewail the robbery by Syrians of the ark sacred to us?" (5.384) **[154]**. *Xoanon* here refers to the image of the god; further, the god Dagon *is* an image—a mere image, for implicit in both context and wording is a comparison to the living and triumphant God of the Jews. Whether the iconoclastic overtones reflect Josephus' Aramaic text, his own general sentiments, or the convictions of his assistants, the passage shows a fairly specialized usage of the term opportunistically employed in a context not specifically devoted to the question of images.[248]

The few other *xoana* that can be dated to the first century A.D. have specialized definitions that will be discussed in the following section. They are few enough, however, that the entire collection of *xoana* from this century can be seen to belie the use of the word found in Philo. He condemns *xoana* so sweepingly that one feels the world must be full of them; yet demonstrable usage reveals no widespread use of the term. The few *xoana* that do appear cannot be marshalled into the kind of horde evoked by Philo's words. The iconoclastic usage of *xoanon* is a rhetorical development and something of an archaeological red herring.

[248] For Manetho: *supra* pp. 43–44 and n. 104. In *Ap.* 2.191 *eikon* is the image of god that the Jews do not make, but the passage concerns the visualization of God rather than actual statues and images. For the date of *Ap.* c. A.D. 100: H. St. J. Thackeray, tr., *Josephus* I (LCL, 1926) xii–xv. For Manetho as a historical source, and for indications that Josephus' copy of the *Aegyptica* was bad, or that he relied on extracts from Manetho in the works of others: W.J. Murnane, rev. of R. Krauss, *Das Ende der Amarnazeit*, *Orientalia* 52 (1983) 279–282. For Josephus' use of assistants and the composition of the *Bellum Judaicum*: Thackeray xi–xvi. For Dagon: E. Ebeling and B. Meissner, eds., *Reallexikon der Assyriologie* II (Berlin and Leipzig, 1938) 91–101 *s.v.* Dagan (H. Schmökel).

The proliferation of *xoana* begins in the second century A.D. Aside from the specialized definitions of the word, which will be treated separately, the literature offers a good array of *xoana*, some new, others met before in quotations from earlier authors, but finding their true context in the later century. It happens that the majority of *xoana* in epigraphical and papyrus texts are concentrated in imperial times. Inscriptions yield several *xoana* that carry on the standard usage found in earlier texts; papyri extend the range of definitions.

The only inscription of these centuries that can be precisely dated comes from Koptos in Egypt [**391**]. It is the record made on August 30, A.D. 103 of the lavish dedication by Didymos, the *rhetor*, of a "*xoanon* of Isis in the Atrium, and the *naos* and everything around it."[249] "Isis in the Atrium" is an iconographical type of nursing Isis. Teucer, a Babylonian astrologer tentatively dated to the first century A.D., mentions "the goddess sitting on a throne and nursing a child, whom some call the goddess Isis in the atrium nursing Horus." Many examples of the type are preserved in a variety of media. During the Ptolemaic period the old Egyptian type became Hellenized, but even in Roman times the Egyptian pedigree is not always completely submerged.[250] The material and size of Didymos' *xoanon* are not mentioned, but surely the image was worthy of its painstaking commemoration. Presumably the *naos* is that of Isis, but an inscription of the second century A.D. from Alexandria attests such an Isis in the Atrium dedicated to Helios-Sarapis.[251] Didymos' usage of *xoanon* differs from that known earlier in Egypt, in the text of the Rosetta Stone [**401**]; his *xoanon* is not a monument of official cult, but instead an image in line with those of earlier inscriptions from the Greek mainland. It can be compared specifically with the *xoana* dedicated together with a *neos* by Dionysius in the Peiraeus [**399**].[252]

[249] Koptos, Alexandria Museum no. 70 [**391**]: *Sammelbuch* V, 8815; Breccia, *Inscrizioni* 46–47 no. 62 (*Cat. gén.* no. 192); *ArchPap* 2 (1903) 439 no. 42; *IGRR* I, 1175 (*signum ligneum aegyptiaco modo factum*).

[250] For Isis in the Atrium: V. Tran Tam Tinh, *Isis Lactans* (Leiden, 1973) *passim*; 18–19 for Teucer, this inscription, and other texts. For Greek and Roman types related to Isis, and additional bibliography: T.H. Price, *Kourotrophos* (Leiden, 1978) 31–40; C.E. Richardson, "Isis Lactans," *OxJArch* 1 (1982) 325–330. It is interesting that this dedication appeared about five years before the proliferation of numismatic examples of the type shown seated in a temple (A.D. 108/109); Tran Tam Tinh, *Isis* 17–18 for these coins as linked to a renovation of the temple of Isis in the wake of a growing popularity of the cult that is already obvious in the first century.

[251] For the Isis in the Atrium dedicated to Helios-Sarapis: *IGRR* I, 1048 (Alexandria, perhaps A.D. II). Tran Tam Tinh, *Isis* (*supra* p. 106 n. 250) 19.

[252] For *IG* II^2, 2948 [**399**]: *supra* pp. 63–64.

A text inscribed on a stone tablet, now lost, from Nicopolis ad Mestum in Thrace [**394**] mentions the dedication of a *xoanon*. On historical grounds the inscription can be dated to the very late first century A.D., perhaps even shortly after the Flavians. It records the dedication of a tripod(?) and a *xoanon* by the *strategos* Flavius Dizalas, son of Ezbenis, and his wife. The gifts were made at the command of Artemis, who seems also to have ordered the couple to perform additional devotions, apparently including the renewal of the cult at Keirpara. The text as transcribed ends with damaged references to a sacrifice.[253]

Scholars concerned with *xoana* in northern Greek inscriptions of this era disagree on the meaning of *xoanon*, some preferring to define it as a wooden image, others, as a primitive image of whatever material. Mihailov, for example, believes that here and in another inscription from Nicopolis [**395**], *xoanon* refers to a figure fashioned "in the most ancient way," but he is unsure whether the material would have been wood or stone. Perdrizet, in contrast, asserts that a *xoanon* is a wooden image made by smoothing a trunk, topping it with a head or a mask, and draping it. He adduces the "*xoana* of Dionysus" shown on fifth-century Attic vases, and supports his definition with independent testimonia for each characteristic: Masurius Sabinus for the debarked trunk; Pausanias for woodenness; and inscriptions from Magnesia and Bargylia for the dressing.[254] Perdrizet's method of combining sources, however, is open to question, since *xoanon* has no uniform definition that can be carried over from text to text. At work too in Perdrizet's analysis is the assumption that *xoana* are primitive, which accounts for his choice of illustrative testimonia; there do exist texts that refer, for instance, to golden *xoana*.

The same kinds of assumptions are clear in Beševliev's comparison of the text from Nicopolis with a Latin inscription found near Kobalitsa, which lay near Drama, along one of the routes controlled by Nicopolis. The inscription concerns a cult of Diana Minervia. To the left of the Latin text is a rough carving of a herm, which seems to wear two necklaces. Salač has asserted that this herm is "without doubt a *xoanon*," an identification that also rests on the assumption of primitive form.[255] There is no strong reason

[253] Mihailov, *Inscriptiones* IV, 287–292 no. 2338 [**394**]; see *SEG* 24, 626. See Mihailov 289 for the suggested restoration at line 10 *θυσίαν καὶ [τὸ ξόα]νον*. For Nicopolis, a Trajanic foundation: R.F. Hoddinott, *Bulgaria in Antiquity* (London and Tonbridge, 1975) 185–186.

[254] Mihailov, *Inscriptiones* IV, 291–292; Perdrizet, "Nikopolis" 226–228. For the Attic figures of Dionysus: *infra* pp. 227–229. For Masurius Sabinus: *infra* p. 163 n. 406. For Pausanias: *infra* pp. 140–147. For Magnesia, Kern 98 [**392**]: *supra* pp. 60–61. For Bargylia [**382**]: *infra* pp. 109–110 and n. 267.

[255] Discussed by Mihailov, *Inscriptiones* IV, 291–292 *ad* line 7. A. Salač, "Inscriptions du Pangée, de la région Drama-Cavalla et de Philippes," *BCH* 47 (1923) 64–69 no. 24.

to identify the cult of Artemis at Nicopolis with that of Diana Minervia, and the triple equation of the herm, the "cult image" of Artemis, and the *xoanon* is not assured.[256] At least two Thessalian parallels for the herm from Kobalitsa exist; the meaning of the one that accompanies the inscription is not clarified by the text, and it seems possible that such figures need not have served as illustrations.[257] Clues to the nature of the *xoanon* of Nicopolis must be sought in the text itself.

Two things are clear about the *xoanon* of Flavius Dizalas: it is a private dedication, and it is an important enough dedication to merit commemoration along with the other gifts and elaborate attentions to the goddess. The family of the *strategos* seems to have been noble; it is, however, only generally probable that the goddess would expect them to provide objects commensurate with their rank and presumable financial capability.[258] The most that can be said about the *xoanon* is that, as a dedication, it is certainly in line with earlier epigraphical *xoana* from the Greek mainland, and that, like them, it is likely to have been a gift worthy of pride.

Several *xoana* appear in epigraphical texts that belong to the Roman period, but have not been assigned precise dates. They are treated in this section partly *faute de mieux*, but also because their divergence from literary usage, as a group, is so marked; in these centuries the major interest lies not so much in the dates of *xoana* as in the contexts in which they appear.

A second inscription from Nicopolis ad Mestum [**395**], also lost, has been assigned to the second century A.D.. It records the fulfillment of another divine command: Dizalas the son of Beithus dedicated to Zeus "the *naos* and the *xoana* in accordance with the oracle" (*τὸν ναὸν καὶ τ[ὰ] ξόανα κατὰ χρηματισμόν*).[259] The nature of the *xoana* is not certain. The plural form suggests that something other than, or perhaps in addition to, the major image of the *naos* is meant. The proud record of their completion, however, clearly places this inscription in line with that of Didymos in Koptos [**391**] and those recording similar gifts; the dedication of Dionysius in the Peiraeus [**399**] seems especially close.[260]

Four inscriptions relating to dedications of *xoana* come from Asia Minor. One, from the area of Baglitsa in eastern Phrygia [**381**], records the

[256] Even the identification of Diana Minervia with the Artemis of Gagoros is not secure: Salač, "Inscriptions" (*supra* p. 107 n. 255) 68–69.

[257] For the Thessalian herms: A. Jardé and M. Laurent, "Inscriptions de la Grèce du Nord," *BCH* 26 (1902) 387–388 no. 95.

[258] For the nobility family: Mihailov, *Inscriptiones* IV, 290.

[259] Mihailov, *Inscriptiones* IV, 293–294 no. 2341; *BullEpig* 1948 *ad* no. 120. Perdrizet, "Nikopolis" 225–228; 225–226 for parallels for the Latin *epsilon* in coinage of A.D. 132–154. For *χρηματισμὸς* here used for an oracle: L. Robert, *Hellenica* 2 (1946) 148.

[260] For IG II^2, 2948 [**399**]: *supra* pp. 62–63.

dedication of a *xoanon* by two brothers who, having become priests, accomplished the setting up "from their own funds."[261] The inscription is carved on a *bomos* of bluish limestone; it recalls the earlier dedication of a *xoanon* on Delos by Charmikos, who had become a priest of Zeus Kynthios and Athena Kynthia **[387]**.[262] The text names no cult, however; the only specific detail is given in the phrase *τῇ γλυκυτάτῃ πατρίδι*. The dear fatherland appears in two more inscriptions about *xoana* from Asia Minor, but does not seem relevant to the question of the statues.[263] More to the point is the reference to the dedicants' own funds, which also reappears, and which implies that the *xoanon* was not cheap. Again, the emphasis on expense can be paralleled in earlier epigraphical references to *xoana*.

A slab carved with a relief from the area of Büyükkadife in Lydia **[383]** repeats the boast about private funding. Trophimos and his daughter "dedicated the *bomos* with the *xuanon* placed on it from their own money." The slab, which may have formed the facing of the *bomos*, shows a female figure in a kalathos, holding a torch and a cornucopia, accompanied by a dog and a drinking serpent.[264] The text recalls the reference in Euripides' *Ion* to the "*xoana* of the altar." It is not clear, however, that an altar is actually meant here; *bomos* can be used of a base, although the usage is rare.[265] Once more, a *xoanon* is a private dedication, apparently costly, and worthy of pride. Its orthography, however, is perhaps the most remarkable quality of this *xoanon*; the form *xuanon* is noted by Tzetzes **[368]** in the twelfth century A.D. as an example of Aeolic dialect.[266]

Bargylia, in Caria, has yielded an inscription announcing the dedication of a *xoanon* of Apollo by a city official **[382]**. The partially preserved name Mar. Aur. . . . suggests a date in the later second century A.D.[267] The

[261] For the dedication from Baglitsa **[381]**: W.M. Calder, ed., *MAMA* I, 220 no. 417; A.E. Kontoleon, "Ἐπιγραφαὶ τῆς Ἐλλάσσονος Ἀσίας," AM 14 (1889) 91 no. 11, notes two holes toward the top of the stone.

[262] Dedication of Charmikos, Delos *ID* 1881 (inv. E. 799) **[387]**: *supra* pp. 64–66.

[263] For γλυκύτατος in private correspondence: *JHS* 101 (1981) 244.

[264] Relief from Büyükkadife **[383]**, in the Cayster valley: J. Keil and A. von Premerstein, *Bericht über eine dritte Reise in Lydien und den angrenzenden Gebieten Ionien* (Vienna, 1914) 99–100 no. 148; the goddess is identified as a fertility goddess, perhaps Demeter or Kore; Papadopoulos, *Xoana* 72 no. 15 suggests Demeter on the basis of the attributes and places the text in the second century A.D. For the relief (reported to be in the Smyrna Museum) and the iconography of the goddess: L. Robert, *Hellenica* 10 (1955) 116–117, pl. 19.1. *Cf. MAMA* I, 146 *ad* no. 279, where the name Trophima is said to suggest Christianity.

[265] For *bomos*: C.G. Yavis, *Greek Altars* (St. Louis, 1949) 54 n. 1. For the *Ion*: *supra* p. 21.

[266] Tze. *Exegesis in Homeri Iliadem* 11 **[368]**; noted also by Papadopoulos, *Xoana* 4.

[267] Inscription from Bargylia **[382]**: G. Cousin and C. Diehl, "Inscriptions de Iasos et de Bargylia," *BCH* 13 (1889) 40 no. 7. For *protos*: D. Magie, *De Romanorum iuris publici sacrique vocabulis sollemnibus in Graecum sermonem conversis* (Leipzig, 1905) 45, 130; P. Veyne, "Augustal de l'an I. Premier pontarque," *BCH* 90 (1966) 149–155, esp. 150 n. 2 for

gift may also have included all the *kosmos*, "adornment," for the *xoanon*, but the phrase is almost wholly restored. The dedication is τῇ γλυκυτάτῃ πατρίδι, the same phrase that appeared in the text from Baglitsa. The publication of the text gives no information about the stone on which it is inscribed; it is not clear even if it might have been the base of the *xoanon*. Presumably the *xoanon* made an impressive dedication. If σὺν τῷ [παντὶ] κό[σμῳ] is correctly restored, the statue would have adornment in common with the *xoana* of Cyzicus and those of the twelve gods at Magnesia. Nonetheless the closest parallels for the inscription remain the other private dedications. The text thus appears to show the usage of *xoanon* that emerged in the inscriptions of the Greek mainland and the areas in its orbit, rather than that attested earlier in Asia Minor.

Another *xoanon* comes from Oenoanda in Lycia [**397**]. *Xoanon* is the last word of the inscription by which Leake identified the site, a long text carved on a pedestal, announcing the pancration victory of Publius Sthenius Fronto and his dedication of a "lovely *xoanon*."[268] The text is not a modest document, managing as it does to mention Publius' glorious earlier victory, for which the town had honored him with a brass *eikon*. On the occasion of this latest victory, he returns the favor by putting up (θῆκ') a *xoanon*. The prominence of the hometown continues one preoccupation of the dedications from Asia Minor. The costliness of the *xoanon* can perhaps be inferred from its comparison with the *klutos*, "glorious," brass *eikon*; it is itself *eratos*, "lovely," a quality not heretofore associated with *xoana*, and not altogether comprehensible.[269] It should not be assumed that the author of these elegiacs has intended to contrast the *eikon* and the *xoanon* by the criterion of material; although the reference to brass might be taken to suggest that the *xoanon* is not made from this metal, such a distinction cannot be demonstrated. The questionable *eratos*, furthermore, casts some doubt on the writer's control of vocabulary. Three possible parallels for *xoanon* used to refer to a portrait come to mind. One occurs in the sixth century A.D., in an epigram of Macedonius the Consul [**167**].[270] In that poem, too, the *xoanon* appears in the context of an athletic victory. Another

---

Robert on πρῶτος τῆς πόλεως as an honorific title; see *IG* XII.5, 292.2 (Paros) for ὁ πρῶτος τῆς πόλεως.

[268] For the dedication from Oenoanda [**397**]: *CIG* III, 4380 m; Addenda p. 1169; Kaibel 944. For the importance of the inscription: *RE* II.17.2 (1937) 2230–2231 *s.v.* Oinoanda (W. Ruge). For the history of the site: A. Hall, "The Oenoanda Survey: 1974–76," *Anatolian Studies* 26 (1976) 191–193. For endowed games, some named for donors, in imperial provinces: D. Magie, *Roman Rule in Asia Minor* (Princeton, 1950) 1392 n. 63; 1522–1523 n. 57 for *agonothetai*; 534–535 for names and games as evidence for the Romanization of Lycia.

[269] LSJ⁹ *s.v.* ἐρατός gives no examples of the word applied to images; songs, hymns, voices, places, and people do not seem wholly equivalent.

[270] See *infra* p. 165.

comparison for the *xoanon* from Oenoanda is one mentioned in an inscription from Adada, modern Karabauli, in Pisidia [**379**].[271] The text, carved on the lintel over a door, records the dedication by Theodoros of "the *neos* from the foundations, with the *xoanon* and the *agalmata*." The devotion of Theodoros to his fatherland is stressed, as is his having paid from his private funds.[272] What separates Theodoros' dedication from the similar texts of Asia Minor is the mention of the *Theoi Sebastoi*, whose chief priest Theodoros is. The possibility arises that the *xoanon* and *agalmata* are monuments of the imperial cult, since no other god is mentioned. *Xoanon* has already been seen in contexts suggestive of imperial cult, and Theodoros' dedication may support the idea of such a connection. It is not clear, however, how the distinction between the *xoanon* and the *agalmata* relates to the personages represented, or even what the two terms denote. Is the *xoanon* the major image of the installation, and if so, what are the *agalmata*? Precise answers may not be possible on the evidence of the inscription alone, because the terminology of the images of the imperial cult reflects a vexing fluidity in concepts and contexts; the firmest information that can be wrested from Theodoros' text is a tentative association of *xoanon* with imperial cult. Finally, an inscription from Qanauat, ancient Canatha, in southern Syria records the dedication of a *xoanon* on behalf of the emperor Elagabalus [**401**]. It is precisely within the cult of emperors that changes in the terminology of images might be expected to take place—in the context of reverence for images of divine beings that were at the same time portraits.[273]

The inscriptions from Asia Minor in the Roman period consistently show *xoana* as expensive private dedications worthy of their donors' pride. This definition corresponds to the earlier epigraphical usage characteristic of the Greek mainland and its orbit, but differs from that of Hellenistic Ionia, carried on in the first century A.D. in Cyzicus, where *xoana* are the focus of official civic cult. The small number of *xoana* emphasizes the rarity of the word in general usage and underscores the difficulty of drawing precise conclusions about its meaning.

[271] *IGRR* III, 336; J.R. Sittington Sterrett, *The Wolfe Expedition to Asia Minor* (Papers of the American School of Classical Studies at Athens III; Boston, 1888) 301 no. 422; Price, *Rituals* 269 no. 121; 176 n. 29.

[272] A date for the inscription in the later second or earlier third century A.D. seems possible. Price, *Rituals* 269 *ad loc.*, suggests this date for two other inscriptions from the site (nos. 119, 120) on the basis of the age of the donor's grandson. He remarks that the three temples of inscriptions nos. 119–121 are standing, and that the suggested date of nos. 119 and 120 "confirms the impression given by the ornamentation of the temples." For Adada: *PECS s.v.*

[273] For the difficulty of establishing categories of images of the imperial cult: Price, *Rituals* 176–180 and *passim*. For the inscription from Qanauat [**401**]: *infra* p. 151. For Philo and the vocabulary of imperial cult: *supra* p. 101.

Two more epigraphical *xoana* come from other areas. An inscription on a block reused in a church in Ḳal 'at Kālôtā [390], in Syria, records a dedication and mentions a *naos* and a golden *xoanon*. The dedication is offered to gods in the plural, Symbaitylos and a lost associate. The fifth-century A.D. church incorporates walls from two separate second-century A.D. temples; the identity of the *xoanon* is therefore not certain.[274] It is reasonable to think that the donors, who have dedicated something (lost) to the gods, are also taking some credit for the *naos* and golden *xoanon*, but because the text preserves only the information that something happened "after completing(?)" the *naos* and *xoanon*, it cannot be said whether the donors' private funds ties this inscription to similar dedications from Asia Minor. That the *xoanon* is golden, however, recalls the golden *xoanon* mentioned in an Egyptian papyrus of A.D.178 (Pap. Oxyrhynchus 1117.1) [375]. The Syrian inscription appears to have divided affinities, and although the image may have been a private dedication of the kind that is well established by this time even in the East, the usage of *xoanon* might be closer to the Hellenistic Egyptian; in that case the image would perhaps be closer to an official "cult image."

The possible connection of the *xoanon* with the god Symbaitylos deserves attention in view of the widespread trendency to equate "baetyls" with aniconic monuments, and hence with primitive *xoana*. The word "baetyl" is a specialized term referring in ancient sources only to the magical, animated stones that gained popularity in the second century A.D.; in antiquity it does not refer to the unworked or non-figural monuments of aniconic cult.[275] It would therefore be incorrect to take the possible connection of *xoanon* with Symbaitylos as proof or suggestion that *xoanon* denotes such an aniconic or formally primitive piece. That this *xoanon* is golden and evidently costly would seem to suggest, furthermore, that the image lay well within the standard traditions of the luxurious fine arts.

One more epigraphical *xoanon* belongs to the imperial age. It appears in a fragmentary text from Portus Ostiae [400] known today only through a transcription. The inscription was discovered in 1793 or 1794, and appears

[274] For the inscription from Ḳal 'at Kālôtā [390]: W.K. Prentice, *Publications of the Princeton University Archaeological Expedition to Syria in 1904–1905 and 1909. Division III. Greek and Latin Inscriptions in Syria. Section B. Northern Syria. Part 6. The Djebel Sim 'ân* (Leiden, 1922) 199–200 no. 1193. For the site (about 25 km. northwest of Aleppo, and not to be confused with Kālôtā, which also has "East" and "West" temples): H.C. Butler, *Syria . . . Division II. Architecture. Section B. Northern Syria* (Leiden, 1920) 318–322; Temple Church built on remains of East and West Temples (A.D. II); the inscription is set into the southern face of the south wall of the Church.

[275] Moore, "Baetylia."

to have come from the Sarapeum.[276] No details about the "*xoanon* of the most holy god Sarapis with Isis in Menouthis" survive. Is the *xoanon* a double image? Is it an image of Sarapis placed in a shrine of Isis? The reference to the Isis of Menouthis suggests an especially close connection with Egypt.

Most of the *xoana* mentioned in inscriptions of the Roman period are private dedications that are evidently costly. This usage continues the epigraphical tradition of the word that was established on the Greek mainland and in areas within its orbit. The association of *xoanon* with images that are the focus of official cult continues in the East, in first-century A.D. Cyzicus and in Egypt, but there too the mainland usage has gained ground. A private individual in Koptos dedicates a *xoanon*, and the majority of inscriptions from Asia Minor in this period are also concerned with private dedications. The marked geographical differences in the usage of the centuries before Christ have greatly diminished. The inscriptions yield no evidence that *xoanon* has narrow typological connotations; some are dedicated together with a *naos*, some not; some are golden; one may even be an honorary statue and not an image of a god. The inscriptions reflect the growing popularity of the word in a variety of contexts.

A *xoanon* in a papyrus text **[375]** of the second century A.D. seems to belong to the traditional world of classical images. It is mentioned in the draft of a letter that is dated c. A.D. 178, written by the superintendents of the golden *xoanon* of Athena-Thoeris.[277] The "great goddess" Thoeris (the Greek version of t3-wrt), an important and popular hippopotamus-goddess, is often mentioned in documents under the name Athena.[278] The superintendents of her *xoanon* appeal to a prefect to grant more favorable arrangements for repaying the gold which they have been convicted of embezzling during the making of the statue. This *xoanon* is a public, rather than a private, project, and in the care of special officials; as such it is comparable to the *xoana* mandated by the Rosetta Stone decree. The tech-

[276] Inscription from Portus Ostiae **[400]**: L. Vidman, ed., *Sylloge inscriptionum religionis Isiacae et Sarapiacae* (RGVV 28; Berlin, 1969) 258 no. 556a; L. Robert, *BullEpig* 1965, 193–194 *ad* 488; L. Moretti, "Sulle inscrizioni greche di Porto," *RendAccLinc* ser. 8, vol. 19 (1964) 197–198, a transcription of Fea, who died in 1836. Moretti (198) argues that *xoanon* means a wooden image; he is refuted by Robert, 193–194. Papadopoulos, *Xoana* 70 no. 1, notes the possibility that an Alexandrian made the dedication and draws attention to the large number of Alexandrians resident in Portus in the second century A.D.

For a *xoanon* dedicated near ancient Phaena, in Syria, between A.D. 165 and 175: *infra* I n. 431.

[277] P.Oxy. 1117 **[375]**, now in the Cairo Museum: *POxy* 8 (1911) 200–202.

[278] For Athena-Thoeris: J. Quaegebeur, W. Clarysse, and B. Van Maele, "Athêna, Nêith and Thoêris in Greek Documents," *ZPE* 60 (1985) 217–232.

nique of the *xoanon* cannot be ascertained from the letter. Solid gold statues, although apparently not the rule in strictly classical practice, are not out of the question here. The only sure information about the *xoanon* is that it was the public image of a goddess and, assuming that the gold was intended to form part of the statue and not as payment for expenses, that it incorporated large amounts of the material.[279] It should be noted that the superintendents use *xoanon* in the heading of their letter, as if it were the official term for the statue. Such application would reflect the use of the word for images of gods in temples that is current in contemporary literature and has roots in Hellenistic times; it may have specific precedents in the use seen in the decree honoring Ptolemy V.

In the literature of the second century A.D. *xoanon* is not a common word, but when it does appear it often refers to temple images and images of gods in general, and in so matter-of-fact a way that one would expect it to be more popular than it is. It seems to carry no connotations of form, age, or material, and simply to denote such images in the most general sense. The best examples of this undifferentiated usage come from Lucian, who uses the word more frequently than almost any other author of the century.[280]

Two passages in Lucian referring to the images of the gods as a class have forerunners in earlier remarks about *xoana*. The comment of Dionysius of Halicarnassus on Romulus' establishment of *hiera*, *temene*, *bomoi*, and *xoana* (2.18.2) [**66**] is reminiscent of Prometheus' description of the state of the world before men existed: "there were no *bomoi* of the gods, or *naoi*—how could there be?—or *agalmata* or *xoana* or anything else of the sort, though they are now to be seen in great numbers everywhere, honored with every form of observance" (*Prom.* 12) [**166**].[281] If there is a difference

[279] The embezzlers are required to repay eighteen talents; Quaegebeur *et al.*, (*supra* p. 113 n. 278) 225, note a loss "amounting to a sum of 18 talents"; Hunt (*POxy* 8, 200) specifies "eighteen talents of silver." According to the ratio of gold to silver in coinage—an imperfect comparison, due to the debasement of silver in coins—the amount would equal about one and one-third talents of gold. The ratio was about 1:13 in the time of Nero, and no change in the imperial system is recorded until Caracalla: H. Mattingly, *Roman Coins* (London, 1967) 123–124. The extremely tentative conclusions that can be drawn from the much earlier Athenian inscriptions concerning the figures of Nikai in which part of the gold reserve in the city in the fifth century B.C. was stored suggest that two talents were enough to make a hollow gold statue six feet high; thus the embezzled gold alone could have made a substantial figure. For the Athenian Nikai: D.B. Thompson, "The Golden Nikai Reconsidered," *Hesperia* 13 (1944) 173–209; 178–181 for the gold and the size of the statue. For golden statues: J.E.G. Whitehorne, "Golden Statues in Greek and Latin Literature," *Greece and Rome* 22 (1975) 109–119. For golden *xoana* in Egypt: F. Preisigke, ed. E. Kiessling, *Wörterbuch der griechischen Papyrusurkunden* Suppl. 1 (Amsterdam, 1969–1971) *s.v.* *ξόανον*.

[280] For a summary of and bibliography on Lucian: *OCD*² *s.v.* Lucian, where his dates are given as c. A.D. 120 to sometime after A.D. 180.

[281] For Greek conceptions of the deep past: *infra* pp. 122–124, 195–205.

here between *agalmata* and *xoana*, it cannot be clarified even by comparing this passage with others. Strabo's reference to the Egyptian temple with no (anthropomorphic) *xoanon* **[352]** is echoed in Lucian's discussion in *De Dea Syria* **[159]** of the establishment of religion by the Egyptians, who built *hiera* and *temene* (compare Herodotus on the same subject **[139]**). The Assyrians learned from them and built *hiera* and *neoi* in which "they both placed *agalmata* and stood up *xoana*." The passage concludes with the interesting observation that "in the past, even among the Egyptians, the *neoi* of the gods were *axoanoi*" (*SyrD* 2–3). It is possible that the combination of *agalmata* and *xoana* owes something to the kind of litany seen in Philo, although its more obvious precedent is Dionysius. In the following section the antiquarian tradition behind these and similar statements will be examined; for the moment it is sufficient to point out the use of *xoanon* for the images that at this time were accepted as the usual and proper fittings of temples.

This general sense of the word also holds in the case of single images. In *Phalaris* I.6 **[164]**, a hypothetical temple robber is imagined entering the *hieron*, pulling down the *anathemata*, and laying hands on the *xoanon*. *Xoana*, then, are standard religious accoutrements, and since the *hieron* apparently has several *anathemata* but only one *xoanon*, the *xoanon* may perhaps be regarded as the major image of the structure. In describing the burgeoning popularity of the sham snake/god Glykon, Lucian says that "next came *graphai* and *eikones*, and *xoana*, some formed of bronze, others of silver" (*Alexander* 18) **[158]**. The proliferation of images of the human-faced snake may have had a comic aspect in that the combination of *graphai*, *eikones*, and *xoana* recalls the kinds of monuments associated with imperial cult; Philo mentions that Augustus was not honored by *agalma* or *xoanon* or *graphe* **[292]**, and there were many imperial *eikones*.[282] That the significance of *xoana* does lie partly in their functions as portrayals is suggested by *De Dea Syria* 34 **[162]**, where the absence of *xoana* of Helios and Selene is explained in this way: "They say that it is a custom to make *xoana* for other gods, for their appearance is not clearly shown to everyone; but Helios and Selene are plain for all to see, and all men see them. What reason is there for the making of *xoana* (*xoanourgia*) for those who appear in the heavens?"

De Dea Syria is filled with *xoana* of a variety of gods. Some have marvelous and uncanny abilities (10 **[160]**; 32 **[162]**); other do not. Some are golden (32, 33 **[162]**) or covered with gems (32 **[162]**). Lucian's descriptions of these *xoana* show that in types and rendering they belong to the repertory of the ordinary figural arts; some are perhaps special in the richness of

[282] Price, *Rituals* 176–177; "imperial *eikones* were common" (177).

their manufacture, being made of precious materials. These and the bronze and silver *xoana* of Glykon recall the golden *xoana* of Egypt and Syria.

Two points of Lucian's usage are of special interest. Although he habitually uses *xoanon* for divine images, in *De Dea Syria* 39 [**163**] he mentions "countless other brazen *xoana* of kings and priests" outside the *neos*. Clearly the term is not always restricted to images that are the focus of worship; it would be possible to argue that monuments of ruler cult are meant, but the images of priests must be explained. That the *xoana* are *μυρία* strongly recalls, furthermore, the dedications that clogged classical sanctuaries. If these *xoana* are honorary statues, they shed light on that of the inscription from Oenoanda.

The most interesting aspect of Lucian's *xoana* is not their definition, however, but their very appearance in *De Dea Syria*. This long description of the sanctuary at Hierapolis imitates Herodotus.[283] One striking anomaly, however, is that whereas Lucian's work is full of *xoana* of many kinds, Herodotus never uses the word at all. There can be no clearer demonstration of the change in the usage of the word since the fifth century B.C.

Two epigrams by Rufinus, who perhaps belongs to the second century A.D., mention *xoana*; both times temple statues are specified, and both times the images are mentioned merely as comparisons—that is to say, their usage could not be more ordinary and free from special interests. In *AnthPal* 5.15 [**327**], Melite is so beautiful that her likeness should be modelled or carved in stone; her loveliness, like a *xoanon* of the blessed, merits its own *neos*. The emphasis here is on beauty and high artistic quality. The same is true in *AnthPal* 5.36 [**328**], in which Rufinus compares features of Rhodoclea's body to glass, and to a *πρωτογλυφές*, "newly-carved," *xoanon* in its *neos*. That this *xoanon* is a new, not an ancient, statue deserves note. The association of both *xoana* with temples recalls the assumption that *neoi* have *xoana* found in Strabo and Lucian; their beauty and high artistic quality recall the precious *xoana* of Lucian and the emphasis on expense that characterizes the epigraphical usage of the word.[284]

[283] For Lucian's imitation of Herodotus, *De Dea Syria*: H.A. Strong, tr. and J. Garstang, ed., *The Syrian Goddess* (London, 1913) 31–32.

[284] *AnthPal* 5.15 [**327**] = *AnthPlan* 7.145 = Rufinus IV in D. Page, ed., *The Epigrams of Rufinus* (Cambridge, 1978). P. Waltz and J. Guillon, eds., *Anthologie Grecque. Première partie. Anthologie Palatine* II (*Livre* V) (Paris, 1928) give the last line with ξοάνοις (Desrousseaux). *AnthPal* 5.36 [**328**] = *AnthPlan* 7.142 (which does not includes lines 5–10; Waltz and Guillon suggest *ad loc.* that the omission is *verecundiae causa*; for censorship as a feature not unexpected in Planudes' productions: Wilson, *Scholars* 231) = Rufinus XII Page. Page, 75 *ad* IV and 82 *ad* XI, notes that the themes of these two poems have no parallels in the *Anthology*. Πρωτογλυφές is a *hapax*; Page (85 *ad* 8) compares the *artiglyphes* of Theocritus(?), for which see *supra* p. 44 n. 105. The peculiarity of Rufinus' vocabulary contributes to the diffi-

Arrian appears to use *xoanon* in the simple sense of "temple image" in his *Periplus of the Euxine Sea* [33], which might perhaps be dated near A.D. 131/2, the year he began his legateship in Cappadocia and prepared a report of his initial inspection of the region.[285] On the island of Leuce are a *neos* of Achilles and a "*xoanon* of old workmanship."[286] The specific reference to the antiquity of the statue speaks against the assumption that *xoanon* has automatic connotations of great age. For his description of the coast, Arrian drew heavily on existing geographies of the area, but it is likely that, whether he borrowed *xoanon* from such a source or used it on his own, he understands it in the way Lucian does, as the image that customarily belongs in a religious structure—here, not of a god, but of a hero with his own *neos*. Such general usage is also attested in an entry of the *Onomasticon* of Pollux [**322**], dated late in the second century A.D.: "These are the things to which we give service: *agalmata*, *xoana*, *hede* of the gods. . . ."[287]

Xoanon meant as a general term for the images of the gods is found in three Sibylline texts that may perhaps be dated to the second century A.D. The first appearance is in the fourth Sibylline book, a composite text whose layers stretch from a Hellenistic foundation through a late first-century A.D. revision, and possibly further.[288] The section in question, lines 24–30 [**174**], predicts an idyllic situation on earth among those who will live piously in the worship of God. They will reject *naoi* and *bomoi* and blood sacrifices. In line 28a they will also have done with "stone *xoana* and handmade *agalmata*," but the verse is not without difficulties.

Geffcken rejects the line because it appears only in Clement's quotation of the oracle (*Protr.* 4.54 P.) [**46**] and because it is identical to a line in Fragment 3 of the Sibyllines [**365**], which he considers to be a Christian forgery.[289] Clement, always the opportunist, tends to seek out the versions

---

culty of dating him. A. Cameron, "Strato and Rufinus," *CQ* 32 (1982) 162–173, argues against Page's suggestion of a date in A.D. IV in favor of one c. A.D. 70–100. Also against the later date: J. and L. Robert, *REG* 95 (1982) 328.

[285] Arrian, *Periplus Ponti Euxini* 21 (32 M) [**33**]. A.G. Roos, ed., *Flavius Arrianus* II. *Scripta minora et fragmenta* (Leipzig, 1967) 21:32. For the date of the *Periplus* as considerably later than the generally accepted A.D. 131/132: A.B. Bosworth, "Arrian's Literary Development," *CQ* 22 n.s. (1972) 183–185. For the authenticity of the work: A.G. Roos, "Ad Ursulum Philippum Boissevain septuagenarium epistula de Arriani Periplo Ponti Euxini," *Mnemosyne* 54 (1926) 101–117.

[286] For this passage [**33**] and Arrian's confusion of the island with the "Course of Achilles" to the northeast: Diller, *Tradition Geographers* 103–104. *Cf.* the anonymous *Periplus Ponti Euxini* 66 [**283**] (A.D. VI): *infra* p. 166.

[287] For Pollux, *On.* I.7 [**322**]: *infra* p. 172 and n. 430.

[288] For the nature and date of Book IV: Collins, "Sibylline Oracles" 381–382.

[289] For line 28a: Geffcken, *Oracula Sibyllina ad loc.*

of texts that best support his arguments; he would have been highly pleased to find a version of the oracle that included *agalmata* and *xoana*.[290] The legitimacy of the line therefore depends on what can be told about its appearance in the Sibylline fragment.

Fragment 3 is preserved in another work of the later second century A.D., Theophilus' *Ad Autolycum* (2.36) [**365**].[291] This apology is the source for three Sibylline fragments, all of which Geffcken considers to be forgeries by Theophilus. The necessity of Christian authorship, however, has not been seen by other scholars, and Fragment 3 is generally thought to belong to a lost second book of the oracles, another part of which is recognized in lines 1–96 of the present Book III. The sentiments of Fragment 3 closely resemble lines 1–45 of Book III, and because both texts are theologically close to Jewish Orphic material, they could be dated as early as the second century B.C. If, however, lines 46–96 are to be associated with verses 1–45, historical considerations would suggest a date for the passage as a whole around the time of Actium.[292] The textual difficulties resulting from the acute fragmentation of Book III make assurance impossible. Because both the overall content of the fragment and the iconoclastic references are so generally suitable for the entire late classical period, the most conservative date for the debated line is to be preferred. The Sibylline *xoana* of Clement and Theophilus both are therefore best considered as examples of the generalized iconoclastic use of the term in the later second century A.D. The suitability of the line for the entire range of Sibylline iconoclasm must be kept in mind, however, and its affiliations with material as early as the second century B.C. underline the persistence of the definition of the word.

A third appearance of *xoana* can be dated on historical grounds c. A.D. 175. In Book VIII, lines 110–130 [**175**], the Sibyl again envisages an idyllic time of peace and social equality. The context is the destruction of Rome and the humbling of the city with its "*xoana* of gold and silver and stone." Following the earlier predictions of doom in Book III, the city has indeed come to a bitter day. The savage vision of the destruction of Rome in particular, however, betrays Christian authorship.[293] Sibylline prophecies tend to exhibit a monotonous awfulness, and here the *xoana* again continue as generalized representatives of idolatry in a conventional vocabulary.

[290] *Cf. supra* p. 97 n. 229 for Clement's role in attaching the authority of "Hecataeus" to [S.] fr. 1126.

[291] For Theophilus, Bishop of Antioch: *ODCC*² *s.v.* For his sole preserved work: R.M. Grant, ed., tr., *Theophilus. Ad Autolycum* (Oxford, 1970).

[292] For the relationship of Fragment 3 to the Sibylline Corpus: Collins, "Sibylline Oracles" 359–361, 469.

[293] For Book VIII: Kurfess, "Christian Sibyllines" (*supra* p. 97 n. 230) 707, and for the "fierce hatred against Rome"; Collins, "Sibylline Oracles" 415–417.

The *xoana* already encountered in Apollodorus [**21–24**] and Antoninus Liberalis [**16–19**] can now be understood in their proper context. Although they appear in passages based on the work of earlier authors such as Acusilaus and Nicander, they reflect the usage current in the later writers' time.[294] *Xoanon* is the word that Apollodorus and Antoninus found natural to use in speaking of images such as the Palladion, the Hera of Argos, and the images of Aspalis and Aphaia. The *xoana* in these summaries are evidence not for the meaning of the word in the fifth and second centuries B.C., but for its sense hundreds of years later. The broad definition lacking typological connotations is the definition of these *xoana*, and they therefore provide no real information about the state of statuary or of its terminology in any period other than the second century A.D. The same is true of Apollodorus' reference to the *xoanon* of Athena set up by Erichthonius (3.14.6) [**23**]. The use of *xoanon* points to no precise facts about the image. Apollodorus seems to mean the statue on the Athenian Acropolis called by Pausanias simply the *agalma* (1.26.6) [**190**] and mentioned briefly by other writers.[295] These independent notices cannot simply be combined to shed light on Apollodorus' usage of *xoanon*, or to derive a true archaeological picture of the statue. Images like this Athena exist to a great extent in the realm of legend; they are cores around which develop traditions that are not always concerned with accurate reporting. Ostensible facts are frequently determined by historical and theoretical conceptions, and context remains the only reliable guide to the terminology.

Conclusions

In the first and second centuries A.D., *xoanon* is more frequently used than in previous times, but it is still rare. The split between epigraphical and literary usage continues, but a certain degree of homogenization is evident in the spread of its application to private dedications, previously restricted to mainland Greece and its immediate sphere, to Asia Minor, Syria, and Egypt. Also to be noted is the connection of the word in literature, and perhaps in inscriptions, with statues of mortals; an especially interesting facet of this usage links *xoana* to the monuments of imperial cult. By and large, however, in literature the word is applied to images of gods, and often particularly to those that stood in temples or were the focus of religious attentions. Apparently the word in this sense lacks any connotations of age, form, or material. As in previous centuries, the expansive use of

[294] For Acusilaus in Apollodorus: *supra* pp. 13–15; for Nicander in Antoninus Liberalis: *supra* pp. 57–59.

[295] For Paus. 1.26.6 [**190**]: *infra* p. 147.

xoanon to refer to so general a category of images contrasts oddly with the rarity of its appearances.

The evidence from literary, epigraphical, and papyrus texts establishes what may be considered the general usage of *xoanon* in the first two centuries after Christ. The following section treats the contemporary definitions that emerged in special contexts and that have influenced the modern understanding of the word.

9. *Xoanon* in the First and Second Centuries A.D.: Iconoclasm and Antiquarianism

Until this point, the discussion of *xoanon* has been able to proceed on a fairly straightforward chronological plan. Because the word appears so rarely, it has been easy to chart its appearances, the greatest difficulty being to identify later usage masquerading as earlier in quotations and extracts. Literary and epigraphical texts have fallen into relatively neat lines, and changes and developments in meaning have shown themselves clearly. The induction of *xoanon* into the vocabulary of iconoclastic polemic, however, complicates its history; by the first century A.D. the word had become established in a context in which it attracted specialized definitions that were at odds with prevailing usage. At the same time, *xoanon* began to appear in another special context: antiquarian research and theory. Because the concerns of antiquarianism and iconoclasm overlap to some extent, it is best to approach the sources in question thematically rather than strictly chronologically. In addition, much of the important material is preserved only in writers of the third and fourth centuries A.D., and some flexibility in chronological treatment is needed in order to sort out the layers of sense. This section, then, attempts to show the development of specialized definitions of *xoanon* in the contexts of iconoclastic and antiquarian writing.

The course of the early Christian iconoclastic controversy cannot be fully discussed here, but the aspects of it that are relevant to the word *xoanon* should be examined in some detail. It is well established that the Christian writers adopted a traditional scheme of Jewish polemic against the pagan gods and their images.[296] Recognizable arguments include the condemnation of the *anaisthesia*, lack of sensation, of the images, and of the baseness of the materials from which they are made. The borrowed elements of Euhemeristic theory also reappear. In general, however, the Christian polemic makes greater use of Greek concepts than does the Jewish, and Christian writers efficiently mined Greek sources for material that could be useful in the struggle against pagan practices.

The development of greatest interest in iconoclastic polemic is the introduction of what amounted to an evolutionary theory of idolatry and statuary. The argument drew heavily on Greek tradition and speculation; under the layers of Christian additions and reinterpretations can still be detected the old Greek scaffolding. The arguments are sometimes difficult to follow because the same points are used by all the authors—Christians

[296] Wallach, "Palestinian Polemic" 402–403. For the Christian adoption of Jewish polemic and the suggestion that the kinds of idolatry mentioned reflect an ethnographic schema: J. Schwartz, "Philon et l'apologétique chrétienne du second siècle," in *Hommages à André Dupont-Sommer* (Paris, 1971) 497–507; *Studia Philonica* 2 (1973) 66.

who oppose images, Christians who approve them, and non-Christians who hold a variety of opinions on the subject—to prove opposing contentions.

The main point of the evolutionary theory is that the urge to symbolize or to depict the gods is a naïve impulse of the kind one might expect in a child or barbarian, barbarians being thought of as the children of the civilized world. This line of thought is not much different from some modern anthropological notions of "primitive" behavior. One of the best expositions of the theory is Dio Chrysostom's defense of idolatry in his twelfth *Oration* **[57]**, which he delivered at Olympia in A.D. 97:

> For certainly no one would maintain that it had been better that no *hidruma* or *eikon* of the gods should have been exhibited among men, on the ground that we should look only at the heavenly objects. For although the intelligent man does indeed reverence all these objects, believing them to be the blessed gods that he sees from a great distance, yet on account of our belief in the divine all men have a strong yearning to honor and worship the deity from close at hand, approaching and laying hold of him with persuasion by offering sacrifice and crowning him with garlands. For just as infant children when torn away from father or mother are filled with terrible longing and desire, and stretch out their hands to their absent parents often in their dreams, so also do men to the gods, rightly loving them for their beneficence and kinship, and being eager in every way to be with them and to hold converse with them. Consequently many of the barbarians, for lack of craftsmanship and difficulty with it, name mountains gods, and unworked trees, too, and shapeless stones, things which are by no means whatever more appropriate in shape than is the human form.[297]

Dio makes no attempt to assert that idolatry is correct or desirable; rather, he excuses it on the grounds of its innocent intention. He compares men and gods outright to children and their parents.[298] Although men exhibit lack of understanding, they commit no impiety. Barbarians are even more pitiful, being doubly deficient in both understanding and art.

Dio's defense of idolatry is based on its theoretical beginnings in the innocent childhood of man, which is a *topos* with a long Greek history. The Greeks habitually characterized both children and barbarians as deficient

[297] Dio Chrysostom, *Or.* 12.60–61 **[57]**: translation adapted from J.W. Cohoon, tr., *Dio Chrysostom* II (LCL, 1939). The title of the oration is "On Man's First Conception of God"; in it, Pheidias is called upon to speak in defense of his Olympian Zeus. Brief comments by Nock, "Posidonius" (*supra* p. 83 n. 201) 7. For Dio's beliefs and career: J.L. Moles, "The Career and Conversion of Dio Chrysostom," *JHS* 98 (1978) 79–100. To Dio's comments on the honor paid to the visible heavenly bodies, *cf.* Luc. *SyrD.* 34 **[162]**, on Helios and Selene, who require no *xoana*.

[298] *Cf.* Strabo 1.2.8 **[334]**: as adults tell pleasant or frightening stories to influence the behavior of children, so mythological stories and representations of them inspire people to good deeds, and indications from the gods deter them from bad ones.

in understanding.[299] One reason for their opinion is the Greek equation of reason with speech, as in the word *logos* itself; certainly young children and *barbaroi* lack at least the latter.[300] The Greeks often conceived the early state of their civilization in terms of the barbarians of their own times: Thucydides (1.6.5) asserts that the early Hellenic world was similar in many ways to the barbarian cultures of his own day, and Plato (*Crat.* 397 C) has Socrates say that the earliest Greeks worshipped what the barbarians do now—the sun and the moon. The religious urge has a place in such contexts; in Protagoras' explanation of the progress of man, for example, the urge to worship the gods seems to be a fundamental, and hence an "early" characteristic.[301] The Stoic Diogenes of Babylon apparently found it παιδαριῶδες, "childish," to say that the gods were human in appearance (ἀνθρωποειδεῖς).[302] The conception appears in a variety of contexts throughout the course of Greek speculation on such subjects.

[299] For the Greek characterization of children as stupid (νήπιος): E. Vermeule, *Aspects of Death in Early Greek Art and Poetry* (Berkeley, Los Angeles, and London, 1979) 113–114; among other possible meanings, she notes "one who cannot yet speak well, or express his thoughts in language." For the word: S.T. Edmunds, "Homeric ΝΗΠΙΟΙΣ," summary of Diss. Harvard University, 1976, *HSCP* 81 (1977) 299–300. The oafish Scythian in Ar. *Th.* is a good example of a Greek view of barbarian stupidity; see Baldry, *Unity* 33 and *passim*. Baldry rightly emphasizes the changes in Greek attitudes toward non-Greeks; it would certainly be wrong to speak of *the* Greek view without qualification. Negative attitudes toward foreigners seem to have been widespread in antiquity. In a Sumerian text called "The Curse of Agade," for example, Amorites are denigrated as people "ignorant of the fundamental institutions of civilization," such as houses, settlements, and agriculture; furthermore, they are criticized as being not only ignorant, but also stupid: see the new edition of the "Curse," J.S. Cooper, *The Curse of Agade* (Baltimore and London, 1983), 30–33 for ethnic jokes and ethnic slurs, which are rare in Sumerian literature. *Cf.* "The Instructions of Suruppak" lines 269–273: "An unknown beast is bad, an unknown man [is horrible]./ On an unknown road, in the front of the foreign country,/ The gods of the foreign countries who eat men,/ Who do not build houses like (civilized) men, who do not build cities like (civilized) men,/ In the . . . of civilized men they come down (from the mountains)": B. Alster, *Studies in Sumerian Proverbs* (*Mesopotamia*, Copenhagen Studies in Assyriology 3; Copenhagen, 1975) 137–138. I thank M. DeJ. Ellis for these references, and for discussing the xenophobic *topos* with me. For the role of agriculture in Greek traditions about the development of civilization: *infra* p. 197 n. 54. For attitudes toward barbarians: B.D. Shaw, "'Eaters of Flesh, Drinkers of Milk': The Ancient Mediterranean Ideology of the Pastoral Nomad," *Ancient Society* 13/14 (1982/1983) 5–31.

[300] For Greek *logos* and related issues: Baldry, *Unity* 22–23.

[301] For the Greek idea that the Greeks of old lived much as present-day barbarians do: Baldry, *Unity* 46–47. For Protagoras and the worship of the gods: Guthrie, *In the Beginning* 87–89; 80–82 for the wild Cyclopes of Homer and their role in Greek theories of the development of civilization. For discussion and bibliography on classical speculation about the early life of man: E. Panofsky, "The Early History of Man in a Cycle of Paintings by Piero di Cosimo," *JWarb* 1 (1937–1938) 16–19. See also *infra* p. 127 n. 307.

[302] Diogenes of Babylon (c. 250 B.C.) *ap.* Philodemus, *De pietate* 15: Arnim, *SVF* III, 217 fr. 33. The text is much restored: π(αι)δ(αριῶ)δες.

Dio's statement that the barbarians, through πενία τε καὶ ἀπορία τέχνης—lack of craftsmanship and difficulty with it—have recourse to found objects and to trees and stones, derives from another Greek conception of the progress of culture, the idea of an age before art. This *topos* appears in several forms, sometimes in straight discussions of artistic progress (*Dieg.* Call. *Aet.* IV fr. 100) [**42**], sometimes in connection with the idea of a past age of greater virtue (Clem.Al. *Protr.* 4.41 P. [**44**]; compare the one hundred seventy years without images in Rome in the context of the Pythagorean-style simplicity of life under Numa: Plut. *Numa* 8.7–8 [**321**]). The invention of art became for some Christian writers the origin of all wickedness, and their enhancements of the basic *topos* go far beyond the original Greek concept.[303]

Sometime during the reign of Commodus, the sophist Maximus of Tyre produced a defense of idolatry [**168, 169**] that follows a course of argument similar to Dio's. Maximus uses the examples of spontaneous forms of worship, children, and barbarians to show that the making of images is a pious, if finally ineffective, effort to honor the gods. He argues that idolatry is a universal and fundamental practice, untaught and unsophisticated, that springs from basic human instincts.

> The gods are the helpers of mankind, all indeed of all; but different gods are considered as giving assistance to different men, according to the rumor of names; and men distribute honors and *agalmata* to them according to the private benefits which they have individually received. Thus sailors dedicate, on a rock undisturbed by the sea, helms to the marine deities. Thus, also, some shepherd dedicates in honor of Pan a fir tree, having chosen a tall one for him, or a deep cavern. Husbandmen, likewise, honor Dionysus, fixing in their garden a wild trunk as a rustic *agalma*. Fountains of water, too, hollow thickets, and flowery meadows, are sacred to Artemis; and the first men consecrated as *agalmata* to Zeus the summits of mountains, such as Olympus and Ida, or any other mountain proximate to the heavens; honor is also paid to rivers, either for the sake of the benefit which they impart, as by the Egyptians to the Nile; or on account of their beauty, as by the Thessalians to Peneus; or on account of their magnitude, as by the Scythians to the Ister; or on account of fabulous tradition, as by the Aetolians to Achelous; or according to law, as the Spartans to Eurotas; or in conformity to the mysteries, as the Athenians to Ilissus. (8.1)

[303] For the *topos* of the age before art: *infra* pp. 195–205. The simplicity of the age of Numa is a variation of the theme. Numa was asked to assume the kingship of Rome partly in the hope that he would civilize the warlike Romans; their basic simplicity has strong aspects of roughness and barbarity, and is not wholly positive. The regime of Numa is characterized in Plutarch's account by elements of Pythagorean nature, and its simplicity has therefore a complex tradition. Note too the one hundred seventy years in which no images were made: *cf.* Varro *ap.* Aug. *DCD* 4.31 [**40**]; *infra* pp. 200–201.

. . . Indeed, it appears to me that external discourse has no need, for its composition, of certain Phoenician, or Ionian, or Attic, or Assyrian, or Egyptian characters, but human weakness devised these marks, in which inserting its dullness, it recovers from them its memory; in like manner a divine nature has no need of *agalmata* or *hidrumata*; but human nature being very weak altogether, and as much distant from divinity as earth from heaven, devised these *semeia*, in which it inserted the names and the renown of the gods. Those, therefore, whose memory is robust, and who are able, by directly extending their soul to heaven, to meet with divinity, have perhaps no need of *agalmata*. This race is, however, rare among men, and in a whole nation you will not find one who recollects divinity, and who is not in want of this kind of assistance, which is the sort that writing-masters devise for boys, who give them obscure marks as copies; by writing over which, their hand being guided by that of the master, they become, through memory, accustomed to the art. It appears to me, therefore, that legislators devised these *agalmata* for men, as if for a certain band of boys, as *semeia* of the honor which should be paid to divinity, and a certain leading by the hand, as it were, and path to remembrance. (8.2)

. . . With respect to the barbarians, all of them in like manner admit the subsistence of divinity, but different nations among these adopt different *semeia*. Hence the Persians adopt fire, an ephemeral *agalma*, insatiable and voracious; and to fire they sacrifice, supplying it with the aliment of fire, and at the same time exclaiming, "O master fire, eat." But it is worth saying to the Persians, "O most stupid of all nations, who, neglecting so many and such mighty *agalmata*, the mild earth, the splendid sun, the navigable sea, prolific rivers, the nourishing air, and the heavens themselves, are especially devoted to one thing, and that most savage and most rapid, not only supplying it with the aliment of wood, with victims, and aromatic fumigations, but by this *agalma* and by this god giving Eretria to be consumed, together with Athens itself, the *hiera* of the Ionians, and the *agalmata* of the Greeks." (8.4) **[168]**

. . . The Celts, indeed, venerate Zeus, but the Celtic *agalma* of Zeus is a lofty oak. The Paeonians venerate Helios, but the Paeonian *agalma* of Helios is a short discus fixed on top of a long pole. The Arabians, indeed, venerate a god whom I do not know; but the *agalma* of him which I have seen is a quadrangular stone. By the Paphians Aphrodite is honored; but you cannot compare her *agalma* to anything else than a white pyramid, the material of which is unknown. Among the Lycians the mountain Olympus creates fire, not like that of Aetna, but peaceful and possessing symmetry; and this fire is to them both *hieron* and *agalma*. The Phrygians who dwell about Celaena venerate two rivers, Marsyas and Maeander, which rivers I have seen. (8.8) **[169]**[304]

[304] F. Dübner, ed., *Theophrasti Characteres . . . Maximi Tyrii Dissertationes* (Paris, 1877). Dübner's no. 8, "Whether Statues Should be Set Up to the Gods," is no. 38 in T. Taylor, tr., *The Dissertations of Maximus Tyrius* (London, 1804), and no. 2 in H. Hobein, ed., *Maximi Tyrii Philosophumena* (Leipzig, 1910). The dates of Maximus are usually given as c. A.D.

Likening idolaters to lovers who cherish every memento of the beloved, applauding the piety of idolaters while regretting their inability to comprehend the nature of the divine, Maximus asserts the necessity of images. "There is not, indeed, any race of men, neither barbarian nor Greek, neither maritime nor continental, neither living a pastoral life, nor dwelling in cities, which can endure to be without some *symbola* of the honor of the gods" (8.9) [**169**]. The universality and multiplicity of images are heavily stressed. "Of *agalmata* there is neither one law, nor one mode, nor one art, nor one matter" (8.3) [**168**]. The proof for this statement is a long ethnographic catalogue in which the images, or the substitutes for images, of various barbarian peoples are listed, interspersed with a chatty commentary.[305] Maximus has provided numerous facts on which to base his emotional plea, and thus brought greater precision to the argument for images. The basic structure of the defense, however, is the same as it was in Dio's oration; children and barbarians continue to justify the making of images.

Convincing as this kind of argument seems in defense of idolatry, it was nonetheless used wholesale to attack the images. Iconoclasts turned every point around, preserving both the theoretical outline and the factual support of the defense, but transforming it into a bleak and unappealing

---

125–185; recently on his dates: R.J. White, tr., *The Interpretation of Dreams. Oneirocritica by Artemidorus* (Park Ridge, New Jersey, 1975) 5. For brief comments on his pretenses to being a follower of Plato: *KP* III, 1115 *s.v.* Maximus II.1. Plato did not face the same issues with respect to idolatry as the writers of the second century A.D., and it is unrealistic to expect a true Platonic prefiguration of these later discussions; *e.g.*, *Leg.* 11.931 A, a passage intended to promote proper tending of aged parents, who are better than any image. To Maximus' ideas *cf.* Plato's disapproval of spontaneous religious acts by men in distress and by women: *Leg.* 10.909 E–910 D. For good descriptions and explanations of similar conflicts between highly organized religious hierarchies and spontaneous religious activity: I.M. Lewis, *Ecstatic Religion* (Penguin, 1971) *passim*. For the simile of schoolboys learning their letters, *cf.* Ar. *Po.* 1448 b: ἐοίκασι δὲ γεννῆσαι μὲν ὅλως τὴν ποιητικὴν αἰτίαι δύο τινὲς καὶ αὗται φυσικαί· τό τε γὰρ μιμεῖσθαι σύμφυτον τοῖς ἀνθρώποις ἐκ παίδων ἐστὶ καὶ τούτῳ διαφέρουσι τῶν ἄλλων ζῴων ὅτι μιμητικώτατόν ἐστι καὶ τὰς μαθήσεις ποιεῖται διὰ μιμήσεως τὰς πρώτας. . . . (Poetry in general seems to have sprung from two causes, each of them lying deep in our nature. First, the instinct of imitation is implanted in man from childhood, one difference between him and other animals being that he is the most imitative of living creatures, and through imitation learns his earliest lessons . . . ; tr. S.H. Butcher).

[305] The ethnographic list seems obviously to originate from the Greek ethnographic tradition, but two of the most popular exempla in the literature relating to idolatry also appear in a Jewish iconoclastic passage, *Jub.* 22.18 (see *supra* p. 96): "they [the gentiles] have no eyes to see what their deeds are, and where they wander astray, saying to the tree 'you are my god,' and to a stone 'you are my lord, and you are my savior.'" It seems possible that the examples found in the polemic on both sides of the iconoclastic controversy entered the fight through Jewish iconoclastic literature: *cf. supra* p. 121 n. 296.

vision of an objectionable practice. In the *Protrepticus* of Clement of Alexandria, a work contemporary with Maximus, the barbarians reappear with their sacred rivers and rocks—but no longer are they charming exemplars of piety. They represent instead the dark ignorance of the past [**44**]:

> In ancient times, then, the Scythians used to worship the dagger, the Arabians their stone, the Persians their river. Other peoples still more ancient erected conspicuous wooden poles and set up pillars of stones, to which they gave the name *xoana* [scraped objects] because the rough surface of the material had been scraped off. Certainly the *agalma* of Artemis in Icarus was an unwrought stock, and that of Cithaeronian Hera in Thespiae was a felled tree-trunk. That of Samian Hera, as Aëthlius says, was at first a *sanis* but afterwards, when Procles was ruler, it became *andriantoeides*. When the *xoana* began to be represented as men, they acquired the additional name *brete*, from *brotoi* [mortals]. In Rome, of old time, according to Varro the prose-writer, the *xoanon* of Ares was a spear, since craftsmen had not yet entered upon the fair-seeming but mischievous art of sculpture. But the moment art flourished, error increased.[306]

In this discussion, Clement refines and spells out in detail the loose evolutionary development by which both supporters and opponents of idolatry asserted that it had come to be. The two sides do not disagree on the raw facts. Clement makes use of the same examples of barbarian practice as Maximus, and presents the same picture of the early world. There is no disagreement on the idea that idolatry developed from primitive practices—chronologically primitive, as proved by the evidence of the past, and inherently primitive, as demonstrated by the customs of barbarians, who, in Greek tradition, are perpetually infantile.[307]

[306] Clem.Al. *Protr.* 4.40 P. [**44**]; translation adapted from Butterworth. For the importance of this passage in the modern evaluation of *xoana*: *supra* p. 5; *infra* pp. 177–194 and *passim*. For the chronology of Clement: J.E.L. Oulton and H. Chadwick, *Alexandrian Christianity* (Philadelphia, 1954) 16–17; J. Quasten, *Patrology* II (Westminster, 1962) 5–9; G.W. Butterworth, tr., *Clement of Alexandria* (LCL, 1919) xi–xii. It is usually thought that Clement was born c. A.D. 150; the *Protrepticus* (*Exhortation to the Greeks*) is dated c. A.D. 190. *Cf. Wi.* 14:27: "For the worship of idols, whose names it is wrong even to mention, is the beginning, cause, and end of every evil" (tr. *New English Bible*).

[307] The conflicting opinions on the early stages of idolatry reflect the two views of the deep past that existed in classical thought: the golden age and the age of savagery. For the characterization of these views as "soft" and "hard" primitivism respectively by A.O. Lovejoy and G. Boas, *Primitivism and Related Ideas in Antiquity* (Baltimore, 1935): E.O. Panofsky, "*Et in Arcadia Ego*: Poussin and the Elegiac Tradition," in *Meaning in the Visual Arts* (Garden City, 1955) 297–300 [repr. from R. Klibansky and H.J. Paton, eds., *Philosophy and History. Essays Presented to Ernst Cassirer* (Oxford, 1936)]. For the position of these theories of the advance of man in the wider scheme of Greek anthropomorphism: G.E.R. Lloyd, "Greek Cosmologies," in C. Blacker and M. Loewe, eds., *Ancient Cosmologies* (London, 1975) 219 and n. 57. To the Greek idea of barbarians as children, *cf.* the famous observation of the

It is interesting to note that for the purpose of this argument the barbarians have become idolaters. Not even the Persians are shown as enemies of Greek religion who have no reverence for any sacred object. In a complete reversal, barbarians do not stand in opposition to the Greek world; instead, they represent an earlier stage in the development of civilization. To the sympatheic observer their odd and touching practices are equated with spontaneous, untaught piety; to the iconoclast, their crude and puny efforts reek of the beastly and stupid. Noble child of nature or wicked savage, each view is pure propaganda.

It is useful to compare these Greek and Christian arguments with Jewish iconoclastic writings. For example, the polemic against idolatry in the apocryphal *Book of Wisdom*, which was probably composed by an Alexandrian Jew in the first century A.D., perhaps c. A.D. 40, touches on several similar points:[308]

> What born fools all men were who lived in ignorance of God, who from the good things before their eyes could not learn to know him who really is, and failed to recognize the artificer though they observed his works! Fire, wind, swift air, the circle of the starry signs, rushing water, or the great lights in heaven that rule the world—these they accounted gods. If it was through delight in the beauty of these things that men supposed them gods, they ought to have understood how much better is the Lord and Master of it all; for it was by the prime author of all beauty that they were created. If it was through astonishment at their power and influence, men should have learnt from these how much more powerful is he who made them. For the greatness and beauty of created things give us a corresponding idea of their Creator. Yet these men are not greatly to be blamed, for when they go astray they may be seeking God and really wishing to find him. Passing their lives among his works and making a close study of them, they are persuaded by appearances because what they see is so beautiful. Yet even so they do not deserve to be excused, for with enough understanding to speculate about the universe, why did they not sooner discover the Lord and Master of it all?
>
> The really degraded ones are those whose hopes are set on dead things, who gave the names of gods to the work of human hands, to gold and silver

---

Egyptian priest that the Greeks, in comparison to the Egyptians, are children: Pl. *Tim.* 22 B. *Cf.* J.A.K. Thomson, *The Art of the Logos* (London, 1935) 59: "In contrast with the Egyptians, reflective Greeks always thought of themselves as a young people"; 59–60 for Hdt. 2.143 and the passage from the *Timaeus*. I thank S.W. Edwards for this reference. See also Groningen, *Grip of the Past* 7–8.

[308] For the *Book of Wisdom*: *ODCC*² *s.v.* Wisdom of Solomon; a date in the reign of Caligula is suggested. Older scholarship tended to place the composition of the book in the second or first century B.C.: the earlier date is given by E.G. Clarke, *The Wisdom of Solomon* (Cambridge, 1973) 1–2. Clarke prints the text of the *New English Bible*, from which the translation given here is taken.

fashioned by art into images of living creatures, or to a useless stone carved by a craftsman long ago. (13:1–10; tr. *New English Bible*)[309]

The iconoclastic polemic of chapters 13–15 stands out as a separate unit within a survey of God's role in the deliverance of the Jews from bondage in Egypt (chs. 10–19), and so may reflect an independent source.[310] The section contains Jewish iconoclastic *topoi*, but is also marked by similarities to Greek discussions of idolatry. The comparatively charitable treatment of earnest, if misguided, worshippers of nature, for example, is not in the spirit of Jewish iconoclasm. To a considerable extent, Jewish and Greek writers influenced each other in the controversy over idolatry, and a common pool of arguments developed.[311]

[309] A. Rahlfs, ed., *Septuaginta* II. *Libri poetici et prophetici* (Fifth ed., Stuttgart, 1935) *Wisdom* 13:1–10:

Μάταιοι μὲν γὰρ πάντες ἄνθρωποι φύσει, οἷς παρῆν θεοῦ ἀγνωσία
καὶ ἐκ τῶν ὁρωμένων ἀγαθῶν οὐκ ἴσχυσαν εἰδέναι τὸν ὄντα
οὔτε τοῖς ἔργοις προσέχοντες ἐπέγνωσαν τὸν τεχνίτην,
ἀλλ' ἢ πῦρ ἢ πνεῦμα ἢ ταχινὸν ἀέρα
ἢ κύκλον ἄστρων ἢ βίαιον ὕδωρ
ἢ φωστῆρας οὐρανοῦ πρυτάνεις κόσμου θεοὺς ἐνόμισαν.
ὧν εἰ μὲν τῇ καλλονῇ τερπόμενοι ταῦτα θεοὺς ὑπελάμβανον,
γνώτωσαν πόσῳ τούτων ὁ δεσπότης ἐστὶ βελτίων,
ὁ γὰρ τοῦ κάλλους γενεσιάρχης ἔκτισεν αὐτά·
εἰ δὲ δύναμιν καὶ ἐνέργειαν ἐκπλαγέντες,
νοησάτωσαν ἀπ' αὐτῶν πόσῳ ὁ κατασκευάσας αὐτὰ δυνατώτερός ἐστιν·
ἐκ γὰρ μεγέθους καὶ καλλονῆς κτισμάτων
ἀναλόγως ὁ γενεσιουργὸς αὐτῶν θεωρεῖται.
ἀλλ' ὅμως ἐπὶ τούτοις μέμψις ἐστὶν ὀλίγη,
καὶ γὰρ αὐτοὶ τάχα πλανῶνται
θεὸν ζητοῦντες καὶ θέλοντες εὑρεῖν·
ἐν γὰρ τοῖς ἔργοις αὐτοῦ ἀναστρεφόμενοι διερευνῶσιν
καὶ πείθονται τῇ ὄψει, ὅτι καλὰ τὰ βλεπόμενα.
πάλιν δ' οὐδ' αὐτοὶ συγγνωστοί·
εἰ γὰρ τοσοῦτον ἴσχυσαν εἰδέναι
ἵνα δύνωνται στοχάσασθαι τὸν αἰῶνα,
τὸν τούτων δεσπότην πῶς τάχιον οὐχ εὗρον;
Ταλαίπωροι δὲ καὶ ἐν νεκροῖς αἱ ἐλπίδες αὐτῶν,
οἵτινες ἐκάλεσαν θεοὺς ἔργα χειρῶν ἀνθρώπων,
χρυσὸν καὶ ἄργυρον τέχνης ἐμμελέτημα
καὶ ἀπεικάσματα ζῴων
ἢ λίθον ἄχρηστον χειρὸς ἔργον ἀρχαίας.

[310] Clarke, *Wisdom* (*supra* p. 128 n. 308) 3, 4 for the possibility that the author of *Wisdom* may have made use of an already-existing iconoclastic polemic.

[311] *Cf.* the connection between idolatry and the worship of the stars in, *e.g.*, 3 Enoch 5 (a celestial component of the practice of idolatry, which traditionally was thought to have originated in the time of Enoch): see *OTP* II, 260. See Urbach, "Rabbinical Laws" (*supra* p. 86 n. 207) 232 n. 74 for "a Greek source for this outlook." For Maimonides (A.D.

It is also useful to consider an example of Jewish iconoclastic polemic that postdates the destruction of the Temple at Jerusalem in A.D. 70. Wallach has analyzed a dialogue, the *Mekilta, Masseket Baḥodesh*, in which a rabbi and a pagan philosopher discuss idolatry.[312] For the most part the arguments center on the traditional Jewish objections to images: their powerlessness, uselessness, and lifelessness, all of which underscore the foolishness of those who worship them. The criticism is put in the mouth of the Patriarch Gamaliel II, but is shown to be anachronistic by the presence of several Greek elements.[313] The most significant of these for this discussion is contained in "Gamaliel"'s question:

> (10) But is it only one object that you worship?
>
> (11) Behold, you worship the sun, the moon, the stars and the constellations, the mountains and the hills, the springs and the glens, and even human beings.

Wallach notes that from the "one object"—which refers to aniconic idols such as wooden posts, stone stelai and cones, and other unshaped objects—the list in section 11 moves up the ladder of idolatry. The progression betrays a graduated scale of idolatry that is wholly at odds with all Jewish conceptions. Heinemann had identified this non-Jewish scheme in another

---

1135–1204) on the origin of idolatry, see *Hilkot Abodah Zarah* 1:1: J. Goldin, "The Magic of Magic and Superstition," in E.S. Fiorenza, ed., *Aspects of Religious Propaganda in Judaism and Early Christianity* (Notre Dame and London, 1976) 130–131:

> In the days of Enosh, the people fell into gross error, and the counsel of the wise men of the generation became foolish. Enosh himself was among those who erred. Their error was as follows: "Since God," they said, "created these stars and spheres to guide the world, set them on high and allotted unto them honour, and since they are ministers who minister before Him, they deserve to be praised and glorified and honour should be rendered them. . . . " When this idea arose in their minds, they began to erect temples to the stars, offered up sacrifices to them, praised and glorified them in speech, and prostrated themselves before them—their purpose, according to their perverse notions, being to obtain the Creator's favour. This was the root of idolatry. . . .

To the gentler condemnation of those who revere the works of nature than of those who manufacture their own objects of worship, *cf.* Tert *Ap.* 16.9 [**360**]: *Alii plane humanius et verisimilius solem credunt deum nostrum.*

The special importance of the worship of natural phenomena such as the stars may be reflected in Vitruvius' account of early man (2.1.2): *et in unum locum plures convenirent habentes ab natura praemium praeter reliqua animalia, ut non proni sed erecti ambularent mundique et astrorum magnificentiam aspicerent* (many came together into one place, having from nature this boon beyond other animals, that they should walk, not with head down, but upright, and should look upon the magnificence of the world and of the stars. Tr. Granger [LCL, 1931]). See also Philo Judaeus, *De dec.* 66 [**287**]; Eus. *PE* 1.6.17 c–d [**99**].

[312] Wallach, "Palestinian Polemic"; 399 and 401 for date after the destruction of the Temple and during the second century A.D. at the latest.

[313] Wallach, "Palestinian Polemic" 392–401 for the ascription of this and other fictitious polemic dialogues to Gamaliel II in an attempt to provide a historical background for an established literary form. The other Greek elements include a sophistic fallacy also found in Plato.

context as Greek; Wallach follows him, adding it to the other indications of Greek literary influence in the dialogue.[314]

The impact of the Greek evolutionary tradition extended, then, even to Jewish literature on idolatry. The children and barbarians stand out ever more clearly as a wholly Hellenic *topos*. In Jewish iconoclasm, the folly of idolatry is not tied to immaturity. Men abruptly go astray; the error begins suddenly, and there is no trace of any evolutionary scheme.[315] The idea of development as seen in Dio, Maximus, and Clement is a new element in iconoclastic thought.

Clement's argument differs from Maximus' in that he has provided a step-by-step explanation of the development of idolatry. It is a twin development that includes both the conceptual and the artistic aspects of the images. Clement outlines what in modern scholarship would be called the evolution of iconic from aniconic worship, and he illustrates each step of the progression with concrete examples and etymological analysis. He has woven information from a variety of sources into an evolutionary scheme of the origin and development of images. The examples of found objects and natural features are paralleled in other writings on idolatry; it is likely that Clement's choice of the *topos* and his selection of particular examples are based on such literature. The information about the Samian Hera, here given to Aëthlius, is also preserved in a commentary on Callimachus **[42]** that seems to go far beyond the scope of the poem to which it is attached.[316] Varro's description of early Roman religion reappears in a slightly different version in Augustine's *De Civitate Dei* **[40]**.[317] Comparable etymological notes on *xoanon* and *bretas* are found in later commentaries and lexica, but their sources are difficult to determine.[318]

Clement's identification of *xoana* as scraped objects that begin the development of images has had immense influence on modern attempts to understand them. His explanation is appealing because it seems logical and well supported by examples. His derivation of *xoanon* from words for scraping agrees so well with modern etymological analysis that the false

---

314 Wallach, "Palestinian Polemic" 400–401; he notes too the mildness of the polemic, which, as has been mentioned, is another characteristic of the Jewish opposition to Greek images. I. Heinemann, *Poseidonios' metaphysische Schriften* I (Breslau, 1921) 147 (the *Book of Wisdom*); 145–147 for Jewish schemata of iconoclasm and polytheism.

315 See, *e.g.*, *Jub.* 11, where the men of Ur are helped along in their sins by "cruel spirits [who] assisted them and led them astray." For ruler cult as the origin of idolatry: Price, *Rituals* 199–200, quoting *Wi.* 14:12–21 (a variant of Euhemerism?). *Cf.* the origin of idolatry in *Wi.* 13:1–10, *supra* pp. 128–129.

316 *Dieg.* to Call. *Aet.* IV, fr. 100 **[42]**: *infra* pp. 195–196.

317 Aug. *DCD* 4.31 **[40]**: *infra* pp. 200–201.

318 *Infra* pp. 169–171. Clement is fond of etymologies: *e.g.*, of Apollo's name: *Strom.* I.164.3 **[47]**.

etymology of *bretas* can be overlooked. There are, however, reasons to inquire more closely into the reliability of Clement's view of *xoanon* and *xoana*.

This passage of the *Protrepticus* is the first appearance of the word *xoanon* in connection with primitive monuments.[319] In making this association it stands alone among both literary and epigraphical texts. The application of *xoanon* to primitive scraped objects contradicts both earlier and contemporary usage. The immediate context of the reference to *xoana* makes it clear that the definition is tendentious. Even a brief examination of the rest of the treatise shows that this special definition differs from Clement's own habitual usage. In the sixth book of the *Stromateis* [**49**], Clement argues that "nothing among created things can be a likeness of God." He condemns the idea that *agalmata* can be *eikones*—likenesses, that is to say, that show the appearance of what is divine. He continues with the assertion that "the race of souls is not in form such as the Greeks fashion their *xoana*." Clearly he means not primitive, unworked monuments here, but the ordinary figural representations that he explicitly criticizes throughout his polemics against idolatry. For the purpose of arguing, then, the impossibility of representing the immaterial, Clement easily conforms to the established iconoclastic vocabulary in which *xoana*, like *agalmata*, are simply the images of the gods in standard pagan practice.

Another clear example of the difference between Clement's special and his usual understanding of *xoanon* is his discussion of the image of Sarapis (*Protr.* 4.42 P.–43 P.) [**44**]. The passage is a patchwork of indirect discourse. Clement names only two of his sources, Isidorus and Athenodorus, to both of whom are attached reports about the *agalma*. Shadowy Somes, Others, and Theys give more information on the work, which is called variously *xoanon*, *agalma*, *andrias*, and *bretas*. While it is possible that Clement faithfully preserves the vocabulary of his informants, it is far more likely, given that he has not even bothered to set down their names, that the variety of terms is a stylistic tool to underline the multiplicity of stories about the image. *Xoanon* takes its place easily among the other terms for statues, with no special remarks by Clement, even though the detailed account of the manufacture of the Sarapis from melted metals and stones shows that it was no hewn image; in form it was far from a shapeless, scraped hulk.

Clement's usual word for an "idol" is *agalma*. Once he couples this word with *xoanon* in a fine phrase reminiscent of Philo when he claims that the most miserable living creatures *ἀμείνους εἰσὶ τῶν ξοάνων τούτων καὶ τῶν ἀγαλμάτων τέλεον ὄντων κωφῶν* (are better than these *xoana* and

[319] Primitive, as opposed to merely rude and rustic; *cf.* Leonidas' *poimenika xoana* [**156**].

agalmata that are entirely dumb; *Protr.* 4.45 P.) [**45**]. The point here seems completely rhetorical.[320]

Clement's ordinary conception of *xoanon* thus seems to fall wide of the definition he devised for it in explaining the history of idolatry. The special definition appears only in this passage, in his attempt to cut the sentimental foundations out from under the images. He needed to turn the arguments of iconophiles to his own use, and he spared no effort in reconditioning their own ammunition to fight them. The task was urgent because by Clement's time the excesses of image worship had reached unprecedented heights. The lush religious climate of the age encouraged exotic practices and beliefs in the magical and miraculous of which the wonder stories of the fourth century B.C. are but the palest of predecessors. Even contemporary pagan writers ridiculed these embarrassing excesses, but Clement's attack was grounded more in dogma than in common sense.[321]

Clement fortified the iconoclastic position with an unparalleled mastery of sources and arguments. He did not, however, originate the scheme of attack; this had its beginnings in earlier, Jewish polemic. The old elements—the uselessness of the images, their *anaisthesia*, lack of sensation, their manufacture by the hands of men from mere materials, and the conception of idolatry as error—all are present.[322] Nor was his version of the development of images unique. He borrowed this, too, applying to his own purpose an idea with an established tradition in Greek thought.

Already by the first century B.C. there had been serious antiquarian efforts to trace the history of statuary, and these attempts involved another special definition of *xoanon*. One such attempt is preserved in a fragment of Plutarch in which *xoana* figure prominently. Eusebius, writing in the fourth century A.D., quotes Plutarch in a passage critical of the making of images, especially from expensive materials (*PE* 3.7.98 d–3.8.99 d) [**108**]:

> These are the statements of this wonderful philosopher, and what could be more unseemly than talking, as they do, in solemn phrase about shameful things, or what more violently unreasonable than to assert that soulless materials, gold and stone and such things, bear *eikones* of the light of the gods and manifestations of their heavenly and ethereal nature? That these are modern sophistries and never entered, even in a dream, into the imagination of the

[320] *Cf. Protr.* 4.42 P. [**44**]: Scyllis and Dipoenus made "the *agalmata* of the Dioscuri at Argos, the *andrias* of Heracles at Tiryns, and the *xoanon* of Munychian Artemis at Sicyon."

[321] For extreme beliefs about images in late classical religion: Nilsson, *GgR* I, 74; Rose, "Images" 46–50. For contemporary attacks on such beliefs: Luc. *Philops.* 19 [**165**]; Plut. *Cam.* 6.2–4 [**316**]; Plut. *Cor.* 37.5–38 [**317**]. For theurgy: E.R. Dodds, *The Greeks and the Irrational* (Berkeley and Los Angeles, 1951) 292–295 (*telestike*).

[322] Uselessness of the idols: 4.45 P.–46 P. (inability of *agalmata* to help worshippers or selves); *anaisthesia* of *agalmata*: 4.45 P. [**45**]; 4.46 P.; manufacture by craftsmen from gold, silver, bronze, stone, earth: 4.50 P.–52 P.; error (πλάνη): 4.41 P. [**44**].

ancients, you may learn, on being informed that *xoana* made of gold, and other material esteemed more precious, were even rejected among the men of former times. Plutarch, at all events, says somewhere thus, word for word:

> The making of *xoana* seems to be something ancient and old, if the first *agalma* sent to Delos to Apollo by Erysichthon on the occasion of the festivals was wooden, and if that of Polias is wooden, the one the autochthonous inhabitants set up, which the Athenians keep to this day. The Samians also had a wooden *hedos* of Hera, as Callimachus says:
>
> > Not yet the well-carved work [of Sclemis], but according to the old custom
> > You were a plank not carved by chisels;
> > For thus did they then set up the gods; and thus
> > At Lindos Danaus placed the simple *hedos* of Athena.
>
> It is said that Peiras, founder of the *hieron* of Argive Hera, having made his own daughter Callithyia priestess, cutting down a straight-grained pear from the trees around Tiryns shaped an *agalma* of Hera. For they did not want to cut stone into a rough and hard to work and soulless *eikon* of a god, and gold and silver they thought to be diseased colors of infertile and corrupt earth and stains breaking out like bruises when it had been struck by fire; and playing with ivory, sometimes they used it for decorating their daintiness.

These things Plutarch [says]; and long before him Plato knew well that there is nothing venerable or suited to the divine nature in gold and ivory, and things manufactured out of soulless material: for hear what sort of directions he gives in the *Laws*:

> The land, therefore, and the household hearth are for all men *hiera* of all the gods; therefore let no one consecrate *hiera* a second time to the gods. Gold and silver in other cities, both in private houses and in *hiera*, are an individious possession, and ivory taken from a dead body is not a pure *anathema*; iron and bronze are implements of war.

It is not easy to determine the context of the Plutarchian fragment. It is generally considered to be part of Plutarch's treatise *On the Festival of the Daedala at Plataea*, but the identification is far from certain; the supposition seems to rest on little more than the appearance of *xoanon* in both this passage and the section that is certainly preserved from the treatise.[323]

One major difficulty in analyzing the fragment is that, despite Eusebius' assurance that it is all Plutarch *kata lexin*, the passage lacks thematic cohesion. The last part, after the section on the *agalma* of Hera at Tiryns, does not seem at all relevant to what immediately precedes it, but obviously harks back to Eusebius' own introduction. In tone and content it is far closer to Judeo-Christian iconoclastic rhetoric, and especially to Eusebius' own

[323] Plut. *Daed. ap.* Eus. *PE* 3.8.1 [**108**]: good discussion and notes in F.H. Sandbach, ed., tr., *Plutarch's Moralia* XV. *Fragments* (LCL, 1969) 282–297 fr. 158.

sentiments in his own voice, than to Plutarch. The similarities can be shown point by point.

The contemptuous reference to the *apsychos eikon* is a stock iconoclastic *topos* that has no good parallel in Plutarch in either vocabulary or sentiment.[324] Eusebius' preliminary remarks criticizing *eikones* made from *apsychos hule*, "soulless material," are, in contrast, a typical example of an iconoclastic preoccupation.[325] Certainly Eusebius has forced the interpretation of the passage from the *Laws* in this direction: the condemnation of soulless material is not the point of Plato's criticism of redundant *hiera* and *anathemata* made from inappropriate substances. The soulless *eikon* has no connection at all with Plutarch's discussion of the earliest of wooden statues; it is, however, a repetition of Eusebius' own sentiments.

The specific attack on gold and silver also has less relevance to Plutarch's list of early wooden statues than to Eusebius' own remarks. Eusebius is attempting to prove that the ancients used simple materials, but because he does not separate this argument from the moral issue of soulless material, his tone is overwrought and far from objectively historical. The castigation of gold and silver that he attributes to Plutarch is closer to his own strident comments than to Plutarch's judicious collection of examples. The best parallel for both tone and content comes from a passage from Philo Judaeus that is preserved in a later chapter of the *Praeparatio*: " . . . because mines of silver and gold are the most useless part of the earth, wholly and utterly inferior to that which is given up to the production of fruits . . . "; a little further on, gold and silver are called *γῆς ὄγκοι*, "lumps of earth," over which men, blinded by love of money, fight incessantly. The *topos* of dead, worthless gold and silver, especially in connection with the idols made from them, can be traced back to Old Testament iconoclasm.[326] There is an obvious difference between these sentiments and those in the

[324] *Cf.*, *e.g.*, Plut. *De Is. Osir.* 71, a less extreme condensation of the treatment of works of art as gods; G. Gwyn Griffiths, ed., tr., *Plutarch's De Iside et Osiride* (Cambridge, 1970) 541–542 for reflections of older Greek ideas in this passage. The condemnation of images as *apsychos* in iconoclastic polemic makes use of definitions of *empsychos* and *apsychos* that differ from earlier and prevailing contemporary usage and may reflect developments in Hellenistic religion that stress magical and prophetic animated images. For *empsychos*: Moore, "Baetylia" 199. *Eikon* in Plutarch applies to images of men and gods both: J. Gwyn Griffiths, rev. H. Engelmann, *The Delian Aretalogy of Sarapis*, *JHS* 96 (1976) 216–217.

[325] *Cf.*, *e.g.*, [Clem.] *Hom.* 10.21 [**54**].

[326] Philo Judaeus, *De providentia* p. 634 (Mang.): Eus. *PE* 8.14.387 d–388 a: *Διότι τὰ μὲν ἀργύρου μέταλλα καὶ χρυσοῦ γῆς ἐστιν ἡ φαυλοτάτη μοῖρα, τῆς πρὸς καρπῶν ἀνειμένης γένεσιν ὅλῳ καὶ τῷ παντὶ λειπομένη.* *Cf.* Clem.Al. *Protr.* 4.50 P.: *τί δ'ἄλλο χρυσὸς ἢ ἄργυρος ἢ ἀδάμας ἢ σίδηρος ἢ χαλκὸς ἢ ἐλέφας ἢ λίθοι τίμιοι; οὐχὶ γῆ τε καὶ ἐκ γῆς;* (What else is gold or silver or adamant or iron or bronze or ivory or precious stones? [Are they] not earth, and [made] from earth?).

passage from Plato that Eusebius adduces as support, and no connection at all with the passage from Plutarch; the iconoclastic *topos* shows itself clearly.

The combination of moral and historical issues in Eusebius' polemic against images has a good parallel in Porphyry's (A.D. III) discussion of the simplicity of ancient works (*De abstinentia* 2.18) **[323]**:

> On account of this they used vessels of clay and wood and wicker, and especially for public sacrifices, believing that divinity takes pleasure in such things. For this reason, too, the older *hede* that are of clay and wood are considered to be more *theia* on account of both the material and the simplicity of the craft. It is said, too, that Aeschylus, when the Delphians [Faber for ms. "brothers"] asked him to write a paean in honor of Apollo, said that the best had been done by Tynnichus; if his own were compared with that man's, the same thing would happen as when new *agalmata* are compared with *archaia* ones; for these, although made simply, are considered *theia*, while the new ones that are elaborately worked, although they are marvelled at, have an inferior notion of god.

It cannot be assumed that these sentiments actually are Aeschylus'. The *topos* of ascribing rustic materials to the distant past belongs to a popular line of Greek thought that also attributed an austere moral superiority to the men of ancient times.[327] The specific example of statues surfaces, for example, in Pausanias' well-known comment that Daedalus' statues, although odd in appearance, have something of the divine about them nonetheless (2.4.5) **[203]**.

The didactic intention of Porphyry's passage is paralleled by Eusebius' comments on the "modern sophistries" of gold and silver images, but is wholly alien to the first part of his quotation from Plutarch. Eusebius seems to be uneasily balancing several concerns: the simplicity of the past, the soulless nature of all materials, and the particularly objectionable character of precious substances. He has forced the interpretation of a not very suitable quotation from Plato to support his argument, and there is reason to

[327] *Theios* can mean "holy," "divine," or "belonging to a god." Guthrie, *In the Beginning* 73–74, notes Porphyry's expression of the accepted view of the moral superiority of the earliest men. *Cf.* Juv. *Sat.* XI.77–129 for an extended contrast between the virtuous simplicity of countrified old Rome and modern, urbanized luxury. To the *topos* of rustic materials used in the past, *cf.* that of the unknown material: *e.g.*, the white pyramid of Aphrodite at Paphos of which the material is unknown: *Max.Tyr.* 8.8 **[169]**; the phiale dedicated to Athena Polias and Zeus Polieus by the hero Lindos ("no one can find out what it is made from"): Lindos Chronicle B I; C. Blinkenberg, *Lindos. Fouilles de l'Acropole 1902–1914* II. *Inscriptions* I (Berlin and Copenhagen, 1941) 161, no. 2, B.I.2–4. The unknown material may recall the magical aspects of ancient, mythical craftsmanship. *Cf.* the following entry in the Chronicle, an offering of the Telchines about which, similarly, "*ουδεις εδυνατο/επιγ[νωμειν εκ] τινος εστι*" (B.II.9–10).

suspect that the passage from Plutarch has been augmented to make it more useful. In any event, the inconsistencies within the quotation as it stands and the close correspondence of its latter part with iconoclastic rhetoric suggest that only the first, historical, remarks at most should be taken as representative of Plutarch's use of *xoanon*.

Plutarch's conception of *xoana* differs in two ways from that of Clement. While Clement's *xoana* are both columns of wood and pillars of stone, Plutarch's are expressly wooden and are equated with wooden *agalmata*. Plutarch does not derive the meaning of *xoanon* from *xeo*. The two *xe-* words in the lines of Callimachus, where the *sanis* is *axoos* and the work of Scelmis *euxoon*, pass without comment. Instead, the word that is stressed is *xulinos*. Plutarch demonstrates the antiquity of *xoana* by examples of *xulinos* statues, an approach which implies that he believes a *xulinos–xoanon* etymology.

Plutarch also differs from Clement in that his *xoana* are not primitive in form. It is important to distinguish between the sense in which Plutarch takes the quotation from Callimachus and the sense of Callimachus himself. Whereas the simplicity of the early images is Callimachus' point, Plutarch cares only that the *sanis* is wooden; this is his only reason for quoting Callimachus. He has interpreted the lines to suit his argument. There are also some indications that Plutarch's idea of early statuary differs from the poet's conception of unworked planks. He says that Peiras "shaped" (*morphosai*) the *agalma* of Hera from wood; it is not, then, an unworked monument. Plutarch neither asserts nor implies that the wooden *agalmata* and *hede* he mentions are not statues in the fullest sense.[328] It would be incorrect to assume that he intended to equate them fully with the unformed pieces described by Callimachus. Wood, and wood alone, is what distinguishes Plutarch's *xoana*, and with this definition of the word, possibly derived from an etymology with *xulinos*, he places the wooden statues in a chronological scheme.

Another *xoanon* is "shaped" from a tree, this time an oak, in Plutarch's account of the Daedala (*Daed.* 6) [**104**]. Eusebius, again, quotes from Plutarch, who relates a "more silly legend" about the origin of the ceremony. In order to win back the affection of Hera, Zeus adopts the plan of Alalcomenes; they cut down a tree, shape it into a dummy, dress it as a bride, name it Daedale, and hold a procession for Zeus' new wife. Hera angrily interrupts the festivity, but, amused by the deception, is reconciled with Zeus. Thus originated the curious ceremony of the Daedala.[329] *Xoanon*

[328] In *De frat. amor.* 1 (*Mor.* 478 A–B) [**318**], Plutarch calls the Spartan *dokana*, the crossed sticks that represented the Dioscuri, *aphidrumata*.

[329] The passage (fr. 157 Sandbach) as given by Eusebius (*PE* 3.1.85 c–86 b) [**104**] ends with the statement that Hera "gave additional honor to the *xoanon*, and called the festival

appears only in this aetiological section of the fragment; the rest is a long discourse on the gods as symbols of nature, and has little relevance to the ceremony. It is Pausanias who adds to the fable a detailed account of the Plataean festival (9.3.1–8) [**271**]. He explains the selection of the trees from which the figures are made, noting that "long ago people called *xoana daedala*" and that in his day "they name the *xoanon* also *daedalon*."

On the basis of the accounts of Plutarch and Pausanias, many theories have been advanced about the Daedala which link the festival to tree-worship and similar, generally "primitive," religious practices.[330] Behind many of these interpretations stands the assumption that a *xoanon* is a crude thing that scarcely deserves to be called a statue, an object that, bereft of the garments put on it, would hardly be recognized as a figure. As will be shown, this belief is not justified in the case of Pausanias; nor does it hold good for Plutarch. The fact that Zeus and Alalcomenes "shape" the tree—*morphosai* again—after cutting it implies that it was more than a stock that was smoothed down. The idea that real garments were placed on crude armatures in order to achieve a complete image owes much to modern theories about the origins of sculpture in which monuments like the Attic figures of Dionysus pieced together from masks and cloth hung on poles are seen as an early stage in sculpture; the validity of such theories, however, is open to question.[331] Certainly there is ample Greek testimony for the

---

Daedala, but nevertheless from jealousy burned it, *καίπερ ἄψυχον* (even though it was soulless)." The *apsychia* of images in connection with the jealousy of God is an iconoclastic idea: Wallach, "Palestinian Polemic" 389–392 for the *Mekilta, Mahesset Baḥodesh* 1–3:

(1) A certain philosopher asked Rabban Gamaliel: It is written in your Law: "For I the Lord Thy God am a jealous God" (Ex. 20.5).

(2) But is there any power in the idol that it should arouse jealousy?

(3) A hero is jealous of another hero, a wise man is jealous of another wise man, a rich man is jealous of another rich man, but has the idol any power that one should be jealous of it?

Wallach (392) notes a parallel Talmudic transmission of the polemic: "He (Gamaliel) replied, I shall give you a parable: To what is the matter like? To a man who marries an additional wife. If the second wife is her superior, the first will not be jealous of her; but if she is her inferior, the first wife will be jealous of her." I am therefore unsure whether the remark about *apsychos* reflects Plutarch's own use of the word or is an enhancement made by Eusebius. Plutarch's usual *apsychos* leans more toward a simple meaning of "alive" in the natural world (*e.g.*, *Cor.* 38.2 [**317**], speech issuing from a thing that is not a living thing), and could make sense here. On the other hand, the combination of a *xoanon* with the idea of Hera's jealousy lends itself to an iconoclastic extra push. For *empsychos* as "animate": Moore, "Baetylia" 199.

[330] *E.g.*, the recent discussions of Burkert, *Structure* 132–134, and A. Schachter, "Some Underlying Cult Patterns in Boeotia," *Proc. Boiotia* 1, 24–25; and *Cults* 1, 242–250.

[331] *Infra* pp. 227–229.

placement of clothing on quite complete statues.[332] In any case, however, Plutarch's story deals with a mythological event and should not, perhaps, be pressed too hard for archaeological facts. It may be that the reader is expected only to imagine very generally the quick preparation of a figure, and not to question the fine points of manufacture. There is every reason to think that for Plutarch the fact that the figure was made from a tree justifies its being called a *xoanon*.

That Plutarch's definition of *xoanon* is wholly determined by the material wood is further suggested by his reference to the sweating statue of Orpheus in *Alexander* 14.8–9 [**313**]. To his mention of the *xoanon* of Orpheus he adds the parenthetical remark ἦν δὲ κυπαρίττινον, "it was made of cypress-wood." Although this somewhat intrusive statement confirms another wooden *xoanon*, it also hints that too much attention is being paid to the definition, almost as if Plutarch were making an effort to use the term precisely. In fact, the four other times that Plutarch uses *xoanon*, it appears that he has fallen into the prevailing usage of his time, as Clement later did, and uses the word as no more than a general term for statues of gods.

In *Lucullus* 13.5 [**319**], for example, men from Pontus plunder the *hieron* of Artemis of Priapus and uproot the *xoanon*. It is impossible to distinguish this usage from that which was established in Hellenistic times, when *xoanon* began to refer to the major statue that was expected to stand in every temple. in *Camillus* 6 [**316**], Plutarch speaks of dubiously miraculous statues—*agalmata* that sweat, and *xoana* that groan and turn and close their eyes. Here too he refers to statues in a wide sense. In listing the memorable sayings of the Spartan Charillus (*Mor.* 232 C) [**315**], Plutarch has someone ask "why all the *xoana* of the gods erected among them [the Spartans] were equipped with weapons." Charillus' somewhat chatty reply leaves no doubt that all statues of the gods are meant: the gods must not be accused of cowardice, and youth must not pray to unarmed gods. Apparently it is the iconography of the gods in general that has been questioned; one may perhaps imagine a visitor to Sparta overwhelmed by armed gods at every turn. Plutarch's last *xoanon* is one of Artemis left behind by the confused Pelasgians, who are sailing to find a new home (*Mor.* 247 D–E) [**320**]. The statue is said to have a long and well-travelled history, but no further information is given about it. That it had been handed down from the Pelasgians' ancestors suggests that Plutarch may have imagined it to be

[332] Fully figural statues are sometimes clothed: see, *e.g.*, the detailed description of the bronze "Satrap," né Poseidon, in Elis (Paus. 6.25.5–6). For clothes placed on statues as votives: Linders, *Studies* 11–12; *cf.* Rouse, *GVO* 274–282.

something like the old wooden statues mentioned in the fragment in Eusebius; on the other hand, it might as easily fit into the general category of images. The word *xoanon* by itself gives no precise idea of the statue.

Like Clement, then, Plutarch has two ideas of what *xoanon* means. Both authors sometimes follow prevailing usage and apply the word to images of gods in general. In certain contexts, however, they adhere to special definitions that are tailored to fit special theories and have nothing in common with ordinary usage. Clement derives *xoanon* from *xeo* and asserts that idolatry began in crudely scraped pillars of stone and wood. Plutarch's *xoana*, in contrast, are *agalmata* of which the principal characteristic is their material, wood; it is possible that the etymology *xulinos–xoanon* stands in the background of this argument for the priority of wooden statuary. The specialized definitions of *xoanon* employed by the two authors are fundamentally incompatible; they are tendentious creations that serve the interests of iconoclasm and antiquarianism respectively.

Another author whose definition of *xoanon* is out of step with prevailing usage is Pausanias. Because he uses the word far more frequently than any other author, and because his work is a guidebook that often gives fairly detailed descriptions of objects, including *xoana*, what has been determined to be his definition of the term has been exceptionally influential for its modern understanding. Pausanias' *xoana*, however, should not unquestioningly be taken as a standard. His application of the word is unique in its purity and consistency. The very frequency with which he employs *xoanon* in contrast to other authors marks his usage as peculiar; the specific interests evident in his guidebook reflect historical convictions that color his conception of the word and the images to which it refers.[333]

The best treatment of *xoanon* in Pausanias is still that of Bennett, who relies heavily on Frazer's comments.[334] Bennett has established beyond question that Pausanias' *xoana* are wooden statues of gods. Her lists show that there are only a few *xoana* of personages such as Orpheus, Trophonius, and Heracles; these, however, receive devotion almost as if they were gods. To this extent Pausanias' *xoanon* is in harmony with general usage. It is exceptional for *xoana* in any context to represent human beings.[335]

The next, and apparently most significant, criterion of a *xoanon* is its material; Pausanias pays special attention to this feature. For him, the word is equivalent to the phrase *ξύλου ἄγαλμα*. He lists the kinds of wood from

[333] These points are noted by Bennett, "Study" 11.

[334] Bennett, "Statues" and "Study."

[335] *Xoana* of Orpheus: 3.20.5 **[237]**; of Trophonius: 9.40.3 **[278]** (*xoanon* only by virtue of following the phrase *ἕτερα ξόανα*); of Heracles: 2.4.5 **[203]**; 2.10.1 **[206]**; 7.26.6 **[255]**; 8.35.2 **[263]**. For the special situation of imperial cult: *supra* p. 111.

which men made *xoana* in the past (8.17.2) [**258**]. Several times he makes a point of contrasting *xoana* with statues made of stone or metal. Even more revealing are his references to statues that are *xoana* except for their faces, feet, and hands, which are of stone—what are now called acroliths.[336] Wood, clearly, is the determining characteristic of a *xoanon*.[337]

Beyond woodenness, there seem to be no physical restrictions on *xoana*. Pausanias describes a wide variety of them: some are large, some small; some are seated, others standing. *Xoana* show gods both nude and clothed, and with many different attributes. The descriptions are more than sufficient to show that Pausanias' *xoana* are fully figural statues in the mainstream of representational art.[338]

One practice that is associated with a very few of Pausanias' *xoana* deserves mention here, as it bears directly on the question of their form. *Xoana* of Eileithyia certainly (1.18.5 [**188**]; 7.23.5–6 [**252**]) and of Dionysus perhaps (1.43.5 [**198**]) are reported to be covered with real garments. This practice has already been encountered in Plutarch's aetiological account of the Plataean Daedala (*Daed.* 6 [**104**]), but the dressing of the *xoanon* as a bride in that story seems to provide no reliable evidence for the form of either *xoana* or early statuary. An anonymous epigram from the *Musa Puerilis* (*AnthPal* 12.40) [**14**], however, raises questions about the form of Pausanias' *xoana* and acroliths with respect to their being draped. The

[336] *Xoana* as wooden statues: Bennett, "Study" 10–11, 16, 17; 17 for word as equivalent of *xulou agalma*; 14, B I and II for citations: I. "*Xoana* contrasted with Marble and Metal Images": with marble: 2.10.7 [**207**]; 2.11.8 [**209**]; 2.37.2 [**228**]; 7.23.5–6 [**252**]; 8.37.12 [**264**]; 8.53.7–8 [**270**]; 9.11.4 [**273**]; with bronze: 4.34.7 [**246**]; 10.19.3 [**281**]; II. "Acrolithic *Xoana*": 2.4.1 [**202**]; 6.24.6 [**248**]; 6.25.4 [**249**]; 7.23.5 [**252**]; 8.31.6 [**260**]; 9.4.1 [**272**]. Section III (p. 14), "Gilded *Xoana*," suggests the possibility that the golden *xoana* of P.Oxy. 1117 [**375**] and the inscription from Ḳal 'at Kālôtā [**390**] might be of gilded wood. This possibility cannot be ruled out, but it seems that without exception Pausanias' gilded *xoana* are only partially gilded (2.2.6–7 [**201**]; 6.24.6 [**248**]; 6.25.4 [**249**]; 8.22.7 [**259**]; 9.4.1 [**272**]), and so there appears not to have been an attempt to create the impression of a completely golden image. Greeks do not seem to have distinguished between "golden" and "gilded" statues: Thompson, "Nikai" (*supra* p. 114 n. 279) 178–180. *Cf.* the descriptions of Pausanias' "acroliths" to those of the *xoana* with stone *protomai* in P.Oxy. 1449 [**376**]: *infra* p. 151.

[337] For the πρόσωπον of Dionysus of Methymna (10.19.3) [**281**]: Lacroix, *Reproductions* 50–54. Lacroix believes that since Pausanias otherwise uses *xoanon* only of (complete) statues, the "mask" was a kind of herm-like, primitive thing (53). The face is made of wood, however, and was recognized as the image of a god, and these two determining characteristics are enough to account for Pausanias' calling the piece a *xoanon*.

[338] Bennett, "Study" 14–16, B IV–IX; on page 17 she argues against the assumption that *xoana* were less than figural: "I have been unable to find any support for the rather popular theory that the term applies specifically to statues either of columnar or board type, and I am inclined to believe that this assumption has rested on the idea that images carved from tree-trunks, shorter logs, and planks must have been the earliest plastic types in Greece."

poem is part of a collection of homoerotic verses compiled by Strato, probably in Hadrianic times.[339] It is the entreaty of a youth to an admirer: "Do not take off my cloak, sir, but consider me thus after the manner of an acrolithic *xoanon* (ἀλλὰ θεώρει / οὕτως ἀκρολίθου κἀμὲ τρόπον ξοάνου). Seeing the naked charm of Antiphilus, you will find the rosebud growing as on thorns." This gem of art-historical dalliance, while a discouragement to the admirer, is an invitation to the modern reader to consider what is meant by an "acrolithic *xoanon*." It is possible that, as in the case of some images mentioned by Pausanias, a wooden statue with stone extremities is meant; on the other hand, since *akrolithos* by itself carries a technical meaning, the broader sense of *xoanon* might be intended. In any case, the implication of the poem is that what lies beneath the covering of an acrolithic *xoanon* does not reward the quest. What comes to mind are the dummies of Dionysus seen in Attic vase-paintings, figures consisting of masks and real garments arranged on posts or armatures. If such figures are the images referred to, the poem would shed an unflattering light on at least the acrolithic *xoana* of Pausanias.

It is impossible, however, to be sure that real clothing is implied. The external covering of a built-up statue may be meant, or perhaps the simile refers more generally to the acrolithic technique. Acroliths have not so far been comprehensively studied, and so comments on them are at most provisional.[340] It seems that one intention in making statues partially in stone—or partially in expensive stone—was to save money; only the visible or important areas of flesh needed to be rendered in good, hard, attractive stone. Intentional contrasts of material seem also to play a part in acrolithic technique. White stone and gilded wood, for example, would be a visually effective combination that would also recall chryselephantine statues. In either case, the non-stone parts of an acrolith need not have been hidden. That Pausanias so readily distinguishes the stone from the wooden parts of composite statues argues against assuming that acroliths were not fully figural. The simile in the epigram, then, probably means that what the disappointed lover would find would be that exquisite extremities belonged to a not-so-lovely body; but it is only the boy who is being undressed, not the *xoanon*.

The reasons for draping *xoana* in real garments should be sought not in their structure, but probably in their cult associations. Garments were

[339] *AnthPal* 12.40 [14]; for Strato: *OCD*[2] *s.v.* Straton (3); Cameron, "Strato and Rufinus" (*supra* p. 116 n. 284) 171 for the possibility of a pre-Hadrianic date for the Μοῦσα παιδική.

[340] I thank C.W. Campbell for helpful discussions about acroliths. For a Roman technique of acrolithic sculpture, see G. Despinis, Ἀκρόλιθα (Athens, 1975); Ridgway, *Fifth Century* 169–170.

placed on other kinds of statues, too: Pausanias notes a bronze image ("Satrap") that wears three garments, one of wool, two of linen (6.25.5–6), and an *agalma* of Asclepius, the white wool chiton and himation of which prevent the material from which it is made from being ascertained (2.11.6). A cult explanation surely accounts for the draping of the *xoana* of Eileithyia; as Bennett points out, deities of childbirth frequently received dedications of clothing.[341] There is no reason to think that Pausanias' *xoana*, acrolithic or no, were less than fully figural.

One obvious way to determine the nature of Pausanias' *xoana* is to examine the archaeological evidence for them. This task, however, is less rewarding in practice than in proposal. For the most part the evidence consists of representations of statues on coins, which are not as helpful as might be expected.[342] The compilation by Imhoof-Blumer and Gardner of coins illustrating monuments in Pausanias has not been superseded. Only about thirty *xoana* are listed, and the evidence for even these is far from satisfactory. The sceptic can object that nine times out of ten it is impossible to be sure that a statue has been correctly identified; even the editors admit that the match between certain coins and the monuments mentioned in the text is not certain. The majority of the statues identified as *xoana* look like quite ordinary classical types, and so would fit well with the emerging picture of Pausanias' definition of the word.[343]

[341] Bennett, "Study" 17–18, emphasizes the rarity of the practice in connection with *xoana*; 18 n. 1 for the dedication of clothing to deities of childbirth; see also *supra* p. 139 n. 332.

[342] *Supra* p. 55 n. 131 for the relief that may reflect the *xoanon* of Athena Nike; p. 80 n. 194 for that of Apollo Smintheus. These are the *xoana* that can be most firmly tied to archaeological evidence, and they show the limitations of an archaeological approach to *xoanon*.

[343] Imhoof-Blumer and Gardner, *NCP*. *Xoana* listed here by page and citation: **5**, 1.43.5; **18**, 2.2.3; **19**, 2.2.6; **24**, 2.4.1; **28**, 2.7.5; **30**, 2.10.7; **36**, 2.19.7; 2.24.3; **37**, 2.19.6; **41**, 2.25.1; **45**, 2.30.1 (Lacroix, *Reproductions* 59, pl. II.1, 2 for a male figure with left leg advanced); 2.30.2; **47**, 2.32.5; **48**, 2.31.6 (Lacroix, *Reproductions* 220–221); **54**, 3.25.3; **56**, 3.16.7; **83**, 7.23.5; **90**, 7.26.4; **96**, 8.13.2; **99**, 8.27.7; **111**, 9.11.4 (Lacroix, *Reproductions* 66, pl. III.1 for V B.C. coins showing a stylistically contemporary piece; Imhoof-Blumer and Gardner suggest that the die-cutters have copied the old *xoanon* of Daedalus only in pose and attributes, and produced an image in contemporary style. Lacroix allows the possibility that the statue itself is fifth-century). For the identification of the image of Athena Polias on Athenian bronze coins of the late third century B.C.: J.H. Kroll, "The Ancient Image of Athena Polias," *Hesperia* Suppl. 20 (1982) 65–76. Kroll makes many interesting observations on the literary sources for this image. He suggests that it was an ancient aniconic stock onto which was added an elaborate *kosmos* consisting of golden ornaments of various kinds, anthropomorphic features, and the woven peplos; " . . . without lifting up the peplos there was nothing to be seen of the true image, except perhaps the face" (75). Kroll emphasizes throughout the "thoroughgoing conventionality of the statue's external form" (76). I see no way to disprove Kroll's argument that the outward conventionality of the statue shown on the coins results completely from added elements—even the feet (76, Addendum). His own analysis of the coin representations, however, speaks against the suggestion. He stresses the "naturalistic" drapery (70–71): "Such

So far, then, Bennett's conclusions are easily confirmed: Pausanias uses *xoanon* to mean wooden statues of gods. That his usage corresponds not to his contemporary Clement's iconoclastic definition, but rather to Plutarch's earlier, antiquarian one is understandable, since the two have similar interests. It seems likely that Pausanias believed a *xulinos–xoanon* etymology, as is probable in the case of Plutarch, but this cannot be demonstrated.

Bennett's last conclusion about Pausanias' definition of *xoanon*, however, is open to question. From her examination of the uses of *xoanon* in his text, she concludes that "Pausanias meant by the word *an ancient wooden statue of a deity* . . . " (Bennett's italics).[344] She states too that "The word *xoanon*, then, at first restricted to images of wood, grew at length to have a meaning synonymous with *ἄγαλμα, εἰκών*, etc., although Pausanias consistently confines it to archaic or archaistic wooden statues of deities."[345] She bases this conclusion on two observations drawn from the raw data in her lists: "the artists named are, except in one instance where Myron is mentioned, either early sculptors who carved ancient *xoana* or later sculptors who made copies of ancient *xoana*"; and "*xoana* were peculiarly venerable, often dating from a remote antiquity, and likewise often connected with heroic legend or mysterious and unusual rites."[346] Although Bennett has recognized that the modern belief that *xoana* are primitive in form derives from modern assumptions about the development of sculpture, she has not looked for similar presuppositions in Pausanias himself.[347] She notes that he is a devoted antiquarian, but seems therefore to assume that the information he gives is objective and reliable. It can be shown, however, that Pausanias does have historical biases and convictions, that they correspond to some extent with those of Plutarch, and that they have some bearing on his ideas about *xoana*.

---

naturalistic dress would of course be quite incongruous on a typical Archaic statue made entirely of stone, bronze, or any other hard material; but it is precisely what we would expect for the old Polias image that was draped in an actual peplos of cloth." The figures on the coins (pl. 11) do indeed show naturalistic drapery effects; but I cannot see how the strong impression of a body with waist, hips, and legs could ever have been achieved by hanging cloth around a pole. The draped Dionysus figures adduced as comparanda by Kroll (74 and n. 42) do show such an arrangement, but look very different from the figure on the coins; none gives a convincing impression of a whole figure. The explanation of the figure shown on the coins might better be sought in the realm of archaistic style, which is suggested by certain elements (*e.g.*, the swallowtail effect below the waist of pl. 11, figs. 7, 9–12). For the idea of anthropomorphic additions to aniconic pieces: *infra* ch. II *passim*.

[344] Bennett, "Study" 16.

[345] Bennett, "Study" 17.

[346] Bennett, "Study" 16.

[347] See *supra* p. 141 n. 338.

The first point to consider is the nature of Pausanias' antiquarianism. Because his text is so vital and universal a tool for classical studies, it is easy to overlook its peculiarity. As Frazer has noted, antiquarianism is not an inevitable preoccupation of a guidebook. A comparison of Pausanias' text with the sprightly commentary preserved under the name of Dicaearchus shows the extent to which modern readers have come to depend on a work that is written not so much about the past as about a vision of the past.[348] Care is needed in distinguishing Pausanias' record of facts from his explanations of them, both to his readers and to himself.

This caution is especially necessary in examining the connection of *xoana* with curious rites. The special venerability that seems to be attached to these images, combined with the peculiarity of the various rites, does appear, as Bennett suggests, to point to the origin of *xoana* in the deepest past. The temptation to use these references as guides into prehistory is strong, but they are not altogether reliable. Pausanias lived in an age when Greece, long under Roman influence and domination, had declined nearly to the state of an open-air museum. Not only was antiquarian interest widespread, but also practices arose that corresponded to contemporary notions about the Greek past. The best-known example of the invention of custom is the infamous rite of Artemis Orthia in Sparta. This vicious ceremony, which is sensationally described by several late authors, seems neither to preserve nor to be based on any Spartan practices from any earlier period, but instead to have been devised to satisfy the Roman appetite for antiquities and the Roman taste for gore.[349] The phenomenon of neo-traditional ceremonies is known from other times and places as well; for instance, an interest in folklore in nineteenth-century Britain appears to have resulted in the institution of new ancestral practices.[350] So it is that even the most ancient-seeming religious activities—the Plataean Daedala, for example—cannot be unquestioningly accepted as authentic survivals that yield reliable evidence about the past.[351]

[348] For Pausanias' antiquarianism and the contrast with Ps.-Dicaearchus: Frazer, *Pausanias* I, xxv ff.; xlii–xlix.

[349] For the rites of Artemis Orthia: H.J. Rose, "The Cult of Artemis Orthia," in R.M. Dawkins, ed., *The Sanctuary of Artemis Orthia at Sparta* (*JHS* Suppl. 5; London, 1929) 399–407.

[350] For antiquarian inspiration in the creation of new traditions: I. and P. Opie, "Tradition and Transmission," *The Times Literary Supplement* 3980 (14 July 1978) 299–300.

[351] For the Daedala: *supra* p. 138 n. 330. F. Frontisi-Ducroux, *Dédale* (Paris, 1975) 197–216; Frazer, *Pausanias* V, 19–20 *ad* 9.3. Hesychius interprets the accounts as showing the decoration of raw stocks: I, 398.55 (Latte): *Δαιδάλου ποίημα . . . καὶ τὸ κοσμούμενον ὑπὸ Πλαταιέων ξύλον*.

Some aspects of Pausanias' particular antiquarianism bear directly on the question of *xoana*. Pausanias shares with Plutarch the idea that statuary developed in a well-defined order. He attempts to put individual works of art into a historical context that owes its structure largely to the concept of inventions and discoveries. For example, in 8.14.7 and 10.38.5–7, he dismisses the claims of certain cast bronze statues to being dedications of Odysseus and spoils of Troy on the grounds that casting was not known before Rhoecus and Theodorus. Technique is an important aspect of the framework of development through discovery.[352]

Pausanias three times mentions the general subject of antiquity in connection with *xoana*. He gives a list (8.17.2) [**258**] of the various woods from which *xoana* were made *τὸ ἀρχαῖον*, in ancient times; the sense of the passage in no way precludes the more recent manufacture of *xoana*, but instead focuses on how they were made in the past. He says of the images in the temple of Aphrodite Areia in Sparta that "the *xoana* here are as *archaia* as any other in Greece" (3.17.5) [**235**]. In 2.19.3 [**213**], he says that he believes that in the age of Danaus all statues were *xoana*, especially the Egyptian ones (*ξόανα γὰρ δὴ τότε εἶναι πείθομαι πάντα καὶ μάλιστα τὰ Αἰγύπτια*). The assertion is much the same as Plutarch's conclusions about the antiquity of wooden statues, *xoana*. Pausanias does not say that all *xoana* are old, but rather that in early times all statuary was made in wood. The old *xoana* in Sparta hold their own among the other old *xoana*, but they do not prove that all *xoana* are ancient. The reference to the Egyptians suggests that Pausanias has been influenced by the line of Greek historical speculation that goes back at least to Herodotus in which the Egyptians, by their own accounting, were believed to have been first in all endeavors (*e.g.*, **139**). Pausanias' own careful observations here seem to fill out his theoretical conception of the progress of history. To this extent, his generalizations about *xoana* place the word in a special context.

The *xoana* in Pausanias' less contemplative passages, however, show a variety that warns against using his theoretical remarks as a strict guide to interpreting the majority of his references. Bennett's lists give about one hundred *xoana*, but only thirty of these are *archaia* or otherwise distinguished by suggestive legendary or cult associations.[353] This total is no more than a third of the pieces, and it is possible that they are exceptional, and hence noteworthy. The kind of internal evidence that makes it clear that woodenness is an invariable characteristic of a *xoana* is lacking for the question of age.

[352] For invention as a *topos* of ancient histories of art: *infra* pp. 197–199.

[353] Bennett, "Study" 12–14 for about one hundred pieces listed by deity in Table A; 15–16, Table B, XVI for "*Xoana* venerable by reason of Antiquity, Association with Heroic Legend, Connection with Unusual Rites, or otherwise noteworthy."

There are omissions and inconsistencies that speak against the assumption that Pausanias' *xoana* are to be associated with a specific stage in the deep past. For example, the image of Athena said to have fallen from the sky onto the Athenian acropolis, which is said by other sources to be of olive wood, is not a *xoanon*, but an *agalma* (1.26.6) [**190**]. Nor do wooden statues have a monopoly on antiquity; there is an *archaion* bronze statue of Athena in Elateis (10.34.6). Pausanias' use of *archaios* in general deserves attention. Its only overlap with a named sculptor that I have found is with Laphaes of Phlius, of whom nothing is known (7.26.6) [**255**]; Daedalus' works, on the other hand, are never called *archaia*. In the same passage in which he calls Laphaes' *xoanon* of Apollo *archaion*, Pausanias stresses the great age of Apollo's *hieron* in Aegira; he calls it ἐς τὰ μάλιστα ἀρχαῖον, τό τε ἱερὸν αὐτὸ καὶ ὁπόσα ἐν τοῖς ἀετοῖς—"exceedingly ancient," as Frazer translates, both the *hieron* itself and whatever is in the pediments. Pedimental decoration—not even sculptures—seems to have appeared in Greece in the early sixth century, with the first preserved evidence for it from Corfu.[354] If Pausanias considered such work to be exceedingly early, something that is merely *archaios* may lie a long way from the legendary past.

Rumpf has emphasized the fact that some of Pausanias' *xoana* are said to be the work of sculptors like Myron, Calamis, Pheidias, and Damophon, and he argues that the word does not denote or connote great age.[355] By Pausanias' time, of course, statues even of Hellenistic times were centuries old, and any made before may have seemed very old indeed; but this is not the issue. Rumpf is correct in stressing that the names of the classical and Hellenistic sculptors pull Pausanias' *xoana* out of the realm of the mythographic and prehistoric and into real history—sometimes fairly late periods at that. The consequence is that the *xoana* of Pausanias cannot simply be assumed to be ancient, whether ancient is conceived in terms of concrete chronology or of theoretical history.

For Pausanias, then, a *xoanon* is a wooden image of a god. To the extent that he limits the term to representations of gods, he conforms to prevailing usage. He resembles Plutarch is making *xoanon* apply only to wooden pieces and in postulating that the earliest sculpture was executed in wood. The consistency of his usage is unique among the ancient writers, and must surely be due to the sober antiquarian purpose of his project, earnestly and conscientiously sustained over ten long books.

The extent to which the specialized definitions of *xoanon* influenced contemporary usage is open to question. The equation of *xoana* with wooden statues may have been accepted by Athenagoras. The antiquarian

[354] For pedimental decoration and sculpture and its transmission to and first appearances in Greece: Ridgway, *Archaic* 187–205, 218.

[355] Rumpf, "Bupalos" 60–62.

connections of the word with theories of the priority of wooden sculpture may perhaps be detected in the Sibylline verses presented by Phlegon of Tralles, but the likelihood is less great.

The *Legatio*, or *Plea on behalf of the Christians*, of the apologist Athenagoras was probably composed between A.D. 176 and 180.[356] The work defends Christians against the charges of atheism and immorality. In section 4 [38], Athenagoras says that the charge of atheism is almost too absurd to bother to deny. If the critics want atheism, they have an example of it close to hand in Diagorus, who denied the existence of God, disclosed every secret doctrine and mystery within his reach, and chopped up a *xoanon* of Heracles "to cook his turnips." The sense of the anecdote demands a wooden *xoanon* (or at least a combustible one). The story is also told by Clement (*Protr.* 2.21 P.) [43], who stresses the material of the Heracles (ἐξ ξύλου, "made from a log"), but uses no word for image. There is a chance that Athenagoras takes the word in a general sense, but it is more likely that he considers *xoanon* to be a wooden image. Another passage in the *Legatio* that concerns images does not clarify Athenagoras' terminology, as it is an imprudent mixture of conflicting sources.[357]

The second century A.D. is the only demonstrable date for the *xoanon* and *xoana* of the Sibylline text given by Phlegon of Tralles [**300**]. In his *De mirabilibus*, a collection of wonder tales, Phlegon records two oracles of the Sibyl which were read on the occasion of the birth of an androgyne in Rome in 125 B.C. The texts in question are extremely important for the study of such Roman prodigies and of the pagan Sibyls. On this account several attempts have been made to establish the nature and date of these complex and imperfectly preserved verses.

One way to approach the texts is through the rituals they prescribe, and a major question is whether these rituals are old—old enough to be connected with the expiation of earlier androgynous births, such as those of 207 and 200 B.C.—or reflect actions taken closer to 125 B.C.[358] Although most scholars prefer to believe that the two oracles preserve material of considerable age, even the date of 125 B.C. is optimistic. Sibylline oracles were often tampered with in antiquity, and the only extant text of the

[356] Schoedel, *Athenagoras* xi; xi–xxv for the nature and plan of the *Legatio*; ix–x for the scanty information preserved about the author.

[357] For *Leg.* 17 [**39**]: *infra* pp. 204–205.

[358] For the prodigy and the oracle: R. Bloch, *Les prodiges dans l'antiquité classique* (Paris, 1963) 126–127. MacBain, *Prodigy* 129–135, believes that the rite described in the oracle cannot be equated with those noted by Livy for the third-century prodigies (27.37.4–15), and argues instead, on the basis of similarities to later expiations, that the oracle was composed for the expiation of 133 B.C.

verses in question depends on Phlegon, who was a freedman of Hadrian.[359] A persistent opinion would identify the Trojan savior in line 69 as Hadrian; even if this suggestion is discounted, it remains that as long as Phlegon is the only witness for the text, the *xoana* can be guaranteed no earlier date.[360]

In line 56, the Sibyl enjoins the people to dedicate a *xoanon* and an *oikos* to Hera according to ancestral customs. Near the end of the oracle (line 64), the Sibyl promises immunity from disaster if her instructions are faithfully observed—if the *oikia* are great in every respect, and if the *xoana* are ξεστά, "carved" or "hewed." The combination of *xesta xoana* and ancestral *nomoi* would seem to guarantee a meaning for *xoanon* close to the hypothetical early wooden hybrid of antiquarianism and Clementine iconoclasm. *Xestos*, however, is used of stone as well as wood, and is therefore not diagnostic with respect to material.[361] It is tempting to see the use of *xoanon* as a deliberate enhancement of the aura of ancient wisdom evoked by Sibylline verses, but there are no grounds to rule out the generalized meaning of the word in both lines. Although in these pagan Sibyllines the prophetess demands *xoana* instead of condemning them as she does in the Jewish and Christian pseudepigrapha, it is likely that that the meaning of the word is not radically different in the two sets of oracles. Pagan *xoana* are merely the customary images that the iconoclasts condemn. If an early date for the verses is accepted, the wide, late-classical definition is required; if the *xoana* reflect textual revisions closer to Phlegon's time, the possibility of antiquarian associations is open, but the older definition cannot be ruled out.[362]

Conclusions

By the end of the second century A.D., *xoanon* had acquired at least two specialized definitions. Plutarch and Pausanias associate the word with wooden statues, and were perhaps influenced by a supposed etymological relationship with *xulinos*. Neither author imposes stylistic or formal restrictions on *xoanon*, but both follow the theory that the earliest statuary was made of wood. Clement explicitly uses the derivation—correct, as it happens—from *xeo* to drive home his point about the origin of idolatry; his *xoana* are crudely scraped pillars of wood and stone. These definitions, one

[359] For Phlegon: *FGrH* 257. For the "interpolation, falsification, and manipulation" of Sibylline oracles—practices notorious even in antiquity—see Collins, "Sibylline Oracles" 320, with references.

[360] For the identity of the Trojan: W. Den Boer, *Private Morality in Greece and Rome. Some Historical Aspects* (Leiden, 1979) 111. Den Boer is among the supporters of Hadrian.

[361] LSJ[9] *s.v.* ξεστός; *cf.* *supra* p. 28 n. 66.

[362] For the Roman Sibyllines: Collins, "Sibylline Oracles" 319–320. For another *xoanon* associated with Phlegon: *infra* p. 166 [**301**].

boldly tendentious, the other less obvious but no less pointed, are incompatible, and their differences clearly reflect the different aims for which they were developed. Both are at odds with the prevailing usage attested in contemporary literature and non-literary texts. Plutarch and Clement do not apply their special definitions consistently, but instead fall often into the common usage; Pausanias alone is faithfully consistent. His work, however, is similarly influenced by theoretical historical considerations, and his general remarks about *xoana* cannot be taken out of that context in order to establish a standard for all *xoana*—not even his own.

In modern studies, the two incompatible special definitions have been combined to yield a picture of *xoana* as a true class of primitive wooden "cult statues." This method, however, yields no more than a composite of polemic and speculation. The explicit remarks of Plutarch, Pausanias, and Clement reflect the authors' own theoretical convictions, and cannot be readily translated into archaeological reality; they need to be examined in context.

10. *Xoanon* in the Third and Fourth Centuries A.D.

In the literary and non-literary texts of the third and fourth centuries A.D., the various meanings of *xoanon* continue to appear, for the most part in the contexts in which they had developed. Inscriptions and other non-literary works again show *xoana* as dedications, and, in two papyri, *xoana* are magical figures; iconoclastic texts offer more *xoana* as generalized idols; other literature still shows a broader use of *xoanon*; and specialized definitions relating to form and material are restricted to scholarly commentary.

At least five *xoana* are listed in a papyrus dated to A.D. 213–217 **[376]** that declares the offerings contained in temples in Oxyrhynchus. One is an acrolith of Demeter (lines 10–11); another, a small bronze image of Neotera (12); there is a second *xoanon* of Neotera, placed on a small basket(?) (13); line 14 lists another acrolithic *xoanon*; and last comes a (largely restored) *xoanon* dedicated in the *hieron* of Kore (52). All are *anathemata*, and so reflect the epigraphical appearance of *xoana* as dedications while testifying to the broad application of the term to images of gods in a variety of materials and sizes. The acrolithic *xoana* are of interest for the question of technique: each is described as a "*xoanon* of which the *protome* is Parian"; of Demeter's, "the other parts of the body" are restored as *xulina*, wooden, while the other *xoanon* has plaster amulets. *Protome* seems to mean "bust," and a design different from that represented by, for instance, Pausanias' *xoana* with various extremities in stone may be indicated.[363]

An inscription found in Qanauat, ancient Canautha, in the Jebel Druse region of Syria, records the dedication of a *xoanon* on behalf of the emperor Elagabalus, his grandmother, and his entire family **[401]**. The welcome brevity of Elagabalus' reign provides equally welcome precision for the date of the dedication (A.D. 218–222), but since even ἡ πόλις ἀνέθηκεν is restored, the text sheds little additional light on the connection of *xoanon* with the imperial cult in the third century.[364]

An elegiac couplet engraved on a stone that is likely to be from Sais **[403]** preserves another Egyptian reference to an offering of a *xoanon*. It commemorates the dedication by Petronios, the *protos* of that city, of a

[363] P.Oxy. 1449 **[376]**; *POxy* 12 (1916) 134–135. Line 10: *xoanon* of Demeter, Parian marble *protome*, other parts of body "ξ . . . " (restored as "wooden"); 12, 13, 14: *xoanon* of Neotera, bronze, small; something on which the *xoanon* of Neotera stands; 52: *xoanon* of Kore. The offerings in question come from the temple of Neotera, or perhaps that of Apollo and Neotera. See LSJ[9] *s.v.* προτομή.

[364] Inscription from Qanauat **[401]**: *IGRR* III, 1228. For the location of the site near Soueida and its history: *Les Guides Bleus. Syrie–Palestine* (Paris, 1932) 353; A.H.M. Jones, *The Cities of the Eastern Roman Provinces*[2] (Oxford, 1971) *passim*, esp. 285–287.

xoanon of Tritogeneia. The couplet gives no other information about the *xoanon*.[365]

The last epigraphical *xoanon* I have found is in a Christian epitaph from Obruk (near ancient Perta in Lycaonia), in Asia Minor [**396**]. The text records the tragic early death of a bride; her husband has written the memorial ἐν λίθῳ ξοάνῳ, "in polished stone." This is the only appearance of the adjective *xoanos* that has been postulated as the source of the noun.[366] No editor has offered a date for this inscription, but several factors and features suggest a date after the middle of the fourth century.[367]

Two papyrus texts of the fourth century A.D. feature *xoana* in connection with magical spells. One, written on the reverse of an earlier text, comes from a grave in Egyptian Thebes and is now in Leiden [**372, 373**].[368] Lines 271 ff. concern a δακτυλίδιον πρὸς ἐπίτευξιν καὶ χάριν καὶ νίκην—"a ring for success and favor and victory." The stone of the ring is described in detail: it is a heliotrope carved with the image of a sun in the following form: a *drakon* holding its tail in its mouth, encircling a holy scarab beetle; a name is to be inscribed on the reverse of the stone (lines 275–277). The text then gives detailed instructions for the rites and invocations which will invest the ring with powers. Lines 301–306 [**372**] of the long invocation call

[365] Alexandria Museum *Cat. gén.* no. 1 [**403**]; Breccia, *Iscrizioni* 71 no. 112; *ArchPap* 2 (1903) 569–570 no. 145; provenance uncertain. For Tritogeneia: *RE* II.7 A1 (1939) 244–245 *s.v.* Tritogeneia (B. Kruse); Cook, *Zeus* III.1, 123–124; the meaning is unknown. For this inscription and Athena in Sais: J.G. Milne, *A History of Egypt Under Roman Rule*³ (London, 1924) 198 (A.D. III).

[366] W.M. Calder, J.M.R. Cormack, *et al.*, eds., *MAMA* VIII (Manchester, 1962) 49 no. 275; stele [**396**]. For the compendium ΧΜΓ: W.K. Prentice, "ΧΜΓ, A Symbol of Christ," *CP* 9 (1914) 410–416; M. Avi-Yonah, *Abbreviations in Greek Inscriptions (The Near East, 200* B.C.–A.D. 1100) (*Quarterly of the Department of Antiquities in Palestine*, suppl. to vol. IX; Jerusalem, 1940) 2, 111; A.C. Bandy, *The Greek Christian Inscriptions of Crete* (Athens, 1970) 10–11; M. Lang, *Graffiti and Dipinti* (*Agora* XXI; Princeton, 1976) 87. For earlier publication of this epitaph: *Hellenica* 13 (1965) 62, also for reference to review of *MAMA* VIII by J. Bingen, *AntCl* 32 (1963) 315, with suggestion that Glykuthyme is a proper name. For the terminology of funerary monuments (here, *mnian, tunbo*) in Asia Minor during A.D. II and III: J. Kubinska, *Les monuments funéraires dans les inscriptions grecques de l'Asie Mineure* (Travaux du Centre d'Archéologie Mediterranéenne de l'Académie Polonaise des Sciences 5; Warsaw, 1968), which does not, however, treat Christian inscriptions.

[367] Christianity seems to have become firmly established in the area after c. A.D. 350. If *glykothyme* is a proper name, it sounds like one of the "significant" names that become very popular among Christians in the fourth century. The elements of carved decoration—Maltese cross in garland, and vine-tendril—do not become popular until around the middle of the fourth century, at least in Phrygia. For the dating of Christian inscriptions in this region: *MAMA* I, xviii–xxii.

[368] Pap. Leiden, Rijksmuseum van Oudheden J. 384 [**372, 373**]: *PGM* II, 57–86, Papyrus XII; Preisendanz dates the text A.D. 300–350 (57). A. Abt, *Die Apologie des Apuleius von Madaura und die antike Zauberei* (RGVV 4.2; Giessen, 1908) 298–299.

upon the greatest god to "give divine and greatest power to this *xoanon*, and make it be strong and powerful over all things." The list of abilities, if attained, is impressive. Equally remarkable is the sense of *xoanon*: it is not a statue, but a gemstone; it does not even bear an image of a god. This singular usage clearly belongs to the specialized vocabulary of magic; there are no parallels for such a meaning in any other context. *Xoanon* may, however, simply refer to the fact that the stone is carved. A passage later in the text extols the power of a spell called "Uphor" to imbue images with life (lines 317–321). By this spell *ζωπυρεῖται πάντα πλάσματα καὶ γλυφαὶ καὶ ξόανα*. It is not clear whether three categories of images are meant, or whether the sense is "all *plasmata*, both carvings and *xoana*."[369] Perhaps *xoana* here refers specifically to carved gems such as the heliotrope in the earlier lines.

A papyrus in the Louvre [374], dated after A.D. 300, gives precise directions for a magical procedure involving a *xoanon* of a different kind. The *xoanon* is a hollow figure of Apollo made from laurel-wood. As it is to be placed on a table, presumably it is small. *Xoanon* here may reflect the role of the word in the vocabulary of magic; on the other hand, it is possible that the broad sense of the term, as seen in prevailing usage, has influenced its selection.[370]

In the literature of the third and fourth centuries, pagan authors adhere to the general usage established in Hellenistic times, while Christian *xoana*, although similarly lacking in specificity, have the negative overtones of iconoclastic polemic. That Christian *xoana* are castigated does not disguise the fact that, like their pagan counterparts, they are not differentiated from other images by formal, technical, or stylistic criteria.

Xoana appear several times in the Pseudo-Clementine *Homilies*. These pseudepigrapha describe the Eastern travels of St. Clement, Bishop of Rome, who lived in the late first century A.D.[371] The text as it is preserved shows signs of several stages of revision and reworking. Even the sources of what is called the basic writing are disputed, but the fundamental text—

[369] For the symbol of the snake eating its own tail: W. Deonna, "Ouroboros," *Artibus Asiae* 15 (1952) 163–170. I have been unable to consult K. Preisendanz, "Aus der Geschichte des Uroboros," *Brauch und Sinnbild. E. Fehrle zum 60. Geburtstag* (Karlsruhe, 1940).

For Uphor: *PGM* II, *ad* XII.316; note the change of gender in line 318. In line 320 the *zopurein* makes it preferable to translate *glyphai* as "carvings" rather than "emblems." The papyrus here reads *γλυφεται και ξοανα*; the suggestion *γλυφαι* is reasonable. *Cf.* the iconography to forms cited in the Mishnah: "If a man found objects on which is a figure of the sun, a figure of the moon, or a figure of a dragon, he must throw them into the Dead Sea"; also a story concerning a ring with the image of a dragon: Urbach, "Rabbinical Laws" (*supra* p. 86 n. 207) 232–233.

[370] Pap. Louvre 2391 (Mimaut) line 301 [374]: *PGM* I, 30–63, Papyrus III.

[371] For Clement of Rome: *ODCC*² *s.v.*

not preserved, but capable of reconstruction—seems to have originated in Syria in the first half of the third century A.D.[372] The *xoana* of the *Homilies* are the standard *xoana* of the iconoclastic tradition. *Xoana* are not gods (*Hom.* 3.3) [**50**]; they are associated with *naoi* and *bomoi* (*Hom.* 9.5) [**51**]; they are worshipped by senseless, error-ridden men (*Hom.* 9.7) [**52**]; they are not living, but daemons adopt their forms (*Hom.* 9.15) [**53**]; and even their own gods do not care for them (*Hom.* 10.23) [**55**]. The Clementines add nothing to what is already known about the *xoana* of iconoclasm, but merely show the persistence of the generalized iconoclastic usage that is rooted in Hellenistic times.[373]

Two Sibylline texts can be dated to the third century A.D. Book XIII, which is probably Jewish or Christian and was probably written in Alexandria, does not mention the deaths of Gallienus or Odenath; in a composition that systematically treats historical events, this fact is enough to date the work c. A.D. 265.[374] In a long section devoted to predicting misery for a long list of peoples and cities, the Sibyl unkindly cheers on the cities of the Arabs to further embellishments of *naoi* and stadia and agoras and *xoana* of gold and silver and ivory, so that they may come to grief (lines 64–68) [**177**]. The wording is close to lines 57–59 of Book III, and the *xoana* are the same generalized images of old Jewish Sibylline iconoclasm.

The *xoana* of lines 487–491 of Sibylline Book VIII [**176**] cannot be precisely dated. The second half of the book, in which they appear, is stylistically similar to the first section, which can be dated c. A.D. 175; the section in question, however, can be given only a *terminus ante quem* of the early fourth century A.D. on the basis of quotations from it in Lactantius.[375] The *xoana* are listed among pagan paraphernalia and practices that Christians shun. Christians are never allowed to pour libations to *xoana*, or to honor them with prayers or flowers or lamps, or even to offer them *anathemata* or incense. The rather saccharine, self-congratulatory tone, so different from the usual Sibylline venom, does not change the meaning of these *xoana*: they are still the images of pagan worship, and are still associated with *naoi* and other pagan trappings.[376]

[372] For the *Pseudo-Clementines* (or *Clementines*, or *Clementina*): J. Irmscher, "The Pseudo-Clementines," in *NTA* II, 532–535; 533 for the "basic writing"; *ODCC*^{2} *s.v.* Clementine Literature.

[373] The *xoana* of Clementine *Recognition* 9.19 and 9.20 may be discounted. The *Recognitions* survive only in the Latin translation of Rufinus which, in combination with Syriac versions, has been used to reconstruct the Greek original: Irmscher, "Pseudo-Clementines" (*supra* p. 154 n. 372) 535; *ODCC*^{2} 304 §2.

[374] For the date of Book XIII: Collins, "Sibylline Oracles" 453.

[375] For the date of the second half of Book VIII: Collins, "Sibylline Oracles" 416–417. For Lactantius' dates (c. 240–c. 320): *ODCC*^{2} *s.v.*

[376] *Cf.* Arn. *Adv.Gen.* 6.3 for another version of the idea that Christians do not frequent *naoi*; *infra* p. 201.

The theologian Origen seems to intend a generalized iconoclastic sense of *xoanon* when he uses the word in his apologetic work *Contra Celsum*, which is dated c. A.D. 249. He speaks of the first setting-up of *xoana* and *neoi* (7.96) **[181]**; he laughs not at "soulless *xoana*," but at the people who worship them (8.41) **[182]**; and he explains that daemons wreak vengeance on Christians "because they drive them out of the *xoana* and human bodies and souls" (8.43) **[183]**. The most interesting feature here is the idea that the pagan images of the gods actually harbor daemons. Clement, for example, asserts simply that the forms (εἴδη) of *agalmata* show the διάθεσις—disposition or characteristics—of the *daimones* (*Protr.* 4.50 P.). Origen's notion adumbrates Eusebius' contention that daemons and powers "lurk" in the images (*e.g.*, *PE* 4.1.131 b **[113]**). *Xoana* keep pace with the evolving *topoi* of iconoclasm. The same generalized meaning if the word holds good in Origen's somewhat gruesome, but not particularly enlightening, explanation of a line in Psalm 105 **[184]**, in which *xoana* are made to figure in connection with necromantic rites.[377]

The continuation of generalized non-iconoclastic usage can be seen in other third-century authors. Diogenes Laertius (1.6) **[64]** speaks of the disapproval of *xoana* by the Magi. Slightly further on in the passage, he mentions several sources who provide information about the beliefs and practices of the group. Although the passage containing *xoana* is often cited among texts related to Aristotle, two of whose works Diogenes names, he is no more likely to have provided the word than any of the others who are named. The meaning of *xoanon* in the passage clearly corresponds with the general definition that develops later than Aristotle, and so it is likely that it is Diogenes himself who simply follows a usage standard for his own time.[378]

Menander Rhetor, instructing a pupil in making a speech on the subject of the Sminthian Apollo, advises him to praise the god's temple and image. He suggests that the pupil compare the *agalma* to the Olympian Zeus and the Athena of the Athenian Acropolis. "Then add, 'What Pheidias, what Daedalus fashioned such a *xoanon*? Perhaps this *agalma* fell from heaven.'" *Agalma* and *xoanon* seem to be interchangeable in this rhe-

[377] For Origen (c. 185–c. 254): *ODCC*² *s.v.*; for the treatise: H. Chadwick, tr., *Origen. Contra Celsum* (Cambridge, 1953).

Origen's explanation of Ps. 105:29 differs substantially from those of other commentators, who interpret "the dead" to mean the pagan gods, in contrast with the true, living God. *Cf.*, *e.g.*, Aug. *ad* Ps. CVI line 30. See M. Buttenwieser, *The Psalms Chronologically Treated with a New Translation* (Library of Biblical Studies; New York, 1938, 1969) 822, 824 *ad* line 30, for "sacrifices offered to the dead" and references to *Wi.* (13:10; 15:17) on the handiwork of men as dead things (see *supra* p. 128). *Cf. Jub.* 22:16–18: *supra* p. 96.

[378] D.L. 1.6 **[64]**; 1.8 for references to Aristotle's *Magicus* and *De philosophia*. For probable date of Diogenes in the earlier third century A.D.: R.L. Hicks, tr., *Diogenes Laertius. Lives of Eminent Philosophers* I (LCL, 1938) xii.

torical fanfare, and devoid of archaeological precision. Although it is possible that an allusion is meant to the discovery of the image in a cave, a tradition apparently pictured on coins, the reference to Pheidias suggests instead that Menander refers simply to the beauty of the statue, which must be due to the skill of some great—if not divine—sculptor.[379]

Pseudo-Callisthenes, whose romance of the life of Alexander the Great is dated around A.D. 300, uses *xoanon*, *agalma*, *andrias*, and *tupos* for images of gods. The study of the terms for images is somewhat complicated by the fact that the romance survives in several recensions and translations which can vary considerably.[380] For example, in the A recension, Alexander adorns a *temenos* for Ammon, while the B recension adds a *xoanon* (1.30.14) **[146]**.[381] In 1.33.5 **[147]**, the episode of the dream oracle of Sarapis connected with the foundation of Alexandria, Alexander finds a *xoanon* of Sarapis. Because of the discrepancies between the several surviving versions of the text, it is not easy to determine the original form of the passage. The *xoanon* is variously in a *naos* or a *bomos* or a *sekos* **[148]**, seated, indescribable, holding a multiform beast and a scepter, and, in the fifth-century Armenian translation, of bronze.[382] Alexander orders a *temenos* prepared for the *xoanon* **[149]**. In a later episode, the sweating statue of Orpheus is both *agalma* and *xoanon*, and the B recension adds more *xoana* to the

[379] Menander Rhetor II.445 **[170]**. For the date of the work in the late third or earlier fourth century A.D.: D.A. Russell and N.G. Wilson, eds., trs., *Menander Rhetor* (Oxford, 1981) xi; xxxviii for emphasis on Alexandria Troas as one of the features indicating the different authorship of Treatises I and II; the author of II would be writing in Athens for a pupil from that city; 358 *ad* II.445.1 for the generalized description of the temple that does not indicate the author's familiarity with the place. The mouse mentioned in other sources does not appear in Menander's treatment. For the image: *supra* p. 80 n. 194.

[380] W. Kroll, ed., *Historia Alexandri Magni (Pseudo-Callisthenes)* I. *Recensio Vetusta* (Berlin, 1926; repr. 1958). Kroll gives the text of Parisinus graec. 1711 (A.D. XI), which is considered, along with parts of the Armenian version and the mid-fourth-century Latin translation of Julius Valerius, to be closest to the lost original.

[381] *Historia Alexandri Magni* 1.30.4, A text: ἀνίσταται οὖν τῶν ὕπνων καὶ μαθῶν τὴν τοῦ θεοῦ ἐνέργειαν κατασκευάζει τὸ τέμενος † ἐκ τῆς ἑαυτοῦ ἐπιγραφῆς (ed. Kroll): "So he arose from his sleep and having witnessed the action of the god, he adorned the *temenos* with an inscription by himself. . . . " (tr. adopted from E.H. Haight, tr., *The Life of Alexander of Macedon* [New York, 1955]).

[382] E.B. Harrison has drawn my attention to the distinction made between κομίζον and κατέχον, suggesting that the god, rather than carrying, is touching the head of and so controlling ("leading") a Cerberus, a standard rendering. The Armenian version gives a bronze image in both this passage and in Alexander's order to Parmeniskos; hence the ξόανον χαλκοῦν in the Greek rendering of the Armenian version by R. Raabe, Ἱστορία Ἀλεξάνδρου: *Die armenische Übersetzung der sagenhaften Alexander-Biographie* (Leipzig, 1896) 23.89; 24–25.94. For the Armenian version and the manuscript tradition of Pseudo-Callisthenes (as summarized above): A.M. Wolohojian, *The Romance of Alexander the Great by Pseudo-Callisthenes* (New York and London, 1969) 1–21; an English translation of the Armenian is given.

passage (1.42.6) [**150, 151**].[383] Candace of Meroe possesses a *naos* and a *xoanon* of Ammon, and has *agalmata* of the barbarian gods in her palace (3.18.3–4 [**152**]; 3.22.4). Alexander in disguise looks to Darius like the *tupoi* of Mithras (2.14.6). In his will, Alexander asks that *andriantes* and *eikones* of himself, his parents, and Ammon and Heracles be dedicated (3.33.23–24). When he dies, the bronze *agalma* of Zeus in Babylon is shaken (3.33.26). *Xoanon* seems to have little special significance.[384]

The Neoplatonist Porphyry, a follower of Plotinus who wrote in the later third century A.D., uses *xoanon* several times.[385] In *De abstinentia*, a tract advocating vegetarianism written c. A.D. 270, he states that the Doumatenes in Arabia bury a sacrificed child under a *bomos* "which they use as a *xoanon*" (2.56.6) [**324**].[386] That *xoanon* here reflects the old iconoclastic meaning is suggested not only by the bald sense of the passage, but also by its similarity to a section of the *Book of Wisdom* concerning the origin of idolatry:

> Some father, overwhelmed with untimely grief for the child suddenly taken from him, made an *eikon* of the child and honored thenceforth as a god what was once a dead human being, handing on to his household the observance of rites and ceremonies. Then this impious custom, established by the passage of time, was observed as a law. (14:15; tr. *New English Bible*)[387]

Porphyry's other *xoana* can be explained by the persistence of the most general definition of the word as a term for images of the gods. In a section of the *Epistle to Anebo the Egyptian* (*ap*. Eus. *PE* 3.4.92 d) [**106**], for instance, Porphyry refers to people whose lives are ruled by the heavens and fate: "ascribing everything to those gods, whom as the only deliverers from fate, they worship in *hiera* and *xoana* and other things." There are Christian overtones here, but the discussion is thoroughly in the Greek philosophical tradition.[388]

[383] To the Pierian *xoanon* of Orpheus *cf*. Plut. *Alex*. 14.5 [**313**].

[384] Images of kings, as well as of gods, are *andriantes* (Necbatanos, 1.3.6; 1.34.4) and *eikones* (Darius, 2.15.11). *Agalmata* are mentioned as riches in the palace of Darius (2.17.2–3), and bronze *andriantes* are heated as weapons against the animals in the Indian battle-line (3.3.3).

[385] A useful, mostly literary introduction to Porphyry is given in the *OCD*² *s.v.*

[386] Porph. *Abst*. 2.56.6 is quoted by Eusebius, *PE* 4.16.156 b [**116**]. For the date of this treatise after A.D. 263 but not much later than A.D. 271: J. Bouffartigue, ed., tr., *Porphyre. De l'abstinence* I. *Livre I* (Paris, 1977) xviii–xix.

[387] *Wi*. 14:15 (Rahlfs, *Septuaginta* II [*supra* p. 129 n. 309]):
ἀώρῳ γὰρ πένθει τρυχόμενος πατὴρ
τοῦ ταχέως ἀφαιρεθέντος τέκνου εἰκόνα ποιήσας
τόν ποτε νεκρὸν ἄνθρωπον νῦν ὡς θεὸν ἐτίμησεν
καὶ παρέδωκεν τοῖς ὑποχειρίοις μυστήρια καὶ τελετάς. . . .

[388] Iamblichus' *De Mysteriis Aegyptiorum* is a reply to Porphyry's *Letter to Anebo*; for this A.D. IV treatise: E. des Places, ed., tr., *Les mystères d'Egypte* (Paris, 1966).

Eusebius preserves substantial fragments of Porphyry's treatise Περὶ ἀγαλμάτων.[389] Porphyry is largely concerned with the symbolic meaning of the images of the gods. In a deft reversal of iconoclastic argument, he contends that only unlearned people regard *xoana* as mere stocks and stones, because they do not know how to read the meaning of their forms (fr. 1) [**107**]. Porphyry uses *xoanon* and *agalma* in the passage as apparently equivalent terms for images, while *eikon* seems to emphasize the ability to show the appearance of the gods and the powers of the gods in visible forms. A *xoanon* of Eileithyia is mentioned in another fragment of the work (fr. 10.66–71: *ap.* Eus. *PE* 3.12.116 d–117 a) [**110**] in the context of an elaborate and labored explanation of iconography in which the images of the gods are interpreted as symbolic *deikela*. The passage in question is comparatively straightforward: "But the city of Eileithyia [Elephantine] worships the third light; the *xoanon* is carved into [the form of] a flying vulture, whose plumage has been contrived of precious stones." This *xoanon*, discussed in the context of symbolic exegesis, is simply an image of a god that represents the deity's appearance.

Three of Porphyry's *xoana* are embedded in quotation sandwiches in the *Praeparatio evangelica*. Section 5.11.199 d–13.201 d [**118**] preserves a passage from Porphyry's *De philosophia ex oraculis haurienda* in which it is explained how the *daimones* instruct their followers in correct ritual procedure. Extracts from such instructions given by Hecate and Sarapis are given; those of Hecate concern the preparation of a magical *xoanon*, which is also called *agalma*. The first spell of Hecate gives elaborate instructions for the consecration of the *xoanon*. The directions are as repellent as they are fitfully obscure, involving lizards and dubious concoctions containing ingredients to be obtained in some unspecified way.[390] The second line of the spell instructs the devotee to make a δέμας, a bodily frame, from wild rue. Hecate gives no specifications regarding the size of this *demas*, but the suppliant is likely to encounter some difficulties no matter how small the image. While it is not easy to match ancient references to plants with modern botanical information, wild rue has an unquestionable reputation of being a stronger herb than the more familiar *Ruta graveolens* of the large family of woody shrubs. Indeed, one Elizabethan description of its action

[389] For Porph. Περὶ ἀγαλμάτων: J. Bidez, *Vie de Porphyre le philosophe néo-platonicien, avec les fragments des traités* Περὶ ἀγαλμάτων *et De regressu anima* (Paris, 1913) 143–157; Appendix I for the text.

[390] Even today, quite obscure materials can be easily purchased at stores specializing in supplies for magic and witchcraft. I have myself seen such shops in Athens and Philadelphia, and can vouch for the availability of dried bats, attractively presented, and of medicinal leeches.

reminds the New World reader of poison ivy.[391] Such trouble scarcely seems rewarded, for the *xoanon* will only have the power to make Hecate appear in dreams—an exceptionally modest ability in comparison to other kinds of magical images.[392] The lines concerning the preparation of the *xoanon* are also found in the collection of Chaldaean oracles which is almost certainly to be associated with a certain Julianus of the era of Marcus Aurelius. The fragment is considered dubious, however, and is best treated with the works of Porphyry.[393] Because *xoanon* is here part of the vocabulary of magic, it may be that it has a specialized definition that cannot be inferred from the passage. A common, garden-variety sense, however, is clearly possible.

In a second verse, Hecate describes a *xoanon* of herself in some detail: her "form is Demeter's," and snakes encircle her. The material is "Parian stone or polished ivory." Unless this *xoanon*, too, has magical connotations, it seems to carry on a generalized meaning of an image of a god.

The *xoanon* in *PE* 1.10.35 d **[102]** may also be assigned to Porphyry, if the passage in question comes not directly from the text of Philo of Byblos, but instead continues Eusebius' quotation of the *Adversus Christianos* of Porphyry, who there quotes Philo, who himself quotes—indeed, has translated from Phoenician into Greek—the work of Sanchuniathon. That Philo's assertion that Sanchuniathon lived before the Trojan War should not be dismissed out of hand is suggested by similarities between the material on Phoenician mythology which Philo insists was taken from his accounts based on documents and temple records, and texts from the second millennium B.C. discovered at Ugarit.[394] The word *xoanon*, of course, belongs to a

[391] J. Gerard, *Gerard's Herball. The Essence thereof distilled by Marcus Woodward from the edition of Th. Johansen, 1636* (London, 1927, 1964) 268: "*Ruta sylvestris* or wild Rue is more vehement both in smel and operation, and therefore the more virulent or pernitious; for sometimes it fometh out a vapor or aire so hurtfull than it scorches the face of him that looketh upon it, raising up blisters, wheals, and other accidents: it venemoth their hands that touch it, and will infect the face also if it be touched before they be clean washed: wherfore it is not to be admitted to meat or medicine."

[392] *Cf.* the hardworking statues described in the Hermetic treatise *Asclepius* III 24 a **[34]**: W. Scott, ed., tr., *Hermetica* I (Oxford, 1924); 76 for the date of the book as a whole of A.D. 268–273; *cf.* Scott, *Hermetica* IV, x–xvi. See *supra* p. 133 n. 321 for extreme beliefs about images in the late classical world.

[393] Hecate's spell **[118]**: *Oracula Chaldaica* 224; E. des Places, ed., tr., *Oracles chaldaïques* (Paris, 1971) no. 224; also quoted by Nicephorus Gregorius (c. A.D. 260–340), *In Synesium de ins.* 539 b–c. For the collection and Kroll's Antonine date: Dodds, *Irrational* (*supra* p. 133 n. 321) 283–284. See also G.G. Stroumsa, "Chaldaean Oracles," *Numen* 22 (1980) 167–172, for a consideration of a new edition of Lewy's *Chaldaean Oracles*.

[394] Sanchuniathon: *FGrH* 794 F 2, F 6; M.S. Drower, "Ugarit," in *CAH*³ II.2, 148, summary with references for suggested dates of c. 1000 and 800–500 B.C. Gifford, *Eusebius* IV, 34–35 *ad* 1.9.30 d 6. *PE* 1.9.31 a–b = Theodoretus, *affect.* 28.10: J. Raeder, ed., *Theodoretus.*

Greek rendering. Eusebius' assertion that he quotes *verbatim* (1.10.31 d) and/or Porphyry's reputation as a scholar may be enough to guarantee the appearance of the word in Philo, who, writing in the later first and earlier second centuries A.D., would have been comfortable using it as a general term for a worshipped image. Eusebius' version of Philo, however, is severely abridged and considerably enhanced by Christian sentiments, and the *xoanon* cannot be securely assigned to any of the earlier authors. The reference is simple enough—Agrueros, or Agrotes, was greatly revered, especially in Byblos, having "both a xoanon, very revered, and a *naos* drawn by yokes of oxen, in Phoenicia."

Another Greek translation involving *xoanon*, this one from a Syriac text, appears in Eusebius (*PE* 6.10.274 d–275 b) **[120, 121]**. The passage is extracted from the treatise *On Fate* by Bardesanes, whose birth is placed by the Chronicle of Edessa in A.D. 155; the work may have been addressed to Marcus Aurelius, and was translated into Greek by Bardesanes' followers.[395] The version given by Eusebius has a Christian flavor, and the *xoana* in it are the *xoana* of idolatry. Among the Seres it is forbidden to murder, steal, or bow to *xoana*, and so their land is free of *naoi*, prostitutes, adultresses, thieves, and murderers. Among the Indians, the Brahmins do not murder, worship *xoana*, eat living food, or drink liquor; in contrast, non-Brahmins murder, fornicate, get drunk, and worship *xoana*, being as they are ruled by fate. The ethnographic lessons are pointed, but seem to be legitimate parts of Bardesanes' argument against the power of the stars and planets to determine fate, since the same stars presumably preside over both the good and the bad halves of particular civilizations. Since the passage is preserved nowhere else, it is impossible to tell whether the *xoana* are Bardesanes' or Eusebius'. Chronologically and thematically, either author is possible.

Eusebius' own *xoana*, as has already been seen in the case of the golden *xoana* in his introduction to Plutarch's discussion of wooden images, are the idols of iconoclastic polemic; most come attached to a *topos*.[396] His conception of these idols is vivid but broad. In *PE* 10.4.469 c **[123]**, Eusebius castigates the *neoi* filled with *agalmata* and *anethemata*, and *xoana* formed

---

Graecarum Affectionum Curatio (Leipzig, 1904; repr. 1969). For Herrenius Philo of Byblos, c. A.D. 54–142: *RE* 8 (1913) 650–651 (A. Gudeman); *FGrH* 790 for fragments of the **Φοινικική** *ἱστορία*; A.I. Baumgarten, *The Phoenician History of Philo of Byblos. A Commentary* (Etudes préliminaires aux religions orientales dans l'empire romain 89; Leiden, 1981).

395 For Bardesanes: Gifford, *Eusebius* IV, 218 *ad* 6.9.273 b.

396 For dates of Eusebius c. A.D. 264–c. 340 and the difficulty of dating his works: D.S. Wallace-Hadrill, *Eusebius of Caesarea* (Westminster, Maryland, 1961) 39–58; 57–58 for chronological table. The *DE* and *PE* are placed c. A.D. 312–318; books I–X of the *Ecc.Hist.* after 318; and *De eccl. theol.* is dated c. A.D. 335.

from every kind of material in the shapes of all kinds of living things. The combinations of terms recalls Philo, and the idols include all forms of images. *Xoana* are the focus of worship: men fall down before them (*PE* 3.14.123 a–b) **[112]**, thinking to revere divine powers within them (*PE* 3.13.122 a) **[111]**; priests are appointed for them (*Ecc.Hist.* 9.4.2) **[96]**; and they are set up along with the other trappings of error. The oldest men in early times did not have these objects; they built no *neoi* and set up no *xoana* because, in a statement similar to Clement's version of Varro (*Protr.* 4.40 P.) **[44]**, the graphic and plastic arts had not been invented (*PE* 1.9.29 d; 1.9.30 b) **[100, 101]**. The first setting-up of *xoana* was inspired by daemons (*PE* 4.16.161 c) **[117]** and introduced to the Greeks as foreign practices by Cadmus (*PE* 10.4.469 b) **[122]**. Again, as in Clement, blame can be laid at the feet of specific leaders into error (*Protr.* 1.4 P.: Orpheus and Methymnion). Eusebius' *xoana* are not old images, but idols that continue to be made (*Ecc.Hist.* 9.11.5–6 **[97]**; *νεοπαγές xoanon* set up in Antioch by Theotecnus). They are infested by daemons who operate through them (*PE* 1.4.12 a **[98]**; 4.1.131 a–b **[113]**; 4.5.141 d **[115]**; *DE* 6.20 **[95]**), but they are soulless (*apsycha*; *De eccl.theol.* 2.22.2–3 **[94]**; *PE* 1.9.30 b **[101]**; 3.3.91 a **[105]**; 4.1.131 a–b **[113]**; 5.14.203 b **[119]**) and, in another passage reminiscent of Clement, *νεκρὰ καὶ κωφά*, "dead and dumb" (*PE* 1.4.12 a **[98]**; compare Clem.Al. *Protr.* 4.45 P. **[45]**). The *xoana* are made from soulless material (*PE* 3.13.122 a **[111]**; *cf.* 3.8.99 d **[108]**); shaped by the hands of workers (*PE* 13.14.691 d **[125]**; *cf.* Clem.Al. *Protr.* 4.45 P. **[45]**). Although they purport to show the appearance of the gods, they are shaped to the form of mortal men (*PE* 1.6.17 c–d **[99]**; 3.10.106 b–c **[109]**; 5.13.201 b **[118]**; 13.14.691 d **[125]**) and, somewhat Euhemeristically, some are *eikones* of men who bore the names of the sun and the elements (*PE* 3.3.90 d–91 a) **[105]**. The *xoana* have long held power, but in the enlightened age of the Gospel their influence is being pushed back (*PE* 1.4.12 a **[98]**; 4.4.140 c **[114]**). Eusebius' *xoana* are generalized idols, catchalls for every iconoclastic *topos*, and have no archaeological value.[397]

[397] I have not attempted to survey patristic literature systematically. Some appearances of *xoanon* in patristic sources are given by G.W.H. Lampe, *A Patristic Greek Lexicon* (Oxford, 1961) *s.v.* with references (M.) to J.P. Migne, *Patrologia Graeca* (Paris, 1857–1866). A.D. IV: *In Nativitam Christi* 6 (2.363 B), doubtfully attributed to Joannes Chrysostomus, with the same meaning; A.D. V: Basilius Seleucensis, *Oration* 1.3 (M. 85.33 B), "statue, form"; basic meaning of "image, idol" used by Theodoretus Cyrrhensis, *Quaestiones in Gen.* 86 (1.95) and *Historia ecclesiastica* 5.22.2 (3.1059); A.D. VII: *Chronicon paschale* p. 285 (M. 92.712 A), uncertain meaning, perhaps referring to "hewn or polished wood or stone"; undated: *Apocalypsis Petri* A 33, "image, idol" that is the object of false worship. *Cf.* W. Bauer (W.F. Arndt and F.W. Gingrich trs.) *A Greek-English Lexicon of the New Testament and Other Early Christian Literature*^{2} (Chicago and London, 1957) *s.v.* *ξόανον* for a sparse selection of examples and the definition "*a* (crude) *wooden image* of idols."

Two authors of the fourth century A.D. exhibit the pagan and Christian usages of *xoanon* respectively. The sophist Libanius, in a speech concerning the arguments that Achilles would have used in carrying off Briseis (*Progymnasmata* 11.15) [**157**], has the hero attempt to convince the Trojans that the abduction was a good thing for the city: "Priam will carve the maiden in stone as an *anathema* bringing the salvation of Ilium; he will set up the *xoanon* near the *temenos* of Tyche."[398] A general rather than a specific meaning seems indicated.

Epiphanius' *Panarion*, written between A.D. 374 and 377, categorizes every heresy then known.[399] *Xoanon* occurs twice in discussions of idolatry: Adam was not an idolater because he bowed neither to *xoana* nor to anything else (2.5) [**73**]; and *xoana* were not the first things that led men into error (3.4) [**74**].[400] Another passage describes a ceremony in the sanctuary of Kore in Alexandria in which "torch-bearers go down into a sort of underground *sekos* and bring up a sort of naked *xoanon* sitting in a litter" (51.22.9–10) [**75**].[401] The *xoanon* has five seals, each bearing a cross interwoven in gold, on its hands, knees, and forehead. The repeated enclitics express the writer's scorn for the *sekos* and *xoanon*; again, the sense of the word reflects the iconoclastic tradition.

A precise definition of *xoanon* does appear in this age, in the fourth-century commentary on Vergil by Servius, who mentions and explains *xoana* three times. Two versions of Servius are preserved. It is thought that the longer one, the *Scholia Danielis*, incorporates a considerable amount of the Vergilian commentary of Aelius Donatus, a grammarian of the fourth century A.D., who was also known and used by Servius.[402]

In the note to *Aeneid* 4.56 [**332**], Servius offers several explanations of the word *delubrum*, "shrine." In the *Scholia Danielis* the last is this: " . . . or, undoubtedly, we call a *simulacrum* a *delubrum*, from *liber* [wood], that is to say, made from scraped wood, which in Greek is called *xoanon*."

[398] For Libanius: *OCD*² *s.v.*; Wilson, *Scholars* 28–29 and *passim*.

[399] For Epiphanius: *ODCC*² *s.v.* For the *Panarion*: G. Vallée, *A Study in Anti-Gnostic Polemics. Irenaeus, Hippolytus, and Epiphanius* (Studies in Christianity and Judaism 1; Waterloo, 1981) 63–91; 66–67 for the title, which refers to an apothecary's box containing remedies for snake-bites; the work "is thought to contain the medications for all illness threatening the true faith" (67).

[400] Sections 1–20 deal with pre-Christian heresies, which are by their nature "errors." Vallée, *Study* (*supra* p. 162 n. 399) 67; 75–76 for Epiphanius' conception of heresy.

[401] Sections 21–25 concern gnostic heresies: Vallée, *Study* (*supra* p. 162 n. 399) 75. For material related to the account of the ceremony: K. Holl, ed., *Epiphanius* I. *Ancoratus und Panarion* (GCS 25; Leipzig, 1915) 286 *ad loc*. For Epiphanius' sources, some heresiological: Vallée, *Study*, *passim* with references.

[402] E.K. Rand, "Is Donatus's Commentary on Virgil Lost?" *CQ* 10 (1916) 158–164. L.D. Reynolds, ed., *Texts and Transmission* (Oxford, 1983) 385–388 (P.K. Marshall).

The shorter version is slightly different: " . . . or, undoubtedly, we call a wooden *simulacrum* a *delubrum* from *liber*, that is to say, made from scraped wood, which in Greek is called *xoanon*."[403] Whatever its origin, the reference to *xoanon* reflects a conflation of Clement's *xeo*-etymology and the application of the word to wooden statues, as found in Plutarch and Pausanias.

A second, more detailed, consideration of *delubrum* precedes the entry for 4.56. The long note on *Aeneid* 2.225 [**331**], in the Laocoon episode, contains this comment near the end: "Masurius Sabinus says that *delubrum* means an *effigies* made by the peeling of bark; for the ancients formed the branches of *felix* [auspicious] trees, the bark having been peeled off, into *effigies* of gods, whence the Greeks say *xoanon*."[404] At least one element of this explanation does not seem to have Greek sources: the distinction between *felix* and *infelix* trees is of considerable antiquity, and the classification appears to be entirely Italian: one list of trees is Etruscan in origin.[405] The explanation differs in several points from that at 4.56 [**332**] and is clearly the fruit of enterprising scholarship. One Masurius Sabinus was a jurist of wide learning who gained the favor of Tiberius and lived into the reign of Nero; this note is Servius' only citation of him.[406] It is difficult to say whether the entire section on scraped images should be attributed to Masurius, or only the first gloss so assigned, with the explanation following *nam* given to another source. The application of the word *delubrum* to images rather than shrines does not seem to occur in literature; it is, however, fairly common for definitions offered by ancient lexica and related works not to travel well.

Something of the same willingness to share dubiously revelant information marks the third appearance of *xoanon* in Servius. The note on *Aeneid* 6.68 [**333**] attempts to explain the phrase *agitataque numina Troiae*, "the shaken divinities of Troy." Servius says; "Either [ones that are] angry with me; or undoubtedly he means *xoana*, that is, small *simulacra*, which were carried in litters and, moved about by themselves, imparted a prophecy; this

[403] Servius *ad Aen.* 4.56 [**332**]: A.F. Stocker and A.H. Travis, eds., *Servianorum in Vergilii Carmina Commentariorum Editio Harvardiana* III (Oxford, 1965) *ad loc.*

[404] Servius *ad Aen.* 2.225 [**331**]: E.K. Rand *et al.*, eds., *Servianorum in Vergilii Carmina Commentariorum Editio Harvardiana* II (Lancaster, Pennsylvania, 1946) *ad loc.*

[405] For the meaning of *arbor felix*: J. André, "Arbor felix, arbor infelix," in *Hommages à Jean Bayet* (Coll. Latomus 70; Brussels, 1964) 35–46; A. Weis, "The Motif of the Adligatus and Tree," *AJA* 86 (1982) 27 n. 48. The distinction was elaborated into a system, and seems to have involved the edibility of fruits. *Cf.* the idea of "good" as "good to eat": Harrison, *Epilegomena* 139.

[406] For Masurius (Massurius) Sabinus: *RE* II.1.2 (1920) 1600–1601 *s.v.* Sabinus (29) (A. Steinwenter); H.J. Rose, *A Handbook of Latin Literature* (New York, 1936) 461. That Servius' Masurius is the one mentioned in Ath. 14.623 e is not certain.

happened among the Egyptians and the Carthaginians." This explanation is entirely different from the etymologically based remarks found in the preceding notes. The information is similar to that given by Diodorus in his account of Alexander's visit to the oracle of Ammon (17.50.6–7) [**62**]. Diodorus' discussion, as has been seen, probably derives not from the histories of Alexander, but rather from a special treatise on oracles.[407] Some such treatise would seem to stand behind Servius' note, since a direct link to Diodorus cannot explain the reference to the Carthaginians.

Servius, then, or his sources, or his improvers, has taken information about *xoana* from different kinds of texts. The etymological references to *xoanon* recall Clement's definition of the images as scraped pillars of wood and stone; the exclusively wooden aspect, however, seems to reflect either a different etymological source or a simple refinement based on the Latin *liber–delubrum* etymology. The latter is more likely, since preserved etymologies of *xoanon* are unanimous in associating it with stone exclusively or, at most, stone and wood. Servius' third reference to *xoana* as oracular statues derives from accounts of the workings of oracles and reflects the broad definition of the word that prevailed during the time in which such works are attested.

Conclusions

In the third and fourth centuries A.D., *xoanon* maintains the meanings it had in earlier times. For the most part these are general and archaeologically uninformative. *Xoana* are dedications in various materials, magical figures, or generalized idols. The specialized, more precise, definitions worked out during the first and second centuries A.D. have little influence; their only trace is in scholarly commentaries. From now on, *xoanon* itself loses what popularity it has gained and appears mostly in lexica, etymologica, and commentaries.

[407] Servius *ad Aen.* 6.68 [**333**]: G. Thilo and H. Hagen, eds., *Servii Grammatici qui feruntur in Vergilii Carmina Commentarii* II (Leipzig, 1884). For D.S. 17.50.6–7 [**62**]: *supra* pp. 75–76.

11. *Xoanon* in the Fifth through Thirteenth Centuries A.D.

In late antiquity, *xoanon* almost ceases to be a living word in literature. Its appearances are almost exclusively in commentaries and lexicographic works. In other contexts it sometimes requires special explanation, showing that it is no longer familiar; in learned works, however, it passes without comment and seems still to be understood as a general term for the image of a god.

The *xoanon* that began this study now finds its true context: this is the Trojan image of Athena mentioned by Proclus in his epitome of Arctinus' *Iliou Persis* [**325**]. The fifth-century plot summary of the epic cycle uses *xoanon* in the way typical of the general literature of the centuries after Christ. It signifies nothing more than the image of a divinity, and cannot be taken as a survival of eighth-century B.C. usage.[408]

In sources of the sixth century A.D., *xoanon* is found as both an independent and a borrowed word. Macedonius the Consul, who lived in the time of Justinian, uses it of a statue set up to honor Thyonichus, a strong and καλὸς παῖς who triumphed over all in athletic competition (*AnthPal* 16.51) [**167**]. It seems that the *xoanon* is a portrait of the boy rather than simply a dedication in his honor: "With this *xoanon* [we honor] the boy Thyonichus, not so that you may see how *kalos* [he was] in the glory of this monument, but so that in you, learning the prize he earned, there may be . . . the desire to emulate this enthusiasm." *Xoana* that may have been portraits have been noted in connection with the imperial cult; Macedonius' epigram, however, seems more closely connected with the dedication at Oenoanda in which a *xoanon* was set up on the occasion of an athletic victory [**397**].[409] The poem may thus continue an earlier usage; it is possible, however, that the application of *xoanon* to portraits not in the realm of imperial cult marks a late expansion of its meaning.

John Philoponus, an Alexandrian scholar working in the first half of the sixth century, produced major commentaries on Aristotle. In a passage of *De anima* (1.3) [**30**], Aristotle mentions a theory about the way in which the soul causes movement in the body; he compares Democritus' opinion with the reference by the comic poet Philippus to Daedalus' use of quicksilver to make a "wooden Aphrodite" move. Themistius [**363**] had added no information on Daedalus' method in his summary of the passage. Philoponus [**153**] expands on Aristotle's remark, explaining in some detail how

[408] For Proclus, *Chrestomathia* 261–263 Severyns [**325**]: *supra* p. 13 n. 25.

[409] For Macedonius and the epigram: R. Aubreton and F. Buffière, eds., trs., *Anthologie Grecque* 13. *Deuxième Partie. Anthologie de Planude* (Paris, 1980) 247 n. 2; *RE* 14.1 (1928) 771–772 (J. Geffcken). For the question of Macedonius' religion: B. Baldwin, "The Christianity of Macedonius Consul," *Mnemosyne* 37 (1984) 451–453.

See *supra* pp. 110–111.

Daedalus prepared hollow places in the image, placing quicksilver in them which, as it rolled about on itself, caused the image to move. To Philoponus, the wooden Aphrodite of Aristotle is a *xoanon*. He evidently thinks that the term denotes a wooden image, and his usage underlines the change in the meaning of the word since Aristotle's time.[410]

The *xoanon* of Achilles mentioned in the anonymous *Periplus Ponti Euxini* [**283**] of the sixth century A.D. is borrowed, along with the rest of the passage, from Arrian's account:[411] "And there is also a *naos* on it [*sc.* the island] of Achilles, and a *xoanon* (or *agalma*) of old workmanship." The gloss *ἤτοι ἄγαλμα* has been added by the compiler to amplify Arrian's *ξόανον*.

Xoana appear in four "codices" of Photius' *Bibliotheca*. The nature and exact date of this mid-ninth-century work are debated; Photius' own title for it is *Inventory and Enumeration of Books That We Have Read, Of Which Our Beloved Brother Tarasius Requested a General Analysis*. The compilation consists of two hundred eighty "codices," each representing the digest of a book. The entries range from short summaries to what appear to be extended excerpts; whether a word has been taken from a source or represents Photius' own usage must be judged by several criteria.[412]

The *xoanon* in codex 97 [**301**], which summarizes the *Compilation of Olympic Victors and Chronicles* by Phlegon of Tralles, is likely to be Photius' own term. In the first place, Photius complains because Phlegon includes too many events; Treadgold surmises that "these seem to have bored Photius so much that he stopped reading in the middle."[413] Furthermore, the reference to the "*xoana* of the so-called gods" in the context of Athenodorus' piratical incursion into Delos of 69 B.C. is a touch of gratuitous Christianity that may reflect an iconoclastic usage. Phlegon could well have used *xoanon*, but the origin of the word in the codex cannot be proved by internal evidence.

The other *xoana* belong to the second part of the *Bibliotheca* (codd. 234–280), which seems to represent a copy of Photius' own reading notes—

[410] Joannes Philoponus *ad* Ar. *de An.* 1.3, 406 b 11 [**153**]. For Philoponus: Wilson, *Scholars* 22, 44–45 and *passim*.

[411] *Periplus Ponti Euxini* 66 [**283**]: K. Müller, *Geographi graeci minores* I (Paris, 1855) 419.66. The work is based on Arrian, Menippus, Pseudo-Scymnus, and Pseudo-Scylax. For the *Periplus*: Diller, *Tradition of Minor Geographers* 102–146; 141 *ad loc.* for this and other glosses; 110–113 for date not before second half of A.D. VI. For Arrian: *supra* p. 117 n. 285.

[412] For the *Bibliotheca*: Treadgold, *Bibliotheca* 4 (title); 12–13, 16–36 (date); 5–7 and *passim* (nature of the summaries). The work is variously dated between A.D. 838 and 875; 855 is widely accepted. Treadgold argues for 845. See also Wilson, *Scholars* 89–119 for Photius; 93–111 for the *Bibliotheca*; and *Speculum* 57 (1982) 943–944 (rev. of Treadgold).

[413] Treadgold, *Bibliotheca* 100–101. Nevertheless, he includes the codex in the class of "Precise Summaries" (183).

the raw material, as it were, of his digests.[414] Photius' methods of work thus come into question; scholars who have studied the text intensively seem almost to look over his shoulder, using lexical clues to distinguish free summary from attempts to excerpt accurately. The codices containing *xoana* fall into a group (codd. 269–277) which, while ranking among the "least coherent," also count among those "in which Photius seems to be keeping as many of the author's words as possible."[415] Three ecclesiastical writers are represented: Asterius of Amasea (cod. 271) [**302**], John Chrysostom (cod. 277) [**304**], and Nilus of Ancyra (cod. 276) [**303**], all of the fourth and fifth centuries A.D. All the *xoana* seem to be understood generally as images. Asterius' *xoanon* is a bronze *agalma*, and John Chrysostom lectures his audience on their need for new eyes so that they will be able, in seeing a naked *xoanon* in a *naos*, to recognize that a stone is a stone and a stock, a stock. "For what benefit are external eyes, when the internal eyes are defective?" A passage from the spurious *Fragmenta ex orationibus de pascha* given to Nilus of Ancyra mentions the creation of living *xoana* from water. It is not a question here of a challenging new archaeological category, but instead of the miracle of life; while human craftsmen must fashion images from clay, the divine creator produces an embryo.

Photius, in his *Lexicon*, uses *xoanon* to refer to an image carried in a procession [**306**] and of an image of Adonis [**307**]. Probably *xoanon* is a general term for a statue with some religious connections. Similar entries in the *Suda* [**356, 357**] repeat Photius' information about the two *xoana*.

Borrowed *xoana* appear in the Homeric commentaries of Eustathius, who was Archbishop of Thessalonica c. A.D. 1175. Eustathius takes information about the image of Apollo Smintheus from Heraclides Ponticus and Strabo (*ad* H. *Il.* 1.39) [**126, 127**]. "For the history says that in Chryse there is a *hieron* of Smintheus, and under the foot of the *xoanon* lies a mouse, the work of Scopas of Paros, the symbol that keeps alive the etymological meaning of the name; that is to say, the etymology of Smintheus."[416] Eustathius mentions an ivory *xoanon* by Colotes (*ad* H. *Il.* 2.603) [**132**] in a passage also derived from Strabo (8.3.4) [**339**], as is his notice of the *xoanon* of Nemesis at Rhamnous which rivals the work of Pheidias (*ad* H. *Il.* 2.556) [**131**] (compare Strabo 9.1.17 [**342**]). Strabo's discussion of the form of the *xoanon* of Athena at Troy (13.1.41) [**343**] is also taken over by Eustathius (*ad* H. *Il.* 6.92) [**135**].

[414] Treadgold, *Bibliotheca* 37–51 for the nature of codd. 234–280, and for the work of Severyns, Hägg, and others.

[415] Treadgold, *Bibliotheca* 43, 44 n. 29.

[416] For Eustathius: Wilson, *Scholars* 196–204; and Strabo: Diller, *Tradition Strabo* 86–87, 182–207. For Strabo on the Apollo Smintheus: *supra* p. 80 n. 194.

Eustathius' last *xoanon* which is a specific image is one which the Ethiopians carry around in a procession (*ad* H. *Il.* 1.423) [**128**]. Because the passage speaks of the "*xoanon* of Zeus and the other gods," the sense is not entirely clear.

Eustathius' remaining *xoana* reflect the fate of the word in lexicographical sources. In discussing the meaning of *agalma*, Eustathius emphasizes that it means anything in which someone takes delight—"even if those of later times apply the word to a *xoanon*" (*ad* H. *Il.* 4.144) [**133**]. Clearly *xoanon* here is understood as a general term for statues; the passage, however, is closely connected with etymological entries concerned with synonyms, and so the comment cannot be assumed to reflect ordinary usage. In three notes, on *Iliad* 1.572 [**129**], 5.730 [**134**], and 14.132 [**136**], Eustathius discusses pairs of nouns and verbs, using *xeo–xoanon* among the examples of derivations. The pairs, including *xeo–xoanon*, appear often in ancient lexica, and are used in modern times by etymologists.[417]

Xoanon appears frequently in the definitions of lexica and etymologica. Frequently these definitions are carried over from lexicon to lexicon; for example, the same list of synonyms appears in the *Suda* [**355**], in Photius' *Lexicon* [**305**], and in the *Synagoge Lexeon Chresimon (Collection of Useful Words)* [**9**]. *Xoanon* also figures in the definitions of *agalma* and *bretas*, two other words for statues for which similar family trees can be drawn up.

There are three basic kinds of definitions of *xoanon*. The first, which has already been mentioned, is the plain list of synonyms. Even this simple list presents difficulties in tracing sources, because the relationships between lexical works are complex.

The list is short: Ξόανον· ἄγαλμα, εἴδωλον, ζῴδιον, ἀνδριάς. The works in which it appears span five centuries. The *Suda* was compiled at the end of the tenth century A.D., and Photius prepared his *Lexicon* at the end of the ninth. Photius depended on a version of the *Synagoge*, the date of which is not certain; it appears to contain material from glossaries compiled in the early fifth century A.D.[418]

[417] For *agalma*: *EtMag s.v.* Ἄγαλμα [**83**]; *EtMagAuc s.v.* ἄγαλμα [**85**]; *SymEt s.v.* ἄγαλμα [**359**]; *AnecBekker* I.334.18 *s.v.* Ἄγαλμα [**11**]. For *xeo–xoanon*, see, *e.g.*, *EtGud s.v.* ξόανον [**81**]; for Chantraine: *supra* p. 12 n. 12.

[418] *Suda s.v.* Ξόανον [**355**]; Photius, *Lexicon s.v.* Ξόανον [**305**]; *Synagoge: AnecBachmann* I.311.8 *s.v.* Ξόανον [**9**]. The *Suda* (ed. A. Adler, *Suidae Lexicon*, 5 vols. [Leipzig, 1928–1938]), sometimes wrongly called Suidas, dates from A.D. X and incorporates material from texts and commentaries as well as from collections of words and excerpts. (Recent summary: Hunger, *Literatur* II, 40–41; Wilson, *Scholars* 145–147.)

For Photius' *Lexicon*: Wilson, *Scholars* 90–93. The date of the work is disputed; some place it after the *Bibliotheca*, thus perhaps as late as after A.D. 846: Hunger, *Literatur* II,

Hesychius, writing in the fifth century A.D., gives essentially the same list [144], but in plurals: *ξόανα· ἀγάλματα, εἴδωλα, ζῴδια.* He adds that "properly" *xoana* are "those carved from wood or stone." The only source that comes to mind for such a comment, combining as it does etymology with the explicit association of *xoana* with wood and stone, is Clement in the *Protrepticus* (4.40 P.) [44]. Evidently the compilers of glossaries do not always study usage independently, but instead rely on information that is already in etymological form.[419]

Hesychius' statement introduces the second general category of definition, of which the major concern is distinguishing among the meanings of synonyms. Three sources preserve definitions of this type: the *Etymologicum Gudianum* [82]; Ammonius [7]; and the so-called *Lexicon of Ptolemaeus of Acalon* [326].

The gloss, according to the *Etymologicum Gudianum*, is this: "*Xoanon* and *bretas* and *eidolon* [Amm.: *agalma*] are different; for a *xoanon* is a carved *eidolon* [Amm.: something carved], stone or ivory or wooden [Amm.: stone or ivory; Ptol.: stone or wooden]; while a *bretas* is something like a *brotos* [mortal], whether bronze, or made out of a similar material; and an *agalma* [*sic*] is fashioned of [marble] [Amm.: poros; Ptol.: Parian] or out of some other stone." The comment on *bretas* can also be traced to Clement (*Protr.* 4.40 P.) [44]. The fullest version of this definition appears in the *Etymologicum* [82], where a *xoanon* may also be of wood. Of these

---

39–40. For the suggestion that the preserved *Lexicon* is an expanded version of an earlier project: Treadgold, *Bibliotheca* 4 n. 15.

Photius appears to have used for his *Lexicon* an augmented version of the *Synagoge*, a version for which he seems to have been in some way responsible. The *Synagoge* itself appears to be based in part on some form of the early A.D. V glossaries connected with St. Cyril; for these: P. Burguière, "Cyrilliana," *REA* 63 (1961) 345–361; 64 (1962) 95–108. Whether these glossaries were made by him or, instead, for use with his works is not clear; at any rate, they were a Christian production. For them: Hunger, *Literatur* II, 37–38; Daly, *Contributions* 68–69; Wilson, *Scholars* 91–92. The *Synagoge* seems to combine material from some such Cyrillian glossary with material from special lexica of the Attic dialect, an epitome of Harpocration, and the like. It is the first of six lexica called the *Lexica Segueriana* that are edited by I. Bekker in *Anecdota Graeca* I (Berlin, 1814). Bekker includes only the A entries; the complete text is given by L. Bachmann in *Anecdota Graeca* (Leipzig, 1828) and the *Synagoge* is sometimes called the *Lexicon Bachmannianum*. For the *Synagoge*: *RE* 12.2 (1925) 2466–2467 s.v. Lexicographie §48 (J. Tolkiehn); H. Stuart Jones, "The Making of a Lexicon," *CR* 55 (1941) 4.

[419] Hesych. *s.v.* *ξόανα* [144]: M. Schmidt, ed., *Hesychii Alexandrini Lexicon* (5 vols.; Jena, 1858–1868; repr. Amsterdam, 1965); *idem*, *Editio minor* (Jena, 1867); K. Latte, ed., *Hesychii Alexandrini Lexicon* (2 vols., never completed; Copenhagen, 1953, 1966). Hesychius survives in a much-abbreviated form. For his sources: Daly, *Contributions* 66–67; Hunger, *Literatur* II, 35–36. *EtGud s.v.* Ἀγάλματα [79] gives a similar list of synonyms in which *xoana* figure. *Cf.* Hesych. *s.v.* *ξέσμα* [143].

works, only the *Etymologicum Gudianum* can be dated, and it is usually placed around A.D. 1100.[420] Ammonius uses material from a first- or second-century A.D. glossary, but incorporates later material in addition, such as Byzantine epitomes.[421] The other *Lexicon* is falsely ascribed to the early imperial grammarian Ptolemy; its true date, however, is not known.[422]

The focus of the third type of definition is etymological. As has already been seen in the case of Eustathius, *xoanon* attracted etymological interest. The twelfth-century scholar Johannes Tzetzes, in another commentary on the Iliad **[368]**, mentions among the features of Aeolic dialect that short "o" becomes "u"; hence *xoanon* is *xuanon*.[423] At least three lexicographical works preserve etymological definitions of *xoanon*: the thirteenth-century *Lexicon* of Pseudo-Zonaras **[371]**; the *Etymologicum Gudianum* **[81]**; and the *Etymologicum* of Orion, a grammarian of the fifth century A.D. Orion gives the fullest version **[185]**: "*Xoanon*: derived from *xeo*, *xeanon*, and by the change of *e* to *o*, *xoanon*." This explanation prefigures the modern concept of vowel gradation. The *Etymologicum Gudianum*, as noted, also includes a discussion of synonyms **[82]**, the second type of definition. The question of the sources of Pseudo-Zonaras is complicated by the existence of longer and shorter versions of the *Lexicon*.[424]

The semantic and etymological definitions are found combined in the twelfth-century *Etymologicum Magnum*. Its entry for *xoanon* **[84]** reads:

420 *EtGud s.v.* Ξόανον 2 **[82]**: F.W. Sturz, ed., *Etymologicum Graecae Linguae Gudianum et alia grammaticorum scripta . . .* (Leipzig, 1818). The edition of E.L. Stefani (Leipzig, 1909, 1920) goes through Z. Note that in the first line, *eidolon* has been substituted for *agalma*, which appears later. The *EtGud* appears to combine material from the *Etymologicum Magnum Genuinum* and the *Etymologicum Parvum* (A.D. IX). *Cf.* the *EtGud* entries for Ἀγάλματα **[79]** and Βρέτας (1) **[80]**, in which *xoanon* figures as synonym and cross-reference. F. Lasserre and N. Livadaras, eds., *Etymologicum Magnum Genuinum, Symeonis Etymologicum una cum Magna Grammatica, Etymologicum Magnum Auctum* I (Rome, 1976). For these: *KP* II, 391–392 *s.v.* Etymologie, and the useful sentence on the *EtMag* in the entry for it in the *OCD*².

421 For Ammonius: *supra* p. 33 n. 80.

422 Ptolemaeus Ascalonita *s.v.* ξόανον **[326]**: G. Heylbut, "Ptolemaeus περὶ διαφορᾶς λέξεων," *Hermes* 22 (1887) 388–410; this entry: 405.23. For the incorrect assignment to the early imperial grammarian: *KP* IV, 1233 s.v. Ptolemaios (4).

423 Tze. *Exegesis in Homeri Iliadem* 11 **[368]**; *cf.* the inscription from Obruk **[396]**. For Tzetzes: Wilson, *Scholars* 190–196.

424 Orion *s.v.* Ξόανον **[185]**: F.W. Sturz, ed., *Orionis Thebani Etymologicon* (Leipzig, 1820) 112.9. This work is preserved only in summary. For its sources: *KP* IV, 345 *s.v.* Orion (3). For vowel gradation: *supra* p. 11 n. 13.

EtGud 415.55 *s.v.* Χόανον (1) **[81]**. [Zonaras] *Lexicon s.v.* ξόανον **[371]** = *AnecPar.* IV.199.17. Some manuscripts give Philo as a source. For Ps.-Zonaras: M. Naoumides, "The Shorter Version of Pseudo-Zonaras, *Lexicon*," in *Serta Turyniana* 436–488; 476.35 for this entry and the mss. variants.

"*Xoanon*: derived from *xeo*, *xeanon* and by a change, *xoanon*. *Xoanon* and *bretas* and *agalma* are different. For a *xoanon* is a carved *eidolon*, stone or ivory or wooden; a *bretas*, on the other hand, is like a *brotos*, either bronze or made of a similar material; while an *agalma* is made of [marble] or of some other stone."[425] While echoes of Clement's explicit etymologies are apparent, this definition displays the characteristic arbitrary details of the genre. The assignment of the materials makes little sense, and is contradicted in other, related, definitions. The entries for *bretas* in both the *Etymologicum Gudianum* **[80]** and the late ninth-century *Etymologicum Genuinum* **[76, 77]** give the same definition of the word, but add that a *bretas* is "especially an *agalma* of a man, made out of wood."[426] There are some correspondences among the definitions of the various words for statues, but little consistency or coherence.[427]

The definitions in question are not like modern dictionary entries. They cannot be relied on to supply reliable information about actual usage in their own or any other period because they rely on existing etymological material. The purpose of the glossaries and lexica that are their sources is also not that of a corresponding modern reference work. Collections of words and terms were always directed to a relatively narrow goal, whether it was to aid the explication of old texts or to ensure accuracy of composition exercises; no non-Attic word, for instance, would be permitted to sully an imitation of Xenophon.[428]

The usefulness of such collections is further reduced by the fact that only rarely did an individual entry survive successive borrowings and abridgments with the name of the illustrative author still attached. One

[425] *EtMag s.v.* *Ξόανον* **[84]**: T. Gaisford, ed., *Etymologicon Magnum* (Oxford, 1848). The ms. reading *παράμηρον* (*παραμήριος*, having to do with the inside of the thighs) is obviously corrupt; for *μαρμάρινον* see Gaisford *ad loc.* I have been unable to consult A. Kopp, *De Ammonii Eranii aliorum distinctionibus synonymicis earumque communi fonte* (Diss. Königsberg, 1883), in which identical passages in the *EtMag* and Ammonius are discussed (72–75): Nickau, *Ammonius* (supra p. 33 n. 80) LXIII.

[426] *EtGen* (A.D. IX) *s.v.* *βρέτας* **[76, 77]**: G. Berger, ed., *Etymologicum Genuinum et Etymologicum Symeonis (β)* (Meisenheim am Glan, 1972) 135 *β* 251; 136 *β* 216. For the *EtGen*: R. Browning, *Studies on Byzantine History, Literature and Education* (London, 1977) XIII, 11. *Cf. EtGud s.v.* Βρέτας (2) **[80]** and *EtMag* 213.2 *s.v.* Βρέτας.

[427] The definitions preserved for *xoanon* are often related to those for *agalma* and *bretas*. For example, the *EtGud*, at the end of its entries for those words **[78, 80]**, refers the reader to *xoanon*. Sometimes *xoanon* figures in definitions as a synonym: *e.g.*, *EtGud s.v.* Βρέτας (1) (115.6) **[80]**; *AnecCramer* II.336.30 *s.v.* *ἀγάλματα*; II.351.9 *s.v.* *βρέτας* **[12]**; [Zonaras] *Lex. s.v.* Ἀγάλματα **[370]**; Amm. *s.v.* *φάσμα* [8]; Sch. Ar. *Lys.* 64 **[29]**. *EtMag s.v.* *ἀγάλματα* (= *EtMagAuc s.v.* *ἀγάλματα*; *cf. SymEt* s.v. *ἄγαλμα* **[359]**) remarks that others call *agalma*, *xoanon*; perhaps the entry is related to the entry for *ἀγάλματα* in the *Suda*, where a list of poets and synonyms is given; *cf.* Eustath. *ad.* H. *Il.* 4.144 **[133]**.

[428] Hunger, *Literatur* II, 33–34 for Atticizing reference books.

instance in which an author's name is preserved is Ammonius' entry on *hiera* [**6**], where it is reported that Theopompus included *xoana* among them.[429] Usually, however, it is impossible to determine the source of a particular usage. Pollux, for example, gives this list of things to which men "give service" (*θεραπεύειν*) [**322**]: "*agalmata*, *xoana*, *hede* of the gods, *eikasmata* of the gods, *eikones*, *mimemata*, [*tupomata*], *eide*, *ideiai*. I myself do not believe that *bretas* is a *deikelon*." The reference to *deikela* recalls the later treatise of Porphyry, Περὶ ἀγαλμάτων, in which images of the gods are explained as symbolic *deikela*.[430] Whether any philosophical aspect is reflected in Pollux's list, however, is difficult to say. In his time, the late second century A.D., *xoanon* was widely used as a general term for a statue of a god. The list does little to illuminate what can be determined of usage from other sources.[431]

Conclusions

The ancient definitions of *xoanon* in lexica and etymologica shed little light on the meaning of the word. They rely on tendentious sources, and the information they derive from earlier works gives no picture of actual usage. Their own additions and amplifications are confusing and contradictory. Although *xoanon* does occur in some Byzantine texts, it is clear that its link with the classical past is all but broken.

[429] For Amm. 241 Nickau [**6**]: *supra* pp. 33–34.

[430] Pollux, *On.* I.7 [**322**]: E. Bethe, ed., *Pollucis Onomasticon* (Lexicographi Graeci IX; Leipzig, 1900; repr. Stuttgart, 1967). For Porphyry's Περὶ ἀγαλμάτων: supra p. 158 n. 389.

[431] The following references to *xoana* have come to my attention:

Iamblichus, *Theol. arith.* 8.7.7.

Dedication of a ξόα[ν]ον [ἐπὶ] Αὐ[ι]δίου Κασσίου ὑπατ[ι]κοῦ from a sanctuary called Manâra Henou: *BullEpig* 1934, p. 253. For Avidius Cassius, governor of Syria under Verus: M. Dunand, *Le musée de Soueïda* (Paris, 1934) 96 no. 197. See *supra* p. 109 n. 267. For nearby Phaena (modern Mismiya), "still merely an important village, a *metrocomia*, in the early third century": Jones, *Cities*[2] (*supra* p. 151 n. 364) 286, 288.

12. Conclusions

Xoanon is a well-established term in classical studies for a wooden "cult statue" of great age and little art. Although this definition is generally thought to rest solidly on the evidence of ancient usage, it is not the meaning of the word in the majority of ancient sources. It is possible to follow the changes in the usage of the word from its first appearances in the later fifth century B.C. down through Byzantine times.

In the beginning, the word connotes a high degree of craftsmanship in a variety of objects. Near the end of the fifth century it becomes associated with splendid images of gods. After that time, with rare exceptions, it is restricted to divine representations, and until the end of its history, it is applied to these, regardless of the material, form, style, or age of the image in question. In Hellenistic times literary and non-literary usage begin to diverge, the *xoana* of inscriptions referring in almost all cases to dedications, while in literature the term most frequently applies to images in temples. The word is never very popular; its somewhat surprising adoption as a term for images of gods in general seems to reflect thinking about divine images in the periphery of the Greek world. There is a good chance that Egyptian influence, transmitted through Alexandrian literature both pagan and Judaeo-Christian, is especially significant in this connection. Only in special contexts, such as iconoclastic polemic and antiquarian studies, does the term seem to be given a precise meaning.

The definitions that have been most significant for the modern interpretations of *xoana* are, not surprisingly, the special ones that are spelled out explicitly. They are: the antiquarian definition, as seen in Plutarch and Pausanias, which may reflect a false etymology with *xulinos* perhaps adopted to harmonize with theories about the historical priority of wooden sculpture; and the definitions related to the iconoclastic debate of Graeco-Roman times. The establishment of *xoanon* as a term for the idol of idolatry owes much to Jewish polemic written in Greek; this usage overlaps to some extent with the widespread application of the term to temple images in general. The negative connotations, however, are wholly iconoclastic. A second iconoclastic definition, one obviously at odds with all other attested meanings of the word, makes *xoanon*, derived (correctly) from *xeo*, into a crudely scraped pillar of stone or wood; this definition is put forward by Clement of Alexandria, who aims to disparage the idols of the heathen by showing that they originate in unappealing primitive practice. Clement's definition did not become widespread.

Because the meaning of *xoanon* varies so greatly from author to author, the collection of *xoana* culled from the ancient written sources has almost no archaeological value. The *xoana* do not constitute a coherent or valid group, and information about one cannot be guaranteed to apply to another. Thus, any attempts at a chronological or geographical treatment of literary *xoana* as objects, as if they were monuments with a generic relationship among themselves, are futile. This is a negative conclusion, but a useful negative.

The second conclusion is that the word *xoanon* does not demonstrate the existence of a group of primitive, ancient, wooden cult images. It is therefore not the helpful tool it has long seemed for the investigation of early Greek art. This too is a negative conclusion, but tonic, in its way, as the disappearance of the literary *xoanon* encourages a closer look at its art-historical counterpart, the theoretical primitive wooden cult statue with which Greek sculpture is often thought to have begun.

CHAPTER II

"*XOANA*" AND THE ORIGINS OF GREEK SCULPTURE

1. Introduction

The examination of *xoanon* as it appears in the ancient written sources has shown that the word by itself neither preserves nor presupposes a tradition of primitive wooden cult statues. This fact alone, however, does not prove that such images never existed under some other name or names. The theory of the primitive wooden cult image plausibly accounts not only for very genesis of Greek statuary, but also for the stylistic deviation of surviving preclassical statues from the naturalistic standards of classical times.[1] It is therefore desirable to ask whether the widely held idea of the "*xoanon*," the primitive wooden cult image, is useful for the study of early Greek sculpture.

A significant contribution to the question of *xoana* has been made by H.-V. Herrmann in an article concerning the origin of Greek monumental sculpture.[2] Herrmann advances persuasive arguments against the idea that Greek monumental sculpture began with crude wooden production. He suggests instead that there existed in the seventh century B.C. wooden statues the scale and formal sophistication of which place them securely in the major line of sculptural development; they were fully accomplished statues, that is to say, not mere forerunners. The evidence of the wooden sculpture preserved from that period confirms this view.

Herrmann's discussion brings into sharp focus the contradiction between the material evidence for early Greek sculpture and the prevailing theoretical assumptions about it. While theory postulates the beginning *ex nihilo* of statuary in the seventh century, a growing number of monuments suggests instead a long artistic continuity to which even the idea of "origins" seems inapplicable. Herrmann considers both the idea of the low artistic position of wood and the theory of evolution from aniconic to figural monuments to be notions built by modern scholars on a thin foundation of literary sources selected to conform to prevailing intellectual convictions. The latter theory he calls "a kind of *Kunst-Darwinismus*."[3]

[1] For the *xoanon* in modern scholarship, see *supra* pp. 1–8.

[2] Herrmann, "Entstehung" 35–48; a shorter version of this article appears, with the same title, in *AA* 1974, 636–638.

[3] Herrmann, "Entstehung" 36–39; 37–38 for *Kunst-Darwinismus*. The basis of Darwinian theory has recently begun to come under scrutiny. An article by W.J. Broad, "Metaphor Getting Its Due as a Wellspring of Science," *New York Times*, July 31, 1983, p. 8 E, reports on several analyses of the origin of scientific theories in contemporary social and economic trends: S.S. Schweber has shown that Darwin "immersed himself in the eonomic works of the

Herrmann's analysis of the material evidence for the early stages of Greek monumental sculpture is cogent, and his demonstration of the gap between archaeology and art-historical theory convincing. His conclusions about the role of the ancient sources, however, can be modified. It is possible to show that the modern concept of *xoana* as the origin of Greek sculpture takes its entire framework, and not simply convenient illustrative material, from theories that are already well developed in ancient literature. The following chapter attempts to show why the ancient sources are not reliable, and to point out some ways in which the material evidence for early Greek sculpture supports neither modern nor ancient theoretical concepts.

---

period just prior to his discovery, imbibing the belief that society functions best when individuals are free to compete and struggle to their own advantage"; S.J. Gould argues that whereas Darwin presented his theory of natural selection as the conclusion of a wholly empirical and objective study, in fact "the political economy of the day" influenced him strongly. The identification of the "Eureka!" *topos* of scientific discovery is more convincing than the assertion that immediate political and economic circumstances determined Darwin's theory. There seems reason to believe that a wider stage was set for the various aspects of "evolutionary" thought in the nineteenth century by the historical conceptions that developed in the eighteenth, many of which depend on concepts borrowed wholesale from classical history. See *infra* p. 190 ns. 38, 39.

2. The Dependence of Modern Theories about the Origins of Greek Sculpture on Ancient Testimony

Modern theories about the origin and early development of Greek sculpture depend on explicit ancient testimony for a primitive stage in Greek art. The basic idea of such a development came, in a sense, ready-made to modern attention. It became, and has remained, a standard element of art history for two reasons: first, until recently, the absence of a reasonably complete archaeological record made it necessary to rely almost entirely on literary sources in treating the preclassical periods; and second, it is desirable in principle to use ancient testimony to illuminate the monuments that are preserved. Both reasons are good reasons, but as it happened, the most promising written sources are also those that need the closest scrutiny. The testimony that forms the foundation of modern theory concerning the origin of Greek sculpture—and that in fact so phrased the question in the first place—is the same testimony that offers atypical and biased information about the word *xoanon*: the iconoclastic polemic of Clement, and the antiquarian speculations of Plutarch and Pausanias.

Modern historical study of ancient art begins with Winckelmann, whose treatment of the origin of Greek sculpture has continued to be influential to this day. The first deployment of the sources in question, however, came before Winckelmann, and in a somewhat different context. The outline of the course of Greek and Roman idolatry provided by the patristic authors proved attractive to Christian authors of later ages who, while ostensibly investigating history, could at the same time voice their disapproval of the pagan practices and so manage to comment on their own times; for the veneration of images continues in Christianity to the present, and has never ceased to be questioned.

The following text comes from the English translation of 1721–1722 of a section of Bernard de Montfaucon's *L'antiquité expliquée—Antiquity Explained, and Represented in Sculptures*—which had appeared in 1719. The passage is part of the introduction to the first volume "Concerning the Origin of Idolatry and the Idea that the Pagans had of the Deities":

> It is certain, one of the Principal Causes of Idolatry arose from hence: Men who had very weak and imperfect Ideas of a Divine Nature, erected statues to some great Personages, who had made themselves Famous by their Actions, or by their Inventions, useful to human life; or lastly of those who had gained the Love and Esteem of all them among whom they lived. Every one made Idols according to his own humour, either of Metals or Wood: as the prophet *Isaiah* says, They made Images of part of the same Wood which they used to make a Fire to warm themselves with, adored them, and put their trust in them. They did not know, as *Horace* speaks, whether they should make a Bench or a God of the Trunk of the Tree; but at last resolv'd it should be a God, and then

adored that Wood which they would have sat on, if it had been their Fancy to have made a Bench. The *Greeks* and the *Romans* had a great Number of these Images; tho' *Varro*, as quoted by St. *Austin*, says, the *Romans* during the space of one hundred and seventy Years, from the building of *Rome*, had no Images of their Gods; but after that time they grew into use, and increased to a vast number in *Rome*, and all over the *Roman* empire.[4]

The idea of the weakness of man's conception of "Divine Nature" comes directly from Maximus of Tyre's comments on the frailty of human powers of mental realization (8.2–3) [**168**]. The Euhemeristic idea that images of gods were in fact no more than images of famous people is an iconoclastic *topos* that appears in the Sibylline Oracles (III.721–732) [**173**] and in the *Letter* of Aristeas (135) [**28**], where the idea is attributed to Moses, and mention is made of the reward for inventing things useful for living.[5] The argument that images of gods are made from materials that might just as well have been put to homelier uses is popular in iconoclastic sources, both Jewish and pagan.[6] Varro is quoted here in the version of Augustine, not of Clement.

Montfaucon was a leading patristic scholar of the Benedictine Congregation of St.-Maur, a group which devoted itself in the seventeenth and eighteenth centuries to historical and literary scholarship. His editions of authors such as Origen were renowned, and it is little wonder that he is thoroughly familiar with sources relevant to the question of idolatry.

In 1738 Abbé Banier produced a work on ancient mythology in which he frankly and vigorously expresses his disapproval of "idolatry." The contemporary English translation carried to another country the Abbé's faith in the importance of his study, "though 'tis our happiness not to live in one of those Ages, when almost the whole World was plunged in an Abyss of Idolatry."[7]

The following passages are quoted from the fourth chapter of Banier's third book, "Of the Progress of Idolatry":

[4] B. de Montfaucon, tr. D. Humphreys, *Antiquity Explained, and Represented in Sculptures* (3 vols., London, 1721–1722; repr. New York and London, 1976). The passage quoted is from the Introduction, I, iv–v (unpaged). For Montfaucon: *ODCC*² *s.v.*

[5] *Supra* p. 88 and n. 211.

[6] Isaiah 44.14–20 (*supra* p. 101 n. 245). Horace, *Sat.* 1.8. *Cf.* Philo, *De vit. cont.* 7 [**296**] for the ignoble destinies of material from which idols are made: *supra* p. 101 and n. 245; Clem.Al. *Protr.* 2.21 P. [**43**] and Athenag. *Leg.* 4 [**38**] for the burning of a wooden Heracles by Diagoras to cook dinner—the hero's thirteenth labor. It is difficult to determine the origin of the conceit in Horace; see E. Fraenkel, *Horace* (Oxford, 1957) 121–122 for the "*olim*" type of introduction in epigrams, and for the class of Priapus epigrams.

[7] Anonymous English translation of Antoine Banier, *The Mythology and Fables of the Ancients Explain'd from History* (London, 1739–40; repr. in the series *The Renaissance and the Gods*, ed. S. Orgel, New York and London, 1976) I, v.

The first Race of Men, some time after their Dispersion, were extremely rude; even the *Greeks*, who became afterwards so polite, were no better at first, if we credit *Diodorus Siculus*, than those whom they were wont to call *Barbarians*. We are not therefore to imagine that Idolatry, in its first setting out, was a study'd system; that Theology was then encumber'd with that Apparatus of Ceremonies they added to it in after-times. Nothing could be more simple, nor at the same time more gross, than the Religion of the primitive Idolaters. . . . The *Scythians*, according to *Clemens Alexandrinus*, in ancient times adored a Scymitar; the *Arabians*, a rough unhewn Stone; and among other Nations, they contented themselves with erecting a Trunk of a Tree, or some Pillar without Ornament. These Pillars they called *Zoara*, because they were peeled when of Timber, and a little smoothed when they were of Stone. In the *Orkneys*, the image of *Diana* was a Log of Wood unwrought; and at *Cytheron*, the *Juno Thespia* was nothing but a Trunk of a Tree cut off; that at *Samos*, but a simple Plank; and so of others.[8]

This section comes directly from Clement's *Protrepticus* (4.40 P.) [44], where the explanation of idolatry reflects the old Greek idea of barbarians as representative of the primitive, early state of mankind, as well as Clement's desire to strip the artistic gloss from idolatry by revealing its origins in low and unappealing practices. The same idea appears in a passage of his *Stromateis* (1.164.1) [47]: "Before, then, the invention of the designs of *agalmata*, the ancients, setting up columns, worshipped them as *aphidrumata* of God."

Banier continues:

At first Sculpture itself was extremely rude. . . . Consequently we may suppose, that the first Statues of the Gods, tho' modelled by this new Art, were still exceeding coarse. The Legs and the Arms were not separated, but joined to the rest of the Matter which they made use of to the Formation of the Figure. They had the Eyes shut, and at most the Arms hanging down, and as it were glued to the Body, and the Feet joined; neither Expression, nor Attitude, nor Gesture. They were mostly square, and like mis-shapen Figures, that ended like those figures called *Termes*. . . . They continued in this state, at least in the West, until *Daedalus*. . . . I shall only say, that he had the art of giving to his Statues, Eyes, Feet, and Hands.[9]

Banier has picked up Clement's remark in the later part of the passage of the *Protrepticus* (4.41 P.) [44] on the origin of idolatry in which he links the invention of art with ever greater folly. The subject of the invention of art leads inevitably to a consideration of Daedalus, about whose achievements there is a considerable amount of ancient testimony—which Banier has

[8] Banier, *Mythology* I, 192–193. Note I of p. 193 cites Clement's "*Orat. ad Gentes.*"

[9] Banier, *Mythology* I, 247; Book III, Ch. IX, "*Of the Statues of the Gods, and of the Manner of representing them.*"

consulted, as is clear from both this passage and his subsequent treatment of the artist:

> nothing signalized him [Daedalus] so much as the Art of making Statues, wherein he succeeded so well, that they were said to be animated, to see and walk: A Fable whose Foundation is not what *Aristotle* alledges, that he made Pieces of Clockwork that walked by means of Quick-silver which he put within them, but that before him the Statues of the *Greeks* were extremely rude, without Eyes, Arms and Legs; they were nothing but shapeless Blocks of Stone, as are still to be seen in the Cabinets of the Curicus. *Daedalus*, as we learn from *Suidas*, *Themistius*, and *Palephatus*, made them Faces according to the Life, formed Arms to them, and separated their Legs, which made him be universally admired.[10]

Banier's account depends largely on the discussion of Daedalus by Diodorus Siculus, an author he quotes in an earlier passage. Diodorus' is today the best known testimony about Daedalus (4.76.1–3) [**59**]:

> In natural ability towering far above all other men, he [*sc.* Daedalus] cultivated the building art, the making of *agalmata*, and the working of stone. He was also the inventor of many devices which contributed to the advancement of his art and built works in many regions of the inhabited world which arouse the wonder of men. In the carving of his *agalmata* he so far excelled all other men that later generations invented the story about him that the *agalmata* of his making were quite like living beings; they could see, they said, and walk, and, in a word, preserved so well the characteristics of the entire body that the statue made by him seemed to be a living being. And since he was the first to represent the open eye and to fashion the legs separated and the arms and hands extended, it was natural that he should have received the admiration of mankind; for the craftsmen before him had carved their *agalmata* with the eyes closed, having hands hanging and attached to the sides.

This explanation enjoyed considerable popularity in antiquity. It is standard in late reference books; for instance, this gloss on the proverb "works of Daedalus" appears in the rhetorical dictionary *Lexeis Rhetorikai* [**10**]:

> For this Daedalus was the first, in making *agalmata*, who carried one foot over the other, and opened up the eyes, and stretched forth the hands; and there were conjectures that he made living works. For before him, *agalmata* were constructed solidly and closed to the sides in a simple way.

Tzetzes, in the twelfth century A.D., gives a similar account (*Chil.* I.19.536–541) [**366**]:

> They say that Daedalus' works moved in this way: before the time of Daedalus they produced *andriantes* that were handless, footless, eyeless. Daedalus

[10] Banier, *Mythology* III, 520; Book II, Ch. X, "*The History of* Dedalus, *and of the Labyrinth of* Crete."

[11] *Lexeis Rhetorikai s.v.* Δαιδάλου ποιημάτων: *AnecBekker* I.240.16 [**10**]. Something seems to have gone wrong with the last sentence: *cf.* D.S. 4.76.3 [**59**].

was the first to separate the hands, feet, fingers, and to arrange the eyelids and other things. Whence grew up the myth, that the works of Daedalus moved.[11]

The explanation even found its way into a more common awareness. For example, Philostratus, in describing the famous statue of Memnon, incorporates it somewhat ambiguously (*VA* 6.4) **[299]**:

The *agalma* faces the morning sun, has no beard, is of black stone, has both feet closed together in the fashion of *agalma*-making in the time of Daedalus, and the hands pressed down on the throne, for it sits in readiness for getting up.

The similarity of expression (ξυμβεβηκέναι δὲ τὼ πόδε ἄμφω) suggests that Philostratus has some knowledge of the accounts of Daedalus' achievements.[12]

The Aristotelian fable with which Banier disagrees belongs to another rationalizing tradition. In Aristophanes and Plato, Daedalus' images move almost by magic, and must be bound to prevent their running away. Aristotle accounts for their mobility by the suggestion that they are powered by quicksilver (*De an.* 1.3, 406 b 9) **[30]**:

Some say that the soul in fact moves the body, in which it is, in the same way in which it moves itself. So, for example, Democritus; and herein he resembled Philippus, the comic poet, who tells us that Daedalus endowed the wooden Aphrodite with motion, simply by pouring in quicksilver: this is very similar to what Democritus says.[13]

Banier, however, prefers the historical kind of rationalizing account. Some of these explanations appear in commentaries, such as these Platonic scholia:

Joannes Tzetzes, *Chiliades* I.19.536–541 **[366]**: T. Kiessling, ed., *Ioannis Tzetzae Historiarum Variarum Chiliades* (Leipzig, 1826).

[12] *Cf.* the translations of V. Mumprecht, ed., tr., *Philostratus. Das Leben des Apollonios von Tyana* (Munich and Zurich, 1983) 585 ("nach der Bildweise des Daidalos") and of C.P. Jones, tr., and G.W. Bowersock, ed., *Philostratus. Life of Apollonius* (Penguin, 1970) 139 ("in the style of Daedalus' statues"). D. del Como, ed., *Vita di Apollonio di Tiana* (Biblioteca Adelphi 82; Milan, 1978) 261 rightly gives "I suoi piedi riuniti come nella statuaria dei tempi di Dedalo." *Cf.* Philostr. *Im.* 1.7. For the date of the *Vita* c. A.D. 220: Bowersock, *Philostratus* 9.

[13] Ar. fr. 194 Kock = Hesych. *s.v.* Δαιδάλεια **[142]**. Philippus *ad* Eubulus fr. 22 Kock = Arist. *de An.* 1.3, 406 b 9; Themistius *ad loc.* **[363]**. *Cf.* Philoponus *ad loc.* **[153]**: *supra* pp. 165–166. Plato, *Euthyphro* 11 B–E **[308]** and *Meno* 97 D–E **[310]** and the related scholia **[309, 311]** are long passages about the need to fasten Daedalean images. See also Sch. E. *Hec.* 838 **[86]** for several approaches to Daedalus' works.

With respect to the practical questions raised by the use of quicksilver, it may be of interest to note a Chinese method described and illustrated by Muschenbroek and reported in J. Beckmann, *A History of Inventions, Discoveries, and Origins*, translated by W. Johnson; 4th ed. revised by W. Francis and J.W. Griffith (London, 1846) II, 134: "What the author [Aristotle] here means I cannot comprehend; but I do not imagine that this Venus threw itself topsy-turvy backwards, like the Chinese puppets."

Sch. Pl. *Meno* 97 D [**311**]: In ancient times craftsmen shaped *zoia* that had closed-up eyes and feet that were not separated, but were set up with their feet together. Daedalus, the finest *agalma*-maker, coming along, was the first who spread apart their eyelids, so that they seemed to see, and set their feet apart, so that they were held to walk; and because of this they were tied, so that they might not flee; since in truth they had now become alive.

Arethas *ad* Pl. *Euthyphro* 11 C [**309**]: . . . Daedalus the Athenian was the most celebrated ever of *andrias*-makers. And he was the first to fashion an *agalma* with the feet apart, those before him having made *brete* whose two feet were joined together. And indeed from this the saying about him is offered by many people, that his masterpieces go about and move, which even now Socrates, jokingly, brings up to Euthyphro.[14]

The dependence of these accounts on Diodorus is clear. They are especially interesting because they give not just information about Daedalus, but also a historical outline of the development of early sculpture. It is this history, quite as much as the facts about Daedalus, that Banier has extracted from the authors he mentions:

Suda, *s.v.* Works of Daedalus [**354**]: with reference to consummate productions of art. Since the ancient craftsmen made the eyes closed up, but Daedalus opened them and separated the feet. And Homer says "who knew how to make all *daedala* with his hands; for Pallas Athena loved him most of all; and who had crafted the even-balanced ships for Alexandros."[15]

Themistius, *Oration* 26.316 a–b [**362**]: Before Daedalus, not only were herms worked in rectangular form, but also all the rest of *andriantes*. Daedalus, because he was the first to separate the two feet of *agalmata*, was thought to make living things.[16]

Palaephatus, *De Incredibilis* 22 [**186**]: Concerning Daedalus. They say about Daedalus that he made *agalmata* that walked of their own accord. But it seems to me impossible that an *andrias* could walk by itself. But the truth is such [as follows]. The *andrias*-makers and the *agalma*-makers in the past made *andriantes* having even the feet joined together. Daedalus was the first

[14] For the scholia attributed to Arethas, Archbishop of Caesarea early in the tenth century: W.C. Greene, "The Platonic Scholia," *TAPA* 68 (1937) 185–186, 192–193. R.S. Bluck, ed., *Plato's Meno* (Cambridge, 1961) 410 *ad* 97 d 5, asserts that the quicksilver of Philippus and the *mechanai*, machines or devices (he suggests clockwork) of Callistratus' *Ekphrasis* 8 "are of course simply rationalistic explanations of the legends about his [Daedalus'] statues 'moving'. The true explanation is probably that given by Diodorus and our scholiast."

[15] *Suda s.v.* Δαιδάλου ποιήματα [**354**]: Adler II.12.110. The quotation from Homer is from the *Iliad*, 5.60–62, and concerns the smith Phereclus.

[16] Themistius, *Or.* 26.316 a–b [**362**]: H. Schenkl, G. Downey, and A.F. Norman, eds., *Themistii Orationes quae supersunt* II (Leipzig, 1971). For Themistius' paraphrase of *de An.* 1.3: L. Spengel, ed., *Themistii Paraphrases Aristotelis librorum quae supersunt* II (Leipzig, 1866) 34–35. Themistius wrote in the fourth century A.D.

who made the one foot separated [*sc.* from the other]. But men said, "This *agalma* that Daedalus made walks around and does not stand still," and even now we speak thus. And there are men depicted as fighting, and horses as galloping, and a ship as being tossed by storms.[17]

The herms and herm-like monuments in collections of antiquities seem to have convinced Banier of the reliability of the ancient testimony. Accordingly, he accepts the ancient judgment of Daedalus and the historical outline that accompanies it.

Banier's method is clear. He has assembled the ancient texts that give explicit information on the subjects of his interest, and accepted both the theories they offer and the evidence they give for those theories. Banier does not recognize the theories as theories, however, but takes Clement's version of the origin of idolatry and the rationalizing accounts of the legend of Daedalus as good solid fact. The authority and coherence of the ancient sources carries over to their new context, where they provide the history of a vanished world.

Although Banier's purpose was to explain the development of pagan idolatry, by following the arguments of his sources he produced at the same time a history of early Greek sculpture. The two subjects are not always completely distinct in the texts that offer developmental theories. It is not surprising, then, that the same texts formed the basis of the first deliberate studies of Greek art. It must be remembered that the corpus of ancient monuments was far less accessible than it is today, when the collection and documentation of archaeological material have made large amounts of it easily available. The pioneers of the eighteenth century had necessarily to rely on literature for their view of the ancient world, and there was no reason not to trust the sources or look to them for guidance and understanding of the monuments that had survived. So it was that the first attempts at a systematic historical treatment of ancient (and especially Greek) art borrowed both approach and premises from literary testimony. The treatise that has proved most influential for the study of ancient art, Winckelmann's *Geschichte der Kunst des Altertums* of 1764, depends completely for its

[17] Palaephatus, *De Incredibilis* 22 [186]: A. Westermann, ed., *Μυθόγραφοι. Scriptores Poeticae Historiae Graeci* (Brunswick, 1843) 286.3. For Palaephatus, dated perhaps to the fourth century B.C.: *OCD*[2] *s.v.* This passage, in form unquestionably an epitome, may not actually reflect a fourth-century B.C. explanation. It differs from the contemporary, mechanistic, explanation of Aristotle and the fifth-century magical idea of images; but these may simply have served the needs of the texts, and the absence of a historical explanation in authors before Diodorus may be an accident of preservation. More telling, however, is the close similarity of the passage to the late versions of the Diodorus-type explanation. It seems possible that the passage given to Palaephatus shows the influence of the later commentaries. The first sentence stands as a gloss on its own, and the part beginning "But it seems to me impossible" may be an addition.

discussion of the origin of sculpture on the sources that so obligingly offer explicit comments, from theory to evidence, on the question.[18]

Winckelmann believes that the art of all nations began in the same way and proceeded along the same line of development. Thus, after some desultory remarks about the early images of the Chaldeans and Egyptians, he sets forth in detail the origins of Greek art, using it at the same time as the model for the universal development of all art. "Among the Greeks the first outlines of these figures were simple, and, for the most part, straight lines; and it is probable that, in the infancy of art, whether among the Egyptians, Etruscans, or Greeks, there was no difference in this respect; and this probability is also confirmed by the testimony of the ancient authors."[19]

He begins with the simplest forms. "For there were already thirty gods worshipped in a visible fashion at the time when one had not yet represented them in the form of men, and was satisfied with indicating them by means of an unworked log or squared stones, as the Arabs and Amazons did. So the Juno at Thespiae and the Diana at Icarus were shaped."[20]

Pausanias, Clement, and Apollonius are the sources of this information. Pausanias discusses the thirty stones (7.22.4) [**251**]: "Closest to the *agalma* stand about thirty square stones; these the people of Pharae revere, selecting for each one the name of some god. In a still older age, among all the Greeks, too, rough stones received the honors of gods, instead of *agalmata*." Clement (*Protr.* 4.40 P.) [**44**] says that "in ancient times, then, the Scythians used to worship the dagger, the Arabians their sacred stone. . . .

[18] J.J. Winckelmann, *Geschichte der Kunst des Altertums* (Vienna, 1934). Editions after 1764 and translations differ from the first edition in the extent of additional explanatory and illustrative material. The edition of W. Senff (Weimer, 1964) 491–502, gives an index of named sources among which do not appear, for example, Clement or Maximus, although Winckelmann's dependence on them is obvious; in the Dresden edition of 1764, however, Winckelmann provided a full index of books cited: see the facsimile of this edition, J.J. Winckelmann, *Kunsttheoretische Schriften* 5 (Studien zur deutschen Kunstgeschichte 343; Baden-Baden and Strasbourg, 1966) XLI–XLVIII. J. Lessing's edition of 1870 supplies many of these references: *Johann Joachim Winckelmann's Geschichte der Kunst des Alterthums* (Berlin, 1870). The English translation of G.H. Lodge, *The History of Ancient Art, translated from the German of John Winckelmann* (Boston, 1872), exists in several editions with different paginations. I follow the Boston edition of 1872. In the following notes the references to the 1934 German text and the English translation are made simply to Winckelmann and Lodge respectively.

[19] "Die ersten Züge dieser Gestalten bei den Griechen waren einfältig und mehrenteils gerade Linien, und unter Ägyptern, Etrurien und Griechen wird beim Ursprunge der Kunst unter jedem Volke kein Unterschied gewesen sein; wie dieses auch die alten Skribenten bezeugen. . . . " Winckelmann 28; Lodge I, 138.

[20] "Denn es waren schon dreissig Gottheiten sichtbar verehrt, da man sie noch nicht in menschlicher Gestalt gebildet hatte und sich begnügte, dieselben durch einen unbearbeiteten Klotz oder durch viereckige Steine, wie die Araber und Amazonen taten, anzudeuten. So war die Juno und [1764: zu] Thespis und die Diana zu Icarus gestaltet." Winckelmann 26–27; *cf.* Lodge, I, 136.

Certainly the *agalma* of Artemis in Icarus was an unwrought stock, and that of Cithaeronian Hera in Thespiae was a felled tree-trunk." (The ellipsis marks the section explaining *xoana* as ancient wooden and stone scraped pillars.) Apollonius of Rhodes speaks of "a holy black stone . . . to which, in the past, all the Amazons prayed" (II.1172–1173).[21]

Winckelmann offers more examples. "Diana Patroa and Jupiter Milichus at Corinth were, like the oldest Venus at Paphos, nothing else than a kind of column. Bacchus was worshipped in the form of a column and Eros himself and the Graces were merely represented by stones."[22]

Pausanias, again, mentions the Artemis and the Zeus. "Beyond the *heroion* of Aratus is an altar to Isthmian Poseidon, and there is a Zeus Meilichios, and an Artemis named Patroa, made without any craft at all; Meilichios looks like a pyramid, she like a column" (2.9.6) **[205]**. Maximus of Tyre illustrates his discussion of idolatry by listing various natural and man-made objects worshipped by various peoples; directly after describing the Arabian stone he notes that "by the Paphians Aphrodite is honored; but you cannot compare her monument to anything else than a white pyramid, the material of which is unknown" (*Diss.* 8.8) **[169]**. Clement quotes Euripides' passage on "a column decked with ivy, of the god Evohe," and cites an oracle saying "a column to the Thebans [is] joy-inspiring Dionysus" (*Strom.* I.163.4–5) **[47]**.[23] Pausanias says of Eros that "of the gods, the Thespians honor Eros especially, from the beginning, and their most *palaion agalma* is a rough stone" (9.27.1) **[276]**.[24] He reports that at Orchomenos "the most *archaion hieron* is of the Graces. They worship the rocks most of all, and [say]

[21] For the *xoana* of Clement: *supra* pp. 127–133. Also for the Arabian stone: Max.Tyr. 8.8 **[169]**: "The Arabians, indeed, venerate a god whom I do not know; but the *agalma* of him which I have seen is a quadrangular stone." Arnobius' version **[31]** of Clem.Al. *Protr.* 4.40 P. **[44]** contains one of the few instances in which he differs from his source. Whereas Clement simply calls the Arabian stone a *lithos*, Arnobius notes that it is unshaped: *informem lapidem*: *Adv.Gen.* 6.11. H. Bryce and H. Campbell, *The Seven Books of Arnobius Adversus Gentes* (Edinburgh, 1871) *ad loc.* Ap.Rhod. *Arg.* 2.1172–1173: εἴσω δὲ μέλας λίθος ἠρήρειστο / ἱερός, ᾧ † ποτε πᾶσαι † Ἀμαζόνες εὐχετόωντο (H. Fraenkel, ed., *Apollonii Rhodii Argonautica* [Oxford, 1970]).

[22] "Diana Patroa und Jupiter Milichus zu Korinth waren, wie die älteste Venus zu Paphos, nichts anders als eine Art Säulen. Bacchus wurde in Gestalt einer Säule verehrt, und selbst die Liebe und die Grazien wurden bloss durch Steine vorgestellt." Winckelmann 27; *cf.* Lodge I, 136. Winckelmann adds here that because of this practice, the word *kion*, "pillar," continued to mean "statue." S. Broc, "L'hermès d'Hiéron à Delphes et le nom de l'hermès en grec," *REG* 76 (1963) 39–51, argues that *kion* was used for herms, citing the lines from the *Phoronis* as evidence (46). On the basis of Themistius, *Or.* 26 **[362]**, she argues that "When statuary began, statues, blocks of stone summarily chipped away, retained the form of a column or pillar at the base" (45). Such a supposition is not necessary to explain the application of *kion* to herms, which is convincingly argued from passages in Plato, Plutarch, and Lucian.

[23] For the Dionysus of Thebes: Schachter, *Cults* 1, 185–192.

[24] For the Eros of Thespiae: Schachter, *Cults* 1, 216–219.

that they fell to Eteocles from heaven. The *agalmata* made with form were dedicated in my time, and they too are of stone" (9.38.1) **[277]**.[25]

Winckelmann concludes the section on the earliest monuments by describing the *dokana* of Sparta. "Among the Spartans, Castor and Pollux were in the form of two parallel blocks of wood, connected by two cross sticks; and this primitive mode of representing the twins is seen in the sign II, by which they were denoted in the zodiac."[26]

Plutarch's remarks on the *dokana* are Winckelmann's source. "The Spartans call the *archaia aphidrumata* of the Dioscuri '*dokana*': they consist of two parallel stocks joined by two other transverse ones placed across them, and this common and indivisible character of the *anathema* seems entirely suitable to the brotherly love of the gods" (*De frat. amor.* 1) **[318]**.[27]

It is important to note that almost none of the various sources from which Winckelmann takes his information about the earliest Greek images is a simple description of a monument, devoid of commentary. The texts are, on the contrary, either actual presentations of the theory of the aniconic origin of idolatry, such as Clement's, or descriptions of pieces to which are attached explicit statements of the author's belief in their antiquity, such as Pausanias' and Plutarch's. Winckelmann, like the writers on pagan antiquity who preceded him, has accepted the ancient testimonia at face value, and has reproduced the scheme of development that they advance, using not only their evidence, but also their theories.

Winckelmann's next comments are of great interest. He asserts that the semi-iconic herm was the next step toward fully representational statues. "In time, heads were placed on these stones; among many others there was such a Neptune in Tricoloni, and a Jupiter in Tegea, both in Arcadia; for in this land more than anywhere else among the Greeks they adhered to the oldest form in art."[28]

[25] For the Charites of Orchomenos: Schachter, *Cults* 1, 140–144.

[26] "Kastor und Pollux hatten bei den Spartanern die Gestalt von zwei Parallelhölzern, welche durch zwei Querhölzer verbunden waren; und diese uralte Bildung derselben erscheint in dem Zeichen II, wodurch diese Zwillinge in dem Tierkreise angedeutet werden." Winckelmann 27; Lodge I, 136–137.

[27] For the *dokana*: M.C. Waites, "The Meaning of the 'Dokana'," *AJA* 23 (1919) 1–18; Cook, *Zeus* I, 767 n. 1; F. Salviat, "Religion populaire et timbres amphoriques; Hermès, Hélène et les ΔOKANA," *BCH* 88 (1964) 492–495. For Sparta Museum no. 588, a relief of the fifth century B.C. with *dokana*: M.N. Tod and A.J.B. Wace, *A Catalogue of the Sparta Museum* (Oxford, 1906) 193 and fig. 68; 114–116 for the *dokana*.

[28] "Auf besagte Steine wurden mit Zeit Köpfe gesetzt; unter vielen anderen war ein solcher Neptunus zu Tricoloni und ein Jupiter zu Tegea, beide in Arkadien: denn in diesem Lande war man unter den Griechen mehr als anderswo bei der ältesten Gestalt in der Kunst geblieben." Winckelmann 27; *cf.* Lodge I, 137. Winckelmann also notes that "among the Greeks, square stones with heads were called, as is well known, Hermae, that is, large stones." His own note refers to the *Suda s.v.* *ἕρμα· λίθος μέγιστος* (Adler II, 411.3020; *cf.* 3021–3022, 3026).

Pausanias, once again, is Winckelmann's source of information. Each of the gods he mentions is said by Pausanias to have an *agalma tetragonon*, a "square image" (8.35.6; 8.48.6 [**269**]; also 8.32.1 and 8.39.6). Pausanias also notes when he mentions the Zeus that "the Arcadians appear to me to be exceedingly fond of this [*sc.* the square] *schema*" (8.48.6) [**269**].

Winckelmann's idea that herms were the middle step between aniconic figures and figural statues has some explicit backing from ancient testimony.[29] Themistius, as has just been seen from his comments on the rectangular form of all *andriantes* before Daedalus [**362**], offers similar information.

Winckelmann follows the ancient traditions in placing Daedalus among the earliest artists. In a later chapter he says that "art was practiced by Daedalus already in the most ancient times, and still in the times of Pausanias there remained images carved of wood from the hand of this famous artist; and he says that their appearance, in spite of all their crudeness, had something of the divine."[30] Here he follows Pausanias, who gives his verdict on the statues of Daedalus after seeing a naked *xoanon* of Heracles in Corinth (2.4.5) [**203**]: " . . . they say it is the craft of Daedalus. Daedalus made things of such a kind, while they are somewhat strange to the eye, still, something divine is also noticeable in them."

Continuing his account of early Greek statuary, Winckelmann describes the achievement of Daedalus in great detail, and stresses his reliance on ancient sources. "Finally Daedalus, according to the most common opinion, began to separate the lower halves of these columnar images into the form of legs; and since it was not understood how to produce an entire human figure from stone, this artist worked in wood, and from him the first statues are said to have received the name Daedali."[31]

[29] Lodge, I, 418 n. 4, cites the comment by Fea (an Italian translator of Winckelmann) on this passage: "Tzetzes (*Chiliad.* XII, *Hist.* 429, v. 593) says that every statue was termed Hermes." The passage, however, is this [**367**]: Ἑρμῆς καὶ σύμπας ἀνδριάς καὶ ὁ σωρὸς τῶν λίθων (Hermes both whole *andrias* and heap of stones); T. Kiessling, ed., *Ioannis Tzetzae Historiarum Variarum Chiliades* (Leipzig, 1826) XII.429.591, page 463. The title of this section is Ἡ περὶ τοῦ Ἑρμοῦ Ἀγοραίου προτυπώματος (The [history] concerning the design of Hermes Agoraios), and so the sense seems rather to be that Hermes is represented by both statues and heaps of stones. The etymology *herma*–Hermes is now doubted: L. Baumbach, "The Mycenaean Contribution to the Study of Greek Religion in the Bronze Age," *SMEA* 20 (1979) 148–149.

[30] "Die Kunst wurde von dem Dädalus an schon in den ältesten Zeiten geübt, und von dieses berühmten Künstlers Hand waren noch zu den Pausanias Zeiten Bildnisse in Holz geschnitzt übrig, und er sagt, dass ihr Anblick bei aller ihrer Unförmlichkeit etwas Göttliches gehabt habe." Winckelmann 296; *cf.* Lodge II, 176.

[31] "Endlich fing Dädalus an, wie die gemeinste Meinung ist, die unterste Hälfte dieser Bildsäulen in Gestalt der Beine voneinander zu sondern; und weil man nicht verstand, aus Stein eine ganze menschliche Figur hervorzubringen, so arbeitete dieser Künstler in Holz,

Pausanias asserts his belief that the statues of the past were all made of wood when he describes the *hieron* of Apollo Lykios in Argos (2.19.3) [**213**]: "The *agalma* in our time was made by Attalus, an Athenian, but in the beginning both the *naos* and the *xoanon* were dedicated by Danaus; for I believe that then they were all *xoana*, and especially the Egyptian ones." In Pausanias' opinion, however, the manufacture of wooden images preceded the career of Daedalus: ". . . long ago, people called *xoana* '*daedala*.' I believe that they called them so even before Daedalus, son of Palamon, was born at Athens, and I think Daedalus was a surname subsequently given to him from the *daedala*, and not a name bestowed on him at birth" (9.3.2) [**271**]. Winckelmann, in contrast, follows the "great man" line of thought, giving the canonical account of the achievements of Daedalus found in Diodorus and other sources.

Thus it is directly from the written sources of antiquity that Winckelmann takes his outline of the beginning of Greek sculpture. That his approach to art is fundamentally literary is only to be expected, given the emphasis placed by the scholarship of his age on the close study of ancient texts and the contrastingly haphazard scattering of actual monuments that could be studied first-hand. In his later "Notes," Winckelmann says that "My greatest satisfaction in elucidating works of ancient art has been when they enabled me to explain or amend an ancient author."[32] The great aim of Winckelmann's work is to show the expression of cultural ideals in art, especially the ideals of classical civilization. Because those ideals were known to his world almost exclusively through literature, it is not surprising that his attitude toward the ancient sources is uncritical. Winckelmann shares little of the aggressive scepticism of the contemporary philologists, whose task was to wring sense from texts full of spurious lines and unsound emendations. His contribution is not primarily the ferreting out of restorations and forgeries; these are matters secondary to his sublime conviction that art, too, is an expression of culture. For Winckelmann there was no question of founding a history of ancient art on purely empirical observation of the monuments alone. Nor had he any reason to question the

---

und von ihm sollen die ersten Statuen den namen Dädali bekommen haben." Winckelmann 27; *cf.* Lodge I, 138.

[32] Lodge I, 126. H. Meyer and J. Schulze, eds., *Winckelmann's Werke* 3. *Geschichte der Kunst des Alterthums* I (Dresden, 1909) XXXII: "Mein grösstes Vergnügen in Erläuterung der Werke alter Kunst ist gewesen, wenn ich durch dieselbe einen alten Scribenten erläutern oder verbessern können." The secondary position of art itself in Winckelmann's writings has often been recognized: *e.g.*, D. Irwin, ed., *Winckelmann. Writings on Art* (London and New York, 1972) 4, 53. The same tendency can be seen in antiquarian writing contemporary with Winckelmann's: *e.g.*, J. Spence, *Polymetis. An Enquiry concerning the Agreement between the Works of the Roman Poets, and the remains of the antient Artists* (London, 1747).

fundamental reliability of his sources. His *History* therefore rests confidently on the traditions of the ancients.

It is important to recognize the extent of Winckelmann's dependence on ancient literary testimony, because his version of the origin of sculpture is similar enough to theories of historical and cultural development widespread in his time to raise the possibility that the ancient sources are secondary, if convenient, elements in a scheme that developed independently. In this case, Winckelmann's *History* would be analogous to the *Kunst-Darwinismus* of the nineteenth century as seen by Herrmann. One likely comparison that comes to mind is Vico's theory of the development of cultures. No link between Winckelmann and Vico can be demonstrated, however, and there are differences between the theories of the two writers that show that the ancient literary sources are the direct inspiration for Winckelmann's discussion of Greek sculpture.[33]

There is a fundamental difference between the causes of cultural development as conceived by Winckelmann and Vico. The most striking is Winckelmann's emphasis on the importance of climate in the development of cultural characteristics, an idea later elaborated by Herder. This idea does not appear in Vico. Its absence is symptomatic of Vico's general conception of early history, which is exclusively concerned with internal social processes—language, law, customs—set on a universal but curiously empty stage. Winckelmann's early people live vigorously in a well-realized natural world; in contrast, Vico never discusses cultural features as concrete as the fine arts.[34]

Other sources than Vico seem more likely to have influenced Winckelmann. One idea that he and Vico do have in common, the independent development of cultures as opposed to the idea of diffusion, is by no means unique to Vico. It is set forth very strongly, for instance, by Shaftesbury, who also does not seem to have been influenced by Vico.[35] Winckelmann's

[33] Giambattistia Vico presented his theory of the universal development of culture in *La scienza nuova* of 1725 and two considerably different editions (*La scienza nuova seconda*) of 1730 and, posthumously, 1744. P. Kidson, "The Figural Arts," in M.I. Finley, ed., *The Legacy of Greece. A New Appraisal* (Oxford, 1981) 402, in discussing eighteenth-century approaches to Greek art, can say at most that Vico "would almost certainly have approved of his [Winckelmann's] approach."

[34] For Winckelmann's discussion of the effect of climate on art: Lodge I, 156–166. For the absence of any consideration of climate in Vico: R.T. Clark, Jr., "Herder, Cesarotti and Vico," *Studies in Philology* 44 (1947) 656, and also for Du Bos, a "geographical determinist" whose *Réflexions critiques sur la poésie et la peinture* of 1719 received wide and immediate recognition; Winckelmann mentions Du Bos (Lodge I, 109) in another context. See also I. Berlin, *Vico and Herder* (New York, 1976) 148.

[35] For disbelief in the diffusion of culture expressed by Shaftesbury and Winckelmann (*cf.* Vico *N.S.* 146): G.A. Wells, "Vico and Herder," *Vico Symposium* 100. For the absence of any

concept of the growth of artistic style from crude youth to accomplished maturity has been traced to Vasari, and from him back to Cicero.[36] Even more significant, the entire outline of the evolution of sculpture from aniconism appears in Banier in 1738, long before any Vichian influence can be found in France.[37] Banier's discussion, too, relies on the ancient theories of idolatry. Finally, similarities in the various historical schemes can be explained by their common, ancient, sources. It has long been recognized that Vico adopted the cyclic theory of history directly from Greek and Roman historians.[38] Some scholars have drawn attention to the fact that he accepts certain ancient theories, and not merely facts, without exposing their biases and unreliability, as is his usual practice. His wholehearted acceptance of some of his ancient sources, especially the Christians, has also been noted. Students of Vico have recognized that certain of his historical conclusions are not his own "inductive generalizations," and that in many ways his methodology is deductive.[39] Although in many ways his work is revolutionary, in his use of the ancient sources Vico appears to have followed the custom of his age. Winckelmann's complete acceptance of the ancient testimony is therefore not anomalous, but is wholly in line with the approach of his contemporaries.

Winckelmann's introductory chapters on the origins of art have a piecemeal quality; geographic determinism coexists uneasily with more universally oriented theories. His treatment of the early stages of Greek sculpture in fact stands out as an independent section, and reflects his reliance on the literary sources of antiquity. This literary bias is the key element in the first modern theories about the development of Greek sculpture. The evolutionary framework was not built by arranging facts scattered in the sources to fit a preconceived pattern. Instead, it resulted from

---

discernible influence of Vico on Shaftesbury, or *vice versa*: R. Wellek, "The Supposed Influence of Vico on England and Scotland in the Eighteenth Century," *Vico Symposium* 216.

[36] For Winckelmann's concept of stylistic development as traceable to Vasari and ultimately to Cicero: P. Gay, *The Enlightenment: An Interpretation* II (New York, 1969) 295–296.

[37] For the absence of Vico's influence in France until the nineteenth century: A. Pons, "Vico and French Thought," *Vico Symposium* 165–171.

[38] For Vico's adoption of the cyclic theory from ancient sources: D. Bidney, "Vico's New Science of Myth," *Vico Symposium* 260–264, esp. 263.

[39] For Vico's "pious and utterly uncritical" attitude toward "the data of Hebrew-Christian history": H. White, "The Tropics of History: The Deep Structure of the *New Science*," in G. Tagliacozzo and D.P. Verene, eds., *Giambattista Vico's Science of Humanity* (Baltimore and London, 1976) 84.

For Vico's methodology, particularly his deductive use of ancient propositions that can be confused with "inductive generalisations": L. Pompa, *Vico. A Study of the 'New Science'* (Cambridge, 1975) 150–151 and *passim*.

the acceptance of the explicit opinions of a small number of ancient authors as to what was early practice, what late, and what was the course of progress. Winckelmann's methodology is consistent with the prevailing contemporary approach to ancient literature. One last observation is of interest: nowhere does Winckelmann offer a comparable rationalistic outline of the origin of the other arts; for none exists in the ancient sources.[40]

The same ancient testimony that furnished Winckelmann with his outline of the development of Greek sculpture has continued to guide scholarship on the subject through the nineteenth century and into the present. The specific points in development identified by the ancient sources—the aniconic age, the transitional stage between aniconic and figural monuments, and the improvements in anthropomorphic statues—have continued to form a relative historical framework within which scholars attempt to interpret the monumental evidence for early Greek art.

The greater part of the ancient testimony for the evolution of sculpture deals specifically with the development of images for worship. It is understandable, then, that attempts to determine the history of early Greek sculpture should often be connected with the study of early religion. This is the case, for example, with Guasco's 1768 treatment of the place of statuary in antiquity, in which he explains the evolution of anthropomorphic forms from aniconic "baetyls."[41] Early religion, not early art, is the subject of Bötticher's fundamental study of tree-worship of 1856, *Der Baumkultus der Hellenen*. In this work, Bötticher argues that the trees worshipped in the aniconic age were subsequently decorated anthropomorphically, and eventually developed into actual anthropomorphic

[40] For post-classical uses of the ancient traditions about the invention of painting: R. Rosenblum, "The Origin of Painting: A Problem in the Iconography of Romantic Classicism," *Art Bulletin* 39 (1957) 279–290.

[41] Octavien, comte de Guasco, *De l'usage des statues chez les anciens. Essai historique* (Brussels, 1768) 3–56. Guasco's theory that the baetyl developed into a herm-like form and then into a true statue is based primarily on Biblical evidence like that incorporated by Clement into his discussion of the origin of idolatry. His essay thus belongs to the class of histories of idolatry by eighteenth-century writers (many associated with churches) who take Scripture as their primary data: *e.g.*, Montfaucon (*supra*) and W. King, *An Historical Account of the Heathen Gods and Heroes necessary for the understanding of the ancient poets* (1710; repr. with introduction by H.R. Williamson, Carbondale, Illinois, 1965) 11–21. Guasco is also called l'Abbé de Guasco. His chapter IV, "De l'Origine des Simulacres des Dieux dans la Grèce," 38–56, collects the monuments named by writers such as Plutarch, Pausanias, Clement, and Tacitus as ancient, and from these references (for the most part, to aniconic pieces such as stones) he fits the Greek evidence into the outline of idolatry which he derives from the Biblical texts. His treatment is almost totally literary; actual art is confined to herm-like representations on coins and medallions. He also believes that the idea of statuary representations of gods came to Greece from Egypt and Phoenicia, again on the basis of the literary sources.

statues.[42] Similar ideas are advanced even today. Burkert, for instance, also relying on literary sources, notably Callimachus' account of the unworked plank that was the earliest Samian Hera, has attempted to identify several examples of a pattern of cult that features "the transition from aniconic to anthropomorphic representation" and "the anthropomorphic image evolving from the tree."[43]

It is also within the context of early Greek religion as revealed by literary sources that art-historical speculations about the first developments of sculpture have been advanced. The classic presentation of the evolutionary theory of early sculpture is Farnell's "The Origins and Earliest Developments of Greek Sculpture" of 1889. Farnell begins by establishing a theoretical framework for his contention that "the free statue was a native Greek development, slowly evolved from the earlier Aniconic object." He derives his framework from the statements of Pausanias, Clement, and others concerning aniconic and ancient images, and from Themistius' account of images before Daedalus.[44] The major new feature of Farnell's argument, which otherwise scarcely differs from Winckelmann's or Bötticher's, is the considerable amount of monumental evidence he brings to bear. Archaeology has provided him with a large array of small terracottas and bronzes and large stone pieces—most notably, the statue dedicated by Nikandre—which to his eye betray unmistakable signs of aniconic ancestry and primitive artistic inability. His discussion of these pieces, ignoring as it does questions of context, and relying as it must on a chronology more relative than precise, is no more than an affirmation of the theory derived from the ancient literature.

The evolutionary theory has travelled from studies of religion and sculpture to other contexts where it is scarcely questioned. For example, Perdrizet draws on the theory of the aniconic origin of images to explain the *xoana* mentioned in an inscription; he speaks of the time when cults were mostly aniconic, and describes *xoana* as worked and smoothed trunks to which were added heads or masks, like the draped pillars of Dionysus seen in vase-paintings, monuments of an old form.[45] Lorimer, in the course of discussing archaeological material in relationship to the Homeric poems,

[42] K. Bötticher, *Der Baumkultus der Hellenen nach dem gottesdienstlichen Gebräuchen und den überlieferten Bildwerken dargestellt* (Berlin, 1856). Nilsson, *GgR* I, 194, notes that Bötticher anticipates Wilhelm Mannhardt's influential collection of folklore, *Wald- und Feldkulte* I. *Der Baumkultus* (Berlin, 1875). Other appearances of the evolutionary theory in works on Greek religion: E. Ehnmark, *The Idea of God in Homer* (Uppsala, 1935) 55; B.C. Dietrich, "Some Evidence from Cyprus of Apolline Cult in the Bronze Age," *RhM* 121 (1978) 10–11.

[43] Burkert, *Structure* 129–132.

[44] Farnell, "Origins"; 167–172 for the literary evidence.

[45] Perdrizet: *supra* p. 107 n. 254.

tacitly accepts the idea of a primitive stage preceding art when she remrks that "to hang a shield on a log or a tree-trunk and even to give the latter a few human traits would not be beyond the powers of a proto-Geometric worshipper."[46]

Sometimes the evolutionary theory is used to interpret a specific monument. Miller, for example, has reconstructed an altar that incorporates herm-like elements. He outlines the evolutionary theory:

> If the reconstruction is valid, then the monument as a whole is not purely aniconic. Rather, it would represent a stage halfway between aniconism and iconism. Such an intermediate stage is well attested elsewhere, particularly with reference to Dionysos. One can, in fact, trace the development of portrayals of Dionysos from a simple aniconic monument [Miller's note 59: Clem.Al. *Strom.* 418 P; *cf.* Paus. 9.12.4] to a complete anthropomorphization. Particularly instructive for the intermediate stage in this evolutionary process are the many instances in vase painting where a pillar, or a column, or even a tree trunk, has a mask of Dionysos affixed to it and [is] wrapped in clothing below. The aniconic image is transformed into a quasi-anthropomorphic statue by the addition of a human head.[47]

The influence of the ancient sources can even be detected in one of the most stylistically and empirically oriented treatments of the origins of Greek sculpture, Ridgway's discussion in *The Archaic Style in Greek Sculpture* of 1977. Ridgway deals specifically with the question of wooden statues, for which the terms *xoana* and *brete* are primary evidence.[48] She summarizes the question this way:

> Large-scale wooden statuary seems to have existed even in prehistoric times and was probably made during the Eighth and Seventh centuries. Presumably ill-shaped at first, it eventually became anthropomorphic but colossal in that the lower part was column-like or shown as if tightly enveloped in a garment. Since religion was probably dominated by female deities, such renderings were highly appropriate for female figures.[49]

Ridgway argues elsewhere that the block-like or plank-like form of the Peplos Kore from the Athenian Acropolis is an intentional reminiscence, or in fact a reproduction, of an early *xoanon* of this column-like type.[50]

In treating the beginning of Archaic, as opposed to Daedalic, stone sculpture, Ridgway suggests that the development of large-scale male statues—the kouroi—is connected with the cult of Apollo, and she outlines

[46] Lorimer, *Homer* 446.

[47] Stephen G. Miller, "The Altar of the Six Goddesses in Thessalian Pherai," *CSCA* 7 (1974) 248.

[48] Ridgway, *Archaic* 23–25.

[49] Ridgway, *Archaic* 37. For "colossal": *supra* p. 27 n. 65.

[50] B.S. Ridgway, "The Peplos Kore, Akropolis 679," *JWAG* 36 (1977) 49–61.

the change from columnar representations of the god to images that have one foot advanced. This advanced foot she believes was meant to indicate action, walking. She suggests too that the ancient stories about Daedalus' moving statues might actually reflect this change from columnar format to images with stretched-out legs.[51]

Even this very brief review shows how strongly the version of the origin of Greek sculpture put forward by antiquarian and patristic sources has influenced modern opinions about early Greek statuary. It has become increasingly clear, however, that the material record of antiquity differs greatly from the view offered by the ancient authors. The reason for the discrepancy can be sought in the particular aims of the ancient sources, which have given rise not only to tendentious arguments that are not always grounded in fact, but also to inconsistencies that further undermine their reliability.

[51] Ridgway, *Archaic* 26–28.

3. Ancient Traditions and Theories about the Beginning of Greek Sculpture

It has been shown that the modern treatments of the origin of Greek sculpture derive from ancient literary testimony. At first view, this testimony appears unanimously to support the idea that statuary evolved from primitive, aniconic monuments. On closer examination, however, it becomes clear that the sources are by no means uniform or consistent. They derive from several different traditions, and the inconsistencies and contradictions among them reflect the particular intentions and concerns of the various writers. The three major lines of ancient thought on the origin of sculpture that are reflected in the sources are antiquarian, art-historical, and iconoclastic. They overlap to some extent, but their differences are clear. None provides reliable evidence about the early stages of statuary.

In the Greek sources that bear on the question of aniconic and figural monuments, images are sharply dissociated from the aniconic past. Pausanias, for example, remarks that in the past the Greeks worshipped not *agalmata*, but unworked stones (7.22.4) [**251**]. Similarly, he says that a Heracles at Hyettus "is not an *agalma* with craft, but a rough stone, according to the *archaios* fashion" (9.24.3) [**275**]. Seven pillars near Sparta are said to be the *agalmata* of the planets, "in accordance, I believe, with an *archaios* fashion" (3.20.9) [**239**].

Pausanias' explicit statement that the aniconic monuments, in contrast to the *agalmata* that are made with *techne*, belong to an *archaios* fashion is significant. His opinion agrees with the lines of Callimachus concerning the Samian Hera and the simplicity of early images (*ap.* Eus. *PE* 3.8.1) [**108**]: "Not yet the well-carved work [of Scelmis]; but according to the old custom you were a plank not carved by chisels; for thus did they then set up the gods." Plutarch used these lines as evidence for the priority of wooden statues, but Callimachus' entire point is the contrast between well-carved work and the simple, uncarved plank of the old fashion.

The few preserved lines of the *Diegesis* to Callimachus' poem shed a somewhat different light on the two monuments of Samian Hera [**42**]:

> . . . the [xoa]non of Hera became [statue-shaped] when Procles was *basileus*; the *xulon* out of which it was worked . . . they say from Argos . . . a very long time ago was carried, planklike, unworked, seeing that the art of carving *agalmata* was not yet advanced.[52]

[52] For *Diegesis* to Callimachus, *Aetia* IV fr. 100 [**42**]: *supra* pp. 47–49 and n. 111. Trypanis, *Callimachus* 75 n. d, gives Procles as the *archon basileus*; see Pfeiffer, *Callimachus* I, 104–105 *ad* IV 25 for references. A Procles had led settlers to Samos in the Ionian migration following the Dorian invasion. This *Diegesis* has been used as evidence for a later Procles ruling on the island (*e.g.*, G.L. Huxley, *The Early Ionians* [London, 1966] 162 n. 48). It seems possible, however, that the original Procles is meant here. For Procles: *RE* II.1.2 (1920) 2209–2212 *s.v.* Samos (L. Burchner). A link with the earlier Procles would give an impossibly high date for the sculptor Smilis, according to the other information preserved about him;

This passage interprets Callimachus' lines literally, seeing not a development in custom, but instead an actual reworking of the monument. The first Hera is the production of people who could do no better, and the *xulon*, "timber," is an uneasy compromise between artist's raw material and aniconic stock. Callimachus himself does not seem to imply such a procedure. It should be noted, too, that immediately after the section on Scelmis, Callimachus mentions Danaus' dedication of the Lindian Athena; there is no room in the poem for the account of the bringing of the wood from Argos to Samos. The *Diegesis* appears, therefore, to incorporate information from some other source. It is an attempt to explain an aniconic monument in terms of ordinary artistic procedure, and, while novel, it is consistent with the idea of an age before art. A comparable confusion exists in the conflicting traditions surrounding the Argive Hera. Different sources mention an aniconic representation and a figural image; there is, however, no attempt to reconcile the two versions of the earliest Argive Hera.[53]

The conception of an age before art that appears in antiquarian authors like Callimachus, Plutarch, and Pausanias corresponds to the widespread idea of the simplicity of the past. Some examples of this *topos* have

---

but it does not seem impossible that the traditions about the first sculptor of the Hera could incorporate legends about two different ages. Certainly Daedalus seems to be a figure of both the Bronze Age and the earliest Archaic world. For a place called *daidaleion* at Mycenaean Knossos: Ventris and Chadwick, *Documents*² 128, 307 (Fp 1.3). For a recent suggestion that the face of the Athena Polias may have been carved from an original aniconic stock: Kroll, "Ancient Image" (*supra* p. 143 n. 343) 75.

[53] For the *bretas* of the Samian Hera: Ath. 15.672 a–e [37]. For the conflicting traditions of the first Hera of Argos: The *Phoronis ap.* Clem.Al. *Strom.* 1.164.2 [47] mentions a *makros kion*, which the context of the fragments shows Clement understood as a column. (For other meanings of *kion*: *supra* p. 185 n. 22.) But Plutarch *ap.* Eus. *PE* 3.8.1 **[108]** speaks of the pear tree that Peiras shaped (*morphosai*) into the *agalma*. See *supra* p. 137. Pausanias saw what he was told was the oldest Hera: a small seated *agalma* dedicated by Pirasus. The differences between the versions have been attributed to the rival claims of Tiryns and Argos to priority in the establishment of the cult of Hera. Whatever historical fact lies in these accounts is not easy to extract. The fragments of the *Phoronis*, perhaps to be dated c. 600 B.C., are not even sufficient to prove the Tirythnian bias of the work, although they strongly suggest it. For this fragment in Clement: *RE* 20.1 (1950) 649–650 *s.v.* Phoronis (2) (F. Stoessl). Pausanias seems to have conflated versions of a tradition that give both Argus and Peiras as the maker of the image; Argus is named as the maker of the pear-wood image of Hera at Tiryns by Demetrius, *Argolica* Book 2, *ap.* Clem.Al. *Protr.* 4.41 P. [44]. It may not be possible to untangle the accounts of the foundation of the cult. The genealogies of the families concerned are hopelessly confused, and the destruction of Tiryns by Argos in the fifth century B.C. is a reminder that the sources of information about the earliest periods are likely to reflect later partisan interests. What can be said is that there are two versions of the history of the earliest Argive Hera, one concerning an aniconic monument, the other a statue made from significant wood. Plutarch's version with the pear tree is reminiscent of Herodotus' account (5.82) of the acquisition of olive wood from Athens for the images of Auxesia and Damia; *cf.* Paus. 2.30.4 **[224]**.

been examined in the context of iconoclastic polemic. Porphyry, for example, stresses the rustic materials with which the men of the past carried on a more devout worship than the luxurious customs of the present [**323**].[54] The vision of an austere but morally superior past is only one of several ideas that the Greeks held about their history.[55] A related conception, which appears in several versions, emphasizes the absence of altars, temples, and images in the deep past, and attributes the institution of these elements of worship to individuals or particular races.[56] The explanation of aniconic worship and its monuments as the custom of the past belongs with this conception of history and cultural development.

It is striking that in the antiquarian idea of the age before art, that era is clearly set off from the age of arts and crafts. Neither a continuous development nor an evolutionary link between the monuments of the two ages is suggested. To this extent the antiquarian conception agrees with the accounts of early sculpture found in writings that are specifically concerned with the history of art. In the small body of such works that is preserved, however, the idea of the primitive or aniconic origin of images does not occur. No writer seems to have thought in terms of the evolution of art from primitive beginnings; instead, the focus of attention is the inspired invention of forms and techniques by individual craftsmen and artists.[57] These accounts of innovations and improvements reflect the well-known aetiological cast of Greek thought. Entire treatises were devoted to the subject of beginnings and discoveries; the Περὶ εὑρημάτων of Scamon of

[54] *Supra* p. 136 and n. 327. For traditions concerning the invention of agriculture as a significant step in the progress of civilization: Shaw, "Eaters of Flesh" (*supra* p. 123 n. 299); L. Lacroix, "Formes de la vie primitive et de la vie civilisée dans les traditions légendaires de la Grèce," in L. Hadermann-Misguich and G. Raepsaet, eds., *Rayonnement grec. Hommages à Charles Delvoye* (Université Libre de Bruxelles. Faculté de Philosophie et Lettres, LXXXIII; Brussels, 1982) 59–67. In some traditions, even Nature herself underwent an evolution: Lacroix 61 for the age before trees existed. Note especially 61–62 for the importance of acorns; *cf. supra* p. 163 n. 405 for the role of the oak in Roman hierarchies of trees.

[55] For such theories: Guthrie, *In the Beginning, passim.*

[56] *E.g.*: Hdt. 2.4 [**139**]; D.H. 2.18.2 [**66**]; Luc. *Prom.* 12 [**166**], 14: for these, *supra* p. 91. *Cf.* Eus. *PE* 1.9.29 d [**100**]: the first and most ancient men did not build temples or set up *xoana* (*cf.* 1.9.30 b [**101**]), since the arts of art and architecture did not yet exist.

Cf. Luc. 5.1448–1457 on the refinement of the inventions of civilization accomplished *paulatim.* C. Bailey, *Titi Lucreti Cari De Rerum Natura Libri Sex* (Oxford, 1947) III, 1548, notes that Lucretius "distinguishes, though not too clearly, between two stages": in the first, necessity gradually "taught men new devices to meet their needs"; in the second, inventiveness "elaborated" these discoveries. Bailey briefly discusses the Epicurean context of these ideas. In line 1541, *picturas et daedala signa polita* have joined the *carmina*, the invention of which he treated previously.

[57] *E.g.*, Pl. *NH* 34.54; 35.15–16; 35.151–153; 36.15; *passim* for first accomplishments within individual craft traditions: *e.g.*, 35.58, Polygnotus the first to show open mouths and teeth.

Mytilene, who lived perhaps in the early fourth century B.C., appears to have been the earliest of these.[58] Such works, by asking about the origin of various arts and techniques, in large part determined the nature of the replies; for the question "Who?" needs to be answered with a name.

The treatises on discoveries and inventions influenced writings on art. Pliny's chapters on art, for example, which preserve information about art history as well as art itself, reflect a considerable variety of sources: alphabetical lists, critical appraisals, guidebooks, anecdotal histories, and so forth. Although in the absence of the treatises themselves it is difficult to recover individual threads of traditions, it is clear that certain ideas about the early stages of art appear consistently, no matter what the specific form in which the subject is treated. The prevailing concept throughout all the discussions is the idea of invention and innovation as the moving forces in historical development. This uniformity does not seem to be the result of Pliny's own predispositions alone, but appears to reflect a general current in Greek thought.[59]

The stories about artistic inventions all have the definite aim of finding Who, When, and How. The greater Why, however, is missing, and seems to need no answer. From the beginning, it appears, figures were conceived whole, completed, and perfect; only technical improvement was needed, and the aims of naturalistic art are taken as universal. The aniconic or primitive stage has no place in these histories of art; unlike the speculations on the early stages of religion, the accounts of the art of the past do not postulate a time in which artistic practice was different. This is so whether the originators of art are plausibly historical or obviously fabulous, as in the case of the Telchines, who are said by Diodorus to have been the first to make images of the gods.[60]

[58] For Scamon of Mytilene: Pfeiffer, *History* I, 21 n. 4, with references. For stories of inventions: A. Kleingünther, Πρῶτος εὑρετής (*Philologus* Suppl. 26.1; Leipzig, 1933). For a long catalogue of inventions by barbarians and a list of writers on inventions: Eus. *PE* 10.5.473 c–476 d (quoting Clem.Al. *Strom.* 1.16). The writers named are Scamon of Mytilene, Theophrastus of Ephesus, Cydippus of Mantinea, Antiphanes, Aristodemus, Aristotle, Philostephanus, and Straton the Peripatetic (*Concerning Inventions*). See also Philo of Byblos: Baumgarten (*supra* p. 159 n. 394) 140–179; and Hyginus, *Fab.* 274, *Quis quid invenit*: H.J. Rose, ed., *Hygini fabulae* (Leiden, n.d.).

[59] Little has survived of ancient treatises on art. They are often referred to in texts, but except for Vitruvius' ten books on architecture they are preserved only in fragments and paraphrases. See Pollitt, *Ancient View* 9–111, esp. 73–111, "Art History in Antiquity." Some of the same ground is treated in more detail by Sellers in Jex-Blake and Sellers, *Pliny* xiv–xciv. For Pliny's alphabetic catalogues of artists: Daly, *Contributions* 37.

[60] *Cf.* Pl. *NH* 35.15 [**312**]: "The origin of painting is obscure, and hardly falls within the scope of this work. The claim of the Egyptians to have discovered the art six thousand years before it reached Greece is obviously an idle boast, while among the Greeks some say that it was first discovered at Sicyon, others at Corinth. All, however, agree that painting began with

It is in the realm of such searches for origins that the rationalizing accounts of the achievements of Daedalus belong.[61] In its emphasis on technique, Diodorus' version is closer to a specialist's tradition than to the popular, magical conception of Daedalus. The technical innovations he describes, however, nonetheless seem more like literary conceits than actual advances in craftsmanship. "And since he was the first to represent the open eye and to fashion legs separated and the arms and hands extended, it was natural that he should have received the admiration of mankind; for the craftsmen before him had carved their *agalmata* with the eyes closed, having hands hanging and attached to the sides" (4.76.3) **[59]**. The mention of the closed eyes betrays the essentially literary nature of the account. What at first appear to be unquestionable technical advances can also be seen as rationalizing explanations of the story that Daedalus' statues lived and moved, and they need not be based in solidly grounded art history. The rationalizing accounts are best treated as evidence not for the history of art, but for its historiography. They cannot safely be used to illuminate the early periods of Greek sculpture, because even in origin they are committed to a definite historical conception, an *a priori* presumption. What the rationalizing version of Daedalus' achievements does show, however, is the conception of statuary as being whole and complete in formal conception from the start. Daedalus simply improved on a schema that was fully figural, but lacked "life." It is iconoclastic rhetoric that pulled this tradition into an evolutionary scheme with which it is fundamentally incompatible, as seen for example in Themistius, where *andriantes* in general are allied with the aniconic stocks of the antiquarian past.

The theory that sculpture evolved from primitive aniconic practice is an iconoclastic invention expressed most clearly by Clement; it is even possible that he devised the idea himself. It has already been seen that both the

---

the outlining of a man's shadow." (Tr. Jex-Blake.) This passage is indicative of the general approach of the Greeks to the subject of the beginnings of art; the same attitude is found repeatedly in Pliny's excerpts and summaries. For the Telchines: D.S. 5.55.1–3: "They say that they were also the first to make *agalmata* of the gods. . . . " This tradition is worth keeping in mind because of the strong overtones of magic, which are reminiscent of the works of Hephaestus in Homer and the uncanny aspects of Daedalus' statues in the fifth-century sources. See also *RE* II.5.1 (1934) 197–224 *s.v.* Telchinen (H. Herter).

[61] Ridgway, *Archaic* 27–28, suggests that the stance of the Archaic kouros indicates movement and that the change from a simple standing position is reflected in the stories about Daedalus' moving statues. See H. Philipp, "Daidalos: Zur schriftlichen Überlieferung," in Museum für Kunst und Gewerbe, Hamburg, *Dädalische Kunst auf Kreta im 7. Jahrhundert v. Chr.* (Mainz, 1970) 5–13 for the possibility that already by the fifth century B.C. a rationalistic explanation was current, and that the lively statues mentioned in comedy were understood to represent Daedalus' achievement in specific connection with seventh-century sculpture. The earliest such explanation, however, appears in Diodorus (*supra* p. 183 n. 17 for Palaephatus), and the explanation of quicksilver is still essentially magical.

defenders of images and their critics based their arguments on an analysis of the past. Iconophiles like Dio Chrysostom and Maximus of Tyre present a sentimental vision of a primitive age of innocent piety; iconoclasts use much of the same illustrative material to show an unpleasant epoch of senseless, deluded barbarism.[62] The origin and development of images are the focus of both schemes.

Dio's conception of the past agrees with the antiquarian idea of an ancient time in which images did not exist (*Or.* 12.60–61) [**57**]: "many of the barbarians, for lack of craftsmanship and difficulty with it, name mountains gods, and unworked trees, too, and shapeless stones, things which are by no means whatever more appropriate in shape than is the human form." Barbarians, as has been seen, represent in Greek tradition the childhood of civilization, and Dio's examples correspond to Clement's list of ancient practices (*Protr.* 4.40 P.) [**44**]. A similar version of the past appears in Eusebius (*PE* 1.9.29 d) [**100**]:

> But that the first and most ancient of men turned their minds neither to building *naoi* nor setting up *xoana*, since then neither graphic nor plastic [nor glyptic] nor modelling arts had been discovered, nor indeed had building nor architecture been established, I think is clear to everyone who considers.

Both iconophile and iconoclast, then, argue their positions on the basis of the idea found in antiquarian contexts of an age before arts.

The absence of arts, however, was not enough to establish the virtue of the past, because idolatry did not consist in images alone. Varro, for example, sees art as merely an extension of error. Augustine quotes and discusses him on this point as follows (*DCD* 4.31) [**40**]:

> He [Varro] also says that for more than one hundred and seventy years the ancient Romans worshipped the gods without an image. "If this usage had continued to our own day," he says, "our worship of the gods would be more devout." And in support of his opinion he adduces, among other things, the testimony of the Jewish race. And he ends with the forthright statement that those who first set up images of the gods for the people diminished reverence in their cities as they added to error, for he wisely judged that gods in the shape of senseless images might easily inspire contempt. And when he says, not "handed down error," but "added to error," he certainly wants it understood that there had been error even without the images.

Clement's version of the same passage is shorter (*Protr.* 4.40 P.) [**44**]:

> In Rome, of old time, according to Varro the prose-writer, the *xoanon* of Ares was a spear, since craftsmen had not yet entered upon the fair-seeming but mischievous art of sculpture. But the moment art flourished, error increased.

[62] *Supra* pp. 121–131.

As it happens, the tradition that the early Romans made no images is probably historically false, and may reflect something of the hoary, old-Roman dislike of foreign fine arts.[63]

Similarly, but with somewhat less composure, Tertullian condemns the entire pagan past (*De idolatria* 3) **[361]**:

> Once, for a time, there were no idols. Before the makers of these monstrosities shot up, the *templa* were solitary and the *aedes* empty, as you may see today in spots where traces of antiquity survive. Of course idolatry was practiced, in fact if not in name. But when the devil brought into the world the makers of statues and portraits and evey kind of image, the practice, untaught as yet but fraught with disaster to mankind, took its name and its developments from the idols.[64]

An allied polemic intention accounts for the curious statement of Arnobius who, insisting that the Christians had no temples, hurries to dissociate his faith from any hint of idolatry (*Adv.Gen.* 6.3): *numquid enim delubris aut templorum eum constructionibus honoramus*? (For do we honor Him with shrines or the building of temples?)[65]

These passages demonstrate the patristic attempt to show Christianity as a complete break with the entire pagan world, past and present. As Eusebius asserts that the power of the demons and the idols has ended today, in the age of the Gospels (*PE* 1.4.12 a **[98]**; 4.4.140 c **[114]**), so Clement, Tertullian, and Arnobius present their faith as an enlightenment.

The iconoclastic writers, then, generally agree in seeing the whole pagan past as a hotbed of idolatry, and in condemning equally all the forms

[63] For Roman aniconic worship: L.R. Taylor, "Aniconic Worship Among the Early Romans," in G.D. Hadzsits, ed., *Classical Studies in Honor of John C. Rolfe* (Philadelphia, 1931) 305–314. The precedence of aniconic worship may not, however, be a historically accurate tradition, but may instead be another invention; for remarks on Varro's assertion of early Roman aniconism and its reflection of Greek romanticism: P. Boyancé, "Les pénates et l'ancienne religion romaine," *REA* 54 (1952) 112–115. *Cf.* Plut. *Num.* 7–8 **[321]** for a Pythagorean version of the golden age before art; *supra* p. 124.

[64] For Tertullian (c. A.D. 160–c. 225): *OCD*[2] *s.v.*; *ODCC*[2] *s.v.*

[65] Arn. *Adv.Gen.* 6.3 defends Christians against the charge of impiety by asserting that they do not insult the pagan gods by refusing to honor them with statues and temples and sacrifices, but instead treat them with the same respect as they do God, for whom they also produce no outward show. The reference to *delubra* and *templa* has caused some difficulties of interpretation, because the early Christians did in fact set aside buildings for worship. Bryce and Campbell, *Arnobius* (*supra* p. 185 n. 21) 273 n. 6, admit that Arnobius here expressly denies that Christians had temples, but they interpret the line to mean that these buildings had "no architectural pretensions." This is also the solution of G.E. McCracken, tr., *Arnobius of Sicca. The Case Against the Pagans* II (Ancient Christian Writers 8; Westminster, Maryland, 1949) 586 n. 9: unostentatious Christian structures were not to be confused with pagan temples and shrines. Nock notes that Christians do not use the words *hieron* and *naos* for their meeting-places: "The Vocabulary of the New Testament," in *Essays* I, 343.

of its worship, past and present. Tertullian, however, touches on a troubling question when he asserts that *idolatria agebatur, non in isto nomine, sed in isto opere*; he flounders in trying to explain how there can be idolatry without idols. His weak answer serves merely to underline the point of theoretical confusion. He and Varro labor to reconcile the idea of the invention of art with the conception of ongoing idolatry. Clement, the boldest of the iconoclasts, devises an entirely new solution: he interprets the worship of non-figural objects as a developmental stage in idolatry, and postulates a continuous evolution from such objects into images in the ordinary sense (*Protr.* 4.40 P.) **[44]**. He attacks images not simply on philosophical, but also on artistic grounds. He attempts to diminish their aesthetic value by tracing their origin to crude and unattractive monuments. This is the only possible answer to arguments that defend images on the basis of their artistic beauty; such a position had been taken by Dio in the case of Pheidias' Olympian Zeus (*Or.* 12). The aesthetic value of images was so strong that it was necessary to diminish it by showing the ugly heritage of the beautiful statues.[66] Clement does this by asserting the existence of a period in which the worship of the gods was carried on with *ad hoc* fetishes and the crudest of monuments, which then evolved into the images of contemporary idolatry. Thus he imposes on the attractive and artistically accomplished statues an unappealing pedigree. By doing so, however, he must contradict the prevailing idea of the complete break between the period before art and the age of the invention of *techne*.

Even Clement, however, falls in with the idea of the age before art. In the *Stromateis* (1.164.1), for example, he explicitly contrasts statues with earlier monuments: *Πρὶν γοῦν ἀκριβωθῆναι τὰς τῶν ἀγαλμάτων σχέσεις κίονας ἱστάντες οἱ παλαιοὶ ἔσεβον τούτοις ὡς ἀφιδρύματα τοῦ θεοῦ* (Before, then, they perfected the fashion of *agalmata*, the ancients, setting up columns, worshipped them as *aphidrumata* of God). There is no hint of any development; instead, as in Pausanias, the columns belong to the old order, over and done with, in an age before art. The point of the passage as a whole is not to explain the origin of idolatry, but instead to detail instances of Greek imitations of the Jews, specifically here in episodes involving pillars of light. Clement has accordingly marshalled his testimony about Greek pillars, but since he is not attempting to give a theoretical account of idolatry, he lapses into the prevailing interpretation of the historical significance of aniconic pieces.

Even in Clement's formal presentation of his theory of idolatry, the more usual conception appears, as for example when he quotes Aëthlius on

[66] *Cf.* Paus. 2.4.5 **[203]** on the works of Daedalus, which look "somewhat strange to the eye."

the history of the Samian Hera (*Protr.* 4.40 P.) [44]: τὸ [ἄγαλμα] τῆς Σαμίας Ἥρας, ὥς φησιν Ἀέθλιος, πρότερον μὲν ἦν σανίς, ὕστερον δὲ ἐπὶ Προκλέους ἄρχοντος ἀνδριαντοειδὲς ἐγένετο (The [*agalma*] of Samian Hera, as Aëthlius says, was at first a *sanis*, but afterwards, when Procles was ruler, it became statue-shaped). At first, the passage appears simply to contrast the aniconic plank with the later anthropomorphic depiction; *sanis* certainly refers to a flat board or plank, and is used regularly of doors and wooden tablets.[67] The sense of the text, however, is slightly different, and corresponds closely to Callimachus' lines on the same image in which he contrasts the uncarved *sanides* of ancient custom with the well-carved work of Scelmis (*ap.* Eus. *PE* 3.8.1) [108]. *Andriantoeides* refers specifically to statues, and here, in its neuter form, it is applied to the *agalma* of Hera (τὸ τῆς Σαμίας Ἥρας, ἄγαλμα supplied from the preceding line). Hera is not anthropomorphic; rather, her *agalma* became *andriantoeides*. The distinction between object and statue could not be clearer. The emphatic *proteron men . . . hysteron de* marks the sharp break between the two forms of the *agalma*. There is no hint of development or evolution. Clement seems to have transmitted the point of Aëthlius' comments accurately, although by doing so he has undercut, ever so slightly, his own theoretical scheme.

It seems, then, that although for the purpose of his argument Clement asserts the continuous evolution of images from aniconic objects, he nonetheless recognizes a break between figural and non-figural monuments. This awareness is indicated even in the sentence in which he describes the change (*Protr.* 4.40 P.) [44]: Ἐπεὶ δὲ ἀνθρώποις ἀπεικονίζεσθαι τὰ ξόανα ἤρξατο, βρέτη τὴν ἐκ βροτῶν ἐπονυμίαν ἐκαρπώσατο (When the *xoana* began to be represented as men, they acquired the additional name *brete*, from *brotoi* [mortals]). Ἤρξατο suggests a change, not a slow development. Although the false etymology with *brotos* shows that the point is the change to an anthropomorphic rendering, the verb *apeikonizesthai* might retain here something of the association with "images" that its active form can have.[68] That is to say, the difference between the *xoana* and the *brete* is not so much what they look like as the fact that the *brete* have the ability to portray at all.

Clement's version of the origin of statuary in aniconic monuments is a special argument devised to prove a specific iconoclastic point. It differs from the prevailing conception of the beginning of art as found in both

[67] LSJ[9] *s.v.* σανίς.

[68] LSJ[9] s.v. ἀπεικονίζω, *represent in a statue*, illustrated by *AnthPal* 12.56; the greater number of examples, however, illustrates more general meanings of representation, description, or expression.

antiquarian writings and writings on art, a conception which he himself appears otherwise to accept.

The conflict between the iconoclastic theory of the origin of sculpture and theories current in other contexts emerges perhaps most clearly in a passage of Athenagoras dealing with the origin of idolatry. Athenagoras was a Christian apologist contemporary with Clement.[69] His discussion of idolatry in his *Embassy* (17) [39] combines the usual Christian arguments against images with startling extracts from treatises on the arts:

> *Eikones* were not in use before the discovery of plastic, graphic, and modelling arts. When came Saurius of Samos, Crato of Sicyon, Cleanthes of Corinth, and the Corinthian maid, tracing out shadows was discovered by Saurius, who drew the outline of a horse in the sun; graphic art was discovered by Crato, who painted in the outlines of the shadows of a man and woman on a whitened tablet; and coroplastic art was discovered by the Corinthian maid (for she fell in love with someone and traced the outline of his shadow on the wall as he slept; then her father—he made pottery—delighted with so precise a likeness, carved out the outline and filled it with clay; the *tupos* is preserved to this very day in Corinth). After these came Daedalus, Theodorus, and Smilis, who went further and discovered modelling and plastic arts. So short, then, is the time since [the introduction of] *eikones* and the making of *eidola* that it is possible to name the craftsman of each god. Endoios, a disciple of Daedalus, made that of Artemis in Ephesus and the old one of Athena from olive-wood (or rather of Athela; for she is Athela, the unsuckled, as those . . . the more mystical sense . . .) and the Seated Athena. The Pythian is the work of Theodorus and Telecles, and the Delian and the Artemis ware the craftsmanship of Tectaeus and Angelion. The Hera in Samos and in Argos are the works of Smilis (and the rest of the *eidola* of Pheidias). The Aphrodite in Cnidus is another work of Praxiteles, the Asclepius in Epidaurus is the work of Pheidias. To put it in a word, not one of them eludes identification as the work of a man. If, then, they are gods, why were they not so from the beginning? Why are they more recent than those who have made them? Why did they need human craftsmanship for their existence? They are earth, stones, matter, and futile craftsmanship.

Athenagoras' discussion falls into two parts. The latter is similar to Clement's list of man-made images (*Protr.* 4.43 P.) [**44**] and presents few difficulties.[70] The first half of the passage, however, the description of the invention of the arts, seems badly out of context, even given Athenagoras' intention of proving that the idols are recent creations of human beings. It is an awkward passage, stuffed with anecdotal detail that contributes little

[69] Schoedel, *Athenagoras* xi for date of the *Legatio* (*Presbeia peri Christianon*) between A.D. 176 and 178. Section 17 is translated in Jex-Blake and Sellers, *Pliny* 224–227. See Schoedel xix–xx for Athenagoras' use of sources and his "not profound" but "generally reliable" information on the history of art.

[70] Only Athenagoras calls the Argive Hera the work of Smilis.

to the argument. Athenagoras seems to quote wholesale some source concerned with the invention of specific media and techniques. At the same point in his argument, Clement had described the development of aniconic pieces into images; Clement's is the more satisfactory presentation. The awkwardness with which Athenagoras, a good writer, has fitted the stories of artists into his iconoclastic argument emphasizes the thorough incompatibility of the traditions about art with the theories about the beginnings of idolatry. The notion of the aniconic origin of images stands out ever more sharply as an iconoclastic invention that has no place outside that context. The traditions about art also emerge as exemplars of a concept of development that are similarly limited in context.

It is clear that the explicit statements in the ancient sources concerning the beginning of Greek sculpture cannot be relied on, either singly or collectively, for accurate information. The idea of the evolution of statuary from primitive aniconic monuments is an argument devised to further the aims of iconoclasm. The idea of an age before art is the product of Greek historical speculation about an idealized past. Even the question itself of the origins of sculpture reflects the aetiological slant of Greek thought, and the accounts of discoveries and advances in the art of sculpture emerge as essentially literary *topoi* that shed little reliable light on the history of the craft. Faulty as the ancient testimony for the early stages of sculpture now appears, however, it remains to be seen whether the ideas contained in that testimony can be proved or disproved by the monumental evidence.

4. Modern Theories about Primitive Wooden Images and the Origins of Greek Sculpture

In modern scholarship there is a variety of theories about the origins of Greek sculpture that involve the concept of primitive wooden images. All rely to some extent on three assumptions: first, that there existed a primitive stage of sculpture in which figural representation was imperfectly achieved; second, that wooden statues of inherently primitive character preceded images carved in stone; and third, that aniconic monuments preceded figural representations and influenced their form. These assumptions can be treated separately.

THE PRIMITIVE STAGE OF SCULPTURE

The idea that Greek sculpture went through a primitive stage in which figural representations were imperfectly conceived and executed can be dismissed on several grounds. In universal terms, there is abundant evidence that genuinely "primitive" cultures can and do produce accomplished and sophisticated figural art. The most familiar example is the art of the European Stone Ages. The work of the cave-dwellers in painting, relief, and sculpture in the round shows what a chronologically early and technically undeveloped culture can achieve in the way of figural representation. Palaeolithic art offers many works in a variety of media that are not only fully representational in intention and conception, but also so competent in execution that one may readily speak of them in terms of naturalism and illusionism.[71]

The monumental record of Greece itself provides no evidence for deficiencies in its earliest known representational art. The well-known "Lady of Lerna" is a fair example of Neolithic naturalism that demonstrates perfect competence in the conception and execution of an anthropomorphic figure.[72] Difficulties still remain in the dating of mainland Neolithic and Chalcolithic anthropomorphic figurines, and so their development cannot

[71] Examples of naturalistic Stone Age art are easily found in handbooks: *e.g.*, N.K. Sandars, *Prehistoric Art in Europe* (Harmondsworth, 1968) pl. 10 (ivory head from Grotte du Pape); pl. 20 (bison in relief from Tuc d'Audoubert); pl. 21 (cows in relief from Fourneau du Diable); pl. 26 (bison in bone from Mas d'Azil). The cave paintings of France and Spain are famous for their naturalism: *e.g.*, pls. 36, 37, 47, 54, 55, 64. Sandars (1) observes that art begins with accomplished productions: "It is therefore the less surprising that what we find is neither crude nor tentative but an ivory figure, a female torso, and a woman's head, . . . which are, I think, works of art by any standard."

[72] Lady of Lerna: J.L. Caskey and M. Eliot, "A Neolithic Figurine from Lerna," *Hesperia* 25 (1956) 175–177; H.-G. Buchholz and V. Karageorghis, *Prehistoric Greece and Cyprus* (London, 1973) no. 1191.

be traced as precisely as would be desirable.[73] A complete sequence is, however, attested for comparable Cycladic figurines. Renfrew has worked out an "evolution" for these figurines from the Neolithic through the Early Cycladic periods, and two important conclusions emerge from his analysis. First, it is clear that in Neolithic times, abstract figural types coexist with highly naturalistic ones.[74] They are separate and contemporary, and are not developmentally related. This fact underlines the importance of aesthetic choice in the tradition of figural representation. Second, the most naturalistic types seem to develop toward abstraction and from naturalistic rendering. It may be that aesthetics are influenced by other factors—the use of the figures, for example, which is not known with certainty. It cannot be doubted, however, that the observable development is the opposite of what would be expected on the assumption that figural representation improves with practice. A similar development can be seen in the Anatolian anthropomorphic figurines of the Neolithic and Early Bronze Age periods.[75] Both the coexistence of more and less naturalistic types and the development of figural types away from naturalism and toward abstraction disprove the theory that figural representation must have evolved from imperfect beginnings.

It might reasonably be objected that the evidence of the earliest cultures of the Greek mainland may not be relevant to the tradition that culminates in classical art because cultural continuity cannot be demonstrated, and in fact seems unlikely. The case for primitive origins is, however, if anything even weaker in the context of Mycenaean art, the first art that can be called Greek with assurance. What is known of Mycenaean art suggests not primitive beginnings, but instead what appears to be the wholesale adoption of sophisticated Cretan figural traditions by a mainland culture whose own lack of interest in representational art seems due not to any incompetence, but rather to a demonstrable aesthetic preference for abstraction. The earliest Cretan figural art, in its turn, follows a course not very different from the Cycladic, and apparently related to it.[76]

[73] For the series of mainland Greek anthropomorphic figurines: P.J. Ucko, *Anthropomorphic Figurines of Predynastic Egypt and Neolithic Crete with Comparative Material from the Prehistoric Near East and Mainland Greece* (Royal Anthropological Institute, Occasional Paper no. 24; London, 1968) 368–372.

[74] For Cycladic figurines: C. Renfrew, "The Development and Chronlogy of the Early Cycladic Figurines," *AJA* 73 (1969) 1–32. For the early coexistence of "both a simplified flattened version of the female form and a more fully elaborated one," see P. Getz-Preziosi, *Early Cycladic Sculpture. An Introduction* (Malibu, 1985) 26 and *passim*.

[75] For Anatolian figurines: Karlsruhe, Badisches Landesmuseum, *Kunst und Kultur der Kykladeninseln im 3. Jahrtausend v. Chr.* (Karlsruhe, 1976) 179 fig. 176 (schematic chart).

[76] For Cretan Neolithic and Early Minoan figurines: Ucko, *Anthropomorphic Figurines* (*supra* p. 207 n. 73) 203–204; Hood, *Arts* 90.

WOOD AS THE MATERIAL OF PRIMITIVE STATUES

The second component of the theory of primitive wooden statues is the preconceptions about the use and characteristics of the material itself. It has often been assumed that wood preceded stone as the material used for statues. The suggestion has been argued on the *a priori* grounds that wood, being easier to acquire and work than stone, would certainly have been used before stone carving was attempted. Another argument is that the earliest known Greek stone statues show traces of formal and stylistic characteristics typical of wooden work, thus proving that stone sculpture had wooden predecessors and models.

Ultimately the idea that wooden sculpture was made before stone depends on ancient testimony that offers on the one hand definite assurances of the historical priority of wooden sculpture, and on the other, references to specific statues that confirm the speculation. Pliny (*NH* 12.1), in discussing the associations between gods and trees, notes that *simulacra* of *numina* had once been made out of trees. Plutarch [**108**], Pausanias [**213**], and Porphyry [**323**] say that they believe that wood was the first material used for statues. Eusebius asserts [**108**] that the ancients did not use stone or metal for their statues. Combined with this tradition of the priority of wood, the modern understanding of the meaning of *xoanon* (which derives in large part from Pausanias, who uses it consistently for wooden statues and who mentions "ancient" *xoana*) has encouraged the belief that the literary references constitute reliable testimony for a real, albeit unpreserved, group of early statues. Many scholars—for example, Müller, Ridgway, and Herrmann—have looked to the literary sources when speculating about the predecessors of the earliest known stone sculpture in Greece.[77]

The argument for the serial exploitation of materials for sculpture was advanced by Winckelmann and elaborated by scholars such as Brunn, who postulated a progressive use of materials and assigned wood a place between soft clay and hard stone. Allied theories, like those of Deonna and de

[77] Pl. *NH* 12.1: *ex arbore et simulacra numinum fuere*. V. Müller, "The Beginnings of Monumental Sculpture in Greece," *MMS* 5 (1934–1936) 167, notes that the literary references show that wood was the most popular material for early statues. Ridgway, *Archaic* 23, suggests that references to *kolossoi* and *xoana* and *brete* "may allow us to postulate that pre-Archaic statues were often, if not always, wooden images represented tightly enveloped in their clothes or with their legs close together." Herrmann, *AA* 1974, 636, summarizes the literary sources that support the idea of large-scale wooden statuary in preclassical times. R.V. Nicholls, "Greek Votive Statuettes and Religious Continuity, *c.* 1200–700 B.C.," in B.F. Harris, ed., *Auckland Classical Essays Presented to E.M. Blaiklock* (Auckland, 1970) 21–22, calls wood "the traditional material for early images of this kind [cult figures] in Greece," citing examples of "wooden figures of remarkable antiquity and crudity [that] seem to have survived even down to Pausanias' day," as well as representations of "primitive cult images" on classical vases.

Ridder, suggested that the increasing dexterity of early sculptors enabled them to extend their work from wood to soft stones and finally to marble. Casson outlined a similar progression from wood to ivory to stone, finding indications in statues made of stone of the use of carpentry tools. Walters explained that "naturally" wood was used for early statues, because it was easy to acquire and work. Herrmann has traced several such theories to the influence of Brunn's systematic scheme.[78]

It should be noted that similar ideas of the priority of wood are advanced by Vitruvius in his speculations about the nature of man's earliest efforts at architecture.[79] The first chapter of his second book is devoted to explaining how early man, advancing from a state like that of the animals (*ut ferae*; 2.1.1), progressed from discovering fire and developing speech to constructing shelters (2.1.1–2). The earliest shelters were made of stakes and twigs and mud (*primumque furcis erectis et virgulis interpositis luto parietes texerunt*; 2.1.3). Following a practice frequent in ancient speculation about the past, Vitruvius uses ethnographic evidence to reconstruct

[78] Herrmann, "Entstehung" 36 and n. 6 for Brunn's theory and its great influence. For remarks on Brunn's belief that "design is inherent in the materials": G.M.A. Hanfmann, rev. F. Matz, *Geschichte der griechischen Kunst* I, *Art Bulletin* 39 (1957) 236 and n. 11. Brunn's theory is dismissed by Poulsen, "Typenbildung" 189–190. For summary of the theory: H. Brunn, *Griechische Kunstgeschichte*, ed. A. Flasch, II (Munich, 1897) 53–56. For the progression of wood to marble as determined by an increasing technical competence and an awakening aesthetic sense: de Ridder and Deonna, *L'art en Grèce* (*supra* p. 3 n. 11) 345–346. See also Casson, *Technique* 83–85. Adam, *Technique* 3–5, refutes Casson, finding no evidence for the use of carpentry tools in stone works. *Cf.* F.R. Grace, *Archaic Sculpture in Boeotia* (Cambridge, Mass., 1939) 53, who believes that the knife was a major tool in early stone carving, but that its use does not prove the origin of such carving in wood; this idea too is criticized by Adam. Walters, *Art of the Greeks* (*supra* p. 3 n. 11) 59 for wood as a common material attested "in many ways" and explained as having been "naturally adopted" because of the ease of acquiring and working it. F. Versakes, "Τὸ ἐν τῇ τέχνῃ τετράγωνον," *AE* 1914, 25–49, argues *passim* against Brunn's theory of the determining importance of the shape—log, beam or plank—used by early wood-carvers, suggesting instead that the angular characteristics of early stone statuary result from the application to stone of techniques for working wood and bone.

[79] John Wood, *The Origin of Building: or, the Plagiarism of the Heathens Detected* (Bath, 1741; repr. Farnborough, 1968) 9–10 and *passim*, compares Vitruvius' account with Biblical passages concerning or touching on the origin and early stages of architecture in an attempt to prove that the classical text, ostensibly based on the writings of Greek architects, "in great Measure, uncontroverted, has its Foundation in the Holy Scriptures" (6–7). *Cf.* Clement of Alexandria's proof of Greek plagiarism from Hebrew teachings: *Strom.* 1.21.101.1 (καὶ περὶ μὲν τοῦ παρ' Ἑβραίων τὰ τῶν φιλοσόφων ἐσκευωρῆσθαι δόγματα . . . διαληψόμεθα)–1.25.166.4. Wood's documentation is scrupulous but not obsessive; he cites secondary sources such as Banier's *Mythology* (45 n. 1), and it is possible that a text like Clement's may have had some influence on his thesis. For Wood's wide classical and ecclesiastical reading attested in "the most peculiar book on architecture written in England during the 18th century": R. W[ittkower], "Federico Zuccari and John Wood of Bath," *JWCI* 6 (1943) 221 and n. 1.

early times: "That these things were so practiced from the beginnings which are described above we can observe, seeing that to this day buildings are constructed of these materials by foreign nations" (*haec autem ex is, quae supra scripta sunt, originibus instituta esse possumus sic animadvertere, quod ad hunc diem nationibus exteris ex his rebus aedificia constituantur*; 2.1.4). He gives examples of timber construction and mud roofing, and assures his readers that "thus by these examples we can form a conclusion about the ancient inventions of buildings, reasoning that they were so" (*ita his signis de antiquis inventionibus aedificiorum, sic ea fuisse ratinocinantes, possumus iudicare*; 2.1.6). As men made progress in skill, they became carpenters, and passed from a state of barbarism to a state of civilization, complete with crafts (2.1.6). Among their achievements was a change from making huts to houses (*non cases sed etiam domos*) with foundations and brick or stone walls and roofs of wood and tiles (2.1.7). Thus timber was still used, but was treated in a careful and sophisticated way; together with the other building materials, it counted as one of the refinements of living (2.1.7). Vitruvius' account is admittedly speculative. It is so similar to the remarks of other writers on the early use of wood for sculpture that one may suspect that some more comprehensive theory of the material and technological advancement of early man underlies the whole range of such assertions. That the basic concern is the question of civilization, with all the philosophical and political concerns attendant on such a concept, must cast doubt on the reliability of the ancient references to the priority of wood as a material in any craft.

Although it seems only common sense to suppose that materials like clay and wood, which are easy to collect and fashion, would have been employed for statuary before stone, which requires considerable effort and technical ability to do either, evidence from specific cultures does not support such a hypothesis of universal development. As has been noted already, Palaeolithic and Neolithic artists were undeterred by the difficulty of working stone. Comparable figures worked from stone and clay are preserved in the series of figurines of the Aegean cultures of the Neolithic through Early Bronze ages.[80] Even a culture that until recently seemed to lack statuary almost completely, the Mycenaean, produced as its one known effort of monumental sculpture the great stone relief of the Lion Gate at Mycenae.

The concern with the ease of working of various materials reflects to some extent the tendency to equate the question of the origins of Greek statuary with that of the origins of monumental stone sculpture as it is

[80] For inconclusive speculations about the relationship of material to the typology of figurines in the early Cretan series: Ucko, *Anthropomorphic Figurines* (*supra* p. 207 n. 73) 336–337; 252–301 for illustrations of 103 figurines in a variety of materials.

typified by Archaic and classical works. The carving of a single large image from a single block is the process used for the earliest known large Greek statues, for example, Nikandre's dedication. It is understandable that the search for the origins of such statues should focus on how sculptors began to extract single figures from individual matrices. There is a sizeable body of evidence, however, for statues that were built up from separate pieces, indicating that both the technical and aesthetic possibilities for early Greek sculpture are greater than the one block–one image idea would allow.

Evidence exists from a variety of times and places for techniques of composite images. For many years, one of the major examples of composite statuary on a large scale in the Bronze Age was the wooden statue with added bronze locks of hair from Knossos, which Evans reconstructed from charred fragments of wood found together with bronze pieces that look like curls of hair. Recently, however, Hägg has examined these bronze remains and reconstructed not one large statue, but several small figures, seeing the bronze curls as individual bronze wigs. Such wigs recall the preserved wigs of steatite which seem to have belonged to composite statues. Bronze pieces that are demonstrably single locks of hair are also known, and there is no doubt that the making of composite figures from a variety of materials was an important technique of Minoan sculpture.[81] The sixth-century B.C. chryselephantine statues found at Delphi are impressive examples of both small and life-size statues built up from many elements.[82] Despinis has reconstructed two Roman statues the stone exteriors of which had been pieced together around wooden cores; these afford a view of one version of the acrolithic images mentioned in literature. There exist many stone heads and extremities that were once attached to wooden bodies.[83] Two limestone Daedalic figures, from Astritsi and Gortyna in Crete, are built up from separate upper and lower pieces.[84] All these techniques go far beyond the addition of details like eyes, or even of extended arms or parts of heads, that

[81] For charred wood and bronze pieces reconstructed as belonging to a large composite (female?) statue: Evans, *PM* III, 522–525; 521 fig. 365 for a drawing of the bronze pieces, interpreted as curls of hair. No photographs of these important pieces for large-scale composite Minoan sculpture were available until the treatment by R. Hägg, "The Bronze Hair-Locks from Knossos. A New Interpretation," *AA* 1983, 543–549.

For comparable wigs of steatite: Evans, *PM* III, 419–422 and Suppl. pl. XXXVI; Hägg 544; Hood, *Arts* 95–96.

[82] For the chryselephantine statues from Delphi: *supra* p. 29 n. 72.

[83] *Supra* p. 142 n. 340.

[84] Figure from Astritsi: C. Davaras, *Die Statue aus Astritsi* (*AK* Beiheft 8; Bern, 1972), esp. 18–20 for the technique; M. Sipsie-Eschbach, "Bemerkungen zum Torso aus Astritsi," *AA* 1982, 487–491, for the possibility that the figure is not seated, but standing. Figure from Gortyna: G. Rizza and V. Santa Maria Scrinari, *Il santuario sull'Acropoli di Gortina* I (Rome, 1968) 156 no. 7; pls. 2–3.

is attested in stone sculpture of various times.[85] Wooden statues might have been constructed in any of these ways. Ridgway has even suggested that the seventh-century Cretan technique of piecing in stone had its origin in woodworking.[86] The evidence of the assembled figures suggests that there may always have been considerable variety in the way statues were made, and that there may not have been a clear-cut progession from wooden to stone productions. While the fact remains that there is still no evidence for sizeable stone statuary before the seventh century B.C., it may be that the questions asked about its origins are slightly off the mark.

Support for the postulated priority of wooden statuary has also been sought in preclassical stone sculpture itself. It has often been said that thin, flat statues like the Nikandre and thin, cylindrical pieces like Cheramyes' dedication display in stone the characteristics of their wooden ancestors, which were carved from planks and poles. This suggestion arose from the unfavorable impression such statues made when they were first compared with the naturalistic works of later Greek art. The explanation of their apparent artistic deficiencies was sought in the theory that they preserved stylistic traces of crude wooden statuary. An important element of this theory was the presumption that sculpture in wood was limited by certain inherent qualities of the material.

The arguments that early stone statues preserve features of wooden ancestors assume that wood as a material has certain inevitable characteristics that betray themselves in style and technique: a round trunk, for example, must yield a round statue, and a flat plank, a flat statue. Thus Brunn, comparing Nikandre's to Cheramyes' dedication, asserted that these stone figures showed their artistic derivation from wooden sculptures, one recalling four-edged beams, the other, rounded tree-trunks. More recently, Cook, believing that because logs were easier to produce than boards, wooden statues would have been carved from rounded logs, dismissed the possibility that wooden statues were the ancestors of the flat-looking Daedalic style.[87] Ridgway, rejecting ideas of wholesale formal dependence, sees instead dependence on wooden prototypes in details like the

[85] For inlaid eyes (*e.g.*, wooden eyes from the Idean cave, bone eyes from Amnisos, inlaid eyes of sixth-century marble statues): L. Adams, *Orientalizing Sculpture in Soft Limestone from Crete and Mainland Greece* (British Archaeological Reports, Suppl. Series 42; Oxford, 1978) 8; 27–28 for the technique of piecing; for separate head as an apparently Milesian characteristic: Ridgway, *Archaic* 93 n. 10; for added arms of korai: Richter, *Korai passim* (*e.g.*, Acr. 673, *Korai* no. 117, which clearly shows the method for attaching arms).

[86] Ridgway, *Archaic* 24–25.

[87] Herrmann discusses Brunn's inference of a wooden origin for early stone statuary on the basis of style, finding in it a new stage in the theory of *xoana*: "Entstehung" 37. *Cf.* R.M. Cook, "Origins of Greek Sculpture," *JHS* 87 (1967) 24–32, esp. 27.

sharp straight lines of profiles and the renderings of hair in some seventh-century terracottas. She suggests further that two technical features of Daedalic statues may have originated in wooden statuary: first, the narrow, columnar outline that might have characterized a statue carved from a wooden board or beam; and second, the technique of piecing a statue together from several parts, which would likely have been expedient in working wood. Herrmann sees a formal continuity between wooden and stone sculpture, again in the sharp precision of carved detail; he asserts that the undercutting of the mantle-hem of the "Dame d'Auxerre" and the carving of her costume were not conceived in stone, but are instead manifestly part of a wooden tradition.[88] Boardman denies that "there is any clear evidence for significant influence on seventh-century statuary from any carpentry styles, other than the purely technical."[89] This statement assumes, however, that there were in fact styles unique to woodworking; it is, furthermore, exactly such technical influence that is a major question.

The idea that specific stylistic characteristics can be explained by the physical nature of materials appears in a variety of studies of Greek and other art.[90] One example of this approach is the application of the distinction between "glyptic" and "plastic" conception—*i.e.*, the carving of statues from hard substances as opposed to their molding in soft ones—to the analysis of the drapery style of the pedimental figures from the Temple of Zeus at Olympia. The "doughy" quality of the drapery has been explained as the result of using clay models for the stone statues. While the suggestion of soft substances does help in visualizing the texture of the drapery, its usefulness stops at description. The theory cannot account for the fact that many contemporary terracotta statues display strongly "glyptic" characteristics. It can be maintained only if, as Ridgway does in her discussion of the question, one postulates a complicated series of deliberate imitations in the

[88] Ridgway, *Archaic* 21–22 for suggestion that "features typical of wood carving can be detected in some of the Daedalic terracottas"; 23–25 for columnar profiles and the technique of piecing. Herrmann, "Entstehung" 40–41 for the formal continuity between wooden and stone sculpture demonstrated by sharp, precise carving. *Cf.* Kyrieleis, "Holzfunde" 102–103.

[89] Boardman, *Archaic* 21.

[90] The material determination of form and style has, for example, recently been elaborately argued by M. Baxandall, *The Limewood Sculptors of Renaissance Germany* (New Haven and London, 1980) 32–38; he explains how the structure of limewood gives it properties that are both good and bad for use in sculpture, and describes the methods used by sculptors to exploit or overcome them. While he proves by contemporary documents that the artists consciously valued limewood, the examples of statues he cites to demonstrate the way form expresses the range of the structural characteristics of the wood do not make this point clear. I am unable to distinguish in the illustrations the formal expression of the stability of the wood from the formal expression of the stress within the wood.

"glyptic" media of the characteristics of "plastic" works, and *vice versa.*[91] It seems better to suggest that stylistic characteristics are not restricted to particular materials.

The idea that form is determined by material appears in other contexts, too. It is often asserted, for example, that certain shapes in pottery copy metal shapes. What is meant is not simply specific features like "rivets" that do indicate that a particular shape has been translated from one material to another, but instead the fundamental formal structure and conception.[92] Hill has demonstrated, however, that some of the Greek vase shapes of which the sharp forms had long been assumed to be inherently metallic could not, in fact, even have been executed in metal with the techniques known at the time they were made.[93]

These examples show the difficulty in assigning specific formal and stylistic features to particular materials. Such attributions are likely to reflect the observer's own experience and convictions about form, which may not hold true in a different aesthetic context. It is even more risky to try to infer the characteristics of statuary that no longer exists in any quantity.

The major difficulty in studying Greek wooden statuary has always been the simple lack of it. Special conditions are needed for the preservation of wood, and until recently only a handful of Greek wooden figures existed.[94] Their number is still comparatively small, but they are varied

[91] B.S. Ridgway, *The Severe Style in Greek Sculpture* (Princeton, 1970) 19–20.

[92] *E.g.*, Hood, *Arts* 27, 34, on the imitation of metal shapes in Middle Minoan eggshell ware; 153–155, where he draws no distinction between the copying of individual details and the imitation of overall shape, form, and decorative intention, and suggests that the "sharply angled profiles" of Minyan Ware shapes are a metallic feature and that the "standard" gray, red, and yellow surfaces may be meant for silver, copper, and gold (155); *cf.* G.E. Mylonas, "The Luvian Invasions of Greece," *Hesperia* 31 (1962) 286–287. See Ventris and Chadwick, *Documents*² 324 for vessel shapes drawn on tablets identified as bronze not only by the BRONZE ideogram, but also by their profiles. An example of a similar theory applied to architecture: N. Leipen, *Athena Parthenos. A Reconstruction* (Toronto, 1971) 38: " . . . since the Corinthian capital is not a form natural to stone, but to metal, it must have been invented for use in connection with some monument where metal, not stone was employed, therefore not for an architectural purpose." See now M. Vickers, "Artful Crafts: The Influence of Metalwork on Athenian Painted Pottery," *JHS* 105 (1985) 108–128: "the fictile vases which have survived from classical antiquity should be regarded as owing not simply their shapes but the very nature of their decoration to metalwork procedures" (128).

[93] D.K. Hill, "The Technique of Greek Metal Vases and Its Bearing on Vase Forms in Metal and Pottery," *AJA* 51 (1947) 248–256. See also Robertson, *History* 18, a warning against postulating "a general metallic influence on Greek pottery," despite occasional such adaptations.

[94] Basic information on the conditions necessary for the preservation of wood is given in H.J. Plenderleith and A.E.A. Werner, *The Conservation of Antiquities and Works of Art*² (London, 1971) 124–125. For Samos: Kyrieleis, "Holzfunde" 87–88, with reference to methods of conservation. For a useful list of preserved wooden objects: *EAA* IV, 530–537 *s.v.* Legno.

enough to show that there are no grounds for postulating a uniform style for wooden sculpture. They do not differ significantly from comparable figural types in other materials, and they display no inevitable stylistic characteristics that can be assigned to wood.

The stylistic variety attainable in wood can be demonstrated by three statuettes that were found in 1934 in a spring sanctuary at Palma Montechiaro, near Gela in Sicily. They were preserved by the sulphurous spring water, and enough of them survives to give a reasonable idea of their appearance, although their bodies have buckled, and the face of the smallest is badly damaged. They are small figures, each under twenty centimeters high. All are females wearing a polos and, apparently, a peplos. They stand on small, projecting bases carved in one piece with the statuettes. Their forearms, which were attached separately, are lost now, but the holes for the tenons by which they were attached are visible.[95]

The smallest statuette is like the figures of the second half of the seventh century in both the sharp constriction of the slender body at the waist and the stiff setting of the head in a pronounced frame of substantial hair. The figure seems formally equivalent to Nikandre's dedication; the careful development of the individual parts of the body and costume and the sharply drawn boundaries between them make both figures exercises in precise and highly decorative articulation. In contrast, the larger wooden statuettes have a smoother silhouette, and the relationship of face and neck to hair is easier, more smoothly and organically coordinated, with little suggestion of a wig. The larger figures find good parallels in Archaic statuary of the later sixth century. The crisp and varied renderings of the wavy hair recall several of the Attic korai. A certain squareness in the face of the smaller figure and a plastic prominence in both faces are reminiscent of the metopes of Temple C at Selinus. The taller of the two compares well in the modelling of her features with the Lyons Kore. The basic peplophoros scheme recalls the Peplos Kore from the Acropolis, but these bodies are more substantial; they are less slender and have greater solidity.[96]

The stylistic similarities of the three wooden statuettes to figures in stone are strong and consistent. It appears, then, that wood is capable of conveying stylistic variations sufficient to allow the figures to be analyzed

[95] Syracuse, National Museum nos. 47134, 47135, 47136: G. Caputo, "Tre xoana e il culto di una sorgente sulfurea in territorio Geloo-Agrigentino," *MonAnt* 37.1 (1938) 586–683. A better photograph is published in *EAA* IV, 531 fig. 624. Richter, *Korai* nos. 31, 53, 54. The tenon of the left arm of 47135 has survived and is clearly visible: *EAA* IV, 531 fig. 624, center.

[96] Convenient illustrations of the pieces mentioned are: Nikandre's dedication: Richter, *Korai* figs. 25–28; Selinus C metopes: L. Giuliani, *Die archaischen Metopen von Selinunt* (Mainz, 1979) 11–33, pls. 1, 4–7; Lyons Kore: Richter, *Korai* figs. 275–281; Peplos Kore: Richter, *Korai* figs. 349–354.

by the chronological and even regional criteria that have been established for sculpture in other materials.

The essential stylistic equivalence of sculpture executed in wood and in other materials can be observed in artistic traditions in which evidence for a variety of media is well preserved. For example, it is recognized that the style of Egyptian sculpture is independent of the materials from which it is made.[97] It is likely that in Greek sculpture, too, stylistic traits are not as closely tied to specific materials as might be supposed purely on the basis of theory. The preserved Greek wooden figures do in fact show a great variety in both overall form and small details of renderings; there seem to be few limits to the effects that can be achieved in wooden work.

The wooden statuary from Samos exhibits a remarkable range of types and styles of figures. This is clear, for example, in a comparison of two female statuettes, the well-known figure of Hera and a nameless kore.[98] The Hera combines the vigorous, well-articulated body that seems typical of the second half of the seventh century B.C. with a great amount of intricately carved ornament. Her tall polos bears rows of carved panels in at least two designs. The edges of her upper garment and the central panel and border of her skirt are richly carved with hatched and diamond patterns. The hair that falls over her shoulders is marked with long, vertical zig-zags; in back, the strands of hair are horizontally hatched.

Both the overall structure and the rich, sharp decorative detail of the Hera are completely different from the simplicity of the kore. This second statuette, dated to the first quarter of the sixth century, is excessively attenuated, and while her forearms, like the Hera's, were separately attached and would have stretched forward, it is unlikely that their presence would have improved the overall impression the figure makes. The head simply seems too large for the body, and there is also a certain crudeness in both the placement and the rendering of the features. That the quality of this figure seems not to be as high as that of the Hera must influence judgment of it.[99]

[97] Discussions of material in Egyptian sculpture concentrate on the techniques by which the materials were made to yield the desired stylistic results: *e.g.*, C. Aldred, *Egyptian Art* (New York and Toronto, 1980) 22–26; 26: " . . . the Egyptian concept of form is imposed on the medium—wood, ivory, metal or stone—with little regard to its inherent qualities." Even in non-stone statues, in which two-dimensional poses may be imitated more closely thanks to the flexibility of the material, there is no alteration in figural conception. Poulsen, "Typenbildung" 190, uses Egyptian wooden statues as evidence against the idea of the insurmountable limitations of wood as a material for sculpture; he notes that early Egyptian wooden statues have no trace of angularity in their rendering of surfaces.

[98] The Hera from Samos: D. Ohly, "Neue Holzfunde aus dem Heraion von Samos. Befund und Rekonstruktion der Herastatuette," *AM* 82 (1967) 89–99, Beil. 43–47; for more recent discoveries: *AM* 82 (1967) 102–107. Kore: *AM* 82 (1967) 107–109 no. 2; Beil. 48–51.

[99] Infelicities noted in *AM* 82 (1967) 108.

The stylistic and formal characteristics of the kore are clear, however, despite its deficiencies. The modelling is generally rounded and slightly soft; note especially the bulging little step from the broad forehead up to the hair. The lips and ears are fleshy, and the planes of the face generous. The silhouette of the overlong lower body lacks visual interest until the bottom, where it flares smoothly and surprisingly gracefully. Nothing about the statuette is sharp or abrupt; its forms are in complete contrast to the crisply articulated Hera.

A third piece from Samos, probably of the later seventh century, differs entirely from both the Hera and the kore. It is a dwarfish, naked figure that squats and holds a smaller figure in its arms.[100] Its body is grossly shaped, with a swelled belly and pneumatic-looking limbs. The depression where a phallus was once attached is clear. The figure it carries is a travesty of a kouros. It is difficult not to think of this figure as primitive; one is inescapably reminded of African tribal carvings and the like, which, despite their vigor, to the Western eye often appear awkward and crude. The overall forms of this Samian figure are brusque and jutting, although individual passages, such as the back of the head, are pleasingly shaped and finely carved. The actual roundness of the parts of the body does not bear out the first impression that the figure has been hacked out. It is, therefore, a piece of good quality, and the reason for its seemingly crude appearance must be sought elsewhere than artistic incompetence. There exists a marble figure in Sparta that is similar to the Samian statuette.[101] Both pieces evidently represent beings who are decidedly outside the usual run of anthropomorphism and whose images have little to do with the ordinary canons of figural art.

It is hard to imagine a piece more unlike the statuettes of conventional seventh- and sixth-century types executed in wood than the Samian daemon; yet all are made from the same material. Clearly wood imposes no inevitable formal characteristics. So well does wood carry out varied stylistic intentions that regional styles can be detected. One statuette from Samos, for example, is a compact and rounded figure with hands folded at the waist who seems like a visitor from the Near East; the ancestry of such a

[100] "Daemon" from Samos: *AM* 82 (1967) 109–112 no. 3; Beil. 52–54, 81.2; R. Hampe and E. Simon, *The Birth of Greek Art* (Fribourg, 1980; tr. New York, 1981) 230, fig. 346.

[101] Female figure from Magula: Tod and Wace, *Catalogue Sparta* (*supra* p. 186 n. 27) 171–172 no. 364; 172 figs. 50, 51; C.A. Christou, Ἀρχαῖα Σπάρτη (Sparta, 1960) 89–91; 90 fig. 21; Boardman, *Archaic* 26 ("perhaps inspired by the east"); 62 fig. 80. To the double-flute player at the right side of the figure, *cf.* the sixth-century figure of Cybele from Boğazköy: K. Bittel, "Phrygisches Kultbild aus Boğazköy," *Antike Plastik* 2 (1963) 7–22; the drapery of this Phrygian work seems to owe something to East Greek forms: J. Boardman, *The Greeks Overseas*[3] (London, 1980) 93 for such influence in the rendering of the costume.

piece lies well outside the Greek sphere.[102] The Hera and a kore that is similar to her find parallels in the material from Gortyna, and a Cretan origin has been suggested for them.[103] Wood can embody not only styles that are fundamentally different, but also variations within individual styles. The kore that is related to the Hera, for instance, is less elaborately carved than the goddess. Although her body and costume are similar, the design of her skirt and the pattern of her hair lack the fine variety that makes the Hera seem a superior work.[104]

The wooden figures that have been examined disappoint any expectation that the literary evidence may have raised that wooden statuary is crude. In spite of variations in style and quality, no piece displays the kind of crudeness that would be helpful to an evolutionary theory. The "daemon" owes its awkward form to iconography; the harshness seems to be intentional, and parts of the figure are finely executed. The only plausibly crude and primitive piece from the wooden material preserved on Samos is a small relief showing an armless little dummy in a niche, and it too can be accounted for in terms of iconography and quality. Kyrieleis has drawn attention to a similar relief from Gortyna. It seems that it and the Samian relief derive from pieces like the niche-reliefs with goddesses known from Sardis, which are very much better executed.[105] The small, crude reliefs do not appear to be the ancestral forms.

This brief examination of some of the wooden statuary preserved from Greek times agrees with Herrmann's conclusion that sculpture in wood, far from being either inherently crude or stylistically sluggish, holds its own with contemporary work in other media.[106] What is less certain is that the material imposes any characteristics of its own. Even the relatively few pieces considered show that wood is versatile enough to carry out a number of different stylistic intentions. Stylistic features like sharp definition of forms and elaborate precision of decoration may perhaps be attributable not to the characteristics of wood as a material, but instead to more general aesthetic preferences. At any rate, the idea that wooden production is inherently crude appears to be invalid.

[102] *AM* 82 (1967) 114–115 no. 5 (Inv. H44); Beil. 56.3, 57.

[103] Kyrieleis, "Holzfunde" 97–99. *Cf.* Adams, *Orientalizing Sculpture* (*supra* p. 212 n. 85) 33, who cites a growing number of monumental female figures in Daedalic dress from East Greece and the islands to which the Auxerre Kore seems indebted.

[104] Kore from Samos: Kyrieleis, "Holzfunde" 94–103 no. 11 (Inv. H. 100); pl. 21.

[105] Relief from Samos: Kyrieleis, "Holzfunde" 105–106 no. 17 (Inv. H. 106); pl. 27.1; 106 and n. 81 for the Gortyna relief: Rizza and Santa Maria Scrinari, *Gortina* (*supra* p. 211 n. 84) 156 no. 4 (*Inv.* 2588); pl. I.4. For the reliefs from Sardis: Kyrieleis, "Holzfunde" 105 and n. 80; G.M.A. Hanfmann and N.H. Ramage, *Sculpture from Sardis* (Archaeological Exploration of Sardis Report 2; Cambridge, Massachusetts, 1978) cat. nos. 4, 6, 7.

[106] Herrmann, "Entstehung" 39.

THE ANICONIC ORIGIN OF GREEK STATUARY

The third and final assumption that has led scholars to postulate a stage of primitive wooden productions in the early development of Greek sculpture is that statues evolved from aniconic representations of the gods. This idea originates directly in the ancient testimony for the origin of idolatry, and is reinforced by ancient references to aniconic pieces that are characteristic of an early stage of worship. The most significant sources are Clement, who explains how aniconic pillars and poles evolved into figural statues, Themistius, who interprets the rationalizing accounts of the achievements of Daedalus in light of that iconoclastic discussion, and the antiquarian authors such as Callimachus, Plutarch, and Pausanias, who assert that in the past, worship was carried on not with *agalmata*, but instead with unworked monuments. These sources, along with other testimonia that support the ideas they present, have already been examined in the context of the historical preconceptions and polemic intentions they embody.[107]

Modern scholars have seized upon this testimony for a variety of ends. Winckelmann uses it chiefly in order to begin his history of ancient art at the very beginning; he presents the speculations in it as facts that can be illustrated by surviving monuments. Farnell uses it to establish a developmental scheme whereby statues such as Nikandre's dedication, which do not conform to the canons of classical naturalism, could be explained as descendants of aniconic ancestors.[108] Some scholars have used it to demonstrate the survival of aniconic practices in later times, being convinced not only by the ancient sources, but also by comparative anthropological evidence, that aniconism preceded the worship of images. Evans, for example, after presenting many examples of such apparent survivals in Mycenaean tree and pillar cults, suggests that the "transition to anthropomorphism" may have occurred in the Mycenaean (that is, in current terms, the Minoan) age, since the traditions about Daedalus, whose statues first broke away from a pillar-like format, associate him with King Minos.[109] Michel, in collecting (mostly literary) evidence for survivals of fetishistic practices in Greece, outlines a progression from unworked sacred stone to worked stone aniconic monuments, which were at last transformed into statues when anthropomorphic gods ousted the older, fetishistic, divinities.[110] Several scholars have focused their attention on the transitional stage between aniconic and iconic forms. Lullies, Curtius, and Deubner, for example,

[107] *Supra* pp. 177–194.

[108] Farnell, "Origins" 167–172.

[109] A.J. Evans, "Mycenaean Tree and Pillar Cult and its Mediterranean Relations," *JHS* 21 (1901) 123–128; 126 for Daedalus.

[110] Ch. Michel, "Les survivances du fétichisme dans les cultes populaires de la Grèce ancienne," *RHR* 60 (1909) 141–160, esp. 141–149.

have argued that herms, a semi-iconic form, had evolved from aniconic pillars. The same argument has recently been advanced by Miller, who sees herms and similar monuments as transitional forms in the evolution of aniconic monuments into anthropomorphic images.[111] Burkert and Dietrich, writing about aspects of the history of Greek religion, take it as given that Greek statuary evolved from aniconic monuments.[112] All these scholars rely heavily on the ancient literary testimony.

There are several reasons to doubt the theory that images evolved from aniconic monuments. What is known of Greek aniconic worship does not support the idea that it is ancestral to the making of images. Nor do semi-iconic forms appear to be evidence for a transitional stage between aniconism and iconism. Most of the information about Greek aniconic worship comes from literary sources, but there are also many representations of such monuments, and a small number of surviving aniconic pieces.[113] A brief review of a representative sampling of this evidence shows the great variety of Greek aniconic worship, and suggests other ways to account for apparently transitional forms ancestral to figural representation.

Tree-trunks and unworked planks are mentioned by several authors. Clement notes such representations of Cithaeronian Hera in Thespiae and a similar Artemis in Icarus; the passage in which these appear, *Protr.* 4.40 P. [**44**], is copied by Arnobius (*Adv.Gen.* 6.11) [**31**], whose references therefore do not count as independent testimony. Callimachus (*ap.* Eus. *PE* 3.8.1) [**108**] mentions simple planks, unworked by chisels, that were the old way of setting up monuments of the gods; he cites the Samian Hera and Danaus' dedication of Athena at Lindos.[114] Tertullian (*Ap.* 16.6) [**360**] notes a similar Ceres in Pharae, as well as the "Attic Pallas." In this category may also be included the Spartan *dokana*, a construction of beams representing the Dioscuri mentioned by Plutarch [**318**] as ancient *aphidrumata*, and pictured on several reliefs of classical times.[115]

[111] For references to and discussion of Lullies, Curtius, and Deubner: Goldman, "Herm" 58. For Miller: *supra* p. 193 n. 47.

[112] *Supra* p. 192 and n. 43. Note also Moore, "Baetylia" 198: "In some places the steps of the further development [of holy stones worked to rectangular blocks to obelisks or pyramids] to rudely iconic forms, and finally to the statue as a work of art, can be traced."

[113] For Greek aniconic practice: M.W. de Visser, *Die nicht menschengestaltigen Götter der Griechen* (Leiden, 1903); Michel, "Survivances" (*supra* p. 219 n. 110); Rose, "Images" *passim*; Miller, "Altar" (*supra* p. 193 n. 47) *passim*; Yalouris, "Bassai"; M.P. Nilsson, *The Minoan-Mycenaean Religion and its Survival in Greek Religion*² (Lund, 1950) 236–261, esp. 254–258 for the Bronze Age.

[114] *Supra* pp. 46–48, 184–185.

[115] *Supra* p. 186 n. 27.

Unworked stones were venerated in several places.[116] The black stone of Cybele at Pessinus, which was moved to Rome in 204 B.C., was famous.[117] Apollonius of Rhodes (2.1172–1173) mentions a black stone venerated in the past by the Amazons. Plutarch (*QG* 13; *Mor.* 294 C) reports that the Thessalian Aenianians revered a stone with which their king Phemius had killed an enemy. This stone is not given the name of a god, but is nonetheless the focus of cult; Plutarch says that the people treat it as *hieros*, sacrificing to it and covering it with the fat from sacrificial victims. This custom recalls the widespread Greek habit of pouring oil on stones; Pausanias (10.24.6) mentions the practice in connection with the stone of Cronus, and Theophrastus satirizes a too-devout man who leaves no roadside stone unoiled (*Char.* 16.4).[118] Pausanias mentions an unworked stone at Thespiae that represents Eros (9.27.1) **[276]** and rocks at Orchomenos that are worshipped "most of all" (9.38.1) **[277]**. Sjöqvist identifies a basalt river-stone found near the altar of the open-air sanctuary at Ayia Irini on Cyprus as the

[116] *RE* 2.1 (1895) 723–728 *s.v.* *ἄργοι λίθοι* (E. Reisch); *supra* p. 220 n. 113 for general treatment of aniconism.

[117] J. Bremmer, "The Legend of Cybele's Arrival in Rome," in M.J. Vermaseren, ed., *Studies in Hellenistic Religions* (Etudes préliminaires aux religions dans l'empire romain 78; Leiden, 1979) 9–22; Griffiths, *Temple Treasures* 19–24; Cook, *Zeus* III, 893–898. A comparatively late tradition seems to make the Cybele a real statue: Herod. 1.11 (*agalma diopetes*).

[118] For Ap. Rhod. *Arg.* 2.1172–1173: *supra* p. 185 n. 21. Plut. *Mor.* 294 B–C:

Ἐκ δὲ τούτου μονομαχοῦσιν οἱ βασιλεῖς, καὶ τὸν τῶν Ἰναχιέων Ὑπέροχον ὁ τῶν Αἰνιάνων Φήμιος ὁρῶν μετὰ κυνὸς αὐτῷ προσφερόμενον οὐκ ἔφη δίκαια ποιεῖν, δεύτερον ἐπάγοντα μαχόμενον· ἀπελαύνοντος δὲ τοῦ Ὑπερόχου τὸν κύνα καὶ μεταστρεφομένου, λίθῳ βαλὼν ὁ Φήμιος αὐτὸν ἀναιρεῖ. κτησάμενοι δὲ τὴν χώραν, τοὺς Ἰναχιεῖς μετὰ τῶν Ἀχαιῶν ἐκβαλόντες, τὸν μὲν λίθον ἐκεῖνον ὡς ἱερὸν σέβονται καὶ θύουσιν αὐτῷ καὶ τοῦ ἱερείου τῷ δημῷ περικαλύπτουσιν. ὅταν δὲ τῷ Ἀπόλλωνι τὴν ἑκατόμβην ἀποδιδῶσι, τῷ Διὶ βοῦν καθιερεύσαντες, μερίδα τοῖς Τέμωνος ἀπογόνοις ἐξαίρετον νέμουσι, καὶ "πτωχικὸν κρέας" ἐπονομάζουσι.

After this affair the two kings engaged in single combat, and Phemius, king of the Aenianians, observing the Inachian king, Hyperochus, advancing to meet him accompanied by a dog, said that Hyperochus was acting unfairly in bringing on a second combatant. But while Hyperochus was driving off the dog and had his back turned, Phemius hit him with a stone and killed him. The Aenianians gained possession of the country, driving out the Inachians together with the Achaeans, and they revere that stone as sacred, and sacrifice to it and cover it round with the fat of the sacrificial victim; and whenever they pay the hecatomb to Apollo, they sacrifice a bull to Zeus; and they set aside a select portion of the flesh for the descendants of Temon, and this they call the "beggar's meat." (Tr. F.C. Babbitt)

W.R. Halliday, *The Greek Questions of Plutarch* (Oxford, 1928) 77–78 *ad loc.* for this stone. For the oiling of stones: Moore, "Baetylia" 202–203; Burkert, *Structure* 41–43. *Supra* p. 39 n. 91 for the oiling of statues.

cult object, suggesting that it may even have been venerated in the earliest installation there, which is dated to Late Cypriot III. He detects on its surface "traces of having been rubbed with ointment and burnt by fire."[119] It is necessary to distinguish carefully between venerated stones and actual "baetyls." "Baetyl" is a term that is often wrongly applied to venerated stones in general; it is in fact a specialized term in antiquity that was used first in Hadrianic times, and it refers to a specific kind of powerful, animated stone.[120] Baetyls are only one aspect of the veneration of stones, and because they are a late development, they are not good evidence for the antiquity of the practice.

Columns and pillars of various kinds are well attested in literature, art, and preserved monuments. The literary evidence has one limitation: frequently it is impossible to be certain what kind of monument is meant. The word *kion* seems usually to mean a pillar, round in section, but by Plato's time it was also used of rectangular herms.[121] That the word *kion* by itself is ambiguous should be kept in mind in reviewing the testimonia for *kiones*. Clement quotes the *Phoronis* and the *Europia* about tall *kiones* of Argive Hera and Apollo at Delphi respectively (*Strom.* 1.164.2; 164.3) [**47**]. Two *styloi* appear in the same passage: an oracle mentions a *stylos* of Dionysus of Thebes, and Euripides refers to a *stylos* of Evohe (*Strom.* 1.163.4; 163.5 = *Ant.* fr. 202 Nauck²). Pausanias mentions an Artemis Patroa in Sicyon fashioned in the shape of a *kion* (2.9.6) [**205**]. In 3.20.9 [**239**], he notes seven *kiones* near Sparta that he supposes to represent the planets in the ancient way—that is, aniconically.[122] Probably the best known of all aniconic cults is the widespread worship of Apollo Agyieus, whose conical pillars stood before the doors of houses and are frequently mentioned in literature. Explanations of Agyieus appear in late lexica and commentaries (*e.g.*, Harpocration *s.v.* and Eusthatius *ad.* H. *Il.* 2.12 [**130**]), and the identification of Agyieus representations in art is secure. These conical pillars appear in vase paintings and on the coins of several cities, notably Megara.[123] On Corfu, in

[119] E. Gjerstad *et al.*, *The Swedish Cyprus Expedition* II (Stockholm, 1935) 702, 796 no. 938; "The stone has been used as cult object." E. Sjöqvist, "Die Kultgeschichte eines cyprischen Temenos," *ARW* 30 (1933) 308–359.

[120] Moore, "Baetylia." I have not been able to consult the dissertation of A. Hubmann, "Der Baitylos" (Archäologisches Institut, Universität Wien, 1978). The broader usage of the word (*e.g.*, Rose, "Images" 35) is misleading.

[121] For *kion* as a name for herms: *supra* p. 185 n. 22.

[122] LSJ⁹ s.v. *κίων*, *στύλος*. For the planets: Rose, "Images" 36–37.

[123] For coins of Byzantium, Ambracia, Apollonia, and Orikos, with remarks on Agyieus: Yalouris, "Bassai" 101 and pl. 45 b. For Agyieus: Farnell, *Cults* I, 15; IV, 307–309, and for the displacement of the "aniconic agalma" by the "anthropomorphic eikon." Frazer, *Pausanias* II, 417; V, 318–319; Rose, "Images" 36; *LIMC* II.1, 188–189 *s.v.* Apollon, I A. Yalouris' suggestion that the Corinthian column at Bassai was the aniconic representation of Apollo

1813, a conical pillar of Agyieus type was found near the temple of Artemis, but it is inscribed as a boundary-stone (*horwos*) of Pythios; still, however, the association is with Apollo.[124] Pausanias mentions an Apollo Agyieus in Megalopolis that is not in the familiar conical shape, but has instead a rectangular design: *σχῆμα τετράγωνον* (8.32.4) [**262**]. Apparently there existed some variation within the representation of Apollo Agyieus, as is the case with other aniconic cults.

Squared shapes were also widespread. Again, it cannot always be told whether the literary sources refer to plain rectangular monuments like stelai, or to herm-like forms. Pausanias mentions statues of the Great Gods in Megalopolis in *τὸ τετράγωνον σχῆμα* (rectangular design; 8.31.7) [**261**]. He notes when speaking of an *agalma tetragonon* of Zeus Teleios that the Arcadians appear to be especially fond of the form (8.48.6) [**269**]. *Tetragonos* is how Pausanias describes what are today called herms (4.33.3) [**245**]; the Athenians gave representations of Hermes *τὸ σχῆμα τὸ τετράγωνον*.

Plain, rectangular stelai that seem to be representations of gods are known from art and from surviving examples. Vase-painting provides many examples of such pillars. Some of the best are found on Apulian red-figured vases; a waist-high stele inscribed ΔΙΟΣ stands between Pelops and Oinomaus as they swear their oath before the race; Aphrodite sits in front of a stele inscribed ΑΦΡΟΔΙΤΗ. A common theme is two youths standing on either side of such pillars; many are plain, but some are marked ΗΡΑΚΛΕΣ, ΝΙΚΑ or ΤΕΡΜΟΝ, suggesting that they are connected with athletics. Most of the stelai are waist-high; some support leaning youths, which makes their identification as representations of gods dubious. Some, however, are as tall as the figures in the scenes.[125]

Epikourios is not convincing; aniconic pillars and poles generally seem to have been set up as independent monuments, and not to have been architectural members; *cf. infra* p. 226 n. 133. Paus. 8.32.4 [**262**] notes an Apollo Agyieus in the form of a herm. Not a vase, but rather a conical pillar seems to be shown in the baldacchino on a hydria by the Painter of Athens 1714, Paris, Cab. Méd. 980: *RVAp* I, 214 no. 169, pl. 68.1. For Apulian vases with representations of aniconic monuments: *infra* p. 223 n. 125.

[124] C.A. Rhomaios, "Les premières fouilles de Corfu," *BCH* 49 (1925) 211–217.

[125] Examples of aniconic monuments on Apulian vases: *Zeus*: London, British Museum F 331, amphora from Ruvo: *AnnInst* 1840, pl. NO; H.B. Walters, *Catalogue of the Greek and Etruscan Vases in the British Museum* IV. *Vases of the Latest Period* (London, 1896) 164–166; L. Séchan, *Etudes sur la tragédie grecque dans ses rapports avec la céramique* (Paris, 1926) 453–454 (F), fig. 129; F. Brommer, *Vasenlisten zur griechischen Heldensage* (Marburg, 1973) 540 D 7; *RVAp* I, 338, pl. 109.2–4, attributed to the Varrese Painter; the scene is identified as "Pelops and Oinomaus making libation at the altar of Zeus." *Aphrodite*: Cleveland 24.534, bell-krater: *CVA* USA 15, Cleveland 1, pl. 43.1, 3 (USA 723), related to the Graz Painter. *Heracles*: London, British Museum F 67, bell-krater: *RVAp* I, 78 no. 85, attributed to the Eton-Nika Painter. *Nika*: Bonn 79, bell-krater: *RVAp* I, 77 no. 83, pl. 27.1, Eton-Nika Painter. *Termon*: London, British Museum F 62, bell-krater: *RVAp* I, 161 no. 215, Graz

Of the stelai that are preserved, the best known are those from Tegea. They range in date from about the fourth century B.C. to the second century A.D. Unlike the plain, squared stelai pictured on the Apulian vases, they are topped by small pyramids; they could be called obelisks. Like the stelai shown on the vases, their inscriptions are varied. While some bear simple dedicatory inscriptions—[K]λεοίτας Ἀγαθôι θεôι ἀνέθηκε and the like—others carry only the nominative form of a divine name—Ἄρτεμις, for example, and Ἥρως. These bear out Pausanias' statement (7.22.4) **[251]** that this kind of monument was in fact given the name of the deity it represented.[126]

Pyramids themselves are another familiar aniconic type. Pausanias notes a pyramidal Zeus Meilichios in Sicyon (2.9.6) **[205]**, and such an Apollo Carinus in Megara (1.44.2) **[199]**. This small, pyramidal stone appears to be shown on Megarian coins, and seems to be related to the common Agyieus form.[127] Zeus Ktesios was commonly represented by pyramids or pillars. Zeus Meilichios is associated in Selinus, in the sanctuary of Demeter Malophoros, with double herm-like figures, two heads topping a plain stele. There seems to be some flexibility in the aniconic representation of deities.[128] Maximus of Tyre (8.8) **[169]** mentions a pyramidal Aphrodite at Paphos made from an unknown material. This monument was famous; on Roman coins, the pyramid is clearly shown standing in the temple. The Cyprus Museum now houses a conical stone found in the sanctuary of Aphrodite in Old Paphos.[129]

Painter; Naples Stg. 657, bell-krater: *RVAp* I, 161 no. 217, pl. 52.4, Graz Painter; a tall pillar is shown. For the setting of these scenes in the palaestra: *RVAp* I, 71, with regard to the Adolphseck Painter, who shows a pillar inscribed with letters. For *termata*: H.M. Lee, "The TEPMA and the Javelin in Pindar, Nemean vii 70–3, and Greek Athletics," *JHS* 96 (1976) 70–79.

[126] Stelai in Tegea: K.A. Rhomaios, "Ἀρκαδικοὶ ἑρμαῖ," *AE* 1911, 149–159; 157–159 for inscribed pillars from other places. Yalouris, "Bassai" 100 for these pillars; he notes that the nominative "implies that the stelai represent the deities themselves and do not simply belong to them." *Cf.* the genitive and dative used on boundary stones (*e.g.*, *supra* p. 223 n. 124) and dedications. See Webster, "Theories" 169 for identifications in the genitive of figures in vase paintings of the sixth and fifth centuries as presupposing a suppressed word for "likeness." Rose, "Images" 35 for ideas about the identification of deities with monuments. For Greek "dolmens": N.C. Moutsopoulos and G. Dimitrokallis, "Further notes on the Megalithic Monuments of Naxos," *Balkan Studies* 18 (1977) 251–259; I owe this reference to B.S. Ridgway.

[127] Megarian coins: Imhoof-Blumer and Gardner, *NCP* 6 no. 7; Head, *Historia Numorum* 393–394; *BMC* Attica 121 nos. 35, 36–39 (IV–III B.C.). For pyramidal monuments: L.E. Lord, "Watchtowers and Fortresses in Argolis," *AJA* 43 (1939) 79 n. 6.

[128] For Zeus Ktesios: Cook, *Zeus* II.2, 1054–1068; III.2, 1180–1181; van Straten, "Did the Greeks Kneel?" (*supra* p. 25 n. 61) 178–180. For Zeus Meilichios: Cook, *Zeus* II.2, 1091–1160; van Straten, 180; Boardman, *Greeks Overseas*[3] (*supra* p. 217 n. 101) 187.

[129] For the Paphian Venus and her shrine: a coin of the third century A.D. shows a conical monument within a shrine: F.G. Maier, "The Paphian Shrine of Aphrodite and Crete," in

The mysterious Chaeronaean δόρυ (spear) mentioned by Pausanias (9.40.11) [**279**] was thought to be the scepter of the Pelopids.[130] Omphaloi were venerated in other contexts than the familiar Delphic: Curtius Rufus (4.3.22) [**56**] describes the bejeweled omphalos of Ammon at Siwa. His description, however, may reflect a confusion between image and shrine. Servius (*ad* V. *Aen.* 1.720) [**330**] mentions an omphalos of Aphrodite on Cyprus, which is likely to be the pyramidal or conical monument already noted. Objects like omphaloi, the most famous example of which is the one at Delphi, and the phallic pillars at Hierapolis (Luc. *SyrD* 16) [**161**] are not wholly aniconic, but nor do they belong completely to the realm of anthropomorphic representation. They seem to be essentially symbolic—a concept that begs many questions.[131]

Even this brief list shows that Greek aniconic monuments are not a patristic or antiquarian invention; they are solidly attested in art and literature, and some have even survived to the present day. The assertion that aniconism was an ancient practice that preceded or was actually ancestral to the making of statues, however, is open to question. This is not the place for an extended discussion of Greek aniconic practice, but some points that bear directly on the relationship of aniconism to the figural representations of the gods can be mentioned.

Perhaps the most serious flaw in the theory of an ancestral aniconic stage as it has been advanced is that it ignores the possibility that religious practice may deliberately adopt aniconism in preference to figural representation.

A case in point is Evans' argument for a "transition to anthropomorphism" in the Bronze Age. Evans explains the existence of figural representations of the gods that are contemporary with aniconic monuments by distinguishing "the actual objects of cult" from the figural "creations of religious fancy": "The idols remained aniconic, but the Gods themselves were naturally pictured to the minds of their worshippers under a more or less human aspect."[132] He makes the distinction, then, between cult practice and artistic practice, but he does not see that this distinction implies that

Acts of the International Archaeological Symposium "The Relations Between Cyprus and Crete, ca. 2000–500 B.C." (1978; Nicosia, 1979) 228–234, pl. 34.1. For the conical stone: P. Dikaios, *A Guide to the Cyprus Museum*³ (Nicosia, 1961) 89–90, from the "area" of the temple.

[130] Rose, "Images" 36; Schachter, *Cults* 1, 199.

[131] For a good collection of references to omphaloi: E. Richards-Mantzoulinou, "Μέλισσα Πότνια," *AAA* 12 (1979) 72–92; she argues that the omphalos is in fact a beehive. For the omphalos of Curtius' description: *supra* pp. 75–76. For processions involving the carrying of a phallus: H.W. Parke, *Festivals of the Athenians* (Ithaca, 1977) 126; 126 n. 154 for the *aition*. See *supra* p. 76 n. 183.

[132] Evans, "Mycenaean Tree and Pillar Cult" (*supra* p. 219 n. 109) 123 for the transition.

aniconism is a religious preference not necessarily connected with art, and not necessarily to be interpreted as a survival. The more recent scholarship on Bronze Age religion tends in fact to approach aniconic monuments as features of particular cults rather than as evidence for a universal stage of religion. Rutkowski, for example, doubts the existence of a widespread cult of pillars such as Evans conceived, and Faure's work on the boulders and the rock formations in caves that were apparently the focus of worship in Crete strongly suggests the need for seeing such monuments in their proper context—that is, to approach them on a cult-by-cult basis.[133]

The evidence for aniconism in classical times also supports the idea that it is a religious choice, rather than a necessity and then a survival. In the first place, the practice appears to go on with considerable vitality and to have a secure place in worship at a time when figural representations of the gods are well established. The Tegean stelai show that aniconic monuments were still being made as late as the second century A.D.; they might be interpreted as a survival, but it should be remembered that this century was also the time when a major new aniconic cult, the magical baetyls, gained popularity.[134] The cult of baetyls evidently satisfied specific religious desires; it was not a continuation, but an innovation.

Another argument for seeing aniconism as a deliberate religious preference is the special affinity that some gods, Zeus Ktesios and Apollo Agyieus, for example, have with aniconic forms. Such affinities suggest that the monuments have specific cult meaning rather than universal developmental significance. The great variety of aniconic forms in general also supports such an idea, pointing as it does to different intentions according to the demands of particular cults.

Aniconism, then, needs to be understood on its own terms. The coexistence of aniconism with the worship of figural representations of the gods has been stressed by scholars such as Picard, Deonna, and Goldman, who see it as a practice valid in itself and not a lingerer in an age when it had been superseded.[135] The meaning of aniconism is not easy to determine. Rose's suggestion that the monuments reflect a belief in *mana*, although

[133] B. Rutkowski, "Mycenaean Pillar Cult in Boiotia," in *Proc. Boiotia* 2, 35–36; he pays special attention to the distinction between freestanding and architectural pillars. For cave sanctuaries and the apparent focus of cult on rock-formations: P. Faure, *Fonctions des cavernes crétoises* (Paris, 1964) *passim*; more recent bibliography in his "Cultes populaires dans la Crète antique," *BCH* 96 (1972) 402–426; 422–424 for sacred boulders.

[134] *Supra* p. 222 n. 120.

[135] Picard, *Man.* I, 48–49; W. Deonna, *Dédale* I (Paris, 1930) 51–56; Goldman, "Herm" 58. Overbeck was convinced of a complete gap between aniconic and iconic forms; his ideas are summarized and rejected by Farnell, "Origins" 168–169. I have not been able to consult Overbeck's own work, "Das Kultusobjekt bei den Griechen in seinem ältesten Gestaltungen," in *Berichte der Sächsischen Gesellschaft d. Wissenschaften* 1864, 15 ff.

perhaps more appropriate to a Roman context, may be closer to the truth than the belief that they were ever the best images that could be managed. It seems likely that no general explanation will hold good for all aniconic monuments. Each cult might best be approached independently, and some attention to the various *aitia* should be paid, without simply dismissing them as inventions masking a universal stage in primitive worship.[136] What seems clear even now is that aniconic practice should not be assumed to be a survival of an evolutionary stage of religion, and that in any event it is independent of developments in art.

The question arises of the interpretation of semi-iconic forms such as herms and the draped pillars that bear masks of Dionysus, which seem to be living fossils preserving transitional forms between aniconic representations and true images. Deonna, arguing against the idea that sculpture evolved from aniconic monuments, emphasizes the danger of assuming that a development which seems logical has chronological validity, and of giving historical value to a purely theoretical scheme.[137] Both the herm and the Dionysus monuments can be explained without resorting to an evolutionary theory.

The best treatment of the origin of the herm is that of Goldman, who believes that the form is an adaptation in stone of the rustic type of Dionysus often seen in vase-paintings. This rustic type, which has been mentioned before as evidence frequently adduced by scholars who favor evolutionary theories of Greek sculpture, is a pillar with brackets at "shoulder-height" that help to hold real garments in place to make a semblance of a body, and a mask that makes the face of the god. According to Goldman, the type was created for Dionysus and transferred to Hermes.[138] Her explanation, which concentrates on the requirements of specific cults, is far more convincing than the evolutionary theory. Some small questions, however, can still be raised.

Perhaps it is not necessary to assume that the two forms—the herm and the "masked pillar" (for convenience)—are related. Although the two look similar, herms are modelled with full heads, not masks. The mask is so closely associated with Dionysus that it seems likely to have iconographic, and not simply practical, significance. The masked pillars, furthermore, are dummy-like constructions that ape full figures, while the herm is an

[136] Rose, "Images" *passim*. For an overview of scholarship on *numen* and similar Roman concepts that are sometimes associated with *mana*: W. Pötscher, "'Numen' und 'numen Augusti'," *ANRW* II.16.1 (Berlin and New York, 1978) 355–374. See also A.D. Nock, "Mana and Roman Religion," in *Essays* II, 603–605. For an *aition* of an aniconic monument: *supra* p. 221 n. 118.

[137] Deonna, *Dédale* I (*supra* p. 226 n. 135) 53.

[138] Goldman, "Herm"; 67 for conclusions.

abstraction that focuses attention on head and genitalia. It does not seem impossible that the two forms might have developed independently.

Evidence from Mycenaean Linear B texts suggests that the etymology *herma–Hermes* is false, and so offers no independent testimony for the development of figures from piles of stones.[139] Since the etymology seems to have been accepted in antiquity, however, perhaps the herm was created with the etymology and the development in mind. There existed a tradition about the origin of herms that differs sharply from the evolutionary theory based on patristic sources. Herodotus (2.51) **[140]** says that the ithyphallic Hermes (by which he appears to mean the herm) was a Pelasgian form taken over by the Athenians and spread by them to the rest of Greece. Pausanias (1.24.3) gives as an example of Athenian religious zeal their invention of the limbless Hermes, and in another place (4.33.3) **[245]** notes, as had Herodotus, that "the squared *schema* for Hermes is the Athenians', and others learned [it] from them." He thinks of the herm as an innovation, not an ancestral form. While this tradition of the history of the herm probably reflects the conventional explanations of origins as borrowings or discoveries, it may be closer to the truth than the evolutionary theory. The herm does indeed appear to be an abstraction that deliberately emphasizes the head and phallus. Burkert has argued that both have apotropaic significance; while his arguments from primate behavior may not be compelling, his explanation has the virtue of considering the function of the herm and its place in cult and life. A less piquant but probably more accurate interpretation can be sought in Onians' demonstration that in Greek thought, the head is considered to be the source of "generative power"; fertility is therefore a possible context for the development of the type.[140] At any rate, it seems clear that both the herm and the masked pillar presuppose the existence of figural representations, specifically statues. One is an abstraction, the other an imitation. Müller has suggested that such semi-iconic figures may be deliberate recollections of aniconic pieces,

[139] *Supra* p. 187 n. 29 for the Linear B evidence.

[140] Paus. 1.24.3 (Rocha-Pereira): *λέλεκται δέ μοι καὶ πρότερον ὡς Ἀθηναίοις περισσότερόν τι ἢ τοῖς ἄλλοις ἐς τὰ θεῖά ἐστι σπουδῆς· πρῶτοι μὲν γὰρ Ἀθηνᾶν ἐπωνόμασαν Ἐργάνην, πρῶτοι δ' ἀκώλους Ἑρμᾶς <ἀνέθεσαν>, ὁμοῦ δέ σφισιν ἐν τῷ ναῷ †σπουδαίων† δαίμων ἐστίν* (I observed even before that the zeal of the Athenians in matters of religion exceeds that of other peoples. For they were the first to give Athena the surname of the Worker and the first <to set up> Hermes without limbs; . . . and in the *naos* with them is a *daimon* [of the zealous]).

Burkert, *Structure* 39–41; *cf*. 43. Onians, *Origins of European Thought* (*supra* p. 39 n. 91) 122. For a summary of the history of the herm, with a list of ancient references: A.B. Lloyd, *Herodotus. Book II. Commentary 1–98* (Etudes préliminaires aux religions orientales dans l'empire romain 43; Leiden, 1976) 239–240 *ad* 2.51.

"compromise-forms" that are not steps in a typological development, but conscious creations.[141] His explanation is attractive in that it breaks away from the idea of the evolution of the aniconic to the figural. It may be wondered, however, if it is necessary to postulate even this kind of deliberate looking back, for there seems to be sufficient freedom within both traditions to explain all the forms that are attested without resorting to developmental ideas of any kind. In any event, it is clear that semi-iconic forms should not be assumed to provide evidence for a developmental transition from aniconic to figural representation.

The idea of the origin of Greek sculpture in aniconic monuments must take its place with the other developmental theories about the beginning of statuary. The assertions of the priority of aniconic worship found in the ancient sources furnished the theoretical framework for the earliest modern treatments of the history of Greek sculpture, and have continued to provide documentary evidence for subsequent studies. These assertions, however, do not represent traditions that necessarily stem from historical truth. They result instead from the tendency to recreate the past along logical lines that is a common feature of Greek historical speculation. Within the traditions of Greek history they serve as examples of conventional explanations. They were exploited outside that tradition by the patristic authors who, drawing at the same time on the conventional polemic of Jewish iconoclasm, sought to strip even the most beautiful idolatrous creations of their aesthetic and emotional appeal by revealing the sticks and stones that ultimately lay beneath. The apparent corroboration of these arguments by supposedly disinterested pagan sources made them seem thoroughly reliable. In the absence of an independent historical record, the combined testimony stood unchallenged.

Plausible as they seem, however, the ancient accounts of the origin of images are simply theories, and do not offer solid evidence for the development of Greek sculpture. Their inadequacy became clear when archaeological evidence began to be examined. While some scholars, as has been seen, attempted to fit the new evidence into the evolutionary scheme outlined by the literary sources, others recognized that the preserved material testified to a different course of development. As early as 1864, Overbeck could find no common conceptual ground between aniconic monuments and figural forms, whether full statues or herms.[142] Poulsen found no evidence to support the evolution of sculpture from crude forms, finding the

[141] Müller, "Kultbild" 499. Such an idea may be true in the case of "aniconic" funerary busts: L. Beschi, "Divinità funerarie cirenaiche," *ASAtene* 31–32 (1969–70) 133–341; M.C. Sturgeon, "Greek Funerary Busts," *Archaeology* 28 (1975) 230–237.

[142] *Supra* p. 226 n. 135.

explanation for clothed and nude types in iconography, and not in a primitive inability to render flesh or drapery.[143] Müller was unable to accept the theory of aniconic origins, and sought to explain the earliest known stone statuary by balancing prehistoric traditions with Oriental sources.[144] Deonna rejected neat schemes of logical developments from primitive forms; believing instead in the completeness of Greek figural vision from the earliest times, he attempted to trace the technical progress in the rendering of the fully realized human form.[145]

It is not likely that any study undertaken today of the origin of Greek sculpture would adopt an approach modelled on that of the literary sources, treating Greek statuary as an undifferentiated production traceable to simple beginnings *ex nihilo*. Current questions focus instead on particular phases of Greek sculpture; one that attracts much attention is the rise of large-scale stone statuary around the middle of the seventh century B.C. There is no evidence so far to suggest that such production was customary or widespread in the Greek world before the seventh century.[146] Its appearance at that time, therefore, is one of the major turning points in the history of Greek art; this is so whether one believes that there is a generally continuous development from what is called Daedalic style through Archaic or, as Ridgway argues, that the Daedalic and the Archaic are fundamentally different styles, the latter primarily dependent on Egyptian sources.[147] There are two major approaches to the question, one that looks for possible antecedents in the Greek past, the other that attempts to trace foreign influence, specifically that of the Near East. Both approaches are essentially archaeological. If an answer is found to the question of when and how Greek monumental statuary in stone came to be, that information can then be used to examine the literary traditions, and it may be possible to explain the course of their development more clearly. Not much illumination is likely to come the other way.

[143] Poulsen, "Typenbildung." Drapery was added separately to the terracotta statuettes produced by a coroplastic workshop in Taras in the second half of the fourth century B.C., but this technique is entirely different from the creation of an individual statue; it is a way to make standardized figurines more individual. For these figures: B.M. Kingsley, "The Master of the Boston Heads," *AJA* 84 (1980) 217.

[144] Müller, "Beginnings" (*supra* p. 208 n. 77).

[145] Deonna, *Dédale* I (*supra* p. 226 n. 135) 53–56; 121–122 for the theory that real drapery was used in early times to achieve clothed figures (*cf.* Poulsen, "Typenbildung").

[146] Cook, "Origins" (*supra* p. 212 n. 87) 27 n. 32 for four works that have been suggested to be pre-Daedalic stone statues, but have not lived up to their promise.

[147] Ridgway, *Archaic* 4 for a definition of Archaic and the beginning of widespread Greek interest in stone statuary only c. 600 B.C.; 26 for a convincing analysis of the Daedalic style as leading not to the Archaic style, but to a dead end.

5. Conclusions

The idea of the *xoanon*, the primitive wooden cult statue that stands at the beginning of Greek sculpture, arose directly from the literary testimony of antiquity. The ancient sources, however, reflecting as they do the concerns of antiquarians, historians of art, and iconoclasts, are neither informative nor reliable.

There is no uniformity of ancient opinion regarding the origin and development of Greek statuary. The theories about the beginning of idolatry in primitive monuments run counter to the prevailing notions about the origins of art in a series of discoveries and inventions. Both traditions prove to be less than reliable sources for the history of early Greek sculpture. One is outright polemic and tendentious; the other is the direct product of a historical *idée fixe*. The accounts of early idolatry are no more correct than those of the invention of painting and sculpture by specific artists or of the simplicity of early civilizations. The assertions of the literary testimony are not borne out by the surviving monumental evidence. The archaeological record offers no confirmation of a primitive stage of sculpture, of the inherent crudeness of wooden production, or of the aniconic stage of worship and representations of the gods. The theories advanced by modern scholars on the basis of the ancient testimony should be laid aside in favor of those based on the increasing amount of monumental evidence, which tells a different story.

Although it is disappointing to find that the literary testimony that seemed so promising a source is not reliable, it is important to understand why, in approaching the question of early Greek sculpture, the written sources must be used with great caution. For the loss of *xoana* there is one consolation: the archaeological view of early Greek sculpture is far more varied and challenging than that provided by the false guides.

CHAPTER III

CONCLUSIONS

The concept of the *xoanon*, the primitive wooden image, has long been an important part of theories about the origin of Greek sculpture. The idea that Greek statuary began with such wooden pieces was based on the literary testimony of antiquity and appeared to be supported by archaeological evidence, insofar as the characteristics of a class of monuments that did not physically exist could be inferred from related material. On closer examination, however, the *xoanon* is not as firm a point in the history of Greek sculpture as has been thought.

The word *xoanon* itself, which had been taken to refer to a particular kind of statue, and so provided both the theoretical foundation and the body of primary evidence for the suggested outline of development, proves not to be a reliable term. The meaning of the word changes radically over time in response to a variety of trends in ancient thought. There is little agreement between its usage in literature and its usage in epigraphical texts, and in some periods there are also noticeable geographical variations in its meaning. Whereas many scholars have tended to take Pausanias' limited and consistent definition as the standard meaning of the word, the examination of its appearance by context and chronology shows that his usage is atypical. *Xoanon* can be borrowed from the ancient sources and used as an archaeological term only at the risk of misinterpreting its meaning in antiquity.

The demonstration that the word *xoanon* has no archaeological value casts doubt on the validity of the concept to which it has been applied—namely, that of the primitive wooden statue. To some extent the question of the "*xoanon*" is separate from that of *xoanon* the word, and involves an examination of a wider range of sources. It can be shown that the idea of the primitive wooden statue as it appears in modern scholarship was borrowed directly from a limited number of ancient sources. The concept of such images developed from a conflation of antiquarian and iconoclastic speculation and theory. Although the idea that statuary originated in crude wooden forms contradicts the prevailing ancient notions about the way sculpture began, and although even in its own milieu it is not free from inconsistencies and contradictions, the explicitness of the sources and their ostensibly scholarly approach made them appear reliable. Once the essentially tendentious basis of the theory is clarified, it can be seen that the archaeological evidence, if left to tell its own story, presents a different picture of early Greek sculpture.

At first these conclusions seem entirely negative and cheerless, especially to those who have believed that the combination of literary testimony and growing archaeological evidence would shed light on the fundamental processes by which Greek sculpture came to be. This is perhaps the place, then, to stress the positive results that have been gained by the foregoing examination of eclectic and often osbscure sources.

There now exists an outline stronger than any that has been constructed before for understanding individual references to *xoana*. As well as being helpful for studies of particular images, this outline may shed light on Greek attitudes toward statues in various times and places. The identification of the intellectual trends involved in the formulation of the concept of primitive images may contribute something to the historiography of art. Some of the material may also be useful for the study of Greek religion; certainly the evidence for the late classical iconoclastic controversy can be examined in greater detail to illuminate the Greek conception of divine images, which is still not well understood.

A positive methodological result of the examination of *xoana* is the reemphasis of the importance of context in the application of literary sources to archaeological questions. Although it is frequently tempting to combine references that bear on particular monuments in order to arrive at comprehensive interpretations and reconstructions, such testimonia need close scrutiny before their documentary value can be assessed. This call for caution is only a secondary issue, however; the case of *xoana* shows how attention to context—in many examples amounting to asking the simple question *Cui bono*?—extends rather than limits the usefulness of the written sources. In place of the old, poorly illustrated catalogue of conjectural *xoana*, there now exists an outline of the concepts and ideas that gave rise to what was for many years a given in archaeological scholarship.

There remains the question of what is to replace *xoana* in the history of Greek art. Ideally, these pages should have provided a new outline of early Greek sculpture, a better alternative to the old ideas. To construct a new history of Greek sculpture, however, is an undertaking not for one worker but for many, and to venture too far in this direction by oneself is to risk putting forward suggestions that are at best short-sighted. Nevertheless there is room here for some observations deriving directly from the subjects that have been treated in detail.

Whatever direction future studies of Greek sculpture may take, one question that can no longer be asked is the old one about the origins of early Greek sculpture. This is a question rooted entirely in the ancient traditions and the scholarship that depended on them in the years before archaeological evidence was available, and neither the concept of "origins" nor the category of "early Greek sculpture" really fits the historical situation as revealed by archaeology. "Early Greek sculpture" has usually meant the first known statuary of monumental size executed in stone that can be seen as part of the series of such sculptures which constitutes one of the major achievements of classical art. The idea of "origins" developed from the expectation that this achievement could be traced to absolute beginnings *ex nihilo*, and that these beginnings embodied a universal order of development. It has become clear, however, that the question of how and when large-scale stone statuary began to appear in the Greek world is a circumscribed, not a universal topic. Monumental stone images are only one part of Greek sculptural production; they need to be considered in the context of statuary in other materials, and cannot be assumed to be the dominant form in all periods. Furthermore, it can no longer be assumed that all monumental stone statuary is part of the same artistic development; for example, Ridgway's arguments for seeing Archaic statues as stemming from a different tradition than do Daedalic are persuasive. The category of "early Greek sculpture" is not precise enough to accommodate the monuments that are now known.

The very idea of "early sculpture" also reflects notions of Greek history that are outmoded; at issue here too is the concept of "origins." Both have been changed by the archaeological recovery of Greek prehistory. The traditions about the Greek past preserved in legendary and literary accounts have been replaced by an outline of events and situations that can be dated more or less absolutely. Instead of a vague period of early civilization in which beginnings *ex nihilo* are conceivable, there now exists the record of a sequence of cultures that can be traced from classical times back to the Neolithic age. The most significant achievement in this area is the demonstration of a continuous Greek culture from the Late Bronze Age through historical times, which was accomplished by the decipherment of Mycenaean Linear B and its identification as a form of Greek. It is no longer possible to look for clean beginnings in an empty field. The history of Greek sculpture has become a series of questions focused on particular points of development. Minoan statuary and statuary created in the Minoan orbit must be taken into account; next, the adoption and adaptation of Minoan forms by the mainland; and finally, the most intriguing question of all—the transmission of second-millennium artistic traditions to the Greek world after the Dark Ages. In addition to these hellenocentric concerns, there are foreign contributions to be considered. All this is a far cry from the simple origins of early statuary envisioned by the Greek traditions and theories and the scholarship derived from them. The gap between tradition and history is one of the most stimulating questions in the history of Greek art.

The retirement of *xoana* from the ranks of Greek sculpture should help clear the way for studies more firmly based in history. It is to be hoped that the evaluation of wooden statuary in general will now proceed free from the misleading influence of the ancient sources, and that new approaches to preclassical sculpture will be made without scholars' feeling obligated to reconcile archaeological fact with impossible information from traditions taken at face value. On another front, it can be noted that a thorough study of Greek words for statues is badly needed. The individual treatments that exist are too limited, and often do not pay sufficient attention to historical context. A study on a grand scale may soon be feasible thanks to the computer banks of the Thesaurus Linguae Graecae project. Such a task, while largely a matter of mechanical drudgery, is sure to yield interesting results and to be important. For no matter what the particular focus of research on Greek sculpture, there is no substitute for knowing what the Greeks thought—or at least said—about their works.

Appendix I
Testimonia

The testimonia assembled in this appendix comprise every text known to me in which the word *xoanon* occurs (with the exception of those which came to my attention too late to be considered in the study: see *supra* p. 172 n. 431), as well as the most important texts, with or without *xoana*, that are discussed in both chapters. The files of the Thesaurus Linguae Graecae available at Harvard University and the University of Pennsylvania as of April 1986 have been searched for *xoana*; it is to be expected that more examples of the word exist. Substantive textual questions are reserved for the discussions of the individual passages and do not affect the readings presented here. The translations are for the most part standard renderings adapted only to highlight the terms under consideration.

The numbers of the testimonia appear in boldface. The testimonia are arranged as follows:

1. Literary and sub-literary texts are presented alphabetically by author and title of work. Ancillary texts (*e.g.*, scholia) are placed with their hosts; for example, the *Diegeseis* appear under Callimachus, *Aetia*.
2. Literary and other texts from papyri are listed by document, alphabetically by corpus or collection (*e.g.*, Pap. Oxyrhynchus; Leiden, Rijksmuseum).
3. Epigraphical texts are listed alphabetically by provenance. Appendix II is a concordance of standard epigraphical sources.

Texts that overlap these categories and texts that are transmitted as quotations in other works are cross-referenced.

The edition of each text is cited at the beginning of the individual entries, except in the case of Pausanias, in which a blanket citation serves for all. When no translator is named, the rendering is my own.

Acusilaus — V B.C.
FGrH 2 F 28
See Apollodorus 2.2.2 [**21**].

1
Aeschylus, *Septem contra Thebas* 217–218 (203–204 Wecklein) — V B.C.
Text: D.L. Page, ed., *Aeschyli septem quae supersunt tragoediae* (Oxford, 1972).

οὔκουν τάδ᾽ ἔσται πρὸς θεῶν· ἀλλ᾽ οὖν θεοὺς
τοὺς τῆς ἁλούσης πόλεος ἐκλείπειν λόγος.

Surely then this will be in the hands of the gods; but there is a saying that the gods of a conquered city abandon [it].

2

Sch. Aeschylus, *Septem contra Thebas* 217 (203 Wecklein)
Text: O.L. Smith, ed., *Scholia graeca in Aeschylum quae exstant omnia* II.2. *Scholia in Aeschylum Septem Adversus Thebas* (Leipzig, 1982) 109, 217 d.

ἀλλὰ λόγος ἐξᾴδεται τοὺς τῆς πόλεως θεοὺς φεύγειν πορθηθείσης αὐτῆς. λέγεται γὰρ ὅτι, ὅταν ἔμελλε πορθηθῆναι ἡ Τροία, ἐφάνησαν οἱ θεοὶ τοῖς Τρωσὶν ἀνελόμενοι ἐκ τῶν ναῶν τὰ ἀγάλματα ἑαυτῶν.

But the saying is sung [that] the gods of a city flee when it is destroyed. For it is said that, when Troy was about to be destroyed, the gods appeared to the Trojans carrying their own *agalmata* out of the temples.

3

Sch. Aeschylus, *Septem contra Thebas* 217 (203 Wecklein)
Text: W. Dindorf, ed., *Aeschylus. Tragoediae superstites et deperditarum fragmenta* III. *Scholia graeca ex codicibus aucta et emendata* (Oxford, 1851; repr. Hildesheim, 1962) 43.217.

ἀλλ' οὖν θεοὺς] οὐκ ἀλόγως λέγει τοὺς τῆς πόλεως θεοὺς φεύγειν, πορθηθείσης αὐτῆς. λέγεται γὰρ ὅτι ὅτε ἔμελλε πορθηθῆναι ἡ Τροία, ἐφάνησαν οἱ θεοὶ τοῖς Τρωσὶν ἀνελόμενοι ἐκ τῶν ναῶν τὰ ἀγάλματα αὐτῶν.
(εἰς τὴν Τροίαν γὰρ τοιοῦτό τι ἐφαίνετο.)

But therefore the gods: Not unreasonably does he say that the gods of a city flee when it has been destroyed. For it is said that when Troy was about to be destroyed, the gods appeared to the Trojans, carrying their own *agalmata* out of the temples. (For in regard to Troy, some such thing appeared.)

4

Aeschylus, *Septem contra Thebas* 304–311 (291–298 Wecklein) V B.C.
Text: D.L. Page, ed., *Aeschyli septem quae supersunt tragoediae* (Oxford, 1972).

ποῖον δ' ἀμείψεσθε γαίας πέδον
τᾶσδ' ἄρειον, ἐχθροῖς
ἀφέντες τὰν βαθύχθον' αἶαν,
ὕδωρ τε Διρκαῖον, εὐτραφέστατον πωμάτων
ὅσων ἵησιν Ποσειδὰν ὁ γαιάοχος
Τηθύος τε παῖδες;

What sort of better ground will you get in exchange for this earth, leaving to enemies the deep-earthed land and the water of Dirce, the most nourishing of the waters that earth-holding Poseidon and the children of Tethys pour forth?

5

Sch. Aeschylus, *Septem contra Thebas* 304 (291 Wecklein) V B.C.
(= Sophocles fr. 452 Radt, Pearson [414 Nauck[2]].)
Text: O.L. Smith, ed., *Scholia graeca in Aeschylum quae exstant omnia* II.2. *Scholia in Septem Adversus Thebas* (Leipzig, 1982) 147–148, 304 a, 304–311 b.

ποῖον δ' ἀμείψεσθε γαίας πέδ(ον)· ἀντὶ τοῦ ποῖον οἰκήσετε δάπεδον ἐντεῦθεν μεταστάντες· εἴρηται δὲ καὶ ἐν Ξοανηφόροις Σοφοκλέους, ὡς οἱ θεοὶ ἀπὸ τῆς Ἰλίου φέρουσιν ἐπὶ τῶν ὤμων τὰ ἑαυτῶν ξόανα εἰδότες ὅτι ἁλίσκεται ἡ πόλις. ἐὰν ταύτην, φησί, τὴν γῆν προδῶτε τοῖς πολεμίοις, ποίαν βελτίονα αὐτῆς εὑρήσετε;

What ground will you get in exchange for this earth: instead of, What ground will you inhabit, migrating thence? It is also said in the *Xoanephoroi* of Sophocles that the gods carry out from Troy on their shoulders their own *xoana*, seeing that the city is being captured. If, he says, you hand over this earth to the enemy, what better than it will you find?

ἄλλως· ποῖον δ' ἀμείψεσθε· ἰστέον ὅτι εἴρηται ἐν Ξοανηφόροις Σοφοκλέους, ὡς οἱ θεοὶ ἀπὸ τῆς Ἰλίου φέρουσιν ἐπὶ τῶν ὤμων τὰ ἑαυτῶν ξόανα εἰδότες ὅτι ἁλίσκεται. ἐὰν οὖν ταύτην τὴν γῆν, φησί, προδῶτε τοῖς πολεμίοις, ποίαν βελτίονα ταύτης εὑρήσετε;

Otherwise: What will you get in exchange: it must be known that it is said in the *Xoanephoroi* of Sophocles that the gods carry out from Troy on their shoulders their own *xoana*, seeing that it is being captured. For if this earth, he says, you give over to the enemy, what better than it will you find?

6

Ammonius *s.v.* *ἱερά*
Text: K. Nickau, ed., *Ammonii qui dicitur liber de adfinium vocabulorum differentia* (Leipzig, 1966) 241.
(= Theopompus *FGrH* 115 F 159.)

ἱερὰ τούς τε περιβόλους τῶν ναῶν καὶ τὰ σφάγια καὶ τὰ ὀστᾶ τῶν ἀνθρώπων, ὡς Ὑπερίδης ἐν τῷ Κατὰ Ἀρχιστρατίδου, καὶ τὰ ξόανα, ὡς Θεόπομπος ἐν εἰκοστῇ ἕκτῃ.

Hiera (sacred things) [are] the *periboloi* of *naoi* and sacrificial offerings and the bones of men, as Hyperides says in *Against Archistratides*; and *xoana*, as Theopompus says in the twenty-sixth book.

7

Ammonius *s.v.* *ξόανον*
Text: K. Nickau, ed., *Ammonii qui dicitur liber de adfinium vocabulorum differentia* (Leipzig, 1966) 338.

ξόανον, βρέτας, ἄγαλμα διαφέρει. ξόανον μὲν γάρ ἐστι τὸ ἐξεσμένον λίθινον ἢ ἐλεφάντινον, βρέτας δὲ τὸ βροτῷ ὅμοιον ἤτοι χαλκοῦν ἢ ἐκ τῆς ἐμφεροῦς ὕλης πεποιημένον, ἄγαλμα δὲ τὸ πώρινον ἢ ἔκ τινος ἑτέρου λίθου κατεσκευασμένον.

Xoanon, *bretas*, and *agalma* are different. For a *xoanon* is something carved, either stone or ivory, while a *bretas* is something like a mortal [*brotos*], either bronze, or made out of a similar material; and an *agalma* is fashioned of poros or out of some other stone.

8

Ammonius *s.v.* *φάσμα*
Text: K. Nickau, ed., *Ammonii qui dicitur liber de adfinium vocabulorum differentia* (Leipzig, 1966) 495.

φάσμα μέν ἐστι τὸ ὅμοιον ἀληθείᾳ, φάντασμα δὲ τὸ ἑτερόμορφον, εἴδωλον δὲ τὸ ὅμοιον τῇ σκιᾷ, τέρας δὲ τὸ ἐναργὲς σῶμα ἑτερόμορφον, βρέτας δὲ τὸ ξόανον.

Phasma is something similar to *alethia*, and *phantasma* is a monstrosity; *eidolon* is similar to a *skia*, and *teras*, a visible body, is a monstrosity; *bretas* is a *xoanon*.

Anecdota Bachmann I.19.5 *s.v.* *Ἄγαλμα*
(= *Synagoge Lexeon Chresimon s.v.*)

See *Anecdota Bekker* I.334.18 [**11**].

9

Anecdota Bachmann I.311.8 *s.v.* *Ξόανον*
(= *Synagoge Lexeon Chresimon s.v.*)
Text: L. Bachmann, ed., *Anecdota Graeca* I (Leipzig, 1828; repr. Hildesheim, 1965).

Ξόανον: ἄγαλμα, εἴδωλον, ζώδιον, ἀνδριάς.

Xoanon: *agalma*; *eidolon*; *zoidion*; *andrias*.

10

Anecdota Bekker I.240.16 *s.v.* Δαιδάλου ποιημάτων
(= *Lexeis Rhetorikai s.v.*)
Text: I. Bekker, ed., *Anecdota Graeca* I. *Lexica Segueriana* (Berlin, 1814).

Δαιδάλου ποιημάτων: παροιμία. ὁ γὰρ Δαίδαλος οὗτος πρῶτος, ποιῶν ἀγάλματα, διεβίβασε τὸν ἕτερον τῶν ποδῶν, καὶ τοὺς ὀφθαλμοὺς ἀνεπέτασε, καὶ τὰς χεῖρας προὔτεινε· καὶ δόξαι ἐγένοντο ὅτι ἔμψυχα ποιεῖ ποιήματα, πρὸ γὰρ αὐτοῦ συμπεπηγότα ἀγάλματα καὶ μεμυκότα πρὸς τὰς πλευρὰς ἁπλῶς.

Works of Daedalus: proverb. For this Daedalus was the first, in making *agalmata*, who carried one foot over the other, and opened up the eyes, and stretched forth the hands; and there were opinions that he made living works. For before him *agalmata* were constructed solidly and closed to the sides in a simple way.

11

Anecdota Bekker I.334.18 *s.v.* Ἄγαλμα
(= *Synagoge Lexeon Chresimon s.v.*)
(= *Anecdota Bachmann* I.19.5.)
Text: I. Bekker, ed., *Anecdota Graeca* I. *Lexica Segueriana* (Berlin, 1814).

Ἄγαλμα: πᾶν ἐφ' ᾧ τις ἀγάλλεται. ἀγάλματα δὲ τὰς γραφὰς καὶ τοὺς ἀνδριάντας λέγουσιν. οἱ δὲ ἁπλῶς ἄγαλμα πᾶν ἀνάθημα καὶ καθιέρωμα, ἢ ξόανον ἤ τι ἄλλο τοιοῦτον εἴη.

Agalma: everything in which someone glories. They call both paintings and statues *agalmata*. Others simply [call] "*agalma*" every offering and dedication, whether it is a *xoanon* or some other such thing.

12

Anecdota Cramer II.351.9 *s.v.* βρέτας
Text: J.A. Cramer, ed., *Anecdota Graeca e codicibus manuscriptis Bibliothecarum Oxoniensium* II (Oxford, 1835; repr. Amsterdam, 1963).

βρέτας: Παρὰ τὸ βροτὸς, βρότας, καὶ βρέτας, τὸ τῷ βροτῷ ὅμοιον, ἤγουν ξόανον· τουτέστιν ὅμοιον ἀνθρώπῳ· τοῦτο παρὰ τὸ μείρω τὸ μερίζω.

Bretas: derived from *brotos* [mortal], *brotas*, and *bretas*, something like a mortal, that is to say *xoanon*; that is, like a man; thus *merizo* is derived from *meiro*.

Anecdota Parisiensis IV.90.1 *s.v.* Ἀγάλματα
See [Zonaras,] *Lexicon s.v.* **[370]**.

Anecdota Parisiensis IV.199.17 *s.v.* *ξόανον*
See [Zonaras,] *Lexicon s.v.* [**371**].

Anthologia Palatina 5.15
See Rufinus [**327**].

Anthologia Palatina 5.36
See Rufinus [**328**].

Anthologia Palatina 6.189
See Moero of Byzantium [**171**].

Anthologia Palatina 9.144
See Anyte of Tegea [**20**].

Anthologia Palatina 9.326
See Leonidas of Tarentum [**156**].

Anthologia Palatina 9.437
See [Theocritus], *Epigram* 4 [**364**].

13
Anthologia Palatina 9.601
Text: H. Beckby, ed., *Anthologia Graeca* III (Munich, 1957).
Translation adapted from W.R. Paton, tr., *The Greek Anthology* III (LCL, 1917).

Τὸ ξόανον τὸ περισσὸν Ἀεξιμένης Ἀφροδίτᾳ
εἵσατο, τῆς πάσης ναυτιλίης φυλακᾷ.
χαῖρ', ὦ πότνια Κύπρι, διδοῦσα δὲ κέρδεα, πλοῦτον
ἄρμενον, εἰδήσεις, ναῦς ὅτι κοινότατον.

This remarkable *xoanon* Aeximenes erected to Aphrodite, the guardian of all navigation. Hail, O sovereign Cypris! and if thou givest gain and welcome wealth thou shalt learn that a ship is most ready to go shares.

14
Anthologia Palatina 12.40
(From the *Musa Puerilis* of Strato)
Text: H. Beckby, ed., *Anthologia Graeca* IV (Munich, 1957)
Translation adapted from W.R. Paton, tr., *The Greek Anthology* IV (LCL, 1918).

Μὴ 'κδύσῃς, ἄνθρωπε, τὸ χλαινίον, ἀλλὰ θεώρει
οὕτως ἀκρολίθου κἀμὲ τρόπον ξοάνου.
γυμνὴν 'Αντιφίλου ζητῶν χάριν, ὡς ἐπ' ἀκάνθαις
εὑρήσεις ῥοδέαν φυομένην κάλυκα.

Do not take off my cloak, sir, but consider me thus after the manner of an acrolithic *xoanon*. Seeing the naked charm of Antiphilus, you will find the rosebud growing as on thorns.

Anthologia Palatina 16.51
See Macedonius the Consul [**167**].

15
Anthologia Palatina 16.249
(= *Anthologia Planudea* 249.)
Text: H. Beckby, ed., *Anthologia Graeca* IV (Munich, 1957).
Translation adapted from W.R. Paton, tr., *The Greek Anthology* V (LCL, 1918).

Δερκόμενος ξόανον καλὸν τόδε, τὰν 'Αφροδίταν,
ὤνθρωφ', ἱλάσκευ πλατίον ἑζόμενος·
αἴνει δὲ Γλυκέραν Διονυσίου, ἅ μ' ἀνέθηκε
πορφυρέας ὀπαλὸν κῦμα παρ' ἠιόνος.

O thou who lookest on this beautiful *xoanon*, seat thee near [it] and worship Aphrodite; and praise Glycera, the daughter of Dionysius, who dedicated me by the gentle wave of the purple shore.

Anthologia Planudea 51
See Macedonius the Consul [**167**].

Anthologia Planudea 249
See *Anthologia Palatina* 16.249 [**15**].

16
Antoninus Liberalis 13.6–7 ? A.D. II
Text: M. Papathomopoulos, ed., tr., *Antoninus Liberalis. Les métamorphoses* (Paris, 1968).

Τὸ δὲ σῶμα τὸ τῆς 'Ασπαλίδος ἐξερευνῶντες πάντα τρόπον, ὅπως κηδεύσωσιν ἐπισήμως, οὐκ ἠδυνήθησαν εὑρεῖν· ἀλλὰ τοῦτο μὲν ἠφανίσθη κατὰ θεόν, ἀντὶ δὲ τοῦ σώματος ἐφάνη ξόανον παρὰ τὸ τῆς 'Αρτέμιδος ἑστηκός. 'Ονομάζεται δὲ παρὰ τοῖς ἐγχωρίοις τοῦτο τὸ ξόανον 'Ασπαλὶς 'Αμειλήτη 'Εκαέργη, ᾧ καθ' ἕκαστον ἔτος αἱ παρθένοι χίμαρον ἄθορον ἐκρήμνων, ὅτι καὶ ἡ 'Ασπαλὶς παρθένος οὖσα ἑαυτὴν ἀπηγχόνισεν.

They searched in every way for the body of Aspalis, in order to give it funeral rites; but they were unable to find it; it had vanished by the act of the god, and in place of the body there appeared a *xoanon* alongside the shrine of Artemis. Among the inhabitants of the region this *xoanon* is called Aspalis Ameilete Hekaerge, and each year the virgins hung from it a virgin kid, since Aspalis had been a virgin when she hung herself.

17

Antoninus Liberalis 40.4 ? A.D. II

Text: M. Papathomopoulos, ed., tr., *Antoninus Liberalis. Les métamorphoses* (Paris, 1968).

Καὶ ὁ μὲν αὐτῇ ἐνεχείρησεν ὀρεγόμενος μιχθῆναι ἡ δὲ Βριτόμαρτις ἀποβᾶσα ἐκ τοῦ πλοίου κατέφυγεν εἰς ἄλσος, ὅθιπέρ ἐστι νῦν αὐτῆς τὸ ἱερόν, κἀνταῦθα ἐγένετο ἀφανὴς καὶ ὠνόμασαν αὐτὴν Ἀφαίαν. Ἐν δὲ τῷ ἱερῷ τῆς Ἀρτέμιδος <ἐφάνη ξόανον>. Τὸν δὲ τόπον, ἐν ᾧ ἀφανὴς ἐγένετο ἡ Βριτόμαρτις, ἀφιέρωσαν Αἰγινῆται καὶ ὠνόμασαν <αὐτὴν> Ἀφαίαν καὶ ἱερὰ ἐπετέλεσαν ὡς θεῷ.

And he, desiring to unite himself with her, attacked her; but Britomartis, having jumped from the boat, fled into a grove, the same one where her sanctuary is now, and there she disappeared, and they called her Aphaia. In the temple of Artemis [appeared a *xoanon*]. The Aiginetans consecrated the place where Britomartis disappeared and named [her] Aphaia and conducted rites as if to a divinity.

18

[Antoninus Liberalis] *Metamorphoses*, Table of Contents 2.13

Text: M. Papathomopoulos, ed., tr., *Antoninus Liberalis. Les métamorphoses* (Paris, 1968).

ιγ'. Ἀσπαλὶς εἰς ξόανον μετὰ θάνατον.

13. Aspalis, into a *xoanon* after death.

19

[Antoninus Liberalis] *Metamorphoses*, Table of Contents 2.40

Text: M. Papathomopoulos, ed., tr., *Antoninus Liberalis. Les métamorphoses* (Paris, 1968).

μ'. Βριτόμαρ<μαρ>τις εἰς ξόανον Ἀφαίαν.

40. Britomartis into the *xoanon* [called] Aphaia.

20

Anyte of Tegea, *Anthologia Palatina* 9.144 III B.C.
Text: H. Beckby, ed., *Anthologia Graeca* III (Munich, 1957).
Translation adapted from W.R. Paton, tr., *The Greek Anthology* III (LCL, 1917).

Κύπριδος οὗτος ὁ χῶρος, ἐπεὶ φίλον ἔπλετο τήνᾳ
αἰὲν ἀπ' ἠπείρου λαμπρὸν ὁρῆν πέλαγος,
ὄφρα φίλον ναύτῃσι τελῇ πλόον· ἀμφὶ δὲ πόντος
δειμαίνει λιπαρὸν δερκόμενος ξόανον.

This is the place of Cypris, for it is dear to her always to look from the land to the bright sea, so that the voyage may end happily for the sailors; the sea trembles around, seeing the shining *xoanon*.

21

Apollodorus 2.2.1–2 ? A.D. II
(= Acusilaus, *FGrH* 2 F 28.)
Text: R. Wagner, ed., *Mythographi Graeci* I. *Apollodori bibliotheca* (1926; repr. Stuttgart, 1965).
Translation adapted from J.G. Frazer, tr., *Apollodorus. The Library* I (LCL, 1921).

Λυγκεὺς δὲ μετὰ Δαναὸν Ἄργους δυναστεύων ἐξ Ὑπερμνήστρας τεκνοῖ παῖδα Ἄβαντα. τούτου δὲ καὶ Ἀγλαΐας τῆς Μαντινέως δίδυμοι παῖδες ἐγένοντο Ἀκρίσιος καὶ Προῖτος. οὗτοι καὶ κατὰ γαστρὸς μὲν ἔτι ὄντες ἐστασίαζον πρὸς ἀλλήλους, ὡς δὲ ἀνετράφησαν, περὶ τῆς βασιλείας ἐπολέμουν, καὶ πολεμοῦντες εὗρον ἀσπίδας πρῶτοι. καὶ κρατήσας Ἀκρίσιος Προῖτον Ἄργους ἐξελαύνει. ὁ δ' ἧκεν εἰς Λυκίαν πρὸς Ἰοβάτην, ὡς δέ τινές φασι, πρὸς Ἀμφιάνακτα· καὶ γαμεῖ τὴν τούτου θυγατέρα, ὡς μὲν Ὅμηρος, Ἄντειαν, ὡς δὲ οἱ τραγικοί, Σθενέβοιαν. κατάγει δὲ αὐτὸν ὁ κηδεστὴς μετὰ στρατοῦ Λυκίων, καὶ καταλαμβάνει Τίρυνθα, ταύτην αὐτῷ Κυκλώπων τειχισάντων. μερισάμενοι δὲ τὴν Ἀργείαν ἅπασαν κατῴκουν, καὶ Ἀκρίσιος μὲν Ἄργους βασιλεύει, Προῖτος δὲ Τίρυνθος. καὶ γίνεται Ἀκρισίῳ μὲν ἐξ Εὐρυδίκης τῆς Λακεδαίμονος Δανάη, Προίτῳ δὲ ἐκ Σθενεβοίας Λυσίππη καὶ Ἰφινόη καὶ Ἰφιάνασσα. αὗται δὲ ὡς ἐτελειώθησαν, ἐμάνησαν, ὡς μὲν Ἡσίοδός φησιν, ὅτι τὰς Διονύσου τελετὰς οὐ κατεδέχοντο, ὡς δὲ Ἀκουσίλαος λέγει, διότι τὸ τῆς Ἥρας ξόανον ἐξηυτέλισαν. γενόμεναι δὲ ἐμμανεῖς ἐπλανῶντο ἀνὰ τὴν Ἀργείαν ἅπασαν, αὖθις δὲ τὴν Ἀρκαδίαν διελθοῦσαι μετ' ἀκοσμίας ἁπάσης διὰ τῆς ἐρημίας ἐτρόχαζον. Μελάμπους δὲ ὁ Ἀμυθάονος καὶ Εἰδομένης τῆς Ἄβαντος, μάντις ὢν καὶ τὴν διὰ φαρμάκων καὶ καθαρμῶν θεραπείαν πρῶτος εὑρηκώς, ὑπισχνεῖται *θεραπεύειν τὰς παρθένους, εἰ λάβοι τὸ τρίτον μέρος τῆς δυναστείας. οὐκ ἐπιτρέποντος δὲ Προίτου θεραπεύειν ἐπὶ μισθοῖς τηλικούτοις, ἔτι μᾶλλον ἐμαίνοντο αἱ παρθένοι καὶ προσέτι μετὰ τούτων αἱ λοιπαὶ γυναῖκες· καὶ γὰρ αὗται τὰς οἰκίας ἀπολιποῦσαι τοὺς ἰδίους ἀπώλλυον παῖδας καὶ εἰς τὴν ἐρημίαν ἐφοίτων. προβαινούσης δὲ ἐπὶ πλεῖστον τῆς συμφορᾶς, τοὺς αἰτηθέντας μισθοὺς ὁ Προῖτος ἐδίδου. ὁ δὲ ὑπέσχετο θεραπεύειν ὅταν ἕτερον τοσοῦτον τῆς γῆς ὁ ἀδελφὸς αὐτοῦ λάβῃ Βίας. Προῖτος δὲ εὐλαβηθεὶς μὴ βραδυνούσης τῆς θεραπείας αἰτηθείη καὶ πλεῖον, θεραπεύειν συνεχώρησεν ἐπὶ τούτοις. Μελάμπους δὲ παραλαβὼν τοὺς δυνατωτάτους τῶν νεανιῶν μετ' ἀλαλαγμοῦ καί τινος ἐνθέου χορείας ἐκ τῶν ὀρῶν αὐτὰς εἰς Σικυῶνα συνεδίωξε. κατὰ δὲ τὸν διωγμὸν ἡ πρεσβυτάτη τῶν θυγατέρων Ἰφινόη μετήλλαξεν· ταῖς δὲ λοιπαῖς τυχούσαις καθαρμῶν σωφρονῆσαι συνέβη. καὶ ταύτας μὲν ἐξέδοτο Προῖτος Μελάμποδι καὶ Βίαντι, παῖδα δ' ὕστερον ἐγέννησε Μεγαπένθην.*

Lynceus reigned over Argos after Danaus and begat a son Abas by Hypermnestra; and Abas had twin sons Acrisius and Proetus by Aglaia, daughter of Mantineus. These two quarreled with each other while they were still in the womb, and when they were grown up they waged war for the kingdom, and in the course of the war they were the first to invent shields. And Acrisius gained the mastery and drove Proetus from Argos; and Proetus went to Lycia to the court of Iobates or, as some say, of Ampianax, and married his daughter, whom Homer calls Antia, but the tragic poets call her Stheneboea. His father-in-law restored him to his own land with an army of Lycians, and he occupied Tiryns, which the Cyclopes had fortified for him. They divided the whole of the Argive territory between them and settled in it, Acrisius reigning over Argos and Proetus over Tiryns. And Acrisius had a daughter Danae by Eurydice, daughter of Lacedaemon, and Proetus had daughters, Lysippe, Iphinoe, and Iphianassa, by Stheneboea. When these were grown up, they went mad, according to Hesiod, because they would not accept the *teletai* [rites] of Dionysus, but as Acusilaus says, because they disparaged the *xoanon* of Hera. Being mad, they roamed over the whole Argive land, and afterwards, passing through Arcadia and the Peloponnese, they ran through the desert in the most disorderly fashion. But Melampus, son of Amythaon by Idomene, daughter of Abas, being a seer and the first to devise the cure by means of drugs and purifications, promised to cure the maidens if he should receive the third part of the sovereignty. When Proetus refused to pay so high a fee for the cure, the maidens raved more than ever, and besides that, the other women raved with them; for they also abandoned their houses, destroyed their own children, and flocked to the desert. Not until the evil had reached a very high pitch did Proetus consent to pay the stipulated fee, and Melampus promised to effect a cure whenever his brother Bias should receive just so much land as himself. Fearing that, if the cure were delayed, yet more would be demanded of him, Proetus agreed to the healing on those terms. So Melampus, taking with him the most stalwart of the young men, chased the women in a bevy from the mountains to Sicyon with shouts and a sort of frenzied dance. In the pursuit Iphinoe, the eldest of the daughters, expired; but the others were lucky enough to be purified and so to recover their wits. Proetus gave them in marriage to Melampus and Bias, and afterwards begat a son, Megapenthes.

22

Apollodorus 3.12.3 ? A.D. II
Text: J.G. Frazer, tr., *Apollodorus. The Library* II (LCL, 1946).
Translation adapted from Frazer.

ἱστορία δὲ ἡ περὶ τοῦ παλλαδίου τοιάδε φέρεται· φασὶ γεννηθεῖσαν τὴν Ἀθηνᾶν παρὰ Τρίτωνι τρέφεσθαι, ᾧ θυγάτηρ ἦν Παλλάς· ἀμφοτέρας δὲ ἀσκούσας τὰ κατὰ πόλεμον εἰς φιλονεικίαν ποτὲ προελθεῖν. μελλούσης δὲ πλήττειν τῆς Παλλάδος τὸν Δία φοβηθέντα τὴν αἰγίδα προτεῖναι, τὴν δὲ εὐλαβηθεῖσαν ἀναβλέψαι, καὶ οὕτως ὑπὸ τῆς Ἀθηνᾶς τρωθεῖσαν πεσεῖν. Ἀθηνᾶν δὲ περίλυπον ἐπ' αὐτῇ γενομένην, ξόανον ἐκείνης ὅμοιον κατασκευάσαι, καὶ περιθεῖναι τοῖς στέρνοις ἣν ἔδεισεν αἰγίδα, καὶ τιμᾶν ἱδρυσαμένην παρὰ τῷ Διί. ὕστερον δὲ Ἠλέκτρας κατὰ τὴν φθορὰν τούτῳ προσφυγούσης, Δία ῥῖψαι [μετ' Ἄτης καὶ] τὸ παλλάδιον εἰς τὴν Ἰλιάδα χώραν, Ἶλον δὲ τούτῳ ναὸν κατασκευάσαντα τιμᾶν. καὶ περὶ μὲν τοῦ παλλαδίου ταῦτα λέγεται.

The story told about the Palladium is as followws: They say that when Athena was born she was brought up by Triton, who had a daughter Pallas; and that both girls practiced the arts of war, but that once on a time they fell out; and when Pallas was about to strike a blow, Zeus in fear interposed the aegis, and Pallas, being afraid, looked up, and so fell wounded by Athena. And being exceedingly grieved for her, Athena made a *xoanon* in her likeness, and wrapped the aegis, which she had feared, about the breast of it, and set it up beside Zeus and honored it. But afterwards Electra, at the time of her violation, took refuge at it, and Zeus threw the Palladion [along with Ate] into the Ilian country; and Ilus built a temple for it, and honored it. And concerning the Palladion this is said.

23

Apollodorus 3.14.6 ? A.D. II
Text: R. Wagner, ed., *Mythographi Graeci* I. *Apollodori Bibliotheca* (1926; repr. Stuttgart, 1965).
Translation adapted from J.G. Frazer, tr., *Apollodorus. The Library* II (LCL, 1946).

ἐν δὲ τῷ τεμένει τραφεὶς ᾿Εριχθόνιος ὑπ᾿ αὐτῆς ᾿Αθηνᾶς, ἐκβαλὼν ᾿Αμφικτύονα ἐβασίλευσεν ᾿Αθηνῶν, καὶ τὸ ἐν ἀκροπόλει ξόανον τῆς ᾿Αθηνᾶς ἱδρύσατο, καὶ τῶν Παναθηναίων τὴν ἑορτὴν συνεστήσατο. . . .

Having been brought up by Athena in her *temenos*, Erichthonius expelled Amphictyon and became king of Athens; and he set up the *xoanon* of Athena on the acropolis, and instituted the festival of the Panathenaia. . . .

24

Apollodorus (*Epitome*) 6.26–27
Text: R. Wagner, ed., *Mythographi Graeci* I. *Apollodori Bibliotheca* (1926; repr. Stuttgart, 1965).
Translation adapted from J.G. Frazer, tr., *Apollodorus. The Library* II (LCL, 1946).

ἐρομένῳ δὲ αὐτῷ, πῶς ἂν ἀπαλλαγείη τῆς νόσου, ὁ θεὸς εἶπεν, εἰ τὸ ἐν Ταύροις ξόανον μετακομίσειεν. οἱ δὲ Ταῦροι μοῖρά ἐστι Σκυθῶν, οἳ τοὺς ξένους φονεύουσι καὶ εἰς τὸ ἱερὸν ῥίπτουσι. τοῦτο ἦν ἐν τῷ τεμένει διά τινος πέτρας ἀναφερόμενον ἐξ ῞Αιδου. παραγενόμενος οὖν εἰς Ταύρους ᾿Ορέστης μετὰ Πυλάδου φωραθεὶς ἑάλω καὶ ἄγεται πρὸς Θόαντα τὸν βασιλέα δέσμοις, ὁ δὲ ἀμφοτέρους πρὸς τὴν ἱέρειαν ἀποστέλλει. ἐπιγνωσθεὶς δὲ ὑπὸ τῆς ἀδελφῆς ἱερὰ ποιούσης ἐν Ταύροις, ἄρας τὸ ξόανον σὺν αὐτῇ φεύγει. κομισθὲν δὲ εἰς ᾿Αθήνας νῦν λέγεται τὸ τῆς Ταυροπόλου.

When he inquired how he should be rid of his disorder, the god answered that he would be rid of it if he should fetch the *xoanon* that was in the land of the Taurians. Now the Taurians are a part of the Scythians, who murder strangers and throw them into the sacred fire, which was in the precinct, being wafted up from Hades through a certain rock. So when Orestes was come with Pylades to the land of the Taurians, he was detected, caught, and carried in bonds before Thoas the king, who sent them both to the priestess. But being recognized by his sister, who acted as priestess among the Taurians, he fled with her, carrying off the *xoanon*. It was conveyed to Athens and is now called the image of Tauropolus.

25

Apollonius Rhodius, *Argonautica* 1.1117–1122 III B.C.
Text: H. Fraenkel, ed., *Apollonii Rhodii Argonautica* (Oxford, 1970).
Translation adapted from R.C. Seaton, tr., *Apollonius Rhodius. The Argonautica* (LCL, 1912; repr. 1980).

ἔσκε δέ τι βριαρὸν στύπος ἀμπέλου ἔντροφον ὕλῃ,
πρόχνυ γεράνδρυον· τὸ μὲν ἔκταμον, ὄφρα πέλοιτο
δαίμονος οὐρείης ἱερὸν βρέτας, ἔξεσε δ᾿ ῎Αργος

εὐκόσμως· καὶ δή μιν ἐπ' ὀκριόεντι κολωνῷ
ἵδρυσαν, φηγοῖσιν ἐπηρεφὲς ἀκροτάτῃσιν
αἵ ῥά τε πασάων πανυπέρταται ἐρρίζωντο·

Now there was a sturdy stump of vine that grew in the forest, a tree exceeding old; this they cut down, to be the *hieron bretas* of the mountain goddess; and Argus smoothed it skillfully, and they set it upon that rugged hill roofed by lofty oaks, which of all trees have their roots highest.

26

Sch. Apollonius Rhodius, *Argonautica* 1.1117
Text: C. Wendel, ed., *Scholia in Apollonium Rhodium Vetera* (Berlin, 1935).

ἔσκε δέ τι στιβα<ρὸν στύπος>: στύπος τὸ πρέμνον καὶ στέλεχος, ἐξ οὗ καὶ <Ἀρχίλοχος 'ὀρέων> ἀπεστύπαζον'. βρέτας δὲ τὸ βροτῷ ἐοικός. καὶ Εὐφορίων δὲ ἐκ τούτου κινηθεὶς τὸ ξόανον τῆς μητρὸς τῶν θεῶν φησιν ἀμπέλινον εἶναι, διὰ τὸ τὴν ἄμπελον ἴσως ἱερὰν εἶναι τῆς 'Ρέας.

There was a certain stur[dy stump]: *stupos* [stump] is the bottom of the trunk of a tree and the crown of the root, from which also [Archilochus, "From the doors] I drove him off." *Bretas* is something like a mortal. And Euphorion, influenced by this, says that the *xoanon* of the Mother of the Gods is made of a grape-vine, because the grape-vine is in like way sacred to Rhea.

27

Apollonius Rhodius, *Argonautica* 4.1277–1289 III B.C.
Text: H. Fraenkel, ed., *Apollonii Rhodii Argonautica* (Oxford, 1970).
Translation adapted from R.C. Seaton, tr., *Apollonius Rhodius. The Argonautica* (LCL, 1912; repr. 1980).

Ὣς φάτο δακρυόεις, σὺν δ' ἔννεπον ἀσχαλόωντι
ὅσσοι ἔσαν νηῶν δεδαημένοι. ἐν δ' ἄρα πᾶσιν
παχνώθη κραδίη, χύτο δὲ χλόος ἀμφὶ παρειάς.
οἷον δ' ἀψύχοισιν ἐοικότες εἰδώλοισιν
ἀνέρες εἱλίσσονται ἀνὰ πτόλιν, ἢ πολέμοιο
ἢ λοιμοῖο τέλος ποτιδέγμενοι ἠέ τιν' ὄμβρον
ἄσπετον, ὅς τε βοῶν κατὰ μυρίος ἔκλυσεν ἔργα,
ὁππότ' ἂν αὐτόματα ξόανα ῥέῃ ἱδρώοντα
αἵματι καὶ μυκαὶ σηκοῖς ἔνι φαντάζωνται,
ἠὲ καὶ ἠέλιος μέσῳ ἤματι νύκτ' ἐπάγῃσιν
οὐρανόθεν, τὰ δὲ λαμπρὰ δι' ἠέρος ἄστρα φαείνῃ—
ὣς τότ' ἀριστῆες δολιχοῦ πρόπαρ αἰγιαλοῖο
ἤλυον ἑρπύζοντες.

Thus he spoke, crying, and all of them that had knowledge of ships agreed but the hearts of all grew numb, and pallor overspread their cheeks. And as, like specters without souls, men roam through a city awaiting the issue of war or of pestilence, or some mighty storm which overwhelms the countless labors of oxen, when the *xoana* of their own accord sweat and run down with blood, and bellowings are heard in *sekoi* or when at mid-day the sun draws on night from heaven, and the stars shine clear through the mist; so at that time along the endless strand the chieftains wandered, groping their way.

Arctinus, *Iliou Persis* ?VIII B.C.
See Proclus, *Chrestomathia* 261–263 Severyns [**325**].

Arethas A.D. IX
See Sch. Plato, *Euthyphro* 11c [**309**].

28

Aristeae epistula 134–135 ?II–I B.C.

Text: H.B. Swete, *An Introduction to the Old Testament in Greek, with an Appendix containing the Letter of Aristeas, edited by H. St J. Thackeray* (Cambridge, 1902; repr. New York, 1968).

Translation adapted from M. Hadas, ed., tr., *Aristeas to Philocrates (Letter of Aristeas)* (New York, 1951).

ποιησάμενος οὖν τὴν καταρχὴν ταύτην, καὶ δείξας ὅτι πάντες οἱ λοιποὶ παρ' ἡμᾶς ἄνθρωποι πολλοὺς θεοὺς εἶναι νομίζουσιν, αὐτοὶ δυναμικώτεροι πολλῷ καθεστῶτες ὧν σέβονται ματαίως—ἀγάλματα γὰρ ποιήσαντες ἐκ λίθων καὶ ξύλων, εἰκόνας φασὶν εἶναι τῶν ἐξευρόντων τι πρὸς τὸ ζῆν αὐτοῖς χρήσιμον, οἷς προσκυνοῦσι, παρὰ πόδας ἔχοντες τὴν ἀναισθησίαν.

After he [Moses] set down these premises he showed that all other men except ourselves believe that there are many gods, though they themselves are much more powerful than the gods they vainly revere. Having made *agalmata* from stones and stocks, they say that they are *eikones* of persons who have made discoveries useful in life, and these they worship, though grasping their lack of sensation.

29

Sch. Aristophanes, *Lysistrata* 64

Text: W.G. Rutherford, ed., *Scholia Aristophanica* II (London and New York, 1896) 156.

θοὐκάτειον: τὸ ἑκ<άτειον>|· ἑκάτειον: <τὸ> τῆς Ἑκάτης ξόανον.

Th'oukateion: the hek[ateion]; *hekateion*: [the] *xoanon* of Hekate.

Aristophanes fr. 194 Kock V B.C.
See Hesychius *s.v.* Δαιδάλεια [**142**].

30

Aristotle, *De anima* 1.3, 406 b 9
(= Eubulus fr. 22 Kock.) IV B.C.
Text and translation: R.D. Hicks, ed., tr., *Aristotle. De Anima* (Cambridge, 1907; repr. Amsterdam, 1965).

ἔνιοι δὲ καὶ κινεῖν φασὶ τὴν ψυχὴν τὸ σῶμα ἐν ᾧ ἐστίν, ὡς αὐτὴ κινεῖται, οἷον Δημόκριτος, παραπλησίως λέγων Φιλίππῳ τῷ κωμῳδοδιδασκάλῳ· φησὶ γὰρ τὸν Δαίδαλον κινουμένην ποιῆσαι τὴν ξυλίνην Ἀφροδίτην, ἐγχέαντ' ἄργυρον χυτόν· ὁμοίως δὲ καὶ Δημόκριτος λέγει· κινουμένας γάρ φησι τὰς ἀδιαιρέτους σφαίρας, διὰ τὸ πεφυκέναι μηδέποτε μένειν, συνεφέλκειν καὶ κινεῖν τὸ σῶμα πᾶν.

Some say that the soul in fact moves the body, in which it is, in the same way in which it moves itself. So, for example, Democritus; and herein he resembled Philippus, the comic poet, who tells us that Daedalus endowed the wooden Aphrodite with motion, simply by pouring in quicksilver: this is very similar to what Democritus says. For according to him the spherical atoms, which from their nature can never remain still, being moved, tend to draw the whole body after them and thus set it in motion.

Aristotle, *Politeia* IV B.C.
See Heraclides Lembus [**138**].

31

Arnobius, *Adversus nationes* 6.8–12 c. A.D. 300
Text: A. Reifferscheid, ed., *Arnobii Adversus Nationes Libri* VII (Corpus Scriptorum Ecclesiasticorum Latinorum IV; Vienna, 1875).
Translation: G.E. McCracken, tr., *Arnobius of Sicca. The Case Against the Pagans* II (Ancient Christian Writers 8; Westminster, Maryland, 1949).

sequitur ut de signis aliquid simulacrisque dicamus, quae multa arte conponitis et religiosa obseruatione curatis. qua in parte si fides est ulla, constituere apud nos ipsos nullis considerationibus possumus, utrumne istud serio et cum proposito faciatis graui an ridendo res ipsas puerili alucinatione ludatis. si enim certum est apud uos deos esse, quos remini atque in summis caeli regionibus degere, quae causa, quae ratio est, ut simulacra ista fingantur a uobis, cum habeatis res certas, quibus preces possitis effundere et auxilium rebus in exigentibus postulare? sin autem non creditis aut, ut mediocriter dicatur, ambigitis, etiam sic ratio quaenam est dubiorum fingere atque instituere simulacra et quod esse non credas uentosa imitatione formare? an numquid dicitis forte, praesentiam uobis quandam his numinum sub exhiberi simulacris, et quia deos uidere non datum est, † eos insolidi et munia officiosa praestari? hoc qui dicit et adserit deos esse non credit, nec habere conuincitur suis religionibus fidem cui opus est uidere quod teneat, ne inane forte sit quod † obscurum non uidetur. 9. deos, inquitis, per simulacra ueneramur. quid ergo? si haec non sint, coli se dii nesciunt nec inpertiri a uobis ullum sibi existimabunt honorem? per tramites ergo quosdam et per quaedam fidei commissa, ut dicitur, uestras sumunt atque accipiunt cultiones, et antequam ii sentiant quibus illud debetur obsequium, simulacris litatis prius et uelut reliquias quasdam aliena ad illos ex auctoritate transmittitis. et quid fieri potis est iniuriosius contumeliosius durius, quam deum alterum scire et rei alteri supplicare? opem sperare de numine et nullius sensus ad effigiem deprecari? nonne illud est, quaeso, quod in uulgaribus prouerbiis dicitur, fabrum caedere cum ferias fullonem, et cum hominis consilium quaeras, ab asellis et porculis agendarum rerum sententias postulare? 10. et unde nouissime scitis, an simulacra haec omnia quae dis immortalibus uicaria substitutione formatis similitudinem referant habeantque diuinam? potest enim fieri, ut barbatus in caelo sit qui esse a uobis effingitur leuis, potest ut senectute prouectior cui puerilem commodatis aetatem, potest ut hic flauus sit * * * qui in ueritate habeat oculos caesios, displosas ut gestitet nares quem esse uos facitis figuratisque nasicam. neque enim rectum est dicere aut appellare simulacrum quod non pariles lineas principali ab ore traducat: quod esse planum et certum manifestis poterit ab rebus agnosci. nam cum omnes homines teretem esse solem indubitabili luminum contemplatione uideamus, os illi uos hominis et mortalium corporum liniamenta donastis. luna semper in motu est et ter denas facies in restitutione accipit menstrua: uobis ducibus et figuratoribus femina est, uultuque est uno quae per habitus mille cottidiana instabilitate mutatur. intellegimus omnes uentos aeris esse fluorem pulsi et mundanis rationibus concitati: per uos hominum formae sent bucinarum animantes tortus intestinis et domesticis flatibus. inter deos uidemus uestros leonis toruissimam faciem mero oblitam minio et nomine † frugiferio nuncupari. si simulacra haec omnia superorum sunt imagines numinum, ergo et in caelo habitare dicendus est deus talis, ad cuius formam et speciem simulacri huius similitudo directa est, et uidelicet ut hic iste, ita illic ille sine reliquo corpore persona est et facies sola, fremibundus hiatibus toruis, dirus sanguineo de colore, † malum dentibus suis comprimens atque ut olim fessi canes linguam ore de patulo † puetuitate proiciens. quod si utique non est, ita ut omnes existimamus non esse, quaenam tanta audacia est. formam tibi quam uolueris fingere ac dicere esse simulacrum dei quam probare non possis ulla esse in parte naturae? 11. ridetis temporibus priscis Persas fluuios coluisse, memoralia ut indicant scripta, informem Arabas lapidem, acinacem Scythiae nationes, ramum pro Cinxia Thespios, lignum Icarios pro Diana indolatum, Pessinuntios silicem pro Deum Matre, pro Marte Romanos hastam, Varronis ut indicant Musae, atque, ut Aethlius memorat, ante usum disciplinamque fictorum pluteum Samios pro Iunone: et abstinetis a risu, cum pro diis immortalibus sigilliolis hominum et formis supplicatis humanis? quinimmo deos esse sigillaria ipsa censetis, nec praeter haec quicquam uim creditis habere diuinam. quid dicitis, o isti? ergone dii caelites habent aures et tempora, ceruices occipitium spinam lumbos latera poplites nates suffragines talos membraque alia cetera, quibus constructi nos sumus et quae prima in parte paulo plenius dicta sunt et scripto uberiore prolata? utinam liceret introspicere sensus uestros recessusque ipsos mentis, quibus uarias uoluitis atque initis obscurissimas cogitationes: reperiremus et uos ipsos eadem sentire quae nos neque alias gerere super numinum figuratione sententias. sed studiis facere quid peruicacibus possumus, quid intentantibus gladios nouasque excogitantibus poenas? minantes adseritis malam scientissimi causam, et quod semel sine ratione fecistis, ne uideamini aliquid aliquando nescisse, defenditis meliusque putatis non uinci quam confessae cedere atque adnuere ueritati. 12. ex huiusmodi causis illud etiam uobis coniuentibus consecutum est, ut in deorum corporibus lasciuiae artificum luderent darentque his formas quae cuilibet tristi possent esse derisui. itaque Hammon cum cornibus iam formatur et fingitur arietinis, Saturnus cum obunca falce custos ruris, ut aliquis ramorum luxuriantium tonsor, cum petaso gnatus Maiae, tamquam uias adgredi praeparet et solem pulueremque declinet, Liber membris cum mollibus et languoris feminei dissolutissimus laxitate, Venus nude et aperta, tamquam si illam dicas publicare, diuendere meritorii corporis formam, cum pilleo Vulcanus et malleo, manu liber sed dextera ut fabrili expeditioni succinctus, cum plectro et fidibus Delius, citharistae gestus seruans, cantaturi et nenias histrionis, cum fuscina rex maris, tamquam illi pugna sit gladiatorii obeunda certaminis: neque ullum est reperire figmentum alicuius numinis, quod non habitus certos ferat fabrorum liberalitate donatos. ecce si aliquis uobis nescientibus et ignaris rex urbanus et callidus ex foribus suis Solem tollat et in Mercurii transferat sedem, Mercurium rursus arripiat atque in Solis faciat commigrare delubrum—uterque enim a uobis glaber atque ore compingitur leui—detque huic radios, Solis capiti petasunculum superponat: quibus modis internoscere poteritis, utrumne Sol iste sit an ille Mercurius, cum habitus uobis deos, non oris soleat proprietas indicare? consimili rursus translatione si nudo Ioui cornua detrahat et Martis temporibus adfigat, Martem armis spoliet et his rursus circumcludat Hammonem: interstinctio fieri quae poterit singulorum, cum qui Iuppiter fuerat idem possit existimari Mars esse et qui Mauors fuerat subintroire speciem Iouis possit

Hammonis? usque adeo ludus est simulacra ista confingere, nomina illis tamquam propria dedicare, quibus si habitum detrahas, tollatur cognitio singulorum, deus pro deo credi, alter uideri pro altero, immo pro utroque utroque possit existimari.

We must next say something about the statues and images which you form with much skill and treat with religious reverence. If in this matter there can be any question of good faith, we can by no amount of reflection determine for ourselves whether you do this in earnest and with serious purpose, or mock those very things and amuse yourselves with childish fancies. For if you are certain of the existence of the gods whom you suppose, and that they live in the lofty regions of heaven, what cause is there, what reason, that you should fashion those images, when you have sure beings to whom you can direct your prayers and request aid in circumstances of need? But, on the other hand, if you do not believe, or to put it more moderately, are in doubt, even so, what reason is there to fashion and set up images of doubtful things? And why produce an inane imitation of something in whose existence you do not believe? Or do you possibly mean to say that by these images the presence, as it were, of these divinities is represented, and because you have not been given the experience of seeing the gods, they are thus concretely worshipped and paid the official services owed them? The man who says this and asserts it, does not believe the gods exist, and he is convicted of having no faith in his own religious beliefs who needs to see what he holds, afraid that a mystery unseen may, after all, be nothing.

9. "We worship the gods," you say, "by means of the images."

Well, if these images do not exist, do the gods not know that they are worshipped and will they think that you show them no honor at all? It is through certain bypaths, then, and certain so-called proxies that they take and receive your tokens of veneration; and before those to whom that duty is owed perceive the homage, you first sacrifice to images and transmit certain remnants, as it were, to them, through outside influence. And what greater injustice, disgrace, and hardship can there be than to know a god on the one hand and on the other to pray to something else? To hope for aid from a deity and to make supplication to a senseless image? Does not this, I ask, amount to what is said in the popular saws, "to hit the carpenter when you strike at the fuller" and "when you seek a man's advice to ask asses and pigs what to do?"

10. And, how, finally, do you know whether all these images you form as substitutions for the immortal gods, reproduce and bear a resemblance to the divine? It may be that one is bearded in heaven who is fashioned by you as beardless. It may be that another is quite advanced in age to whom you give a boy's years. It may be that here one who really has blue eyes has

brown ones; that he has a pug nose whom you make and fashion with a pointed nose. And certainly it is not right to speak of, or call, a 'likeness' something which does not derive a uniformity of features from the face that is its prototype—an obvious certainty which can be gathered from manifest realities.

While, for instance, all of us human beings see by the indubitable sight of our eyes that the sun is round, you have given it the countenance of a man and the features of mortal bodies. The moon is ever in motion and in the course of its monthly restoration puts on thirty faces: under your guidance and designing, it is a woman and has but one countenance, she whose physiognomy changes a thousand times each day in the instability that is hers. We understand that all the winds are a flow of air set in motion by physical phenonema: with you they are human forms blowing twisted trumpets, the blasts of air coming from their own insides.

Among your gods we see the fierce face of a lion smeared with pure vermilion and named Frugiferius. If all these images are likenesses of the divinities above, then one must say there dwells also in heaven such a god, whose form and appearance have served as a model for the present; and, of course, as here that figure of yours, so there that divinity himself is merely a mask and face without a corresponding body, growling and opening his fierce jaws, gruesome in his bloody dye, his teeth sunk in an apple and, as street urchins sometimes childishly do, sticking his tongue out of his gaping mouth!

But if it is not so, as all think it is not, how do you explain this brashness—to fashion to yourself whatever form you please and to call it an image of a god whom you cannot prove exists anywhere in the universe?

11. You laugh at the fact that in ancient times the Persians worshipped rivers, as the written tradition states; the Arabs, an unformed stone; the Scythian nations a sabre; the Thespians a branch instead of Cinxia; the Icarians an unhewn log in place of Diana; the Pessinuntians a piece of flint in place of the Mother of the Gods; the Romans instead of Mars a spear, as the Muses of Varro point out; and, as Aethlius relates, the Samians, before they were acquainted with the statuary's art, a board instead of Juno: and you keep from laughing when instead of the immortal gods you pray to statuettes of men and to human forms? Indeed, you even regard these little statuettes themselves as gods and outside of these you do not believe that anything has divine power.

What do you say, you—? So the gods in heaven have ears and temples, necks, an occiput, spine, loins, sides, knees, buttocks, thighs, ankles, and all the other parts with which we are formed, and which were mentioned in the first part somewhat more fully and described in greater detail? Would that we might peer into your feelings and deep into into your minds in which you reflect on and entertain all your most secret thoughts! We should find that you, too, feel the same regarding the physical appearance of the divinities as we do. But what can we do in the face of the obstinate bias of people threatening us with swords and devising new penalties? By your threats you shield a cause, of the bad state of which you are aware, and once you have gone through with something irrational, that you may not leave the impression that on a given occasion you were uninformed, you defend it; and you think it better to have it your way than to give in and consent to acknowledged truth.

12. From causes of this kind it has also resulted with your connivance that the wanton fancy of artisans have played on the bodies of the gods and given them forms which could serve as a laughing stock to anyone, however strait-laced. Thus, in fact, Hammon is formed and fashioned with goats' horns. Saturn with his crooked sickle is guardian of the countryside like some pruner of the too luxurious branches. The son of Maia wears a broad-brimmed hat, as if he were prepared to take to the roads, and protecting himself against the sun and dust. There is Liber with his delicate limbs and utterly enervated by the languor of effeminacy. Venus is naked and uncovered, as if to say that she offered for sale, auctioned off the beauty of her meretricious body. Vulcan has his cap and hammer, and his right hand free and his garment tucked up ready for the smithy. The Delian has his plectrum and his lyre, making the gestures of a guitar player and of an actor about to sing dirges. The King of the Sea holds his trident, as if he had to fight in a gladiatorial contest; and no representation of any divinity can be found which does not have certain characteristics attributed to it by the generosity of its craftsmen.

Now listen, if without your knowing anything about it some witty and clever ruler were to remove the Sun from the gate and transfer it to the place of Mercury and, conversely, were to carry off Mercury and make him emigrate to the shrine of the Sun—both of them, as you know, are represented by you as beardless and smooth-shaven—and were to give the latter rays and to place on the head of the Sun the little travelling hat, how would you be able to know them apart, whether this one is the Sun or that one Mercury, since their dress, not the facial characteristics, usually identifies the gods for you?

Again, if he were, by a similar transfer, to remove the horns from the unclad Jupiter, and fasten them to the sides of Mars, and strip Mars of his weapons and so again furnish Hammon with them, how can they be distinguished from each other, since he who was Jupiter can be taken to be the same as Mars, and he who was Mavors can assume the appearance of Jupiter Hammon? Such tomfoolery it is to fashion those images of yours, to dedicate names to them as if they were their own: if you took away their trappings, the possibility of recognizing individuals would be eliminated, god would be confused with god, one would seem to be other—yes, both could be taken to be both.

32

Arrian, *Anabasis* 2.18.1 A.D. II

Text: A.G. Roos, ed., *Flavii Arriani quae exstant omnia* I. *Alexandri Anabasis* (Leipzig, 1967).

Translation adapted from E.I. Robson, tr., *Arrian. Anabasis Alexandri Books I–IV* (LCL, 1929).

Ταῦτα λέγων οὐ χαλεπῶς ἔπειθεν ἐπιχειρεῖν τῇ Τύρῳ· καί τι καὶ θεῖον ἀνέπειθεν αὐτόν, ὅτι ἐνύπνιον αὐτῆς ἐκείνης τῆς νυκτὸς ἐδόκει αὐτὸς μὲν τείχει προσάγειν τῶν Τυρίων, τὸν δὲ Ἡρακλέα δεξιοῦσθαί τε αὐτὸν καὶ ἀνάγειν ἐς τὴν πόλιν. καὶ τοῦτο ἐξηγεῖτο Ἀρίστανδρος ὡς ξὺν πόνῳ ἁλωσομένην τὴν Τύρον, ὅτι καὶ τὰ τοῦ Ἡρακλέους ἔργα ξὺν πόνῳ ἐγένετο.

Saying these things Alexander easily won over his staff to the attack on Tyre, and he had an omen to help him, for in a dream that night it seemed he was approaching the wall of Tyre; [and] Heracles was stretching out to him his right hand and conducting him into the city. Aristandros interpreted the dream thus: Tyre would be taken, but with much toil, for toil was the mark of Heracles' achievements.

33

Arrian, *Periplus Ponti Euxini* 21 (32 M) c. A.D. 131/2

Text: A.G. Roos, ed., *Flavius Arrianus* II. *Scripta Minora* (Leipzig, 1967).

ταύτην λέγεται Θέτις ἀνεῖναι τῷ παιδί, καὶ ταύτην οἰκεῖν τὸν Ἀχιλλέα. καὶ νεώς ἐστιν ἐν αὐτῇ τοῦ Ἀχιλλέως, καὶ ξόανον τῆς παλαιᾶς ἐργασίας.

(Leuce)

It is said that Thetis left it [the island] to her son, and that Achilles inhabits it. And on it there is a *neos* of Achilles, and a *xoanon* of old workmanship.

34

Asclepius III.24 a ? A.D. III

Text and translation: W. Scott, ed., tr., *Hermetica* I (Oxford, 1924).

Asclepius: Statuas dicis, o Trismegiste?

Trismegistus: Statuas, o Asclepi. Videsne quatenus tu ipse diffidas? Statuas animatas sensu et spiritu plenas, tantaque facientes et talia, statuas futurorum praescias, eaque sorte, vate, somniis, multisque aliis rebus praedicentes, inbecillitates hominibus facientes easque curantes, tristitiam laetitiamque pro meritis <dispensantes>.

Asclepius: Do you mean statues, Trismegistus?
Trismegistus: Yes, Asclepius. See how even you give way to doubt! I mean statues, but statues living and conscious, filled with the breath of life, and doing many mighty works; statues which have foreknowledge, and predict future events by the drawing of lots, and by prophetic inspiration, and by dreams, and in many other ways; statues which inflict diseases and heal them, dispensing sorrow and joy according to men's deserts.

Asterius of Amasea A.D. IV–V
See Photius, *Bibliotheca* 271 [**302**].

35
Athenaeus 13.606 a–b
(= Philemon fr. 139 Kock.) A.D. II–III
Text: G. Kaibel, ed., *Athenaei Naucratitae Dipnosophistarum libri XV*, III (Leipzig, 1890; repr. Stuttgart, 1962).
Translation adapted from C.B. Gulick, tr., *Athenaeus. The Deipnosophists* VI (LCL, 1937).

τῆς πράξεως ταύτης μνημονεύει καὶ Ἄλεξις ὁ ποιητὴς ἐν τῷ ἐπιγραφομένῳ δράματι Γραφῇ λέγων ὧδε·

γεγένηται δ', ὡς λέγουσιν, κἀν Σάμῳ τοιοῦθ' ἕτερον. λιθίνης
ἐπεθύμησεν κόρης ἄνθρωπος ἐγκατέκλεισέ θ' αὑτὸν τῷ νεῷ.

καὶ Φιλήμων τοῦ αὐτοῦ μνημονεύων φησίν·

ἀλλ' ἐν Σάμῳ μὲν τοῦ λιθίνου ζῴου ποτὲ ἄνθρωπος ἠράσθη τις· εἶτ'
εἰς τὸν νεὼν κατέκλεισεν αὑτόν.

Κτησικλέους δ' ἐστὶν ἔργον τὸ ἄγαλμα, ὥς φησιν Ἀδαῖος ὁ Μιτυληναῖος ἐν τῷ περὶ Ἀγαλματοποιῶν. Πολέμων δὲ ἢ ὁ ποιήσας τὸν ἐπιγραφόμενον Ἑλλαδικὸν 'ἐν Δελφοῖς, φησίν, ἐν τῷ Σπινατῶν θησαυρῷ παῖδές εἰσιν λίθινοι δύο, ὧν τοῦ ἑτέρου Δελφοί φασι τῶν θεωρῶν ἐπιθυμήσαντά τινα συγκατακλεισθῆναι καὶ τῆς ὁμιλίας . . . καταλιπεῖν στέφανον. φωραθέντος δ' αὐτοῦ τὸν θεὸν χρωμένοις τοῖς Δελφοῖς συντάξαι ἀφεῖναι τὸν ἄνθρωπον· δεδωκέναι γὰρ αὐτὸν μισθόν.'

The poet Alexis mentions this deed in the play entitled *A Picture*, commenting as follows: "Another case of a like sort occurred, they say, in Samos. A man conceived a passion for a stone maiden, and locked himself up in the *neos*." And Philemon, mentioning the same, says, "Why, once on a time, in Samos, a certain man fell in love with a stone *zoion*; thereupon he locked himself in the *neos*."

This *agalma* is the work of Ctesicles, as Adaeus of Mytilene says in his work *On Agalma-Makers*. But Polemon or whoever wrote the work

Heladicon says, "In Delphi, in the treasury of the Spinatae, are two stone boys, for one of which, the Delphians say, a certain pilgrim to the shrine once conceived a passion and locked himself up with it, leaving behind him a wreath as the price of the intercourse. When his act was detected the god ordained to the Delphians who consulted his oracle that they should release the man; for he had paid the price."

36

Athenaeus 14.636 f–637 a A.D. II–III
(= Sophocles fr. 238 Radt, Pearson [217 Nauck[2]].)
Text: G. Kaibel, ed., *Athenaei Naucratitae Dipnosophistarum libri XV*, III (Leipzig, 1890; repr. Stuttgart, 1962).
Translation adapted from C.B. Gulick, tr., *Athenaeus. The Deipnosophists* VI (LCL, 1937).

Δοῦρις δ' ἐν τῷ περὶ Τραγῳδίας ὠνομάσθαι φησὶ τὴν μάγαδιν ἀπὸ Μάγδιος Θρᾳκὸς γένος. Ἀπολλόδωρος δ' ἐν τῇ πρὸς τὴν Ἀριστοκλέους Ἐπιστολὴν Ἀντιγραφῇ 'ὃ νῦν, φησίν, ἡμεῖς λέγομεν ψαλτήριον, τοῦτ' εἶναι μάγαδιν, ὁ δὲ κλεψίαμβος κληθείς, ἔτι δ' ὁ τρίγωνος καὶ ὁ ἔλυμος καὶ τὸ ἐννεάχορδον ἀμαυρότερα τῇ χρείᾳ καθέστηκεν. καὶ Ἀλκμὰν δέ φησιν· 'μάγαδιν δ' ἀποθέσθαι.' Σοφοκλῆς δὲ ἐν Θαμύρᾳ·

πηκταὶ δὲ λύραι καὶ μαγάδιδες
τά τ' ἐν Ἕλλησι ξόαν' ἡδυμελῆ.

Duris in his work *On Tragedy* says that the *magadis* takes its name from Magdus, a Thracian by birth. Apollodorus in his *Answer to Aristocles' Letter* says, "What we today call a psalterium is the magadis but the clepsiambus, as it was called, the triangle, the elymus, and the nine-stringed have become rather obsolete in use." And so Alcman says: "To lay aside the magadis." Sophocles in *Thamyras*: "Well-built lyres and magadides/ and the melodius *xoana* among the Greeks."

37

Athenaeus 15.672 a–e A.D. II–III
Text: G. Kaibel, ed., *Athenaei Naucratitae Dipnosophistarum libri XV*, III (Leipzig, 1890; repr. Stuttgart, 1962).
Translation adapted from C.B. Gulick, tr., *Athenaeus. The Deipnosophists* VII (LCL, 1941).

ἐγὼ δ' ἐντυχὼν τῷ Μηνοδότου τοῦ Σαμίου συγγράμματι, ὅπερ ἐπιγράφεται Τῶν κατὰ τὴν Σάμον ἐνδόξων ἀναγραφή, εὗρον τὸ ζητούμενον. Ἀδμήτην γάρ φησιν τὴν Εὐρυσθέως ἐξ Ἄργους φυγοῦσαν ἐλθεῖν εἰς Σάμον, θεασαμένην δὲ τὴν τῆς Ἥρας ἐπιφάνειαν καὶ τῆς οἴκοθεν σωτηρίας *χαριστήριον βουλομένην ἀποδοῦναι ἐπιμεληθῆναι τοῦ ἱεροῦ τοῦ καὶ νῦν ὑπάρχοντος, πρότερον δὲ ὑπὸ Λελέγων καὶ Νυμφῶν καθιδρυμένου· τοὺς δ' Ἀργείους πυθομένους καὶ χαλεπαίνοντας πεῖσαι χρημάτων ὑποσχέσει Τυρρηνοὺς ληστρικῷ [τε] βίῳ χρωμένους ἁρπάσαι τὸ βρέτας, πεπεισμένους τοὺς Ἀργείους ὡς, εἰ τοῦτο γένοιτο, πάντως τι κακὸν πρὸς τῶν τὴν Σάμον κατοικούντων ἡ Ἀδμήτη πείσεται. τοὺς δὲ Τυρρηνοὺς ἐλθόντας εἰς τὸν Ἡραίτην ὅρμον καὶ ἀποβάντας εὐθέως ἔχεσθαι τῆς πράξεως. ἀθύρου δὲ ὄντος τότε τοῦ νεὼ ταχέως ἀνελέσθαι τὸ βρέτας καὶ διακομίσαντας ἐπὶ θάλασσαν εἰς τὸ σκάφος ἐμβαλέσθαι· λυσαμένους δ' αὐτοὺς τὰ πρυμνήσια καὶ τὰς ἀγκύρας ἀνελομένους εἰρεσίᾳ τε πάσῃ χρωμένους ἀπαίρειν οὐ δύνασθαι. ἡγησαμένους οὖν θεῖόν τι τοῦτ' εἶναι πάλιν ἐξενεγκαμένους τῆς νεὼς τὸ βρέτας ἀποθέσθαι παρὰ τὸν αἰγιαλὸν· καὶ ψαιστὰ αὐτῷ ποιήσαντας περιδεεῖς ἀπαλλάττεσθαι. τῆς δὲ Ἀδμήτης ἕωθεν δηλωσάσης ὅτι τὸ βρέτας ἠφανίσθη καὶ ζητήσεως γενομένης εὑρεῖν μὲν αὐτὸ τοὺς ζητοῦντας ἐπὶ τῆς ᾐόνος, ὡς δὲ δὴ βαρβάρους Κᾶρας ὑπονοήσαντας αὐτόματον ἀποδεδρακέναι πρός τι λύγου θωράκιον ἀπερείσασθαι καὶ τοὺς εὐμηκεστάτους τῶν κλάδων ἑκατέρωθεν ἐπισπασαμένους περιειλῆσαι πάντοθεν. τὴν δὲ Ἀδμήτην λύσασαν αὐτὸ ἁγνίσαι καὶ στῆσαι πάλιν ἐπὶ τοῦ βάθρου, καθάπερ πρότερον ἵδρυτο. διόπερ ἐξ ἐκείνου καθ' ἕκαστον ἔτος ἀποκομίζεσθαι τὸ βρέτας εἰς τὴν ᾐόνα καὶ ἀφαγνίζεσθαι ψαιστά τε αὐτῷ παρατίθεσθαι· καὶ καλεῖσθαι Τόναια τὴν ἑορτήν, ὅτι συντόνως συνέβη περιειληθῆναι τὸ βρέτας ὑπὸ τῶν τὴν πρώτην αὐτοῦ ζήτησιν ποιησαμένων.*

But I have lighted on the treatise of Menodotus of Samos, the one entitled *Register of Notable Things in Samos*, and have found the object of our search. He says that Admete, the daughter of Eurystheus, went in flight from Argos to Samos, and after seeing Hera in a vision she wished to render a thank-offering for her escape from home, and so undertook the care of the temple which is there today, founded earlier by Leleges and the Nymphs; but the Argives, hearing of this, in their anger promised money to the Tyrrhenians, who lived the life of pirates, if they would carry off the *bretas* of Hera, being themselves convinced that if that happened Admete would surely suffer some harm at the hands of the people of Samos. So the Tyrrhenians made for the port of Hera, and disembarking set to work at once. Since the *neos* had no door at that time, they soon picked up the *bretas* and carried it to the sea, where they placed it in their ship; but though they loosed the cables, pulled up the anchors, and rowed with all their might, they could not get under way. Thinking, therefore that this was a divine portent, they carried the *bretas* out of the ship again and deposited it on the shore; and setting barley-cakes beside it they departed in great fear. Next morning Admete disclosed that the *bretas* had disappeared, and starting in search the seekers found it on the beach; but the Carians, as one would expect of barbarians, surmised that the image had run away of its own accord, and so they fastened it to a mat of withes, pulling the longest branches tightly on both sides of it, and so wrapping it round. Admete unfastened it and purified it and set it once more on its pedestal, just as it had stood before. Wherefore, ever since, they have carried the *bretas* every year to the sea-beach and purged it and set offerings of barley-cakes beside it; the festival is called the Tonaia, because the *bretas*, as it happened, had been so tightly wrapped about by the men who made the first search for it.

38

Athenagoras, *Legatio* 4 c. A.D. 176–180

Text: W.R. Schoedel, ed., tr., *Athenagoras. Legatio and de resurrectione* (Oxford, 1972).

Translation adapted from Schoedel.

Ὅτι μὲν οὖν οὐκ ἐσμὲν ἄθεοι (πρὸς ἓν ἕκαστον ἀπαντήσω τῶν ἐγκλημάτων), μὴ καὶ γελοῖον ᾖ τοὺς λέγοντας [μὴ] ἐλέγχειν. Διαγόρᾳ μὲν γὰρ εἰκότως ἀθεότητα ἐπεκάλουν Ἀθηναῖοι, μὴ μόνον τὸν Ὀρφικὸν εἰς μέσον κατατιθέντι λόγον καὶ τὰ ἐν Ἐλευσῖνι καὶ τὰ τῶν Καβίρων δημεύοντι μυστήρια καὶ τὸ τοῦ Ἡρακλέους ἵνα τὰς γογγύλας ἕψοι κατακόπτοντι ξόανον, ἄντικρυς δὲ ἀποφαινομένῳ μηδὲ ὅλως εἶναι θεόν· ἡμῖν δὲ διαιροῦσιν ἀπὸ τῆς ὕλης τὸν θεὸν καὶ δεικνύουσιν ἕτερον μέν τι εἶναι τὴν ὕλην ἄλλο δὲ τὸν θεὸν καὶ τὸ διὰ μέσου πολὺ (τὸ μὲν γὰρ θεῖον ἀγένητον εἶναι καὶ ἀίδιον, νῷ μόνῳ καὶ λόγῳ θεωρούμενον, τὴν δὲ ὕλην γενητὴν καὶ φθαρτήν), μή τι οὐκ ἀλόγως τὸ τῆς ἀθεότητος ἐπικαλοῦσιν ὄνομα. . . .

I shall now meet each charge separately. It is so obvious that we are not atheists that it seems ridiculous even to undertake the refutation of those who make the claim. It was right for the Athenians to charge Diagoras with atheism; for not only did he disclose Orphic doctrine, divulge the mysteries of Eleusis and those of the Cabiri, and chop up the *xoanon* of Heracles to cook his turnips, but he bluntly declared that there is no god at all. But surely it is not rational for them to apply the term atheism to us who distinguish God from matter and show that matter is one thing and God another and the difference between them immense; for the divine is uncreated and eternal and can be contemplated only by thought and reason, whereas matter is created and perishable.

39

Athenagoras, *Legatio* 17 c. A.D. 176–180

Text: W.R. Schoedel, ed., tr., *Athenagoras. Legatio and de resurrectione* (Oxford, 1972).

Translation adapted from Schoedel.

Σκέψασθε δέ μοι διὰ βραχέων (ἀνάγκη δὲ ἀπολογούμενον ἀκριβεστέρους παρέχειν τοὺς λογισμοὺς καὶ περὶ τῶν ὀνομάτων, ὅτι νεώτερα, καὶ περὶ τῶν εἰκόνων, ὅτι χθὲς καὶ πρῴην γεγόνασιν ὡς λόγῳ εἰπεῖν· ἴστε δὲ καὶ ὑμεῖς ταῦτα ἀξιολογώτερον ὡς ἂν ἐν πᾶσιν καὶ ὑπὲρ πάντας τοῖς παλαιοῖς συγγιγνόμενοι)· φημὶ οὖν Ὀρφέα *καὶ* Ὅμηρον *καὶ* Ἡσίοδον *εἶναι τοὺς καὶ γένη καὶ ὀνόματα δόντας τοῖς ὑπ' αὐτῶν λεγομένοις θεοῖς. μαρτυρεῖ δὲ καὶ* Ἡρόδοτος· "Ἡσίοδον *γὰρ καὶ* Ὅμηρον *ἡλικίην τετρακοσίοισι ἔτεσι δοκέω πρεσβυτέρους ἐμοῦ γενέσθαι, καὶ οὐ πλείοσι· οὗτοι δέ εἰσιν οἱ ποιήσαντες θεογονίην* Ἕλλησι *καὶ τοῖσι θεοῖσι τὰς ἐπωνυμίας δόντες καὶ τιμάς τε καὶ τέχνας διελόντες καὶ εἴδεα αὐτῶν σημήναντες." αἱ δ' εἰκόνες μέχρι μήπω πλαστικὴ καὶ γραφικὴ καὶ ἀνδριαντοποιητικὴ ἦσαν, οὐδὲ ἐνομίζοντο·* Σαυρίου *δὲ τοῦ* Σαμίου *καὶ* Κράτωνος *τοῦ* Σικυωνίου *καὶ* Κλεάνθους *τοῦ* Κορινθίου *καὶ κόρης* Κορινθίας *ἐπιγενομένων καὶ σκιαγραφίας μὲν εὑρεθείσης ὑπὸ* Σαυρίου *ἵππον ἐν ἡλίῳ περιγράψαντος, γραφικῆς δὲ ὑπὸ* Κράτωνος *ἐν πίνακι λελευκωμένῳ σκιὰς ἀνδρὸς καὶ γυναικὸς ἐναλείψαντος,—ἀπὸ δὲ τῆς κόρης ἡ κοροπλαθικὴ εὑρέθη (ἐρωτικῶς γάρ τινος ἔχουσα περιέγραψεν αὐτοῦ κοιμωμένου ἐν τοίχῳ τὴν σκιάν, εἶθ' ὁ πατὴρ ἡσθεὶς ἀπαραλλάκτῳ οὔσῃ τῇ ὁμοιότητι—κέραμον δὲ εἰργάζετο—ἀναγλύψας τὴν περιγραφὴν πηλῷ προσανεπλήρωσεν· ὁ τύπος ἔτι καὶ νῦν ἐν* Κορίνθῳ *σῴζεται),—τούτοις δὲ ἐπιγενόμενοι* Δαίδαλος, Θεόδωρος, Σμῖλις *ἀνδριαντοποιητικὴν καὶ πλαστικὴν προσεξεῦρον. ὁ μὲν δὴ χρόνος ὀλίγος τοσοῦτος ταῖς εἰκόσι καὶ τῇ περὶ τὰ εἴδωλα πραγματείᾳ, ὡς ἔχειν εἰπεῖν τὸν ἑκάστου τεχνίτην θεοῦ. τὸ μὲν γὰρ ἐν* Ἐφέσῳ *τῆς* Ἀρτέμιδος *καὶ τὸ τῆς* Ἀθηνᾶς *(μᾶλλον δὲ* Ἀθηλᾶς·† *ἀθήλη γὰρ ὡς οἱ μυστικώτερον οὕτω γὰρ*†) *τὸ ἀπὸ τῆς ἐλαίας τὸ παλαιὸν καὶ τὴν* Καθημένην Ἔνδοιος *εἰργάσατο μαθητὴς* Δαιδάλου, *ὁ δὲ* Πύθιος *ἔργον* Θεοδώρου *καὶ* Τηλεκλέους *καὶ ὁ* Δήλιος *καὶ ἡ* Ἄρτεμις Τεκταίου *καὶ* Ἀγγελίωνος *τέχνη, ἡ δὲ ἐν* Σάμῳ Ἥρα *καὶ ἐν* Ἄργει Σμίλιδος *χεῖρες καὶ* †Φειδίου *τὰ λοιπὰ εἴδωλα*† *ἡ* Ἀφροδίτη *ἐν* Κνίδῳ *ἑτέρα* Πραξιτέλους *τέχνη, ὁ ἐν* Ἐπιδαύρῳ Ἀσκληπιὸς *ἔργον* Φειδίου. *συνελόντα φάναι, οὐδὲν αὐτῶν διαπέφευγεν τὸ μὴ ὑπ' ἀνθρώπου γεγονέναι. εἰ τοίνυν θεοί, τί οὐκ ἦσαν ἐξ ἀρχῆς; τί δέ εἰσιν νεώτεροι τῶν πεποιηκότων; τί δὲ ἔδει αὐτοῖς πρὸς τὸ γενέσθαι ἀνθρώπων καὶ τέχνης; γῆ ταῦτα καὶ λίθοι καὶ ὕλη καὶ περίεργος τέχνη.*

I ask you to examine them briefly. For it is necessary in defending my cause to make precise observations both about their names, showing that they are very recent, and about their *eikones*, showing that they were made, so to speak, only yesterday or the day before. You yourselves know these things better than I, since you are deeply versed beyond all others in the ancients. I say, then, that it was Orpheus, Homer, and Hesiod who gave genealogies and names to those they called gods. Herodotus also provides proof of this: "For I think that Hesiod and Homer preceded me in age by four hundred years, and not more. They are the ones who provided the Greeks with a genealogy of the gods, gave names to the gods, distributed to them their honors and crafts, and described their *eidea*." *Eikones* were not in use before the discovery of the plastic, graphic, and modelling arts. When came Saurius of Samos, Crato of Sicyon, Cleanthes of Corinth, and the Corinthian maid, tracing out shadows was discovered by Saurius, who drew the outline of a horse in the sun; graphic art was discovered by Crato, who painted in the outlines of the shadows of a man and woman on a whitened tablet; and coroplastic art was discovered by the Corinthian maid (for she fell in love with someone and traced the outline of his shadow on the wall as he slept; then her father—he made pottery—delighted with so precise a likeness, carved out the outline and filled it with clay; the *tupos* is preserved to this very day in Corinth). After these came Daedalus, Theodorus, and Smilis, who went further and discovered modelling and plastic arts. So short, then, is the time since [the introduction of] *eikones* and the making of *eidola* that it is possible to name the craftsman of each god. Endoios, a disciple of Daedalus, made that of Artemis in Ephesus and the old one of Athena from olive-wood (or rather of Athela; for she is Athela, the unsuckled, as those . . . the more mystical sense . . .) and the Seated Athena. The Pythian is the work of Theodorus and Telecles, and the Delian and the Artemis are the craftsmanship of Tectaeus and Angelion. The Hera in Samos and in Argos are the works of Smilis (and the rest of the *eidola* of Pheidias). The Aphrodite in Cnidus is another work of Praxiteles, the Asclepius in Epidaurus is the work of Pheidias. To put it in a word, not one of them eludes identification as the work of a man. If, then, they are gods, why were they not so from the beginning? Why are they more recent than those who have made them? Why did they need human craftsmanship for their existence? They are earth, stones, matter, and futile craftsmanship.

40

Augustine, *De Civitate Dei* 4.31 A.D. IV–V

Text and translation: W.M. Green, tr., *Saint Augustine. The City of God Against the Pagans* II (LCL, 1963, 1978).

Dicit etiam antiquos Romanos plus annos centum et septuginta deos sine simulacro colisse. "Quod si adhuc," inquit, "mansisset, castius dii observarentur." Cui sententiae suae testem adhibet inter cetera etiam gentem Iudaeam; nec dubitat eum locum ita concludere ut dicat qui primi simulacra deorum populis posuerunt eos civitatibus suis et metum dempsisse et errorem addidisse, prudenter existimans deos facile posse in simulacrorum stoliditate contemni. Quod vero non ait "errorem tradiderunt," sed "addideunt," iam utique fuisse etiam sine simulacris vult intellegi errorem.

Quapropter cum solos dicit animadvertisse quid esset Deus qui eum crederent animam mundum gubernantem, castiusque existimat sine simulacris observari religionem, quis non videat quantum propinquaverit veritati? Si enim aliquid contra vetustatem tanti posset erroris, profecto et unum Deum, a quo mundum crederet gubernari, et sine simulacro colendum esse censeret; atque in tam proximo inventus facile fortasse de animae mutabilitate commoneretur ut naturam potius incommutabilem, quae ipsam quoque animam condidisset, Deum verum esse sentiret.

He [Varro] also says that for more than one hundred and seventy years the ancient Romans worhipped the gods without an image. "If this usage had continued to our own day," he says, "our worship of the gods would be more devout." And in support of his opinion he adduces, among other things, the testimony of the Jewish race. And he ends with the forthright statement that those who first set up images of the gods for the people diminished reverence in their cities as they added to error, for he wisely judged that gods in the shape of senseless images might easily inspire contempt. And when he says, not "handed down error," but "added to error," he certainly wants it understood that there had been error even without the images. Hence when he says that only those who believe God to be the soul which governs the world have discovered that he really is, and when he thinks that worship is more devout without images, who can fail to see how near he comes to the truth? If he had had the strength to resist so ancient an error, assuredly he would have held that one God should be worshipped, by whom the world is governed, and worshipped without an image. And being found so near the truth, he might perhaps have yielded easily to correction in regard to the mutability of the soul, so that he would perceive that the true God is rather an unchanging being, who also created the soul itself.

Bardesanes, *On Fate* A.D. III
See Eusebius, *Praeparatio evangelica* 6.10.274 d–275 b [**120–121**].

41
Callimachus, *Aetia* I fr. 7.9–14 III B.C.
Text: R. Pfeiffer, ed., *Callimachus* I (Oxford, 1949) 14–15.
Translation: C.A. Trypanis, ed., tr., *Callimachus. Aetia. Iambi. Lyric Poems . . .* (LCL, 1958, 1975).

]ες ἀνείμον[ες Ἰώ]ς ἀπὸ κ̣όλ̣πο̣υ̣
μητρὸς Ἐλειθυίη]ς̣ ἤλθετ[ε β]ο[υλομένης,
ἐν δὲ Πάρῳ κάλλη τ]ε καὶ αἰόλα β̣ε[ῦδε᾽ ἔχουσαι
. . . . .ἀπ᾽ ὀστλί]γγων δ᾽ αἰὲν ἄλειφα ῥέει,
ἔλλατε νῦν,] ἐ̣[λέ]γ̣ο̣ι̣σ̣ι̣ [δ]᾽ ἐνιψήσασθ[ε] λιπώσ[ας
χεῖρ]α̣ς ἐμ̣[οῖς, ἵνα μο]ι πουλὺ μένωσ[ι]ν ἔτος.

. . . naked as with the goodwill of Eileithyia you came forth from your mother's womb, but in Paros you stand wearing fineries and shimmering tunics, and ointment always flows from your locks. Come now and wipe your anointed hands upon my elegies that they may live for many a year.

Diegesis to Callimachus, *Aetia* I fr. 31 B (Pfeiffer)
See Pap. Oxyrhynchus 2263 fr. I [**378**].

Callimachus, *Aetia* IV fr. 100 (Pfeiffer)
See Eusebius, *Praeparatio evangelica* 3.8.99b [**108**]. III B.C.

42
Diegesis to Callimachus, *Aetia* IV fr. 100 (Pfeiffer)
Text: R. Pfeiffer, ed., *Callimachus* I (Oxford, 1949) 105.
Translation adapted from Trypanis, ed., tr., *Callimachus. Aetia. Iambi. Lyric Poems* . . . (LCL, 1958, 1975).

]γ̣ι̣ α̣φ[
. . . . . . τὸ ξόα]νον τῆς Ἥρας [ἀνδρι-
αντοειδὲ]ς̣ ἐ[γέ]νετο ἐπὶ β̣ασ̣ι̣λέως
Προκ[λέους· τὸ] δὲ ξύ̣[λο]ν, ἐ̣ξ̣ οὗ εἰργάσθη
ε̣. .η̣[. . . .].αμ̣[.]ς..ν, ἐ̣ξ̣ Ἄργους δὲ φασι[. . . . . . .]ο̣τ̣α̣ς ἔτι πάλαι σανιδῶ-
δες [κομι]σθῆναι κάταργον ἅτε μηδέ-
πω π[ροκ]ε̣κοφυίας τῆς ἀγαλματομικῆς.

[The *xoa*]*non* of Hera became [statue-shaped] when Proc[les] was *basileus*; the *xulon* out of which it was worked . . . they say from Argos . . . a very long time ago was carried, planklike, unworked, seeing that the art of carving *agalmata* was not yet advanced.

Callimachus, *Iambus* VI fr. 196.29–31 (Pfeiffer) III B.C.
See Pap. Oxyrhynchus 2171 Fr. 2 [**377**].

43
Clement of Alexandria, *Protrepticus* 2.21 P. c. A.D. 190
Text: G.W. Butterworth, tr., *Clement of Alexandria* (LCL, 1919).
Translation adapted from Butterworth.

ὁ δ' Ἡρακλέα ἐκ ξύλου λαβὼν κατεσκευασμένον (ἔτυχε δὲ ἕψων τι οἴκοι, οἷα εἰκός) "εἶα δή, ὦ Ἡράκλεις", εἶπεν· "νῦν σοι ἤδη καιρός, ὥσπερ Εὐρυσθεῖ, ἀτὰρ δὴ καὶ ἡμῖν ὑπουργῆσαι τὸν τρισκαιδέκατον τοῦτον ἆθλον καὶ Διαγόρᾳ τοὔψον παρασκευάσαι", κἆτ' αὐτὸν εἰς τὸ πῦρ ἐνέθηκεν ὡς ξύλον.

Another, having taken hold of a Heracles made from a log—he happened, likely enough, to be cooking something at home—said, "Come, Heracles, now is your time to undertake this thirteenth labour for me, as you did [the twelve] for Eurystheus, and prepare Diagoras his dish!" Then he put him into the fire like a log.

44

Clement of Alexandria, *Protrepticus* 4.40 P.–43 P. c. A.D. 190
Text: G.W. Butterworth, tr., *Clement of Alexandria* (LCL, 1919).
Translation adapted from Butterworth.

Εἰ δ' ἔτι πρὸς τούτοις φέρων ὑμῖν τὰ ἀγάλματα αὐτὰ ἐπισκοπεῖν παραθείην, ἐπιόντες ὡς ἀληθῶς λῆρον εὑρήσετε τὴν συνήθειαν, "ἔργα χειρῶν ἀνθρώπων" ἀναίσθητα προστρεπόμενοι. πάλαι μὲν οὖν οἱ Σκύθαι τὸν ἀκινάκην, οἱ Ἄραβες τὸν λίθον, οἱ Πέρσαι τὸν ποταμὸν προσεκύνουν, καὶ τῶν ἄλλων ἀνθρώπων οἱ ἔτι παλαιότεροι ξύλα ἱδρύοντο περιφανῆ καὶ κίονας ἵστων ἐκ λίθων· ἃ δὴ καὶ ξόανα προσηγορεύετο διὰ τὸ ἀπεξέσθαι τῆς ὕλης. ἀμέλει ἐν Ἰκάρῳ τῆς Ἀρτέμιδος τὸ ἄγαλμα ξύλον ἦν οὐκ εἰργασμένον, καὶ τῆς Κιθαιρωνίας Ἥρας ἐν Θεσπείᾳ πρέμνον ἐκκεκομμένον· καὶ τὸ τῆς Σαμίας Ἥρας, ὥς φησιν Ἀέθλιος, πρότερον μὲν ἦν σανίς, ὕστερον δὲ ἐπὶ Προκλέους ἄρχοντος ἀνδριαντοειδὲς ἐγένετο. Ἐπεὶ δὲ ἀνθρώποις (41 P.) ἀπεικονίζεσθαι τὰ ξόανα ἤρξατο, βρέτη τὴν ἐκ βροτῶν ἐπωνυμίαν ἐκαρπώσατο. ἐν Ῥώμῃ δὲ τὸ παλαιὸν δόρυ φησὶ γεγονέναι τοῦ Ἄρεως τὸ ξόανον Οὐάρρων ὁ συγγραφεύς, οὐδέπω τῶν τεχνιτῶν ἐπὶ τὴν εὐπρόσωπον ταύτην κακοτεχνίαν ὡρμηκότων. ἐπειδὴ δὲ ἤνθησεν ἡ τέχνη, ηὔξησεν ἡ πλάνη.

Ὡς μὲν οὖν τοὺς λίθους καὶ τὰ ξύλα καὶ συνελόντι φάναι τὴν ὕλην ἀγάλματα ἀνδρείκελα ἐποιήσαντο, οἷς ἐπιμορφάζετε εὐσέβειαν συκοφαντοῦντες τὴν ἀλήθειαν, ἤδη μὲν αὐτόθεν δῆλον· οὐ μὴν ἀλλὰ καὶ ἀποδείξεως ποσῆς ἐπιδεομένου τοῦ τόπου οὐ παραιτητέον. τὸν μὲν οὖν Ὀλυμπίασι Δία καὶ τὴν Ἀθήνησι Πολιάδα ἐκ χρυσοῦ καὶ ἐλέφαντος κατασκευάσαι Φειδίαν παντί που σαφές· τὸ δὲ ἐν Σάμῳ τῆς Ἥρας ξόανον Σμίλιδι τῷ Εὐκλείδου πεποιῆσθαι Ὀλύμπιχος ἐν Σαμιακοῖς ἱστορεῖ. μὴ οὖν ἀμφιβάλλετε, εἰ τῶν Σεμνῶν Ἀθήνησι καλουμένων θεῶν τὰς μὲν δύο Σκόπας ἐποίησεν ἐκ τοῦ καλουμένου λυχνέως λίθου, Κάλως δὲ τὴν μέσην αὐταῖν· ἱστοροῦντα ἔχω σοι Πολέμωνα δεικνύναι ἐν τῇ τετάρτῃ τῶν Πρὸς Τίμαιον· μηδ' εἰ τὰ ἐν Παταροις τῆς Λυκίας ἀγάλματα Διὸς καὶ Ἀπόλλωνος Φειδίας πάλιν ἐκεῖνος [τὰ ἀγάλματα] καθάπερ τοὺς λέοντας τοὺς σὺν αὐτοῖς ἀνακειμένους εἴργασται· εἰ δέ, ὥς φασί τινες, Βρυάξιος ἡ τέχνη, οὐ διαφέρομαι· ἔχεις καὶ τοῦτον ἀγαλματουργόν· ὁπότερον αὐτοῖν βούλει ἐπίγραφε. καὶ μὴν Τελεσίου τοῦ Ἀθηναίου, ὥς φησι Φιλόχορος, ἔργον εἰσὶν ἀγάλματα ἐννεαπήχη Ποσειδῶνος καὶ Ἀμφιτρίτης ἐν Τήνῳ προσκυνούμενα. Δημήτριος γὰρ ἐν δευτέρῳ τῶν Ἀργολικῶν τοῦ ἐν Τίρυνθι τῆς Ἥρας ξοάνου καὶ τὴν ὕλην ὄγχνην καὶ τὸν ποιητὴν Ἄργον ἀναγράφει. πολλοὶ δ' ἂν τάχα που θαυμάσειαν, εἰ μάθοιεν τὸ Παλλάδιον τὸ διοπετὲς καλούμενον, (42 P.) ὃ Διομήδης καὶ Ὀδυσσεὺς ἱστοροῦνται μὲν ὑφελέσθαι ἀπὸ Ἰλίου, παρακαταθέσθαι δὲ Δημοφῶντι, ἐκ τῶν Πέλοπος ὀστῶν κατεσκευάσθαι, καθάπερ τὸν Ὀλύμπιον ἐξ ἄλλων ὀστῶν Ἰνδικοῦ θηρίου. καὶ δὴ τὸν ἱστοροῦντα Διονύσιον ἐν τῷ πέμπτῳ μέρει τοῦ Κύκλου παρίστημι. Ἀπελλᾶς δὲ ἐν τοῖς Δελφικοῖς δύο φησὶ γεγονέναι τὰ Παλλάδια, ἄμφω δ' ὑπ' ἀνθρώπων δεδημιουργῆσθαι. ἀλλ' ὅπως μηδεὶς ὑπολάβῃ καὶ ταῦτά με ἀγνοίᾳ παρεικέναι, παραθήσομαι τοῦ Μορύχου Διονύσου τὸ ἄγαλμα Ἀθήνησι γεγονέναι μὲν ἐκ τοῦ φελλάτα καλουμένου λίθου, ἔργον δὲ εἶναι Σίκωνος τοῦ Εὐπαλάμου, ὥς φησι Πολέμων ἔν τινι ἐπιστολῇ. ἐγενέσθην δὲ καὶ ἄλλω τινὲ δύο Κρητικὼ οἶμαι ἀνδριαντοποιὼ (Σκύλλις καὶ Δίποινος ὠνομαζέσθην)· τούτω δὲ τὰ ἐν Ἄργει τοῖν Διοσκούροιν ἀγάλματα κατεσκευασάτην καὶ τὸν ἐν Τίρυνθι Ἡρακλέους ἀνδριάντα καὶ τὸ τῆς Μουνυχίας Ἀρτέμιδος ξόανον ἐν Σικυῶνι.

Καὶ τί περὶ ταῦτα διατρίβω, ἐξὸν αὐτὸν τὸν μεγαλοδαίμονα ὑμῖν ἐπιδεῖξαι ὅστις ἦν, ὃν δὴ κατ' ἐξοχὴν πρὸς πάντων σεβασμοῦ κατηξιωμένον ἀκούομεν, τοῦτον <ὃν> ἀχειροποίητον εἰπεῖν τετολμήκασιν, τὸν Αἰγύπτιον Σάραπιν; οἱ μὲν γὰρ αὐτὸν ἱστοροῦσιν χαριστήριον ὑπὸ Σινωπέων Πτολεμαίῳ τῷ Φιλαδέλφῳ τῷ Αἰγυπτίων πεμφθῆναι βασιλεῖ, ὃς λιμῷ τρυχομένους αὐτοὺς ἀπ' Αἰγύπτου μεταπεμψαμένους σῖτον [ὁ Πτολεμαῖος] ἀνεκτήσατο, εἶναι δὲ τὸ ξόανον τοῦτο ἄγαλμα Πλούτωνος· ὁ δὲ δεξάμενος τὸν ἀνδριάντα καθίδρυσεν ἐπὶ τῆς ἄκρας, ἣν νῦν Ῥακῶτιν καλοῦσιν, ἔνθα καὶ τὸ ἱερὸν τετίμηται τοῦ Σαράπιδος, γειτνιᾷ δὲ τοῖς τόποις τὸ χωρίον. Βλιστίχην δὲ τὴν παλλακίδα τελευτήσασαν ἐν Κανώβῳ μεταγαγὼν ὁ Πτολεμαῖος ἔθαψεν ὑπὸ τὸν προδεδηλωμένον σηκόν. ἄλλοι δέ φασι Ποντικὸν εἶναι βρέτας τὸν Σάραπιν, μετῆχθαι δὲ εἰς Ἀλεξάνδρειαν μετὰ τιμῆς πανηγυρικῆς. Ἰσίδωρος μόνος παρὰ Σελευκέων τῶν πρὸς Ἀντιοχείᾳ τὸ ἄγαλμα μεταχθῆναι λέγει, ἐν σιτοδείᾳ καὶ αὐτῶν γενομένων καὶ ὑπὸ Πτολεμαίου διατραφέντων. Ἀλλ' ὅ γε Ἀθηνόδωρος (43 P.) ὁ τοῦ Σάνδωνος ἀρχαΐζειν τὸν Σάραπιν βουληθεὶς οὐκ οἶδ' ὅπως περιέπεσεν, ἐλέγξας αὐτὸν ἄγαλμα εἶναι γενητόν· Σέσωστρίν φησι τὸν Αἰγύπτιον βασιλέα, τὰ πλεῖστα τῶν παρ' Ἕλλησι παραστησάμενον ἐθνῶν, ἐπανελθόντα εἰς Αἴγυπτον ἐπαγαγέσθαι τεχνίτας ἱκανούς· τὸν οὖν Ὄσιριν τὸν προπάτορα τὸν αὐτοῦ δαιδαλθῆναι ἐκέλευσεν αὐτὸς πολυτελῶς, κατασκευάζει δὲ αὐτὸν Βρύαξις ὁ δημιουργός, οὐχ ὁ Ἀθηναῖος, ἄλλος δέ τις ὁμώνυμος ἐκείνῳ τῷ Βρυάξιδι· ὃς ὕλῃ κατακέχρηται εἰς δημιουργίαν μικτῇ καὶ ποικίλῃ. ῥίνημα γὰρ χρυσοῦ ἦν αὐτῷ καὶ ἀργύρου χαλκοῦ τε καὶ σιδήρου καὶ μολίβδου, πρὸς δὲ καὶ κασσιτέρου, λίθων δὲ Αἰγυπτίων ἐνέδει οὐδὲ εἷς, σαπφείρου καὶ αἱματίτου θραύσματα σμαράγδου τε, ἀλλὰ καὶ τοπαζίου. λεάνας οὖν τὰ πάντα καὶ ἀναμίξας ἔχρωσε κυάνῳ, οὗ δὴ χάριν μελάντερον τὸ χρῶμα τοῦ ἀγάλματος, καὶ τῷ ἐκ τῆς Ὀσίριδος καὶ τοῦ Ἄπιος κηδείας ὑπολελειμμένῳ *φαρμάκῳ φυράσας τὰ πάντα διέπλασεν τὸν Σάραπιν· οὗ καὶ τοὔνομα αἰνίττεται τὴν κοινωνίαν τῆς κηδείας καὶ τὴν ἐκ τῆς ταφῆς δημιουργίαν, σύνθετον ἀπό τε Ὀσίριδος καὶ Ἄπιος γενόμενον Ὀσίραπις.*

If, in addition to this, I bring the *agalmata* themselves and place them by your side for inspection, you will find on going through them that custom is truly futile, when it leads you to adore senseless things, "the works of men's hands." In ancient times, then, the Scythians used to worship the dagger, the Arabians their stone, the Persians their river. Other peoples still more ancient erected conspicuous wooden poles and set up pillars of stones, to which they gave the name *xoana* [scraped objects] because the rough surface of the material had been scraped off. Certainly the *agalma* of Artemis in Icarus was an unwrought stock, and that of Cithaeronian Hera in Thespiae was a felled tree-trunk. That of Samian Hera, as Aëthlius says, was at first a *sanis* but afterwards, when Procles was ruler, it became *andriantoeides*. When the *xoana* began to be represented as men, they acquired the additional name *brete*, from *brotoi* [mortals]. In Rome, of old time, according to Varro the prose-writer, the *xoanon* of Ares was a spear, since craftsmen had not yet entered upon the fair-seeming but mischievous art of sculpture. But the moment art flourished, error increased.

It is now, therefore, self-evident that out of stones and blocks of wood, and, in one word, out of matter, men fashioned *agalmata* resembling the human form, to which you offer a semblance of piety, calumniating the truth. Still, since the point calls for a certain amount of argument, we must not decline to furnish it. Now everyone, I suppose, will admit that Zeus at Olympia and Athena Polias at Athens were wrought of gold and ivory by Pheidias; and Olympichus in his *Samian History* relates that the *xoanon* of Hera in Samos was made by Smilis the son of Eucleides. Do not doubt, then, that of the goddesses at Athens called "venerable" two were made by Scopas out of the stone called *lychneus*, and the middle one by Calos; I can point out to you the account given by Polemon in the fourth volume of his work *Against Timaeus*. Neither doubt that the *agalmata* of Zeus and Apollo in Lycian Patara were also wrought by the great Pheidias, just as were the lions that are dedicated along with them. But if, as some say, the art is that of Bryaxis, I do not contradict. He also is one of your sculptors; put down which of the two you like. Further, the nine-cubit *agalmata* of Poseidon and Amphitrite worshipped in Tenos are the work of the Athenian Telesius, as Philochorus tells us. Demetrius in his second book of *Argolic History*, speaking of the *xoanon* of Hera in Tiryns, records both its material, pear-tree wood, and its maker, Argus. Many would perhaps be astonished to learn that the Palladion called "heaven sent" [because it fell from heaven], which Diomedes and Odysseus are related to have stolen away from Troy, and to have entrusted to the keeping of Demophon, is made out of the bones of Pelops, just as the Olympian Zeus is also made out of bones—those of an Indian beast. I give you, too, my authority for this, namely Dionysius, who relates the story in the fifth section of his *Cycle*. Apellas in his *Delphic History* says that there are two such Palladia, and that both are of human workmanship. I will also mention the *agalma* of Morychian Dionysus at Athens—in order that no one may suppose me to have omitted these facts through ignorance—that it is made out of the stone called *phellatas* and is the work of Sicon the son of Eupalamus, as Polemon says in a certain letter. There were also two other sculptors, Cretans I believe, whose names were Scyllis and Dipoenus. This pair made the *agalmata* of the Dioscuri at Argos, the *andrias* of Heracles at Tiryns, and the *xoanon* of Munychian Artemis at Sicyon.

But why do I linger over these, when I can show you the origin of the arch-daemon himself, the one who, we are told, is pre-eminently worthy of veneration by all men, whom they have dared to say is made without hands, the Egyptian Sarapis? Some relate that he was sent by the people of Sinope as a thank-offering to Ptolemy Philadelphus, king of Egypt, who had earned their gratitude at a time when they were worn out with hunger and had sent for grain from Egypt; and that this *xoanon* was an *agalma* of Pluto. On receiving the *andrias*, the king set it up on the promontory which they now call Rhacotis, where stands the honored temple of Sarapis; and the spot is close to the burial places. And they say that Ptolemy had his mistress Blistiche, who had died in Canobus, brought here and buried under the before-mentioned shrine. Others say that Sarapis was a *bretas* from Pontus, and that it was conveyed to Alexandria with the honor of a solemn festival. Isidorus alone states that the *agalma* was brought from the people of Seleucia near Antioch, when they too had been suffering from the dearth of grain and had been sustained by Ptolemy. But Athenodorus the son of Sandon, while intending to establish the antiquity of Sarapis, stumbled in some unaccountable way, for he has proved him to be an *agalma* made by man. He says that Sesostris the Egyptian king, having subdued most of the nations of Greece, brought back on his return to Egypt a number of skillful craftsmen. He gave personal orders, therefore, that Osiris his own ancestor should be elaborately wrought at great expense; and [the image] was made by the artist Bryaxis—not the famous Athenian, but another of the same name—who has used a mixture of various materials in its construction. He had filings of gold, silver, bronze, iron, lead, and even tin; and not a single Egyptian stone was lacking, there being pieces of sapphire, hematite, emerald, and topaz also. Having reduced them all to powder and mixed them, he stained the mixture dark blue (on account of which the color of the statue is nearly black), and, mingling the whole with the pigment left over from the funeral rites of Osiris and Apis, he moulded Sarapis; whose very name implies this connection with the funeral rites, and the construction out of material for burial, Osirapis being a compound formed from Osiris and Apis.

45

Clement of Alexandria, *Protrepticus* 4.44 P.–45 P. c. A.D. 190
Text: G.W. Butterworth, tr., *Clement of Alexandria* (LCL, 1919).
Translation adapted from Butterworth.

σὺ δὲ ἀλλ' εἰ μὴ προφήτιδος ἐπακούεις, τοῦ γε σοῦ ἄκουσον φιλοσόφου, τοῦ Ἐφεσίου Ἡρακλείτου, τὴν ἀναισθησίαν ὀνειδίζοντος τοῖς ἀγάλμασι· "καὶ τοῖς ἀγάλμασι τουτέοισιν εὔχονται, ὁκοῖον εἴ τις <τοῖς> δόμοις λεσχηνεύοιτο". ἦ γὰρ οὐχὶ τερατώδεις οἱ λίθους προστρεπόμενοι, εἶτα μέντοι καὶ πρὸ τῶν πυλῶν ἱστάντες αὐτοὺς ὡς ἐνεργεῖς, Ἑρμῆν προσκυνοῦντες ὡς θεὸν καὶ τὸν Ἀγυιέα θυρωρὸν ἱστάντες; εἰ γὰρ ὡς ἀναισθήτους ὑβρίζουσιν, τί προσκυνοῦσιν ὡς θεούς; εἰ δὲ αἰσθήσεως αὐτοὺς μετέχειν οἴονται, τί τούτους ἱστᾶσι θυρωρούς; Ῥωμαῖοι δὲ τὰ μέγιστα κατορθώματα τῇ Τύχῃ ἀνατιθέντες καὶ ταύτην μεγίστην οἰόμενοι θεόν, φέροντες εἰς τὸν κο(45 P.)πρῶνα ἀνέθηκαν αὐτήν, ἄξιον νεὼν τὸν ἀφεδρῶνα νείμαντες τῇ θεῷ.

Ἀλλὰ γὰρ ἀναισθήτῳ λίθῳ καὶ ξύλῳ καὶ χρυσίῳ πλουσίῳ οὐδ' ὁτιοῦν μέλει, οὐ κνίσης, οὐχ αἵματος, οὐ καπνοῦ, ᾧ δὴ τιμώμενοι καὶ τυφόμενοι ἐκμελαίνονται· ἀλλ' οὐδὲ τιμῆς, οὐχ ὕβρεως· τὰ δὲ καὶ παντός ἐστιν ἀτιμότερα ζῴου, τὰ ἀγάλματα. καὶ ὅπως γε τεθείασται τὰ ἀναίσθητα, ἀπορεῖν ἔπεισί μοι καὶ κατελεεῖν τοὺς πλανωμένους τῆς ἀνοίας ὡς δειλαίους· εἰ γὰρ καί τινα τῶν ζῴων οὐχὶ πάσας ἔχει τὰς αἰσθήσεις, ὥσπερ εὐλαὶ καὶ κάμπαι καὶ ὅσα διὰ τῆς πρώτης γενέσεως εὐθὺς ἀνάπηρα φαίνεται, καθάπερ οἱ σπάλακες καὶ ἡ μυγαλῆ, ἥν φησιν ὁ Νίκανδρος "τυφλήν τε σμερδνήν τε"· ἀλλά γε ἀμείνους εἰσὶ τῶν ξοάνων τούτων καὶ τῶν ἀγαλμάτων τέλεον ὄντων κωφῶν· ἔχουσιν γὰρ αἴσθησιν μίαν γέ τινα, φέρε εἰπεῖν ἀκουστικὴν ἢ ἁπτικὴν ἢ τὴν ἀναλογοῦσαν τῇ ὀσφρήσει ἢ τῇ γεύσει· τὰ δὲ οὐδὲ μιᾶς αἰσθήσεως μετέχει, τὰ ἀγάλματα. πολλὰ δέ ἐστι τῶν ζῴων, ὅσα οὔτε ὅρασιν ἔχει οὔτε ἀκοὴν ουδὲ μὴν φωνήν, οἷον καὶ τὸ τῶν ὀστρέων γένος, ἀλλὰ ζῇ γε καὶ αὔξεται, πρὸς δὲ καὶ τῇ σελήνῃ συμπάσχει· τὰ δὲ ἀγάλματα ἀργά, ἄπρακτα, ἀναίσθητα, προσδεῖται καὶ προσκαθηλοῦται καὶ προσπήγνυται, χωνεύεται, ῥινᾶται, πρίεται, περιξέεται, γλύφεται. κωφὴν μὲν δὴ γαῖαν ἀεικίζουσιν οἱ ἀγαλματοποιοί, τῆς οἰκείας ἐξιστάντες φύσεως, ὑπὸ τῆς τέχνης προσκυνεῖν ἀναπείθοντες· προσκυνοῦσιν δὲ οἱ θεοποιοὶ οὐ θεοὺς καὶ δαίμονας κατά γε αἴσθησιν τὴν ἐμήν, γῆν δὲ καὶ τέχνην, τὰ ἀγάλματα ὅπερ ἐστίν. ἔστιν γὰρ ὡς ἀληθῶς τὸ ἄγαλμα ὕλη νεκρὰ τεχνίτου χειρὶ μεμορφωμένη· ἡμῖν δὲ οὐχ *ὕλης αἰσθητῆς αἰσθητόν, νοητὸν δὲ τὸ ἄγαλμά ἐστιν. νοητόν, οὐκ αἰσθητόν ἐστι [τὸ ἄγαλμα] ὁ θεός, ὁ μόνος ὄντως θεός.*

If, however, you refuse to listen to the prophetess, hear at least your own philosopher, Heraclitus of Ephesus, when he taunts the *agalmata* for their want of feeling: "and they pray to these *agalmata* just as if someone were to chatter to his house." Are they not amazing, these men who make supplication to stones, and yet set them up before their gates as if alive and active, worshipping the Hermes as a god, and setting up the "god of the ways" as door-keeper? For if they treat them with contumely as being without feeling, why do they worship them as gods? But if they believe them to partake of feeling, why do they set them up as door-keepers? The Romans, although they ascribe their greatest successes to Fortuna, and believe her to be the greatest deity, carry her to the privy and set her up there, thus assigning her a fit temple.

But indeed the senseless wood and stone and precious gold pay not the smallest regard to the steam, the blood, and the smoke, They are blackened by the cloud of smoke which is meant to honor them, but [they heed] neither the honor nor the insult. There is not a single living creature that is not more worthy of honor than these *agalmata*; and how it comes to pass that senseless things have been deified I am at a loss to know, and I deeply pity for their lack of understanding the men who are thus miserably wandering in error. For even though there are some living creatures which do not possess all the senses, as worms and caterpillars, and all those that appear to be imperfect from the first through the conditions of their birth, such as moles and the field mouse, which Nicander calls "blind and terrible"; yet these are better than those *xoana* and *agalmata* that are entirely dumb. For they have at any rate some one sense, that of hearing, let us say, or of touch, or something corresponding to smell or taste; but these *agalmata* do not even partake of one sense. There are also many kinds of living creatures, such as the oyster family, which possess neither sight nor hearing nor yet speech; nevertheless they live and grow and are even affected by the moon. But the *agalmata* are motionless things incapable of action or sensation; they are bound and nailed and fastened, melted, filed, sawn, polished, carved. The dumb earth is dishonored when sculptors pervert its peculiar nature and by their art entice men to worship it; while the god-makers, if there is any sense in me, worship not gods and daemons, but earth and art, which is all the *agalmata* are. For an *agalma* is really lifeless matter shaped by a craftsman's hand; but in our view the image of God is not an object of sense made from matter perceived by ther senses, but a mental object. God, that is, the only true God, is percevied not by the senses but by the mind.

46

Clement of Alexandria, *Protrepticus* 4.54 P. c. A.D. 190
(= *Oracula Sibyllina* IV.27–30.)
Text: G.W. Butterworth, tr., *Clement of Alexandria* (LCL, 1919).
Translation adapted from Butterworth.

« "Ὄλβιοι" μόνοι τοίνυν, ὡς ἔπος εἰπεῖν, ὁμοθυμαδὸν ἐκεῖνοι πάντες κατὰ τὴν Σίβυλλαν

οἳ ναοὺς <μὲν> πάντας ἀπαρνήσονται ἰδόντες
καὶ βωμούς, εἰκαῖα λίθων ἱδρύματα κωφῶν,
καὶ λίθινα ξόανα καὶ ἀγάλματα χειροποίητα,
αἵματι ἐμψύχῳ μεμιασμένα καὶ θυσίαισι
τετραπόδων, διπόδων, πτηνῶν θηρῶν τε φόνοισιν.

The only men, therefore, who can with one consent, so to speak, be called "blessed," are all those whom the Sibyl describes,

Who, seeing the *naoi*,will reject them all,
and *bomoi*, useless foundations of dumb stones
and stone *xoana* and handmade *agalmata*,
defiled with animate blood and with sacrifices
of four-footed, two-footed, and winged [creatures] and cries of beasts.

47

Clement of Alexandria, *Stromateis* 1.163.4–164.4 c. A.D. 200
(418 P.–419 P.)
(= Euripides fr. 203 Nauck[2].)
Text: O. Stählin, ed., *Clemens Alexandrinus* II. *Stromata Buch I–VI* (GCS 15; Leipzig, 1906).
Translation adapted from W. Wilson, tr., *The Writings of Clement of Alexandria* I (Ante-Nicene Christian Library 4; Edinburgh, 1867).

λέγεται δὲ καὶ ἐν χρησμῷ τινι·
στῦλος Θηβαίοισι Διώνυσος πολυγηθής,
ἐκ τῆς παρ' Ἑβραίοις ἱστορίας. ἀλλὰ καὶ Εὐριπίδης ἐν Ἀντιόπῃ φησίν·
ἔνδον δὲ θαλάμοις βουκόλων
κομῶντα κισσῷ στῦλον Εὐίου θεοῦ.
σημαίνει δὲ ὁ στῦλος τὸ ἀνεικόνιστον τοῦ θεοῦ, ὁ δὲ πεφωτισμένος στῦλος πρὸς τῷ τὸ ἀνεικόνιστον σημαίνειν δηλοῖ τὸ ἑστὸς καὶ μόνιμον τοῦ θεοῦ καὶ τὸ ἄτρεπτον αὐτοῦ φῶς καὶ ἀσχημάτιστον. πρὶν γοῦν ἀκριβωθῆναι τὰς τῶν ἀγαλμάτων σχέσεις κίονας ἱστάντες οἱ παλαιοὶ ἔσεβον τούτους ὡς ἀφιδρύματα τοῦ θεοῦ. γράφει γοῦν ὁ τὴν Φορωνίδα ποιήσας·
Καλλιθόη κλειδοῦχος Ὀλυμπιάδος βασιλείης,
Ἥρης Ἀργείης, ἣ στέμμασι καὶ θυσάνοισι
πρώτη ἐκόσμησε<ν> περὶ κίονα μακρὸν ἀνάσσης.

ἀλλὰ καὶ ὁ τὴν Εὐρωπίαν ποιήσας ἱστορεῖ τὸ ἐν Δελφοῖς ἄγαλμα Ἀπόλλωνος κίονα εἶναι διὰ τῶνδε·

ὄφρα θεῷ δεκάτην ἀκροθίνιά τε κρεμάσαιμεν
σταθμῶν ἐκ ζαθέων καὶ κίονος ὑψηλοῖο.

Ἀπόλλων μέντοι μυστικῶς κατὰ στέρησιν τῶν πολλῶν νοούμενος ὁ εἷς ἐστι θεός. ἀλλ᾽ οὖν τὸ πῦρ ἐκεῖνο τὸ ἐοικὸς στύλῳ καὶ πῦρ τὸ διὰ βάτου σύμβολόν ἐστι φωτὸς ἁγίου τοῦ διαβαίνοντος ἐκ γῆς καὶ ἀνατρέχοντος αὖθις εἰς οὐρανὸν διὰ τοῦ ξύλου, δι᾽ οὗ καὶ τὸ βλέπειν ἡμῖν νοητῶς δεδώρηται.

It is said also in a certain oracle:

"A column to the Thebans [is] joy-inspiring Dionysus,"

from the history of the Hebrews. 5. Also, Euripides says in *Antiope*:

"In the chambers within, the herdsman,
a column decked with ivy, of the god Evohe."

6. The pillar indicates the unportrayability of God; the pillar of light, in addition to the unportrayability, shows also the stability and the permanent duration of God, and his unchangeable and inexpressible light. 164.1. Before, then, they perfected the fashion of *agalmata*, the ancients, setting up columns, worshipped them as *aphidrumata* of God.
2. Thus he who composed the *Phoronis* writes:

"Callithoe, priestess [lit. "key-bearer"] of the Olympian queen,
Argive Hera, who first with fillets and with fringes
adorned the queen's tall column all around."

3. Furthermore, he who composed the *Europia* tells that the *agalma* of Apollo in Delphi is a pillar in these words:

"That to the god first-fruits and tithes we may
hang on sacred pillars and on high column."

Apollo, interpreted mystically by "privation of many," means the One God. 4. But, thus, the fire like a pillar, and the fire in the desert, is the symbol of the holy light which passed through from the earth and returned again to heaven, by the wood [*sc.* of the cross], by which also the gift of mental vision was given to us.

48

Clement of Alexandria, *Stromateis* 5.14.113.1–2 (717 P.) c. A.D. 200
(= [Sophocles] fr. 1126 Radt, Pearson [1025 Nauck[2]].)
See also: Clement of Alexandria, *Protrepticus* 7.7.63 P.; Eusebius, *Praeparatio evangelica* 13.13.40; Ps.-Justin, *Cohortatio ad Gentiles* 18 and *De monarchia* 2.
Text: O. Stählin, ed., *Clemens Alexandrinus* II. *Stromata Buch I–VI* (GCS 15; Leipzig, 1906).

Translation adapted from A. Attridge, "Fragments of Pseudo-Greek Poets," in J.H. Charlesworth, ed., *The Old Testament Pseudepigrapha* II (Garden City, 1985) 825–826.

Ὁ μὲν Σοφοκλῆς, ὥς φησιν Ἑκαταῖος ὁ τὰς ἱστορίας συνταξάμενος ἐν τῷ Κατ' Ἄβραμον καὶ τοὺς Αἰγυπτίους, ἄντικρυς ἐπὶ τῆς σκηνῆς ἐκβοᾷ·

εἷς ταῖς ἀληθείαισιν, εἷς ἐστι<ν> θεός,
ὃς οὐρανόν τε ἔτευξε καὶ γαῖαν μακρὴν
πόντου τε χαροπὸν οἶδμα καὶ ἀνέμων βίαν.
θνητοὶ δὲ πολλοὶ καρδίαν πλανώμενοι,
ἱδρυσάμεσθα πημάτων παραψυχὴν
θεῶν ἀγάλματα ἐκ λίθων, ἢ χαλκέων
ἢ χρυσοτεύκτων ἢ ἐλεφαντίνων τύπους·
θυσίας τε τούτοις καὶ κακὰς πανηγύρεις
στέφοντες, οὕτως εὐσεβεῖν νομίζομεν.

As Hecataeus the historian said in *On Abraham and the Egyptians*, Sophocles openly cries out on the stage:

God is one, one in very truth,
who fashioned heaven and the broad earth,
the depth's gray swell and the winds' might.
But many of us mortals, erring in our heart,
have set up consolation for calamities,
agalmata of gods from stones or bronzes
or *tupoi* of goldwork or ivories;
sacrifices do we grace with these, and
evil festivals, and think we act thus piously.

49

Clement of Alexandria, *Stromateis* 6.18.163.1–2 (825 P.) c. A.D. 200
Text: O. Stählin, ed., *Clemens Alexandrinus* II. *Stromata Buch I–VI* (GCS 15; Leipzig, 1906).
Translation adapted from W. Wilson, tr., *The Writings of Clement of Alexandria* II (Ante-Nicene Christian Library 12; Edinburgh, 1869).

Τούτων οὕτως ἐχόντων τοὺς Ἕλληνας χρὴ διὰ νόμου καὶ προφητῶν ἐκμανθάνειν ἕνα μόνον σέβειν θεόν, τὸν ὄντως ὄντα παντοκράτορα, ἔπειτα διὰ τοῦ ἀποστόλου διδάσκεσθαι τοῦτο· "ἡμῖν δὲ οὐδὲν εἴδωλον ἐν κόσμῳ", ἐπεὶ μηδὲν ἀπεικόνισμα τοῦ θεοῦ οἷόν τε ἐν γενητοῖς εἶναι, προσεπιδιδάσκεσθαι δὲ ὡς οὐδὲ τούτων ὧν σέβουσι τὰ ἀγάλματα εἶεν ἂν αἱ εἰκόνες· οὐ γάρ πω τοιοῦτον κατὰ τὸ σχῆμα τὸ τῶν ψυχῶν γένος ὁποῖα διαπλάσσουσιν Ἕλληνες τὰ ξόανα. ψυχαὶ μὲν γὰρ ἀόρατοι, οὐ μόνον αἱ λογικαί, ἀλλὰ καὶ αἱ τῶν ἀλόγων ζῴων, τὰ δὲ σώματα αὐτῶν μέρη μὲν αὐτῶν οὐδέποτε γίνεται τῶν ψυχῶν, ὄργανα δὲ ὧν μὲν ἐνιζήματα, ὧν δὲ ὀχήματα, ἄλλων δὲ *ἄλλον τρόπον κτήματα. ἀλλ' οὐδὲ τῶν ὀργάνων τὰς εἰκόνας οἷόν τε ἀπομιμεῖσθαι ἐναργῶς, ἐπεὶ καὶ τὸν ἥλιόν τις, ὡς ὁρᾶται, πλασσέτω καὶ τὴν ἶριν τοῖς χρώμασιν ἀπεικαζέτω.*

Such, then, being the case, the Greeks ought by the Law and the Prophets to learn to worship one God only, the only Sovereign; then to be taught by the Apostle, "but to us an *eidolon* is nothing in the world," since nothing among created things can be a likeness of God; and further, to be taught that none of those *agalmata* which they worship can be similitudes: for the race of souls is not in form such as the Greeks fashion their *xoana*. For souls are invisible; not only those that are rational, but those also of the other animals. And their bodies never become parts of the souls themselves, but organs—partly as seats, partly as vehicles—and in other cases possessions in various ways. But it is not possible to copy accurately even the *eikones* of the organs; since, were it so, one might model the sun, as it is seen, and take the likeness of the rainbow in colours.

50

[Clement of Rome], *Homiliae* 3.3 A.D. I–VI

Text: P. de Lagarde, ed., *Clementina* (Leipzig, 1865).

Translation adapted from T. Smith, P. Peterson, and J. Donaldson, trs., *The Clementine Homilies* (Ante-Nicene Christian Library 17; Edinburgh, 1870).

ταῦτα ἀκούσας πῶς οὐκ ἂν ἠθύμησα; διὸ καὶ ὑμᾶς τοὺς συνόντας μοι ἀδελφοὺς εἰδέναι ἠθέλησα ὡς οὐ μετρίως τὴν ψυχὴν ἀλγῶ, ἐνορῶν τὸν μὲν πονηρὸν πρὸς δοκιμὴν ἀνθρώπων ἐγρηγορότα, τοὺς δὲ ἀνθρώπους τῆς ἑαυτῶν σωτηρίας πάνυ ἀμελοῦντας. ἐμηχανήσατο γὰρ τοῖς ἀπὸ ἐθνῶν μέλλουσιν περὶ τῶν ἐπιγείων ξοάνων πείθεσθαι ὅτι οὐκ εἰσὶν θεοί, ἑτέρων πολλῶν θεῶν δόξας εἰσενεγκεῖν, ὅπως ἐὰν παύσωνται τῆς κάτω πολυθέου μανίας, ἑτέρως ἢ καὶ χεῖρον κατὰ τῆς τοῦ θεοῦ μοναρχίας λέγειν ἀπατηθήσονται, ἵνα μηδέποτε τὰ τῆς μοναρχίας προτιμήσαντες οὐπώποτε ἐλέους τυχεῖν δυνηθῶσιν. ταύτης δὲ τῆς τόλμης ἕνεκα ὁ Σίμων ταῖς ψευδέσιν τῶν γραφῶν περικοπαῖς ὡπλισμένος πολεμεῖν ἡμῖν προσέρχεται. καὶ τὸ δεινότερον ὅτι ἀφ' ὧν οὐ πεπίστευκε προφητῶν τοιαῦτα δογματίζειν κατὰ τοῦ ὄντως θεοῦ οὐ πεφόβηται.

When I heard this, how was I not disheartened! Wherefore I wished you also, my brethren, who associate with me, to know that I am beyond measure grieved in my soul, seeing the wicked one awake for the temptation of men, and men wholly indifferent about their own salvation. For to those from amongst the Gentiles who were about being persuaded respecting the earthly *xoana* that they are no gods, he has contrived to bring in opinions of many other gods, in order that, if they cease from the polytheo-mania, they may be deceived to speak otherwise, and even worse [than they now do], against the sole government of God, so that they may not yet value the truths connected with that monarchy, and may never be able to obtain mercy. And for the sake of this attempt Simon comes to do battle with us, armed with the false chapters of the Scriptures. And what is more dreadful, he is not afraid to dogmatize thus against the true God from the prophets whom he does not [in fact] believe.

51

[Clement of Rome], *Homiliae* 9.5 A.D. I–VI

Text: P. de Lagarde, ed., *Clementina* (Leipzig, 1865).

Translation adapted from T. Smith, P. Peterson, and J. Donaldson, trs., *The Clementine Homilies* (Ante-Nicene Christian Library 17; Edinburgh, 1870).

ἐκ ταύτης οὖν τῆς ἐξ οὐρανοῦ χαμαὶ πεσούσης ἀστραπῆς ὁ μάγος ἀναιρεθεὶς Νεβρώδ, ἐκ τοῦ συμβάντος πράγματος Ζωροάστρης μετωνομάσθη διὰ τὸ τὴν τοῦ ἀστέρος κατ᾽ αὐτοῦ ζῶσαν ἐνεχθῆναι ῥοήν. οἱ δὲ ἀνόητοι τῶν τότε ἀνθρώπων ὡς διὰ τὴν εἰς θεὸν φιλίαν κεραυνῷ μεταπεμφθεῖσαν τὴν ψυχὴν νομίσαντες, τοῦ σώματος τὸ λείψανον κατορύξαντες, τὸν μὲν τάφον ναῷ ἐτίμησαν ἐν Πέρσαις, ἔνθα ἡ τοῦ πυρὸς καταφορὰ γέγονεν, αὐτὸν δὲ ὡς θεὸν ἐθρήσκευσαν. τούτῳ τῷ ὑποδείγματι καὶ οἱ λοιποὶ ἐκεῖσε τοὺς κεραυνῷ θνήσκοντας ὡς θεοφιλεῖς θάπτοντες ναοῖς τιμῶσιν καὶ τῶν τεθνεώτων ἰδίων μορφῶν ἱστᾶσιν ἀγάλματα. ἐντεῦθεν ὁμοίως ἐζήλωσαν καὶ τῶν κατὰ τόπους οἱ δυναστεύσαντες, ὧν οἱ πλεῖστοι τῶν αὐτοῖς ἠγαπημένων καὶ μὴ κεραυνῷ θνησκόντων τοὺς τάφους ναοῖς καὶ ξοάνοις τιμῶντες καὶ βωμοὺς ἀνάπτοντες ὡς θεοὺς προσκυνεῖσθαι προσέταξαν. πολλῷ δὲ ὕστερον διὰ τὸν πολὺν χρόνον ὑπὸ τῶν μεταγενεστέρων ὄντως θεοὶ εἶναι ἐνομίσθησαν.

Therefore the magician Nebrod, being destroyed by this lightning falling on earth from heaven, for this circumstance had his name changed to Zoroaster, on account of the living (*zosan*) stream of the star (*asteros*) being poured upon him. But the unintelligent amongst the men who then were, thinking that through the love of God his soul had been sent for by lightning, buried the remains of his body, and honoured his burial-place with a *naos* among the Persians, where the descent of the fire occurred, and worshipped him as a god. By this example also, others there bury those who die by lightning as beloved of God, and honour them with *naoi*, and erect *agalmata* of the dead in their own forms. Thence, in like manner, the rulers in different places were emulous [of like honour], and very many of them honoured the tombs of those who were beloved of them, though not dying by lightning, with *naoi* and *xoana*, and lighted up *bomoi*, and ordered them to be adored as gods. And long after, by the lapse of time, they were thought by posterity to be really gods.

52

[Clement of Rome], *Homiliae* 9.7 A.D. I–IV
Text: P. de Lagarde, ed., *Clementina* (Leipzig, 1865).
Translation adapted from T. Smith, P. Peterson, and J. Donaldson, trs., *The Clementine Homilies* (Ante-Nicene Christian Library 17; Edinburgh, 1870).

τοῦ δὲ τὰ ξόανα σέβειν οὐκ ἐπαύσαντο διὰ τὴν κακὴν τῶν μάγων ἐπίνοιαν, εὑρόντων αὐτοῖς προφάσεις κρατεῖν αὐτοὺς πρὸς τὴν ματαίαν λατρείαν δυναμένας· ἱδρύσαντες γὰρ αὐτὰ μαγικαῖς τελεταῖς ἑορτὰς αὐτοῖς ὥρισαν ἔκ τε θυμάτων, σπονδῶν, αὐλῶν τε καὶ κρότων, ὧν προφάσει οἱ ἀνόητοι ἀπατώμενοι, καίτοι τῆς βασιλείας αὐτῶν ἀφαιρεθείσης, αὐτοὶ τῶν συνελθουσῶν θρησκειῶν οὐκ ἀπολείπονται· ἐπὶ τοσοῦτον τῆς ἀληθείας διὰ τὴν ἡδυπάθειαν προετίμησαν τὴν πλάνην. οἳ καὶ μετὰ μέθην παραβώμιον ἐπολολύζουσιν, τῆς ψυχῆς ἐκ βάθους ὥσπερ δι' ὀνείρων αὐτοῖς τὴν μέλλουσαν ἐπὶ ταῖς τοιαύταις αὐτῶν πράξεσιν προαγγελλούσης τιμωρίαν.

But they did not cease to worship *xoana*, by reason of the evil intelligence of the magicians, who found excuses for them, which had power to constrain them to the foolish worship. For, establishing these things by magical ceremonies, they assigned them feasts from sacrifices, libations, flutes, and shoutings, by means of which senseless men, being deceived, and their kingdom being taken from them, yet did not desist from worship that they had taken up with. To such an extent did they prefer error, on account of its pleasantness, before truth. They also howl after their sacrificial surfeit, their soul from the depth, as it were by dreams, forewarning them of the punishment that is to befall such deeds of theirs.

53

[Clement of Rome], *Homiliae* 9.15 A.D. I–IV
Text: P. de Lagarde, ed., *Clementina* (Leipzig, 1865).
Translation adapted from T. Smith, P. Peterson, and J. Donaldson, trs., *The Clementine Homilies* (Ante-Nicene Christian Library 17; Edinburgh, 1870).

ὡς γὰρ οἱ δεινοὶ ὄφεις τοῖς αὐτῶν πνεύμασιν τοὺς στρουθοὺς ἐπισπῶνται, οὕτω καὶ αὐτοὶ τοὺς μεταλαμβάνοντας τῆς αὐτῶν τραπέζης (διά γε τῶν βρωτῶν καὶ ποτῶν ἀνακραθέντες αὐτῶν τῷ νῷ) εἰς τὸ ἴδιον αὐτῶν ἐπισπῶνται βούλημα, μεταμορφοῦντες ἑαυτοὺς κατ' ὄναρ κατὰ τὰς τῶν ξοάνων ἰδέας, ἵνα τὴν πλάνην αὐξήσωσιν. τὸ γὰρ ξόανον οὔτε ζῷόν ἐστιν οὔτε θεῖον ἔχει πνεῦμα, ὁ δὲ ὀφθεὶς δαίμων τῇ μορφῇ ἀπεχρήσατο. πόσοις κατ' ὄναρ ὁμοίως ἄλλοις ὤφθησαν καὶ ὕπαρ συναντήσαντες ἀλλήλοις πρὸς τὸ κατ' ὄναρ ἀντιβάλλοντες οὐ συνεφώνησαν; ὥστε οὐκέτι ὄναρ ἐπιφανείη ἐκεῖνό ἐστιν, ἀλλ' ἢ δαίμονός ἐστιν ἢ ψυχῆς τὰ ἐπιγενήματα τοῖς παρία φόβοις καὶ ἐπιθυμίᾳ ἀποδιδούσης τὰς ἰδέας· ἡ γὰρ φόβῳ τὸν νοῦν πληγεῖσα, διὰ ὀνείρων τὰς ἰδέας ἀποκυΐσκει. εἰ δὲ τὰ ξόανα οἴεσθε ὡς ἔνπνοα ὑπάρχοντα τὰ ποιαῦτα ἐνεργεῖν δύνασθαι, ἐπὶ ζυγοῦ ἐπιστήσαντες αὐτά, ἴσου ὄντος τοῦ κανόνος, τὸ ἀντίρροπον ἐπὶ τῆς ἑτέρας πλάστιγγος θέντες, ἀξιώσατε αὐτὰ ἢ ὁλκότερα γενέσθαι ἢ κουφότερα, καὶ οὕτως ἐὰν γένηται, ἔνπνοά ἐστιν· ἀλλ' οὐ γίνεται· εἰ δὲ ἔσται, οὔπω τὸ τοιοῦτο θεός ἐστιν. καὶ γὰρ δακτύλῳ δαίμονος τοῦτο γενέσθαι δύναται. καὶ σκώληκες κινοῦνται, καὶ θεοὶ οὐ λέγονται.

For as dire serpents draw sparrows to them by their breath, so also these draw to their own will those who partake of their table, being mixed up with their understanding by means of food and drink, changing themselves in dreams according to the forms of the *xoana*, that they may increase error. For the *xoanon* is neither a living creature, nor has it a divine spirit, but the demon that appeared abused the form. How many, in like manner, have been seen by others in dreams; and when they have met one another when awake, and compared them with what they saw in their dream, they have not accorded; so that the dream is not a manifestation, but is either the production of a demon or of the soul, giving forms to present fears and desire. For the soul, being struck with fear, conceives forms in dreams. But if you think that *xoana*, as being alive, can accomplish such things, place them on a beam accurately balanced, and place an equipoise in the other scale, then ask them to become either heavier or lighter; and if this be done, then they are alive. But it does not so happen. But if it were so, this would not prove them to be gods. For this might be accomplished by the finger of the demon. Even maggots move, yet they are not called gods.

54

[Clement of Rome], *Homiliae* 10.21 A.D. I–IV

Text: P. de Lagarde, ed., *Clementina* (Leipzig, 1865).

Translation adapted from T. Smith, P. Peterson, and J. Donaldson, trs., *The Clementine Homilies* (Ante-Nicene Christian Library 17; Edinburgh, 1870).

λέγουσι γὰρ οἱ πολλοί· Τῶν σεβασμάτων ἡμῶν σέβομεν οὐ τὸν χρυσὸν οὐδὲ τὸν ἄργυρον οὐδὲ ξύλον ἢ λίθον (ἴσμεν γὰρ καὶ ἡμεῖς ὅτι ταῦτα οὐδέν ἐστιν ἢ ἄψυχος ὕλη καὶ ἀνθρώπου θνητοῦ τέχνη), ἀλλὰ τὸ κατοικοῦν ἐν αὐτοῖς πνεῦμα, τοῦτο θεὸν λέγομεν. ὁρᾶτ' οὖν τῶν ταῦτα λεγόντων τὴν κακοήθειαν. ἐπεὶ γὰρ τὸ φαινόμενον εὐέλεγκτόν ἐστιν ὅτι οὐδέν ἐστιν, κατέφυγον ἐπὶ τὸ ἀόρατον, ὡς ἐπ' ἀδήλῳ τινὶ ἐλεγχθῆναι μὴ δυνάμενοι. πλὴν συνομολογοῦσιν ἡμῖν οἱ τοιοῦτοι ἐπὶ μέρους ὅτι τὸ ἥμισυ τῶν παρ' αὐτοῖς ἱδρυμάτων θεὸς οὐκ ἔστιν, ἀλλ' ἀναίσθητος ὕλη. λοιπὸν δὲ περιλείπεται δεῖξαι αὐτοῖς πῶς πιστεύομεν ὅτι θεῖον ἔχει πνεῦμα. ἀλλ' ἐπιδεῖξαι ἡμῖν οὐ δύνανται ὅτι ἔστιν, ἐπεὶ μὴ ἔστιν—καὶ αὐτοῖς ἑωρακέναι οὐ πιστεύομεν. ἡμεῖς αὐτοῖς ὅτι θεῖον οὐκ ἔχει πνεῦμα τὰς ἀποδείξεις παρέξομεν, ὅπως τοῦ δοκεῖν αὐτὰ ἔνπνοα εἶναι οἱ φιλαλήθεις τὸν ἔλεγχον ἀκούσαντες τῆς λυσσώδους ὑπονοίας ἀποτράπωνται.

For many say, we do not worship the gold or the silver, the wood or the stone, of the objects of our worship. For we also know that these are nothing but soulless matter and the craft of mortal man. But the spirit that dwells in them, that we call God. Behold the immorality of those who speak thus! For when that which appears is easily proved to be nothing, they have recourse to the invisible, as not being able to be convicted in respect of what is nonapparent. However, they agree with us in part, that one half of their *hidrumata* is not God, but matter without sensation. It remains for them to show how we are to believe that [these images] have a divine spirit. But they cannot prove to us that it is so, for it is not so; and we do not believe them [when they say that they] have seen it. We shall afford them proofs that they have not a divine spirit, that lovers of truth, hearing the refutation of the thought that they are animated, may turn away from the hurtful delusion.

55

[Clement of Rome], *Homiliae* 10.23 A.D. I–IV

Text: P. de Lagarde, ed., *Clementina* (Leipzig, 1865).

Translation adapted from T. Smith, P. Peterson, and J. Donaldson, trs., *The Clementine Homilies* (Ante-Nicene Christian Library 17; Edinburgh, 1870).

ναί φησιν, ἀλλὰ προνοίᾳ αὐτῶν ἐφωράθησαν. ψεῦδός ἐστιν. πόσοι γὰρ οὐκ ἐφωράθησαν αὐτῶν; εἰ δὲ διὰ τὸ ἐνίους συνειλῆφθαι δύναμιν αὐτοὺς ἔχειν λέγουσιν, πεπλάνηνται. καὶ γὰρ τῶν τυμβωρύχων τινὲς μὲν εὑρίσκονται, τινὲς δὲ λανθάνουσιν, καὶ οὐ δήπου γε τῇ τῶν νεκρῶν δυνάμει οἱ συλληφθέντες ἐφωράθησαν. τοιοῦτόν τι καὶ περὶ τοὺς κλεπτομένους καὶ συλωμένους θεοὺς ἔστιν ἡμῖν νοεῖν. ἀλλά (φησίν) οὐ πεφροντίκασιν τῶν ξοάνων αὐτῶν οἱ ἐν αὐτοῖς ὄντες θεοί. τί οὖν αὐτὰ ὑμεῖς τημελεῖτε σμήχοντες καὶ πλύνοντες καὶ καθαίροντες, στεφανοῦντες, ἐπιθύοντες; διόπερ ἐντεῦθεν συννοήσατε μηδὲ ὀρθῷ λογισμῷ ποιοῦντες. ὡς γὰρ τοῖς νεκροῖς ἐπικλαίετε, οὕτω καὶ τοῖς θεοῖς ὑμῶν ἐπιθύετε καὶ σπένδετε.

Nay, it will be said; but they are detected by their foresight. It is false; for how many of them have not been detected? And if on account of the capture of some it be said that they have power, it is a mistake. For of those who rob tombs, some are found out and some escape; but it is not by the power of the dead that those who are apprehended are detected. And such ought to be our conclusion with respect to those who steal and pilfer the gods. But it will be said, The gods that are in them take no care of their *xoana*. Why, then, do you tend them, wiping them, and washing them, and scouring them, crowning them and sacrificing to them? Wherefore agree with me that you act altogether without right reason. For as you lament over the dead, so you sacrifice and make libations to your gods.

56

Quintus Curtius Rufus 4.3.21–22 A.D. I

Text and translation: J.C. Rolfe, tr., *Quintus Curtius* I (LCL, 1946).

Cumque unus e civibus in contione indicasset, oblatam esse per somnum sibi speciem Apollinis, quem eximia religione colerent, urbem deserentis molemque a Macedonibus in salo iactam in silvestrem saltum esse mutatum, quamquam auctor levis erat, tamen ad deteriora credenda proni metu aurea catena devinxere simulacrum araeque Herculis, cuius numini urbem dicaverant, inseruere vinculum quasi illo deo Apollinem retenturo. Syracusis id simulacrum devexerant Poeni et in maiore locaverant patria multisque aliis spoliis urbium a semet captarum non Carthaginem magis quam Tyrum ornaverant.

And when one of their citizens declared in a public assembly that a vision of Apollo, whom they worshipped with special veneration, had appeared to him in his sleep as deserting the city, and that the causeway which the Macedonians had constructed in the sea had changed into a forest tract, although the author of the tale was a man of slight importance, yet, inclined through fear to believe the worst, they bound the *simulacrum* of Apollo with a chain of gold to its base, and attached the chain to the altar of Hercules, to whose divine power they had dedicated their city, supposing that the god would hold Apollo back. The Carthaginians had carried off that *simulacrum* from Syracuse and had placed it in their ancestral fatherland, and with many other spoils of the cities which they had captured they had adorned Tyre rather than Carthage.

St. Cyril, *Lexicon s.v. ξόανον*
(= *Anecdota Parisiensis* IV.119.17.)
See [Zonaras], *Lexicon s.v.* [**371**].

Demetrius of Troezen *FGrH* 304 F 1 IV B.C.
See Clement of Alexandria, *Protrepticus* 4.41 P. [**44**].

Diegeseis to Callimachus
See Callimachus *ad loc.*

57

Dio Chrysostom, *Oration* 12.60–61 A.D. 97
Text: J. von Arnim, ed., *Dionis Prusaensis quem vocant Chrysostomum quae exstant omnia* I (Berlin, 1893).
Translation adapted from J.W. Cohoon, tr., *Dio Chrysostom* II (LCL, 1939).

οὐδὲ γὰρ ὡς βέλτιον ὑπῆρχε μηδὲν ἵδρυμα μηδὲ εἰκόνα θεῶν ἀποδεδεῖχθαι παρ' ἀνθρώποις φαίη τις ἄν, ὡς πρὸς μόνα ὁρᾶν δέον τὰ οὐράνια. ταῦτα μὲν γὰρ ξύμπαντα ὅ γε νοῦν ἔχων σέβει, θεοὺς ἐγούμενος μακαρίους μακρόθεν ὁρῶν· διὰ δὲ τὴν πρὸς τὸ δαιμόνιον ὁρμὴν ἰσχυρὸς ἔρως πᾶσιν ἀνθρώποις ἐγγύθεν τιμᾶν καὶ θεραπεύειν τὸ θεῖον, προσιόντας καὶ ἁπτομένους μετὰ πειθοῦς, θύοντας καὶ στεφανοῦντας. ἀτεχνῶς γὰρ ὥσπερ νήπιοι παῖδες πατρὸς ἢ μητρὸς ἀπεσπασμένοι δεινὸν ἵμερον ἔχοντες καὶ πόθον ὀρέγουσι χεῖρας οὐ παροῦσι πολλάκις ὀνειρώττοντες, οὕτω καὶ θεοῖς ἄνθρωποι ἀγαπῶντες δικαίως διά τε εὐεργεσίαν καὶ συγγένειαν, προθυμούμενοι πάντα τρόπον συνεῖναί τε καὶ ὁμιλεῖν· ὥστε καὶ πολλοὶ τῶν βαρβάρων πενίᾳ τε καὶ ἀπορίᾳ τέχνης ὄρη θεοὺς ἐπονομάζουσι καὶ δένδρα ἀργὰ καὶ ἀσήμους λίθους, οὐδαμῇ [οὐδαμῶς] οἰκειότερα τῆς μορφῆς.

For certainly no one would maintain that it had been better that no *hidruma* or *eikon* of the gods should have been exhibited among men, on the ground that we should look only at the heavenly objects. For although the intelligent man does indeed reverence all these objects, believing them to be the blessed gods that he sees from a great distance, yet on account of our belief in the divine all men have a strong yearning to honor and worship the deity from close at hand, approaching and laying hold of him with persuasion by offering sacrifice and crowning him with garlands. For just as infant children when torn away from father or mother are filled with terrible longing and desire, and stretch out their hands to their absent parents often in their dreams, so also do men to the gods, rightly loving them for their beneficence and kinship, and being eager in every way to be with them and to hold converse with them. Consequently many of the barbarians, for lack of craftsmanship and difficulty with it, name mountains gods, and unworked trees, too, and shapeless stones, things which are by no means whatever more appropriate in shape than is the human form.

58

Diodorus Siculus 1.98.5–9 I B.C.

Text: F. Vogel, ed., *Diodori bibliotheca historica* I (third ed.; Leipzig, 1888; repr. Stuttgart, 1964).

Translation adapted from C.H. Oldfather, tr., *Diodorus of Sicily* I (LCL, 1933).

See also Eusebius, *Praeparatio evangelica* 10.8.482 c [**124**].

Ἕλληνας ἐκδόντα τυχεῖν ἀξιολόγου δόξης. τῶν τε ἀγαλματοποιῶν τῶν παλαιῶν τοὺς μάλιστα διωνομασμένους διατετριφέναι παρ᾽ αὐτοῖς Τηλεκλέα καὶ Θεόδωρον, τοὺς Ῥοίκου μὲν υἱούς, κατασκευάσαντας δὲ τοῖς Σαμίοις τὸ τοῦ Ἀπόλλωνος τοῦ Πυθίου ξόανον. τοῦ γὰρ ἀγάλματος ἐν Σάμῳ μὲν ὑπὸ Τηλεκλέους ἱστορεῖται τὸ ἥμισυ δημιουργηθῆναι, κατὰ δὲ τὴν Ἔφεσον ὑπὸ τἀδελφοῦ Θεοδώρου τὸ ἕτερον μέρος συντελεσθῆναι· συντεθέντα δὲ πρὸς ἄλληλα τὰ μέρη συμφωνεῖν οὕτως ὥστε δοκεῖν ὑφ᾽ ἑνὸς τὸ πᾶν ἔργον συντετελέσθαι. τοῦτο δὲ τὸ γένος τῆς ἐργασίας παρὰ μὲν τοῖς Ἕλλησι μηδαμῶς ἐπιτηδεύεσθαι, παρὰ δὲ τοῖς Αἰγυπτίοις μάλιστα συντελεῖσθαι. παρ᾽ ἐκείνοις γὰρ οὐκ ἀπὸ τῆς κατὰ τὴν ὅρασιν φαντασίας τὴν συμμετρίαν τῶν ἀγαλμάτων κρίνεσθαι, καθάπερ παρὰ τοῖς Ἕλλησιν, ἀλλ᾽ ἐπειδὰν τοὺς λίθους κατακλίνωσι καὶ μερίσαντες κατεργάσωνται, τὸ τηνικαῦτα τὸ ἀνάλογον ἀπὸ τῶν ἐλαχίστων ἐπὶ τὰ μέγιστα λαμβάνεσθαι· τοῦ γὰρ παντὸς σώματος τὴν κατασκευὴν εἰς ἓν καὶ εἴκοσι μέρη καὶ προσέτι τέταρτον διαιρουμένους τὴν ὅλην ἀποδιδόναι συμμετρίαν τοῦ ζῴου. διόπερ ὅταν περὶ τοῦ μεγέθους οἱ τεχνῖται πρὸς ἀλλήλους σύνθωνται, χωρισθέντες ἀπ᾽ ἀλλήλων σύμφωνα κατασκευάζουσι τὰ μεγέθη τῶν ἔργων οὕτως ἀκριβῶς ὥστε ἔκπληξιν παρέχειν τὴν ἰδιότητα τῆς πραγματείας αὐτῶν. τὸ δ᾽ ἐν τῷ Σάμῳ ξόανον συμφώνως τῇ τῶν Αἰγυπτίων φιλοτεχνίᾳ κατὰ τὴν κορυφὴν διχοτομούμενον διορίζειν τοῦ ζῴου τὸ μέσον μέχρι τῶν αἰδοίων, ἰσάζον ὁμοίως ἑαυτῷ πάντοθεν· εἶναι δ᾽ αὐτὸ λέγουσι κατὰ τὸ πλεῖστον παρεμφερὲς τοῖς Αἰγυπτίοις, ὡς ἂν τὰς μὲν χεῖρας ἔχον παρατεταμένας, τὰ δὲ σκέλη διαβεβηκότα.

Also of the ancient *agalma*-makers the most renowned sojourned among them, namely, Telecles and Theodorus, the sons of Rhoecus, who executed for the people of Samos the *xoanon* of the Pythian Apollo. For it is related that one half of the *agalma* was worked by Telecles in Samos, and the other half was finished by his brother Theodorus at Ephesus; and when the two parts were brought together they fitted so perfectly that the whole work had the appearance of having been done by one man. This method of working is practiced nowhere among the Greeks, but is followed generally among the Egyptians. For with them the symmetrical proportions of the *agalmata* are not fixed in accordance with the appearance they present to the eye, as is done among the Greeks, but as soon as they lay out the stones and, after apportioning them, are ready work on them, at that stage they take the proportions, from the smallest parts to the largest; for, dividing the structure of the entire body into twenty-one parts and one-fourth in addition, they express in this way the complete figure in its symmetrical proportions. Consequently, so soon as the artisans agree as to the size [*sc.* of the statue], they separate and proceed to turn out the various sizes assigned to them, in such a way that they correspond, and they do it so accurately that the peculiarity of the system excites amazement. And the *xoanon* in Samos, in conformity with the ingenious method of the Egyptians, was cut into two parts from the top of the head down to the private parts and the *zoion* was divided in the middle, each part exactly matching the other at every point. And they say that it is for the most part similar to Egyptian ones, as having the arms stretched stiffly down the sides and the legs separated.

59

Diodorus Siculus 4.76.1–3 I B.C.

Text: F. Vogel, ed., *Diodori bibliotheca historica* I (third ed.; Leipzig, 1888; repr. Stuttgart, 1964).

Translation adapted from C.H. Oldfather, tr., *Diodorus of Sicily* III (LCL, 1939).

Δαίδαλος ἦν τὸ μὲν γένος Ἀθηναῖος, εἷς τῶν Ἐρεχθειδῶν ὀνομαζόμενος· ἦν γὰρ υἱὸς Μητίονος τοῦ Εὐπαλάμου τοῦ Ἐρεχθέως· φύσει δὲ πολὺ τοὺς ἄλλους ἅπαντας ὑπεραίρων ἐζήλωσε τά τε περὶ τὴν τεκτονικὴν τέχνην καὶ τὴν τῶν ἀγαλμάτων κατασκευὴν καὶ λιθουργίαν. εὑρετὴς δὲ γενόμενος πολλῶν τῶν συνεργούντων εἰς τὴν τέχνην, κατεσκεύασεν ἔργα θαυμαζόμενα κατὰ πολλοὺς τόπους τῆς οἰκουμένης. κατὰ δὲ τὴν τῶν ἀγαλμάτων κατασκευὴν τοσοῦτο τῶν ἁπάντων ἀνθρώπων διήνεγκεν ὥστε τοὺς μεταγενεστέρους μυθολογῆσαι περὶ αὐτοῦ διότι τὰ κατασκευαζόμενα τῶν ἀγαλμάτων ὁμοιότατα τοῖς ἐμψύχοις ὑπάρχει· βλέπειν τε γὰρ αὐτὰ καὶ περιπατεῖν, καὶ καθόλου τηρεῖν τὴν τοῦ ὅλου σώματος διάθεσιν, ὥστε δοκεῖν εἶναι τὸ κατασκευασθὲν ἔμψυχον ζῷον. πρῶτος δ' ὀμματώσας καὶ διαβεβηκότα τὰ σκέλη ποιήσας, ἔτι δὲ τὰς χεῖρας διατεταμένας ποιῶν, εἰκότως ἐθαυμάζετο παρὰ τοῖς ἀνθρώποις· οἱ γὰρ πρὸ τούτου τεχνῖται κατεσκεύαζον τὰ ἀγάλματα τοῖς μὲν ὄμμασι μεμυκότα, τὰς δὲ χεῖρας ἔχοντα καθειμένας καὶ ταῖς πλευραῖς κεκολλημένας.

Daedalus was an Athenian by birth and was known as one of the clan named Erechthids, since he was the son of Metion, the son of Eupalamus, the son of Erechtheus. In natural ability towering far above all other men, he cultivated the building art, the making of *agalmata*, and the working of stone. He was also the inventor of many devices which contributed to the advancement of his art and built works in many regions of the inhabited world which arouse the wonder of men. In the carving of his *agalmata* he so far excelled all other men that later generations invented the story about him that the *agalmata* of his making were quite like living beings; they could see, they said, and walk, and, in a word, preserved so well the characteristics of the entire body that the statue made by him seemed to be a living being. And since he was the first to represent the open eye and to fashion the legs separated and the arms and hands extended, it was natural that he should have received the admiration of mankind; for the craftsmen before him had carved their *agalmata* with the eyes closed, having hands hanging and attached to the sides.

60

Diodorus Siculus 17.10 I B.C.

Text: K.T. Fischer, ed., *Diodori bibliotheca historica* IV (third ed.; Leipzig, 1906; repr. Stuttgart, 1964).

Translation adapted from C.B. Welles, tr., *Diodorus of Sicily* VIII (LCL, 1963).

οὗτος μὲν οὖν ἀποθηριωθεὶς τὴν ψυχὴν μηχανάς τε πολιορκητικὰς συνεστήσατο καὶ τἄλλα πρὸς τὸν κίνδυνον παρεσκευάζετο, οἱ δ' Ἕλληνες πυνθανόμενοι τὸ μέγεθος τῶν περὶ τοὺς Θηβαίους κινδύνων ἐδυσφόρουν ἐπὶ ταῖς προσδοκωμέναις περὶ αὐτῶν συμφοραῖς, οὐ μὴν βοηθεῖν γ' ἐτόλμων τῇ πόλει διὰ τὸ προπετῶς καὶ ἀβούλως εἰς ὁμολογουμένην ἀπώλειαν ἑαυτὴν δεδωκέναι. οἱ δὲ Θηβαῖοι ταῖς μὲν εὐτολμίαις προθύμως ἀνεδέχοντο τοὺς κινδύνους, φήμαις δέ τισι μάντεων καὶ θεῶν σημείοις ἠποροῦντο. πρῶτον μὲν γὰρ ἐν τῷ τῆς Δήμητρος ἱερῷ λεπτὸν ἀράχνης ὕφασμά τι διαπεπετασμένον ὤφθη, τὸ μὲν μέγεθος ἔχον ἱματίου, κύκλῳ δὲ περιφαῖνον ἶριν τῇ κατ' οὐρανὸν ἐοικυῖαν. περὶ οὗ τὸ μὲν ἐν Δελφοῖς χρηστήριον ἔδωκεν αὐτοῖς τόνδε τὸν χρησμόν·

σημεῖον τόδε πᾶσι θεοὶ φαίνουσι βροτοῖσι,
Βοιωτοῖς δὲ μάλιστα καὶ οἳ περιναιετάουσι.

τὸ δὲ πάτριον τῶν Θηβαίων μαντεῖον τοῦτον ἐξήνεγκε τὸν χρησμόν·

ἱστὸς ὑφαινόμενος ἄλλῳ κακόν, ἄλλῳ ἄμεινον.

τοῦτο μὲν οὖν τὸ σημεῖον ἐγένετο τρισὶ μησὶν ἀνωτέρω τῆς Ἀλεξάνδρου παρουσίας ἐπὶ τὰς Θήβας, ὑπ' αὐτὴν δὲ τὴν ἔφοδον τοῦ βασιλέως οἱ κατὰ τὴν ἀγορὰν ἀνδριάντες ἐφάνησαν ἱδρῶτας ἀφιέντες καὶ μεστοὶ σταλαγμῶν μεγάλων. χωρὶς δὲ τούτων ἧκόν τινες τοῖς ἄρχουσιν ἀπαγγέλλοντες τὴν ἐν Ὀγχηστῷ λίμνην μυκήματι παραπλήσιον φωνὴν ἀφιέναι, τῇ δὲ Δίρκῃ κατὰ τὴν ἐπιφάνειαν τοῦ ὕδατος αἱματοειδῆ φρίκην ἐπιτρέχειν. ἕτεροι δὲ ἧκον ἐκ Δελφῶν μηνύοντες ὅτι ὁ ἀπὸ Φωκέων ναός, ὃν ἱδρύσαντο Θηβαῖοι, ᾑματωμένην ἔχων τὴν ὀροφὴν ὁρᾶται. οἱ δὲ περὶ τὴν τῶν σημείων διάκρισιν ἀσχολούμενοι σημαίνειν ἔφασαν τὸ μὲν ὕφασμα θεῶν ἀπὸ τῆς πόλεως χωρισμόν, τὸ δὲ τῆς ἴριδος χρῶμα πραγμάτων ποικίλων χειμῶνα, τὸν δὲ τῶν ἀνδριάντων ἱδρῶτα ὑπερβάλλουσαν κακοπάθειαν, τὸ δ᾿ ἐν πλείοσι τόποις φαινόμενον αἷμα φόνον πολὺν κατὰ τὴν πόλιν ἐσόμενον. συνεβούλευον οὖν τῶν θεῶν φανερῶς σημαινόντων τὴν ἐσομένην τῇ πόλει συμφορὰν μὴ συγκαταβαίνειν εἰς τὸ διὰ μάχης κρίνειν τὸν πόλεμον, ἑτέραν δὲ διάλυσιν ζητεῖν διὰ λόγων ἀσφαλεστέραν.

Raging in his heart, [Alexander] set to constructing siege machines and to preparing whatever else was necessary for the attack.

Elsewhere in Greece, as people learned the seriousness of the danger hanging over the Thebans, they were distressed at their expected disaster but had no heart to help them, feeling that the city by precipitate and ill-considered action had consigned itself to evident annihilation. In Thebes itself, however, men accepted their risk willingly and with good courage, but they were puzzled by certain sayings of *manteis* and portents of the gods.

First there was the light spider's web in the temple of Demeter which was observed to have spread itself out to the size of a himation, and which all about shone like a rainbow in the sky. About this, the oracle at Delphi gave them the response:

"The gods to mortals all have sent this sign;
To the Boeotians especially, and to their neighbors."

The ancestral oracle of Thebes itself had given this reponse:

"The woven web is something bad to one, to one a better thing."

This sign had occurred three months before Alexander's descent on the city, but at the very moment of the king's arrival the *andriantes* in the *agora* were seen to burst into perspiration and be full of great drops of moisture. More than this, people reported to the city officials that the marsh at Onchestus was emitting a sound very like a bellow, while at Dirce a bloody ripple ran along the surface of the water. Finally, travellers coming from Delphi told how the temple which the Thebans had dedicated from the Phocian spoils was observed to have bloodstains on its roof.

Those who made a business of interpreting such portents stated that the spider web signified the departure of the gods from the city, its iridescence meant a storm of mixed troubles, the sweating of the *andriantes* was the sign of an overwhelming catastrophe, and the appearance of blood in many places foretold a vast slaughter throughout the city. They counselled that the gods were clearly predicting disaster for the city and recommended that the outcome of the war should not be risked upon the battlefield, but that a safer solution should be sought for in conversation.

61

Diodorus Siculus 17.41.7–8 I B.C.

Text: K.T. Fischer, ed., *Diodori bibliotheca historica* IV (third ed.; Leipzig, 1906; repr. Stuttgart, 1964).

Translation adapted from C.B. Welles, tr., *Diodorus of Sicily* VIII (LCL, 1963).

ἐγίνετο δὲ καὶ ἄλλα σημεῖα παράδοξα, δυνάμενα διατροπὴν καὶ φόβον τοῖς ὄχλοις παρασχέσθαι. κατὰ γὰρ τὰς τροφὰς παρὰ τοῖς Μακεδόσιν οἱ διακλώμενοι τῶν ἄρτων αἱματοειδῆ τὴν πρόσοψιν εἶχον. ἑωρακέναι δέ τις ἔφησεν ὄψιν καθ' ἣν ὁ Ἀπόλλων ἔλεγε μέλλειν ἑαυτὸν ἐκλιπεῖν τὴν πόλιν. τοῦ δὲ πλήθους ὑπονοήσαντος ὅτι πεπλακὼς εἴη τὸν λόγον χαριζόμενος Ἀλεξάνδρῳ καὶ διὰ τοῦτο τῶν νεωτέρων ὁρμησάντων ἐπὶ τὸ λιθοβολῆσαι τὸν ἄνθρωπον οὗτος μὲν διὰ τῶν ἀρχόντων <ἐκ>κλαπεὶς καὶ καταφυγὼν εἰς τὸ τοῦ Ἡρακλέους ἱερὸν διέφυγε τὴν τιμωρίαν διὰ τὴν ἱκεσίαν, οἱ δὲ Τύριοι δεισιδαιμονήσαντες χρυσαῖς σειραῖς προσέδησαν τὸ τοῦ Ἀπόλλωνος ξόανον τῇ βάσει, ἐμποδίζοντες, ὡς ᾤοντο, τοῦ θεοῦ τὸν ἐκ τῆς πόλεως χωρισμόν.

There were other incredible happenings, too, capable of spreading confusion and terror among people. At the distribution of rations on the Macedonian side, the broken pieces of bread had a bloody look. Someone reported [on the Tyrian side] that he had seen a vision in which Apollo told him that he would leave the city. Everyone suspected that the man had made the story up in order to curry favor with Alexander, and on account of this some of the younger citizens set out to stone him; he was, however, spirited away by the magistrates and took refuge in the *hieron* of Heracles, where as a suppliant he escaped the people's wrath, but the Tyrians were so superstitious that they tied the *xoanon* of Apollo to its base with golden cords, preventing, as they thought, the god from leaving the city.

62

Diodorus Siculus 17.50.6–7 I B.C.

Text: K.T. Fischer, ed., *Diodori bibliotheca historica* IV (third ed.; Leipzig, 1906; repr. Stuttgart, 1964).

Translation adapted from C.B. Welles, tr., *Diodorus of Sicily* VIII (LCL, 1963).

τὸ δὲ τοῦ θεοῦ ξόανον ἐκ σμαράγδων καί τινων ἄλλων <πολυτελῶν λίθων> περιέχεται καὶ τὴν μαντείαν ἰδιάζουσαν παντελῶς ποιεῖται. ἐπὶ νεὼς γὰρ περιφέρεται χρυσῆς ὑπὸ ἱερέων ὀγδοήκοντα· οὗτοι δ' ἐπὶ τῶν ὤμων φέροντες τὸν θεὸν προάγουσιν αὐτομάτως ὅποι ποτ' ἂν ἄγῃ τὸ τοῦ θεοῦ νεῦμα τὴν πορείαν. συνακολουθεῖ δὲ πλῆθος παρθένων καὶ γυναικῶν παιᾶνας ᾀδουσῶν κατὰ πᾶσαν τὴν ὁδὸν καὶ πατρίῳ καθυμνουσῶν ᾠδῇ τὸν θεόν.

The *xoanon* of the god is surrounded by emeralds and other precious stones, and answers those who consult the oracle in quite a peculiar fashion. It is carried about on a golden boat by eighty priests, and these, with the god on their shoulders, go without their own volition wherever the god directs their path. A multitude of girls and women follows them singing paeans along the entire path and praising the god in a traditional hymn.

63

Diodorus Siculus 31.35 I B.C.
(= *Excerpta Constantiniana* 2(1) pp. 289–290.)
Text: F.R. Walton, ed., tr., *Diodorus of Sicily* XI (LCL, 1957).
Translation adapted from Walton.

"Ὅτι Προυσίας ὁ Βιθυνῶν βασιλεὺς ἀποτυχὼν τῆς ἐπιβολῆς τῆς περὶ τὸν Ἄτταλον τὸ πρὸ τῆς πόλεως τέμενος τὸ καλούμενον Νικηφόριον διέφθειρεν καὶ τὸν νεὼν ἐλυμήνατο. ἐσύλησε δὲ καὶ τοὺς ἀνδριάντας καὶ τὰ τῶν θεῶν ξόανα καὶ τὸ περιβόητον ἄγαλμα τοῦ Ἀσκληπιοῦ, δοκοῦν ἔργον εἶναι Φυρομάχου, περιττῶς κατεσκευασμένον, καὶ τὰ ἱερὰ πάντ' ἐσύλα.

King Prusias of Bithynia, having failed in his design on Attalus, destroyed the *temenos* before the city that was called the Nicephorium, and despoiled the *neos*. He plundered the *andriantes* and the *xoana* of the gods and the famous *agalma* of Ascelpius, reported to be the work of Phyromachus, a piece of extraordinary workmanship, and he plundered all the *hiera*.

64

Diogenes Laertius 1.6 A.D. III
Text: H.S. Long, ed., *Diogenes Laertii vitae philosophorum* I (Oxford, 1964; repr. 1966).
Translation adapted from R.D. Hicks, tr., *Diogenes Laertius. Lives of Eminent Philosophers* I (LCL, 1938).

Οἱ δὲ φάσκοντες ἀπὸ βαρβάρων ἄρξαι φιλοσοφίαν καὶ τὸν τρόπον παρ' ἑκάστοις αὐτῆς ἐκτίθενται· καί φασι τοὺς μὲν γυμνοσοφιστὰς καὶ Δρυΐδας αἰνιγματωδῶς ἀποφθεγγομένους φιλοσοφῆσαι, σέβειν θεοὺς καὶ μηδὲν κακὸν δρᾶν καὶ ἀνδρείαν ἀσκεῖν. τοὺς γοῦν γυμνοσοφιστὰς καὶ θανάτου καταφρονεῖν φησι Κλείταρχος ἐν τῇ δωδεκάτῃ· τοὺς δὲ Χαλδαίους περὶ ἀστρονομίαν καὶ πρόρρησιν ἀσχολεῖσθαι· τοὺς δὲ Μάγους περί τε θεραπείας θεῶν διατρίβειν καὶ θυσίας καὶ εὐχάς, ὡς αὐτοὺς μόνους ἀκουομένους. ἀποφαίνεσθαί τε περὶ οὐσίας θεῶν καὶ γενέσεως, οὓς καὶ πῦρ εἶναι καὶ γῆν καὶ ὕδωρ· τῶν δὲ ξοάνων καταγινώσκειν, καὶ μάλιστα τῶν λεγόντων ἄρρενας εἶναι θεοὺς καὶ θηλείας.

But the advocates of the theory that philosophy took its rise among the barbarians go on to explain the different forms it assumed in different countries. As to the Gymnosophists and Druids, we are told that they uttered their philosophy in riddles, bidding men to reverence the gods, to abstain from wrongdoing, and to practice courage. That the Gymnosophists at all events despise even death itself is affirmed by Clitarchus in his twelfth book; he also says that the Chaldaeans apply themselves to astronomy and forecasting the future; while the Magi spend their time in worship of the gods, in sacrifices and in prayers, on the grounds that none but themselves have the ear of the gods. They propound their views concerning the being and origin of the gods, whom they hold to be fire, earth, and water; they condemn the use of *xoana*, and especially the error of attributing to the divinities the difference of sex.

65

Dionysius of Halicarnassus 1.50.3–4 I B.C.–A.D. I
Text: K. Jacoby, ed., *Dionysii Halicarnasei antiquitatum romanarum quae supersunt* I (Leipzig, 1885; repr. Stuttgart, 1967).
Translation adapted from E. Cary, tr., *The Roman Antiquities of Dionysius of Halicarnassus* I (LCL, 1937).

ταύτης τε δὴ τῆς συγγενείας ἀναμνήσει καὶ φιλοφροσύνῃ τῶν ἐπιχωρίων διατρίβοντες αὐτόθι καὶ ἅμα ἀπλοίᾳ κατειργόμενοι θύουσιν Ἀφροδίτῃ πρὸς τῷ κατασκευασθέντι ἱερῷ θυσίαν, ἣν εἰς τόδε χρόνου συντελοῦσι κοινῇ Ζακύνθιοι, καὶ ἀγῶνα ποιοῦσιν ἐφήβοις τῶν τε ἄλλων ἀγωνισμάτων καὶ δρόμου· τὸ δὲ νικητήριον ὁ πρῶτος ἐλθὼν εἰς τὸν νεὼν λαμβάνει· λέγεται δὲ Αἰνείου καὶ Ἀφροδίτης ὁ δρόμος, καὶ ξόανα τούτων ἕστηκεν ἀμφοτέρων. ἐκεῖθεν δὲ πελάγιον ποιησάμενοι τὸν πλοῦν εἰς Λευκάδα κατάγονται, κατεχόντων ἔτι τὸ χωρίον Ἀκαρνάνων. κἀν ταύτῃ πάλιν ἱερὸν Ἀφροδίτης ἱδρύονται τοῦτο, ὃ νῦν ἐστιν ἐν τῇ νησῖδι τῇ μεταξὺ τοῦ Διορύκτου τε καὶ τῆς πόλεως, καλεῖται δὲ Ἀφροδίτης Αἰνειάδος. ἄραντες δὲ αὐτόθεν ἐπί τε Ἄκτιον ἐλθόντες ὁρμίζονται τοῦ Ἀμβρακικοῦ κόλπου πρὸς τὸ ἀκρωτήριον. κἀκεῖθεν εἰς Ἀμβρακίαν ἀφικνοῦνται πόλιν, ἧς ἐβασίλευεν Ἄμβραξ ὁ Δεξαμενοῦ τοῦ Ἡρακλέους, καὶ ὑπολείπονται ἑκατέρωθι μνημεῖα τῆς ἀφίξεως· ἐν Ἀκτίῳ μὲν Ἀφροδίτης Αἰνειάδος ἱερὸν καὶ πλησίον αὐτοῦ θεῶν μεγάλων, ἃ καὶ εἰς ἐμὲ ἦν· ἐν δὲ Ἀμβρακίᾳ ἱερόν τε τῆς αὐτῆς θεοῦ καὶ ἡρῷον Αἰνείου πλησίον τοῦ μικροῦ θεάτρου, ἐν ᾧ καὶ ξόανον μικρὸν ἀρχαϊκὸν Αἰνείου λεγόμενον, καὶ αὐτὸ θυσίαις ἐγέραιρον αἱ καλούμεναι παρ' αὐτοῖς ἀμφίπολοι.

In memory, therefore, of this kinship and by reason of the kindness of the inhabitants they stayed there some time, being also detained by unfavorable weather; and they offered to Aphrodite at the *hieron* they had built to her a sacrifice which the Zacynthians perform in common to this day, and instituted games for young men, consisting among other events of a footrace in which the one who comes first to the *neos* gains the prize. This is called the course of Aeneas and Aphrodite, and *xoana* of both are erected there. From there, after a voyage through the open sea, they landed at Leucas, which was still in the possession of the Acarnanians. Here again they built a *hieron* to Aphrodite, which stands today on the little island between Dioryctus and the city; it is called the [*hieron*] of Aphrodite Aeneias. And departing thence, they sailed to Actium and anchored off the promontory of the Ambracian Gulf; and from there they came to the city of Ambracia, which was then ruled by Ambrax, the son of Dexamenus, the son of Heracles. Monuments of their coming are left in both places: at Actium, the *hieron* of Aphrodite Aeneias, and near to it that of the Great Gods, both of which existed even to my time; and in Ambracia, a *hieron* of the same goddess and a *heroon* of Aeneas near the little theater, in which there was a small, *archaikon xoanon* said to be of Aeneas, that was honored with sacrifices by the priestesses they called *amphipoloi.*

66

Dionysius of Halicarnassus 2.18.2 I B.C.–A.D. I

Text: K. Jacoby, ed., *Dionysii Halicarnasei antiquitatum romanarum quae supersunt* I (Leipzig, 1885; repr. Stuttgart, 1967).

Translation adapted from E. Cary, tr., *The Roman Antiquities of Dionysius of Halicarnassus* I (LCL, 1937).

(See also Eusebius, *Praeparatio evangelica* 2.8.78 b [**103**].)

ἱερὰ μὲν οὖν καὶ τεμένη καὶ βωμοὺς καὶ ξοάνων ἱδρύσεις μορφάς τε αὐτῶν καὶ σύμβολα καὶ δυνάμεις καὶ δωρεάς, αἷς τὸ γένος ἡμῶν εὐηργέτησαν, ἑορτάς τε ὁποίας τινὰς ἑκάστῳ θεῶν ἢ δαιμόνων ἄγεσθαι προσήκει καὶ θυσίας, αἷς χαίρουσι γεραιρόμενοι πρὸς ἀνθρώπων, ἐκεχειρίας τε αὖ καὶ πανηγύρεις καὶ πόνων ἀναπαύλας καὶ πάντα τὰ τοιαῦτα ὁμοίως κατεστήσατο τοῖς κρατίστοις τῶν παρ' Ἕλλησι νομίμων. . . .

He [Romulus] established *hiera* and *temene* and *bomoi*, arranged for the setting up of *xoana*, determined the shapes and symbols of [the gods], and declared their powers, the beneficent gifts which they have made to mankind, the particular festivals that should be celebrated in honor of each god or *daimon*, the sacrifices with which they delight to be honored by men, as well as the holidays, festal assemblies, days of rest, and everything alike of that nature, in all of which he followed the best customs in use among the Greeks.

67

Dionysius of Halicarnassus 4.40.7 I B.C.–A.D. I

Text: K. Jacoby, ed., *Dionysii Halicarnasei antiquitatum romanarum quae supersunt* II (Leipzig, 1888; repr. Stuttgart, 1967).

Translation adapted from E. Cary, tr., *The Roman Antiquities of Dionysius of Halicarnassus* II (LCL, 1939).

ἐδήλωσε δέ τι καὶ ἄλλο δαιμόνιον ἔργον, ὅτι θεοφιλὴς ἦν ἀνήρ, ἐξ οὗ καὶ ἡ περὶ τῆς γενέσεως αὐτοῦ μυθικὴ καὶ ἄπιστος ὑπόληψις, ὥσπερ εἴρηταί μοι πρότερον, ἀληθὴς εἶναι ὑπὸ πολλῶν ἐπιστεύθη. ἐν γὰρ τῷ ναῷ τῆς Τύχης, ὃν αὐτὸς κατεσκεύασεν, εἰκὼν αὐτοῦ κειμένη ξυλίνη κατάχρυσος ἐμπρήσεως γενομένης καὶ τῶν ἄλλων ἁπάντων διαφθαρέντων μόνη διέμεινεν οὐδὲν λωβηθεῖσα ὑπὸ τοῦ πυρός. καὶ ἔτι νῦν ὁ μὲν νεὼς καὶ τὰ ἐν αὐτῷ πάντα, ὅσα μετὰ τὴν ἔμπρησιν εἰς τὸν ἀρχαῖον κόσμον ἐπετελέσθη φανερά, ὅτι τῆς καινῆς ἐστι τέχνης, ἡ δ' εἰκών, οἵα πρότερον ἦν, ἀρχαικὴ τὴν κατασκευήν· διαμένει γὰρ ἔτι σεβασμοῦ τυγχάνουσα ὑπὸ Ῥωμαίων. καὶ περὶ μὲν Τυλλίου τοσαῦτα παρελάβομεν.

And it was made clear by another prodigy that this man was dear to the gods; in consequence of which that fabulous and incredible opinion I have already mentioned concerning his birth also came to be regarded by many as true. For in the *naos* of Fortune which he himself had built there stood a gilded wooden *eikon* of Tullius, and when a conflagration occurred and everything else was destroyed, it alone remained uninjured by the flames. And even to this day, although the *neos* itself and all the objects in it, which were restored to their former condition after the fire, are obviously the products of modern art, the *eikon*, as aforetime, is of *archaike* workmanship; for it still remains an object of veneration by the Romans. Concerning Tullius these are all the facts that have been handed down to us.

68

Dionysius of Halicarnassus 6.69.1 — I B.C.–A.D. I

Text: K. Jacoby, ed., *Dionysii Halicarnasei antiquitatum romanarum quae supersunt* II (Leipzig, 1888; repr. Stuttgart, 1967).

Translation adapted from E. Cary, tr., *The Roman Antiquities of Dionysius of Halicarnassus* IV (LCL, 1943).

Ταῦτ' εἰπὼν ἐπαύσατο. ἐπεὶ δ' αἱ τῶν πρεσβυτέρων γνῶμαι τῇ Μενηνίου προσέθεντο, καὶ καθῆκεν ὁ λόγος ἐπὶ τοὺς νεωτέρους, ὀρθῆς οὔσης ἁπάσης τῆς βουλῆς ἀνίσταται Σπόριος Ναύτιος, οἰκίας ἐν τοῖς πάνυ λαμπροτάτης διάδοχος· ὁ γὰρ ἡγεμὼν αὐτῶν τοῦ γένους Ναύτιος ἀπὸ τῶν σὺν Αἰνείᾳ στειλάντων τὴν ἀποικίαν, ὃς ἦν Ἀθηνᾶς ἱερεὺς Πολιάδος καὶ τὸ ξόανον ἀπηνέγκατο τῆς θεᾶς μετανιστάμενος, ὃ διεφύλαττον ἄλλοι παρ' ἄλλων μεταλαμβάνοντες οἱ τοῦ γένους ὄντες τοῦ Ναυτίων· ὃς ἐδόκει καὶ διὰ τὴν οἰκείαν ἀρετὴν λαμπρότατος εἶναι τῶν νέων, καὶ οὐκ εἰς μακρὰν τῆς ὑπατικῆς ἐξουσίας τεύξεσθαι.

Having said this, he ended. When the opinions of the older senators agreed with that of Menenius and it came to the turn of the younger members to speak, the whole senate being on tip-toe with suspense, Spurius Nautius rose up, the heir of a most illustrious family. For Nautius, the founder of the line, was one of those who took out the colony with the Aeneas, being a priest of Athena Polias; and when he removed it [from Troy], he brought with him the *xoanon* of the goddess, which the family of the Nautii guarded thereafter, receiving it in succession from one another. This man was esteemed the most illustrious of all the younger senators for his own merit as well, and it was expected that he would soon obtain the consulship.

69

Dionysius of Halicarnassus 8.39.1 I B.C.–A.D. I

Text: K. Jacoby, ed., *Dionysii Halicarnasei antiquitatum romanarum quae supersunt* III (Leipzig, 1891; repr. Stuttgart, 1967).

Translation adapted from E. Cary, tr., *The Roman Antiquities of Dionysius of Halicarnassus* V (LCL, 1945).

Αἱ δὲ γυναῖκες αὐτῶν, ὡς ἐγγὺς ὄντος ἤδη τοῦ δεινοῦ, καταλιποῦσαι τῆς οἴκοι μονῆς τὸ εὐπρεπὲς ἔθεον ἐπὶ τὰ τεμένη τῶν θεῶν ὀλοφυρόμεναί τε καὶ προκυλιόμεναι τῶν ξοάνων· καὶ ἦν ἅπας μὲν ἱερὸς τόπος οἰμωγῆς τε καὶ ἱκετείας γυναικῶν ἀνάπλεως, μάλιστα δὲ τὸ τοῦ Καπετωλίου Διὸς ἱερόν.

In the meantime their wives, seeing the danger now at hand and abandoning the sense of propriety that kept them in the seclusion of their homes, ran to the *temene* of the gods with lamentations and threw themselves at the feet of the of the *xoana*. And every holy place, particularly the *hieron* of Jupiter Capitolinus, was filled with the cries and supplications of women.

70

Dionysius of Halicarnassus 8.55.3–4 I B.C.–A.D. I

Text: K. Jacoby, ed., *Dionysii Halicarnasei antiquitatum romanarum quae supersunt* III (Leipzig, 1891; repr. Stuttgart, 1967).

Translation adapted from E. Cary, tr., *The Roman Antiquities of Dionysius of Halicarnassus* V (LCL, 1945).

ταῖς δὲ γυναιξὶ βουλευσαμέναις εἰσῆλθεν ἐπιφθόνου μὲν δωρεᾶς μηδεμιᾶς δεῖσθαι, ἀξιοῦν δ' ἐπιτρέψαι σφίσι τὴν βουλὴν ἐπὶ τύχης γυναικῶν ἱδρύσασθαι ἱερόν, ἐν ᾧ τὰς περὶ τῆς πόλεως ἐποιήσαντο λιτὰς χωρίῳ, θυσίας τε καθ' ἕκαστον ἔτος αὐτῇ συνιούσας ἐπιτελεῖν ἐν ᾗ τὸν πόλεμον ἔλυσαν ἡμέρᾳ. ἡ μέντοι βουλὴ καὶ ὁ δῆμος ἀπὸ τῶν κοινῶν ἐψηφίσαντο χρημάτων τέμενός τ' ὠνηθὲν καθιερωθῆναι τῇ θεῷ, καὶ ἐν αὐτῷ νεὼν καὶ βωμόν, ὡς ἂν οἱ ἱερομνήμονες ἐξηγῶνται, συντελεσθῆναι, θυσίας τε προσάγεσθαι δημοτελεῖς καταρχομένης τῶν ἱερῶν γυναικός, ἣν ἂν ἀποδείξωσιν αὐταὶ λειτουργὸν τῶν ἱερῶν. ταῦτα τῆς βουλῆς ψηφισαμένης ἱέρεια μὲν ὑπὸ τῶν γυναικῶν ἀπεδείχθη τότε πρῶτον ἡ τὴν γνώμην αὐταῖς εἰσηγησαμένη περὶ τῆς πρεσβείας Οὐαλερία καὶ τὴν μητέρα τοῦ Μαρκίου πείσασα συλλαβέσθαι σφίσι τῆς ἐξόδου. θυσίαν δὲ πρώτην αἱ γυναῖκες ἔθυσαν ὑπὲρ τοῦ δήμου καταρχομένης τῶν ἱερῶν τῆς Οὐαλερίας ἐπὶ τοῦ κατασκευασθέντος ἐν τῷ τεμένει βωμοῦ, πρὶν ἢ τὸν νεὼν καὶ τὸ ξόανον ἀνασταθῆναι, μηνὶ Δεκεμβρίῳ τοῦ κατόπιν ἐνιαυτοῦ, τῇ νέᾳ σελήνῃ, ἣν Ἕλληνες μὲν νουμηνίαν, Ῥωμαῖοι δὲ καλάνδας καλοῦσιν· αὕτη γὰρ ἦν ἡ λύσασα τὸν πόλεμον ἡμέρα.

It occurred to the women after some deliberation to ask for no indivious gift, but to request of the senate permission to found a *hieron* to Fortuna Muliebris on the spot where they had interceded for their country, and to assemble and perform annual sacrifices to her on the day on which they had put an end to the war. However, the senate and the people decreed that from the public funds a *temenos* should be purchased and consecrated to the goddess, and a *neos* and *bomos* erected in it, in such manner as the pontiffs should direct, and that sacrifices should be performed at the public expense, the initial ceremonies to be conducted by a woman, whichever one the women themselves should choose to officiate at the rites. The senate having passed this decree, the woman then chosen by the others to be priestess for the first time was Valeria, who had proposed to them the embassy and had persuaded the mother of Marcius to join the others in going out of the city. The first sacrifice was performed on behalf of the city by the women, Valeria beginning the rites, upon the altar raised in the *temenos*, before the *neos* and the *xoanon* were erected, in the month of December of the following year, on the day of the new moon, which the Greeks call *noumenia* and the Romans *calends*; for this was the day that had put an end to the war.

71

Dionysius of Halicarnassus 8.56.2–4 I B.C.–A.D. I

Text: K. Jacoby, ed., *Dionysii Halicarnasei antiquitatum romanarum quae supersunt* III (Leipzig, 1891; repr. Stuttgart, 1967).

Translation adapted from E. Cary, tr., *The Roman Antiquities of Dionysius of Halicarnassus* V (LCL, 1945).

ἱστορεῖται τοίνυν, ὅτι τῆς βουλῆς ψηφισαμένης ἐκ τοῦ δημοσίου πάσας ἐπιχορηγηθῆναι τὰς εἰς τὸν νεών τε καὶ τὸ ξόανον δαπάνας, ἕτερον δ' ἄγαλμα κατασκευασαμένων τῶν γυναικῶν ἀφ' ὧν αὐταὶ συνήνεγκαν χρημάτων, ἀνατεθέντων τ' αὐτῶν ἀμφοτέρων ἅμα ἐν τῇ πρώτῃ τῆς ἀνιερώσεως ἡμέρᾳ, θάτερον τῶν ἀφιδρυμάτων, ὃ κατεσκευάσανθ' αἱ γυναῖκες, ἐφθέγξατο πολλῶν παρουσῶν γλώττῃ Λατίνῃ φωνὴν εὐσύνετόν τε καὶ γεγωνόν· ἧς ἐστι φωνῆς ἐξερμηνευόμενος ὁ νοῦς εἰς τὴν Ἑλλάδα διάλεκτον τοιόσδε· Ὁσίῳ πόλεως νόμῳ γυναῖκες γαμεταὶ δεδώκατέ με. οἷα δὲ φιλεῖ γίνεσθαι περὶ τὰς παραδόξους φωνάς τε καὶ ὄψεις, πολλὴ ταῖς παρούσαις ἐνέπιπτεν ἀπιστία, μή ποτ' οὐ τὸ ξόανον εἴη τὸ φθεγξάμενον, ἀνθρωπίνη δέ τις φωνή· μάλιστα δ' ὅσαι πρὸς ἄλλῳ τινὶ τὸν νοῦν ἔχουσαι τηνικαῦτα ἔτυχον, οὐκ ἰδοῦσαι τὸ φθεγγόμενον, ὅ τι ποτ' ἦν, ταύτην εἶχον τὴν πρὸς τὰς ἰδούσας ἀπιστίαν. ἔπειτ' αὖθις πληθύοντος τοῦ νεὼ καὶ σιωπῆς πλείστης κατὰ δαίμονα γενομένης ἐν μείζονι φωνῇ ταὐτὸ ξόανον ἐφθέγξατο τὴν αὐτὴν λέξιν, ὥστε μηδὲν ἔτι εἶναι τὸ ἀμφίλογον. ἡ μὲν οὖν βουλὴ ὡς ταῦτ' ἔμαθεν ἐψηφίσατο θυσίας ἄλλας καὶ σεβασμούς, οὓς ἂν οἱ τῶν ἱερῶν ἐξηγηταὶ παραδῶσι καθ' ἕκαστον ἔτος ἐπιτελεῖν. αἱ δὲ γυναῖκες ἐν ἔθει κατεστήσαντο τῇ τῆς ἱερείας χρησάμεναι γνώμῃ, τῷ ξοάνῳ τούτῳ μήτε στεφάνους ἐπιτιθέναι μήτε χεῖρας προσφέρειν γυναῖκας, ὅσαι δευτέρων ἐπειράθησαν γάμων, τὴν δὲ τιμὴν καὶ θεραπείαν αὐτοῦ πᾶσαν ἀποδεδόσθαι ταῖς νεογάμοις. ἀλλὰ περὶ μὲν τούτων οὔτε παρελθεῖν τὴν ἐπιχώριον ἱστορίαν καλῶς εἶχεν, οὔτε πλείονα περὶ αὐτῆς ποιεῖσθαι λόγον. ἐπάνειμι δ', ὅθεν εἰς τοῦτον ἐξέβην τὸν λόγον.

It is related, then, that when the senate had ordered that the whole expense of both the *neos* and the *xoanon* should be defrayed from the public treasury, and the women had caused another *agalma* to be made with the money they themselves had contributed, and both *agalmata* had been set up together on the first day of the dedication, one of them, the one which the women had provided, uttered some words in Latin in a voice both distinct and loud, when many were present. The meaning of the words when translated into the Greek language is as follows: "You have conformed to the holy law of the city, matrons, in dedicating me." The women who were present were very incredulous, as usually happens in the case of unusual voices and sights, believing that it was not the *xoanon* that had spoken, but some human voice; and those particularly who happened at the moment to have their mind on something else and did not see what it was that spoke, showed this incredulity toward those who had seen it. Later, on a second occasion, when the *neos* was full and there chanced to be a profound silence, the same *xoanon* pronounced the same words in a louder voice, so that there was no longer any doubt about it. The senate, upon hearing what had passed, ordered other sacrifices and rites to be performed every year, such as the interpreters of religious rites should direct. And the women upon the advice of their priestess established it as a custom that no women who had been married a second time should crown this *xoanon* with garlands or touch it with their hands, but that all the honor and worship paid to it should be committed to the newly-married women. But concerning these matters it was fitting that I should neither omit the native account nor dwell too long upon it. I return now to the point from which I digressed.

72

Dionysius of Halicarnassus 13.III.(3) I B.C.–A.D. I
Text: K. Jacoby, ed., *Dionysii Halicarnasei antiquitatum romanarum quae supersunt* IV (Leipzig, 1905; repr. Stuttgart, 1967).
Translation adapted from E. Cary, tr., *The Roman Antiquities of Dionysius of Halicarnassus* VII (LCL, 1950).

Ὁ αὐτὸς Κάμιλλος ἐπὶ τὴν Οὐιεντανῶν πόλιν στρατεύων ηὔξατο τῇ βασιλείᾳ Ἥρᾳ τῇ ἐν Οὐιεντανοῖς, ἐὰν κρατήσῃ τῆς πόλεως τό τε ξόανον αὐτῆς ἐν Ῥώμῃ καθιδρύσειν καὶ σεβασμοὺς αὐτῇ καταστήσεσθαι πολυτελεῖς. ἁλούσης δὲ τῆς πόλεως ἀπέστειλε τῶν ἱππέων τοὺς ἐπιφανεστάτους ἀρουμένους ἐκ τῶν βάθρων τὸ ἕδος· ὡς δὲ παρῆλθον οἱ πεμφθέντες εἰς τὸν νεών, καί τις ἐξ αὐτῶν εἴτε μετὰ παιδιᾶς καὶ γέλωτος εἴτε οἰωνοῦ δεόμενος, εἰ βούλοιτο μετελθεῖν εἰς Ῥώμην ἡ θεός, ἤρετο, φωνῇ γεγωνῷ τὸ ξόανον ἐφθέγξατο, ὅτι βούλεται. τοῦτο καὶ δὶς γέγονεν· ἀπιστοῦντες γὰρ οἱ νεανίσκοι, εἰ τὸ ξόανον ἦν τὸ φθεγξάμενον, πάλιν ἤροντο τὸ αὐτὸ καὶ τὴν αὐτὴν φωνὴν ἤκουσαν.

This same Camillus, when conducting his campaign against Veii, made a vow to Queen Hera of the Veientes that if he should take the city he would set up her *xoanon* in Rome and establish costly rites in her honor. Upon the capture of the city, accordingly, he sent the most distinguished of the *hippeis* to remove the *hedos* from its pedestal; and when those who had been sent came into the *neos* and one of them, either in jest and sport or desiring an omen, asked whether the goddess wished to remove to Rome, the *xoanon* answered in a loud voice that she did. This happened twice; for the young men, doubting whether it was the *xoanon* that had spoken, asked the same question again and heard the same reply.

73

Epiphanius, *Panarion* (= *Adversus haereses*) 2.4–5 A.D. 374–377
Text: K. Holl, ed., *Epiphanius* I. *Ancoratus und Panarion* (GCS 25; Leipzig, 1915) 174.21–175.5.

Ἀδὰμ γὰρ <ὁ> πρωτόπλαστος πέπλασται οὐκ ἐμπερίτομος, ἀλλ᾽ ἀκροβύστης μὲν τῇ σαρκί, οὐκ εἰδωλολάτρης δὲ ἦν καὶ ᾔδει πατέρα θεὸν καὶ υἱὸν καὶ ἅγιον πνεῦμα· προφήτης γὰρ ἦν. οὐκ ἔχων τοίνυν περιτομὴν οὐκ ἦν Ἰουδαῖος, ξόανα δὲ μὴ προσκυνῶν ἢ ἄλλο τι οὐκ ἦν εἰδωλολάτρης· προφήτης γὰρ <ἦν> ὁ Ἀδὰμ καὶ ᾔδει ὅτι ὁ πατὴρ εἶπε τῷ υἱῷ "ποιήσωμεν ἄνθρωπον".

For Adam the first-formed was formed not circumcised, but uncircumcised in the flesh; and he was not an idolater and knew God the Father and Son and Holy Spirit; for he was a prophet. Therefore, not having circumcision he was not a Jew, and not worshipping *xoana* or any other thing he was not an idolater; for Adam [was] a prophet and knew that the Father said to the Son, "We shall make man."

74

Epiphanius, *Panarion* (= *Adversus haereses*) 3.4 A.D. 374–377
Text: K. Holl, ed., *Epiphanius* I. *Ancoratus und Panarion* (GCS 25; Leipzig, 1915) 177.11–18.

Φαλὲκ δὲ γεννᾷ τὸν Ῥαγαῦ, Ῥαγαῦ τὸν Σεροὺχ τὸν ἑρμηνευόνενον ἐρεθισμόν, ἀφ' οὗ ἤρξατο εἰς ἀνθρώπους ἡ εἰδωλολατρεία τε καὶ ὁ Ἑλληνισμός, ὡς ἡ ἐλθοῦσα εἰς ἡμᾶς γνῶσις περιέχει. οὔπω δὲ ἐν ξοάνοις καὶ ἐν τορείαις λίθων ἢ ξύλων ἢ ἀργυροτεύκτων ἢ <ἐκ> χρυσοῦ ἢ ἄλλης τινὸς ὕλης πεποιημέναις, μόνον δὲ διὰ χρωμάτων καὶ εἰκόνων ἡ τοῦ ἀνθρώπου διάνοια ἑαυτῇ ἐφηύρατο τὴν κακίαν καὶ διὰ τοῦ αὐτεξουσίου καὶ λογιότητος καὶ νοῦ ἀντὶ τῆς ἀγαθότητος τὸ παράνομον ἐφηύρατο.

And Phalek begat Rhagau, [and] Rhagau [begat] Serouch who proclaimed rebelliousness, from which began among men both idolatry and Hellenism, as the knowledge that has come among us says. But not yet in the *xoana* and in the carvings in relief that have been made of stones or stocks or wrought silver things or [out of] gold or any other material, but only through colors and *eikones* has the mind of man discovered evil, and through a free and very learned mind discovered the unlawful instead of the best.

75

Epiphanius, *Panarion* (= *Adversus haereses*) 51.22.9–10 A.D. 374–377
Text: K. Holl, ed., *Epiphanius* I. *Ancoratus und Panarion* (GCS 25; Leipzig, 1915) 285.12–286.7.

πρῶτον μὲν ἐν Ἀλεξανδρείᾳ ἐν τῷ Κορείῳ <οὕ>τω καλουμένῳ· ναὸς δέ ἐστι μέγιστος τουτέστιν τὸ τέμενος τῆς Κόρης. ὅλην γὰρ τὴν νύκτα ἀγρυπνήσαντες ἐν ᾄσμασί τισι καὶ αὐλοῖς τῷ εἰδώλῳ ᾄδοντες καὶ παννυχίδα διατελέσαντες μετὰ τὴν τῶν ἀλεκτρυόνων κλαγγὴν κατέρχονται λαμπαδηφόροι εἰς σηκόν τινα ὑπόγαιον καὶ ἀναφέρουσι ξόανόν τι ξύλινον <ἐν> φορείῳ καθεζόμενον γυμνόν, ἔχον σφραγῖδά τινα σταυροῦ ἐπὶ τοῦ μετώπου διάχρυσον καὶ ἐπὶ ταῖς ἑκατέραις χερσὶν ἄλλας δύο τοιαύτας σφραγῖδας καὶ ἐπ' αὐτοῖς τοῖς δυσὶ γονάτοις ἄλλας δύο, ὁμοῦ δὲ [τὰς] πέντε σφραγῖδας ἀπὸ χρυσοῦ τετυπωμένας, καὶ περιφέρουσιν αὐτὸ τὸ ξόανον ἑπτάκις κυκλώσαντες τὸν μεσαίτατον ναὸν μετὰ αὐλῶν καὶ τυμπάνων καὶ ὕμνων καὶ κωμάσαντες καταφέρουσιν αὐτὸ αὖθις εἰς τὸν ὑπόγαιον τόπον. ἐρωτώμενοι δὲ ὅτι τί ἐστι τοῦτο τὸ μυστήριον ἀποκρίνονται καὶ λέγουσιν ὅτι ταύτῃ τῇ ὥρᾳ σήμερον ἡ Κόρη (τουτέστιν ἡ παρθένος) ἐγέννησε τὸν Αἰῶνα.

At first in Alexandria in the so-called *Koreion*; there is a very large *neos*, that is to say the *temenos* of Kore. For, passing an entire sleepless night in some sort of hymns and worshipping the *eidolon* with flutes and continuing in an all-night festival, after the crow of the cocks the torch-bearers go down into a sort of underground *sekos* and bring up a sort of naked wooden *xoanon* sitting [in] a litter, which has a kind of seal of a cross interwoven in gold on its forehead, and in each of its hands two such other seals, and on its two knees another two, the five seals alike having been modelled out of gold, and they carry this *xoanon* around seven times, circling the innermost *naos*, with flutes and drums and hymns, and, having revelled, they bring it back down again into the underground place. When they have been asked why this secret rite is, they reply and say that at this same hour Kore (that is to say the virgin) brought forth Aion.

76

Etymologicum Genuinum s.v. βρέτας A.D. IX

Text: G. Berger, ed., *Etymologicum Genuinum et Etymologicum Symeonis* (*β*) (R. Merkelbach, ed., Beiträge zur klassischen Philologie 45; Meisenheim am Glan, 1972) 136. *β*216.

βρέτας· παρὰ τὸ βροτὸς βρέτας κατὰ τροπήν, τὸ βροτοειδὲς ἄγαλμα. κυρίως δὲ τὸ ἀπὸ ξύλου πεποιημένον ἀνθρώπου ἄγαλμα.

Bretas: Derived from *brotos* [mortal], *bretas* by a change, an *agalma* looking like a mortal. Especially an *agalma* of a man made out of wood.

77

Etymologicum Genuinum s.v. βρέτας A.D. IX

Text: G. Berger, ed., *Etymologicum Genuinum et Etymologicum Symeonis* (*β*) (R. Merkelbach, ed., Beiträge zur klassischen Philologie 45; Meisenheim am Glan, 1972) 135. *β*251.

βρέτας· εἴρηται παρὰ τὸ βροτὸς βρέτας κατὰ τροπήν, οἷον τὸ βροτοειδὲς ἄγαλμα. κυρίως δὲ τὸ ἀπὸ ξύλου πεποιημένον ἀνθρώπου ἄγαλμα.

Bretas: It is said to be derived from *brotos* [mortal], *bretas* by a change, a kind of *agalma* that looks like a mortal. Especially an *agalma* of a man made out of wood.

78

Etymologicum Gudianum s.v. Ἄγαλμα C. A.D. 1100

Text: E.L. de Stefani, ed., *Etymologicum Gudianum quod vocatur* I (Leipzig, 1909) 6.21.

Ἄγαλμα· ἐκ τοῦ ἀγάλλω· ἐν ᾧ ἀγάλλεταί τις κἄν τε ἱμάτιον ᾖ κἄν τε εἰκών. καὶ εἰς τὸ Ξόανον.

Agalma: From *agallo* [to glory]; something in which one glories, whether it be a *himation* or an *eikon*. See also *Xoanon*.

79

Etymologicum Gudianum s.v. Ἀγάλματα c. A.D. 1100
Text: E.L. de Stefani, ed., *Etymologicum Gudianum quod vocatur* I (Leipzig, 1909) 6.15.

Ἀγάλματα· ξόανα, ἀφομοιώματα, εἰκόνες ἢ ἀνδριάντες κεράμειοι, κολοσ<σ>οί, βρέτας, χαρακτήρ, [ὅ ἐστιν] εἴδωλον.

Agalmata: *xoana*, copies, *eikones* or terracotta *andriantes*, *kolossoi*, *bretas*, *character*, [which is] *eidolon*.

80

Etymologicum Gudianum s.v. Βρέτας (1) c. A.D. 1100
Text: E.L. de Stefani, ed., *Etymologicum Gudianum quod vocatur* I (Leipzig, 1909) 286.12.
(= F.W. Sturz, ed., *Etymologicum graecae linguae Gudianum et alia grammaticorum scripta* [Leipzig, 1818] 115.6.)

N̄ Βρέτας· εἴδωλον ἢ ξόανον σημαίνει, καὶ γέγονεν οὕτως· ἔστι βρ[ετ]ῶ, τὸ σημαῖνον τὸ φθείρω, ἐξ οὗ βροτός, καὶ ἐκ τοῦ βροτός βρέτας. ἔστι δὲ ἄκλιτον. καὶ εἰς τὸ Ξόανον.

Bretas means *eidolon* or *xoanon*, and it comes about in this way: there is *breto*, which means "destroy," from which comes *brotos* [mortal], and from *brotos* comes *bretas*. It is indeclinable. See also *Xoanon*.

Etymologicum Gudianum s.v. Βρέτας (2) c. A.D. 1100
Text: F.W. Sturz, ed., *Etymologicum graecae linguae Gudianum et alia grammaticorum scripta* (Leipzig, 1818) 115.10.

Βρέτας, παρὰ τὸ βροτῷ ἐοικέναι, ἢ παρὰ τὸ βροτοῖς ἀπεικονίζεσθαι. κυρίως δὲ τὸ ἀπὸ ξύλου πεποιημένον ἀνθρώπου ἄγαλμα.

Bretas, derived from looking like a *brotos* [mortal], or from representing mortals. Especially an *agalma* of a man made out of wood.

81

Etymologicum Gudianum s.v. Ξόανον (1) c. A.D. 1100
Text: F.W. Sturz, ed., *Etymologicum graecae linguae Gudianum et alia grammaticorum scripta* (Leipzig, 1818) 415.55.

Ξόανον, παρὰ τὸ ξέω ξέανον καὶ ξόανον.

Xoanon, derived from *xeo*, *xeanon* and *xoanon*.

82

Etymologicum Gudianum s.v. Ξόανον (2) c. A.D. 1100
Text: F.W. Sturz, ed., *Etymologicum graecae linguae Gudianum et alia grammaticorum scripta* (Leipzig, 1818) 415.56.

Ξόανον, καὶ βρέτας καὶ εἴδωλον διαφέρει· ξόανον μὲν γὰρ ἐστι τὸ ἐξεσμένον εἴδωλον, λίθινον ἢ ἐλεφάντινον ἢ ξύλινον· βρέτας δὲ τῷ βροτῷ ὅμοιον, ἤτοι χαλκοῦν, ἢ ἐξ ἐμφεροῦς ὕλης πεποιημένον· ἄγαλμα δὲ τὸ παρὰ μηρὸν, ἢ ἐκ τινὸς ἑτέρου λίθου κατασκευασμένον.

Xoanon, and *bretas* and *eidolon* are different; for a *xoanon* is a carved *eidolon*, stone or ivory or wooden; while a *bretas* is something like a *brotos* [mortal], whether bronze, or made out of a similar material; and an *agalma* is fashioned of [marble] or out of some other stone.

83

Etymologicum Magnum s.v. Ἄγαλμα ? A.D. XII
Text: T. Gaisford, ed., *Etymologicon Magnum* (Oxford, 1848) 5.35.

Ἄγαλμα: Ἀγαλλίαμα, καλλώπισμα, [παν] ἐφ' ᾧ τὶς ἀγάλλεται καὶ χαίρει, κἄν τε ἱμάτιον ᾖ, κἄν τε εἰκών· οἱ δὲ μεθ' Ὅμηρον ποιηταὶ ἄγαλμα εἶπον τὸ ξόανον. [Τὸ δὲ ἄγαλμα παρὰ τὸ ἀγάλλω].

Agalma: Transport of joy, ornament, [everything] in which one glories and takes pleasure, whether it be a *himation* or an *eikon*. The poets after Homer call an *agalma* a *xoanon*.
[*Agalma* is derived from *agallo*].

84

Etymologicum Magnum s.v. Ξόανον ? A.D. XII
Text: T. Gaisford, ed., *Etymologicon Magnum* (Oxford, 1848) 611.12.

Ξόανον: Παρὰ τὸ ξέω ξέανον· καὶ τροπῇ, ξόανον. Διαφέρει δὲ ξόανον, καὶ βρέτας, καὶ ἄγαλμα. Ξόανον μὲν γάρ ἐστι τὸ ἐξεσμένον εἴδωλον, λίθινον, ἢ ἐλεφάντινον, ἢ ξύλινον· Βρέτας δὲ, τὸ βροτῷ ὅμοιον, ἤτοι χαλκοῦν, ἢ ἐξ ἐμφεροῦς ὕλης πεποιημένον· Ἄγαλμα δὲ, τὸ παράμηρον, ἢ ἔκ τινος ἑτέρου λίθου κατεσκευασμένον.

Xoanon: derived from *xeo*, *xeanon* and by a change, *xoanon*. *Xoanon* and *bretas* and *agalma* are different. For *xoanon* is a carved *eidolon*, stone or ivory or wooden; a *bretas*, on the other hand, is like a *brotos* [mortal], either bronze or made of a similar material; while an *agalma* is made of [marble] or of some other stone.

85
Etymologicum Magnum Auctum s.v. *ἄγαλμα*
Text: F. Lasserre and N. Livadaras, eds., *Etymologicum Magnum Genuinum. Symeonis Etymologicum una cum magna grammatica Etymologicum Magnum Auctum* I (Rome, 1976) 19.49.

ἄγαλμα· ἀγαλλίαμα, καλλώπισμα, ἐφ' ᾧ τις ἀγάλλεται καὶ χαίρει κἄν τε ἱμάτιον ᾖ, κἄν τε εἰκών. οἱ δὲ μεθ' Ὅμηρον ποιηταὶ ἄγαλμα εἶπον τὸ ξόανον.

Agalma: Transport of joy, ornament, in which one glories and takes pleasure, whether it be a *himation* or an *eikon*. The poets after Homer call an *agalma* a *xoanon*.

Eubulus fr. 22 Kock
See Aristotle, *De anima* 1.3, 406 b 9 [**30**], and Themistius *ad loc.* [**363**].

Euphorion III B.C.
See Sch. Apollonius Rhodius I.1117 [**26**].

86
Sch. Euripides, *Hecuba* 838
Text: W. Dindorf, ed., *Scholia Graeca in Euripidis Tragoedias* I (Oxford, 1863).

Δαιδάλου τέχναισι: περὶ τῶν Δαιδάλου ἔργων ὅτι ἐκινεῖτο καὶ προΐει φωνὴν αὐτός τε ὁ Εὐριπίδης ἐν Εὐρυσθεῖ λέγει,

οὐκ ἔστιν, ὦ γεραιέ, μὴ δείσῃς τάδε·
τὰ Δαιδάλεια πάντα κινεῖσθαι δοκεῖ
βλέπειν τ' ἀγάλμαθ'· ὧδ' ἀνὴρ κεῖνος σοφός.

καὶ Κρατῖνος ἐν Θρᾴτταις "Πανὶ κακὸν δεῦρο μαστεύων τινὰ ποτὲ χαλκοῦν ἢ ξύλινον καὶ χρύσεον προσῆν, οὐδαμῶς ξύλινος ἐκεῖνος, ἀλλὰ χαλκοῦς ὢν ἀπέδρα. πότερον Δαιδάλειος ἦν, ἢ τίς ἐξέκλεψεν αὐτόν;" καὶ Πλάτων

A. *οὗτος, τίς εἶ; λέγε ταχύ· τί σιγᾷς; οὐκ ἐρεῖς:*
B. *Ἑρμῆς ἔγωγε Δαιδάλου φωνὴν ἔχων*
ξύλινος βαδίζων αὐτόματος ἐλήλυθα.

Δαιδάλου τέχναισι: ἀγαλματοποιὸς ὁ Δαίδαλος, ποιῶν ἀγάλματα οὕτω κάλλιστα ὡς ἱστορηθῆναι περὶ τούτων τοῖς ποιηταῖς ὅτι φωνὴν ἠφίεσαν καὶ ἐκινοῦντο. οὗτος δὲ ὁ Δαίδαλος καὶ πτερὰ, ὅτε ἐβούλετο, περιετίθει ἑαυτῷ καὶ ἵπτατο. ἐπεὶ καὶ τὸν υἱὸν Ἴκαρον, ἐκ κηροῦ πτερὰ πλασάμενος καὶ περιθεὶς αὐτῷ, ἐποίησεν ἐναέριον κομισθῆναι. διαλυθέντος δὲ τοῦ κηροῦ πέπτωκεν εἰς τὸ νῦν ἀπ' αὐτοῦ καλούμενον Ἰκάριον πέλαγος. φασὶ γὰρ ἀμυνόνεμον τὸν Ἥλιον Δαίδαλον, ὡς πεποιηκότα τὴν θυγατέρα αὐτοῦ Πασιφάην, ἐρασθεῖσαν ταύρου, μιγῆναι αὐτῷ, ἐπεὶ τότε πετόμενον εἶδε τὸν υἱὸν αὐτοῦ Ἴκαρον, ἐκ κηροῦ πτεροῖς χρώμενον, σφοδρῶς ἐμπεσεῖν τοῖς πτεροῖς, καὶ διαλυθῆναι ταῦτα παρασκευάσαι, καὶ τὸν ἐν τούτοις κουφιζόμενον Ἴκαρον κατενεχθέντα πεπνίχθαι. Δαιδάλου: ὃς καὶ τὰ εἴδωλα ἐποίει καὶ κινεῖσθαι καὶ λαλεῖν. ὁ Δαίδαλος ἀνὴρ ἦν ἀγαλματοποιός· ἐποίει δὲ ἀγάλματα ξύλινα, καὶ ἐκινοῦντο καὶ ἐλάλουν. πῶς δὲ μέλλει γίνεσθαι τοῦτο. τὸν Δαίδαλον λέγουσι μεταμείβειν ἑαυτὸν εἰς ποικίλα εἴδη καὶ μορφάς, καὶ ἀγάλματα ποιεῖν βαδίζοντα. ἔστι δὲ μῦθος, λέγεται δὲ οὕτως διὰ τὸ ποικίλας ὑπὲρ πάντας καὶ παρηλλαγμένας μορφὰς προσφέρειν τοῖς ἀγάλμασι, καὶ διὰ τὸ διαλελυμένους τοὺς πόδας τῶν ἀγαλμάτων ποιοῦντα, τῶν ἄλλων συνημμένους ποιούντων.

By works of Daedalus: Referring to the works of Daedalus, that they moved and emitted a voice, Euripides himself also says in the *Eurystheus*, "O honored sir, it is not possible, that you fear these things; all *agalmata* made by Daedalus seem to see and move; that man is in this way ingenious." And Cratinus in the *Thracians*: "Pan . . . hither seeking some . . . bronze or wood and gold added, in no way wood, that one, but being bronze wandered away. Whether it was Daedalean, or someone stole it?" And Plato: "A: Who are you? Speak promptly; why are you silent? Don't you talk? B: I am a Hermes of Daedalus, with a voice, made of wood, and I have come, walking of my own accord." By works of Daedalus: Daedalus was a maker of *agalmata*, making *agalmata* so very beautiful that the story was told about them by the poets that they emitted a voice and moved. And this Daedalus also, when he wished, put on wings and flew. When, having fashioned wings and put them on his son Icarus too, he made him travel in the air. But when the wax gave way, he fell into the sea that is now called Icarian after him. For they say that Helios had his revenge on Daedalus, since he had made his daughter Pasiphae, who was in love with a bull, have intercourse with it; when he saw Daedalus' son Icarus flying, using wax wings, he shone violently down upon the wings, and caused them to break apart, and Icarus, who was buoyed up by them, having tumbled down, drowned. Of Daedalus: he who also used to make *eidola* both move and talk. Daedalus was a man who made *agalmata*. He used to make wooden *agalmata*, and they used to move and talk. How this came to be. They say that Daedalus changes himself into various forms and shapes, and makes *agalmata* that walk around. There is an account: it is said as follows: [that] on account of his giving *agalmata* forms that are more complex than all others, and different, and on account of his making the feet of *agalmata* separated, others making them joined together.

87
Sch. Euripides, *Hippolytus* 73
(= Euripides fr. 372 Nauck².)
Text: W. Dindorf, ed., *Scholia Graeca in Euripidis Tragoedias* I (Oxford, 1863).

σοὶ τόνδε πλεκτόν: πρὸς τὸν χειροποίητον στέφανον, ὃν ἔφερε τῷ ξοάνῳ. τινὲς μέντοι καὶ τοῦτο ἐπὶ τῆς αὐτῆς ἀλληγορίας ἀκούουσι, λέγοντες τὸν ὕμνον κόσμον εἰρῆσθαι αὐτῆς. τοῦτον ἂν λέγοι τὸν ὕμνον δεικτικῶς πρὸς τὸ εἰρημένον "πότνια." Ἄλλως. διαβεβόηται τοῦτο τὸ ζήτημα. καὶ οἱ μὲν ὑπέλαβον τὸν Ἱππόλυτον στέφειν τὴν Ἄρτεμιν ἀνθίνῳ στεφάνῳ· ὁ δὲ Φιλόχορος τὴν ἐν Ἄργαις Ἄρτεμιν τῷ μὲν λόγῳ στέφεσθαί φησιν, ἐφ' ἑαυτοῦ δὲ τὸν Ἱππόλυτον ταῦτα λέγειν, ὅτι ἐμαυτὸν σοὶ ἀνατίθημι, ὦ θεὰ, στέφανον, τουτέστι κόσμον ἀνθηρότατον· κόσμον γὰρ εἶναι τῇ παρθένῳ τὸ μετὰ τοῦ σωφρονεστάτου τῶν νέων διημερεύειν. ἄλλοι δὲ μηδὲν αἰνίττεσθαι τὸν ποιητὴν φασι καὶ μηδὲν ἀλληγορεῖν, ἀλλὰ κυρίως λέγειν, καὶ τῷ ὄντι στέφανον φέρειν τὸν Ἱππόλυτον. τοῦτον δὲ ἐκ τοιούτον λειμῶνος, καθ' ὃν οὐκ ἔστιν ἡμῖν ὅσιον οὐδὲ δρέπεσθαι τῶν ἀνθέων· τὸ γὰρ "οὐδ' ἦλθέ πω σίδηρος" εἰς τοῦτο καταστρέφει, ὅτι οὐδὲ δρέπεται ὑπό τινος, οὐδὲ εἴργασται. ἄλλοι δέ φασι τὸν Εὐριπίδην τροπικώτερον τὸν ἐπὶ τῇ Ἀρτέμιδι ὕμνον στέφανον λέγειν. καὶ γὰρ δὴ παράλογον εἶναι καὶ πολλὴν ἀτοπίαν ἔχον, καὶ δοκεῖν ἄνθιμον λειμῶνα εἶναι, ὅθεν ἐδρέφθη τὰ ἄνθη, καὶ τοιούτον, εἰς ὃν οἱ εἰσιόντες ἐξετάζονται πότερον διδακτὴν ἔχουσι τὴν σωφροσύνην ἢ ἐκ φύσεως, καὶ κατάρδεσθαι αὐτόν. Φιλόχορος δέ φησι τῷ μὲν ξοάνῳ πλεκτὸν στέφανον προσφέρειν, τῇ δὲ θεῷ τὸν ὕμνον. ἐξ ἀκηράτου δὲ, τῆς ἀδόλου καὶ ἀφθάρτου διανοίας. Ἄλλως. ἐπιεικῶς οἱ ποιηταὶ τὰς μὲν ἰδίας φύσεις λειμῶσιν, ἢ ποταμοῖς, ἢ μελίσσαις εἰκαζουσι, τὴν δὲ ποίησιν στεφάνοις, διὰ μὲν τῶν ἀνθέων τὸ ποικίλον καὶ τὸ κάλλος αὐτῆς παριστῶντες, διὰ δὲ τῶν ποταμῶν τὴν πληθὺν καὶ τὴν εἰς τὸ ποιεῖν ὁρμὴν, διὰ δὲ τῶν μελισσῶν τὸ μελιχρὸν, διὰ δὲ τῶν στεφάνων τὸν κόσμον τῶν ὑμνουμένων. ταῦτα δὴ πάντα συνελὼν ὁ ποιητὴς ἐφαίδρυνε τῆς ἀλληγορίας τὸν τρόπον. τὸ δὲ "ἐξ ἀκηράτου λειμῶνος," ἐπειδὴ δεῖ πάντως τὸν μετιόντα μουσικὴν καθαράν τε καὶ ἀκήρατον ἔχειν τὴν ψυχὴν πάντοτε καὶ ἄχραντον ἀπὸ κακοῦ, καὶ μάλιστα τῆς αἰδοῦς μεμοιραμένην. διὰ γάρ τοι τὸ αἰδέσιμον καὶ παρθένους ὑποτίθενται τὰς Μούσας, γονιμωτάτας οὔσας.

Ἄλλως. καθόλου μέν ἐστι τῆς διανοίας καὶ στέφανον αὐτὸν προσφέροντα, ἅτε δὴ σοφόν· τῷ μὲν ξοάνῳ ἄρα τὸν χειροποίητον στέφανον προσφέρει, τῇ δὲ θεῷ τὸν ὕμνον. πλεκτὸν τοίνυν στέφανον λέγει τὸν ὕμνον, δίκην πλοκῆς συντεθέντας τοὺς λόγους ἀποτελεῖν τὸν ὕμνον.

To you the plaited thing: refers to the handmade crown, which he brought to the *xoanon*. Some, however, also take this to be an allegory, saying that the hymn is strung together as an ornament for her. This would mean that the hymn is demonstrably addressed to the "Mistress" who is mentioned. Alternatively: This is a famous question. And some interpret Hippolytus crowning Artemis with a flower wreath. But Philochorus says that Artemis in Agrai is crowned with a speech, but according to the same author Hippolytus means this, that I dedicate to you, O goddess, myself as a crown, that is to say, the most splendid ornament; for it is an ornament for the maiden to pass the day with the wisest of young men. But others say that the poet is not at all speaking in riddles and not using allegories, but speaks precisely, and that Hippolytus in reality brings a crown. This is from the kind of meadow in which divine law does not permit us to be, nor to gather flowers; for the phrase "nor came iron there ever" points to this, that it is neither culled by anyone, nor worked. But others say that Euripides figuratively calls the hymn to Artemis a crown. For also it is indeed unreasonable and a great absurdity, both to think that the meadow is flowery, whence the flowers were gathered, and such that those entering it are examined as to whether their prudence has been taught or comes from nature, and besprinkle it with praise. But Philochorus says that he offers a plaited wreath to the *xoanon*, but a hymn to the goddess. From an unknown place, and from genuine and undefiled intention. Alternatively: Poets usually liken characteristic natures to meadows, or rivers, or bees, and poetry to wreaths, on the one hand expressing its beauty and intricacy in terms of flowers, and on the other, the abundance and impulse to create it in terms of rivers, and its sweetness in terms of bees, and the honor to those who are celebrated in terms of crowns. The poet, drawing all these things together, was illuminating the manner of the allegory. But the phrase "from an unknown meadow," since it is necessary for him who pursues poetry to have a pure and undefiled spirit always, and especially one that has reverence as its lot. For surely it is by reason of venerability that they enjoin even the maiden Muses, who are most fertile.

Alternatively: In general it is (a matter) of intention and him offering a wreath, as though indeed wise; on the one hand, it seems, he offers a handmade wreath to the *xoanon*, but a hymn to the goddess. The plaited wreath, accordingly, means the hymn, after the manner of plaiting, putting words together to produce a hymn.

88

Euripides, *Ion* 1397–1403 c. 412 B.C.
Text: W. Biehl, ed., *Euripides. Ion* (Leipzig, 1979).
Translation adapted from A.S. Way, tr., *Euripides* IV (LCL, 1912).

[Κρ.] οὐκ ἐν σιωπῇ τἀμά· μή με νουθέτει.
ὁρῶ γὰρ ἄγγος οὑξέθηκ' ἐγώ ποτε —
σέ γ', ὦ τέκνον μοι, βρέφος ἔτ' ὄντα νήπιον,

Κέκροπος ἐς ἄντρα καὶ Μακρὰς πετρηρεφεῖς.
λείψω δὲ βωμὸν τόνδε, κεἰ θανεῖν με χρή.
[Ιω.] λάζυσθε τήνδε· θεομανὴς γὰρ ἥλατο
βωμοῦ λιποῦσα ξόανα· δεῖτε δ᾽ ὠλένας.

Creusa: Not for me silence! Teach me not my part!
For I see the cradle in which I set you out,
O my child, still an infant baby,
Into the cave of Cecrops and the Long Rocks.
I will leave this altar, even if I must die.
Ion: Seize her; for maddened by a god she leaped,
Having left the *xoana* of the altar; bind her arms.

89

Hypothesis of Euripides, *Iphigenia in Tauris*
Text: D. Sansone, ed., *Euripides. Iphigenia in Tauris* (Leipzig, 1981).

Ὀρέστης κατὰ χρησμὸν ἐλθὼν εἰς Ταύρους τῆς Σκυθίας μετὰ Πυλάδου παραγενηθεὶς τὸ παρ᾽ αὐτοῖς τιμώμενον τῆς Ἀρτέμιδος ξόανον ὑφελέσθαι προῃρεῖτο.

In accordance with an oracle, Orestes, coming with Pylades to the Taurians of Scythia, determined to steal away the *xoanon* of Artemis that is honored among them.

90

Euripides, *Iphigenia in Tauris* 1358–1359 c. 412 B.C.
Text: D. Sansone, ed., *Euripides. Iphigenia in Tauris* (Leipzig, 1981).

λόγοι δ᾽ ἐχώρουν· τίνι λόγῳ πορθμεύετε
κλέπτοντες ἐκ γῆς ξόανα καὶ θυηπόλους;

And our words went out: By what *logos* do you, stealing *xoana* and priestesses from the land, carry [them away]?

91

Euripides, *Troiades* 511–530 415 B.C.
Text: W. Biehl, ed., *Euripides. Troades* (Leipzig, 1970).
Translation adapted from A.S. Way, tr., *Euripides* I (LCL, 1916).

[Χο.] Ἀμφί μοι Ἴλιον, ὦ
Μοῦσα καινῶν ὕμνων,
ἄεισον ἐν δακρύοις ᾠ-
δὰν ἐπικήδειον·
νῦν γὰρ μέλος ἐς Τροί-
αν ἰα<κ>χήσω,

τετραβάμονος ὡς ὑπ' ἀπήνας
'Αργείων ὀλό{ι}μαν τά-
λαινα δοριάλωτος,
ὅτ' ἔλιπον ἵππον οὐράνια
βρέμοντα χρυσεοφάλαρον ἔνο-
πλον ἐν πύλαις 'Αχαιοί·
ἀνὰ δ' ἐβόασεν λεὼς
Τρῳάδος ἀπὸ πέτρας σταθείς·
"Ἴτ', ὦ πεπαυμένοι πόνων,
τόδ' ἱερὸν ἀνάγετε ξόανον
'Ιλιάδι Διογενεῖ κόρᾳ."
τίς οὐκ ἔβα νεανίδων,
τίς οὐ γεραιὸς ἐκ δόμων;
κεχαρμένοι δ' ἀοιδαῖς
δόλιον ἔσχον ἄταν.

Chorus: O Muse, sing to me of Ilium,
With new songs
Sing in tears
A dirge;
For now the song about Troy
I will cry,
How by the four-footed vehicle
Of the Argives I was ruined, a suffering captive,
When the Achaeans left the
Horse, clamoring to heaven,
Decked with gold *phalara*, crammed with men,
At the gates;
Thereupon the people of Troy
Cried aloud from the citadel:
Come, O you who have been given rest from troubles,
Lead up this *hieron xoanon*
To the Ilian maiden born of Zeus.
Who of the youths did not come?
What elder was not outside his home?
Rejoicing with songs at
The snare holding ruin.

92

Sch. Euripides, *Troiades* 525
Text: E. Schwartz, ed., *Scholia in Euripidem* II (Berlin, 1891) 361.

τόδ' ἱερόν: *πρὸς ἑαυτοὺς δὲ. φησὶ. παρεκελεύοντο οἱ* Τρῶες· *τοῦτο τὸ ἱερὸν ξόανον. τὸν ἵππον, ἄγετε τῇ* 'Αθηνᾷ;—

This holy: but towards themselves, he says, the Trojans were exhorting; this holy *xoanon*, the horse, bring to Athena.

93

Euripides, *Troiades* 1071–1076 415 B.C.

Text: W. Biehl, ed., *Euripides. Troades* (Leipzig, 1970).

φροῦδαί σοι θυσίαι χορῶν τ'
εὔφημοι κέλαδοι κατ' ὄρ-
  φναν τε παννυχίδες θεῶν,
χρυσέων τε ξοάνων τύποι
Φρυγῶν τε ζάθεοι σελᾶ-
  ναι συνδώδεκα πλήθει.

Chorus: Your sacrifices are vanished, and
the fair voices of choruses,
and at night, the all-night festivals of the gods,
and the *tupoi* of golden *xoana*,
and the holy *selanai* of the Phrygians,
twelve in number.

Euripides fr. 203 Nauck[2] (*Antiope*) V B.C.

See Clement of Alexandria, *Stromateis* 1.163.5 [**47**].

Euripides fr. 372 Nauck[2] V B.C.

See Sch. Euripides, *Hecuba* 838 [**87**].

Europia

See Clement of Alexandria, *Stromateis* 1.164.3 [**47**].

94

Eusebius, *De ecclesiastica theologia* 2.22.2–3 C. A.D. 335

Text: E. Klostermann, ed., *Eusebius Werke* IV. *Gegen Marcell, Über die kirchliche Theologie, Die Fragmente Marcellus* (GCS 14; Leipzig, 1906).

αὐτὸς οὖν ὁ ἀληθινὸς ἦν θεός, ὁ εἷς μόνος καὶ ἕτερος οὐκ ἔστιν πλὴν αὐτοῦ, ὁ μὴ μόνον διὰ τῶν προφητῶν ἀλλὰ διὰ τοῦ ἰδίου υἱοῦ ταῦτα κατ' ἐκεῖνο καιροῦ εἰδωλολατρεύοντι τῷ Ἰουδαίων ἐγκελευόμενος ἔθνει. αὐτίκα δ' οὖν ὁ Ἡσαΐας (μᾶλλον δὲ ὁ θεὸς δι' αὐτοῦ) εἰπὼν "πλὴν ἐμοῦ οὐκ ἔστιν θεός. τίς ὥσπερ ἐγώ;" καὶ ἑξῆς "μάρτυρες ὑμεῖς ἐστε εἰ ἔστιν θεὸς πλὴν ἐμοῦ", ἐπήγαγεν τὸ "καὶ οὐκ ἦσαν τότε. οἱ πλάσσοντες καὶ οἱ γλύφοντες πάντες μάταιοι, ποιοῦντες τὰ καταθύμια αὐτῶν". καὶ δι' ὅλης δὲ τῆς αὐτοῦ προφητείας εὕροις ἂν κοπτόμενα τὰ ἄψυχα ξόανα, καὶ παρ' ἑκάστῳ δὲ προφήτῃ ὁμοίως εἰς ἀποτροπὴν τῆς πολυθέου πλάνης τὸν ἕνα θεὸν κηρυττόμενον εὑρήσεις.

He therefore was the real God, the one [and] only, and there is no other except him, he who not only through the prophets but through his own son at that time commanded these things to the idolatrous nation of the Jews. At once, therefore, Isaiah (or rather, God through him) saying, "Except for me there is no God. Who is there like unto me?" and then "Be you witnesses, if there is a God except me," he brought in the [statement], "and there were not then. The modellers and the carvers, all [are] foolish, making things according to their own minds." And in his entire prophecy you would find the soulless *xoana* struck down, and in each prophetic utterance likewise you would find the one God proclaimed as a dissuasion from the error of polytheism.

95

Eusebius, *Demonstratio evangelica* 6.20 — c. A.D. 312–318

Text: A. Heikel, ed., *Eusebius Werke* 6. *Die Demonstratio Evangelica* (GCS 23; Leipzig, 1913).

Οἱ πρὶν τὴν Αἴγυπτον οἰκοῦντες φαῦλοι καὶ μοχθηροὶ δαίμονες, ἐξ αἰῶνος μακροῦ τοῖς ξοάνοις ἐμφωλεύοντες καὶ τὰς τῶν Αἰγυπτίων ψυχὰς πάσῃ δεισιδαιμονίας πλάνῃ καταδουλούμενοι, συναισθόμενοι ξίνης τινὸς καὶ ἐνθέου δυνάμεως ἐπιδημούσης αὐτοῖς, αὐτίκα συνεκινοῦντο, σάλον καὶ κλόνον ἐν ἑαυτοῖς πάσχοντες, ἥ τε καρδία αὐτῶν καὶ ἡ διανοητικὴ δύναμις ἡττᾶτο ἔνδον ἐν ἑαυτοῖς, ὑποχωροῦσα καὶ νικωμένη ὑπὸ τῆς ἀοράτως συνελαυνούσης καὶ πυρὸς δίκην ἀρρήτῳ λόγῳ φλεγούσης αὐτοὺς δυνάμεως.

The bad and rascally demons that formerly inhabited Egypt, from a long time past lurking in *xoana* and enslaving the souls of the Egyptians with every deceit of supersition, when they perceived within themselves some strange and divinely inspired power coming to stay among them, they straightway moved off together, suffering perplexity and agitation within themselves; both their heart and their power of thought were broken inside them, having given way to and been defeated by a weapon matched in combat, and the power of fire lighting up justice to them with the unutterable word.

96

Eusebius, *Historia ecclesiastica* 9.4.2 — post A.D. 318

Text: E. Schwartz, ed., *Eusebius Werke* II.2. *Die Kirchengeschichte* (GCS 9; Leipzig, 1908).

Translation adapted from J.E.L. Oulton, tr., *Eusebius. The Ecclesiastical History* II (LCL, 1932).

ἱερεῖς δῆτα κατὰ πόλιν τῶν ξοάνων καὶ ἐπὶ τούτοις ἀρχιερεῖς πρὸς αὐτοῦ Μαξιμίνου οἱ μάλιστα ταῖς πολιτείαις διαπρέψαντες καὶ διὰ πασῶν ἔνδοξοι γενόμενοι καθίσταντο, οἷς καὶ πολλή τις εἰσήγετο σπουδὴ περὶ τὴν τῶν θεραπευομένων πρὸς αὐτῶν θρησκείαν.

Maximin himself appointed as priests of the *xoana* in each city and, moreover, as high priests, those who were especially distinguished in the public services and had made their mark in the entire course thereof, by whom great zeal was brought to bear on the worship of the gods whom they served.

97

Eusebius, *Historia ecclesiastica* 9.11.5–6 post A.D. 318
Text: E. Schwartz, ed., *Eusebius Werke* II.2. *Die Kirchengeschichte* (GCS 9; Leipzig, 1908).
Translation adapted from J.E.L. Oulton, tr., *Eusebius. The Ecclesiastical History* II (LCL, 1932).

ἐκάλει δὲ ἄρα καὶ Θεότεκνον ἡ δίκη, οὐδαμῶς τὰ κατὰ Χριστιανῶν αὐτῷ πεπραγμένα λήθῃ παραδιδοῦσα. ἐπὶ μὲν γὰρ τῷ κατ' Ἀντιόχειαν ἱδρυθέντι πρὸς αὐτοῦ ξοάνῳ δόξας εὐημερεῖν, ἤδη καὶ ἡγεμονίας ἠξίωτο παρὰ Μαξιμίνου, Λικίννιος δ' ἐπιβὰς τῆς Ἀντιοχέων πόλεως φώραν τε γοήτων ποιησάμενος, τοὺς τοῦ νεοπαγοῦς ξοάνου προφήτας καὶ ἱερεῖς βασάνοις ᾐκίζετο, τίνι λόγῳ τὴν ἀπάτην καθυποκρίνοιντο. πυνθανόμενος· ὡς δ' ἐπικρύπτεσθαι αὐτοῖς πρὸς τῶν βασάνων συνελαυνομένοις ἀδύνατον ἦν, ἐδήλουν δὲ τὸ πᾶν μυστήριον ἀπάτην τυγχάνειν τέχνῃ τῇ Θεοτέκνου μεμηχανημένην, τοῖς πᾶσιν τὴν ἀξίαν ἐπιθεὶς δίκην, πρῶτον αὐτὸν Θεότεκνον, εἶτα δὲ καὶ τοὺς τῆς γοητείας κοινωνοὺς μετὰ πλείστας ὅσας αἰκίας θανάτῳ παραδίδωσιν.

So it was that Theotecnus also was summoned by Justice, who in no wise consigned to oblivion what he did against the Christians. For after he had set up the *xoanon* at Antioch, he seemed to be prospering, and had actually been deemed worthy of a governorship by Maximin; but when Licinius came to the city of the Antiochenes, he made a search for charlatans, and plied with tortures the prophets and priests of the new-made *xoanon*, to find out by what contrivance they were practising this deceit. And when the infliction of the tortures made concealment impossible for them, and they revealed that the whole *mysterion* was a deceit manufactured by the art of Theotecnus, he inflicted a just punishment on them all, putting to death, after a long series of tortures, first Theotecnus himself, and then also the partners in his charlatanry.

98

Eusebius, *Praeparatio evangelica* 1.4.12 a–c A.D. 312–318
Text: E.H. Gifford, ed., tr., *Eusebii Pamphili evangelicae praeparationis libri XV* (Oxford, 1903) I.
Translation adapted from Gifford (vol. III).

Ἀλλὰ ταῦτα μὲν πάλαι ἦν πρότερον, νυνὶ δὲ οὐκέθ' ὁμοίως ἐστίν, ἑνὸς τοῦ σωτηρίου νόμου τῆς εὐαγγελικῆς δυνάμεως τὴν θηριώδη καὶ ἀπάνθρωπον τούτων ὅλων καταλύσαντος νόσον. Τὸ δὲ μηκέτι θεοὺς ἡγεῖσθαι ἤτοι τὰ νεκρὰ καὶ κωφὰ ξόανα, ἢ τοὺς ἐν τούτοις ἐνεργοῦντας πονηροὺς δαίμονας, ἢ τὰ μέρη τοῦ φαινομένου κόσμου, ἢ τας τῶν πάλαι κατοιχομένων θηντῶν ψυχάς, ἢ τῶν ἀλόγων ζώων τὰ βλαπτικώτατα, ἀντὶ δὲ τούτων ἁπάντων διὰ μιᾶς τῆς εὐαγγελικῆς τοῦ σωτῆρος ἡμῶν διδασκαλίας Ἕλληνας ὁμοῦ καὶ βαρβάρους τοὺς γνησίως ἀλλ' οὐκ ἐπιπλάστως αὐτοῦ τῷ λόγῳ προσανέχοντας εἰς τοσοῦτον ἄκρας φιλοσοφίας ἐλθεῖν, ὡς μόνον τὸν ἀνωτάτω Θεόν, αὐτὸν ἐκεῖνον τὸν ἐπέκεινα τῶν ὅλων, τὸν παμβασιλέα καὶ κύριον οὐρανοῦ τε καὶ γῆς, ἡλίου τε καὶ ἄστρων, καὶ τοῦ σύμπαντος κόσμου δημιουργόν, σέβειν καὶ ὑμνεῖν καὶ θεολογεῖν, βιοῦν τε ἀκριβῶς καὶ οὕτως μανθάνειν ὡς μέχρι καὶ τοῦ ἐμβλέπειν τοῖς ὀφθαλμοῖς παιδαγωγεῖσθαι, καὶ μηδὲν ἀκόλαστον ἐκ τοῦ μετ' ἐπιθυμίας ὁρᾶν ἐννοεῖν, πρόρριζον δὲ ἐξ αὐτῆς διανοίας πᾶν αἰσχρὸν ὑποτέμνεσθαι πάθος,—ταῦτα πάντα πῶς οὐκ ἂν τοῖς πᾶσι συμβάλλοιτο πρὸς εὐζωΐαν;

But these [*i.e.*, live burial, *etc.*] were customs of a former age, and are now no longer practiced in the same manner, the salutary law of the power of the Gospel having alone abolished the savage and inhuman pest of all these evils. Then there is the fact that men no longer regard as gods either the dead and dumb *xoana*, or the evil daemons operating in them, or the parts of the visible world, or the souls of mortals long since departed, or the most hurtful of irrational animals; but instead of all these, surely by the teaching of our Savior in the Gospel, Greeks and barbarians together, who sincerely and unfeignedly adhere to His word, have reached such a point of high philosophy, as to worship and praise and acknowledge as divine none but the highest God, the very same who is above the universe, the absolute monarch and lord of heaven and earth, and sun and stars, creator of the whole world. They have also learned to live a strict life, so as to be guided even in looking with their eyes, and to conceive no licentious thought from a lustful look, but to cut away the very roots of every base passion from the mind itself. Must not then all these things help all men towards a virtuous and happy life?

99

Eusebius, *Praeparatio evangelica* 1.6.17 c–d A.D. 312–318
Text: E.H. Gifford, ed., tr., *Eusebii Pamphili evangelicae praeparationis libri XV* (Oxford, 1903) I.
Translation adapted from Gifford (vol. III).

Οἵ γε μὴν λοιποὶ τῶν ἀνθρώπων τῆσδε τῆς μόνης καὶ ἀληθοῦς ἀποπεσόντες εὐσεβείας, τὰ φωσφόρα τῶν οὐρανίων σαρκὸς ὀφθαλμοῖς, οἷα νήπιοι *τὰς ψυχάς, καταπλαγέντες, θεούς τε ἀνεῖπον, καὶ θυσίαις τε καὶ προσκυνήσεσιν ἐγέραιρον, οὐ νεὼς δειμάμενοι, οὐδ' ἀφιδρύμασι καὶ ξοάνοις θνητῶν εἰκόνας πλασμάμενοι, πρὸς αἰθέρα δὲ καὶ αὐτὸν οὐρανὸν ἀποβλέποντες καὶ μέχρι τῶν τῇδε ὁρωμένων ταῖς ψυχαῖς ἐφικνούμενοι.*

The rest of mankind, however, having fallen away from this, the only true worship, and gazing in awe on the luminaries of the heavens with eyes of flesh, as if infantile in their souls, proclaimed them gods, and honored them with sacrifices and *proskyneses*, although they had not built *neoi*, nor formed *eikones* of mortals with *hidrumata* and *xoana*, but looked up to the aether and to heaven itself and reached up with their souls to the things there.

100

Eusebius, *Praeparatio evangelica* 1.9.29 d — A.D. 312–318
Text: E.H. Gifford, ed., tr., *Eusebii Pamphili evangelicae praeparationis libri XV* (Oxford, 1903) I.
Translation adapted from Gifford (vol. III).

Ἀλλ' ὅτι μὲν οἱ πρῶτοι καὶ παλαίτατοι τῶν ἀνθρώπων οὔτε ναῶν οἰκοδομίαις προσεῖχον οὔτε ξοάνων ἀφιδρύμασιν, οὔπω τότε γραφικῆς οὐδὲ πλαστικῆς [ἢ γλυπτικῆς] ἢ ἀνδριαντοποιητικῆς τέχνης ἐφευρημένης, οὐδὲ μὴν οἰκοδομικῆς οὐδὲ ἀρχιτεκτονικῆς πω συνεστώσης, παντί τῳ οἶμαι συλλογιζομένῳ δῆλον εἶναι.

But that the first and most ancient of men turned their minds neither to building *naoi* nor setting up *xoana*, since then neither graphic nor plastic [nor glyptic] nor modelling arts had been discovered, nor indeed had building or architecture yet been established, I think is clear to everyone who considers.

101

Eusebius, *Praeparatio evangelica* 1.9.30 b — A.D. 312–318
Text: E.H. Gifford, ed., tr., *Eusebii Pamphili evangelicae praeparationis libri XV* (Oxford, 1903) I.
Translation adapted from Gifford (vol. III).

Οὐκ ἄρα τις ἦν θεογονίας Ἑλληνικῆς ἢ βαρβαρικῆς τοῖς παλαιοτάτοις τῶν ἀνθρώπων λόγος, οὐδὲ ξοάνων ἀψύχων ἵδρυσις, οὐδ' ἡ νῦν πολλὴ φλυαρία τῆς τῶν θεῶν ἀρρένων τε καὶ θηλειῶν ὀνομασίας.

So then there was no mention of a theogony, either Greek or barbarian, among the oldest of men, nor the setting up of soulless *xoana*, nor much silly talk there is now about the naming of gods male and female.

102

Eusebius, *Praeparatio evangelica* 1.10.35 d A.D. 312–318
(= Porphyry, *Adversus Christianos*, quoting Philo Byblius, quoting in turn Sanchuniathon.)
Text: E.H. Gifford, ed., tr., *Eusebii Pamphili evangelicae praeparationis libri XV* (Oxford, 1903) I.
Translation adapted from Gifford (vol. III).

Μετὰ ταῦτ᾽ ἐκ τοῦ γένους τούτων γενέσθαι νεανίας δύο, καλεῖσθαι δὲ αὐτῶν τὸν μὲν Τεχνίτην, τὸν δὲ Γήϊνον Αὐτόχθονα. Οὗτοι ἐπενόησαν τῷ πηλῷ τῆς πλίνθου συμμιγνύειν φορυτόν, καὶ τῷ ἡλίῳ αὐτὰς τερσαίνειν, ἀλλὰ καὶ στέγας ἐξεῦρον. Ἀπὸ τούτων ἐγένοντο ἕτεροι, ὧν ὁ μὲν Ἀργὸς ἐκαλεῖτο, ὁ δὲ Ἀγρούηρος ἢ Ἀγρότης, οὗ καὶ ξόανον εἶναι μάλα σεβάσμιον καὶ ναὸν ζυγοφορούμενον ἐν Φοινίκῃ· παρὰ δὲ Βυβλίοις ἐξαιρέτως θεῶν ὁ μέγιστος ὀνομάζεται.

Afterwards there were born from this race two young men, one of them called Technites, the other Geinon Autochton. These devised the mixing of straw with the mud of bricks, and drying them by the sun, and also invented roofs. From them were born others, of whom one was called Argos, the other Agrueros or Agrotes, of whom there is both a *xoanon*, very revered, and a *naos* drawn by yokes of oxen, in Phoenicia; among the people of Byblos he is specially named the greatest of gods.

103

Eusebius, *Praeparatio evangelica* 2.8.78 b A.D. 312–318
(= Dionysius of Halicarnassus 2.18 [**66**].)
Text: E.H. Gifford, ed., tr., *Eusebii Pamphili evangelicae praeparationis libri XV* (Oxford, 1903) I.
Translation adapted from E. Cary, tr., *The Roman Antiquities of Dionysius of Halicarnassus* I (LCL, 1937).

Ἱερὰ μὲν οὖν καὶ τεμένη καὶ βωμοὺς καὶ ξοάνων ἱδρύσεις μορφάς τε αὐτῶν καὶ σύμβολα καὶ δυνάμεις καὶ δωρεάς αἷς τὸ γένος ἡμῶν εὐηργέτησαν, ἑορτάς τε ὁποίας τινὰς ἑκάστῳ θεῶν ἢ δαιμόνων ἄγεσθαι προσήκει, καὶ θυσίας αἷς χαίρουσι γεραιρόμενοι πρὸς ἀνθρώπων, ἐκεχειρίας τε αὖ καὶ πανηγύρεις καὶ πόνων ἀναπαύλας, καὶ πάντα τὰ τοιαῦτα ὁμοίως κατεστήσατο τοῖς κρατίστοις τῶν παρὰ τοῖς Ἕλλησι νομίμων.

He [Romulus] established *hiera* and *temene* and *bomoi*, arranged for the setting up of *xoana*, determined the shapes and symbols of [the gods], and declared their powers, the beneficent gifts which they have made to mankind, the particular festivals that should be celebrated in honor of each god or *daimon*, the sacrifices with which they delight to be honored by men, as well as the holidays, festal assemblies, days of rest, and everything alike of that nature, in all of which he followed the best customs in use among the Greeks.

104

Eusebius, *Praeparatio evangelica* 3.1.85 c–86 b A.D. 312–318
(= Plutarch, *De Daedalis Plataeensibus* 6 [*Moralia* fr. 157 Sandbach].)
Text: E.H. Gifford, ed., tr., *Eusebii Pamphili evangelicae praeparationis libri* XV (Oxford, 1903) I.
Translation adapted from Gifford (vol. III).

Δεῖ δὲ ἴσως καὶ τὸν εὐηθέστερον μῦθον εἰπεῖν. λέγεται γὰρ ὁ Ζεύς, τῆς Ἥρας αὐτῷ διαφερομένης καὶ μηκέτι φοιτᾶν εἰς τὸ αὐτὸ βουλομένης ἀλλὰ κρυπτούσης ἑαυτήν, ἀμηχανῶν καὶ πλανώμενος Ἀλαλκομένει τῷ αὐτόχθονι συντυχεῖν, καὶ διδαχθῆναι ὑπὸ τούτου ὡς ἐξαπατητέον τὴν Ἥραν σκηψάμενον γαμεῖν ἑτέραν. Συνεργοῦντος δὲ τοῦ Ἀλαλκομένους, κρύφα τεμόντας αὐτοὺς εὐκτέανον καὶ παγκάλην δρῦν μορφῶσαί τε αὐτὴν καὶ καταστεῖλαι νυμφικῶς, Δαιδάλην προσαγορεύσαντας· εἶτα οὕτως ἀναμέλπεσθαι μὲν τὸν ὑμέναιον, λουτρὰ δὲ κομίζειν τὰς Τριτωνίδας νύμφας, αὐλοὺς δὲ καὶ κώμους τὴν Βοιωτίαν παρασχεῖν· περαινομένων δὲ τούτων, οὐκέτι τὴν Ἥραν καρτερεῖν, ἀλλὰ καταβᾶσαν ἐκ τοῦ Κιθαιρῶνος, τῶν Πλαταιάδων αὐτῇ γυναικῶν ἑπομένων, ὑπ' ὀργῆς καὶ ζηλοτυπίας θέουσαν ἐλθεῖν πρὸς τὸν Δία, καὶ τοῦ πλάσματος φανεροῦ γενομένου διαλλαγεῖσαν μετὰ χαρᾶς καὶ γέλωτος αὐτὴν νυμφαγωγεῖν· τιμὴν δὲ τῷ ξοάνῳ προσθεῖναι, καὶ Δαίδαλα τὴν ἑορτὴν προσαγορεῦσαι, κατακαῦσαι δὲ ὅμως αὐτὸ καίπερ ἄψυχον ὂν ἀπὸ ζηλοτυπίας.

But perhaps we ought also to mention the more silly legend. For Zeus is said when Hera was at variance with him, and was no longer willing to consort with him, but hid herself, to have been wandering about in perplexity and to have fallen in with Alalcomenes the earth-born, and was taught by him that, to deceive Hera, he must pretend to wed another wife. So Alalcomenes helped him, and they secretly, having cut down a tall and beautiful oak, shaped it and dressed it in bridal array, having called it by name Daedale; then the hymenaeal was duly chanted, and the nymphs of Triton brought lustral water, and Boeotia supplied flutes and festal processions. But when these performances went on, Hera could bear it no longer, but came down from Cithaeron, followed by the women of Plataea, and from anger and jealousy came running up to Zeus, and when the counterfeit became manifest, she was reconciled to him and with joy and laughter herself led the bridal procession, and gave additional honor to the *xoanon*, and called the festival Daedala, but nevertheless from jealousy burned it, even though it was soulless.

105

Eusebius, *Praeparatio evangelica* 3.3.90 d–91 a A.D. 312–318
Text: E.H. Gifford, ed., tr., *Eusebii Pamphili evangelicae praeparationis libri XV* (Oxford, 1903) I.
Translation adapted from Gifford (vol. III).

Ταῦτα καὶ τὰ τοιαῦτα εἰπών, πάλιν εἰς δαίμονας ἀναφέρει τοὺς περὶ τῶν δηλουμένων θεῶν μύθους· καὶ πάλιν ἄλλως ἀποδίδωσι, καὶ αὖθις ἑτέρως ἀλληγορῶν. Ἦν δ' ἂν κατὰ λόγον πυθέσθαι ὁποτέρων θεῶν τὰ ξόανα τὰς ἐντετυπωμένας μορφὰς σώζειν φήσουσιν. Πότερα δαιμόνων; ἀλλὰ πυρὸς καὶ ἀέρος καὶ γῆς καὶ ὕδατος, ἢ ἀνδρῶν καὶ γυναικῶν εἰκόνας, καὶ ζώων ἀλόγων καὶ θηρίων σχήματα; Ἐπεὶ γὰρ καὶ πρὸς αὐτῶν συγκεχώρηται ὁμωνύμως ἡλίῳ καὶ τοῖς καθόλου στοιχείοις θηντοὺς ἄνδρας τινὰς γεγονέναι, καὶ τούτους θεοὺς ἀνηγορεῦσθαι, τίνων εἰκὸς ἂν εἴη λέγειν μορφὰς εἶναι καὶ εἰκόνας τὰς ἐν τοῖς ἀψύχοις ξοάνοις γλυφάς; Πότερον τῶν καθόλου στοιχείων, ἤ, ὅπερ καὶ τὸ ἐναργὲς τῆς ὄψεως ἐπιδείκνυσι, τῶν ἐν νεκροῖς κειμένων θνητῶν;

Saying these and suchlike things, he refers back to the daemons the *mythoi* concerning the aforementioned gods and again gives first one allegorical rendering and then another. It would have been reasonable to inquire of which gods they will say the *xoana* preserve the *morphai* that have been impressed. Or of what daemons? Or are they *eikones* of fire and air and earth and water, or of men and women? Or *schemata* of irrational animals and beasts? For since even to themselves it has been admitted that there have been certain mortal men with the same names as the sun and the universal elements, and that these have been proclaimed gods, of whom would it be reasonable to say that the *morphai* are, and the *eikones* carved in the soulless *xoana*? Of the universal elements, or, as also the clarity of sight shows, of mortals lying among the dead?

106

Eusebius, *Praeparatio evangelica* 3.4.92 c–d A.D. 312–318
(= Porphyry, *Epistle to Anebo the Egyptian*.)
Text: E.H. Gifford, ed., tr., *Eusebii Pamphili evangelicae praeparationis libri XV* (Oxford, 1903) I.
Translation adapted from Gifford (vol. III).

Ἑώρα γὰρ τοὺς τὸν Ἥλιον δημιουργὸν φαμένους, καὶ τὰ περὶ τὸν Ὄσιριν καὶ τὴν Ἶσιν, καὶ πάντας τοὺς ἱερατικοὺς μύθους ἢ εἰς τοὺς ἀστέρας καὶ τὰς τούτων φάνσεις καὶ κρύψεις καὶ ἐπιτολὰς ἑλιττομένους, ἢ εἰς τὰς τῆς σελήνης αὐξήσεις καὶ μειώσεις, ἢ εἰς τὴν τοῦ ἡλίου πορείαν, ἢ τό γε νυκτερινὸν ἡμισφαίριον ἢ τὸ ἡμερινόν, ἢ τόν γε ποταμόν· καὶ ὅλως πάντα εἰς τὰ φυσικὰ καὶ οὐδὲν εἰς ἀσωμάτους καὶ ζώσας οὐσίας ἑρμηνεύοντας. Ὧν οἱ πλείους καὶ τὸ ἐφ' ἡμῖν ἐκ τῆς τῶν ἀστέρων ἀνῆψαν κινήσεως, οὐκ οἶδ' ὅπως δεσμοῖς ἀλύτοις ἀνάγκῃ, ἣν εἱμαρμένην λέγουσιν, πάντα καταδήσαντες, καὶ πάντα τούτοις ἀνάψαντες τοῖς θεοῖς, οὓς ὡς λυτῆρας τῆς εἱμαρμένης μόνους ἔν τε ἱεροῖς καὶ ξοάνοις καὶ τοῖς ἄλλοις θεραπεύουσι.

For he saw that those who say that Helios is the *demiourgos*, turn both the stories about Osiris and Isis, and all the priestly *muthoi*, either to bear on the stars and their appearances and vanishings and risings, or on the waxings and wanings of the moon, or on the course of the sun, or the nighttime hemisphere, or the daytime one, or the river; and altogether, explaining everything in terms of physical things, and nothing to do with incorporeal and living beings. And most of them even ascribed our own activity to the movement of the stars, nor do I know how, binding with unloosable bonds by necessity, which they call fate, everything, and ascribing everything to those gods, whom as the only deliverers from fate, they worship in *hiera* both *xoana* and other things.

107

Eusebius, *Praeparatio evangelica* 3.6.97 d–7.98 a A.D. 312–318
(= Porphyry, Περὶ ἀγαλμάτων fr. 1 Bidez.)
Text: E.H. Gifford, ed., tr., *Eusebii Pamphili evangelicae praeparationis libri XV* (Oxford, 1903) I.
Translation adapted from Gifford (vol. III).

Ἄκουε δ' οὖν καὶ τῆς τούτων φυσιολογίας, μεθ' οἵας ἐξενήνεκται τῷ Πορφυρίῳ ἀλαζονείας·

> *Φθέγξομαι οἷς θέμις ἐστί, θύρας δ' ἐπίθεσθε βέβηλοι.*
>
> *Σοφίας θεολόγου νοήματα δεικνύς, οἷς τὸν θεὸν καὶ τοῦ θεοῦ τὰς δυνάμεις διὰ εἰκόνων συμφύλων αἰσθήσει ἐμήνυσαν ἄνδρες τὰ ἀφανῆ φανεροῖς ὑποτυπώσαντες πλάσμασι τοῖς καθάπερ ἐκ βίβλων τῶν ἀγαλμάτων ἀναλέγειν τὰ περὶ θεῶν μεμαθηκόσι γράμματα. Θαυμαστὸν δὲ οὐδὲν ξύλα καὶ λίθους ἡγεῖσθαι τὰ ξόανα τοὺς ἀμαθεστάτους, καθὰ δὴ καὶ τῶν γραμμάτων οἱ ἀνόητοι λίθους μὲν ὁρῶσι τὰς στήλας, ξύλα δὲ τὰς δέλτους, ἐξυφασμένην δὲ πάπυρον τὰς βίβλους.*

Listen then to their physiology also, and observe with what boastfulness it has been published by Porphyry.

"I speak to those who lawfully may hear;
Depart all ye profane, and close the doors."

The thoughts of a wise theology, wherein men indicated God and God's powers by *eikones* akin to sense, and sketched invisible things in visible forms, I will show to those who have learned to read from the *agalmata* as from books the things there written concerning the gods. Nor is it any wonder that the utterly unlearned regard these *xoana* as stocks and stones, just as also those who do not understand the written letters look upon the the stelae as mere stones, and on the tablets as bits of wood, and on books as woven papyrus.

108

Eusebius, *Praeparatio evangelica* 3.7.98 d–8.99 d A.D. 312–318
(= Plutarch, *De Daedalis Plataeensibus* [*Moralia* fr. 158 Sandbach].)
(= Callimachus, *Aetia* IV fr. 100 Pfeiffer.)
Text: E.H. Gifford, ed., tr., *Eusebii Pamphili evangelicae praeparationis libri XV* (Oxford, 1903) I.
Translation adapted from Gifford (vol. III).

Ταῦτα ὁ θαυμαστὸς φιλόσοφος, ὧν τί ἂν γένοιτο ἀσχημονέστερον τὰ αἰσχρὰ σεμνολογοῦσιν, τί δὲ βιαιότερον <ἢ> τὰς ἀψύχους ὕλας, χρυσὸν καὶ λίθον καὶ τὰ τοιαῦτα, εἰκόνας φέρειν τοῦ φωτὸς τῶν θεῶν καὶ τῆς οὐρανίου καὶ αἰθερίου φύσεως δηλώματα φάσκειν; Ὅτι δὲ τῶν νέων ἐστὶ ταῦτα σοφίσματα, μηδ' ὄναρ τῶν παλαιῶν εἰς ἐνθύμησιν ἐλθόντα, γνοίης ἂν μαθὼν ὅτι καὶ ἀπόβλητα ἦν παρὰ τοῖς προτέροις τὰ διὰ χρυσοῦ καὶ τῆς νομιζομένης πολυτελεστέρας ὕλης ξόανα. Λέγει δ' οὖν Πλούταρχος ὧδέ πη κατὰ λέξιν·

Ἡ δὲ τῶν ξοάνων ποίησις ἀρχαῖον ἔοικεν εἶναί τι καὶ παλαιόν, εἴ γε ξύλινον μὲν ἦν τὸ πρῶτον εἰς Δῆλον ὑπὸ Ἐρυσίχθονος Ἀπόλλωνι ἐπὶ τῶν θεωριῶν ἄγαλμα, ξύλινον δὲ τὸ τῆς Πολιάδος ὑπὸ τῶν αὐτοχθόνων ἱδρυθέν, ὃ μέχρι νῦν Ἀθηναῖοι διαφυλάττουσιν. Ἥρας δὲ καὶ Σάμιοι ξύλινον εἶχον εἶδος, ὥς φησι Καλλίμαχος,

Οὔπω <Σμίλιδος> ἔργον ἐΰξοον, ἀλλ' ἐπὶ τεθμὸν
δηναιὸν γλυφάνων ἄξοος ἦσθα σανίς.
ὧδε γὰρ ἱδρύοντο θεοὺς τότε· καὶ γὰρ Ἀθήνης
ἐν Λίνδῳ Δαναὸς λιτὸν ἔθηκεν ἕδος.

Λέγεται δὲ Πείρας ὁ πρῶτος Ἀργολίδος Ἥρας ἱερὸν εἰσάμενος, τὴν ἑαυτοῦ θυγατέρα Καλλίθυιαν ἱέρειαν καταστήσας, ἐκ τῶν περὶ Τίρυνθα δένδρων ὄγχνην τεμὼν εὐκτέανον, Ἥρας ἄγαλμα μορφῶσαι. Πέτραν μὲν γὰρ εἰς θεοῦ κοπῆναι εἰκόνα σκληρὰν καὶ δύσεργον καὶ ἄψυχον οὐκ ἐβούλοντο· χρυσὸν δὲ καὶ ἄργυρον ἡγοῦντο γῆς ἀκάρπου καὶ διεφθαρμένης χρώματα νοσώδη καὶ κηλῖδας ἐξανθεῖν ὥσπερ μώλωπας ὑπὸ πυρὸς ῥαπισθείσης· ἐλέφαντι δὲ παίζοντες μὲν ἔσθ' ὅπου προσεχρῶντο, ποικίλματι τρυφῆς.

Ταῦτα ὁ Πλούταρχος· καὶ τούτου δὲ πολὺ πρότερον ὁ Πλάτων οὐδὲν εἶναι σεμνὸν οὐδὲ προσεοικὸς θείᾳ φύσει ἐν χρυσῷ καὶ ἐλέφαντι τοῖς τε ἐξ ὕλης ἀψύχου κατασκευάσμασιν εὖ μάλα εἰδὼς ἐπάκουσον ἐν τοῖς Νόμοις ὁποῖα διατάττεται·

> Γῆ μὲν οὖν ἑστία τε οἰκήσεως ἱερὰ πᾶσι πάντων θεῶν· μηδεὶς οὖν δευτέρως ἱερὰ καθιερούτω θεοῖς. Χρυσὸς δὲ καὶ ἄργυρος ἐν ἄλλαις πόλεσιν ἰδίᾳ τε καὶ ἐν ἱεροῖς ἐστιν ἐπίφθονον κτῆμα, ἐλέφας δὲ ἀπολελοιπότος ψυχὴν σώματος οὐκ εὐαγὲς ἀνάθημα· σίδηρος δὲ καὶ χαλκὸς πολέμων ὄργανα.

These are the statements of this wonderful philosopher, and what could be more unseemly than talking, as they do, in solemn phrase about shameful things, or what more violently unreasonable than to assert that soulless materials, gold and stone and such things, bear *eikones* of the light of the gods and manifestations of their heavenly and ethereal nature? That these are modern sophistries, and never entered, even in a dream, into the imagination of the ancients, you may learn, on being informed that *xoana* made of gold, and other material esteemed more precious, were even rejected among the men of former times. Plutarch, at all events, says somewhere thus, word for word:

> The making of *xoana* seems to be something ancient and old, if the first *agalma* sent to Delos to Apollo by Erysichthon on the occasion of the festivals was wooden, and if that of Polias is wooden, the one the autochthonous inhabitants set up, which the Athenians keep to this day. The Samians also had a wooden *hedos* of Hera, as Callimachus says:
>
> > Not yet the well-carved work [of Smilis], but according to the old custom
> > You were a plank not carved by chisels;
> > For thus did they then set up the gods; and thus
> > At Lindos Danaus placed the simple *hedos* of Athena.
>
> It is said that Peiras, founder of the *hieron* of Argive Hera, having made his own daughter Callithyia priestess, cutting down a straight-grained pear from the trees around Tiryns shaped an *agalma* of Hera. For they did not want to cut stone into a rough and hard to work and soulless *eikon* of a god, and gold and silver they thought to be diseased colors of infertile and corrupt earth and stains breaking out like bruises when it had been struck by fire; and playing with ivory, sometimes they used it for decorating their daintiness.

These things Plutarch [says]; and long before him Plato knew well that there is nothing venerable or suited to the divine nature in gold and ivory, and things manufactured out of soulless material: for hear what sort of directions he gives in the *Laws*:

> The land, therefore, and the household hearth are for all men *hiera* of all the gods; therefore let no one consecrate *hiera* a second time to the gods. Gold and silver in other cities, both in private houses and in *hiera*, are an individious possession, and ivory taken from a dead body is not a pure *anathema*; iron and bronze are implements of war.

109

Eusebius, *Praeparatio evangelica* 3.10.106 b–c A.D. 312–318
Text: E.H. Gifford, ed., tr., *Eusebii Pamphili evangelicae praeparationis libri* XV (Oxford, 1903) I.
Translation adapted from Gifford (vol. III).

Ψυχὴ μὲν οὖν λογικὴ καὶ ἀθάνατος καὶ νοῦς ἀπαθὴς ἐν ἀνθρώπου φύσει εὖ μοι δοκεῖ λέγεσθαι εἰκόνα καὶ ὁμοίωσιν ἀποσώζειν θεοῦ, καθ' ὅσον ἄϋλος καὶ ἀσώματος νοερά τε καὶ λογικὴ τὴν οὐσίαν συνέστηκεν, ἀρετῆς οὖσα καὶ σοφίας δεκτική. Εἰ δή τις εἴη δυνατὸς ψυχῆς ἄγαλμα καὶ μορφὴν ἐν εἰκόνι τεκτήνασθαι, δύναιτ' ἂν οὗτος καί τι τῶν κρειττόνων· εἰ δὲ ἄμορφος καὶ ἀειδὴς καὶ ἀσχημάτιστος, οὔτε ὁράσει θεωρητὸς οὔτε λόγῳ καὶ ἀκοῇ τὴν οὐσίαν καταληπτὸς ὁ ἀνθρώπινος νοῦς, τίς ἂν μανείη τοσοῦτον ὡς τὸ ἀνδρείκελον ξόανον Θεοῦ τοῦ ἀνωτάτω μορφὴν καὶ εἰκόνα φέρειν ἀποφήνασθαι;

Thus the rational and immortal soul and the unaffected mind in the nature of man seem to me well to be said to preserve the *eikon* and *homoiosis* [image and likeness] of God, since it has been composed immaterial and incorporeal and intellectual and logical in its being, being capable of virtue and wisdom. Thus if anyone were able to contrive an *agalma* and *morphe* of the soul in an *eikon*, such a person would also make something of the higher natures; but if the *nous* of man is formless and invisible and unfigurable, neither visible by seeing nor by speech and hearing graspable in its being, who could be mad enough that he would declare that a *xoanon* that is like a man bears the *morphe* and *eikon* of God, the highest?

110

Eusebius, *Praeparatio evangelica* 3.12.116 d– 117 a A.D. 312–318
(= Porphyry, *Περὶ ἀγαλμάτων* 10.67 Bidez.)
Text: E.H. Gifford, ed., tr., *Eusebii Pamphili evangelicae praeparationis libri* XV (Oxford, 1903) I.
Translation adapted from Gifford (vol. III).

Ἡ δὲ τῆς Εἰλειθυίας πόλις τὸ τρίτον φῶς θεραπεύει· τὸ δὲ ξόανον τετύπωται εἰς γῦπα πετομένην, ἧς τὸ πτέρωμα ἐκ σπουδαίων συνέστηκε λίθων. Σημαίνει δὲ τὸ μὲν γυποειδὲς αὐτῆς τὴν γεννητικὴν πνευμάτων σελήνην· ἐκ γὰρ τοῦ πνεύματος οἴονται συλλαμβάνειν τὸν γῦπα, θηλείας πάσας ἀποφαινόμενοι.

But the city of Eileithuia worships the third light; the *xoanon* is carved into [the form of] a flying vulture, whose plumage has been contrived of precious stones. Her vulture form indicates that the moon is the engenderer of winds; for they think the vulture conceives from the wind, declaring that they are all female.

111
Eusebius, *Praeparatio evangelica* 3.13.122 a–b A.D. 312–318
Text: E.H. Gifford, ed., tr., *Eusebii Pamphili evangelicae praeparationis libri XV* (Oxford, 1903) I.
Translation adapted from Gifford (vol. III).

Τοῦτο γὰρ δέον ἦν ποιεῖν τοῖς τἀληθὲς ἐπεγνωκόσι, μηδὲ κατάγειν καὶ καταβάλλειν εἰς αἰσχρὰς καὶ ἐμπαθεῖς ἀρρητολογίας τὴν σεβάσμιον τοῦ Θεοῦ πρόσρησιν· ἀλλὰ μηδ' ἐν οἰκίσκοις καὶ σκότου μυχοῖς ἀνδρῶν τε οἰκοδομίαις σφᾶς αὐτοὺς ἐναποκλείειν, ὡς ἔνδον εὑρήσοντας τὸν Θεόν, μηδ' ἐν ξοάνοις ἐξ ἀψύχου πεποιημένοις ὕλης τὰς θείας τιμᾶν οἴεσθαι δυνάμεις, μηδὲ μὴν γεώδεσιν ἀτμοῖς αἱμάτων καὶ λύθρου καὶ νεκρῶν ζώων αἵμασι κεχαρισμένα τῷ Θεῷ πράττειν νομίζειν.

For this was what those who had known the truth ought to do, and not to degrade and debase the venerable name of God into foul and lustful fables of unspeakable things; not yet to shut themselves up in cells and dark recesses and buildings made by men, as if they would find God inside, nor to think that they were worshipping the divine powers in *xoana* made out of soulless material, nor to suppose that by vapors of gore and filth steaming from the earth, and by the blood of slain animals they are doing things pleasing to God.

112
Eusebius, *Praeparatio evangelica* 3.14.123 a–b A.D. 312–318
Text: E.H. Gifford, ed., tr., *Eusebii Pamphili evangelicae praeparationis libri XV* (Oxford, 1903) I.
Translation adapted from Gifford (vol. III).

Μετὰ γοῦν τὴν μακρὰν καὶ πολλὴν φιλοσοφίαν καὶ μετὰ τὰς σεμνὰς μετεωρολογίας καὶ φυσιολογίας, ἄνωθέν ποθεν ὡς ἀφ' ὑψηλοτάτης ἀκρωρείας καταπίπτοντες σὺν τοῖς πλήθεσι κατεσύροντο, καὶ τῇ τῶν παλαιῶν πολυθέῳ πλάνῃ συνεφύροντο, τὰ τοῖς πολλοῖς ὅμοια, διὰ τοῦ θύειν καὶ τοῖς ξοάνοις προσπίπτειν, δοξάζειν ὑποκρινόμενοι αὔξοντές τε καὶ ἔτι μᾶλλον κρατύνοντες τὴν δημώδη τῶν μυθικῶν διηγημάτων περὶ θεῶν ὑπόληψιν.

So after their long and important philosophical speculation, and after their solemn systems of meteorology and physiology, they fell down from their high place, as it were from the loftiest mountain top, and were dragged down with the common herd, and swept away with the polytheistic delusion of the ancients, pretending that they glorified the like deities by sacrificing and falling down before *xoana*, and increasing, and still further strengthening, the vulgar opinion of the legendary stories about the gods.

113

Eusebius, *Praeparatio evangelica* 4.1.131 a–b A.D. 312–318
Text: E.H. Gifford, ed., tr., *Eusebii Pamphili evangelicae praeparationis libri XV* (Oxford, 1903) I.
Translation adapted from Gifford (vol. III).

Ὅτι μὲν οὖν οὐ θεοὶ τὰ ἄψυχα ξόανα προφανὲς καὶ αὐτοῖς, ὅτι δ' οὐδὲ τὰ τῆς μυθικῆς αὐτῶν θεολογίας φέρει τινὰ σεμνὸν καὶ θεοπρεπῆ λόγον ἐν τῷ πρώτῳ δέδεικται συγγράμματι, ὥσπερ οὖν καὶ ἐν τῷ δευτέρῳ καὶ τῷ τρίτῳ ὅτι μηδὲ τὰ τῆς φυσικωτέρας καὶ φιλοσόφου τῶν μύθων ἑρμηνείας ἀβίαστον αὐτοῖς περιέχει τὴν ἐξήγησιν. Τὸ δὴ τρίτον φέρε σκεψώμεθα, τί ποτε χρὴ νομίζειν τὰς ἐν τοῖς ξοάνοις φωλευούσας δυνάμεις, πότερα τὸν τρόπον ἀστείας καὶ ἀγαθὰς καὶ ὡς ἀληθῶς θείας, ἢ τούτων ἁπάντων τὰ ἐναντία.

Thus, that the soulless *xoana* are not gods is evident even to themselves, and that their mythical theology offers no explanation that is respectable and appropriate to a god, has been shown in the first book [of the *PE*], as likewise in the second and third it has been shown that neither does their more physical and philosophical interpretation of the legends contain an unforced explanation. Come, let us examine the third point, how it is necessary to consider the powers that lurk in the *xoana*, whether civilized and good and truly divine in character, or thoroughly the opposite of these.

114

Eusebius, *Praeparatio evangelica* 4.4.140 a–d A.D. 312–318
Text: E.H. Gifford, ed., tr., *Eusebii Pamphili evangelicae praeparationis libri XV* (Oxford, 1903) I.
Translation adapted from Gifford (vol. III).

Οἶμαι δὲ παντί τῳ εἶναι σαφές, ὡς ὁ τῶν προκειμένων ἔλεγχος οὐ μικρὸν ἀλλὰ καὶ μέγιστον ὁμοῦ καὶ ἀναγκαιότατον περιέξει μέρος τῆς εὐαγγελικῆς ὑποθέσεως. Εἰ γὰρ οἱ πρὸ τῆς τοῦ σωτῆρος ἡμῶν Ἰησοῦ Χριστοῦ παρουσίας πανταχοῦ πάντες, Ἕλληνες καὶ βάρβαροι, δειχθεῖεν μὴ τὸν ἀληθῆ Θεὸν ἐπεγνωκότες, ἀλλ' ἤτοι τὰ μὴ ὄντα ὡς ὄντα δοξάζοντες, ἢ ὑπό τινων μοχθηρῶν καὶ θεομάχων πνευμάτων δαιμόνων τε πονηρῶν καὶ ἀκαθάρτων τυφλῶν δίκην ὧδε κἀκεῖσε περιηγμένοι, καὶ βυθῷ κακίας πρὸς αὐτῶν καθειλκυσμένοι· (καὶ τί γὰρ ἄλλ' ἢ δαιμονῶντες;) πῶς οὐ μειζόνως ἂν ὀφθείη τὸ μέγα τῆς εὐαγγελικῆς οἰκονομίας μυστήριον, πάντας πανταχόθεν ἐκ τῆς πατροπαραδότου πλάνης τῆς τῶν δαιμόνων καταδυναστείας διὰ τῆς τοῦ σωτῆρος φωνῆς ἀνακεκλημένους, καὶ τοὺς μέχρις ἐσχατιῶν γῆς οἰκοῦντας ἀνθρώπους τῆς ἐξ αἰῶνος κατασχούσης τὸν πάντα βίον ἀπάτης λελυτρωμένους, ὥστε ἐξ ἐκείνου καὶ εἰς δεῦρο λελύσθαι μὲν καὶ καθῃρῆσθαι αὐτοῖς ναοῖς καὶ ξοάνοις τὰ πεπαλαιωμένα τῆς τῶν ἐθνῶν ἁπάντων πλάνης ἱδρύματα, ἱερὰ δὲ ὄντως σεμνὰ καὶ εὐσεβείας διδασκαλεῖα τῷ παμβασιλεῖ καὶ δημιουργῷ τῶν ὅλων ἐν μέσαις πόλεσί τε καὶ κώμαις δυνάμει καὶ ἀρετῇ τοῦ σωτῆρος ἡμῶν ἀνὰ τὸν σύμπαντα κόσμον ἀνεγηγέρθαι, θυσίας τε τὰς θεοπρεπεῖς εὐχαῖς ὁσίων διακεκαθάρθαι κακίας ἁπάσης, ἔν τε ἀπαθείᾳ ψυχῆς καὶ πάσης ἀρετῆς ἀναλήψει κατὰ τὰ θεῖα καὶ σωτηριώδη παιδεύματα ἐξ ἁπάντων ὁσημέραι διηνεκῶς τῶν ἐθνῶν ἐπιτελεῖσθαι, τὰς δὴ καὶ μόνας ἀρεστὰς οὔσας καὶ προσηνεῖς θυσίας τῷ ἐπὶ πάντων Θεῷ;

Now I think it is plain to every one that the proof of the matters before us will embrace not a small part, but a very great and at the same time very necessary part of the evangelic argument. For suppose it should be shown that all men everywhere, both Greeks and barbarians, before the advent of our savior Jesus Christ, had no knowledge of the true God, but either regarded "the things that are not as though they were," or were led about hither and thither like blind men by certain wicked spirits fighting against God, and by evil and impure daemons, and were by them dragged down into an abyss of wickedness (for what else ailed them but possession by daemons?)—how can the great mystery of the Gospel dispensation fail to be seen in a higher light? I mean, that all men from all quarters have been called back by our savior's voice from the delusion handed down by their fathers about the tyranny of daemons, and that the men who dwell as far off as the ends of the earth have been released from the deception which from the earliest age oppressed their whole life, for since His time and up to the present have been broken up and destroyed the antiquated *hidrumata* of delusion of all the nations, in their *naoi* and *xoana*, and *hiera* that are holy, and schools of worship have been raised up in honor of the universal king and creator of all things, in the midst of cities and villages and by the power and goodness of our savior through the entire world, and by prayers of holy men and sacrifices which are worthy of God have been purified from all wickedness, and in freedom of soul from all passions, and in the acquirement of every virtue, according to the divine doctrines of salvation, are day by day continually offered up by all nations—those sacrifices which alone are acceptable and pleasing to the God who is over all?

115

Eusebius, *Praeparatio evangelica* 4.5.141 d A.D. 312–318

Text: E.H. Gifford, ed., tr., *Eusebii Pamphili evangelicae praeparationis libri XV* (Oxford, 1903) I.

Translation adapted from Gifford (vol. III).

Πάρεστι γοῦν σοι τὰς διὰ τῶν ξοάνων ἐνεργούσας δυνάμεις ὁποίας χρῆν ἀποφαίνεσθαι σκοπεῖν, πότερα θεοὺς ἢ δαίμονας, καὶ εἴτε φαύλους εἴτε ἀγαθούς, ἐκ τῶν παρατεθησομένων.

It is within your power, at any rate, to consider in what way ought to be viewed the powers that operate through the *xoana*, whether as gods or as daemons, and whether evil or good, on the basis of what will be led before you.

116

Eusebius, *Praeparatio evangelica* 4.16.156 b A.D. 312–318
(= Porphyry, *De abstinentia* 2.56.6 [**324**].)
Text: E.H. Gifford, ed., tr., *Eusebii Pamphili evangelicae praeparationis libri XV* (Oxford, 1903) I.
Translation adapted from Gifford (vol. III).

Καὶ Δουματηνοὶ δὲ τῆς Ἀραβίας κατ᾽ ἔτος ἕκαστον ἔθυον παῖδα, ὃν ὑπὸ βωμὸν ἔθαπτον, ᾧ χρῶνται ὡς ξοάνῳ.

And the Doumatenes of Arabia each year sacrificed a child, whom they buried under the altar, which they use as a *xoanon*.

117

Eusebius, *Praeparatio evangelica* 4.16.161 b–d A.D. 312–318
Text: E.H. Gifford, ed., tr., *Eusebii Pamphili evangelicae praeparationis libri XV* (Oxford, 1903) I.
Translation adapted from Gifford (vol. III).

Τοιαῦτα δὴ καὶ οὗτος διὰ τῆς οἰκείας ἱστορίας παρέδωκεν. Εἰκότως ἄρα καὶ ἡ παρ᾽ Ἑβραίοις γραφὴ καταμέμφεται τοῖς τὰ τοιαῦτα ζηλώσασι τῶν ἐκ περιτομῆς, φάσκουσα, Καὶ ἔθυον τοὺς υἱοὺς αὐτῶν καὶ τὰς θυγατέρας αὐτῶν τοῖς δαιμονίοις· καὶ ἐφονοκτονήθη ἡ γῆ ἐν τοῖς αἵμασι, καὶ ἐμιάνθη ἐν τοῖς ἔργοις αὐτῶν. Ἀλλὰ γὰρ ἡγοῦμαι διὰ τούτων ἀπεληλέγχθαι σαφῶς δαιμονικήν τινα γεγονέναι τὴν παλαιτάτην καὶ πρώτην τῶν ξοάνων ἵδρυσιν, καὶ πᾶσαν τὴν εἰδωλικὴν τῶν ἐθνῶν θεοποιίαν καὶ δαιμόνων οὐκ ἀγαθῶν ἀλλὰ πάντα μοχθηροτάτων καὶ φαύλων· ὡς ἐπαληθεύειν τὸ φάσκον ἐν προφητείαις λόγιον, Πάντες οἱ θεοὶ τῶν ἐθνῶν δαιμόνια· τό τε ἀποστολικόν, δι᾽ οὗ φησιν, Ὅτι ἃ θύουσι, δαιμονίοις καὶ οὐ Θεῷ θύουσιν.

Such things indeed this man [Diodorus Siculus] handed down in his own history. With good reason then does the scripture of the Hebrews lay blame upon those of the circumcision who emulated such practices, saying: "They sacrificed their sons and daughters to the daemons, and the land was defiled with their blood, and was polluted with their works [*Ps.* 105(106):37]." But in fact I believe it is clearly proved by this that the most ancient and first setting up of *xoana*, and all the idolatrous making of gods by the nations was something inspired by daemons, and not good daemons, but thoroughly worthless and wicked ones; so that the oracle speaks truth that says: "All the gods of the nations are daemons" [*Ps.* 95(96):5]; and the passage of the Apostle, where he says, that "the things which they sacrifice, they sacrifice to daemons and not to God [1 *Cor.* 10:20]."

118

Eusebius, *Praeparatio evangelica* 5.11.199 d–13.201 d A.D. 312–318
(= Porphyry, *De philosophia ex oraculis haurienda.*)
(= *Oracula Chaldaica* 224.)
Text: E.H. Gifford, ed., tr., *Eusebii Pamphili evangelicae praeparationis libri XV* (Oxford, 1903) I.
Translation adapted from Gifford (vol. III).

Οὐ μόνον δὲ τὴν πολιτείαν αὐτῶν αὐτοὶ μεμηνύκασι καὶ τὰ ἄλλα τὰ εἰρημένα, ἀλλὰ καὶ οἷστισι χαίρουσι καὶ κρατοῦνται ὑπηγόρευσαν, καὶ μὴν καὶ τίσιν ἀναγκάζονται, τίνα δὲ δεῖ θύειν, καὶ ἐκ ποίας ἡμέρας ἐκτρέπεσθαι, τό τε σχῆμα τῶν ἀγαλμάτων ποταπὸν δεῖ ποιεῖν, αὐτοί τε ποίοις σχήμασι φαίνονται ἔν τε ποίοις διατρίβουσι τόποις· καὶ ὅλως ἓν οὐδέν ἐστιν, ὃ μὴ παρ' αὐτῶν μαθόντες ἄνθρωποι οὕτως αὐτοὺς ἐτίμησαν. Πολλῶν δ' ὄντων ἃ τούτων ἐστὶ παραστατικά, ὀλίγα ἐκ τῶν πολλῶν παραθησόμεθα, ἵνα μὴ ἀμάρτυρον τὸν λόγον καταλείπωμεν.

Ὅτι δὲ καὶ τὰ ἀγάλματα αὐτοὶ ὑπέθεντο πῶς χρὴ ποιεῖν καὶ ἐκ ποίας ὕλης δηλώσει τὰ τῆς Ἑκάτης ἔχοντα τοῦτον τὸν τρόπον·

Ἀλλὰ τέλει ξόανον, κεκαθαρμένον, ὥς σε διδάξω·
πηγάνου ἐξ ἀγρίοιο δέμας ποίει, ἠδ' ἐπικόσμει
ζώοισιν λεπτοῖσι κατοικιδίοις σκαλαβώταις·
σμύρνης καὶ στύρακος λιβάνοιό τε μίγματα τρίψας
σὺν κείνοις ζώοισι, καὶ <αἰθριάσας> ὑπὸ μήνην
αὔξουσαν, τέλει αὐτὸς ἐπευχόμενος τήνδ' εὐχήν.

Εἶτ' ἐξέδωκεν εὐχήν, ἐδίδαξέ τε, πόσους ληπτέον σκαλαβώτας.

Ὅσσαι μορφαί μοι, τόσσοις ζώοις σε κελεύω
καὶ σφόδρα ταῦτα <τελεῖν>· δάφνης δέ μοι αὐτογενέθλου
οἴκου ἐμοῦ χώρημα ποιεῖν· καὶ ἀγάλματι πολλὸν
κείνῳ ἐπευχόμενος δι' ὕπνων ἐμέ τοι ἀναθηρήσεις.

καὶ πάλιν ἄλλοτε ἄγαλμα ἑαυτῆς ἐξέδωκε τοιοῦτον.

Καὶ περὶ τῶν σχημάτων ὅπως φαντάζονται αὐτοὶ μεμηνύκασιν, ἀφ' ὧν καὶ τὰ ἀγάλματα οὕτω καθιδρύνθη. Λέγει γοῦν ὁ Σάραπις ἰδὼν τὸν Πᾶνα περὶ ἑαυτοῦ·

Φαιδρὴ μὲν κατὰ δῶμα θεοῦ καταλάμπεται αὐγή·
ἦλθε γάρ, ἠντιβόλησε θεὸς μέγας· εἶδεν ἐμεῖο

κάρτος ἀμαιμάκετον, λαμπηδόνα φλογμοτύραννον,
βόστρυχον ἐκ κεφαλῆς νεάτης χαροποῖσι μετώποις
ἀμφὶς ἰαινόμενον, πλοχμοῖς θ' ἱεροῖσι γενείου.

Καὶ ὁ Πὰν ὕμνον περὶ ἑαυτοῦ ἐκδιδοὺς ἐδίδαξε λέγειν οὕτως·

Εὔχομαι βροτὸς γεγὼς
Πανὶ σύμφυτῳ θεῷ,
Δισσοκέρατι, δισσόποδι,
τραγοσκελεῖ, τρυφῶντι,

καὶ τὰ ἀκολουθα. Καὶ ἡ Ἑκάτη δὲ περὶ ἑαυτῆς οὕτω φησίν·

Ἤδη μοι σύ γε πάντα ποίει· ξόανον δὲ ἐν αὐτῷ,
μορφή μοι πέλεται Δημήτερος ἀγλαοκάρπου,
εἵμασι παλλεύκοις, περὶ ποσσὶ δὲ χρυσοπέδιλος·
ἀμφὶ δὲ τῇ ζώνῃ δολιχοὶ προθέουσι δράκοντες,
ἴχνεσιν ἀχράντοισιν ἐφερπύζοντες, ἄνωθεν
αὐτῆς ἐκ κεφαλῆς ἀρτώμενοι ἐς πόδας ἄκρους,
σπειρηδὸν περὶ πᾶσαν ἑλισσόμενοι κατὰ κόσμον.

Ὕλη δέ, φησιν,

ἢ Παρίοιο λίθου, ἢ εὐξέστου ἐλέφαντος.

But not only have they themselves informed us of their mode of life and the other things that have been mentioned, but they have also suggested by what kinds of things they are pleased and prevailed upon, and indeed also by what they are compelled, what is necessary to sacrifice, and what day to avoid, and what *schema* of *agalmata* it is necessary to make, and in what *schemata* they appear, and in what places they reside; and altogether, there is no one thing, by which men honor them, that they have not learned from them. As the proofs which confirm this are many, we will bring forward a few from the many, so that we shall not leave our statement without witness.

That they [*sc.* daemons] themselves suggested how even their *agalmata* ought to be made, and of what kind of material, shall be shown by the response of Hecate in the following form:

But consecrate a *xoanon* that has been purified, in the way I will teach you;
make a body out of wild rue, deck it with
little animals, with household lizards,
and having brewed myrrh, glue, incense
with these animals, and gone into the fresh air when
the moon is crescent, perform this rite, making this prayer.

Then she sets forth the prayer, and showed how many lizards must be taken:

As many as my forms are, with so many animals I order you
to do these things, and carefully; with self-planted laurel
make a spacious house for me; and to that *agalma*
having offered many a prayer you will see me in dreams.

And again in another place she described an *agalma* of herself of this kind.

And they themselves have indicated how they appear with respect to their *schemata*, from which their *agalmata* too were set up. Sarapis for example says of himself, after seeing Pan:

A brilliant light shone through the god's own house;
He came, the mighty god, and met me there.
My matchless strength, and glow of lordly fire,
And waving curls he saw, which from my head
On either side play round my radiant brows,
And mingle with the red beard's sacred locks.

Pan also taught men a hymn concerning himself, which runs as follows:

To Pan, a god of kindred race,
A mortal born my vows I pay;
Whose horned brows and cloven feet
And goat-like legs his lust betray,

and the rest, and Hecate speaks thus about herself:

Make everything for me anon; a *xoanon* in it;
My form is Demeter's, bright with autumn fruits,
White robes, and golden sandals around the feet,
Around the waist long snakes run to and fro,
Gliding o'er all with undefiled track,
And from the head down to the tips of the feet
Wrapping me fairly round with spiral coils.

And the material, she says,

Or of Parian stone or polished ivory.

119

Eusebius, *Praeparatio evangelica* 5.14.203 a–b A.D. 312–318

Text: E.H. Gifford, ed., tr., *Eusebii Pamphili evangelicae praeparationis libri XV* (Oxford, 1903) I.

Translation adapted from Gifford (vol. III).

Διὰ τούτων καὶ τῶν τούτοις ὁμοίων ὁ γενναῖος Ἑλλήνων φιλόσοφος, ὁ θαυμαστὸς θεολόγος, ὁ τῶν ἀπορρήτων μύστης, τὴν ἐκ λογίων φιλοσοφίαν ὡς ἀπόρρητα θεῶν περιέχουσαν λόγια παραφαίνει, ἄντικρυς τῆς πονηρᾶς καὶ δαιμονικῆς ἀληθῶς δυνάμεως ἐξαγορεύων τὰς κατ' ἀνθρώπων ἐνέδρας.

Τί γὰρ ἂν γένοιτο βιωφελὲς ἀνθρώποις ἐκ τῆς κακοτέχνου γοητείας; Τί δ' ἂν ἔχοι θεοφιλὲς ἡ τῶν ἀψύχων ξοάνων περιεργία; Ποίας δ' ἂν εἰκὼν γένοιτ' ἂν ἐνθέου δυνάμεως ἡ τῶν τοιῶνδε σχημάτων μόρφωσις;

By these [quotations] and ones like them, the noble philosopher of the Greeks [Porphyry], the marvellous theologian, the initiate of secret things, exhibits the philosophy from the oracles as containing secret oracles of the gods, while openly declaring the plots against men of their evil and truly daemonic power. For what benefit for men could there be from sorcery, the evil craft? Or what love of God does the fussing about with soulless *xoana* have? Of what divine power could be an *eikon* in the shape of such *schemata*?

120

Eusebius, *Praeparatio evangelica* 6.10.274 d–275 a A.D. 312–318
(= Bardesanes, *On Fate* [Greek translation from Syriac].)
Text: E.H. Gifford, ed., tr., *Eusebii Pamphili evangelicae praeparationis libri XV* (Oxford, 1903) I.
Translation adapted from Gifford (vol. III).

Νόμος ἐστὶ παρὰ Σήραις μηδένα φονεύειν, μήτε πορνεύειν, μήτε κλέπτειν, μήτε ξόανα προσκυνεῖν· καὶ ἐν ἐκείνῃ τῇ μέγιστῃ χώρᾳ οὐ ναόν ἐστιν ἰδεῖν, οὐ γυναῖκα πορνικήν, οὐ μοιχαλίδα ὀνομαζομένην, οὐ κλέπτην ἑλκόμενον ἐπὶ δίκην, οὐκ ἀνδροφόνον, οὐ πεφονευμένον.

It is the law among the Seres that no one is to murder, nor to be a prostitute, nor to steal, nor to bow to *xoana*; and in that very large country there is no *naos* to see, no prostitute, no woman named adultress, no thief dragged away for justice, no murderer, no victim of murder.

121

Eusebius, *Praeparatio evangelica* 6.10.275 a–b A.D. 312–318
(= Bardesanes, *On Fate* [Greek translation from Syriac].)
Text: E.H. Gifford, ed., tr., *Eusebii Pamphili evangelicae praeparationis libri XV* (Oxford, 1903) I.
Translation adapted from Gifford (vol. III).

Παρὰ Ἰνδοῖς καὶ Βακτρίοις εἰσὶ χιλιάδες πολλαὶ τῶν λεγομένων Βραχμάνων, οἵτινες κατὰ παράδοσιν τῶν προγόνων καὶ νόμων οὔτε φονεύουσιν, οὔτε ξόανα σέβονται, οὐκ ἐμψύχου γεύονται, οὐ μεθύσκονταί ποτε, οἴνου καὶ σίκερος μὴ γευόμενοι, οὐ κακίᾳ τινὶ κοινωνοῦσι προσέχοντες τῷ Θεῷ, τῶν ἄλλων Ἰνδῶν φονευόντων, καὶ ἑταιρευόντων, καὶ μεθυσκομένων, καὶ σεβομένων ξόανα, καὶ πάντα σχεδὸν καθ' εἱμαρμένην φερομένων.

Among the Indians and the Bactrians, there are many ten-thousands of those called Brahmins, who according to the tradition of their ancestors and their laws neither murder, nor worship *xoana*, nor taste of living food, nor ever get drunk, since they do not taste of wine or fermented liquor, nor have any contact with any evil, for they devote themselves to God, while other Indians murder, and fornicate, and get drunk, and worship *xoana*, and carry on almost everything according to the dictates of fate.

122

Eusebius, *Praeparatio evangelica* 10.4.469 b A.D. 312–318

Text: E.H. Gifford, ed., tr., *Eusebii Pamphili evangelicae praeparationis libri XV* (Oxford, 1903) II.

Translation adapted from Gifford (vol. III).

Οἷς τὰ μὲν ἐκ Φοινίκης Κάδμος ὁ Ἀγήνορος, τὰ δ' ἐξ Αἰγύπτου περὶ θεῶν, ἢ καί ποθεν ἄλλοθεν, μυστήρια καὶ τελετάς, ξοάνων τε ἱδρύσεις, καὶ ὕμνους, ᾠδάς τε καὶ ἐπῳδάς, ἤτοι ὁ Θρᾴκιος Ὀρφεύς, ἢ καί τις ἕτερος Ἕλλην ἢ βάρβαρος, τῆς πλάνης ἀρχηγοὶ γενόμενοι, συνεστήσαντο· τούτων γὰρ οὐδένας καὶ αὐτοὶ ἂν ὁμολογήσαιεν Ἕλληνες παλαιοτέρους εἰδέναι.

Cadmus the son of Agenor introduced to them [the ancient Greeks] practices from Phoenicia, and practices from Egypt concerning the gods, or also from someplace else, mysteries and rites, and the setting up of *xoana*, and hymns, and odes and epodes, either the Thracian Orpheus [introduced to them] or some other Greek or barbarian, who became the leaders in delusion; for even the Greeks themselves would acknowledge that they know no one more ancient than these men.

123

Eusebius, *Praeparatio evangelica* 10.4.469 c A.D. 312–318

Text: E.H. Gifford, ed., tr., *Eusebii Pamphili evangelicae praeparationis libri XV* (Oxford, 1903) II.

Translation adapted from Gifford (vol. III).

Πολὺς γοῦν παρὰ τοῖς πᾶσιν ὁ προδηλωθεὶς περὶ θεῶν ἐκράτει λόγος· νεῴ τε περικαλλεῖς, παντοίοις ἀγάλμασι καὶ ἀναθήμασι κεκοσμημένοι, παρὰ τοῖς πᾶσιν ἐξήσκηντο· ἀτὰρ δὴ καὶ ξόανα παντοίας ὕλης εἰς πᾶσαν θνητῶν ζώων ἰδέαν τετυπωμένα φιλοκάλως ἐξείργαστο.

At all events, the aforesaid doctrine concerning the gods gained power among all men in large part; and among all men beautiful *neoi* were furnished, decked out with all kinds of *agalmata* and *anathemata*; and furthermore *xoana* formed of all kinds of material into every image of mortal *zoia* were aesthetically worked.

124

Eusebius, *Praeparatio evangelica* 10.8.482 c A.D. 312–318
(= Diodorus Siculus 1.98.5 [58].)
Text: E.H. Gifford, ed., tr., *Eusebii Pamphili evangelicae praeparationis libri XV* (Oxford, 1903) II.
Translation adapted from Gifford (vol. III).

Πάντων δὲ τῶν παλαιῶν ἀγαλματοποιῶν τοὺς μάλιστα διωνομασμένους διατετριφέναι παρ' αὐτοῖς, Τηλεκλέα καὶ Θεόδωρον, τοὺς Ῥοίκου μὲν υἱούς, κατασκευάσαντας δὲ τοῖς Σαμίοις τὸ τοῦ Ἀπόλλωνος τοῦ Πυθίου ξόανον.

Of all the ancient *agalma*-makers, the most famous had sojourned among them, Telecles and Theodorus, the sons of Rhoecus, having made the *xoanon* of Pythian Apollo for the Samians.

125

Eusebius, *Praeparatio evangelica* 13.14.691 d–692 b A.D. 312–318
Text: E.H. Gifford, ed., tr., *Eusebii Pamphili evangelicae praeparationis libri XV* (Oxford, 1903) II.
Translation adapted from Gifford (vol. III).

Αὐτίκα γοῦν βραχύ τι τῆς φιλαυτίας εἰ ἐθελήσιας ὑφεῖναι, καὶ φῶς αὐτὸ δυνάμει λογικῆς οὐσίας ἐπιθεωρῆσαι, γνοίης ἂν τὸν θαυμάσιον φιλόσοφον αὐτὸν ἐκεῖνον, τὸν δὴ μόνον πάντων Ἑλλήνων ἀληθείας προθύρων ψαύσαντα, ὕλῃ φθαρτῇ καὶ ξοάνοις βαναύσων χερσὶν εἰς ἀνδρείκελον σχῆμα κατεσκευασμένοις τὴν τῶν θεῶν προσηγορίαν καταισχύνοντα, καὶ μετὰ τὸ μέγα τῆς μεγαλοφωνίας ὕψος, δι' ἧς τὸν πατέρα καὶ δημιουργὸν εἰδέναι τοῦδε τοῦ παντὸς διετείνατο, ἄνωθέν ποθεν ἐξ ὑπερκοσμίων ἁψίδων εἰς τὸν κατωτάτω βυθὸν τῆς θεομισοῦς εἰδωλολατρείας τῷ δήμῳ τῶν Ἀθηναίων συνωθούμενων· ὡς μὴ διατρέπεσθαι τὸν Σωκράτην καταβῆναι φάντα εἰς Πειραῖα προσευξόμενον τῇ θεῷ, καὶ τὴν βάρβαρον ἑορτὴν τοὺς πολίτας τότε πρῶτον ἐπιτελοῦντας θεασόμενον, καὶ τὸν ἀλεκτρυόνα τῷ Ἀσκληπιῷ θῦσαι ὁμολογοῦντα προστάξαι, τόν τε πάτριον Ἑλλήνων ἐξηγητήν, τὸν ἐγκαθήμενον ἐν Δελφοῖς δαίμονα, θειάζοντα.

Now, for example, if you would suppress a little of this self-admiration, and contemplate the true light itself by the power of reason, you would know that even that wonderful philosopher, who alone of all the Greeks touched the front doors of truth, dishonors the name of the gods by applying it to perishable matter and *xoana* manufactured by the hands of workers into a man-shaped *schema*, even after the great height of his magniloquence, in which he contended that he knew the father and creator of everything, he is thrust down from his place on high among the supramundane circles, and sinks with the common people of Athens into the lowest depth of their God-detested idolatry; so that he does not shrink from saying that Socrates had gone down to the Peiraeus to pray to the goddesss, and to see his fellow citizens then for the first time celebrating their barbarous festival; acknowledging also that he had enjoined the offering of a cock to Aesclepius, and regarded as a god the ancestal prophet of the Greeks, the daemon who sits enshrined at Delphi.

126

Eustathius *ad* Homer, *Iliad* 1.39 A.D. XII

Text: M. van der Valk, ed., *Eustathius archiepiscopi Thessalonicensis commentarii ad Homeri Iliadem pertinentes* I (Leiden, 1971) 56.7–9.

φησὶ γὰρ ἡ ἱστορία, ὅτι ἐν τῇ Χρύσῃ Σμινθέως ἐστὶν ἱερὸν καὶ μῦς ὑπόκειται τῷ ποδὶ τοῦ ξοάνου, Σκόπα ἔργον τοῦ Παρίου, τὸ σύμβολον τὸ τὴν ἐτυμότητα σῷζον τοῦ ὀνόματος, ἤγουν ἐν ᾧ κεῖται ἡ τοῦ Σμινθέως ἐτυμολογία.

For the history says that in Chryse there is a *hieron* of Smintheus, and under the foot of the *xoanon* lies a mouse, the work of Scopas of Paros, the symbol that keeps alive the etymological meaning of the name; that is to say, in which the etymology of Smintheus lies.

127

Eustathius *ad* Homer, *Iliad* 1.39 A.D. XII

Text: M. van der Valk, ed., *Eustathius archiepiscopi Thessalonicensis commentarii ad Homeri Iliadem pertinentes* I (Leiden, 1971) 57.14–16.

Ἡρακλέων δ' ὁ Ποντικὸς πληθύοντάς φησι τοὺς παρὰ τὸ ἱερὸν μύας νομισθῆναι ἱεροὺς καὶ τὸ ξόανον οὕτω κατασκευασθῆναι βεβηκὸς ἐπὶ τὺ μυΐ.

Heracleon Ponticus says that the mice around the *hieron* are considered sacred and that the *xoanon* thus has been fashioned standing on a mouse.

128

Eustathius *ad* Homer, *Iliad* 1.423 A.D. XII

Text: M. van der Valk, ed., *Eustathius archiepiscopi Thessalonicensis commentarii ad Homeri Iliadem pertinentes* I (Leiden, 1971) 196.22–28.

Ὅτι τὸ τὸν Δία εἰς Ὠκεανὸν ἔρχεσθαι ἐπὶ τοὺς ἀμύμονας Αἰθιοπῆας, θεοὺς δ' ἅμα πάντας ἕπεσθαι, δωδεκάτῃ δὲ αὖθις ἔρχεσθαι εἰς Ὄλυμπον, τινὲς μὲν ἱστορικῶς θεραπεύουσι λέγοντες, ὅτι ἐν Διοσπόλει μέγιστόν ἐστι Διὸς ἱερόν, ἀφ' οὗ λαβόντες Αἰθίοπες Διὸς ξόανον καὶ ἄλλων δαιμόνων σὺν αὐτῷ κατά τινα καιρὸν τεταγμένον περινοστοῦσι τὰ κατὰ τὴν Λιβύην καὶ πανηγυρίζουσι πολυτελῶς ἐπὶ δώδεκα ἡμέρας, ἐπεὶ καὶ τοσοῦτοι παρ' αὐτοῖς οἱ θεοί.

That Zeus went to Ocean among the blameless Ethiopians, and all the gods followed, at the same time, and on the twelfth day he comes back to Olympus, some foster [this] as historical, saying that in Diospolis there is a very large *hieron* of Zeus, from which the Ethiopians, taking a *xoanon* of Zeus and of the other divinities with him, at a certain arranged time, go around the area around the land of Libya, and they celebrate a festival lavishly for twelve days, because such gods [are] among them.

129

Eustathius *ad* Homer, *Iliad* 1.572 A.D. XII
Text: M. van der Valk, ed., *Eustathius archiepiscopi Thessalonicensis commentarii ad Homeri Iliadem pertinentes* I (Leiden, 1971) 233.37–234.5.

Ὅτι ἐπίηρα παρὰ τοῖς νεωτέροις τὰ ἐπιθυμητὰ παρὰ τὸ ἐρᾶν, ὡς ἀπὸ εὐθείας τῆς τὸ ἐπίηρον. οἱ δὲ παλαιοὶ ἐπίηρά φασι τὴν μετὰ ἐπικουρίας χάριν καὶ παράγουσι τὴν λέξιν οὕτως· ὥσπερ κόπτω κόπανον καὶ ἔχω ὄχανον, τὸ τῆς ἀσπίδος κράτημα, [δρέπω δρέπανον, ἥδω καὶ ἐν συστολῇ ἕδω ἕδανον καὶ ἕδνον κατὰ συγκοπήν, φρύγω φρύγανον, πέττω ἢ πέπτω πόπανον, ξέω ξόανον], οὕτως ἐρῶ, τὸ ἐπιθυμῶ, ἔρανον καὶ ἐκτάσει ἤρανον καὶ ἐπιήρανον, οὗ πληθυντικὸν ἐπιήρανα καὶ ἀποκοπῇ ἐπίηρα.

That *epiēra* [acceptable gift] among the more recent commentators means *epithumata* [cravings], derived from *eran*, as from its nominative *epiēron*. The ancients say that *epiēra* is the grace of aid and they derive the word thus: as *kopto–kopanon* and *echo–ochanon*, the handle of a shield, [*drepo–drepanon*, *hēdo* and in contraction *hĕdo–hedanon* and *hednon* by syncope, *phrygo–phryganon*, *petto* or *pepto–popanon*, *xeo–xoanon*], thus *ero*, to desire, *eranon* and by lengthening the short syllable, *ēranon* and *epiēranon*, whose plural is *epiērana* and by *apocope*, *epiēra*.

130

Eustathius *ad* Homer, *Iliad* 2.12 A.D. XII
Text: M. van der Valk, ed., *Eustathius archiepiscopi Thessalonicensis commentarii ad Homeri Iliadem pertinentes* I (Leiden, 1971) 256.24–257.1.

Ὅτι τὴν Τροίαν περιφράζων πόλιν εὐρυάγυιαν Τρώων καλεῖ. ἔστι δὲ εὐρυάγυια ἡ πλατύρρυμος· ἀγυιὰ γὰρ ἡ κοινῶς λεγομένη ῥύμη, ἀφ' ἧς καὶ ἀγυιεὺς κίων ἱερὸς Ἀπόλλωνος πρὸ θυρῶν ἑστώς, λήγων εἰς ὀξύ. γίνεται δὲ παρὰ τὸ ἄγειν· ὅθεν καὶ ὁ ἀγὼν καὶ ἡ ἀγορά. ἐναντία δὲ ἡ εὐρυάγυια ταῖς στενωποῖς. ἔφη δέ τις καὶ "ἀγυιάτιδας θεράπνας" τοὺς πρὸ τῶν θυρῶν βωμούς, [οἳ πρὸς χάριν Ἀγυιέως Ἀπόλλωνος ἵδρυντο, τιμωμένου πρὸ πυλῶν ὡς ἀλεξικάκου.

That, making a periphrasis, he calls Troy the "wide-wayed city of the Trojans." "Wide-wayed" means "with broad streets"; for "*anguia*" is what is commonly called an alley, from which the column sacred to Apollo that stands before doors is called "*agyieus*," ending in a point. It is derived from "*agein*." Whence also "*agon*" and "*agora*." On the other hand "wide-wayed" refers to straits. But someone says also that "wide-wayed abodes" are the altars in front of doors, [which are set up for the worship of Agyieus Apollo, who is honored in front of doors as an averter of evil.]

131

Eustathius *ad* Homer, *Iliad* 2.556 A.D. XII
Text: M. van der Valk, ed., *Eustathius archiepiscopi Thessalonicensis commentarii ad Homeri Iliadem pertinentes* I (Leiden, 1971) 437.23–26.

Μαραθὼν δὲ ὕστερον μὲν τὸν Περσικὸν ἀγῶνα, πρὸ δὲ Ὁμήρου τὸν Μαραθώνιον ταῦρον, ὃν ἀνεῖλε Θησεύς· Ῥαμνοῦς δὲ τὸ τῆς Νεμέσεως ξόανον μεγέθει καὶ κάλλει κατωρθωμένον καὶ τοῖς τοῦ Φειδίου ἐνάμιλλον. . . .

Marathon [was] later [the site of] the Persian conquest, and before Homer [the home of] the Marathonian bull, which Theseus bound up; Rhamnus [has] the *xoanon* of Nemesis set up, in size and beauty a match even for the [works] of Pheidias.

132

Eustathius *ad* Homer, *Iliad* 2.603 A.D. XII
Text: M. van der Valk, ed., *Eustathius archiepiscopi Thessalonicensis commentarii ad Homeri Iliadem pertinentes* I (Leiden, 1971) 465.13–15.

ἔστι δὲ καὶ κώμη μετρία ἔχουσα τὸν Κολώτου Ἀσκληπιὸν ξόανον θαυμαστόν, φησίν, ἰδεῖν, ἐλεφάντινον.

There is also a village of middling size having a *xoanon* of Asclepius by Colotes, wondrous, he says, to see, of ivory.

133

Eustathius *ad* Homer, *Iliad* 4.144 A.D. XII
Text: M. van der Valk, ed., *Eustathius archiepiscopi Thessalonicensis commentarii ad Homeri Iliadem pertinentes* I (Leiden, 1971) 722.2–4.

Ἄγαλμα δὲ πανταχοῦ παρὰ τῷ ποιητῇ πᾶν, ἐφ' ᾧ τις ἀγάλλεται, ὡς δηλοῖ καὶ ἡ Ὀδύσσεια, εἰ καὶ οἱ μεταγενέστεροι ἐπὶ ξοάνου τὴν λέξιν τεθείκασι.

An *agalma*, everywhere in the author, [is] everything in which someone glories, as the *Odyssey* also shows, even if those of later times apply the word to a *xoanon*.

134

Eustathius *ad* Homer, *Iliad* 5.730 s A.D. XII
Text: M. van der Valk, ed., *Eustathius archiepiscopi Thessalonicensis commentarii ad Homeri Iliadem pertinentes* II (Leiden, 1976) 181.9–12.

Τὸ δ' αὐτὸ νοητέον καὶ εἰς τὰ χρυσᾶ λέπαδνα. λέπαδνα γὰρ κυρίως πλατεῖς ἱμάντες, οἷς ἀναδεσμοῦνται οἱ τράχηλοι τῶν ἵππων πρὸς τὸν ζυγόν, παρὰ τὸ λέπω, τὸ λεπίζω, λέπανον, ὡς ξέω ξόανον καὶ κόπτω κόπανον, καὶ πλεονασμῷ |τοῦ δ λέπαδνον.

This passage must be considered also with respect to the gold yoke-straps. For *lepadna* [are] properly flat straps, by which are fastened the necks of the horses to the yoke; [the word] is derived from *lepo*, *lepizo*, *lepanon*, as *xeo–xoanon* and *kopto–kopanon*, and by pleonasm of *d*, *lepadnon*.

135

Eustathius *ad* Homer, *Iliad* 6.92 A.D. XII
Text: M. van der Valk, ed., *Eustathius archiepiscopi Thessalonicensis commentarii ad Homeri Iliadem pertinentes* II (Leiden, 1976) 251.20–252.6.

Φασὶ δὲ τὸ ἐν Τροίᾳ Παλλάδιον διοπετὲς μὲν εἶναι, ἤγουν ἐξ ἀέρος ἄνωθεν οὐρανόθεν πεσόν, ἀνδρὸς δὲ δορὰν ἠμφιέσθαι στέμμα τε ἔχειν καὶ ἠλακάτην, ἐν δὲ τῇ κεφαλῇ πῖλον καὶ δόρυ ἐν τῇ δεξιᾷ. Ἐνταῦθα δὲ τὸ ἀναθεῖναι, ἀφ' οὗ γίνεται τὸ ἀνάθημα, θεῖναι λέγει χωρὶς προθέσεως. Θεῖναι γάρ, φησίν, Ἀθηνᾶς ἐπὶ γούνασιν, ὡς καθημένου δηλαδὴ τοῦ Παλλαδίου, ἢ θεῖναι παρὰ γόνασιν, εἴπερ ἵσταται. Δύναται δέ, φασί, τὸ ἐπὶ γούνασι νοηθῆναι καὶ ἀντὶ τοῦ ἐπὶ γουνασμῷ καὶ ἱκετείᾳ. ὁ δὲ Γεωγράφος, ὅπου λέγει τὴν μὲν παλαιὰν Ἴλιον ἠφανίσθαι, τὴν δὲ νῦν βλεπομένην νεωτέραν εἶναι, μὴ ἀποδεχόμενος τοὺς νοοῦντας τὸ ἐπὶ γούνασιν ἀντὶ τοῦ παρὰ τοῖς γούνασι, φησίν, ὅτι τὸ τῆς Ἀθηνᾶς ξόανον νῦν μὲν ἑστηκὸς ὁρᾶται, Ὅμηρος δὲ καθήμενον ἐμφαίνει ἐν τῷ "πέπλον θεῖναι Ἀθηναίης ἐπὶ γούνασιν", ὡς καὶ τὸ "γούνασιν ἐφέζεσθαι φίλον υἱόν". βέλτιον γὰρ οὕτως ἢ παρὰ τοῖς γόνασιν, ὡς τὸ "ἡ δ' ἧσται ἐπ' ἐσχάρῃ ἐν πυρὸς αὐγῇ". κάθηνται δὲ Ἀθηνᾶς ξόανα καὶ ἐν Φωκαίᾳ καὶ Μασσαλίᾳ καὶ Ῥώμῃ καὶ Χίῳ.

They say that in Troy is the Palladium that fell from the sky, that is to say, fallen from above out of the air, from heaven; and it is debated whether it has a man's spear and wreath and distaff, on the head a cap and a spear in the right [hand]. And here [the passage refers to] the dedication, from which comes the *anathema*, he says they performed away from public view. For they placed [it], he says, on the knees of Athena, since clearly the Palladium is seated, or they place [it] by her knees, if indeed [the Palladium] is standing. And he says that the phrase "on the knees" can also mean "on the occasion of the supplication and *hiketeia* [supplication]." And the Geographer somewhere or other says that the old [image of Athena in] Ilium was seated, but the one which is visible now is more recent; he does not accept the idea that they say "on the knees" instead of "by the knees"; he says that the *xoanon* of Athena is now seen standing, but Homer indicated [a] seated [image] in the line "placed the peplos on the knees of Athena," as also the line "should set a dear son on his knees." For it is better thus than "by the knees," as the line "she who sits by the hearth in the gleam of the fire." The *xoana* of Athena are seated in Phocaea and Massalia and Rome and Chios.

136

Eustathius *ad* Homer, *Iliad* 14.132 A.D. XII

Text: M. van der Valk, ed., *Eustathius archiepiscopi Thessalonicensis commentarii ad Homeri Iliadem pertinentes* III (Leiden, 1979) 594.8–13.

Τὸ δὲ "θυμῷ ἦρα φέροντες" ἀντὶ τοῦ χαριζόμενοι ἑαυτοῖς. Ὅτι δὲ ἦρα τὴν χάριν λέγει καὶ τὸ ἐραστὸν δέ, [καὶ ὅτι ἐκ τοῦ ἦρ ἡ χάρις ἡ τοιαύτη λέξις γίνεται, ἢ μᾶλλον ἐκ τοῦ ἐρῶ, τὸ ἐπιθυμῶ, ἵνα ὥσπερ ἐκ τοῦ κόπτω καὶ ξέω καὶ τρυπῶ κόπανα καὶ ξόανα καὶ τρύπανα, οὕτω καὶ ἐρῶ ἤρανα καὶ κατὰ ἀποκοπὴν ἦρα], προδεδήλωται.

The phrase "bringing gratification to their wrath" instead of "gratifying themselves." That *era* means "gratification" and the thing desired [and that from *er*, *charis*, such a word comes, or rather from *ero*, "to desire," so that just as from *kopto* and *xeo* and *trypo* (come) *kopana* and *xoana* and *trypana*, thus too: *ero*, *erane*, and, by *apocope*, *era*] is shown plainly.

Excerpta Constantiniana 2(1) pp. 289–290

See Diodorus Siculus 31.35 Walton [**63**].

137

Harpocration *s.v.* Νίκη Ἀθηνᾶ A.D. II

(= Lycurgus fr. VI.13 [40] [Conomis] [Περὶ τῆς ἱερείας].)

Text: W. Dindorf, ed., *Harpocrationis Lexicon in Decem Oratores atticos* (Oxford, 1853) I, 214.6.

Νίκη Ἀθηνᾶ: Λυκοῦργος ἐν τῷ περὶ τῆς ἱερείας. ὅτι δὲ Νίκης Ἀθηνᾶς ξόανον ἄπτερον, ἔχον ἐν μὲν τῇ δεξιᾷ ῥόαν, ἐν δὲ τῇ εὐωνύμῳ κράνος, ἐτιμᾶτο παρ' Ἀθηναίοις δεδήλωκεν Ἡλιόδωρος ὁ περιηγητὴς ἐν α' περὶ ἀκροπόλεως.

Nike Athena: Lycurgus, in *On the Priestess.* Heliodorus the periegete, in the first book of *On the Acropolis*, discloses that the *xoanon* of Nike Athena is without wings, has a pomegranate in her right hand, a helmet in her left, and is honored by the Athenians.

Heliodorus, *On the Acropolis* I ? II B.C.
See Harpocration *s.v.* Νίκη Ἀθηνᾶ [**137**].

138
Heraclides Lembus 45 Dilts (17 Schneidewin) II B.C.
Text: M.R. Dilts, ed., tr., *Heraclidis Lembi Excerpta Politiarum* (Greek, Roman and Byzantine Monographs 5; Durham, 1971).

Μολοττῶν: Μολοττοὶ δὲ τῆς Ἀρτέμιδος συλήσαντες τὸ ἱερὸν καὶ τοῦ ξοάνου χρυσοῦν ἀφελόμενοι στέφανον θυσίαν ἐτίθεσαν ἀντ' αὐτοῦ. τῶν δὲ Κεφαλλήνων ἄλλον ἐπιθέντων, τοῦτον ἀπέβαλεν ἡ θεὸς καὶ χαμαὶ κείμενος εὑρέθη. Κεφαλλῆνες δὲ ἀπὸ Κεφάλου ἐκλήθησαν.

The Molossians, having pillaged the *hieron* of Artemis and torn away the golden crown of the *xoanon*, made a sacrifice in return for it; when the Cephallenians put on another [crown], the goddess threw it off and it was found lying on the ground. The Cephallenians were named after Cephalus.

Heraclides Ponticus IV B.C.
See Eustathius *ad* Homer, *Iliad* 1.39 [**126**, **127**], and Strabo 13.1.48 [**345**].

139
Herodotus 2.4 V B.C.
Text: P.-E. Legrand, ed., tr., *Hérodote. Histoires* II (Paris, 1936).
Translation adapted from A.D. Godley, tr., *Herodotus* I (LCL, 1931).

Δυώδεκά τε θεῶν ἐπωνυμίας ἔλεγον πρώτους Αἰγυπτίους νομίσαι καὶ Ἕλληνας παρὰ σφέων ἀναλαβεῖν, βωμούς τε καὶ ἀγάλματα καὶ νηοὺς θεοῖσι ἀπονεῖμαι σφέας πρώτους καὶ ζῷα ἐν λίθοισι ἐγγλύψαι. [Καὶ] *τούτων μέν νυν τὰ πλέω ἔργῳ ἐδήλουν οὕτω γενόμενα.*

Further, they said the Egyptians first used the appellations of the twelve gods, which the Greeks afterwards borrowed from them; and it was they who first assigned to the several gods their *bomoi* and *agalmata* and *neoi*, and first carved figures on stone. They showed me most of this by plain proof.

140
Herodotus 2.51 V B.C.
Text: P.-E. Legrand, ed., tr., *Hérodote. Histoires* II (Paris, 1936).
Translation adapted from A.D. Godley, tr., *Herodotus* I (LCL, 1931).

Ταῦτα μέν νυν καὶ ἄλλα πρὸς τούτοισι, τὰ ἐγὼ φράσω, Ἕλληνες ἀπ' Αἰγυπτίων νενομίκασι· τοῦ δὲ Ἑρμέω τὰ ἀγάλματα ὀρθὰ ἔχειν τὰ αἰδοῖα ποιεῦντες οὐκ ἀπ' Αἰγυπτίων μεμαθήκασι, ἀλλ' ἀπὸ Πελασγῶν πρῶτοι *μὲν Ἑλλήνων ἁπάντων Ἀθηναῖοι παραλαβόντες, παρὰ δὲ τούτων ὦλλοι. Ἀθηναίοισι γὰρ ἤδη τηνικαῦτα ἐς Ἕλληνας τελέουσι Πελασγοὶ σύνοικοι ἐγένοντο ἐν τῇ χώρῃ, ὅθεν περ καὶ Ἕλληνες ἤρξαντο <αὐτοὶ> νομισθῆναι. Ὅστις δὲ τὰ Καβείρων ὄργια μεμύηται, τὰ Σαμοθρήικες ἐπιτελέουσι παραλαβόντες παρὰ Πελασγῶν, οὗτος ὡνὴρ οἶδε τὸ λέγω· τὴν γὰρ Σαμοθρηίκην οἴκεον πρότερον Πελασγοὶ οὗτοι οἵ περ Ἀθηναίοισι σύνοικοι ἐγένοντο, καὶ παρὰ τούτων Σαμοθρήικες τὰ ὄργια παραλαμβάνουσι. Ὀρθὰ ὦν ἔχειν τὰ αἰδοῖα τἀγάλματα τοῦ Ἑρμέω Ἀθηναῖοι πρῶτοι Ἑλλήνων μαθόντες παρὰ Πελασγῶν ἐποιήσαντο. Οἱ δὲ Πελασγοὶ ἱρόν τινα λόγον περὶ αὐτοῦ ἔλεξαν, τὰ ἐν τοῖσι ἐν Σαμοθρηίκῃ μυστηρίοισι δεδήλωται.*

These customs now and others besides, which I shall show, were taken by the Greeks from the Egyptians. It was not so with the ithyphallic *agalmata* of Hermes; the making of these came from the Pelasgians, from whom the Athenians were the first of all Greeks to take it, and then handed it on to others. For the Athenians were then already counted as Greeks when the Pelasgians came to dwell in the land with them, and thereby began to be considered as Greeks. Whoever has been initiated into the rites of the Cabeiri, which the Samothracians learned from the Pelasgians and now practice, he understands what my meaning is. Samothrace was formerly inhabited by those Pelasgians who came to dwell among the Athenians, and it is from them that the Samothracians take their rites. The Athenians, then, were the first Greeks to make ithyphallic *agalmata* of Hermes, and this they did because the Pelasgians had taught them. The Pelasgians told a certain sacred tale about this, which is set forth in the Samothracian mysteries.

141

Herodotus 4.108 V B.C.

Text: P.-E. Legrand, ed., tr., *Hérodote. Histoires* IV (Paris, 1949).
Translation adapted from A.D. Godley, tr., *Herodotus* II (LCL, 1950).

Βουδῖνοι δέ, ἔθνος ἐὸν μέγα καὶ πολλόν, γλαυκόν τε πᾶν ἰσχυρῶς ἐστι καὶ πυρρόν. Πόλις δὲ ἐν αὐτοῖσι πεπόλισται ξυλίνη, οὔνομα δὲ τῇ πόλι ἐστὶ Γελωνός· τοῦ δὲ τείχεος μέγαθος κῶλον ἕκαστον τριήκοντα σταδίων ἐστί, ὑψηλὸν δὲ καὶ πᾶν ξύλινον, καὶ <αἱ> οἰκίαι αὐτῶν ξύλιναι καὶ τὰ ἱρά. Ἔστι γὰρ δὴ αὐτόθι Ἑλληνικῶν θεῶν ἱρὰ ἑλληνικῶς κατεσκευασμένα ἀγάλμασί τε καὶ βωμοῖσι καὶ νηοῖσι ξυλίνοισι, καὶ τῷ Διονύσῳ τριετηρίδας ἀνάγουσι καὶ βακχεύουσι. Εἰσὶ γὰρ οἱ Γελωνοὶ τὸ ἀρχαῖον Ἕλληνες, ἐκ τῶν δὲ ἐμπορίων ἐξαναστάντες οἴκησαν ἐν τοῖσι Βουδίνοισι· καὶ γλώσσῃ τὰ μὲν Σκυθικῇ, τὰ δὲ Ἑλληνικῇ χρέωνται. Βουδῖνοι δὲ οὐ τῇ αὐτῇ γλώσσῃ χρέωνται καὶ Γελωνοί, οὐδὲ δίαιτα ἡ αὐτή.

The Budini are a great and numerous nation; the eyes of all of them are very bright, and they are ruddy. They have a city built of wood called

Gelonus. The wall of it is thirty furlongs in length on each side of the city; the wall is high and all of wood; and their houses are wooden, and their *hira*; for there are among them *hira* of Greek gods, furnished in Greek fashion with *agalmata* and *bomoi* and *neoi* of wood; and they honor Dionysus every two years with festivals and revels. For the Geloni are by their origin Greeks, who left their trading ports to settle among the Budini; and they speak a language half Greek and half Scythian. But the Budini speak not the same language as the Geloni, nor is their manner of life the same.

142
Hesychius *s.v.* *Δαιδάλεια* A.D. V
(= Aristophanes fr. 194 Kock.)
Text: K. Latte, ed., *Hesychii Alexandrini lexicon* I (Copenhagen, 1953) 398.48.

Ἀριστοφάνες τὸν ὑπὸ Δαιδάλου κατασκευασθέντα ἀνδριάντα, ὡς διὰ τὸ ἀποδιδράσκειν δεδεμένον.

Aristophanes [uses the word for] the *andrias* made by Daedalus, as it was bound because it would run away.

143
Hesychius *s.v.* *ξέσμα* A.D. V
Text: K. Latte, ed., *Hesychii Alexandrini lexicon* II (Copenhagen, 1966) 726.58.

ξέσμα· ξόανον

Xesma: *xoanon*.

144
Hesychius *s.v.* *ξόανα* A.D. V
Text: K. Latte, ed., *Hesychii Alexandrini lexicon* II (Copenhagen, 1966) 727.84.

ξόανα· ἀγάλματα, εἴδωλα, ζῴδια. κυρίως δὲ τὰ ἐκ ξύλων ἐξεσμένα, ἢ λίθων.

Xoana: *agalmata*, *eidola*, *zoidia*: properly, those carved from wood or stone.

145
Hesychius *s.v.* *ξοάνων* A.D. V
Text: M. Schmidt, ed., *Hesychii Alexandrini lexicon* (ed. minor; Jena, 1867) 1101.32.

ξοάνων· προθύρων ἐξεσμένων

Xoanōn: carved doors.

146

Historia Alexandri Magni (Pseudo-Callisthenes) 1.30.13–14
Text: C. Müller, ed., *Pseudo-Callisthenes*, in *Reliqua Arriani et scriptorum de rebus Alexandri M.*, published with F. Dübner, ed., *Arriani Anabasis et Indica* (Paris, 1846).

Μαθὼν δὲ τὴν ἐνέργειαν τοῦ Ἄμμωνος Ἀλέξανδρος [ἐπισκευάζει αὐτοῦ τὸ τέμενος καὶ τὸ ξόανον αὐτοῦ περιεχρύσωσε, καὶ τῇ αὐτοῦ ἐπιγραφῇ ἀφιέρωσε· "Πατρὶ θεῷ Ἄμμωνι Ἀλέξανδρος."].

Learning of this action of Ammon, Alexander [restored his *temenos* and gilded his *xoanon*, and consecrated (it) with his inscription: "To his father, the god Ammon, Alexander (dedicated this)"].

147

Historia Alexandria Magni (Pseudo-Callisthenes) 1.33.5
Text: W. Kroll, ed., *Historia Alexandri Magni* I (Berlin, 1926, 1958).
Translation adapted from E.H. Haight, tr., *The Life of Alexander of Macedon* (New York, 1955).

ὁ δὲ τάχιον ἐκεῖ παραγενόμενος εἶδε τὰ σπλάγχνα ἐπὶ τοῦ βωμοῦ κείμενα καὶ ναὸν ὑπὸ ἀρχαιότητος καθιδρυμένον, ξόανον δὲ ἔνδον καθεζόμενον, ὃ θνητὴ φύσις οὐχ εὗρεν ἀπαγγεῖλαι· παρειστήκει δὲ τῷ ἀφράστῳ ξοάνῳ κόρης ἄγαλμα μέγιστον.

He went there in haste and saw the viscera lying on the altar and a *naos* built in antiquity and a seated *xoanon* inside, which mortal tongue could not describe; and beside the indescribable *xoanon* there stood a huge *agalma* of a maiden.

148

Historia Alexandri Magni (Pseudo-Callisthenes) 1.33.10–11
Text: C. Müller, ed., *Pseudo-Callisthenes*, in *Reliqua Arriani et scriptorum de rebus Alexandri M.*, published with F. Dübner, ed., *Arriani Anabasis et Indica* (Paris, 1846).

εἶδε τὰ σπλάγχνα ἐπὶ τοῦ βωμοῦ κείμενα, τὸν δὲ βωμὸν ὑπὸ ἀρχαίων καθιδρυθέντα καὶ σηκὸν καὶ ξόανον ἔνδον προκαθεζόμενον, καὶ τῇ δεξιᾷ χειρὶ κομίζοντα θηρίον πολύμορφον, τῇ δὲ εὐωνύμῳ σκῆπτρον κατέχον, καὶ παρεστήκει τῷ ξοάνῳ κόρης ἄγαλμα μέγιστον.

[Alexander] saw the entrails lying on an altar; an altar built in ancient times and a *sekos* and a *xoanon* inside, seated, and it had a multiform beast in its right hand, and in its left a scepter; and next to the *xoanon* stood a very large *agalma* of Kore.

149

Historia Alexandri Magni (Pseudo-Callisthenes) 1.33.13
Text: W. Kroll, ed., *Historia Alexandri Magni* I (Berlin, 1926, 1958).
Translation adapted from E.H. Haight, tr., *The Life of Alexander of Macedon* (New York, 1955).

Κελεύει δὲ καὶ Παρμενίωνι ἀρχιτέκτονι ξόανον κατασκευάσαι δωμησάμενον τέμενος ἐμφερὲς τοῖς Ὁμηρικοῖς στίχοις, ὡς εἶπεν ἐκεῖνος ὡδί που <ὁ> ἀοίδιμος Ὅμηρος. . . .

He ordered also Parmenion the architect to prepare a suitable *temenos* for the *xoanon*, corresponding to the Homeric verses, as that poet Homer said thus somewhere.

150

Historia Alexandri Magni (Pseudo-Callisthenes) 1.42.6
Text: W. Kroll, ed., *Historia Alexandri Magni* I (Berlin, 1926, 1958).
Translation adapted from E.H. Haight, tr., *The Life of Alexander of Macedon* (New York, 1955).

Παραγίνεται οὖν εἰς τὴν Πιερίαν πόλιν τῆς Βεβρυκίας, ἔνθα ἦν ναὸς καὶ ἄγαλμα τοῦ Ὀρφέως καὶ αἱ Πιερίδες Μοῦσαι καὶ τὰ θηρία αὐτῷ παρεστῶτα. βλέποντος δὲ τοῦ Ἀλεξάνδρου εἰς τὸ ἄγαλμα τοῦ Ὀρφέως ἵδρωσε τὸ ξόανον ἐν τῷ προσώπῳ καὶ ἐν ὅλῳ τῷ σώματι.

Then he went to the Pierian city of Bebrycia where there was a *naos* and an *agalma* of Orpheus, and the Pierian Muses and the wild beasts standing by him. When Alexander looked at the *agalma* of Orpheus, the *xoanon* sweated on the face and the entire body.

151

Historia Alexandri Magni (Pseudo-Callisthenes) 1.42.6–7 (B′)
Text: C. Müller, ed., *Pseudo-Callisthenes*, in *Reliqua Arriani et scriptorum de rebus Alexandri M.*, published with F. Dübner, ed., *Arriani Anabasis et Indica* (Paris, 1846).
Translation adapted from E.H. Haight, tr., *The Life of Alexander of Macedon* (New York, 1955).

Παραγίνεται οὖν εἰς τὴν Πιερίαν πόλιν τῆς Βεβρυκίας, ἔνθα ἦν ναὸς καὶ ἄγαλμα τοῦ Ὀρφέως καὶ αἱ Πιερίδες Μοῦσαι καὶ τὰ θηρία αὐτῶν περιεστῶτα τὰ ξόανα. Βλέποντος δὲ τοῦ Ἀλεξάνδρου εἰς τὸ ἄγαλμα τοῦ Ὀρφέως, ἵδρωσε τὸ ξόανον αὐτοῦ ὅλον.

Then he went to the Pierian city of Bebrycia, in which was a *naos* and an *agalma* of Orpheus and the Pierian Muses and the wild beasts standing around their *xoana*. When Alexander looked at the *agalma* of Orpheus, his *xoanon* sweated all over.

152
Historia Alexandri Magni (Pseudo-Callisthenes) 3.18.3–4
Text: W. Kroll, ed., *Historia Alexandri Magni* I (Berlin, 1926, 1958).
Translation adapted from E.H. Haight, tr., *The Life of Alexander of Macedon* (New York, 1955).

[Ἐπιστολὴ Ἀλεξάνδρου Κανδάκῃ.]
"Βασιλεὺς Ἀλέξανδρος βασιλίσσῃ Κανδάκῃ τῇ ἐν Μερόῃ καὶ τοῖς ὑπ' αὐτὴν τυράννοις χαίρειν. παραγενάμενος εἰς Αἴγυπτον ἤκουσα παρὰ τῶν ἐκεῖ ἱερέων † εἶδον ὑμῶν τάφους καὶ οἰκητήρια δηλοῦντα, ὅτι χρόνον τινὰ ἐκυριεύσατε Αἰγύπτου καὶ Ἄμμων μεθ' ὑμῶν ἐστράτευσε, μετὰ δὲ ὀλίγον χρόνον πάλιν χρηματίσαντος Ἄμμωνος ἀνελύσατε εἰς τὴν ἰδίαν πόλιν. διὸ ἔπεμψα πρὸς ὑμᾶς· τόν τε ναὸν καὶ <τὸ> ξόανον τοῦ Ἄμμωνος ἀγάγετε ἐπὶ τὰ ὅρια, ἵνα θύσωμεν αὐτῷ. εἰ δὲ μὴ βούλεσθε ἔρχεσθαι σὺν αὐτῷ, συμμίξαντες ἐν τάχει ἐν Μερόῃ συμβουλευσώμεθα. πέμψατε ἡμῖν ἐνθάδε ἃ ἂν φαίνηται."

(Letter of Alexander to Candace)
"King Alexander sends greeting to Queen Candace in Meroe and to the rulers under her. When I was in Egypt, I heard of you from the priests there and saw your graves and dwellings, which showed that for some time you had ruled Egypt. I heard that Ammon made an expedition with you, and after a short time on Ammon's advice you returned to your own city. This is the point of my sending a letter to you. Bring the *naos* and the *xoanon* of Ammon to the frontier that we may make a sacrifice to it. But if you do not wish to come with it, let us meet soon in Meroe and have a conference. Let me know your wish there."

153
Joannes Philoponus *ad* Aristotle, *De Anima* 1.3, 406 b 11 A.D. VI
Text: M. Hayduck, ed., *Ioannis Philoponi in Aristotelis de anima libros commentaria* (Commentaria in Aristotelem Graeca 15; Berlin, 1897) 114.28–29; 114.35–115.3.

ἔνιοι δέ φασι καὶ κινεῖν τὸ σῶμα ἐν ᾧ ἐστιν, ὡς αὐτὴ κινεῖται. ἔλεγον γάρ, φησί, τὰς σφαιρικὰς ἀτόμους εὐκινήτους οὔσας συγκινεῖν ἑαυταῖς τὸ σῶμα, τὸ αὐτό, φησί, λέγοντες τῷ κωμικῷ Φιλίππῳ, ὃς ἔλεγε τὸν Δαίδαλον ποιῆσαι ξυλίνην Ἀφροδίτην κινουμένην· κοιλώματα γάρ τινα ποιήσας ἐν τῷ ξοάνῳ ὁ Δαίδαλος ἐνέχεεν ὑδράργυρον, ἵνα κινούμενος ὁ ὑδράργυρος (εὐκίνητος γὰρ καὶ συνεχῶς μετακυλιόμενος καὶ τῇ ἑαυτοῦ ὤσει κινῶν τὸ ξόανον) φαίνεσθαι ποιῇ ἐξ αὐτοῦ κινούμενον τὸ τῆς Ἀφροδίτης ξόανον.

Some say that it [the soul] also moves the body in which it is, as it moves itself.
For, he says, they said that spherical atoms, being quickly moving, move along with themselves the body, he says, saying the same thing as the comic poet Philippus, who said that Daedalus made a wooden Aphrodite move. For, having made some hollow places in the *xoanon*, Daedalus held quicksilver inside, so that the quicksilver when it was moved (for it is easily moved, and [being in an] enclosed [situation], rolling over and with the push itself moving the *xoanon*) made the *xoanon* of Aphrodite appear to be moving by itself.

John Chrysostom, *Sermons* A.D. VI
See Photius, *Bibliotheca* 277 [**304**].

154
Josephus, *Bellum Judaicum* 5.375–385 A.D. I
Text: H. St. J. Thackeray, tr., *Josephus* III. *The Jewish War, Books IV–VII* (LCL, 1928).
Translation adapted from Thackeray.

Ταῦτα τὸν Ἰώσηπον παραινοῦντα πολλοὶ μὲν ἔσκωπτον ἀπὸ τοῦ τείχους, πολλοὶ δ' ἐβλασφήμουν, ἔνιοι δ' ἔβαλλον. ὁ δ' ὡς ταῖς φανεραῖς οὐκ ἔπειθε συμβουλίαις, ἐπὶ τὰς ὁμοφύλους μετέβαινεν ἱστορίας, "ἆ δειλοί," βοῶν, "καὶ τῶν ἰδίων ἀμνήμονες συμμάχων, ὅπλοις καὶ χερσὶ πολεμεῖτε Ῥωμαίοις; τίνα γὰρ ἄλλον οὕτως ἐνικήσαμεν; πότε δ' οὐ θεὸς ὁ κτίσας, ἂν ἀδικῶνται, Ἰουδαίων ἔκδικος; οὐκ ἐπιστραφέντες ὄψεσθε πόθεν ὁρμώμενοι μάχεσθε καὶ πηλίκον ἐμιάνατε σύμμαχον; οὐκ ἀναμνήσεσθε πατέρων ἔργα δαιμόνια, καὶ τὸν ἅγιον τόνδε χῶρον ἡλίκους ἡμῖν πάλαι πολέμους καθεῖλεν; ἐγὼ μὲν φρίττω τὰ ἔργα τοῦ θεοῦ λέγων εἰς ἀναξίους ἀκοάς· ἀκούετε δ' ὅμως, ἵνα γνῶτε μὴ μόνον Ῥωμαίοις πολεμοῦντες ἀλλὰ καὶ τῷ θεῷ. βασιλεὺς ὁ τότε Νεχαὼς Αἰγυπτίων, ὁ δ' αὐτὸς ἐκαλεῖτο καὶ Φαραώ, μυρίᾳ χειρὶ καταβὰς ἥρπασε Σάρραν βασιλίδα, τὴν μητέρα τοῦ γένους ἡμῶν. τί οὖν ὁ ταύτης ἀνὴρ Ἀβραάμ, προπάτωρ δὲ ἡμέτερος; ἆρα τὸν ὑβριστὴν ἠμύνατο τοῖς ὅπλοις, καίτοι ὀκτωκαίδεκα μὲν καὶ τριακοσίους ὑπάρχους ἔχων, δύναμιν δὲ ὑφ' ἑκάστῳ τούτων ἄπειρον; ἢ αὐτοὺς μὲν ἐρημίαν ἡγήσατο μὴ συμπαρόντος θεοῦ, καθαρὰς δ' ἀνατείνας τὰς χεῖρας εἰς ὃν νῦν ἐμιάνατε χῶρον ὑμεῖς, τὸν ἀνίκητον αὐτῷ βοηθὸν ἐστρατολόγησεν; οὐ μετὰ μίαν ἑσπέραν ἄχραντος μὲν ἡ βασίλισσα ἀνεπέμφθη πρὸς τὸν ἄνδρα, προσκυνῶν δὲ τὸν ὑφ' ὑμῶν αἱμαχθέντα χῶρον ὁμοφύλῳ φόνῳ καὶ τρέμων ἀπὸ τῶν ἐν νυκτὶ φαντασμάτων ἔφευγεν ὁ Αἰγύπτιος, ἀργύρῳ δὲ καὶ χρυσῷ τοὺς θεοφιλεῖς Ἑβραίους ἐδωρεῖτο; εἴπω τὴν εἰς Αἴγυπτον μετοικίαν τῶν πατέρων; οὐ τυραννούμενοι καὶ βασιλεῦσιν ἀλλοφύλοις ὑποπεπτωκότες τετρακοσίοις ἔτεσι, παρὸν ὅπλοις ἀμύνεσθαι καὶ χερσί, σφᾶς αὐτοὺς ἐπέτρεψαν τῷ θεῷ; τίς οὐκ οἶδεν τὴν παντὸς θηρίου καταπλησθεῖσαν Αἴγυπτον καὶ πάσῃ φθαρεῖσαν νόσῳ, τὴν ἄκαρπον γῆν, τὸν ἐπιλείποντα Νεῖλον, τὰς ἐπαλλήλους δέκα πληγάς, τοὺς διὰ ταῦτα μετὰ φρουρᾶς προπεμπομένους πατέρας ἡμῶν ἀναιμάκτους ἀκινδύνους, οὓς ὁ θεὸς αὐτῷ νεωκόρους ἦγεν; ἀλλὰ τὴν ὑπὸ Σύρων ἁρπαγεῖσαν ἁγίαν ἡμῖν λάρνακα οὐκ ἐστέναξε μὲν ἡ Παλαιστίνη καὶ Δαγὼν τὸ ξόανον, ἐστέναξε δὲ πᾶν τὸ τῶν ἁρπασαμένων ἔθνος, σηπόμενοι δὲ τὰ κρυπτὰ τοῦ σώματος καὶ δι' αὐτῶν τὰ σπλάγχνα μετὰ τῶν σιτίων καταφέροντες, χερσὶ ταῖς λῃσαμέναις ἀνεκόμισαν κυμβάλων καὶ τυμπάνων ἤχῳ καὶ πᾶσι μειλικτηρίοις ἱλασκόμενοι τὸ ἅγιον;

Josephus, during this exhortation, was derided by many from the ramparts, by many execrated, and by some assailed with missiles. Failing to move them by this direct advice, he passed to reminiscences of their nation's history.

"Ah, miserable wretches," he cried, "unmindful of your own true allies, would you make war on the Romans with arms and might of hand? What other foe have we conquered thus, and when did God, who created, fail to avenge the Jews, if they were wronged? Will you not turn your eyes and mark what place is that whence you issue to battle and reflect how mighty an Ally you have outraged? Will you not recall your fathers' superhuman exploits and what mighty wars this holy places has quelled for us in days of old? For myself, I shudder at recounting the works of God to unworthy ears; yet listen, that you may learn that you are warring not against the Romans only, but also against God.

"Nechaos, also called Pharaoh, the reigning king of Egypt, came down with a prodigious host and carried off Sarah, a princess and the mother of our race. What action, then, did her husband, Abraham, our forefather, take? Did he avenge himself on the ravisher with the sword? He had, to be sure, three hundred and eighteen officers under him, each in command of a boundless army. Or did he not rather count these as nothing, if unaided by God, and uplifting pure hands towards this spot which you have now polluted enlist the invincible Ally on his side? And was not the Queen, after one night's absence, sent back immaculate to her lord, while the Egyptian, in awe of the spot which you have stained with the blood of your countrymen and trembling at his visions of the night, fled, bestowing silver and gold upon those Hebrews beloved of God?

"Need I speak of the migration of our fathers to Egypt? Oppressed and in subjection to foreign monarchs for four hundred years, though they might have defended themselves by resort to arms and violence, did they not commit themselves to God? Who has not heard tell of Egypt overrun with all manner of beasts and wasted with every disease, of the barren land, the failing Nile, the ten successive plagues, and how in consequence our fathers were sent forth under escort, without bloodshed, without risk, God conducting them as the future guardians of his shrine?

"Or again did not Palestine and Dagon the *xoanon* bewail the robbery by Syrians of the ark sacred to us? Did not the whole nation of those raiders bewail the deed, ulcerated in their secret parts and excreting their entrails along with their food, until with the hands which stole it they restored it, to the sound of cymbals and timbrels, and with all manner of expiations propitiating the *hagion*?"

155

Josephus. *Contra Apionem* 1.243–244, 248–250 A.D. I
Text: R. Reinach, ed., L. Blum, tr., *Flavius Josephe. Contre Apion* (Paris, 1930).
Translation adapted from H. St. J. Thackeray, tr., *Josephus* I (LCL, 1926).

'Αμένωφις δ' ὁ τῶν Αἰγυπτίων βασιλεύς, ὡς ἐπύθετο τὰ κατὰ τὴν ἐκείνων ἔφοδον, οὐ μετρίως συνεχύθη τῆς παρὰ 'Αμενώφεως τοῦ Παάπιος μνησθεὶς προδηλώσεως. Καὶ πρῶτον συναγαγὼν πλῆθος Αἰγυπτίων καὶ βουλευσάμενος μετὰ τῶν ἐν τούτοις ἡγεμόνων τά τε ἱερὰ ζῷα τὰ [πρῶτα] μάλιστα ἐν τοῖς ἱεροῖς τιμώμενα ὡς ἑαυτὸν μετεπέμψατο καὶ τοῖς κατὰ μέρος ἱερεῦσι παρήγγελλεν ὡς ἀσφαλέστατα τῶν θεῶν συγκρύψαι τὰ ξόανα.

The news of their invasion sorely perturbed Amenophis, the king of the Egyptians, who recalled the prediction of Amenophis son of Paapis. He began by assembling the population of the Egyptians, and, after deliberation with the leaders among them, sent for the sacred animals that were held in greatest reverence in the *hiera*, and instructed the priests in each district to conceal the *xoana* of the gods as securely as possible.

Καὶ τὰ μὲν κατὰ τὴν Αἰθιοπίαν τοιαῦτα. Οἱ δὲ Σολυμῖται κατελθόντες σὺν τοῖς μιαροῖς τῶν Αἰγυπτίων οὕτως ἀνοσίως καὶ <ὠμῶς> τοῖς ἀνθρώποις προσηνέχθησαν, ὥστε τὴν τῶν προειρημένων <ποιμένων> κράτησιν χρυσὸν φαίνεσθαι τοῖς τότε τὰ τούτων ἀσεβήματα θεωμένοις· καὶ γὰρ οὐ μόνον πόλεις καὶ κώμας ἐνέπρησαν, οὐδὲ ἱεροσυλοῦντες οὐδὲ λυμαινόμενοι ξόανα *θεῶν ἠρκοῦντο, ἀλλὰ καὶ τοῖς ἀδύτοις ὀπτανίοις τῶν σεβαστευομένων ἱερῶν ζῴων χρώμενοι διετέλουν, καὶ θύτας καὶ σφαγεῖς τούτων ἱερεῖς καὶ προφήτας ἠνάγκαζον γίνεσθαι καὶ γυμνοὺς ἐξέβαλλον. Λέγεται δέ, ὅτι <ὁ> τὴν πολιτείαν καὶ τοὺς νόμους αὐτοῖς καταβαλόμενος ἱερεύς, τὸ γένος Ἡλιοπολίτης, ὄνομα <δὲ> Ὀσάρσηφ ἀπὸ τοῦ ἐν Ἡλιουπόλει θεοῦ Ὀσίρεως, ὡς μετέβη εἰς τοῦτο τὸ γένος, μετετέθη τοὔνομα καὶ προσηγορεύθη* Μωυσῆς.

Such was the condition of affairs in Ethiopia. Meanwhile the Solymites came down with the polluted Egyptians, and treated the inhabitants in so sacrilegious a manner that the regime of the shepherds seemed like a golden age to those who now beheld the impieties of their present enemies. Not only did they set cities and villages on fire, not only did they pillage the *hiera* and mutilate the *xoana* of the gods, but, not content with that, they habitually used the very *adyta* [as kitchens] for roasting the venerated sacred animals, and forced the priests and prophets to become sacrificers and slaughterers, and then turned them out naked. It is said that the priest who gave them a constitution and laws was a native of Heliopolis, named Osarsiph after the Heliopolitan god Osiris, and that when he went over to this people he changed his name and was called Moses.

156

Leonidas of Tarentum, *Anthologia Palatina* 9.326 III B.C.
Text: H. Beckby, ed., *Anthologia Graeca* III (Munich, 1957).
Translation adapted from W.R. Paton, tr., *The Greek Anthology* III (LCL, 1917).

Πέτρης ἐκ δισσῆς ψυχρὸν κατεπάλμενον ὕδωρ,
χαίροις, καὶ Νυμφέων ποιμενικὰ ξόανα
πέτραι τε κρηνέων καὶ ἐν ὕδασι κόσμια ταῦτα
ὑμέων, ὦ κοῦραι, μυρία τεγγόμενα,
χαίρετ'· Ἀριστοκλέης ὅδ' ὁδοιπόρος, ᾧπερ ἀπῶσα
δίψαν βαψάμενος, τοῦτο δίδωμι γέρας.

Hail, thou cold water that leaps down from the cloven rock, and you rustic *xoana* of the Nymphs! Hail, you drinking troughs and your thousand little dolls, you Maidens of the spring, that lie drenched in its waters! Hail! And I, Aristocles, the wayfarer, give you this cup which I dipped in your stream to quench my thirst.

Letter of Aristeas 134–135
See *Aristeae epistula* [28].

Lexeis Rhetorikai s.v. Δαιδάλου ποιημάτων
See *Anecdota Bekker* I.240.16 [**10**].

157
Libanius, *Progymnasmata* 11.15.3 A.D. IV
Text: R. Foerster, ed., *Libanii opera* VIII (Leipzig, 1915).

Τίνας ἂν εἴποι λόγους Ἀχιλλεὺς ἀφαιρούμενος τὴν Βρισηίδα; ἐκέρδανας, ὦ Τροία, διὰ τὴν Βρισηΐδα τὴν ἅλωσιν. ξέσει Πρίαμος ἐν λίθῳ τὴν κόρην ἀνάθημα τῆς Ἰλίου σωτήριον, παρὰ τὸ τῆς Τύχης τέμενος ἀνορθώσει ταύτης τὸ ξόανον.

What Arguments Would Achilles, Carrying Off Briseis, Have Spoken? You have gained an advantage, O Troy, by the capture of Briseis. Priam will carve the maiden in stone as an *anathema* bringing the salvation of Ilium; he will set up the *xoanon* near the *temenos* of Tyche.

158
Lucian, *Alexander* 18 A.D. II
Text: M.D. Macleod, ed., *Luciani Opera* II (Oxford, 1974).
Translation adapted from A.M. Harmon, tr., *Lucian* IV (LCL, 1923).

Κατ' ὀλίγον οὖν καὶ ἡ Βιθυνία καὶ ἡ Γαλατία καὶ ἡ Θρᾴκη συνέρρει, ἑκάστου τῶν ἀπαγγελλόντων κατὰ τὸ εἰκὸς λέγοντος ὡς καὶ γεννώμενον ἴδοι τὸν θεὸν καὶ ὕστερον ἅψαιτο μετ' ὀλίγον παμμεγέθους αὐτοῦ γεγενημένου καὶ τὸ πρόσωπον ἀνθρώπῳ ἐοικότος. γραφαί τε ἐπὶ τούτῳ καὶ εἰκόνες καὶ ξόανα, τὰ μὲν ἐκ χαλκοῦ, τὰ δὲ ἐξ ἀργύρου εἰκασμένα, καὶ ὄνομά γε τῷ θεῷ ἐπιτεθέν· Γλύκων γὰρ ἐκαλεῖτο ἔκ τινος ἐμμέτρου καὶ θείου προστάγματος. ἀνεφώνησε γὰρ ὁ Ἀλέξανδρος

Εἰμὶ Γλύκων, τρίτον αἷμα Διός, φάος ἀνθρώποισιν.

Little by little, Bithynia, Galatia, and Thrace came pouring in, for everyone who carried the news very likely said that he had not only had seen the god but had subsequently touched him, after he had grown very great in a short time and had a face that looked like a man's. Next came *graphai* and *eikones*, and *xoana*, some formed of bronze, others of silver, and naturally a name was bestowed upon the god. He was called Glycon in consequence of a divine behest in meter; for Alexander proclaimed: "I am Glycon, third blood of Zeus, bright light to men."

159
Lucian, *De Dea Syria* 2–3 A.D. II
Text: M.D. Macleod, ed., *Luciani Opera* III (Oxford, 1980).
Translation adapted from H.A. Strong, tr. and J. Garstang, ed., *The Syrian Goddess* (London, 1913).

Πρῶτοι μὲν ὦν ἀνθρώπων τῶν ἡμεῖς ἴδμεν Αἰγύπτιοι λέγονται θεῶν τε ἐννοίην λαβεῖν καὶ ἱρὰ εἴσασθαι καὶ τεμένεα καὶ πανηγύριας ἀποδεῖξαι. πρῶτοι δὲ καὶ οὐνόματα ἱρὰ ἔγνωσαν καὶ λόγους ἱροὺς ἔλεξαν. μετὰ δὲ οὐ πολλοστῷ χρόνῳ παρ' Αἰγυπτίων λόγον Ἀσσύριοι ἐς θεοὺς ἤκουσαν, καὶ ἱρὰ καὶ νηοὺς ἤγειραν, ἐν τοῖς καὶ ἀγάλματα ἔθεντο καὶ ξόανα ἐστήσαντο. τὸ δὲ παλαιὸν καὶ παρ' Αἰγυπτίοισιν ἀξόανοι νηοὶ ἔσαν.

The first men among us to receive knowledge of the gods, and to build *hiera* and *temene* and to summon meetings for religious observances are said to have been the Egyptians. They were the first, too, to take cognizance of holy names, and to repeat sacred traditions. Not long after them the Assyrians heard from the Egyptians their doctrine as to the gods, and they reared *hiera* and *neoi*: in these they both placed *agalmata* and stood up *xoana*. In the past, even among the Egyptians, the *neoi* of the gods were *axoanoi* [without *xoana*].

160

Lucian, *De Dea Syria* 10 A.D. II

Text: M.D. Macleod, ed., *Luciani Opera* III (Oxford, 1980).

Translation adapted from H.A. Strong, tr. and J. Garstang, ed., *The Syrian Goddess* (London, 1913).

Τάδε μέν ἐστι τὰ ἐν τῇ Συρίῃ ἀρχαῖα καὶ μεγάλα ἱρά. τοσούτων δὲ ἐόντων ἐμοὶ δοκέει οὐδὲν τῶν ἐν τῇ ἱρῇ πόλει μέζον ἔμμεναι οὐδὲ νηὸς ἄλλος ἁγιώτερος οὐδὲ χώρη ἄλλη ἱερωτέρη. ἔνι δὲ ἐν αὐτῷ καὶ ἔργα πολυτελέα καὶ ἀρχαῖα ἀναθήματα καὶ πολλὰ θωύματα καὶ ξόανα θεοπρεπέα. καὶ θεοὶ δὲ κάρτα αὐτοῖσιν ἐμφανέες· ἱδρώει γὰρ δὴ ὦν παρὰ σφίσι τὰ ξόανα καὶ κινέεται καὶ χρησμηγορέει, καὶ βοὴ δὲ πολλάκις ἐγένετο ἐν τῷ νηῷ κλεισθέντος τοῦ ἱεροῦ, καὶ πολλοὶ ἤκουσαν. ναὶ μὴν καὶ ὄλβου πέρι ἐν τοῖσιν ἐγὼ οἶδα πρῶτόν ἐστιν· πολλὰ γὰρ αὐτοῖσιν ἀπικνέεται χρήματα ἔκ τε Ἀραβίης καὶ Φοινίκων καὶ Βαβυλωνίων καὶ ἄλλα ἐκ Καππαδοκίης, τὰ δὲ καὶ Κίλικες φέρουσι, τὰ δὲ καὶ Ἀσσύριοι [φέρουσιν]. εἶδον δὲ ἐγὼ καὶ τὰ ἐν τῷ νηῷ λάθρῃ ἀποκέαται, ἐσθῆτα πολλὴν καὶ ἄλλα ὁκόσα ἐς ἄργυρον ἢ ἐς χρυσὸν ἀποκέκριται. ἑορταὶ μὲν γὰρ καὶ πανηγύριες οὐδαμοῖσιν ἄλλοισιν ἀνθρώπων τοσαίδε ἀποδεδέχαται.

These are the ancient and great *hiera* in Syria. Of these, none seems to me greater than those found in the sacred city; no *neos* seems to me more holy, no region more sacred. They possess splendid works and ancient *anathemata* and many sights and marvelous *xoana*. And the gods make their presence known in no doubtful way. The *xoana* sweat and move and deliver oracles, and a shout has often been raised in the *neos* when the *hieron* was closed, and many heard it. And indeed I know that this [*sc. hieron*] is first in wealth among them; for much money comes to them from Arabia and from the Phoenicians and the Babylonians, and other money from Cappadocia, and the Cilians bring it money, and the Assyrians., And I saw the things stored privately in the *neos*, many garments and other valuables, which are exchanged for silver or gold. Nowhere among mankind are so many festivals and sacred assemblies instituted as among them.

161

Lucian, *De Dea Syria* 16 A.D. II

Text: M.D. Macleod, ed., *Luciani Opera* III (Oxford, 1980).

Translation adapted from H.A. Strong, tr. and J. Garstang, ed., *The Syrian Goddess* (London, 1913).

ἁνδάνει δέ μοι ἃ λέγουσιν τοῦ ἱροῦ πέρι τοῖσι Ἕλλησι τὰ πολλὰ ὁμολογέοντες, τὴν μὲν θεὸν Ἥρην δοκέοντες, τὸ δ' ἔργον Διονύσου τοῦ Σεμέλης ποίημα· καὶ γὰρ δὴ Διόνυσος ἐς Συρίην ἀπίκετο κείνην ὁδὸν τὴν ἦλθεν ἐς Αἰθιοπίην. καὶ ἔστι πολλὰ ἐν τῷ ἱρῷ Διονύσου ποιητέω σήματα, ἐν τοῖσι καὶ ἐσθῆτες βάρβαροι καὶ λίθοι Ἰνδοὶ καὶ ἐλεφάντων κέρεα, τὰ Διόνυσος ἐξ Αἰθιόπων ἤνεικεν, καὶ φαλλοὶ δὲ ἑστᾶσι ἐν τοῖσι προπυλαίοισι δύο κάρτα μεγάλοι, ἐπὶ τῶν ἐπίγραμμα τοιόνδε ἐπιγέγραπται, "Τούσδε φαλλοὺς Διόνυσος Ἥρῃ μητρυιῇ ἀνέθηκα." τὸ ἐμοὶ μέν νυν καὶ τάδε ἀρκέει, ἐρέω δὲ καὶ ἄλλ' ὅ τι ἐστὶν ἐν τῷ νηῷ Διονύσου ὄργιον. φαλλοὺς Ἕλληνες Διονύσῳ ἐγείρουσιν, ἐπὶ τῶν καὶ τοιόνδε τι φέρουσιν, ἄνδρας μικροὺς ἐκ ξύλου πεποιημένους, μεγάλα αἰδοῖα ἔχοντας· καλέεται δὲ τάδε νευρόσπαστα. ἔστι δὲ καὶ τόδε ἐν τῷ ἱρῷ· ἐν δεξιᾷ τοῦ νηοῦ κάθηται μικρὸς ἀνὴρ χάλκεος ἔχων αἰδοῖον μέγα.

I approve of the remarks about the *hieron* made by those who in the main accept the theories of the Greeks: according to these the goddess is Hera, but the work was carried out by Dionysus, the son of Semele: Dionysus visited Syria on his journey to Aethiopia. And there are in the *hieron* many *semata* [signs] that Dionysus was its actual founder: among them, barbaric raiment, Indian stones, and elephants' tusks brought by Dionysus from the Aethiopians. Further, a pair of phalli of great size are standing in the *propylaia*, on which this epigram is inscribed: "Dionysus dedicated these phalloi to Hera my stepmother." This proof satisfies me, and I will describe another *orgion* of Dionysus that is in the *neos*. The Greeks erect phalli to Dionysus, and on these they carry, singular to say, small men made of wood, with enormous pudenda; they call these *neurospasta*. There is also this in the *neos*; on the right of the *neos* sits a small bronze man who has large private parts.

162
Lucian, *De Dea Syria* 32–35 A.D. II
Text: M.D. Macleod, ed., *Luciani Opera* III (Oxford, 1980).
Translation adapted from H.A. Strong, tr. and J. Garstang, ed., *The Syrian Goddess* (London, 1913).

Καὶ δῆτα τὸ μὲν τοῦ Διὸς ἄγαλμα ἐς Δία πάντα ὁρῇ καὶ κεφαλὴν καὶ εἵματα καὶ ἕδρην, καί μιν οὐδὲ ἐθέλων ἄλλως εἰκάσεις. ἡ δὲ Ἥρη σκοπέοντί τοι πολυειδέα μορφὴν ἐκφανέει· καὶ τὰ μὲν ξύμπαντα ἀτρεκέϊ λόγῳ Ἥρη ἐστίν, ἔχει δέ τι καὶ Ἀθηναίης καὶ Ἀφροδίτης καὶ Σεληναίης καὶ Ῥέης καὶ Ἀρτέμιδος καὶ Νεμέσιος καὶ Μοιρέων. χειρὶ δὲ τῇ μὲν ἑτέρῃ σκῆπτρον ἔχει, τῇ ἑτέρῃ δὲ ἄτρακτον, καὶ ἐπὶ τῇ κεφαλῇ ἀκτῖνάς τε φορέει καὶ πύργον καὶ κεστὸν τῷ μούνην τὴν Οὐρανίαν κοσμέουσιν. ἔκτοσθεν δέ οἱ χρυσός τε ἄλλος περικέαται καὶ λίθοι κάρτα πολυτελέες, τῶν οἱ μὲν λευκοί, οἱ δὲ ὑδατώδεες, πολλοὶ δὲ οἰνώδεες, πολλοὶ δὲ πυρώδεες, ἔτι δὲ ὄνυχες οἱ Σαρδῷοι πολλοὶ καὶ ὑάκινθοι καὶ σμάραγδοι, τὰ φέρουσιν Αἰγύπτιοι καὶ Ἰνδοὶ καὶ Αἰθίοπες καὶ Μῆδοι καὶ Ἀρμένιοι καὶ Βαβυλώνιοι. τὸ δὲ δὴ μέζονος λόγου ἄξιον, τοῦτο ἀπηγήσομαι· λίθον ἐπὶ τῇ κεφαλῇ φορέει· λυχνὶς καλέεται, οὔνομα δὲ οἱ τοῦ ἔργου ἡ συντυχίη. ἀπὸ τούτου ἐν νυκτὶ σέλας πολλὸν ἀπολάμπεται, ὑπὸ δέ οἱ καὶ ὁ νηὸς ἅπας οἷον ὑπὸ λύχνοισι φαείνεται. ἐν ἡμέρῃ δὲ τὸ μὲν φέγγος ἀσθενέει, ἰδέην δὲ ἔχει κάρτα πυρώδεα. καὶ ἄλλο θωυμαστόν ἐστιν ἐν τῷ ξοάνῳ. ἢν ἑστεὼς ἀντίος ἐσορέῃς, εἰς σὲ ὁρῇ καὶ μεταβαίνοντι τὸ βλέμμα ἀκολουθέει· καὶ ἢν ἄλλος ἑτέρωθεν ἱστορέῃ, ἴσα καὶ ἐς ἐκεῖνον ἐκτελέει.

Ἐν μέσῳ δὲ ἀμφοτέρων ἕστηκεν ξόανον ἄλλο χρύσεον, οὐδαμὰ τοῖσι ἄλλοισι ξοάνοισι ἴκελον. τὸ δὲ μορφὴν μὲν ἰδίην οὐκ ἔχει, φορέει δὲ τῶν ἄλλων θεῶν εἴδεα. καλέεται δὲ σημήιον καὶ ὑπ' αὐτῶν Ἀσσυρίων, οὐδέ τι οὔνομα ἴδιον αὐτῷ ἔθεντο, ἀλλ' οὐδὲ γενέσιος αὐτοῦ καὶ εἴδεος λέγουσιν. καί μιν οἱ μὲν ἐς Διόνυσον, ἄλλοι δὲ ἐς Δευκαλίωνα, οἱ δὲ ἐς Σεμίραμιν ἄγουσιν· καὶ γὰρ δὴ ὦν ἐπὶ τῇ κορυφῇ αὐτοῦ περιστερὴ χρυσέη ἐφέστηκεν, τοὔνεκα δὴ μυθέονται Σεμιράμιος ἔμμεναι τόδε σημήιον. ἀποδημέει δὲ δὶς ἑκάστου ἔτεος ἐς θάλασσαν ἐς κομιδὴν τοῦ εἶπον ὕδατος.

Ἐν αὐτῷ δὲ τῷ νηῷ ἐσιόντων ἐν ἀριστερᾷ κέαται πρῶτα μὲν θρόνος Ἠελίου, αὐτοῦ δὲ ἕδος οὐκ ἔνι· μούνου γὰρ Ἠελίου καὶ Σεληναίης ξόανα οὐ δεικνύουσιν. ὅτευ δὲ εἵνεκα ὧδε νομίζουσιν, ἐγὼ καὶ τόδε ἔμαθον. λέγουσι τοῖσι μὲν ἄλλοισι θεοῖσιν ὅσιον ἔμμεναι ξόανα ποιέεσθαι, οὐ γὰρ σφέων ἐμφανέα πάντεσι τὰ εἴδεα· Ἠέλιος δὲ καὶ Σεληναίη πάμπαν ἐναργέες καὶ σφέας πάντες ὁρέουσι. κοίη ὦν αἰτίη ξοανουργίης τοῖσι ἐν τῷ ἠέρι φαινομένοισι;

Μετὰ δὲ τὸν θρόνον τοῦτον κέαται ξόανον Ἀπόλλωνος, οὐκ οἷον ἐώθεε ποιέεσθαι· οἱ μὲν γὰρ ἄλλοι πάντες Ἀπόλλωνα νέον τε ἥγηνται καὶ πρωθήβην ποιέουσιν, μοῦνοι δὲ οὗτοι Ἀπόλλωνος γενειήτεω ξόανον δεικνύουσιν. καὶ τάδε ποιέοντες ἑωυτοὺς μὲν ἐπαινέουσιν, Ἑλλήνων δὲ κατηγορέουσιν καὶ ἄλλων ὁκόσοι Ἀπόλλωνα παῖδα θέμενοι ἱλάσκονται. αἰτίη δὲ ἥδε· δοκέει αὐτέοισι ἀσοφίη μεγάλη ἔμμεναι ἀτελέα ποιέεσθαι τοῖσι θεοῖσι τὰ εἴδεα, τὸ δὲ νέον ἀτελὲς ἔτι νομίζουσιν. ἐν δὲ καὶ ἄλλο τῷ σφετέρῳ Ἀπόλλωνι καινουργέουσι· μοῦνοι Ἀπόλλωνα εἵμασι κοσμέουσιν.

The *agalma* of Zeus recalls Zeus in all its details—head, robes, throne; and not even wanting to could one conjecture him otherwise. Hera, however, as you look at her will recall to you a variety of forms. Speaking generally she is undoubtedly Hera, but she has something of the attributes of Athena, and of Aphrodite, and of Selene, and of Rhea, and of Artemis, and of Nemesis, and of the Fates. In one of her hands she has a sceptre, in the other, a distaff; on her head she bears rays and a tower and she has a girdle with which they adorn only Aphrodite Ourania. And on the outside she is gilded, and expensive stones adorn her, some white, some sea-green, many wine-dark, many flashing like fire, and in addition there are many onyxes from Sardinia and the jacinth and emeralds, the things that the Egyptians bring, and the Indians and the Ethiopians and the Medes and the Armenians and the Babylonians. But the thing that is more worthy of note, this I will report: she wears a stone on her head; it is called *lychnis*, and it takes its name from its attribute. From it at night a great light shines forth, so that the whole *neos* gleams brightly as by the light of lamps. But in the day the brightness grows faint, it has the likeness of a bright fire. And there is another marvel in this *xoanon*: if you stand over against it, it looks you in the face, and as you pass it the gaze still follows you, and if another approaching from a different quarter looks at it, he is similarly affected.

33. In the middle of the two stands another golden *xoanon*, in no way similar to the other *xoana*. This has no form of its own, but bears the characteristics of other gods. It is called a *semeion* by the Assyrians themselves, nor have they given it any name of its own, but they speak not of its origin and appearance. Some refer it to Dionysus, others to Deucalion, some to Semiramis; for its summit is crowned by a golden pigeon, and this is why they allege that it is the *semeion* of Semiramis. It is taken down to the sea twice each year to bring up the water of which I have spoken.

34. In this *neos*, as you enter, on the left there stands a throne of Helios but there is no *hedos* on it, for they do not show the *xoana* of Helios alone and of Selene. I have learned the reason of this practice. They say that it is a custom to make *xoana* for other gods, for their appearance is not clearly shown to everyone; but Helios and Selene are plain for all to see, and all

men see them. What reason is there for the making of *xoana* for those who appear in the heavens?
35. Behind this throne stands a *xoanon* of Apollo of an unusual character. All others think of Apollo as a youth, and represent him in the flower of his age. These alone show the *xoanon* of Apollo with a beard. They justify their action, and criticize the Greeks and others who set up Apollo as a boy, and appease him in that guise. This is the reason: it seems to them a mark of ignorance to assign imperfect forms to the gods, and they consider youth an imperfection. They have also introduced another strange novelty in their Apollo; they alone represent Apollo as robed.

163

Lucian, *De Dea Syria* 38–39 A.D. II
Text: M.D. Macleod, ed., *Luciani Opera* III (Oxford, 1980).
Translation adapted from H.A. Strong, tr. and J. Garstang, ed., *The Syrian Goddess* (London, 1913).

μετὰ δὲ τὸν Ἀπόλλωνα ξόανόν ἐστιν Ἄτλαντος, μετὰ δὲ Ἑρμέω καὶ Εἰλειθυίης.

Τὰ μὲν ὦν ἐντὸς τοῦ νηοῦ ὧδε κεκοσμέαται· ἔξω δὲ βωμός τε κέαται μέγας χάλκεος, ἐν δὲ καὶ ἄλλα ξόανα μυρία χάλκεα βασιλέων τε καὶ ἱερέων· καταλέξω δὲ τῶν μάλιστα ἄξιον μνήσασθαι. ἐν ἀριστερῇ τοῦ νεὼ Σεμιράμεως ξόανον ἕστηκεν ἐν δεξιῇ τὸν νηὸν ἐπιδεικνύουσα. ἀνέστη δὲ δι᾽ αἰτίην τοιήνδε. ἀνθρώποισιν ὁκόσοι Συρίην οἰκέουσιν νόμον ἐποιέετο ἑαυτὴν μὲν ὅκως θεὸν ἱλάσκεσθαι, θεῶν δὲ τῶν ἄλλων καὶ αὐτῆς Ἥρης ἀλογέειν. καὶ ὧδε ἐποίεον. μετὰ δὲ ὥς οἱ θεόθεν ἀφίκοντο νοῦσοί τε καὶ συμφορὴ καὶ ἄλγεα, μανίης μὲν ἐκείνης ἀπεπαύσατο καὶ θνητὴν ἑωυτὴν ὁμολόγεεν καὶ τοῖσιν ὑπηκόοισιν αὖτις ἐκέλευεν ἐς Ἥρην τρέπεσθαι. τούνεκα δὴ ἔτι τοιήδε ἀνέστηκεν, τοῖσιν ἀπικνεομένοισι τὴν Ἥρην ἱλάσκεσθαι δεικνύουσα, καὶ θεὸν οὐκέτι ἑωυτὴν ἀλλ᾽ ἐκείνην ὁμολογέουσα.

Behind Apollo is the *xoanon* of Atlas; behind that, of Hermes and Eileithuia.
39. Such, then, are the interior decorations of the *neos*; outside stands a great altar of brass, and countless other brazen *xoana* of kings and priests. I will mention those which seem most worthy of remembrance. To the left of the *neos* stands a *xoanon* of Semiramis, pointing with her right hand to the *neos*. It was erected for this reason. The queen had issued a decree that all the Syrians should worship her as a deity, adding that they were to take no count of the others, not excepting even Hera; and they obeyed her decree. Afterwards, however, when disease and misfortune and grief were inflicted on her from heaven, she calmed down from her frenzied infatuation, and admitted herself a mere mortal and ordered her subjects to turn again to

Hera. This is why she stands today in this posture, pointing out to those who come Hera as the goddess whose grace is to be won, and admitting that she is not a goddess, but that Hera is indeed.

164

Lucian, *Phalaris* I.6 A.D. II
Text: M.D. Macleod, ed., *Luciani Opera* I (Oxford, 1972).
Translation adapted from A.M. Harmon, tr., *Lucian* I (LCL, 1913).

ὅμοιον ὡς εἴ τις παρ' ὑμῖν ἱερόσυλόν τινα ἰδὼν ἀπὸ τῆς πέτρας ῥιπτόμενον ἃ μὲν ἐτόλμησε μὴ λογίζοιτο, ὡς νύκτωρ ἐς τὸ ἱερὸν παρῆλθε καὶ κατέσπασε τὰ ἀναθήματα καὶ τοῦ ξοάνου ἥψατο, κατηγοροίη δὲ ὑμῶν πολλὴν τὴν ἀγριότητα, ὅτι Ἕλληνές τε καὶ ἱεροὶ εἶναι λέγοντες ὑπεμείνατε ἄνθρωπον Ἕλληνα πλησίον τοῦ ἱεροῦ—καὶ γὰρ οὐ πάνυ πόρρω τῆς πόλεως εἶναι λέγεται ἡ πέτρα—κολάσει τοιαύτῃ περιβαλεῖν.

. . . it is as if someone among yourselves should see someone guilty of sacrilege thrown over the cliff, and should not take into account what he had dared to do, how at night he had entered the *hieron* and pulled down the *anathemata* and laid hands on the *xoanon*, but should accuse you of great barbarity on the ground that you, who call yourselves Greeks and priests, countenanced the infliction of such a punishment on a fellow Greek near the *hieron*—for they say that the cliff is not very far from the city.

165

Lucian, *Philopseudes* 19 A.D. II
Text: M.D. Macleod, ed., *Luciani Opera* II (Oxford, 1974).
Translation: A.M. Harmon, tr., *Lucian* III (LCL, 1921).

Ἐπειδὰν τάχιστα, ἔφη, νὺξ γένηται, ὁ δὲ καταβὰς ἀπὸ τῆς βάσεως ἐφ' ᾗ ἕστηκε περίεισιν ἐν κύκλῳ τὴν οἰκίαν, καὶ πάντες ἐντυγχάνομεν αὐτῷ ἐνίοτε καὶ ᾄδοντι, καὶ οὐκ ἔστιν ὅντινα ἠδίκησεν· ἐκτρέπεσθαι γὰρ χρὴ μόνον· ὁ δὲ παρέρχεται μηδὲν ἐνοχλήσας τοὺς ἰδόντας. καὶ μὴν καὶ λούεται τὰ πολλὰ καὶ παίζει δι' ὅλης τῆς νυκτός, ὥστε ἀκούειν τοῦ ὕδατος ψοφοῦντος.

Ὅρα τοίνυν, ἦν δ' ἐγώ, μὴ οὐχὶ Πέλλιχος ὁ ἀνδριάς, ἀλλὰ Τάλως ὁ Κρὴς ὁ τοῦ Μίνωος ᾖ· καὶ γὰρ ἐκεῖνος χαλκοῦς τις ἦν τῆς Κρήτης περίπολος. εἰ δὲ μὴ χαλκοῦ, ὦ Εὔκρατες, ἀλλὰ ξύλου πεποίητο, οὐδὲν αὐτὸν ἐκώλυεν οὐ Δημητρίου ἔργον εἶναι, ἀλλὰ τῶν Δαιδάλου τεχνημάτων· δραπετεύει γοῦν, ὡς φῄς, ἀπὸ τῆς βάσεως καὶ οὗτος.

"As soon as night comes," he said, "he gets down from the pedestal on which he stands and goes all about the house; we all encounter him, sometimes singing, and he has never harmed anybody. One has but to turn aside, and he passes without molesting in any way those who saw him. Upon my word, he often takes baths and disports himself all night, so that the water can be heard splashing." "See here, then," said I, "perhaps the *andrias* is not Pellichus but Talos the Cretan, the son of Minos: he was a bronze man, you know, and made the rounds in Crete. If he were made of wood instead of bronze, O Eucrates, there would be nothing to hinder his being one of the devices of Daedalus instead of a work of Demetrius; anyhow he is like them in playing truant from his pedestal, by what you say."

166

Lucian, *Prometheus* 12 A.D. II
Text: M.D. Macleod, ed., *Luciani Opera* I (Oxford, 1972).
Translation adapted from A.M. Harmon, tr., *Lucian* II (LCL, 1915).

ἦν τοίνυν πάλαι—ῥᾷον γὰρ οὕτω δῆλον ἂν γένοιτο, εἴ τι ἠδίκηκα ἐγὼ μετακοσμήσας καὶ νεωτερίσας τὰ περὶ τοὺς ἀνθρώπους—ἦν οὖν τὸ θεῖον μόνον καὶ τὸ ἐπουράνιον γένος, ἡ γῆ δὲ ἄγριόν τι χρῆμα καὶ ἄμορφον, ὕλαις ἅπασα καὶ ταύταις ἀνημέροις λάσιος, οὔτε δὲ βωμοὶ θεῶν ἢ ναοί—πόθεν γάρ;—ἢ ἀγάλματα ἢ ξόανα ἤ τι ἄλλο τοιοῦτον, οἷα πολλὰ νῦν ἁπανταχόθι φαίνεται μετὰ πάσης ἐπιμελείας τιμώμενα·

There existed, then, a long time ago—for if I begin there it will be easier to see whether I have done any wrong in my alterations and innovations with regard to men—there existed, then, only the divine and heavenly race. The earth was a rude and shapeless thing, all shaggy with woods, and wild woods at that, and there were no *bomoi* [altars] of the gods, or *naoi*—how could there be?—or *agalmata* or *xoana* or anything else of the sort, though they are now to be seen in great numbers everywhere, honored with every form of observance.

Lycurgus fr. VI.13 (40) (Conomis) (Περὶ τῆς ἱερείας) IV B.C.
See Harpocration *s.v.* Νίκη Ἀθηνᾶ [137].

167

Macedonius the Consul, *Anthologia Palatina* 16.51 A.D. VI
(= *Anthologia Planudea* 51.)
Text: H. Beckby, ed., *Anthologia Graeca* 4 (Munich, 1957).
Translation adapted from W.R. Paton, tr., *The Greek Anthology* V (LCL, 1918).

Τῷ ξοάνῳ τὸν παῖδα Θυώνιχον, οὐχ ἵνα λεύσσῃς,
  ὡς καλὸς ἐν τῇδε μνάματος ἀγλαΐᾳ,
ἀλλ' ἵνα σοὶ τὸν ἄεθλον, ὃν ἐξεπόνησε, μαθόντι,
  ὠγαθέ, τᾶς αὐτᾶς ζᾶλος ἔοι μανίας.
οὗτος ὁ μὴ κλίνας καμάτῳ πόδα, πάντα δ' ἀγῶνι
  ἅλικα νικήσας, ὁπλότερον, πρότερον.

With this *xoanon* [we honor] the boy Thyonichus, not so that you may see how *kalos* [he was] in the glory of this monument, but so that in you, learning the prize he earned, there may be, O good Sir, the desire to emulate this enthusiasm. This is he whose legs never gave way owing to fatigue, who won over everyone in the contest, his own age, younger, and older.

Manetho III B.C.
See Josephus, *Contra Apionem* [**154, 155**].

168
Maximus of Tyre 8.1–4 A.D. II
Text: H. Hobein, ed., *Maximi Tyrii Philosophumena* (Leipzig, 1910).
Translation adapted from T. Taylor, tr., *The Dissertations of Maximus Tyrius* (London, 1804) No. 38.

Εἰ θεοῖς ἀγάλματα ἱδρυτέον.

1. *Ἀρωγοὶ ἀνθρώποις θεοί, πάντες μὲν πᾶσιν, ἄλλοι δὲ ἄλλοις ἐνομίσθησαν κατὰ τὴν φήμην τῶν ὀνομάτων, καὶ διένειμαν αὐτοῖς οἱ ἄνθρωποι τιμὰς καὶ ἀγάλματα, οἱ ἐς τὰ ἴδια ἕκαστοι ὠφεληθέντες. Οὕτω μὲν ναῦται ἐπὶ ἀκλύστου πέτρας ἀνέθηκαν οἴακας θαλαττίοις· οὕτω δέ τις ποιημένων τὸν Πᾶνα τιμᾷ ἐλάτην αὐτῷ ὑψηλὴν ἐξελόμενος, ἢ ἄντρον βαθύ· καὶ γεωργοὶ Διόνυσον τιμῶσιν, πήξαντες ἐν ὀρχάτῳ αὐτοφυὲς πρέμνον, ἀγροικικὸν ἄγαλμα· ἱερὰ δὲ Ἀρτέμιδος, πηγαὶ ναμάτων, καὶ κοῖλαι νάπαι, καὶ εὔθηροι λειμῶνες· ἐπεφήμισαν δὲ καὶ Διὶ ἀγάλματα οἱ πρῶτοι ἄνθρωποι, κορυφὰς ὀρῶν, Ὄλυμπον, καὶ Ἴδην, καὶ εἴ τι ἄλλο ὄρος πλησιάζει τῷ οὐρανῷ· ἔστιν που καὶ ποταμῶν τιμή, ἢ κατὰ ὠφέλειαν, ὥσπερ Αἰγυπτίοις πρὸς τὸν Νεῖλον· ἢ κατὰ κάλλος, ὡς Θετταλοῖς πρὸς τὸν Πηνειόν· ἢ κατὰ μέγεθος, ὡς Σκύθαις πρὸς τὸν Ἴστρον· ἢ κατὰ μῦθον, ὡς Αἰτωλοῖς πρὸς Ἀχελῷον· ἢ κατὰ νόμον, ὡς Σπαρτιάταις πρὸς τὸν Εὐρώταν· ἢ κατὰ τελετήν, ὡς Ἀθηναίοις πρὸς Ἰλισσόν. Εἶτα ποταμοὶ μὲν διέλαχον τὰς τιμὰς κατὰ τὴν χρείαν τῶν ὠφελουμένων, καὶ αἱ τέχναι τιμῆς θεῶν ἑκάστη εὔπορος, ἄλλο ἄλλη προστησαμένη ἄγαλμα· εἰ δέ που τὶ γένος ἀνθρώπων ἐστὶν οὐ θαλάττιον οὐδὲ γεωργικόν, ἀλλ' ἀστυπολοῦν καὶ ἀνακεκραμένον κοινωνίᾳ πολιτικῇ νόμου καὶ λόγου, ἆρα τούτοις ἀγέραστον ἔσται τὸ θεῖον καὶ ἀτίμητον; ἢ τιμήσουσιν μέν, τῇ δὲ φήμῃ μόνῃ· ἀγαλμάτων δὲ καὶ ἱδρυμάτων οὐκ οἰήσονται δεῖν τοῖς θεοῖς; οὐδὲ γὰρ δεῖ τοῖς θεοῖς ἀγαλμάτων οὐδὲ ἱδρυμάτων μᾶλλον, ἢ εἰκόνων ἀγαθοῖς ἀνδράσιν.*

2. *Ὥσπερ δέ, οἶμαι, τῷ κατὰ τὰς φωνὰς λόγῳ οὐδὲν δεῖ πρὸς σύστασιν χαρακτήρων Φοινικίων τινῶν, ἢ Ἰωνικῶν, ἢ Ἀττικῶν, ἢ Ἀσσυρίων, ἢ Αἰγυπτίων, ἀλλ' ἡ ἀνθρωπίνη ἀσθένεια ἐξεῦρεν σημεῖα ταῦτα, ἐν οἷς ἀποτιθεμένη τὴν αὐτῆς ἀμβλύτητα ἐξ αὐτῶν ἀναμάττεται τὴν αὖθις μνήμην·*

οὕτως ἀμέλει καὶ τῇ τοῦ θείου φύσει δεῖ μὲν οὐδὲν ἀγαλμάτων οὐδὲ ἱδρυμάτων, ἀλλὰ ἀσθενὲς ὂν κομιδῇ τὸ ἀνθρώπειον, καὶ διεστὸς τοῦ θείου ὅσον 'οὐρανὸς γῆς', σημεῖα ταῦτα ἐμηχανήσατο, ἐν οἷς ἀποθήσεται τὰ τῶν θεῶν ὀνόματα καὶ τὰς φήμας αὐτῶν. Οἷς μὲν οὖν ἡ μνήμη ἔρρωται, καὶ δύνανται εὐθὺ τοῦ οὐρανοῦ ἀνατεινόμενοι τῇ ψυχῇ τῷ θείῳ ἐντυγχάνειν, οὐδὲν ἴσως δεῖ τούτοις ἀγαλμάτων· σπάνιον δὲ ἐν ἀνθρώποις τὸ τοιοῦτο γένος, καὶ οὐκ ἂν ἐντύχοις δήμῳ ἀθρόῳ τοῦ θείου μνήμονι, καὶ μὴ δεομένῳ τοιαύτης ἐπικουρίας· οἷον καὶ τοῖς παισὶν οἱ γραμματισταὶ μηχανῶνται ὑποχαράττοντες αὐτοῖς σημεῖα ἀμυδρά, οἷς ἐπάγοντες τὴν χειρουργίαν, ἐθίζονται τῇ μνήμῃ πρὸς τὴν τέχνην. Δοκοῦσιν δή μοι καὶ οἱ νομοθέται, καθάπέρ τινι παίδων ἀγέλῃ, ἐξευρεῖν τοῖς ἀνθρώποις ταυτὶ τὰ ἀγάλματα, σημεῖα τῆς πρὸς τὸ θεῖον τιμῆς, καὶ ὥσπερ χειραγωγίαν τινὰ καὶ ὁδὸν πρὸς ἀνάμνησιν.

3. Ἀγαλμάτων δὲ οὐχ εἷς νόμος, οὐδὲ εἷς τρόπος, οὐδὲ τέχνη μία, οὐδὲ ὕλη μία· ἀλλὰ τὸ μὲν Ἑλληνικόν, τιμᾶν τοὺς θεοὺς ἐνόμισαν τῶν ἐν γῇ τοῖς καλλίστοις, ὕλῃ μὲν καθαρᾷ, μορφῇ δὲ ἀνθρωπίνῃ, τέχνῃ δὲ ἀκριβεῖ. Καὶ οὐκ ἄλογος ἡ ἀξίωσις τῶν τὰ ἀγάλματα εἰς ἀνθρωπίνην ὁμοιότητα καταστησαμένων· εἰ γὰρ ἀνθρώπου ψυχὴ ἐγγύτατον θεῷ καὶ ἐμφερέστατον, οὐ δήπου εἰκὸς τὸ ὁμοιότατον αὐτῷ περιβαλεῖν, τὸν θεόν, σκήνει ἀτοπωτάτῳ, ἀλλ' ὅπερ ἔμελλεν ψυχῆς ἀθανάτοις εὔφορόν τε ἔσεσθαι καὶ κοῦφον καὶ εὐκίνητον μόνον, τοῦτο τῶν ἐν γῇ σωμάτων ἀνατεῖνον τὴν κορυφὴν ὑψοῦ, σοβαρὸν, καὶ γαῦρον, καὶ σύμμετρον, οὔτε διὰ μέγεθος ἐκπληκτικόν, οὔτε διὰ χαίτην φοβερόν, οὔτε διὰ βάρος δυσκίνητον, οὔτε διὰ λειότητα ὀλισθηρόν, οὔτε διὰ τραχύτητα ἀντίτυπον, οὔτε διὰ ψυχρότητα ἑρπηστικόν, οὔτε ἰταμὸν διὰ θερμότητα, οὔτε νηκτὸν διὰ μανότητα, οὐκ ὠμοφάγον δι' ἀγριότητα, οὐ ποιηφάγον δι' ἀσθένειαν, ἀλλὰ κεκραμένον μουσικῶς πρὸς τὰ αὐτοῦ ἔργα· φοβερὸν μὲν δειλοῖς, ἥμερον δὲ ἀγαθοῖς, βαδιστικὸν μὲν τῇ φύσει, πτηνὸν δὲ τῷ λόγῳ, νηκτὸν δὲ τέχνῃ, σιτοφάγον καὶ γεωπόνον καὶ καρποφάγον καὶ εὔχρουν καὶ εὐσταλὲς καὶ εὐωπὸν καὶ εὐγένειον, διὰ τοιούτου σώματος τύπων τοὺς θεοὺς τιμᾶν ἐνόμισαν οἱ Ἕλληνες.

4. Τὸ δὲ βαρβαρικόν, ὁμοίως μὲν ἅπαντες ξυνετοὶ τοῦ θεοῦ, κατεστήσαντο δὲ αὐτοῖς σημεῖα ἄλλοι ἄλλα. Πέρσαι μὲν πῦρ, ἄγαλμα ἐφήμερον, ἀκόρεστον καὶ ἀδηφάγον· καὶ θύουσιν Πέρσαι πυρί, ἐπιφοροῦντες αὐτῷ τὴν πυρὸς τροφήν, ἐπιλέγοντες·

πῦρ δέσποτα, ἔσθιε.

Ἄξιον δὲ πρὸς τοὺς Πέρσας εἰπεῖν, Ὦ πάντων γενῶν ἀνοητότατον, οἱ τοσούτων καὶ τηλικούτων ἀγαλμάτων ἀμελήσαντες, γῆς ἡμέρου, καὶ ἡλίου λαμπροῦ, καὶ θαλάττης πλοΐμου, καὶ ποταμῶν γονίμων, καὶ ἀέρος τροφίμου, καὶ αὐτοῦ οὐρανοῦ, περὶ ἓν μάλιστα ἀσχολεῖσθε τὸ ἀγριώτατον καὶ ὀξύτατον, οὐ ξύλων αὐτῷ τροφὴν χορηγοῦντες μόνον, οὐδὲ ἱερείων, οὐδὲ θυμιαμάτων· ἀλλὰ τούτῳ τῷ ἀγάλματι καὶ τούτῳ τῷ θεῷ καὶ τὴν Ἐρετρίαν ἀναλῶσαι δεδώκατε, καὶ τὰς Ἀθήνας αὐτάς, καὶ τὰ Ἰώνων ἱερά, καὶ τὰ Ἑλλήνων ἀγάλματα.

Whether *Agalmata* Should Be Set Up to the Gods

1. The gods are the helpers of mankind, all indeed of all; but different gods are considered as giving assistance to different men, according to the rumor of names; and men distribute honors and *agalmata* to them according to the private benefits which they have individually received. Thus sailors dedicate, on a rock undisturbed by the sea, helms to the marine deities. Thus, also, some shepherd dedicates in honor of Pan a fir tree, having chosen a tall one for him, or a deep cavern. Husbandmen likewise honor Dionysus, fixing in their garden a wild trunk as a rustic *agalma*. Fountains of water, too, hollow thickets, and flowery meadows, are sacred to Artemis; and the first men consecrated as *agalmata* to Zeus the summits of mountains, such as Olympus and Ida, or any other mountain proximate to the heavens; honor is also paid to rivers, either for the sake of the benefit which they impart, as by the Egyptians to the Nile; or on account of their beauty, as by the Thessalians to Peneus; or on account of their magnitude, as by the Scythians to the Ister; or on account of fabulous tradition, as by the Aetolians to Achelous; or according to law, as the Spartans to Eurotas; or in conformity to the mysteries, as the Athenians to Ilissus. Shall, therefore, rivers be allotted honors, according to the indigence of those whom they benefit, and shall every art honor its patron deity, dedicating a different *agalma* to a different god? but if there is a certain race of men, not marine, nor rustic, but inhabitants of cities, and mingled with the political communion of law and reason, will divinity be ungifted, and unhonored by these? or will they honor him, indeed, but with words alone, and think that the gods have no need of *agalmata* and *hidrumata*? For the gods are not more in want of *agalmata* and *hidrumata* than good men are of *eikones*.

2. Indeed, it appears to me that external discourse has no need, for its composition, of certain Phoenician, or Ionian, or Attic, or Assyrian, or Egyptian characters, but human weakness devised these marks, in which inserting its dullness, it recovers from them its memory; in like manner a divine nature has no need of *agalmata* or *hidrumata*; but human nature being very weak altogether, and as much distant from divinity as earth from heaven, devised these *semeia*, in which it inserted the names and the renown of the gods. Those, therefore, whose memory is robust, and who are able, by directly extending their soul to heaven, to meet with divinity, have perhaps no need of *agalmata*. This race is, however, rare among men, and in a whole nation you will not find one who recollects divinity, and who is not in want of this kind of assistance, which is the sort that writing-masters devise

for boys, who give them obscure marks as copies; by writing over which, their hand being guided by that of the master, they become, through memory, accustomed to the art. It appears to me, therefore, that legislators devised these *agalmata* for men, as if for a certain band of boys, as *semeia* of the honor which should be paid to divinity, and a certain leading by the hand, as it were, and path to remembrance.

3. Of *agalmata*, however, there is neither one law, nor one mode, nor one art, nor one matter. For with respect to the Greeks, they think it fit to honor the gods from things the most beautiful in the earth, from a pure matter, the human form, and accurate art. And their opinion is not irrational, who fashion *agalmata* in the human resemblance. For if the human soul is most near and most similar to divinity it is not reasonable to suppose that the divinity would invest that which is most similar to himself with a most deformed body, but rather with one which would be an easy vehicle to immortal souls, light, and adapted to motion. For this alone, of all the bodies on the earth, raises its summit on high, is magnificent, superb, and full of symmetry, neither astonishing through its magnitude, nor terrible through its strength, nor moved with difficulty through its weight, nor slippery through its smoothness, nor repercussive through its hardness, nor grovelling through its coldness, nor precipitate through its heat, nor inclined to swim through its laxity, nor feeding on raw flesh through its ferocity, nor on grass through its imbecility; but is harmonically composed for its proper works, and is dreadful to timid animals, but mild to such as are brave; it is also adapted to walk by nature, but winged by reason, capable of swimming by art, feeds on corn and fruits, and cultivates the earth, is of a good color, stands firm, has a pleasing countenance, and a graceful beard. In the resemblance of such a body the Greeks think fit to honor the gods.

4. With respect to the barbarians, all of them in like manner admit the subsistence of divinity, but different nations among these adopt different *semeia*. Hence the Persians adopt fire, an ephemeral *agalma*, insatiable and voracious; and to fire they sacrifice, supplying it with the aliment of fire, and at the same time exclaiming, "O master fire, eat." But it is worth saying to the Persians, "O most stupid of all nations, who, neglecting so many and such mighty *agalmata*, the mild earth, the splendid sun, the navigable sea, prolific rivers, the nourishing air, and the heavens themselves, are especially devoted to one thing, and that most savage and most rapid, not only supplying it with the aliment of wood, with victims, and aromatic fumigations, but by this *agalma* and by this god giving Eretria to be consumed, together with Athens itself, the *hiera* of the Ionians, and the *agalmata* of the Greeks."

169

Maximus of Tyre 8.8–9 A.D. II

Text: H. Hobein, ed., *Maxini Tyrii Philosophumena* (Leipzig, 1910). Translation adapted from T. Taylor, tr., *The Dissertations of Maximus Tyrius* (London, 1804) No. 38.

8. Κελτοὶ σέβουσιν μὲν Δία, ἄγαλμα δὲ Διὸς Κελτικὸν ὑψηλὴ δρῦς. Παίονες σέβουσιν μὲν Ἥλιον, ἄγαλμα δὲ Ἡλίου Παιονικὸν δίσκος βραχὺς ὑπὲρ μακροῦ ξύλου. Ἀράβιοι σέβουσι μέν, ὅντινα δέ, οὐκ οἶδα· τὸ δὲ ἄγαλμα εἶδον, λίθος ἦν τετράγωνος. Παφίοις ἡ μὲν Ἀφροδίτη τὰς τιμὰς ἔχει· τὸ δὲ ἄγαλμα οὐκ ἂν εἰκάσαις ἄλλῳ τῷ ἢ πυραμίδι λευκῇ, ἡ δὲ ὕλη ἀγνοεῖται. Λυκίοις ὁ Ὄλυμπος πῦρ ἐκδιδοῖ, οὐχ ὅμοιον τῷ Αἰτναίῳ, ἀλλ' εἰρηνικὸν καὶ σύμμετρον· καὶ ἐστὶν αὐτοῖς τὸ πῦρ τοῦτο καὶ ἱερὸν καὶ ἄγαλμα. Φρύγες οἱ περὶ Κελαινὰς νεμόμενοι τιμῶσιν ποταμοὺς δύο, Μαρσύαν καὶ Μαίανδρον· εἶδον τοὺς ποταμούς· ἀφίησιν αὐτοὺς πηγὴ μία, ἣ προελθοῦσα ἐπὶ τὸ ὄρος ἀφανίζεται κατὰ νώτου τῆς πόλεως, καὖθις ἐκδιδοῖ ἐκ τοῦ ἄστεος, διελοῦσα τοῖς ποταμοῖς καὶ τὸ ὕδωρ καὶ τὰ ὀνόματα· ὁ μὲν ἐπὶ Λυδίας ῥεῖ, ὁ Μαίανδρος· ὁ δὲ αὐτοῦ περὶ τὰ πεδία ἀναλίσκεται. Θύουσιν Φρύγες τοῖς ποταμοῖς, οἱ μὲν ἀμφοτέροις, οἱ δὲ τῷ Μαιάνδρῳ, οἱ δὲ τῷ Μαρσύᾳ· καὶ ἐμβάλλουσιν τὰ μηρία εἰς τὰς πηγάς, ἐπιφημίσαντες τοὔνομα τοῦ ποταμοῦ, ὁποτέρῳ ἔθυσαν· ἀπενεχθέντα δὲ ἐπὶ τὸ ὄρος, καὶ ὑποδύντα ὄρος σὺν τῷ ὕδατι, οὔτ' ἂν ἐπὶ τὸν Μαρσύαν ἐκδοθείη τὰ τοῦ Μαιάνδρου, οὔτ' ἐπὶ τὸν Μαίανδρον τὰ του Μαρσύου· εἰ δὲ ἀμφοῖν εἴη, διαιροῦνται τὸ δῶρον. Ὄρος Καππαδόκαις καὶ θεὸς καὶ ὅρκος καὶ ἄγαλμα, Μαιώτοις λίμνη, Τάναϊς Μασσαγέταις.

9. Ὦ πολλῶν καὶ παντοδαπῶν ἀγαλμάτων· ὧν τὰ μὲν ὑπὸ τέχνης ἐγένετο, τὰ δὲ διὰ χρείαν ἠγαπήθη, τὰ δὲ δι' ὠφέλειαν ἐτιμήθη, τὰ δὲ δι' ἔκπληξιν ἐθαυμάσθη, τὰ δὲ διὰ μέγεθος ἐθειάσθη, τὰ δὲ διὰ κάλλος ἐπῃνέθη. Πλὴν οὐδὲν γένος, οὐ βάρβαρον, οὐχ Ἑλληνικόν, οὐ θαλάττιον, οὐκ ἠπειωτικόν, οὐ νομαδικόν, οὐκ ἀστυπολοῦν, ἀνέχεται τὸ μὴ καταστήσασθαι σύμβολα ἄττα τῆς τῶν θεῶν τιμῆς. Πῶς ἂν οὖν τις διαιτήσαι τὸν λόγον, εἴτε χρὴ ποιεισθαι ἀγάλματα θεῶν, εἴτε μή; Εἰ μὲν γὰρ ἄλλοις τισὶν νομοθετοῦμεν ὑπερορίοις ἀνθρώποις ἔξω τοῦ καθ' ἡμᾶς αἰθέρος, ἄρτι ἐκ γῆς ἀναφυομένοις, ἢ ὑπό τινος προμηθείας πλαττομένοις, ἀπείροις βίου καὶ νόμου καὶ λόγου, δέοι ἂν ἴσως τοῦ σκέμματος· πότερα ἐατέον τουτὶ τὸ γένος, ἐπεὶ τῶν αὐτοφυῶν τούτων ἀγαλμάτων προσκυν<εῖν αἰρ>οῦνται, οὐκ ἐλέφαντα, οὐδὲ χρυσόν, οὐδὲ δρῦν, οὐδὲ κέδρον, οὐδὲ ποταμόν, οὐδὲ ὄρνιθα, ἀλλὰ τὸν ἥλιον ἀνίσχοντα, καὶ τὴν σελήνην λάμπουσαν, καὶ τὸν οὐρανὸν πεποικιλμένον, καὶ γῆν αὐτήν, καὶ ἀέρα αὐτόν, καὶ πῦρ πᾶν, καὶ ὕδωρ πᾶν· <ἢ> καὶ τούτους καθείρξομεν εἰς ἀνάγκην τιμῆς ξύλων ἢ λίθων ἢ τύπων; εἰ δέ ἐστιν οὗτος ἱκανὸς ὁ πάντων νόμος, τὰ κείμενα ἐῶμεν, τὰς φήμας τῶν θεῶν ἀποδεχόμεονι, καὶ φυλάττοντες αὐτῶν τὰ σύμβολα, ὥσπερ καὶ τὰ ὀνόματα.

8. The Celts, indeed, venerate Zeus, but the Celtic *agalma* of Zeus is a lofty oak. The Paeonians venerate Helios, but the Paeonian *agalma* of Helios is a short discus fixed on top of a long pole. The Arabians, indeed, venerate a god whom I do not know; but the *agalma* of him which I have seen is a quadrangular stone. By the Paphians Aphrodite is honored; but you cannot compare her *agalma* to anything else than a white pyramid, the material of which is unknown. Among the Lycians the mountain Olympus creates fire, not like that of Aetna, but peaceful and possessing symmetry; and this fire is to them both *hieron* and *agalma*. The Phrygians who dwell about Celaena venerate two rivers, Marsyas and Maeander, which rivers I have seen. One fountain is the source of these, which proceeding as far as to the mountain disappears at the back of the city, and again emerges from the city, separating both the water and the names of the rivers. And Maeander, indeed, flows to Lydia, but the waters of Marsyas are consumed about the plains. The Phrygians sacrifice to these rivers, some indeed to both, but others to Maeander, and others to Marsyas alone. They also throw the thighs of the victims into the fountains, and invoking by name the river to which they sacrifice; and these thighs are carried as far as to the mountain and go under the water. The things too which are sacrificed to one of these rivers are never carried by the stream into the other; but if the sacrifice is to both these they divide the gift. A mountain is to the Cappadocians a god, an oath, and an *agalma*; a lake to the Maeotae; and the Tanais to the Massagetae.

9. O many and all-various *agalmata*! of which some are fashioned by art, and others are embraced by indigence; some are honored through utility, and others are venerated through the astonishment which they excite; some are considered as divine through their magnitude, and others are celebrated for their beauty! There is not, indeed, any race of men, neither barbarian nor Greek, neither maritime nor continental, neither living a pastoral life, nor dwelling in citites, which can endure to be without some *symbola* of the honor of the gods. How, therefore, shall anyone discuss the question whether it is proper that *agalmata* of the gods should be made or not? For if we were to give laws to other men recently sprung from the earth, and dwelling beyond our boundaries and our air, or who were fashioned by a certain Prometheus, ignorant of life, and law, and reason, it might, perhaps, demand consideration whether this race should be permitted to adore these spontaneous *agalmata* alone, which are not fashioned from ivory nor gold, and which are neither oaks nor cedars, nor rivers nor birds, but the rising sun, the splendid moon, the variegated heaven, the earth itself and the air, all fire and all water; or shall we constrain these also to the necessity of honoring timbers, or stones, or *tupoi*? But if this is the common law of all men, let us make no innovations, let us admit the conceptions concerning the gods, and preserve their *symbola* as well as their names.

170

Menander Rhetor II.445 A.D. III–IV

Text: D.A. Russell and N.G. Wilson, eds., trs., *Menander Rhetor* (Oxford, 1981) 445.15–24.

Translation adapted from Russell and Wilson.

ἐπὶ τούτοις ἐκφράσεις τὸ ἄγαλμα τοῦ θεοῦ παραβάλλων τῷ Ὀλυμπίῳ Διΐ, καὶ Ἀθηνᾷ τῇ ἐν ἀκροπόλει τῶν Ἀθηναίων. εἶτα ἐπάξεις, ποῖος Φειδίας, τίς Δαίδαλος τοσοῦτον ἐδημιούργησε ξόανον; τάχα που ἐξ οὐρανοῦ τὸ ἄγαλμα τοῦτ' ἐρρύη. καὶ ὅτι ἐστεφάνωται δάφναις, φυτῷ προσήκοντι τῷ θεῷ κατὰ Δελφούς. καὶ τὸ ἄλσος ἐκφράσεις καὶ ποταμοὺς τοὺς ἐγγὺς καὶ τὰς πηγάς· καὶ ὅτι οὐ πολὺ τὸ διάστημα, καὶ ὅτι πᾶσα ἡ ἄνοδος ἡ ἐπὶ τὸ ἱερὸν ἱερὰ καὶ ἀνακειμένη Ἀπόλλωνι.

After this, you should describe the *agalma* of the god, comparing it with Zeus at Olympia and Athena on the acropolis of the Athenians. Then add, "What Pheidias, what Daedalus fashioned such a *xoanon*? Perhaps this *agalma* fell from heaven." And [say] that "It is garlanded with bay, a plant belonging to the god, as the Delphians say." You should also describe the grove, the rivers near by and the spring, and say that the distance is not great, and all the road up to the *hieron* is sacred and dedicated to Apollo.

171

Moero of Byzantium, *Anthologia Palatina* 6.189 III B.C.

Text: H. Beckby, ed., *Anthologia Graeca* 1 (Munich, 1957).

Translation adapted from W.R. Paton, tr., *The Greek Anthology* I (LCL, 1916).

Νύμφαι Ἁμαδρυάδες, ποταμοῦ κόραι, αἳ τάδε βένθη
ἀμβρόσιαι ῥοδέοις στείβετε ποσσὶν ἀεί,
χαίρετε καὶ σῴζοιτε Κλεώνυμον, ὃς τάδε καλὰ
εἵσαθ' ὑπαὶ πιτύων ὔμμι, θεαί, ξόανα.

Hamadryad nymphs, ambrosial daughters of the river who forever tread these depths with rosy feet, hail, and save the life of Cleonymus, who set up these beautiful *xoana* under the pines for you, goddesses.

Nicander, *Heteroioumena* Book 2 II B.C.

See Antoninus Liberalis 13.6–7 [**16**].

Olympichus ? IV–III B.C.

FGrH 537 F 1

See Clement of Alexandria, *Protrepticus* 4.41 P. [**44**].

Oracula Chaldaica 224
See Eusebius, *Praeparatio evangelica* 5.12 [**118**].

Nilus of Ancyra, *On Easter* A.D. V
See Photius, *Bibliotheca* 276 [**303**].

172
Oracula Sibyllina III.57–59 c. 31 B.C.
Text: J. Geffcken, ed., *Die Oracula Sibyllina* (GCS 8; Leipzig, 1902).
Translation adapted from J.J. Collins, "Sibylline Oracles," in J.H. Charlesworth, ed., *The Old Testament Pseudepigrapha* I (Garden City, 1983) 363.

ἄρτι δ' ἔτι κτίζεσθε, πόλεις, κοσμεῖσθέ τε πᾶσαι
ναοῖς καὶ σταδίοις ἀγοραῖς χρυσοῖς ξοάνοις τε
ἀργυρέοις λιθίνοις τε, ἵν' ἔλθητ' εἰς πικρὸν ἦμαρ.

Yet, just for today, cities, build, and all adorn yourselves with *naoi* and *stadia* and agoras and golden *xoana*, and silver ones, and stone ones, so that you will come to the bitter day.

173
Oracula Sibyllina III.721–723 II–I B.C.
Text: J. Geffcken, ed., *Die Oracula Sibyllina* (GCS 8; Leipzig, 1902).
Translation adapted from J.J. Collins, "Sibylline Oracles," in J.H. Charlesworth, ed., *The Old Testament Pseudepigrapha* I (Garden City, 1983) 378.

ἡμεῖς δ' ἀθανάτοιο τρίβου πεπλανημένοι ἦμεν,
ἔργα δὲ χειροποίητα σεβάσμεθα ἄφρονι θυμῷ
εἴδωλα ξόανά τε καταφθιμένων ἀνθρώπων.

Wandering, we had gone far from the path of the immortal, we revered with senseless spirit works made by hand, *eidola* and *xoana* of men who have perished.

174
Oracula Sibyllina IV.24–30 late A.D. I
(= Clement of Alexandria, *Protrepticus* 4.54 P.)
Text: J. Geffcken, ed., *Die Oracula Sibyllina* (GCS 8; Leipzig, 1902).
Translation adapted from J.J. Collins, "Sibylline Oracles," in J.H. Charlesworth, ed., *The Old Testament Pseudepigrapha* I (Garden City, 1983) 384.

ὄλβιοι ἀνθρώπων κεῖνοι κατὰ γαῖαν ἔσονται,
ὅσσοι δὴ στέρξουσι μέγαν θεὸν εὐλογέοντες
πρὶν πιέειν φαγέειν τε πεποιθότες εὐσεβίῃσιν·
οἳ νηοὺς μὲν ἅπαντας ἀπαρνήσονται ἰδόντες
καὶ βωμούς, εἰκαῖα λίθων ἀφιδρύματα κωφῶν,
[καὶ λίθινα ξόανα καὶ ἀγάλματα χειροποίητα] (28a)
αἵμασιν ἐμψύχων μεμιασμένα καὶ θυσίῃσιν
τετραπόδων. . . .

Happy will be those of mankind on earth
who will love the great God, blessing him
before drinking and eating, putting their trust in piety.
They will reject all *neoi* when they see them,
bomoi too, useless *aphidrumata* of dumb stones
(and stone *xoana* and handmade *agalmata*)
defiled with the blood of animate creatures, and sacrifices
of four-footed animals. . . .

175
Oracula Sibyllina VIII.122–125 c. A.D. 175
Text: J. Geffcken, ed., *Die Oracula Sibyllina* (GCS 8; Leipzig, 1902). Translation adapted from J.J. Collins, "Sibylline Oracles," in J.H. Charlesworth, ed., *The Old Testament Pseudepigrapha* I (Garden City, 1983) 420–421.

κλειδοφύλαξ εἱρκτῆς μεγάλης ἐπὶ βῆμα θεοῖο.
— — — — — — — — — — — — — — — —
χρυσοῖς τε °ξοάνοισιν ἀργυρέοις λιθίνοισιν°
ὡραῖαι γίνεσθε, ἵν' ἔλθητ' εἰς πικρὸν ἦμαρ
σὴν πρώτην κόλασιν, Ῥώμη, καὶ βρυγμὸν ὁρῶσαι.

Guardian of the key of the great enclosure on the tribunal of God. . . .
and with *xoana* of gold and silver and stone,
be beautiful, so that you may come to a bitter day,
to see your punishment first, Rome, and the gnashing of teeth.

176
Oracula Sibyllina VIII.487–491 before A.D. 300
Text: J. Geffcken, ed., *Die Oracula Sibyllina* (GCS 8; Leipzig, 1902). Translation adapted from J.J. Collins, "Sibylline Oracles," in J.H. Charlesworth, ed., *The Old Testament Pseudepigrapha* I (Garden City, 1983) 429.

οὔποτε πρὸς νηῶν ἀδύτοις ἐώμεσθα πελάζειν,
οὐ ξοάνοις σπένδειν, οὐδ' εὐχωλῇσι γεραίρειν,

οὐδ' ὀδμαῖς ἀνθῶν πολυτερπέσιν οὐδὲ μὲν αὐγαῖς
λαμπτήρων, ἀτὰρ οὐδ' °ἄρα τοὺς° ἀναθήμασι κοσμεῖν,
οὐ λιβάνου ἀτμοῖσιν ἀνιεῖσιν φλόγα °βωμόν°. . . .

We are never allowed to approach the *adyta* of *neoi*,
nor to pour libations to *xoana* nor to honor them with prayers,
nor with the delightful scents of flowers nor with gleams
of lamps, nor even to embellish them with *anathemata*,
nor with breaths of incense sending up a flame on the *bomos*.

177

Oracula Sibyllina XIII.64–68 c. A.D. 265

Text: J. Geffcken, ed., *Die Oracula Sibyllina* (GCS 8; Leipzig, 1902).
Translation adapted from J.J. Collins, "Sibylline Oracles," in J.H. Charlesworth, ed., *The Old Testament Pseudepigrapha* I (Garden City, 1983) 455.

νῦν κοσμεῖσθε, πόλεις Ἀράβων, ναοῖς σταδίοις τε
ἠδ' ἀγοραῖς πλατείαις τε καὶ ἀγλαοφεγγέι πλούτῳ
καὶ ξοάνοις χρυσῷ τε καὶ ἀργύρῳ ἠδ' ἐλέφαντι·
ἐκ πάντων δὲ μάλιστα μαθηματική περ ἐοῦσα
Βόστρα Φιλιππόπολίς <τε>, ἵν' ἔλθῃς εἰς μέγα πένθος. . . .

Now cities of Arabs, be embellished with *naoi* and stadia
and broad marketplaces and resplendent wealth,
and *xoana* of gold and silver and ivory,
but above all Bostra and Philippopolis, though given to learning,
that you may come to great grief.

Oracula Sibyllina fr. 3.21–31
See Theophilus, *Ad Autolycum* 2.36 [**365**].

Oracula Sibyllina
See also Phlegon of Tralles, *Mirabilia* X [**300**].

178

Origen, *Contra Celsum* 1.5 c. A.D. 249

Text: P. Koetschau, ed., *Origenes Werke* I. *Die Schrift vom Martyrium. Buch I–IV Gegen Celsus* (GCS 2; Leipzig, 1899).
Translation adapted from H. Chadwick, tr., *Origen: Contra Celsum* (Cambridge, 1953).

Τὰ δὲ περὶ τῆς εἰδωλολατρείας ὡς ἴδια τῶν ἀπὸ τοῦ λόγου ἐκτιθέμενος καὶ ὑποκατασκευάζει λέγων αὐτοὺς διὰ τοῦτο μὴ νομίζειν αὐτοὺς χειροποιήτους θεοὺς, ἐπεὶ μὴ εὔλογόν ἐστι τὰ ὑπὸ φαυλοτάτων δημιουργῶν καὶ *μοχθηρῶν τὸ ἦθος εἰργασμένα εἶναι θεούς, πολλάκις καὶ ὑπὸ ἀδίκων ἀνθρώπων κατασκευασθέντα. ἐν τοῖς ἑξῆς οὖν θέλων αὐτὸ κοινοποιῆσαι ὡς οὐ πρῶτον ὑπὸ τούτου εὑρεθὲν ἐκτίθεται Ἡρακλείτου λέξιν τὴν λέγουσαν· "ὅμοια, ὡς εἴ τις τοῖς δόμοις λεσχηνεύοιτο, ποιεῖν τοὺς προσιόντας ὡς θεοῖς τοῖς ἀψύχοις." οὐκοῦν καὶ περὶ τούτου λεκτέον ὅτι ὁμοίως τῷ ἄλλῳ ἠθικῷ τόπῳ ἐγκατεσπάρησαν τοῖς ἀνθρώποις ἔννοιαι, ἀφ' ὧν καὶ ὁ Ἡράκλειτος καὶ εἴ τις ἄλλος Ἑλλήνων ἢ βαρβάρων τοῦτ' ἐνενόησε κατασκευάσαι. ἐκτίθεται γὰρ καὶ Πέρσας τοῦτο φρονοῦντας, παρατιθέμενος Ἡρόδοτον ἱστοροῦντα αὐτό. προσθήσομεν δὲ καὶ ἡμεῖς ὅτι καὶ Ζήνων ὁ Κιτιεὺς ἐν τῇ Πολιτείᾳ φησίν· "ἱερά τε οἰκοδομεῖν οὐδὲν δεήσει· ἱερὸν γὰρ οὐδὲν χρὴ νομίζειν οὐδὲ πολλοῦ ἄξιον καὶ ἅγιον, οἰκοδόμων τε ἔργον καὶ βαναύσων." σαφὲς οὖν ὅτι καὶ περὶ τούτου τοῦ δόγματος γέγραπται "ἐν ταῖς καρδίαις" τῶν ἀνθρώπων γράμμασι θεοῦ τὸ πρακτέον.*

In giving an account of the attitude to idolatry as characteristic of them [Christians] he even supports that view, saying: "Because of this they would not regard as gods those that are made by hands, since it is irrational that things should be gods which are customarily made by craftsmen of the lowest kind who are morally wicked. For often they have been made by bad men." Later, when he wants to make out that the idea is commonplace and that it was not discovered first by [Christianity], he quotes the saying of Heraclitus which says: "Those who approach soulless things as gods act like a man who holds conversation with houses." I would reply in this instance also, as in that of the other ethical principles, that moral ideas have been inplanted in men, and that it was from these that Heraclitus and any other Greek or barbarian conceived the notion of maintaining this doctrine. He also quotes the Persians as holding this view, adducing Herodotus as authority for this. We will also add that Zeno of Citium says in his Republic: "There will be no need to build *hiera*; for nothing ought to be thought sacred, or of great value, and holy, which is the work of builders and artisans." Obviously, therefore, in respect of this doctrine also, the knowledge of what is right conduct was written by God in the hearts of men.

179

Origen, *Contra Celsum* 7.62 c. A.D. 249
(= Herodotus 1.131.)
Text: P. Koetschau, ed., *Origenes Werke* II. *Buch V–VIII Gegen Celsus. Die Schrift vom Gebet* (GCS 3; Leipzig, 1899).
Translation adapted from H. Chadwick, tr., *Origen: Contra Celsum* (Cambridge, 1953).

Φέρε δὲ ἴδωμεν καὶ τὰ ἑξῆς, ἐν οἷς ταῦτά φησι· στῶμεν δ' ἐκεῖθεν· οὐκ ἀνέχονται νεὼς ὁρῶντες καὶ βωμοὺς καὶ ἀγάλματα. οὐδὲ γὰρ Σκύθαι τοῦτο οὐδὲ Λιβύων οἱ Νομάδες οὐδὲ Σῆρες οἱ ἄθεοι οὐδ' ἄλλα ἔθνη τὰ δυσαγέστατα καὶ ἀνομώτατα. ὅτι δὲ καὶ Πέρσαι οὕτως νομίζουσιν, Ἡρόδοτος ἐν τοῖσδε ἱστορεῖ· "Πέρσας δὲ οἶδα νόμοισι τοῖσδε χρεωμένους, ἀγάλματα μὲν καὶ βωμοὺς καὶ ναοὺς οὐκ ἐν νόμῳ ποιευμένους ἱδρύεσθαι, ἀλλὰ καὶ τοῖσι ποιεῦσι μωρίην ἐπιφέρουσιν· ὡς μὲν ἐμοὶ δοκέει, διότι οὐκ ἀνθρωποφυέας ἐνόμισαν τοὺς θεοὺς καθάπερ οἱ Ἕλληνες εἶναι." καὶ μὴν καὶ Ἡράκλειτος ὧδέ πως ἀποφαίνεται· "καὶ τοῖς ἀγάλμασι τουτέοισιν εὔχονται, ὁκοῖον εἴ τις τοῖς δόμοισι λεσχηνεύοιτο, οὔ τι γινώσκων θεοὺς οὐδ' ἥρωας, οἵτινές εἰσι." τί γοῦν σοφώτερον τοῦ Ἡρακλείτου ἡμᾶς διδάσκουσιν; ὁ μέν γε μάλα ἀπορρήτως ὑποσημαίνει ἠλίθιον τὸ "τοῖς ἀγάλμασιν" εὔχεσθαι, ἐὰν μὴ γινώσκῃ τις "θεοὺς καὶ ἥρωας, οἵτινές εἰσιν".

Ἡράκλειτος μὲν οὕτως· οἱ δὲ ἄντικρυς τὰ ἀγάλματα ἀτιμάζουσιν. εἰ μὲν ὅτι λίθος ἢ ξύλον ἢ χαλκὸς ἢ χρυσὸς, ὃν ὁ δεῖνα ἢ ὁ δεῖνα εἰργάσατο, οὐκ ἂν εἴη θεὸς, γελοία ἡ σοφία. τίς γὰρ καὶ ἄλλος εἰ μὴ πάντῃ νήπιος ταῦτα ἡγεῖται θεοὺς ἀλλὰ θεῶν ἀναθήματα καὶ ἀγάλματα; εἰ δ' ὅτι μηδὲ θείας εἰκόνας ὑποληπτέον, ἄλλην γὰρ εἶναι θεοῦ μορφήν, ὥσπερ καὶ Πέρσαις δοκεῖ· λελήθασιν αὐτοὶ σφᾶς αὐτοὺς ἐλέγχοντες, ὅταν φῶσιν ὅτι "ὁ θεὸς ἐποίησε τὸν ἄνθρωπον" ἰδίαν "εἰκόνα" τὸ δὲ εἶδος ὅμοιον ἑαυτῷ. ἀλλὰ συνθήσονται μὲν εἶναι ταῦτα ἐπὶ τιμῇ τινων, ἢ ὁμοίων ἢ ἀνομοίων τὸ εἶδος, οὔτε δὲ θεοὺς εἶναι, οἷς ταῦτα ἀνάκειται, ἀλλὰ δαίμονας, οὐδὲ χρῆναι θεραπεύειν δαίμονας ὅστις σέβει θεόν.

But let us look at the next passage where he says this: "However, let us leave this point. They cannot bear to see *neoi* and *bomoi* and *agalmata*. The Scythians also do not tolerate this, nor do the Nomads of Libya, nor the Seres who believe in no gods, nor other nations that are most impious and have no regard for law. And that this view is taken by the Persians also is related by Herodotus in these words: 'Now I know that the Persians follow these laws, and do not hold it legal for *agalmata* and *bomoi* and *naoi* when they are made to be established, but even attribute stupidity to people who do so. The reason for this, it seems to me, is that they did not regard the gods as possessing a nature like that of men as the Greeks did.' Moreover, Heraclitus somewhere affirms: 'And they pray to these *agalmata* just as if someone were to have conversation with houses, not knowing the gods nor the heroes, who they are.' What indeed do they teach us which is wiser than Heraclitus? At all events he hints in very obscure language that it is silly for anyone to pray to *agalmata* if he does not know who the gods and heroes are.

"Such is Heraclitus' meaning. But they openly dishonor the *agalmata*. If what they mean is that something stone or wood or bronze or gold which some man or other wrought cannot be a god, their wisdom is ludicrous. Who but an utter infant imagines that these things are gods and not *anathemata* and *agalmata* of gods? But if they mean that we ought not to suppose that *eikones* are divine because God has a different shape, as the

Persians also maintain, they have unwittingly refuted themselves. For they say that 'God made man in the same *eikon*, with an appearance like his own.' But, although they will agree that these things are intended for the honor of certain beings, whether they resemble their appearance or not, yet they think that those to whom they are dedicated are not gods but daemons, and that no one who worships God ought to serve daemons."

180

Origen, *Contra Celsum* 7.65 c. A.D. 249
Text: P. Koetschau, ed., *Origenes Werke* II. *Buch V–VIII Gegen Celsus. Die Schrift vom Gebet* (GCS 3; Leipzig, 1899).
Translation adapted from H. Chadwick, tr., *Origen: Contra Celsum* (Cambridge, 1953).

ἐπεὶ δὲ καὶ τὴν Ἡρακλείτου παρέθετο λέξιν, ὑποδιηγησάμενος αὐτὴν ὑποσημαίνουσαν ἠλίθιον εἶναι τὸ "τοῖς ἀγάλμασιν" εὔχεσθαι. ἐὰν μὴ γινώσκῃ τις "θεοὺς καὶ ἥρωας, οἵτινές εἰσι," λεκτέον ὅτι γινώσκειν μὲν ἔστι θεὸν καὶ τὸν μονογενῆ αὐτοῦ καὶ τοὺς τετιμημένους ὑπὸ θεοῦ τῇ θεὸς προσηγορίᾳ καὶ μετέχοντας τῆς θεότητος αὐτοῦ, ἑτέρους ὄντας παρὰ πάντας τοὺς θεοὺς "τῶν ἐθνῶν," "οἵτινές εἰσι" "δαιμόνια"· οὐ μὴν δυνατόν ἐστι καὶ γινώσκειν τὸν θεὸν καὶ "τοῖς ἀγάλμασιν" εὔχεσθαι.

Then he quotes the saying of Heraclitus which he interpreted as meaning that it is silly for anyone to pray to *agalmata* if he does not know the gods and heroes, who they are. My reply is that it is possible to know God and His only-begotten Son and those beings who have been honored by God with the title of God and who partake of His divinity, who are different from all the gods of the heathen, who are daemons; but it is quite impossible both to know God and to pray to *agalmata*.

181

Origen, *Contra Celsum* 7.69 c. A.D. 249
Text: P. Koetschau, ed., *Origenes Werke* II. *Buch V–VIII Gegen Celsus. Die Schrift vom Gebet* (GCS 3; Leipzig, 1899).
Translation adapted from H. Chadwick, tr., *Origen: Contra Celsum* (Cambridge, 1953).

"πάντες" γὰρ "οἱ θεοὶ τῶν ἐθνῶν δαιμόνια." δῆλον δὲ καὶ τοῦτο ἐκ τοῦ εἰς τὰ δοκοῦντα ἐνεργέστερα τῶν νομιζομένων ἱερῶν κατακλίσεις περιέργους γεγονέναι καὶ κατὰ τὰς ἀρχὰς τῆς ἱδρύσεως τῶν τοιῶνδε ξοάνων καὶ νεῶν, ἅστινας κατακλίσεις οἱ τῇ τῶν δαιμόνων διὰ μαγγανειῶν θεραπείᾳ σχολάζοντες πεποίηνται.

For "all the gods of the heathen are daemons." [*Ps.* 95.5.] This is also clear from the fact that, for these supposed holy places which seem to be more powerful, curious spells were used at the time when such *xoana* and *neoi* were first set up; and these were performed by those who devote their time to worshipping daemons by means of incantations.

182

Origen, *Contra Celsum* 8.41 c. A.D. 249

Text: P. Koetschau, ed., *Origenes Werke* II. *Buch V–VIII Gegen Celsus. Die Schrift vom Gebet* (GCS 3; Leipzig, 1899).

Translation adapted from H. Chadwick, tr., *Origen: Contra Celsum* (Cambridge, 1953).

ἐπ' ἴσης δὲ ἠλίθιον τὸ λοιδορεῖσθαι λίθῳ ἢ χρυσῷ ἢ ἀργύρῳ, τοῖς μεμορφωμένοις εἰς τὴν νενομισμένην τοῖς μακρὰν θειότητος τυγχάνουσι θεῶν μορφήν. οὕτω δὲ οὐδὲ καταγελῶμεν τῶν ἀψύχων ξοάνων ἀλλ' εἰ ἄρα τῶν προσκυνούντων αὐτοῖς.

It is equally silly to pour abuse on stone or gold or silver, which are shaped into the customary shape of gods by people who are far from God. So also we do not laugh at soulless *xoana*, but, if at all, only at people who worship them.

183

Origen, *Contra Celsum* 8.43 c. A.D. 249

Text: P. Koetschau, ed., *Origenes Werke* II. *Buch V–VIII Gegen Celsus. Die Schrift vom Gebet* (GCS 3; Leipzig, 1899).

Translation adapted from H. Chadwick, tr., *Origen: Contra Celsum* (Cambridge, 1953).

εἶτα μετὰ ταῦτα ὁ Κέλσος, ἐπαναλαμβάνων τὸν πρὸς τοὺς βλασφημοῦντας τὰ ἀγάλματα λόγον, φησίν· οἶδε δέ, οὓς σὺ βλασφημεῖς, ἐνῆν μὲν εἰπεῖν ὅτι καὶ αὐτοὶ βούλονται <καὶ> διὰ τοῦτ' ἀνέχονται βλασφημούμενοι· τὰ γὰρ ἴσα τοῖς ἴσοις παραβαλεῖν κράτιστον· ἀλλ' οὗτοί γε καὶ σφόδρα ἀμύνονται τὸν βλασφημοῦντα, ἤτοι γε φεύγοντα διὰ τοῦτο καὶ κρυπτόμενον ἢ ἁλισκόμενον καὶ ἀπολλύμενον. οὐ βλασφημοῦντας οὖν ἀλλ' ἀπελαύνοντας ἀπὸ τῶν ξοάνων καὶ τῶν ἀνθρωπίνων σωμάτων καὶ ψυχῶν Χριστιανοὺς ἀμύνεσθαι νομίζουσιν οἱ δαίμονες. μὴ νοῶν γὰρ τὸ γινόμενον ἀληθές τι κατὰ τὸν τόπον ὁ Κέλσος εἴρηκεν· ἀληθὲς γὰρ τὸ φαύλων δαιμόνων πληρουμένας τὰς τῶν καταδικαζόντων Χριστιανοὺς ψυχὰς καὶ τῶν προδιδόντων καὶ τῶν εὐδοκούντων Χριστιανοῖς προσπολεμεῖν.

Then after this Celsus repeats his words to those who blaspheme *agalmata*, saying: "But these gods whom you blaspheme could say that this too was their will, and that this is why they endure it when they are blasphemed. Where the matters are equal, it is best to compare them fairly on the same level. The latter, however, actually do take severe revenge on anyone who blasphemes them; for either he runs away and hides himself on account of what he has done, or he is caught and destroyed." The daemons are accustomed to taking vengeance on Christians not because Christians blaspheme them, but because they drive them out of the *xoana* and human bodies and souls. Although Celsus did not realize what he was doing, he did say something true on this point. For it is true that the souls of people who condemn Christians and betray them, and delight in fighting against them are filled by evil daemons.

184

Origen, *Fragmenta in Psalmos* 105.29 A.D. III
Text: J.B. Pitra, ed., *Analecta sacra spicilegio Solesmensi parata* III. *Patres antenicaeni* (Venice, 1883) 214.
Καὶ ἔφαγον θυσίας νεκρῶν.
Ἢ διὰ τὸ νεκρομαντείας τὰ περὶ τὰ ξόανα τελετὰς ποιεῖν, ἢ διὰ τὸ νεκρῶν ἀνδρῶν μνήμας ποιεῖσθαι. Νεκροὶ γὰρ, οἱ περὶ τὸν Κρόνον.

And they ate the sacrifices of the dead.
Either by performing necromantic rites, those concerning *xoana*, or by making memorials of dead men for themselves. For the dead [are] those who have to do with Cronus.

185

Orion of Thebes, *Etymologicon s.v. Ξόανον* A.D.V
Text: F.W. Sturz, ed., *Orionis Thebani Etymologicon* (Leipzig, 1820) 112.9.

Ξόανον, παρὰ τὸ ξέω ξέανον, καὶ τροπῇ τοῦ ε̄ εἰς ο̄ , ξόανον.

Xoanon: derived from *xeo*, *xeanon*, and by the change of *e* to *o*, *xoanon*.

186

Palaephatus, *De Incredibilis* 22 ? IV B.C.
Text: A. Westermann, ed., Μυθόγραφοι. *Scriptores Poeticae Historiae Graeci* (Brunswick, 1843) 286.3.

Περὶ Δαιδάλου. Λέγουσι περὶ Δαιδάλου ὡς ἀγάλματα κατεσκεύαζε δι' ἑαυτῶν πορευόμενα. τὸ δὲ ἀνδριάντα δι' αὑτοῦ βαδίζειν ἀδύνατον εἶναι δοκεῖ ἔμοιγε. τὸ δὲ ἀληθὲς τοιοῦτον. οἱ τότε ἀνδριαντοποιοὶ καὶ ἀγαλματοποιοὶ κατεσκεύαζον ἀνδριάντας συμπεφυκότας ἔχοντας καὶ τοὺς πόδας. Δαίδαλος δὲ πρῶτος ἐποίει διαβεβηκότας τὸν ἕνα πόδα. οἱ δὲ ἄνθρωποι ἔλεγον "ὁδοιποροῦν τοῦτο τὸ ἄγαλμα, ὃ εἰργάσατο Δαίδαλος, ἀλλ' οὐχὶ ἑστηκός," ὡς καὶ νῦν λέγομεν· εἰσί γε καὶ μαχόμενοι ἄνδρες γεγραμμένοι καὶ τρέχοντες ἵπποι καὶ χειμαζομένη ναῦς.

Concerning Daedalus.They say about Daedalus that he made *agalmata* that walked of their own accord. But it seems to me impossible that an *andrias* could walk by itself. But the truth is such [as follows]. The *andrias*-makers and the *agalma*-makers in the past made *andriantes* having even the feet joined together. Daedalus was the first who made the one foot separated [*sc.* from the other]. But men said, "This *agalma* that Daedalus made walks around and does not stand still," and even now we speak thus. And there are men depicted as fighting, and horses as galloping, and a ship as being tossed by storms.

Pausanias A.D. II

Text: The text of all the passages of Pausanias is taken from the edition of F. Spiro, ed., *Pausaniae Graeciae descriptio* (3 vols.; Leipzig, 1903; repr. Stuttgart, 1967).

Translations are adapted from the edition of J.G. Fraser, tr., *Pausanias's Description of Greece* I (London, 1913).

187

Pausanias 1.3.5

ᾠκοδόμηται δὲ καὶ Μητρὸς θεῶν ἱερόν, ἣν Φειδίας εἰργάσατο, καὶ πλησίον τῶν πεντακοσίων καλουμένων βουλευτήριον, οἳ βουλεύουσιν ἐνιαυτὸν Ἀθηναίοις· Βουλαίου δὲ ἐν αὐτῷ κεῖται ξόανον Διὸς καὶ Ἀπόλλων τέχνη Πεισίου καὶ Δῆμος ἔργον Λύσωνος.

(Athens)

There was built also a *hieron* of the Mother of the Gods, whom Pheidias worked. Near it is the Bouleuterion of the Five Hundred, as they are called, who form the annual council of Athens. In this Bouleuterion are a *xoanon* of Zeus Boulaios and an Apollo, craft of Peisios, and a Demos, work of Lyson.

188

Pausanias 1.18.5

μόνοις δὲ Ἀθηναίοις τῆς Εἰλειθυίας κεκάλυπται τὰ ξόανα ἐς ἄκρους τοὺς πόδας. τὰ μὲν δὴ δύο εἶναι Κρητικὰ καὶ Φαίδρας ἀναθήματα ἔλεγον αἱ γυναῖκες, τὸ δὲ ἀρχαιότατον Ἐρυσίχθονα ἐκ Δήλου κομίσαι.

The Athenians are the only people whose *xoana* of Eileithyia are draped to the tips of the feet. The women said that two were Cretan, *anathemata* of Phaedra, but that Erysichton brought the oldest from Delos.

189
Pausanias 1.23.7

καὶ Ἀρτέμιδος ἱερόν ἐστι Βραυρωνίας, Πραξιτέλους μὲν τέχνη τὸ ἄγαλμα, τῇ θεῷ δέ ἐστιν ἀπὸ Βραυρῶνος δήμου τὸ ὄνομα· καὶ τὸ ἀρχαῖον ξόανόν ἐστιν ἐν Βραυρῶνι, Ἄρτεμις ὡς λέγουσιν ἡ Ταυρική.

There is also a *hieron* of Brauronian Artemis, the *agalma* is the craft of Praxiteles, but the goddess gets her name from the deme Brauron; and the *archaion xoanon* is in Brauron, which they say is the Tauric Artemis.

190
Pausanias 1.26.6

τὸ δὲ ἁγιώτατον ἐν κοινῷ πολλοῖς πρότερον νομισθὲν ἔτεσιν <ἢ> συνῆλθον ἀπὸ τῶν δήμων ἐστὶν Ἀθηνᾶς ἄγαλμα ἐν τῇ νῦν ἀκροπόλει, τότε δὲ ὀνομαζομένῃ πόλει· φήμη δὲ ἐς αὐτὸ ἔχει πεσεῖν ἐκ τοῦ οὐρανοῦ. καὶ τοῦτο μὲν οὐκ ἐπέξειμι εἴτε οὕτως εἴτε ἄλλως ἔχει. . . .

But the object which was universally deemed the most holy many years before the union of demes is an *agalma* of Athena in what is now called the Acropolis, but was then called the Polis. The legend is that it fell from heaven, but whether this was so or not I will not go through in detail. . . .

191
Pausanias 1.29.2

Ἀθηναίοις δὲ καὶ ἔξω πόλεως ἐν τοῖς δήμοις καὶ κατὰ τὰς ὁδοὺς θεῶν ἐστιν ἱερὰ καὶ ἡρώων καὶ ἀνδρῶν τάφοι· ἐγγυτάτω δὲ Ἀκαδημία, χωρίον ποτὲ ἀνδρὸς ἰδιώτου, γυμνάσιον δὲ ἐπ᾽ ἐμοῦ. κατιοῦσι δ᾽ ἐς αὐτὴν περίβολός ἐστιν Ἀρτέμιδος καὶ ξόανα Ἀρίστης καὶ Καλλίστης· ὡς μὲν ἐγὼ δοκῶ καὶ ὁμολογεῖ τὰ ἔπη τὰ Πάμφω, τῆς Ἀρτέμιδός εἰσιν ἐπικλήσεις αὗται, λεγόμενον δὲ καὶ ἄλλον ἐς αὐτὰς λόγον εἰδὼς ὑπερβήσομαι.

Outside of the city, in the demes and along the roads, the Athenians have *hiera* of the gods and graves of heroes and men. Nearest the city is the Academy, once the property of a private man, but in my time a gymnasium. On the way to it there is a *peribolos* sacred to Artemis, with *xoana* of Ariste ("best") and Calliste ("fairest"). In my opinion, confirmed by the verses of Sappho, these names are epithets of Artemis. I know that another explanation of them is given, but I shall pass it over.

192
Pausanias 1.31.4

τὸ δὲ ἐν Μυρρινοῦντι ξόανόν ἐστι Κολαινίδος.

The *xoanon* in Myrrhinus is of Colaenis.

193
Pausanias 1.33.1

Μαραθῶνος δὲ ἀπέχει τι μὲν Βραυρών, ἔνθα Ἰφιγένειαν τὴν Ἀγαμέμνονος ἐκ Ταύρων φεύγουσαν τὸ ἄγαλμα ἀγομένην τὸ Ἀρτέμιδος ἀποβῆναι λέγουσι, καταλιποῦσαν δὲ τὸ ἄγαλμα ταύτῃ καὶ ἐς Ἀθήνας καὶ ὕστερον ἐς Ἄργος ἀφικέσθαι· ξόανον μὲν δὴ καὶ αὐτόθι ἐστὶν Ἀρτέμιδος ἀρχαῖον, τὸ δὲ ἐκ τῶν βαρβάρων οἵτινες κατὰ γνώμην ἔχουσι τὴν ἐμήν, ἐν ἑτέρῳ λόγῳ δηλώσω. . . .

Some way from Marathon is Brauron, where they say that Iphigeneia, daughter of Agamemnon, fleeing from the Taurians, landed with the *agalma* of Artemis. Here, it is said, she left the *agalma* and went to Athens, afterwards to Argos. There is indeed an *archaion xoanon* of Artemis here; but in another place I shall show who, in my opinion, possess that which was brought from the barbarians. . . .

194
Pausanias 1.33.7

πτερὰ δ' ἔχον οὔτε τοῦτο τὸ ἄγαλμα Νεμέσεως οὔτε ἄλλο πεποίηται τῶν ἀρχαίων, ἐπεὶ μηδὲ Σμυρναίοις τὰ ἁγιώτατα ξόανα ἔχει πτερά· οἱ δὲ ὕστερον—ἐπιφαίνεσθαι γὰρ τὴν θεὸν μάλιστα ἐπὶ τῷ ἐρᾶν ἐθέλουσιν—ἐπὶ τούτῳ Νεμέσει πτερὰ ὥσπερ Ἔρωτι ποιοῦσι.

Neither this *agalma* of Nemesis nor any other made by the ancients has wings, for not even do the most holy *xoana* at Smyrna have wings; but later men—because they held that the goddess mostly appears around love—have made wings on this Nemesis just as on Eros.

195
Pausanias 1.36.2

νῆσος δὲ πρὸ Σαλαμῖνός ἐστι καλουμένη Ψυττάλεια· ἐς ταύτην τῶν βαρβάρων ὅσον τετρακοσίους ἀποβῆναι λέγουσιν, ἡττωμένου δὲ τοῦ Ξέρξου ναυτικοῦ καὶ τούτους ἀπολέσθαι φασὶν ἐπιδιαβάντων ἐς τὴν Ψυττάλειαν τῶν Ἑλλήνων. ἄγαλμα δὲ ἐν τῇ νήσῳ σὺν τέχνῃ μέν ἐστιν οὐδέν, Πανὸς δὲ ὡς ἕκαστον ἔτυχε ξόανα πεποιημένα.

There is an island in front of Salamis called Psyttalia. They say that about four hundred barbarians landed on it, and that, when the fleet of Xerxes was worsted, they were destroyed when the Greeks crossed over to Psyttalia. There is on the island no *agalma* with craft, but there happen to be *xoana* of Pan made each by itself.

196
Pausanias 1.38.8

ἐν τούτῳ τῷ πεδίῳ ναός ἐστι Διονύσου, καὶ τὸ ξόανον ἐντεῦθεν Ἀθηναίοις ἐκομίσθη τὸ ἀρχαῖον· τὸ δὲ ἐν Ἐλευθεραῖς <τὸ> ἐφ' ἡμῶν ἐς μίμησιν ἐκείνου πεποίηται.

In this plain there is a *naos* of Dionysus, and from here the *archaion xoanon* was brought to Athens; the one in Eleutherae in our own time is made as a copy of it.

197
Pausanias 1.42.5

τοῦ δὲ Ἀπόλλωνος πλίνθου μὲν ἦν ὁ ἀρχαῖος ναός· ὕστερον δὲ βασιλεὺς ᾠκοδόμησεν Ἀδριανὸς λίθου λευκοῦ. ὁ μὲν δὴ Πύθιος καλούμενος καὶ ὁ Δεκατηφόρος τοῖς Αἰγυπτίοις μάλιστα ἐοίκασι ξοάνοις, ὃν δὲ Ἀρχηγέτην ἐπονομάζουσιν, Αἰγινητικοῖς ἔργοις ἐστὶν ὅμοιος· ἐβένου δὲ πάντα ὁμοίως πεποίηται.

The *archaios naos* of Apollo was of brick, but afterwards the Emperor Hadrian built it of white marble. The one called the Pythian, and the Receiver of Tithes, look much like Egyptian *xoana*, but the one they surname Founder is like Aeginetan works; all alike are made of ebony.

198
Pausanias 1.43.5

ᾠκοδόμησε δὴ καὶ τῷ Διονύσῳ τὸ ἱερὸν Πολύιδος καὶ ξόανον ἀνέθηκεν ἀποκεκρυμμένον ἐφ' ἡμῶν πλὴν τοῦ προσώπου· τοῦτο δέ ἐστι τὸ φανερόν.

(Megara)
Polyidus also built the *hieron* of Dionysus, and dedicated a *xoanon*, which in our time is all hidden except the face, the only visible part of it.

199
Pausanias 1.44.2

ἔστι δὲ ἐν τῷ γυμνασίῳ τῷ ἀρχαίῳ πλησίον πυλῶν καλουμένων Νυμφάδων λίθος παρεχόμενος πυραμίδος σχῆμα οὐ μεγάλης· τοῦτον Ἀπόλλωνα ὀνομάζουσι Καρινόν, καὶ Εἰλειθυιῶν ἐστιν ἐνταῦθα ἱερόν.

(Megara)
In the *archaion* gymnasium, near the gate called "of the Nymphs," is a stone in the shape of a small pyramid; this they call Apollo Carinus, and there is a *hieron* of the Eileithyias here.

200
Pausanias 2.2.3

ἔστι δὲ ἐν Λεχαίῳ μὲν Ποσειδῶνος ἱερὸν καὶ ἄγαλμα χαλκοῦν, τὴν δὲ ἐς Κεγχρέας ἰόντων ἐξ ἰσθμοῦ ναὸς Ἀρτέμιδος καὶ ξόανον ἀρχαῖον.

In Lechaeum there is a *hieron* of Poseidon with a bronze *agalma*. On the way from the Isthmus to Cenchreae there is a *naos* of Artemis and an *archaion xoanon*.

201
Pausanias 2.2.6–7

λόγου δὲ ἄξια ἐν τῇ πόλει τὰ μὲν λειπόμενα ἔτι τῶν ἀρχαίων ἐστίν, τὰ δὲ πολλὰ αὐτῶν ἐπὶ τῆς ἀκμῆς ἐποιήθη τῆς ὕστερον. ἔστιν οὖν ἐπὶ τῆς ἀγορᾶς—ἐνταῦθα γὰρ πλεῖστά ἐστι τῶν ἱερῶν—Ἄρτεμίς τε ἐπίκλησιν Ἐφεσία καὶ Διονύσου ξόανα ἐπίχρυσα πλὴν τῶν προσώπων· τὰ δὲ πρόσωπα ἀλοιφῇ σφισιν ἐρυθρᾷ κεκόσμηται· Λύσιον δέ, τὸν δὲ Βάκχειον ὀνομάζουσι. τὰ δὲ λεγόμενα ἐς τὰ ξόανα καὶ ἐγὼ γράφω. Πενθέα ὑβρίζοντα ἐς Διόνυσον καὶ ἄλλα τολμᾶν λέγουσι καὶ τέλος ἐς τὸν Κιθαιρῶνα ἐλθεῖν ἐπὶ κατασκοπῇ τῶν γυναικῶν, ἀναβάντα δὲ ἐς δένδρον θεάσασθαι τὰ ποιούμενα· τὰς δέ, ὡς ἐφώρασαν, καθελκύσαι τε αὐτίκα Πενθέα καὶ ζῶντος ἀποσπᾶν ἄλλο ἄλλην τοῦ σώματος. ὕστερον δέ, ὡς Κορίνθιοι λέγουσιν, ἡ Πυθία χρᾷ σφισιν ἀνευρόντας τὸ δένδρον ἐκεῖνο ἴσα τῷ θεῷ σέβειν· καὶ ἀπ᾽ αὐτοῦ διὰ τόδε τὰς εἰκόνας πεποίηνται ταύτας.

The remarkable objects in the city include some remains of ancient Corinth, but most of them date from the period of the restoration. In the agora (for most of the *hiera* are there) is an Artemis surnamed Ephesian; also *xoana* of Dionysus gilded all over except the faces, which are adorned with red paint. One of these is named the Deliverer, the other, Bacchius. The story told about these *xoana* I, too, will record. They say that among the insults which Pentheus dared to offer Dionysus he at last went to Mount Cithaeron to spy upon the women, and getting up into a tree watched their doings; but the women discovered him, dragged him instantly down, and tore him limb from limb. Afterwards, as the Corinthians say, the Pythia ordered them in an oracle to find the tree and worship it as much as the god himself; so they had these *eikones* made out of the tree.

202

Pausanias 2.4.1

τοῦ μνήματος δέ ἐστιν οὐ πόρρω Χαλινίτιδος Ἀθηνᾶς ἱερόν· Ἀθηνᾶν γὰρ θεῶν μάλιστα συγκατεργάσασθαι τά τε ἄλλα Βελλεροφόντῃ φασὶ καὶ ὡς τὸν Πήγασόν οἱ παραδοίη χειρωσαμένη τε καὶ ἐνθεῖσα αὐτῃ τῷ ἵππῳ χαλινόν. τὸ δὲ ἄγαλμα τοῦτο ξόανόν ἐστι, πρόσωπον δὲ καὶ χεῖρες καὶ ἀκρόποδες εἰσὶ λευκοῦ λίθου.

(Corinth)

Not far from the tomb [of Medea's children] is a *hieron* of Athena the Bridler; for they say that Athena above all the gods helped Bellerophon in his exploits, and that in particular she handed over to him Pegasus, tamed and bridled with her own hands. This *agalma* is a *xoanon*, but the face and hands and feet are of white stone.

203

Pausanias 2.4.5

τὸ δὲ ἱερὸν τῆς Ἀθηνᾶς τῆς Χαλινίτιδος πρὸς τῷ θεάτρῳ σφίσιν ἐστὶν καὶ πλησίον ξόανον γυμνὸν Ἡρακλέους, Δαιδάλου δὲ αὐτό φασιν εἶναι τέχνην. Δαίδαλος δὲ ὁπόσα εἰργάσατο, ἀτοπώτερα μέν ἐστιν ἐς τὴν ὄψιν, ἐπιπρέπει δὲ ὅμως τι καὶ ἔνθεον τούτοις.

(Corinth)

The *hieron* of Athena the Bridler is beside the theater, and near it is a naked *xoanon* of Heracles, they say it is the craft of Daedalus. Daedalus made things of such a kind, while they are somewhat strange to the eye, still, something divine is also noticeable in them.

204

Pausanias 2.7.5

ἐν δὲ τῇ νῦν ἀκροπόλει Τύχης ἱερόν ἐστιν Ἀκραίας, μετὰ δὲ αὐτὸ Διοσκούρων· ξόανα δὲ οὗτοί τε καὶ τὸ ἄγαλμα τῆς Τύχης ἐστί.

(Sicyon)

In the present acropolis there is a *hieron* of Fortune of the Height, and beyond it, of the Dioscuri. These and the *agalma* of Fortune are *xoana*.

205
Pausanias 2.9.6

μετὰ δὲ <τὸ> Ἀράτου ἡρῷον ἔστι μὲν Ποσειδῶνι Ἰσθμίῳ βωμός, ἔστι δὲ Ζεὺς Μειλίχιος καὶ Ἄρτεμις ὀνομαζομένη Πατρῴα, σὺν τέχνῃ πεποιημένα οὐδεμιᾷ· πυραμίδι δὲ ὁ Μειλίχιος, ἡ δὲ κίονί ἐστιν εἰκασμένη.

(Sicyon)
Beyond the *heroion* of Aratus is an altar to Isthmian Poseidon, and there is a Zeus Meilichios, and an Artemis named Patroa, made without any craft at all; Meilichios looks like a pyramid, she like a column.

206
Pausanias 2.10.1

ἔστι δὲ καὶ ἑτέρωθι ἱερὸν Ἡρακλέους· τὸν μὲν πάντα ἐνταῦθα περίβολον Παιδιζὴν ὀνομάζουσιν, ἐν μέσῳ δέ ἐστι τῷ περιβόλῳ τὸ ἱερόν, ἐν δὲ αὐτῷ ξόανον ἀρχαῖον, τέχνη Φλιασίου Λαφάους.

(Sicyon)
Elsewhere there is a *hieron* of Heracles; the entire *peribolos* there they name Paedize, in the middle of the *peribolos* is a *hieron*, and in it is an *archaion xoanon*, the craft of Laphaes, a Phliasian.

207
Pausanias 2.10.7

ἀπὸ τούτων δὲ ἀνιοῦσιν ἐς τὸ γυμνάσιον ἔστιν ἐν δεξιᾷ Φεραίας ἱερὸν Ἀρτέμιδος· κομισθῆναι δὲ τὸ ξόανον λέγουσιν ἐκ Φερῶν.

(Sicyon)
Going up from here to the gymnasium there is on the right a *hieron* of Pheraean Artemis; they say that the *xoanon* was brought from Pherae.

208
Pausanias 2.11.7

τῆς δὲ Κορωνίδος ἔστι μὲν καὶ ταύτης ξόανον, καθίδρυται δὲ οὐδαμοῦ τοῦ ναοῦ· θυομένων δὲ τῷ θεῷ ταύρου καὶ ἀρνὸς καὶ ὑὸς ἐς Ἀθηνᾶς ἱερὸν τὴν Κορωνίδα μετενεγκόντες ἐνταῦθα τιμῶσιν.

(Titane, Sanctuary of Asclepius)
There is also a *xoanon* of Coronis. It does not stand in the *naos*; but when they are sacrificing a bull, a lamb, and a pig to the god, after they have brought Coronis to the *hieron* of Athena they honor her there.

209
Pausanias 2.11.8

ἀνάκειται δὲ ἀγάλματα ἐν τῇ στοᾷ Διονύσου καὶ Ἑκάτης, Ἀφροδίτη τε καὶ Μήτηρ θεῶν καὶ Τύχη· ταῦτα μὲν ξόανα, λίθου δὲ Ἀσκληπιὸς ἐπίκλησιν Γορτύνιος.

(Titane, Sanctuary of Asclepius)
In the stoa there are dedicated *agalmata* of Dionysus and of Hecate, and Aphrodite and the Mother of the Gods, and Fortune; these are *xoana*, but Asclepius, surnamed Gortynian, is of stone.

210
Pausanias 2.12.1

ἐν δὲ Τιτάνῃ καὶ Ἀθηνᾶς ἱερόν ἐστιν, ἐς ὃ τὴν Κορωνίδα ἀνάγουσιν· ἐν δὲ αὐτῷ ξόανον Ἀθηνᾶς ἐστιν ἀρχαῖον, κεραυνωθῆναι δὲ καὶ τοῦτο ἐλέγετο. . . .

In Titane there is also a *hieron* of Athena, to which they carry up Coronis; in it is an *archaion xoanon* of Athena, which is also said to have been struck by lightning.

211
Pausanias 2.17.4–5

τὸ δὲ ἄγαλμα τῆς Ἥρας ἐπὶ θρόνου κάθηται μεγέθει μέγα, χρυσοῦ μὲν καὶ ἐλέφαντος, Πολυκλείτου δὲ ἔργον· ἔπεστι δέ οἱ στέφανος Χάριτας ἔχων καὶ Ὥρας ἐπειργασμένας, καὶ τῶν χειρῶν τῇ μὲν καρπὸν φέρει ῥοιᾶς, τῇ δὲ σκῆπτρον. τὰ μὲν οὖν ἐς τὴν ῥοιὰν—ἀπορρητότερος γάρ ἐστιν ὁ λόγος—ἀφείσθω μοι· κόκκυγα δὲ ἐπὶ τῷ σκήπτρῳ καθῆσθαί φασι λέγοντες τὸν Δία, ὅτε ἤρα παρθένου τῆς Ἥρας, ἐς τοῦτον τὸν ὄρνιθα ἀλλαγῆναι, τὴν δὲ ἅτε παίγνιον θηρᾶσαι. τοῦτον τὸν λόγον καὶ ὅσα ἐοικότα εἴρηται περὶ θεῶν οὐκ ἀποδεχόμενος γράφω, γράφω δὲ οὐδὲν ἧσσον. λέγεται δὲ παρεστηκέναι τῇ Ἥρᾳ τέχνῃ Ναυκύδους ἄγαλμα Ἥβης, ἐλέφαντος καὶ τοῦτο καὶ χρυσοῦ· παρὰ δὲ αὐτήν ἐστιν ἐπὶ κίονος ἄγαλμα Ἥρας ἀρχαῖον. τὸ δὲ ἀρχαιότατον πεποίηται μὲν ἐξ ἀχράδος, ἀνετέθη δὲ ἐς Τίρυνθα ὑπὸ Πειράσου τοῦ Ἄργου, Τίρυνθα δὲ ἀνελόντες Ἀργεῖοι κομίζουσιν ἐς τὸ Ἡραῖον· ὃ δὴ καὶ αὐτὸς εἶδον, καθήμενον ἄγαλμα οὐ μέγα.

(Argive Heraeum)
The *agalma* of Hera is seated on a throne, and is large in size, of gold and ivory, and the work of Polyclitus; on her [head] is a *stephanos* with the Charites and the Horai wrought on it and in one hand she carries a pomegranate, in the other a scepter. The story about the pomegranate—for it is a somewhat mystic *logos*—I shall omit; but the cuckoo perched on the scepter is explained by a story, that when Zeus was in love with the maiden

Hera he changed himself into this bird, and that Hera caught the bird as a plaything. This and similar stories of the gods I record, though I do not accept them. It is said that beside the Hera once stood an *agalma* of Hebe, also of ivory and gold, the craft of Naucydes. Beside her is an *archaion agalma* of Hera on a column. But the most *archaion* one is made of the wild pear tree; it was dedicated in Tiryns by Pirasus, son of Argus,and when the Argives destroyed Tiryns they brought [it] to the Heraeum; I saw it myself, a seated *agalma*, not large.

212
Pausanias 2.18.3

ἀπὸ δὲ τῶν Κριῶν—οὕτω γὰρ τοῦ Θυέστου τὸ μνῆμα ὀνομάζουσι—προελθοῦσιν ὀλίγον ἐστὶν ἐν ἀριστερᾷ χωρίον Μυσία καὶ Δήμητρος Μυσίας ἱερὸν ἀπὸ ἀνδρὸς Μυσίου τὸ ὄνομα, γενομένου καὶ τούτου, καθάπερ λέγουσιν Ἀργεῖοι, ξένου τῇ Δήμητρι. τούτῳ μὲν οὖν οὐκ ἔπεστιν ὄροφος· ἐν δὲ αὐτῷ ναός ἐστιν ἄλλος ὀπτῆς πλίνθου, ξόανα δὲ Κόρης καὶ Πλούτωνος καὶ Δήμητρός ἐστι.

A little beyond the Rams—for so they name the tomb of Thyestes—there is on the left a place Mysis and a *hieron* of Demeter Mysia. The name is derived from Mysius, one of those men, the Argives say, who entertained Demeter. It has no roof; but in it is another *naos*, built of burnt bricks, and *xoana* of the Maid and Pluto and Demeter.

213
Pausanias 2.19.3

Ἀργείοις δὲ τῶν ἐν τῇ πόλει τὸ ἐπιφανέστατόν ἐστιν Ἀπόλλωνος ἱερὸν Λυκίου. τὸ μὲν οὖν ἄγαλμα τὸ ἐφ' ἡμῶν Ἀττάλου ποίημα ἦν Ἀθηναίου, τὸ δὲ ἐξ ἀρχῆς Δαναοῦ καὶ ὁ ναὸς καὶ τὸ ξόανον ἀνάθημα ἦν· ξόανα γὰρ δὴ τότε εἶναι πείθομαι πάντα καὶ μάλιστα τὰ Αἰγύπτια.

The most famous building in Argos is a *hieron* of Apollo Lykios. The *agalma* in our time was made by Attalus, an Athenian, but in the beginning both the *naos* and the *xoanon* were dedicated by Danaus; for I believe that then they were all *xoana*, and especially the Egyptian ones.

214
Pausanias 2.19.6

τὰ δὲ ξόανα Ἀφροδίτης καὶ Ἑρμοῦ, τὸ μὲν Ἐπειοῦ λέγουσιν ἔργον εἶναι, τὸ δὲ Ὑπερμήστρας ἀνάθημα. ταύτην γὰρ τῶν θυγατέρων μόνην τὸ πρόσταγμα ὑπεριδοῦσαν ὑπήγαγεν ὁ Δαναὸς ἐς δικαστήριον, τοῦ τε Λυγκέως οὐκ ἀκίνδυνον αὑτῷ τὴν σωτηρίαν ἡγούμενος καὶ ὅτι τοῦ τολμήματος οὐ μετασχοῦσα ταῖς ἀδελφαῖς καὶ τῷ βουλεύσαντι τὸ ὄνειδος ηὔξησε. κριθεῖσα δὲ ἐν τοῖς Ἀργείοις ἀποφεύγει τε καὶ Ἀφροδίτην ἐπὶ τῷδε ἀνέθηκε Νικηφόρον.

(Argos, Sanctuary of Apollo Lykios)
Of the *xoana* of Aphrodite and Hermes, they say that one is a work of Epius, the other, an *anathema* of Hypermnestra. For Danaus brought her to trial, the only one of his daughters who disregarded his command, thinking his own safety imperilled by the escape of Lynceus and that by not sharing the crime of her sisters she had inflamed the infamy that attached to himself as the contriver of the deed. Being tried by the Argives, she was acquitted and dedicated a Victory-bringing Aphrodite on this occasion.

215
Pausanias 2.19.7

Δαναὸς δὲ ταῦτά τε ἀνέθηκε καὶ πλησίον κίονας καὶ Διὸς καὶ Ἀρτέμιδος ξόανον.

Danaus dedicated these, also some pillars near from . . . of Zeus and a *xoanon* of Artemis.

216
Pausanias 2.23.1

ἐντεῦθεν ἐρχομένοις ὁδὸν καλουμένην <Κοίλην> ναός ἐστιν ἐν δεξιᾷ Διονύσου· τὸ δὲ ἄγαλμα εἶναι λέγουσιν ἐξ Εὐβοίας. συμβάσης γὰρ τοῖς Ἕλλησιν, ὡς ἐκομίζοντο ἐξ Ἰλίου, τῆς πρὸς τῷ Καφηρεῖ ναυαγίας, τοὺς δυνηθέντας ἐς τὴν γῆν διαφυγεῖν τῶν Ἀργείων ῥῖγός τε πιέζει καὶ λιμός. εὐξαμένοις δὲ θεῶν τινα ἐν τοῖς παροῦσιν ἀπόροις γενέσθαι σωτῆρα, αὐτίκα ὡς προήεσαν ἐφάνη σφίσι Διονύσου σπήλαιον, καὶ ἄγαλμα ἦν ἐν τῷ σπηλαίῳ τοῦ θεοῦ· τότε δὲ αἶγες ἄγριαι φεύγουσαι τὸν χειμῶνα ἐς αὐτὸ ἦσαν ἠθροισμέναι. ταύτας οἱ Ἀργεῖοι σφάξαντες τά τε κρέα ἐδείπνησαν καὶ δέρμασιν ἐχρήσαντο ἀντὶ ἐσθῆτος. ἐπεὶ δὲ ὁ χειμὼν ἐπαύσατο καὶ ἐπισκευάσαντες τὰς ναῦς οἴκαδε ἐκομίζοντο, ἐπάγονται τὸ ἐκ τοῦ σπηλαίου ξόανον· καὶ διατελοῦσιν ἐς τόδε τιμῶντες ἔτι.

(Argos)
Going from here along <Hollow> Street, as it is called, there is on the right a *naos* of Dionysus; they say that the *agalma* came from Euboea. For when the Greeks, returning from Ilium, were shipwrecked at Caphereus, those of the Argives who contrived to escape to land were distressed by cold and hunger. So they prayed that one of the gods would save them in their present strait; and straightway as they went forward they spied a cave of

Dionysus, and in the cave was an *agalma* of the god and some wild goats, which had sought shelter there from the storm. These the Argives killed and ate, and used their skins as garments. And when the storm was over, and they had refitted their ships and were sailing for home, they took with them the *xoanon* from the cave; and they worship it to this day.

217
Pausanias 2.24.3–4

επ' ἄκρᾳ δέ ἐστι τῇ Λαρίσῃ Διὸς ἐπίκλησιν Λαρισαίου ναός, οὐκ ἔχων ὄροφον· τὸ δὲ ἄγαλμα ξύλου πεποιημένον οὐκέτι ἑστηκὸς ἦν ἐπὶ τῷ βάθρῳ. καὶ Ἀθηνᾶς δὲ ναός ἐστι θέας ἄξιος· ἐνταῦθα ἀναθήματα κεῖται καὶ ἄλλα καὶ Ζεὺς ξόανον, δύο μὲν ᾗ πεφύκαμεν ἔχον ὀφθαλμούς, τρίτον δὲ ἐπὶ τοῦ μετώπου. τοῦτον τὸν Δία Πριάμῳ φασὶν εἶναι τῷ Λαομέδοντος πατρῷον ἐν ὑπαίθρῳ τῆς αὐλῆς ἱδρυμένον, καὶ ὅτε ἡλίσκετο ὑπὸ Ἑλλήνων Ἴλιον, ἐπὶ τούτου κατέφυγεν ὁ Πρίαμος τὸν βωμόν. ἐπεὶ δὲ τὰ λάφυρα ἐνέμοντο, λαμβάνει Σθένελος ὁ Καπανέως αὐτόν, καὶ ἀνάκειται μὲν διὰ τοῦτο ἐνταῦθα· τρεῖς δὲ ὀφθαλμοὺς ἔχειν ἐπὶ τῷδε ἄν τις τεκμαίροιτο αὐτόν. Δία γὰρ ἐν οὐρανῷ βασιλεύειν, οὗτος μὲν λόγος κοινὸς πάντων ἐστὶν ἀνθρώπων. ὃν δὲ ἄρχειν φασὶν ὑπὸ γῆς, ἔστιν ἔπος τῶν Ὁμήρου Δία ὀνομάζον καὶ τοῦτον·

Ζεύς τε καταχθόνιος καὶ ἐπαινὴ Περσεφόνεια.

Αἰσχύλος δὲ ὁ Εὐφορίωνος καλεῖ Δία καὶ τὸν ἐν θαλάσσῃ. τρισὶν οὖν ὁρῶντα ἐποίησεν ὀφθαλμοῖς, ὅστις δὴ ἦν ὁ ποιήσας, ἅτε ἐν ταῖς τρισὶ ταῖς λεγομέναις λήξεσιν ἄρχοντα τὸν αὐτὸν τοῦτον θεόν.

On the summit of Larisa is a *naos* of Larisian Zeus. The roof is gone, and the *agalma*, which is made of wood, no longer stands on its pedestal. There is also a *naos* of Athena which is worth seeing. Among the *anathemata* which it contains is a *xoanon* of Zeus with two eyes in the usual place, and a third eye on the forehead. They say that this Zeus was the paternal god of Priam, son of Laomedon, and stood in the *aule* under the open sky; and when Ilium was taken by the Greeks, Priam fled for refuge to this god's altar. In the division of the spoils, Sthenelus, son of Capaneus, got it, and that is why it stands here. The reason why it has three eyes may be conjectured to be the following. All men agree that Zeus reigns in heaven, and there is a verse of Homer which gives the name of Zeus to the god who is said to rule under the earth: "Both underground Zeus and Persephone." Further, Aeschylus, son of Euphorion, applies the name also to the god in the sea. So the artist, whoever he was, represented Zeus with three eyes, because it is one and the same Zeus who reigns in three realms of nature, as they are called.

218
Pausanias 2.25.1

ἐπὶ δὲ τῆς ὁδοῦ ταύτης ἱερὸν διπλοῦν πεποίηται, καὶ πρὸς ἡλίου δύνοντος ἔσοδον καὶ κατὰ ἀνατολὰς ἑτέραν ἔχον. κατὰ μὲν δὴ τοῦτο Ἀφροδίτης κεῖται ξόανον, πρὸς δὲ ἡλίου δυσμὰς Ἄρεως· εἶναι δὲ τὰ ἀγάλματα· Πολυνείκους λέγουσιν ἀναθήματα καὶ Ἀργείων, ὅσοι τιμωρήσοντες αὐτῷ συνεστρατεύοντο.

(Road from Argos to Mantinea)
On this road a double *hieron* has been made, with one entrance on the west and the other on the east. In the one there is a *xoanon* of Aphrodite, in the western one, of Ares; they say that the *agalmata* are dedications of Polynices and the Argives, who took the field in his cause.

219
Pausanias 2.25.6

ἔστι δὲ ἐν ταῖς Ὀρνεαῖς Ἀρτέμιδός τε ἱερὸν καὶ ξόανον ὀρθὸν καὶ ἕτερος ναὸς θεοῖς πᾶσιν ἐς κοινὸν ἀνειμένος.

In Orneae there is is a *hieron* of Artemis with a standing *xoanon*, and there is another *naos* dedicated to all the gods in common.

220
Pausanias 2.25.10

κατὰ δὲ τὴν ἐς Ἐπίδαυρον εὐθεῖάν ἐστι κώμη Λῆσσα, ναὸς δὲ Ἀθηνᾶς ἐν αὐτῇ καὶ ξόανον οὐδέν τι διάφορον ἢ τὸ ἐν ἀκροπόλει τῇ Λαρίσῃ.

On the straight road to Epidaurus is a village, Lessa, a *naos* of Athena in it and a *xoanon* in no way different from that on Larisa the acropolis.

221
Pausanias 2.29.1

τὴν δὲ Ἀθηνᾶν ἐν τῇ ἀκροπόλει, ξόανον θέας ἄξιον, Κισσαίαν ἐπονομάζουσιν.

(Epidaurus)
They call Athena on the acropolis, a *xoanon* of the goddess worth seeing, Cissaean.

222
Pausanias 2.30.1

Ἀπόλλωνι μὲν δὴ ξόανον γυμνόν ἐστι τέχνης τῆς ἐπιχωρίου, τῇ δὲ Ἀρτέμιδί ἐστιν ἐσθής, κατὰ ταὐτὰ δὲ καὶ τῷ Διονύσῳ· καὶ γένεια Διόνυσος ἔχων πεποίηται.

(Aegina)
The naked *xoanon* of Apollo is of native craft; Artemis has clothing, and so does Dionysus; and Dionysus is made having a beard.

223
Pausanias 2.30.2

τοῦ περιβόλου δὲ ἐντὸς ναός ἐστι, ξόανον δὲ ἔργον Μύρωνος, ὁμοίως ἓν πρόσωπόν τε καὶ τὸ λοιπὸν σῶμα.

(Aegina; Hecate)
Within the *peribolos* is a *naos*, a *xoanon*, a work of Myron, similarly one, in face and the rest of the body.

224
Pausanias 2.30.4

τὸ δὲ Πανελλήνιον, ὅτι μὴ τοῦ Διὸς τὸ ἱερόν, ἄλλο τὸ ὄρος ἀξιόλογον εἶχεν οὐδέν. τοῦτο δὲ τὸ ἱερὸν λέγουσιν Αἰακὸν ποιῆσαι τῷ Διί· τὰ δὲ ἐς τὴν Αὐξησίαν καὶ Δαμίαν, ὡς οὐχ ὗεν ὁ θεὸς Ἐπιδαυρίοις, ὡς τὰ ξόανα ταῦτα ἐκ μαντείας ἐποιήσαντο ἐλαίας παρ' Ἀθηναίων λαβόντες, ὡς Ἐπιδαύριοι μὲν οὐκ ἀπέφερον ἔτι Ἀθηναίοις ἃ ἐτάξαντο οἷα Αἰγινητῶν ἐχόντων τὰ ἀγάλματα, Ἀθηναίων δὲ ἀπώλοντο οἱ διαβάντες διὰ ταῦτα ἐς Αἴγιναν, ταῦτα εἰπόντος Ἡροδότου καθ' ἕκαστον αὐτῶν ἐπ' ἀκριβὲς οὔ μοι γράφειν κατὰ γνώμην ἦν εὖ προειρημένα, πλὴν τοσοῦτό γε ὅτι εἶδόν τε τὰ ἀγάλματα καὶ ἔθυσά σφισι κατὰ <τὰ> αὐτὰ καθὰ δὴ καὶ Ἐλευσῖνι θύειν νομίζουσιν.

(Aegina)
There is nothing worth mention on Panhellenius except the *hieron* of Zeus. They say that Aeacus made this *hieron* for Zeus. But the story of Auxesia and Damia, how no rain fell on the Epidaurians, how they made these *xoana* as the result of an oracle, taking olive trees from the Athenians, how the Epidaurians did not remit to the Athenians what they agreed to pay, since the Aeginetans were holding the *agalmata*, and the Athenians who

crossed over to Aegina to get them were destroyed, these things Herodotus having told in detail and accurately, it is not for me to write what has well been told, except that I saw the *agalmata* and sacrificed to them according to the ritual observed in sacrificing at Eleusis.

225
Pausanias 2.31.6

ἄγαλμα δέ ἐστι τὸ ἐφ' ἡμῶν ἀνάθημα Αὐλίσκου, τέχνη δὲ Ἕρμωνος Τροιζηνίου· τοῦ δὲ Ἕρμωνος τούτου καὶ τὰ τῶν Διοσκούρων ξόανά ἐστι.

(Troezen)
The *agalma* of our time is an *anathema* of Auliscus, the craft of Hermon of Troezen. The *xoana* of the Dioscuri are also by this Hermon.

226
Pausanias 2.32.5

ἐν δὲ τῇ ἀκροπόλει τῆς Σθενιάδος καλουμένης ναός ἐστιν Ἀθηνᾶς, αὐτὸ δὲ εἰργάσατο τῆς θεοῦ τὸ ξόανον Κάλλων Αἰγινήτης· μαθητὴς δὲ ὁ Κάλλων ἦν Τεκταίου καὶ Ἀγγελίωνος, οἳ Δηλίοις ἐποίησαν τὸ ἄγαλμα τοῦ Ἀπόλλωνος· ὁ δὲ Ἀγγελίων καὶ Τεκταῖος παρὰ Διποίνῳ καὶ Σκύλλιδι ἐδιδάχθησαν.

(Troezen)
In the acropolis there is a *naos* of Athena, who is called Sthenias. Callon of Aegina worked the *xoanon* of the goddess. Callon was a pupil of Tectaeus and Angelion, who made the *agalma* of Apollo for the Delians; Angelion and Tectaeus were themselves trained in the school of Dipoenus and Scyllis.

227
Pausanias 2.36.6

ἀπὸ δὲ Ἐρασίνου τραπεῖσιν ἐς ἀριστερὰ σταδίους ὅσον ὀκτώ, Διοσκούρων ἱερόν ἐστιν Ἀνάκτων· πεποίηται δέ σφισι κατὰ ταὐτὰ καὶ ἐν τῇ πόλει τὰ ξόανα.

(Lerna)
Turning to the left from the Erasinus for about eight furlongs, there is a *hieron* of the Lords Dioscuri; their *xoana* are made in the same way as those in the city.

228
Pausanias 2.37.1–2

ἐντὸς δὲ τοῦ ἄλσους ἀγάλματα ἔστι μὲν Δήμητρος Προσύμνης, ἔστι δὲ Διονύσου, καὶ Δήμητρος καθήμενον ἄγαλμα οὐ μέγα· ταῦτα μὲν λίθου πεποιημένα, ἑτέρωθι δ' ἐν ναῷ Διόνυσος Σαώτης καθήμενον ξόανον καὶ Ἀφροδίτης ἄγαλμα ἐπὶ θαλάσσῃ λίθου. . . .

(Lerna)
In the grove are *agalmata* of Demeter Prosymna, and there is one of Dionysus, and also a not large, seated *agalma* of Demeter. These are made of stone, but on the other side in a *naos* there is a seated *xoanon* of Savior Dionysus and an *agalma* of stone of Aphrodite beside the sea.

229
Pausanias 3.13.9

ξόανον δὲ ἀρχαῖον καλοῦσιν Ἀφροδίτης Ἥρας· ἐπὶ δὲ θυγατρὶ γαμουμένῃ νενομίκασι τὰς μητέρας τῇ θεῷ θύειν.

(Sparta)
They call the *archaion xoanon* of Aphrodite Hera; at the marriage of her daughter, it is the custom for a mother to sacrifice to the goddess.

230
Pausanias 3.14.4–5

τὸ δὲ ἱερὸν τῆς Θέτιδος κατασκευασθῆναί φασιν ἐπ' αἰτίᾳ τοιαύτῃ· πολεμεῖν μὲν πρὸς Μεσσηνίους ἀφεστηκότας, τὸν δὲ βασιλέα σφῶν Ἀνάξανδρον ἐσβαλόντα ἐς τὴν Μεσσηνίαν λαβεῖν αἰχμαλώτους γυναῖκας, ἐν δὲ αὐταῖς εἶναι Κλεώ, Θέτιδος δὲ αὐτὴν ἱέρειαν εἶναι. ταύτην ἡ τοῦ Ἀναξάνδρου γυνὴ τὴν Κλεὼ παρὰ τοῦ Ἀναξάνδρου αἰτεῖ, καὶ τό τε ξόανον τῆς Θέτιδος ἀνεῦρεν ἔχουσαν καὶ ναὸν μετ' αὐτῆς ἱδρύσατο τῇ θεῷ· ἐποίει δὲ ταῦτα ἡ Λεανδρὶς κατὰ ὄψιν ὀνείρατος. τὸ μὲν δὴ ξόανον τῆς Θέτιδος ἐν ἀπορρήτῳ φυλάσσουσι. . . .

(Sparta)
They say the *hieron* of Thetis was constructed for the following cause. In the war with the Messenian rebels, King Anaxander invaded Messenia and among the women who fell into his hands was Cleo, priestess of Thetis. Anaxander's wife (Leandris) asked him to give her Cleo, and she found that she (Cleo) had the *xoanon* of Thetis, and with her she founded a *naos* to the

goddess; Leandris did this, because of a vision in a dream. The *xoanon* of Thetis they still preserve in secret. . . .

231
Pausanias 3.14.7

τὸ δὲ τοῦ Ἀγνίτα πεποίηται μὲν ἐν δεξιᾷ τοῦ Δρόμου, Ἀσκληπιοῦ δέ ἐστιν ἐπίκλησις ὁ Ἀγνίτας, ὅτι ἦν ἄγνου τῷ θεῷ ξόανον· ἡ δὲ ἄγνος λύγος καὶ αὐτὴ κατὰ ταὐτά ἐστι τῇ ῥάμνῳ.

(Sparta)
The [sanctuary] of Agnitas is built on the right of the Dromos. Agnitas is a surname of Asclepius, because the *xoanon* of the god was of *agnos*. The *agnos* is a kind of willow just like the *rhamnos*.

232
Pausanias 3.15.7

τοῦ ναοῦ δὲ ἀπαντικρὺ πέδας ἐστὶν ἔχων Ἐνυάλιος, ἄγαλμα ἀρχαῖον. γνώμη δὲ Λακεδαιμονίων τε ἐς τοῦτό ἐστιν ἄγαλμα καὶ Ἀθηναίων ἐς τὴν Ἄπτερον καλουμένην Νίκην, τῶν μὲν οὔποτε τὸν Ἐνυάλιον φεύγοντα οἰχήσεσθαί σφισιν ἐνεχόμενον ταῖς πέδαις, Ἀθηναίων δὲ τὴν Νίκην αὐτόθι ἀεὶ μενεῖν οὐκ ὄντων πτερῶν. τόνδε μέν εἰσιν αἱ πόλεις αὗται τὰ ξόανα τὸν τρόπον ἱδρυμέναι καὶ ἐπὶ δόξῃ τοιαύτῃ. . . .

(Sparta)
Opposite this *naos* there is an Enyalius in fetters, an *archaion agalma*. The notion of both the Lacedaemonians about this *agalma*, and of the Athenians about the Nike called Apteros, is that never will Enyalius, fleeing, go away from them, being held fast by fetters; and of the Athenians, that Nike will always stay there, being without wings. That is why these cities have set up these *xoana* in this way and on the grounds of this belief.

233
Pausanias 3.15.10–11

προελθοῦσι δὲ οὐ πολὺ λόφος ἐστὶν οὐ μέγας, ἐπὶ δὲ αὐτῷ ναὸς ἀρχαῖος καὶ Ἀφροδίτης ξόανον ὡπλισμένης. ναῶν δὲ ὧν οἶδα μόνῳ τούτῳ καὶ ὑπερῷον ἄλλο ἐπῳκοδόμηται Μορφοῦς ἱερόν. ἐπίκλησις μὲν δὴ τῆς Ἀφροδίτης ἐστὶν ἡ Μορφώ, κάθηται δὲ καλύπτραν τε ἔχουσα καὶ πέδας περὶ τοῖς ποσί· περιθεῖναι δέ οἱ Τυνδάρεων τὰς πέδας φασὶν ἀφομοιοῦντα τοῖς δεσμοῖς τὸ ἐς τοὺς συνοικοῦντας τῶν γυναικῶν βέβαιον. τὸν γὰρ δὴ ἕτερον λόγον, ὡς τὴν θεὸν πέδαις ἐτιμωρεῖτο ὁ Τυνδάρεως, γενέσθαι ταῖς θυγατράσιν ἐξ

Ἀφροδίτης ἡγούμενος τὰ ὀνείδη, τοῦτον οὐδὲ ἀρχὴν προσίεμαι· ἦν γὰρ δὴ παντάπασιν εὔηθες κέδρου ποιησάμενον ζῴδιον καὶ ὄνομα Ἀφροδίτην θέμενον ἐλπίζειν ἀμύνεσθαι τὴν θεόν.

(Sparta)
A little way further on is a not large hill, on it an *archaios naos* and a *xoanon* of armed Aphrodite. This is the only *naos* I know that has an upper storey, sacred to Morpho. Morpho is a surname of Aphrodite, she is seated, wearing a veil, with fetters on her feet. They say that Tyndareus put the fetters on her, meaning to symbolize by these bonds the fidelity of women to their husbands. The other explanation, that Tyndareus punished the goddess with fetters because he thought it was she who had brought his daughters to shame, is one that I cannot accept for a moment. It would have been too silly to imagine that by making a cedar-wood *zoidion* and dubbing it Aphrodite, he could punish the goddess.

234
Pausanias 3.16.7–11

τὸ δὲ χωρίον τὸ ἐπονομαζόμενον Λιμναῖον Ὀρθίας ἱερόν ἐστιν Ἀρτέμιδος. τὸ ξόανον δὲ ἐκεῖνο εἶναι λέγουσιν ὅ ποτε [καὶ] Ὀρέστης καὶ Ἰφιγένεια ἐκ τῆς Ταυρικῆς ἐκκλέπτουσιν· ἐς δὲ τὴν σφετέραν Λακεδαιμόνιοι κομισθῆναί φασιν Ὀρέστου καὶ ἐνταῦθα βασιλεύοντος. καί μοι εἰκότα λέγειν μᾶλλόν τι δοκοῦσιν ἢ Ἀθηναῖοι. ποίῳ γὰρ δὴ λόγῳ κατέλιπεν ἂν ἐν Βραυρῶνι Ἰφιγένεια τὸ ἄγαλμα; ἢ πῶς, ἡνίκα Ἀθηναῖοι τὴν χώραν ἐκλιπεῖν παρεσκευάζοντο, οὐκ ἐσέθεντο καὶ τοῦτο ἐς τὰς ναῦς; καίτοι διαμεμένηκεν ἔτι καὶ νῦν τηλικοῦτο ὄνομα τῇ Ταυρικῇ θεῷ, ὥστε ἀμφισβητοῦσι μὲν Καππάδοκες καὶ οἱ τὸν Εὔξεινον οἰκοῦντες τὸ ἄγαλμα εἶναι παρὰ σφίσιν, ἀμφισβητοῦσι δὲ καὶ Λυδῶν οἷς ἐστιν Ἀρτέμιδος ἱερὸν Ἀναιίτιδος. Ἀθηναίοις δὲ ἄρα παρώφθη γενόμενον λάφυρον τῷ Μήδῳ· τὸ γὰρ ἐκ Βραυρῶνος ἐκομίσθη τε ἐς Σοῦσα καὶ ὕστερον Σελεύκου δόντος Σύροι Λαοδικεῖς ἐφ' ἡμῶν ἔχουσι. μαρτύρια δέ μοι καὶ τάδε, τὴν ἐν Λακεδαίμονι Ὀρθίαν τὸ ἐκ τῶν βαρβάρων εἶναι ξόανον· τοῦτο μὲν γὰρ Ἀστράβακος καὶ Ἀλώπεκος οἱ Ἴρβου τοῦ Ἀμφισθένους τοῦ Ἀμφικλέους τοῦ Ἄγιδος τὸ ἄγαλμα εὑρόντες αὐτίκα παρεφρόνησαν· τοῦτο δὲ οἱ Λιμνᾶται Σπαρτιατῶν καὶ Κυνοσουρεῖς καὶ <οἱ> ἐκ Μεσόας τε καὶ Πιτάνης θύοντες τῇ Ἀρτέμιδι ἐς διαφοράν, ἀπὸ δὲ αὐτῆς καὶ ἐς φόνους προήχθησαν, ἀποθανόντων δὲ ἐπὶ τῷ βωμῷ πολλῶν νόσος ἔφθειρε τοὺς λοιπούς. καί σφισιν ἐπὶ τούτῳ γίνεται λόγιον αἵματι ἀνθρώπων τὸν βωμὸν αἱμάσσειν· θυομένου δὲ ὅντινα ὁ κλῆρος ἐπελάμβανε, Λυκοῦργος μετέβαλεν ἐς τὰς ἐπὶ τοῖς ἐφήβοις μάστιγας, ἐμπίπλαταί τε οὕτως ἀνθρώπων αἵματι ὁ βωμός. ἡ δὲ ἱέρεια τὸ ξόανον ἔχουσά σφισιν ἐφέστηκε· τὸ δέ ἐστιν ἄλλως μὲν κοῦφον ὑπὸ σμικρότητος, *ἣν δὲ οἱ μαστιγοῦντές ποτε ὑποφειδόμενοι παίωσι κατὰ ἐφήβου κάλλος ἢ ἀξίωμα, τότε ἤδη τῇ γυναικὶ τὸ ξόανον γίνεται βαρὺ καὶ οὐκέτι εὔφορον, ἡ δὲ ἐν αἰτίᾳ τοὺς μαστιγοῦντας ποιεῖται καὶ πιέζεσθαι δι' αὐτούς φησιν. οὕτω τῷ ἀγάλματι ἀπὸ τῶν ἐν τῇ Ταυρικῇ θυσιῶν ἐμμεμένηκεν ἀνθρώπων αἵματι ἥδεσθαι· καλοῦσι δὲ οὐκ 'Ορθίαν μόνον ἀλλὰ καὶ Λυγοδέσμαν τὴν αὐτήν, ὅτι ἐν θάμνῳ λύγων εὑρέθη, περιειληθεῖσα δὲ ἡ λύγος ἐποίησε τὸ ἄγαλμα ὀρθόν.*

The place called Limnaeum is a *hieron* of Artemis Orthia. They say that the *xoanon* is the one which Orestes and Iphigenia once stole from the Tauric land. The Lacedaemonians say it was brought to their land because Orestes was king of the country. This story seems to me more likely than the one which the Athenians tell. For what could have induced Iphigenia to leave the *agalma* at Brauron? or why, when the Athenians were preparing to evacuate the country, did they not take it with them on board ship? To this day the name of the Tauric goddess stands so high that the Cappadocians who inhabit the Euxine claim to possess the *agalma*, and a like claim is set up by the Lydians who own the *hieron* of Artemis Anaeitis. And yet we are asked to believe that the Athenians calmly allowed it to fall into the hands of the Mede! For the one at Brauron was carried to Susa, and was afterwards presented by Seleucus to the Syrians of Laodicea, who possess it to this day. There are, besides, the following proofs that the Orthia at Lacedaemon is the very *xoanon* that was brought from the land of the barbarians. In the first place, Astrabacus and Alopecus, the sons of Irbus, who was the son of Amphisthenes, who was the son of Amphicles, who was the son of Agis, went mad as soon as they found the *agalma*. In the second place, when the Spartan Limnatians, the Cynosaurians, and the people of Mesoa and Pitane were sacrificing to Artemis they fell out, and from words they came to bloodshed, and after many had been slain on the altar a plague wasted the rest. Thereupon they were bidden by an oracle to wet the altar with human blood. A man upon whom the lot fell was sacrificed; but Lycurgus changed the custom into that of scourging the lads, and so the altar reeks with human blood. The priestess stands by them holding the *xoanon*. It is small and light; but if the scourgers lay on lightly because a lad is handsome or noble, then the *xoanon* grows so heavy in the woman's hands that she can hardly hold it, and she lays the blame on the scourgers, saying they are weighing her down. Thus has the relish for human blood continued ingrained in the *agalma* since the days when the sacrifices were offered to it in the Tauric land. They call her not only Orthia, but also Lygodesma, because it was found in a thicket of willows, and the willows twining round it kept the *agalma* upright.

235
Pausanias 3.17.5

ὄπισθεν δὲ τῆς Χαλκιοίκου ναός ἐστιν Ἀφροδίτης Ἀρείας· τὰ δὲ ξόανα ἀρχαῖα εἴπερ τι ἄλλο ἐν Ἕλλησιν.

(Sparta)
Behind [the sanctuary of Athena] of the Brazen House is a *naos* of Aphrodite Areias; the *xoana* here are as *archaia* as any other in Greece.

236
Pausanias 3.19.7

ἑτέρα δὲ ἐκ τῆς πόλεως ὁδὸς ἐς Θεράπνην ἄγει· κατὰ δὲ τὴν ὁδὸν Ἀθηνᾶς ξόανόν ἐστιν Ἀλέας.

(Sparta)
Another road leads from the city to Therapne; on this road there is a *xoanon* of Athena Alea.

237
Pausanias 3.20.5

Δήμητρος ἐπίκλησιν Ἐλευσινίας ἐστὶν ἱερόν· ἐνταῦθα Ἡρακλέα Λακεδαιμόνιοι κρυφθῆναί φασιν ὑπὸ Ἀσκληπιοῦ τὸ τραῦμα ἰώμενον· καὶ Ὀρφέως ἐστὶν ἐν αὐτῷ ξόανον, Πελασγῶν ὥς φασιν ἔργον.

(Taygetus)
There is a *hieron* of Demeter surnamed Eleusinian; here, the Lacedaemonians say, Heracles was hidden by Asclepius while he was being healed of his wound; and there is a *xoanon* of Orpheus in it, a work, they say, of the Pelasgians.

238
Pausanias 3.20.7

ἐκ τούτου δὴ τοῦ Ἕλους ξόανον Κόρης τῆς Δήμητρος ἐν ἡμέραις ῥηταῖς ἀνάγουσιν ἐς τὸ Ἐλευσίνιον.

. . . from this Helos they bring up the *xoanon* of Kore, the daughter of Demeter, on stated days to the Eleusinion.

239
Pausanias 3.20.9

κίονες δὲ ἑπτὰ [οἳ] τοῦ μνήματος τούτου διέχουσιν οὐ πολύ, κατὰ τρόπον οἶμαι τὸν ἀρχαῖον, οὓς ἀστέρων τῶν πλανητῶν φασιν ἀγάλματα.

(Road from Sparta to Arcadia)
The seven pillars (which) are not far from this tomb . . . in accordance, I believe, with an *archaios* fashion, which they say are the *agalmata* of the planets.

240
Pausanias 3.23.1

τὸ δὲ ἱερὸν τῆς Οὐρανίας ἁγιώτατον καὶ ἱερῶν ὁπόσα Ἀφροδίτης παρ' Ἕλλησίν ἐστιν ἀρχαιότατον· αὐτὴ δὲ ἡ θεὸς ξόανον ὡπλισμένον.

(Cythera)
The *hieron* of Ourania is most holy, and of *hiera*, however many of Aphrodite [there are] among the Greeks, this is the most *archaion*; the goddess herself is an armed *xoanon*.

241
Pausanias 3.23.2–5

περιπλεύσαντι δὲ τὴν ἄκραν τῆς Μαλέας καὶ ἑκατὸν στάδια ἀποσχόντι, ἐπὶ θαλάσσῃ χωρίον ἐν ὅροις Βοιατῶν Ἀπόλλωνος μὲν ἱερόν ἐστιν, Ἐπιδήλιον δὲ ὀνομαζόμενον· τὸ γὰρ τοῦ Ἀπόλλωνος ξόανον, ὃ νῦν ἐστιν ἐνταῦθα, ἐν Δήλῳ ποτὲ ἵδρυτο. τῆς γὰρ Δήλου τότε ἐμπορίου τοῖς Ἕλλησιν οὔσης καὶ ἄδειαν τοῖς ἐργαζομένοις διὰ τὸν θεὸν δοκούσης παρέχειν, Μηνοφάνης Μιθριδάτου στρατηγὸς εἴτε αὐτὸς ὑπερφρονήσας εἴτε καὶ ὑπὸ Μιθριδάτου προστεταγμένον—ἀνθρώπῳ γὰρ ἀφορῶντι ἐς κέρδος τὰ θεῖα ὕστερα λημμάτων—οὗτος οὖν ὁ Μηνοφάνης, ἅτε οὔσης ἀτειχίστου τῆς Δήλου καὶ ὅπλα οὐ κεκτημένων <τῶν> ἀνδρῶν, τριήρεσιν ἐσπλεύσας ἐφόνευσε μὲν τοὺς ἐπιδημοῦντας τῶν ξένων, ἐφόνευσε δὲ αὐτοὺς τοὺς Δηλίους· κατασύρας δὲ πολλὰ μὲν ἐμπόρων χρήματα, πάντα δὲ <τὰ> ἀναθήματα, προσεξανδραποδισαμένος δὲ καὶ γυναῖκας καὶ τέκνα, καὶ αὐτὴν ἐς ἔδαφος κατέβαλε τὴν Δῆλον. ἅτε δὲ πορθουμένης τε καὶ ἁρπαζομένης, τῶν τις βαρβάρων ὑπὸ ὕβρεως τὸ ξόανον τοῦτο ἀπέρριψεν ἐς τὴν θάλασσαν· ὑπολαβὼν δὲ ὁ κλύδων ἐνταῦθα τῆς Βοιατῶν ἀπήνεγκε, καὶ τὸ χωρίον διὰ τοῦτο Ἐπιδήλιον ὀνομάζουσι. τὸ μέντοι μήνιμα <τὸ> ἐκ τοῦ θεοῦ διέφυγεν οὔτε Μηνοφάνης οὔτε αὐτὸς Μιθριδάτης· ἀλλὰ Μηνοφάνην μὲν παραυτίκα, ὡς ἀνήγετο ἐρημώσας τὴν Δῆλον, λοχήσαντες ναυσὶν οἱ διαπεφευγότες τῶν ἐμπόρων καταδύουσι, Μιθριδάτην δὲ ὕστερον τούτων ἠνάγκασεν ὁ θεὸς αὐτόχειρα αὑτοῦ καταστῆναι, τῆς τε ἀρχῆς οἱ καθῃρημένης καὶ ἐλαυνόμενον πανταχόθεν ὑπὸ Ῥωμαίων· εἰσὶ δὲ οἵ φασιν αὐτὸν παρά του τῶν μισθοφόρων θάνατον βίαιον ἐν μέρει χάριτος εὕρασθαι. τούτοις μὲν τοιαῦτα ἀπήντησεν ἀσεβήσασι. . . .

After sailing around the tip of Malea, a hundred stadia away, a place on the coast on the borders of Boeae is a *hieron* of Apollo, called Epidelion; for the *xoanon* of Apollo, which now is there, once was set up in Delos. Since Delos at that time was the emporium of Greece and was thought to offer safe conduct for traders on account of the god's being there, Menophanes, general of Mithridates, knowing that the island was unfortified and the people unarmed, sailed to it with a fleet, massacred the population, foreigners and natives alike, looted much of the merchandise and all the *anathemata*, sold the women and children into slavery, and razed the town of Delos to the ground. Whether he did it out of pure wantonness or by the express orders of Mithridates, who can tell? A covetous man thinks more of gain than of godliness. In the hurly-burly of the sack a saucy barbarian hurled this *xoanon* into the sea; and the waves took it and carried it off to this spot in the territory of Boeae, and therefore they name the place Epidelion. Nevertheless, neither Menophanes nor Mithridates himself eluded the wrath of the god. Menophanes was overtaken by it immediately; for when he put out to sea after the sack of Delos the merchants who had escaped lay in wait for him and sent him to the bottom. At a later time Mithridates, shorn of his kingdom and hounded from land to land by the Romans, was driven by the god to lay hands on himself. Some say, however, that one of his mercenaries dealt him, as a favor, the fatal stroke. Such was fate that befell these impious men.

242
Pausanias 3.25.3

θεῶν δὲ ἐν τῇ γῇ σφισιν ἱερά ἐστιν Ἀρτέμιδός τε ἐπίκλησιν Ἀστρατείας, ὅτι τῆς ἐς τὸ πρόσω στρατείας ἐνταῦθα ἐπαύσαντο Ἀμαζόνες, καὶ Ἀπόλλων Ἀμαζόνιος· ξόανα μὲν ἀμφότερα, ἀναθεῖναι δὲ λέγουσιν αὐτὰ τὰς ἀπὸ Θερμώδοντος γυναῖκας.

(Pyrrichus)
In their land there are *hiera* of the gods, of Artemis surnamed Astratea, because here the Amazons ceased from their *strateia* (forward march); and of Amazonian Apollo. Both are *xoana*, and they say the women who came from Thermodon dedicated them.

243
Pausanias 3.25.10

θέας δὲ ἄξια ἐν Οἰτύλῳ Σαράπιδός ἐστιν ἱερὸν καὶ ἐν τῇ ἀγορᾷ Καρνείου ξόανον Ἀπόλλωνος.

Worth seeing in Oetylus are a *hieron* of Sarapis, and in the agora a *xoanon* of Carnean Apollo.

244

Pausanias 3.26.5

καὶ Ἀπόλλωνος Καρνείου ξόανά ἐστι κατὰ ταὐτὰ καθὰ δὴ καὶ Λακεδαιμονίων νομίζουσιν οἱ Σπάρτην ἔχοντες.

(Leuctra)

There are also *xoana* of Carnean Apollo, in exactly the way the Lacedaemonians who hold Sparta customarily have them.

245

Pausanias 4.33.3

ἰόντι δὲ τὴν ἐπ' Ἀρκαδίας ἐς Μεγάλην πόλιν ἐστὶν ἐν ταῖς πύλαις Ἑρμῆς τέχνης τῆς Ἀττικῆς· Ἀθηναίων γὰρ τὸ σχῆμα τὸ τετράγωνόν ἐστιν ἐπὶ τοῖς Ἑρμαῖς, καὶ παρὰ τούτων μεμαθήκασιν οἱ ἄλλοι.

Following the Arcadian road that leads to Megalopolis, there is at the gates a Hermes of Attic craft; for the squared *schema* for Hermes is the Athenians', and others learned [it] from them.

246

Pausanias 4.34.7

ἐκ Κορώνης δὲ ὡς ὀγδοήκοντα σταδίους προελθόντι Ἀπόλλωνός ἐστιν ἱερὸν πρὸς θαλάσσῃ τιμὰς ἔχον· ἀρχαιότατόν τε γὰρ λόγῳ τῷ Μεσσηνίων ἐστὶ καὶ νοσήματα ὁ θεὸς ἰᾶται, Κόρυνθον δὲ Ἀπόλλωνα ὀνομάζουσι. τοῦτο μὲν δὴ ξόανον, τοῦ Ἀργεώτα δὲ χαλκοῦν ἐστι τὸ ἄγαλμα· ἀναθεῖναι δέ φασι τοὺς ἐν τῇ Ἀργοῖ πλεύσαντας·

Going from Corone about eighty stadia there is a *hieron* of Apollo beside the sea that is held in honor; for according to the word of the Messenians it is very *archaion* and the god heals diseases, and they call him Crested-Lark Apollo. This is a *xoanon*, but the *agalma* of Argeot (Apollo) is of bronze; they say that those who sailed in the Argo dedicated it.

247

Pausanias 5.26.6

παρὰ δὲ τὴν Ἀθηνᾶν πεποίηται Νίκη· ταύτην Μαντινεῖς ἀνέθεσαν, τὸν πόλεμον δὲ οὐ δηλοῦσιν ἐν τῷ ἐπιγράμματι· Κάλαμις δὲ οὐκ ἔχουσαν πτερὰ ποιῆσαι λέγεται ἀπομιμούμενος τὸ Ἀθήνησι τῆς Ἀπτέρου καλουμένης ξόανον.

(Olympia)
Beside Athena is made Victory; the Mantineans dedicated her, but they did not mention the war in the inscription; they say Calamis made it without wings, in imitation of the *xoanon* of her called Wingless in Athens.

248
Pausanias 6.24.6–7

ἔστι δὲ καὶ Χάρισιν ἱερὸν καὶ ξόανα ἐπίχρυσα τὰ ἐς ἐσθῆτα, πρόσωπα δὲ καὶ χεῖρες καὶ πόδες λίθου λευκοῦ· ἔχουσι δὲ ἡ μὲν αὐτῶν ῥόδον, ἀστράγαλον δὲ ἡ μέση, καὶ ἡ τρίτη κλῶνα οὐ μέγαν μυρσίνης. ἔχειν δὲ αὐτὰς ἐπὶ τοιῷδε εἰκάζοι τις ἂν τὰ εἰρημένα, ῥόδον μὲν καὶ μυρσίνην Ἀφροδίτης τε ἱερὰ εἶναι καὶ οἰκεῖα τῷ ἐς Ἄδωνιν λόγῳ, Χάριτας δὲ Ἀφροδίτῃ μάλιστα <φίλας> εἶναι θεῶν· ἀστράγαλον δὲ μειρακίων τε καὶ παρθένων, οἷς ἄχαρι οὐδέν πω πρόσεστιν ἐκ γήρως, τούτων εἶναι τὸν ἀστράγαλον παίγνιον. τῶν Χαρίτων δὲ ἐν δεξιᾷ ἄγαλμά ἐστιν Ἔρωτος· ἕστηκε δὲ ἐπὶ βάθρου τοῦ αὐτοῦ.

There is also a *hieron* of the Graces and *xoana* that are gilded on the drapery, but the faces, hands, and feet are of white stone; one of them holds a rose, the middle one a die, and the third a sprig of myrtle. The reason why they hold these things may be conjectured to be this: As the rose and the myrtle are sacred to Aphrodite, and associated with the story of Adonis, so of all the deities the Graces are most akin to Aphrodite; and the die is a plaything of youths and maidens whom age has not yet robbed of youthful grace. On the right of the Graces is an *agalma* of Eros; but it stands on the same base.

249
Pausanias 6.25.4

τοῖς δὲ Ἠλείοις καὶ Τύχης <ἐστὶν> [τὸ] ἱερόν· ἐν στοᾷ δὲ τοῦ ἱεροῦ μεγέθει μέγα ἄγαλμα ἀνάκειται, ξόανον ἐπίχρυσον πλὴν προσώπου καὶ χειρῶν τε ἄκρων καὶ ποδῶν, ταῦτα δέ οἱ ἐστι λίθου λευκοῦ.

The Eleans have also a *hieron* of Fortune; in a stoa of the *hieron* is dedicated an *agalma* large in size, a *xoanon* gilded except the face, hands, and feet, which are of white stone.

250
Pausanias 7.20.7–8

τῆς δὲ ἀγορᾶς ἄντικρυς κατὰ ταύτην τὴν διέξοδον τέμενός ἐστιν Ἀρτέμιδος καὶ ναὸς Λιμνάτιδος. ἐχόντων δὲ ἤδη Λακεδαίμονα καὶ Ἄργος Δωριέων, ὑφελέσθαι Πρευγένην τῆς Λιμνάτιδος τὸ ἄγαλμα κατὰ ὄψιν ὀνείρατος λέγουσιν ἐκ Σπάρτης, κοινωνῆσαι δὲ αὐτῷ τοῦ ἐγχειρήματος τῶν δούλων τὸν εὐνούστατον. τὸ δὲ ἄγαλμα τὸ ἐκ τῆς Λακεδαίμονος τὸν μὲν ἄλλον χρόνον ἔχουσιν ἐν Μεσόᾳ, ὅτι καὶ ἐξ ἀρχῆς ὑπὸ τοῦ Πρευγένους ἐς τοῦτο ἐκομίσθη τὸ χωρίον· ἐπειδὰν δὲ τῇ Λιμνάτιδι τὴν ἑορτὴν ἄγωσι, τῆς θεοῦ τις τῶν οἰκετῶν ἐκ Μεσόας ἔρχεται τὸ ξόανον κομίζων τὸ ἀρχαῖον ἐς τὸ τέμενος τὸ ἐν τῇ πόλει.

(Patrae)
Facing the agora, just at the way out of it, there is a *temenos* of Artemis and a *naos* of the Lady of the Lake. When the Dorians were now in possession of Lacedaemon and Argos, it is said that Preugenes, in obedience to a dream, stole the *agalma* of the Lady of the Lake from Sparta, being assisted in the enterprise by the most devoted of his slaves. The *agalma* thus brought from Lacedaemon is generally kept at Mesoa, because that was the place to which Preugenes brought it originally; but when they celebrate the festival in honor of the Lady of the Lake, one of the slaves of the goddess fetches the *archaion xoanon* from Mesoa to the *temenos* in the city.

251
Pausanias 7.22.4

ἑστήκασι δὲ ἐγγύτατα τοῦ ἀγάλματος τετράγωνοι λίθοι τριάκοντα μάλιστα ἀριθμόν· τούτους σέβουσιν οἱ Φαρεῖς, ἑκάστῳ θεοῦ τινὸς ὄνομα ἐπιλέγοντες. τὰ δὲ ἔτι παλαιότερα καὶ τοῖς πᾶσιν Ἕλλησι τιμὰς θεῶν ἀντὶ ἀγαλμάτων εἶχον ἀργοὶ λίθοι.

(Pharae)
Closest to the *agalma* stand about thirty square stones; these the people of Pharae revere, selecting for each one the name of some god. In a still older age, among all the Greeks, too, rough stones received the honors of gods, instead of *agalmata*.

252
Pausanias 7.23.5–6

Αἰγιεῦσι δὲ Εἰλειθυίας ἱερόν ἐστιν ἀρχαῖον, καὶ ἡ Εἰλείθυια ἐς ἄκρους ἐκ κεφαλῆς τοὺς πόδας ὑφάσματι κεκάλυπται λεπτῷ, ξόανον πλὴν προσώπου τε καὶ χειρῶν ἄκρων καὶ ποδῶν, ταῦτα δὲ τοῦ Πεντελησίου λίθου πεποίηται· καὶ ταῖς χερσὶ τῇ μὲν ἐς εὐθὺ ἐκτέταται, τῇ δὲ ἀνέχει δᾷδα. Εἰλειθυίᾳ δὲ εἰκάσαι τις ἂν εἶναι δᾷδας, ὅτι γυναιξὶν ἐν ἴσῳ καὶ πῦρ εἰσιν αἱ ὠδῖνες· ἔχοιεν δ' ἂν λόγον καὶ ἐπὶ τοιῷδε αἱ δᾷδες, ὅτι Εἰλείθυιά ἐστιν ἡ ἐς φῶς ἄγουσα τοὺς παῖδας. ἔργον δὲ τοῦ Μεσσηνίου Δαμοφῶντός ἐστι τὸ ἄγαλμα.

At Aegium there is an *archaion hieron* of Eileithyia, and Eileithyia is draped from head to foot in a robe of fine texture, a *xoanon* except the face, tips of the hands, and feet; these, however, are made of Pentelic stone. And of the hands, one is stretched straight out, and in the other she holds a torch. Torches may be supposed to be an attribute of Eileithyia, because the labor pains of women are like fire, or their meaning may be that Eileithyia is she who brings children to light. The *agalma* is a work of Damophon the Messenian.

253
Pausanias 7.25.13

ὁδὸς δὲ ἀπὸ τοῦ τάφου σταδίων ὅσον τριάκοντα ἐπὶ τὸν καλούμενον Γαῖον· Γῆς δὲ ἱερόν ἐστιν ὁ Γαῖος ἐπίκλησιν Εὐρυστέρνου, ξόανον δὲ τοῖς μάλιστα ὁμοίως ἐστὶν ἀρχαῖον.

(Road near Helice)
The road from the grave is about thirty stadia to the Gaeus, as it is called. The Gaeus is a sanctuary of Ge, who here bears the surname of Broad-bosomed; the *xoanon* in it is equally *archaion*.

254
Pausanias 7.26.4

ἐν τούτῳ τῷ ἱερῷ καὶ Ἀθηνᾶς ἄγαλμα ἕστηκε· πρόσωπόν τε καὶ ἄκραι χεῖρες ἐλέφαντος καὶ οἱ πόδες, τὸ δὲ ἄλλο ξόανον χρυσῷ τε ἐπιπολῆς διηνθισμένον ἐστὶ καὶ φαρμάκοις.

(Aegira, Sanctuary of Zeus)
In this *hieron* there stands also an *agalma* of Athena; the face, hands, and feet are of ivory, but the rest is a *xoanon* adorned with gilding and colors.

255
Pausanias 7.26.6

ἔστι καὶ Ἀπόλλωνος ἱερὸν ἐς τὰ μάλιστα ἀρχαῖον τό τε ἱερὸν αὐτὸ καὶ ὁπόσα ἐν τοῖς ἀετοῖς, ἀρχαῖον δὲ καὶ τοῦ θεοῦ τὸ ξόανον, γυμνός, μεγέθει μέγας· τὸν ποιήσαντα δὲ εἶχεν οὐδεὶς τῶν ἐπιχωρίων εἰπεῖν· ὅστις δὲ ἤδη τὸν Ἡρακλέα τὸν ἐν Σικυῶνι ἐθεάσατο, τεκμαίροιτο ἂν καὶ ἐν Αἰγείρᾳ τὸν Ἀπόλλωνα ἔργον εἶναι τοῦ αὐτοῦ Φλιασίου Λαφάους.

(Aegira)
There is also an exceedingly *archaion hieron* of Apollo, both the *hieron* itself and whatever is in the gables, and the *xoanon* of the god is also *archaion*, naked and large in size; none of the natives could tell the maker; but anyone who has seen the Heracles at Sicyon would infer that the Apollo in Aegira is also a work of this same Laphaes the Phliasian.

256
Pausanias 8.5.8

ἐπὶ δὲ Σίμου τοῦ Φιάλου βασιλεύοντος ἠφανίσθη Φιγαλεῦσιν ὑπὸ πυρὸς τῆς Μελαίνης Δήμητρος τὸ ἀρχαῖον ξόανον· ἐσήμαινε δὲ ἄρα οὐ μετὰ πολὺ ἔσεσθαι καὶ αὐτῷ Σίμῳ τοῦ βίου τὴν τελευτήν.

In the reign of Simus, son of Phialus, the *archaion xoanon* of Black Demeter at Phigalia was destroyed by fire; as it turned out, this signified the end of life for Simus himself after not much more time.

257
Pausanias 8.13.2

πρὸς δὲ τῇ πόλει ξόανόν ἐστιν Ἀρτέμιδος· ἵδρυται δὲ ἐν κέδρῳ μεγάλῃ, καὶ τὴν θεὸν ὀνομάζουσιν ἀπὸ τῆς κέδρου Κεδρεᾶτιν.

(Orchomenos)
Close to the city is as *xoanon* of Artemis; it is set in a great cedar, and they name the goddess the Cedar Goddess after the cedar.

258
Pausanias 8.17.2

τοῖς δὲ ἀνθρώποις τὸ ἀρχαῖον, ὁπόσα καὶ ἡμεῖς καταμαθεῖν ἐδυνήθημεν, τοσάδε ἦν ἀφ' ὧν τὰ ξόανα ἐποιοῦντο, ἔβενος, κυπάρισσος, αἱ κέδροι, τὰ δρύινα, ἡ μῖλαξ, ὁ λωτός· τῷ δὲ Ἑρμῇ τῷ Κυλληνίῳ τούτων μὲν ἀπὸ οὐδενός, θύου δὲ πεποιημένον τὸ ἄγαλμά ἐστιν, ὀκτὼ δὲ εἶναι ποδῶν μάλιστα αὐτὸ εἰκάζομεν.

(Arcadia, Mt. Cyllene)
The kinds of wood out of which men of old made *xoana* for themselves were, so far as we have been able to learn: ebony, cypress, the cedars, the oaks, yew, and lotus. However, the *agalma* of Cyllenian Hermes is made of none of these, but of juniper; we guessed it to be about eight feet high.

259
Pausanias 8.22.7

ἐν Στυμφάλῳ δὲ καὶ ἱερὸν Ἀρτέμιδός ἐστιν ἀρχαῖον Στυμφαλίας· τὸ δὲ ἄγαλμα ξόανόν ἐστι τὰ πολλὰ ἐπίχρυσον.

In Stymphalus there is also an *archaion hieron* of Stymphalian Artemis; the *agalma* is a *xoanon*, mostly gilded.

260
Pausanias 8.31.5–6

ἔστι δὲ ἐντὸς τοῦ περιβόλου τῶν Μεγάλων θεῶν καὶ Ἀφροδίτης ἱερόν. πρὸ μὲν δὴ τῆς ἐσόδου ξόανά ἐστιν ἀρχαῖα, Ἥρα καὶ Ἀπόλλων τε καὶ Μοῦσαι—ταῦτα κομισθῆναί φασιν ἐκ Τραπεζοῦντος—, ἀγάλματα δὲ ἐν τῷ ναῷ Δαμοφῶν ἐποίησεν Ἑρμῆν ξύλου καὶ Ἀφροδίτης ξόανον· καὶ ταύτης χεῖρές εἰσι λίθου καὶ πρόσωπόν τε καὶ ἄκροι πόδες.

(Megalopolis)
Within the *peribolos* of the Great Goddesses there is also a *hieron* of Aphrodite. In front of the entrance are *archaia xoana* of Hera, Apollo, and the Muses, which they say were brought from Trapezus. Damophon made the agalmata in the *naos*, a Hermes of wood and a *xoanon* of Aphrodite; and her hands are of stone, and her face and feet.

261
Pausanias 8.31.7

κεῖται δὲ ἐντὸς τοῦ περιβόλου θεῶν τοσάδε ἄλλων ἀγάλματα τὸ τετράγωνον παρεχόμενα σχῆμα, Ἑρμῆς τε ἐπίκλησιν Ἀγήτωρ καὶ Ἀπόλλων καὶ Ἀθηνᾶ τε καὶ Ποσειδῶν, ἔτι δὲ Ἥλιος ἐπωνυμίαν ἔχων Σωτὴρ [δὲ] εἶναι καὶ Ἡρακλῆς.

(Megalopolis)
Within the *peribolos* of the goddesses there are also these *agalmata* exhibiting the square *schema*: Hermes surnamed Leader, Apollo, Athena, Poseidon, and also Helios with the surname Savior, and Heracles.

262
Pausanias 8.32.4

τῆς δὲ Ἀγροτέρας ἐστὶν ἐν δεξιᾷ τέμενος· ἐνταῦθα ἔστι μὲν ἱερὸν Ἀσκληπιοῦ καὶ ἀγάλματα αὐτός τε καὶ Ὑγεία, εἰσὶ δὲ ὑποκαταβάντι ὀλίγον θεοὶ—παρέχονται δὲ καὶ οὗτοι σχῆμα τετράγωνον, Ἐργάται δέ ἐστιν αὐτοῖς ἐπίκλησις—Ἀθηνᾶ τε Ἐργάνη καὶ Ἀπόλλων Ἀγυιεύς. . . .

(Megalopolis)
On the right of the *naos* of the Huntress is a *temenos*; here there is a *hieron* of Asclepius, and *agalmata* of himself and Health; a little lower down are gods—they also are made in the square *schema*, and surnamed Worker—Athena Ergane and Apollo Agyieus.

263
Pausanias 8.35.2

δοκεῖν δέ μοι καὶ τὸ ὑπὸ Δαιδάλου ποιηθὲν τῷ Ἡρακλεῖ ξόανον ἐν μεθορίῳ τῆς Μεσσηνίας καὶ Ἀρκάδων ἐνταῦθα εἱστήκει.

I believe, too, that the *xoanon* that was made by Daedalus for Heracles stood here in the borders between Messenia and Arcadia.

264
Pausanias 8.37.12

ἐνταῦθα ἔστι μὲν βωμὸς Ἄρεως, ἔστι δὲ ἀγάλματα Ἀφροδίτης ἐν ναῷ, λίθου τὸ ἕτερον λευκοῦ, τὸ δὲ ἀρχαιότερον αὐτῶν ξύλου. ὡσαύτως δὲ καὶ Ἀπόλλωνός τε καὶ Ἀθηνᾶς ξόανά ἐστι· τῇ δὲ Ἀθηνᾷ καὶ ἱερὸν πεποίηται.

(Lycosoura)
Here there is an altar of Ares, and there are *agalmata* of Aphrodite in the *naos*, the one of white stone, the more *archaion* of them of wood. Likewise there are *xoana* of Apollo and Athena; and also a *hieron* of Athena has been made.

265
Pausanias 8.41.5–6

ἡμέρᾳ δὲ τῇ αὐτῇ κατὰ ἔτος ἕκαστον τὸ ἱερὸν ἀνοιγνύουσι τῆς Εὐρυνόμης, τὸν δὲ ἄλλον χρόνον οὔ σφισιν ἀνοιγνύναι καθέστηκε· τηνικαῦτα δὲ καὶ θυσίας δημοσίᾳ τε καὶ ἰδιῶται θύουσιν. ἀφικέσθαι μὲν δή μοι τῆς ἑορτῆς οὐκ ἐξεγένετο ἐς καιρὸν οὐδὲ τῆς Εὐρυνόμης τὸ ἄγαλμα εἶδον· τῶν Φιγαλέων <δ'> ἤκουσα ὡς χρυσαῖ τε τὸ ξόανον συνδέουσιν ἁλύσεις καὶ εἰκὼν γυναικὸς τὰ ἄχρι τῶν γλουτῶν, τὸ ἀπὸ τούτου δέ ἐστιν ἰχθύς.

(Phigalia)
On the same day every year they open the *hieron* of Eurynome, but it is against their rule to open it at any other time. On that occasion they offer both public and private sacrifice. I did not happen to arrive at the season of the festival, nor did I see the *agalma* of Eurynome; but I heard from the Phigalians that the *xoanon* is bound fast by golden chains, and that it is the *eikon* of a woman to the hips, but below that it is a fish.

266
Pausanias 8.42.1–13

τὸ δὲ ἕτερον τῶν ὀρῶν τὸ Ἐλάιον ἀπωτέρω μὲν Φιγαλίας ὅσον τε σταδίοις τριάκοντά ἐστι, Δήμητρος δὲ ἄντρον αὐτόθι ἱερὸν ἐπίκλησιν Μελαίνης.

ὅσα μὲν δὴ οἱ ἐν Θελπούσῃ λέγουσιν ἐς μῖξιν τὴν Ποσειδῶνός τε καὶ Δήμητρος, κατὰ ταὐτά σφισιν οἱ Φιγαλεῖς νομίζουσι, τεχθῆναι δὲ ὑπὸ τῆς Δήμητρος οἱ Φιγαλεῖς φασιν οὐχ ἵππον ἀλλὰ τὴν Δέσποιναν ἐπονομαζομένην ὑπὸ Ἀρκάδων· τὸ δὲ ἀπὸ τούτου λέγουσι θυμῷ τε ἅμα ἐς τὸν Ποσειδῶνα αὐτὴν καὶ ἐπὶ τῆς Περσεφόνης τῇ ἁρπαγῇ πένθει χρωμένην μέλαιναν ἐσθῆτα ἐνδῦναι καὶ ἐς τὸ σπήλαιον τοῦτο ἐλθοῦσαν ἐπὶ χρόνον ἀπεῖναι πολύν. ὡς δὲ ἐφθείρετο μὲν πάντα ὅσα ἡ γῆ τρέφει, τὸ δὲ ἀνθρώπων γένος καὶ ἐς πλέον ἀπώλλυτο ὑπὸ τοῦ λιμοῦ, θεῶν μὲν ἄλλων ἠπίστατο ἄρα οὐδεὶς ἔνθα ἀπεκέκρυπτο ἡ Δημήτηρ, τὸν δὲ Πᾶνα ἐπιέναι μὲν τὴν Ἀρκαδίαν καὶ ἄλλοτε αὐτὸν ἐν ἄλλῳ θηρεύειν τῶν ὀρῶν, ἀφικόμενον δὲ καὶ πρὸς τὸ Ἐλάιον κατοπτεῦσαι τὴν Δήμητρα σχήματός τε ὡς εἶχε καὶ ἐσθῆτα ἐνεδέδυτο ποίαν· πυθέσθαι δὴ τὸν Δία ταῦτα παρὰ τοῦ Πανὸς καὶ οὕτως ὑπ' αὐτοῦ πεμφθῆναι τὰς Μοίρας παρὰ τὴν Δήμητρα, τὴν δὲ πεισθῆναί τε ταῖς Μοίραις καὶ ἀποθέσθαι μὲν τὴν ὀργήν, ὑφεῖναι δὲ καὶ τῆς λύπης. σφᾶς δὲ ἀντὶ τούτων φασὶν οἱ Φιγαλεῖς τό τε σπήλαιον νομίσαι τοῦτο ἱερὸν Δήμητρος καὶ ἐς αὐτὸ ἄγαλμα ἀναθεῖναι ξύλου. πεποιῆσθαι δὲ οὕτω σφίσι τὸ ἄγαλμα· καθέζεσθαι μὲν ἐπὶ πέτρᾳ, γυναικὶ δὲ ἐοικέναι τἄλλα πλὴν κεφαλήν· κεφαλὴν δὲ καὶ κόμην εἶχεν ἵππου, καὶ δρακόντων τε καὶ ἄλλων θηρίων εἰκόνες προσεπεφύκεσαν τῇ κεφαλῇ· χιτῶνα δὲ ἐνεδέδυτο καὶ <ἐς> ἄκρους τοὺς πόδας· δελφὶς δὲ ἐπὶ τῆς χειρὸς ἦν αὐτῇ, περιστερὰ δὲ ἡ ὄρνις ἐπὶ τῇ ἑτέρᾳ. ἐφ' ὅτῳ μὲν δὴ τὸ ξόανον ἐποιήσαντο οὕτως, ἀνδρὶ οὐκ ἀσυνέτῳ γνώμην ἀγαθῷ δὲ καὶ τὰ ἐς μνήμην δῆλά ἐστι· Μέλαιναν δὲ ἐπονομάσαι φασὶν αὐτήν, ὅτι καὶ ἡ θεὸς μέλαιναν τὴν ἐσθῆτα εἶχε. τοῦτο μὲν δὴ τὸ ξόανον οὔτε ὅτου ποίημα ἦν οὔτε ἡ φλὸξ τρόπον ὅντινα ἐπέλαβεν αὐτό, μνημονεύουσιν· ἀφανισθέντος δὲ τοῦ ἀρχαίου Φιγαλεῖς οὔτε ἄγαλμα ἄλλο ἀπεδίδοσαν τῇ θεῷ καὶ ὁπόσα ἐς ἑορτὰς καὶ θυσίας τὰ πολλὰ δὴ παρῶπτό σφισιν, ἐς ὃ ἡ ἀκαρπία ἐπιλαμβάνει τὴν γῆν· καὶ ἱκετεύσασιν αὐτοῖς χρᾷ τάδε ἡ Πυθία·

> Ἀρκάδες Ἀζᾶνες βαλανηφάγοι, οἳ Φιγάλειαν
> νάσσασθ', ἱππολεχοῦς Δηοῦς κρυπτήριον ἄντρον,
> ἥκετε πευσόμενοι λιμοῦ λύσιν ἀλγινόεντος,
> μοῦνοι δὶς νομάδες, μοῦνοι πάλιν ἀγριοδαῖται.
> Δηὼ μέν σε ἔπαυσε νομῆς, Δηὼ δὲ νομῆας
> ἐκ δησισταχύων καὶ ἀναστοφάγων πάλι θῆκε,
> νοσφισθεῖσα γέρα προτέρων τιμάς τε παλαιάς.
> καί σ' ἀλληλοφάγον θήσει τάχα καὶ τεκνοδαίτην,
> εἰ μὴ πανδήμοις λοιβαῖς χόλον ἱλάσσεσθε
> σήραγγός τε μυχὸν θείαις κοσμήσετε τιμαῖς.

ὡς δὲ οἱ Φιγαλεῖς ἀνακομισθὲν τὸ μάντευμα ἤκουσαν, τά τε ἄλλα ἐς πλέον τιμῆς ἢ τὰ πρότερα τὴν Δήμητρα ἦγον καὶ Ὀνάταν τὸν Μίκωνος Αἰγινήτην πείθουσιν ἐφ' ὅσῳ δὴ μισθῷ ποιῆσαί σφισιν ἄγαλμα Δήμητρος· τοῦ δὲ

᾿Ονάτα τούτου Περγαμηνοῖς ἐστιν ᾿Απόλλων χαλκοῦς, θαῦμα ἐν τοῖς μάλιστα μεγέθους τε ἕνεκα καὶ ἐπὶ τῇ τέχνῃ. τότε δὴ ὁ ἀνὴρ οὗτος ἀνευρὼν γραφὴν ἢ μίμημα τοῦ ἀρχαίου ξοάνου—τὰ πλείω δέ, ὡς λέγεται, καὶ κατὰ ὀνειράτων ὄψιν—ἐποίησε χαλκοῦν Φιγαλεῦσιν ἄγαλμα, γενεῖ μάλιστα <δυσὶν> ὕστερον τῆς ἐπὶ τὴν ῾Ελλάδα ἐπιστρατείας τοῦ Μήδου. μαρτυρεῖ δέ μοι τῷ λόγῳ· κατὰ γὰρ τὴν Ξέρξου διάβασιν ἐς τὴν Εὐρώπην Συρακουσῶν τε ἐτυράννει καὶ Σικελίας τῆς ἄλλης Γέλων ὁ Δεινομένους· ἐπεὶ δὲ ἐτελεύτησε Γέλων, ἐς ῾Ιέρωνα ἀδελφὸν Γέλωνος περιῆλθεν ἡ ἀρχή· ῾Ιέρωνος δὲ ἀποθανόντος πρότερον πρὶν ἢ τῷ ᾿Ολυμπίῳ Διὶ ἀναθεῖναι τὰ ἀναθήματα ἃ εὔξατο ἐπὶ τῶν ἵππων ταῖς νίκαις, οὕτω Δεινομένης ὁ ῾Ιέρωνος ἀπέδωκεν ὑπὲρ τοῦ πατρός. ᾿Ονάτα καὶ ταῦτα ποιήματα, καὶ ἐπιγράμματα ἐν ᾿Ολυμπίᾳ, τὸ μὲν ὑπὲρ τοῦ ἀναθήματός ἐστιν αὐτῶν,

σόν ποτε νικήσας, Ζεῦ ᾿Ολύμπιε, σεμνὸν ἀγῶνα
τεθρίππῳ μὲν ἅπαξ, μουνοκέλητι δὲ δίς,
δῶρα ῾Ιέρων τάδε σοι ἐχαρίσσατο· παῖς δ᾿ ἀνέθηκε
Δεινομένης πατρὸς μνῆμα Συρακοσίου·

τὸ δὲ ἕτερον λέγει τῶν ἐπιγραμμάτων·

υἱὸς <μέν> με Μίκωνος ᾿Ονάτας ἐξετέλεσσεν,
νάσῳ ἐν Αἰγίνᾳ δώματα ναιετάων.

ἡ δὲ ἡλικία τοῦ ᾿Ονάτα κατὰ τὸν ᾿Αθηναῖον ῾Ηγίαν καὶ ᾿Αγελάδαν συμβαίνει τὸν ᾿Αργεῖον.

ταύτης μάλιστα ἐγὼ τῆς Δήμητρος ἕνεκα ἐς Φιγαλίαν ἀφικόμην. καὶ ἔθυσα τῇ θεῷ, καθὰ καὶ οἱ ἐπιχώριοι νομίζουσιν, οὐδέν· τὰ δὲ ἀπὸ τῶν δένδρων τῶν ἡμέρων τά τε ἄλλα καὶ ἀμπέλου καρπὸν καὶ μελισσῶν τε κηρία καὶ ἐρίων τὰ μὴ ἐς ἐργασίαν πω ἥκοντα ἀλλὰ ἔτι ἀνάπλεα τοῦ οἰσύπου {ἃ} τιθέασιν ἐπὶ τὸν βωμὸν <τὸν> ᾠκοδομημένον πρὸ τοῦ σπηλαίου, θέντες δὲ καταχέουσιν αὐτῶν ἔλαιον. ταῦτα ἰδιώταις τε ἀνδράσι καὶ ἀνὰ πᾶν ἔτος Φιγαλέων τῷ κοινῷ καθέστηκεν ἐς τὴν θυσίαν. ἱέρεια δέ σφισίν ἐστιν ἡ δρῶσα, σὺν δὲ αὐτῇ καὶ τῶν ἱεροθυτῶν καλουμένων ὁ νεώτατος· οἱ δέ εἰσι τῶν ἀστῶν τρεῖς ἀριθμόν. ἔστι δὲ δρυῶν τε ἄλσος περὶ τὸ σπήλαιον καὶ ὕδωρ ψυχρὸν ἄνεισιν ἐκ τῆς γῆς. τὸ δὲ ἄγαλμα τὸ ὑπὸ τοῦ ᾿Ονάτα ποιηθὲν οὔτε ἦν κατ᾿ ἐμὲ οὔτε εἰ ἐγένετο ἀρχὴν Φιγαλεῦσιν ἠπίσταντο οἱ πολλοί· τῶν δὲ ἐντυχόντων ἡμῖν ἔλεγεν ὁ πρεσβύτατος γενεαῖς πρότερον τρισὶν ἢ κατ᾿ αὐτὸν ἐμπεσεῖν ἐς τὸ ἄγαλμα ἐκ τοῦ ὀρόφου πέτρας, ὑπὸ τούτων δὲ καταγῆναι καὶ ἐς ἅπαν ἔφασκεν αὐτὸ ἀφανισθῆναι· καὶ ἔν γε τῷ ὀρόφῳ δῆλα καὶ ἡμῖν ἔτι ἦν, καθὰ ἀπερρώγεσαν αἱ πέτραι.

The other mountain, Mt. Elaius, is about thirty stadia from Phigalia; there is a cave there sacred to Demeter surnamed the Black. All that the people of Thelpusa say touching the loves of Poseidon and Demeter is believed by the Phigalians; but the Phigalians say that Demeter gave birth, not to a horse, but to her whom the Arcadians name the Mistress, and they say that afterwards Demeter, wroth with Poseidon, and mourning the rape of Persephone, put on black raiment, and entering this grotto tarried there in seclusion a long while. But when all the fruits of the earth were wasting away, and the race of men was perishing still more of hunger, none of the other gods, it would seem, knew where Demeter was hid; but Pan, roving over Arcadia, and hunting now on one mountain, now on another, came at last to Mount Elaius, and spied Demeter, and saw the plight she was in, and what sort of garb she wore. So Zeus learned of this from Pan, and sent the Fates to Demeter, and she harkened to the Fates, and put aside her wrath, and abated even from her grief.

For that reason the Phigalians say that they accounted the grotto sacred to Demeter, and set up in it an *agalma* of wood. The *agalma*, they say, was made thus: it was seated on a rock, and was in the likeness of a woman, all but the head; the head and the hair were those of a horse, and attached to the head were *eikones* of serpents and other wild beasts; she was clad in a tunic that reached even to the ends of her feet; on one of her hands was a dolphin, and on the other a bird. Why they made the *xoanon* thus is plain to any man not witless in judgement and good at remembering things.

They say they surnamed her Black, because the garb the goddess wore was black. They do not remember who made this *xoanon*, nor how it caught fire. When the *archaion agalma* disappeared the Phigalians did not give the goddess another in its stead, and as to the festivals and sacrifices, why they neglected most of them, until a dearth came upon the land; then they besought the god, and the Pythian priestess answered them as follows:

Arcadians, Azanians, acorn-eaters, who inhabit
Phigalia, the cave where the Horse-mother Deo lay hid,
You come to learn a riddance of grievous famine,
You who alone have been nomads twice, and twice tasted the berries wild.
'Twas Deo who stopped your pasturing, and 'twas Deo caused you again
To go without the cakes of herdsmen who drag the ripe ears home,
Because she was robbed of privileges that men of old bestowed on her and of her ancient honors.
And soon shall she make you to eat each other, and to feast on your children,
If you appease not her wrath with libations offered of the whole people,
And if you adorn not the nook of the tunnel with honors divine.

When the oracle was reported to them, the Phigalians held Demeter in higher honor than before, and in particular they induced Onatas, the Aeginetan, son of Micon, to make them an *agalma* of Demeter for so much. There is a bronze Apollo at Pergamus by this Onatas, which is one of the greatest marvels both for size and workmanship. Then this man, discovering a *graphe* or *mimema* [copy] of the *archaion xoanon*—but mostly, it is said, according to a dream vision—made a bronze *agalma* for the Phigalians, about a generation after the expedition of the Medes against Greece. For this statement I have evidence. For at the time when Xerxes crossed into Europe, Gelo, son of Dinomanes, was tyrant of Syracuse and all the rest of Sicily; but when Gelo died, the sovereignty devolved on his brother Hiero; and as Hiero died before he dedicated to Olympian Zeus the *anathemata* he had vowed for his victories in the chariot-race, they were offered by his son Dinomanes in his stead. These offerings are also works of Onatas; and there are inscriptions at Olympia. The one over the *anathema* is this:

For his victories in thy august contests, Olympian Zeus,
One victory with the four-horse car, and two with the racehorse,
Hiero bestowed these gifts on thee; they were dedicated by his son,
Dinomenes, in memory of his Syracusan sire.

The other inscription runs:

Onatas, son of Micon, wrought me,
He dwelt in a house in the isle of Aegina.

Onatas may have been a contemporary of the Athenian Hegias, and of Ageladas the Argive.

Chiefly on account of this Demeter I went to Phigalia, but I sacrificed no victim to the goddess, such being the custom of the natives; instead, they bring the fruit of the vine and of other cultivated trees, also honeycombs, and wool which is yet unspun and full of grease; these they lay on the altar, which is built in front of the grotto, and having laid them on it they pour oil on them. Such is the rule of sacrifice observed both by private persons, and throughout the year by the Phigalian community. They have a priestess who performs the rites, and she is assisted by the youngest of the sacrificers, as they are called, who are citizens, three in number. There is a grove of oaks round about the grotto, and cold water wells up from the earth. The *agalma* made by Onatas was no longer in existence in my time, and most of the Phigalians were not aware that it had ever existed; but the oldest man we met said that three generations before his time some stones from the roof had fallen on the *agalma*, smashing and annihilating it; and sure enough in the roof we could still clearly see the places from which the stones had broken off.

267
Pausanias 8.46.2

Ἰλίου τε γὰρ ἁλούσης καὶ νεμομένων τὰ λάφυρα Ἑλλήνων, Σθενέλῳ τῷ Καπανέως τὸ ξόανον τοῦ Διὸς ἐδόθη τοῦ Ἑρκείου. . . .

(Concerning the long history of plundering)
For when Ilium was taken and the Greeks were dividing up the spoils, the *xoanon* of Zeus of the Courtyard was given to Stheneleus, son of Capaneus.

268
Pausanias 8.46.3

Ἀργείοις δὲ τὰ ἐκ Τίρυνθος ἔτι καὶ ἐς ἐμὲ τὸ μὲν παρὰ τῇ Ἥρᾳ ξόανον, τὸ δὲ ἐν τοῦ Ἀπόλλωνός ἐστιν ἀνακείμενον τοῦ Λυκίου. . . .

But down to my time the Argives still preserve those they took from Tiryns, the one *xoanon* beside Hera, the other is set up in the [sanctuary] of Apollo Lukios.

269
Pausanias 8.48.6

ἀντὶ τούτων μὲν τῷ Ἄρει γέγονεν <ἡ> ἐπίκλησις· πεποίηται δὲ καὶ Διὸς Τελείου βωμὸς καὶ ἄγαλμα τετράγωνον· περισσῶς γὰρ δή τι τῷ σχήματι τούτῳ φαίνονταί μοι χαίρειν οἱ Ἀρκάδες.

(Tegea)
That is why Ares got his surname; there is also an altar of Full-grown Zeus and a square *agalma*; for the Arcadians appear to me to be exceedingly fond of this *schema*.

270
Pausanias 8.53.7–8

τούτου δέ ἐστιν οὐ πόρρω Διονύσου τε ἱερὰ δύο καὶ Κόρης βωμὸς καὶ Ἀπόλλωνος ναὸς καὶ ἄγαλμα ἐπίχρυσον· Χειρίσοφος δὲ ἐποίησε, Κρὴς μὲν γένος, ἡλικίαν δὲ αὐτοῦ καὶ τὸν διδάξαντα οὐκ ἴσμεν· ἡ δὲ δίαιτα ἡ ἐν Κνωσσῷ Δαιδάλῳ παρὰ Μίνῳ συμβᾶσα ἐπὶ μακρότερον δόξαν τοῖς Κρησὶ καὶ ἐπὶ ξοάνων ποιήσει παρεσκεύασε.

(Tegea)
Not far from it are two *hiera* of Dionysus, an altar of Kore, and a *naos* of Apollo and a gilded *agalma*. Chirisophus made [it], a Cretan by birth, but his date and master we do not know; the residence of Daedalus in Knossos, at the court of Minos, conferred on the Cretans for a long time a reputation for the making of *xoana*.

271

Pausanias 9.3.1–9

Ἥραν ἐφ᾽ ὅτῳ δὴ πρὸς τὸν Δία ὠργισμένην ἐς Εὔβοιάν φασιν ἀναχωρῆσαι, Δία δέ, ὡς οὐκ ἔπειθεν αὐτήν, παρὰ Κιθαιρῶνα λέγουσιν ἐλθεῖν δυναστεύοντα ἐν Πλαταιαῖς τότε· εἶναι γὰρ τὸν Κιθαιρῶνα οὐδενὸς σοφίαν ὕστερον. οὗτος οὖν κελεύει τὸν Δία ἄγαλμα ξύλου ποιησάμενον ἄγειν ἐπὶ βοῶν ζεύγους ἐγκεκαλυμμένον, λέγειν δὲ ὡς ἄγοιτο γυναῖκα Πλάταιαν τὴν Ἀσωποῦ. καὶ ὁ μὲν ἔπρασσε κατὰ τὴν παραίνεσιν τοῦ Κιθαιρῶνος· Ἥρα δὲ ἐπέπυστό τε αὐτίκα καὶ αὐτίκα ἀφίκετο. ὡς δὲ ἐπλησίαζε τῇ ἁμάξῃ καὶ τοῦ ἀγάλματος τὴν ἐσθῆτα περιέρρηξεν, ἥσθη τε τῇ ἀπάτῃ ξόανον εὑροῦσα ἀντὶ νύμφης γυναικὸς καὶ διαλλαγὰς ποιεῖται πρὸς τὸν Δία. ἐπὶ ταύταις ταῖς διαλλαγαῖς Δαίδαλα ἑορτὴν ἄγουσιν, ὅτι οἱ πάλαι τὰ ξόανα ἐκάλουν δαίδαλα· ἐκάλουν δὲ ἐμοὶ δοκεῖν πρότερον ἔτι ἢ Δαίδαλος ὁ Παλαμάονος ἐγένετο Ἀθήνησι, τούτῳ δὲ ὕστερον ἀπὸ τῶν δαιδάλων ἐπίκλησιν γενέσθαι δοκῶ καὶ οὐκ ἐκ γενετῆς τεθῆναι τὸ ὄνομα. Δαίδαλα οὖν ἄγουσιν οἱ Πλαταιεῖς ἑορτὴν δι᾽ ἔτους ἑβδόμου μέν, ὡς ἔφασκεν ὁ τῶν ἐπιχωρίων ἐξηγητής, ἀληθεῖ μέντοι λόγῳ δι᾽ ἐλάσσονος καὶ οὐ τοσούτου χρόνου· ἐθελήσαντες δὲ ἀπὸ Δαιδάλων ἐς Δαίδαλα ἕτερα ἀναριθμῆσαι τὸν μεταξὺ χρόνον ἐς τὸ ἀκριβέστατον οὐκ ἐγενόμεθα οἷοί τε. ἄγουσι δὲ οὕτω τὴν ἑορτήν. δρυμός ἐστιν Ἀλαλκομενῶν οὐ πόρρω· μέγιστα τῶν ἐν Βοιωτίᾳ στελέχη δρυῶν ἐστιν ἐνταῦθα. ἐς τοῦτον οἱ Πλαταιεῖς ἀφικόμενοι τὸν δρυμὸν προτίθενται μοίρας κρεῶν ἑφθῶν. ὄρνιθες δὲ οἱ μὲν ἄλλοι σφίσιν ἥκιστά εἰσι δι᾽ ὄχλου, τῶν κοράκων δὲ—οὗτοι γάρ σφισιν ἐπιφοιτῶσιν—ἔχουσιν ἀκριβῆ τὴν φρουράν. τὸν δὲ αὐτῶν ἁρπάσαντα κρέας, ἐφ᾽ ὅτῳ τῶν δένδρων καθεδεῖται, φυλάσσουσιν. ἐφ᾽ οὗ δ᾽ ἂν καθεσθῇ, τεμόντες ποιοῦσιν ἀπὸ τούτου τὸ δαίδαλον· δαίδαλον γὰρ δὴ καὶ τὸ ξόανον αὐτὸ ὀνομάζουσι. ταύτην μὲν ἰδίᾳ οἱ Πλαταιεῖς ἑορτὴν ἄγουσι, Δαίδαλα μικρὰ ὀνομάζοντες· Δαιδάλων δὲ ἑορτὴν τῶν μεγάλων καὶ Βοιωτοί σφισι συνεορτάζουσι, δι᾽ ἑξηκοστοῦ δὲ ἄγουσιν ἔτους· ἐκλιπεῖν γὰρ τοσοῦτον χρόνον τὴν ἑορτήν φασιν, ἡνίκα οἱ Πλαταιεῖς ἔφευγον. ξόανα δὲ τεσσαρεσκαίδεκα ἕτοιμά σφισίν ἐστι κατ᾽ ἐνιαυτὸν ἕκαστον παρασκευασθέντα ἐν Δαιδάλοις τοῖς μικροῖς. ταῦτα ἀναιροῦνται κλήρῳ Πλαταιεῖς Κορωναῖοι Θεσπιεῖς Ταναγραῖοι Χαιρωνεῖς Ὀρχομένιοι Λεβαδεῖς Θηβαῖοι· διαλλαγῆναι γὰρ καὶ οὗτοι Πλαταιεῦσιν ἠξίωσαν καὶ συλλόγου μετασχεῖν κοινοῦ καὶ ἐς Δαίδαλα θυσίαν ἀποστέλλειν, ὅτε Κάσσανδρος ὁ Ἀντιπάτρου τὰς Θήβας ἀνῴκισε. τῶν δὲ πολισμάτων ὁπόσα ἐστὶν ἐλάσσονος λόγου, συντελῆ ἀναιροῦνται. τὸ δὲ ἄγαλμα κομίσαντες παρὰ τὸν Ἀσωπὸν καὶ ἀναθέντες ἐπὶ ἅμαξαν, γυναῖκα ἐφιστᾶσι νυμφεύτριαν· οἱ δὲ αὖθις κληροῦνται καθ᾽ ἥντινα τάξιν τὴν πομπὴν ἀνάξουσι· τὸ δὲ ἐντεῦθεν τὰς ἁμάξας ἀπὸ τοῦ ποταμοῦ πρὸς ἄκρον τὸν Κιθαιρῶνα ἐλαύνουσιν. εὐτρέπισται δέ σφισιν ἐπὶ τῇ κορυφῇ *τοῦ ὄρους βωμός, ποιοῦσι δὲ τρόπῳ τοιῷδε τὸν βωμόν· ξύλα τετράγωνα ἁρμόζοντες πρὸς ἄλληλα συντιθέασι κατὰ ταὐτὰ καὶ εἰ λίθων ἐποιοῦντο οἰκοδομίαν, ἐξάραντες δὲ ἐς ὕψος φρύγανα ἐπιφέρουσιν. αἱ μὲν δὴ πόλεις καὶ τὰ τέλη θήλειαν θύσαντες τῇ Ἥρᾳ βοῦν ἕκαστοι καὶ ταῦρον τῷ Διὶ τὰ ἱερεῖα οἴνου καὶ θυμιαμάτων πλήρη καὶ τὰ δαίδαλα ὁμοῦ καθαγίζουσιν ἐπὶ τοῦ βωμοῦ, ἰδιῶται δὲ ὁπόσα <δὴ> θύουσιν οἱ πλούσιοι· τοῖς δὲ οὐχ ὁμοίως δυναμ<ένο>ις τὰ λεπτότερα τῶν προβάτων θύειν καθέστηκε, καθαγίζειν δὲ τὰ ἱερεῖα ὁμοίως πάντα. σὺν δέ σφισι καὶ αὐτὸν τὸν βωμὸν ἐπιλαβὸν τὸ πῦρ ἐξανήλωσε· μεγίστην δὲ ταύτην φλόγα καὶ ἐκ μακροτάτου σύνοπτον οἶδα ἀρθεῖσαν. ὑπὸ δὲ τῆς κορυφῆς, ἐφ᾽ ᾗ τὸν βωμὸν ποιοῦνται, πέντε που μάλιστα καὶ δέκα ὑποκαταβάντι σταδίους νυμφῶν ἐστιν ἄντρον* Κιθαιρωνίδων, *Σφραγίδιον μὲν ὀνομαζόμενον, μαντεύεσθαι δὲ τὰς νύμφας τὸ ἀρχαῖον αὐτόθι ἔχει λόγος.*

They say that Hera, enraged at Zeus for some reason, retired to Euboea; and that Zeus, when he could not persuade her, came to Cithaeron, who then ruled in Plataea; for Cithaeron was second to none in craft. He accordingly advised Zeus to have an *agalma* made of wood, to convey it, wrapped up, in a bullock cart, and to say that he was taking to wife Plataea, daughter of Asopus. And Zeus did as Cithaeron advised him, and no sooner had Hera heard of it than she flew to the spot. Going up to the wagon she tore the dress off the *agalma*, and finding a *xoanon* instead of a bride, she was pleased with the trick, and made it up with Zeus. In memory of this reconciliation they celebrate a festival called Daedala, because long ago, people called *xoana* "*daedala*." I believe that they called them so even before Daedalus, son of Palamaon, was born at Athens, and I think Daedalus was a surname subsequently given to him from the *daedala*, and not a name bestowed on him at birth. So the Plataeans hold the festival of the Daedala, the local guide said, every sixth year, but really the celebrations take place at shorter intervals. We tried to reckon the exact interval between one Daedala and another, but we could not do it. They hold the festival thus. There is an oak wood not far from Alalcomenae; the trunks of the oak trees in it are the largest in Boeotia. To this wood come the Plataeans, set out pieces of boiled flesh, and keep a sharp watch on the crows, which come flocking to them; the other birds do not trouble them in the least. They observe the crow which pounces on the flesh and the tree on which he perches. Then they fell the tree on which he perched, and make the *daedalon* out of it; for they name the *xoanon* also *daedalon*. This festival the Plataeans hold by themselves, and name it the Little Daedala; but the festival of the Great Daedala is held by them conjointly with the Boeotians every sixtieth year; for they say that the festival remained in abeyance for that time, when the Plataeans were in exile. There are fourteen *xoana* made ready, these having been provided year by year at the Little Daedala. Lots are drawn for these by the Plataeans, Coroneans, Thespians, Tanagraeans, Chaeroneans, Orchomenians, Lebadeans, and Thebans; for at the time when Cassander, son of Antipater, restored Thebes, the Thebans desired to be reconciled to the Plataeans, to share in the common assembly, and to send a sacrifice to the Daedala. The towns of less note club together. Having decked the *agalma* . . . to the Asopus, and having set it up on a wagon, they place a bridesmaid on the wagon. The representatives of the different cities again cast lots for the places they are to have in the procession. Then they drive the wagons from the river to the top of Cithaeron. On the summit of the mountain an altar has been got ready. They make it in this fasion: they put together quadrangular blocks of wood, fitting them into each other, just in the same way as if they were constructing an edifice of stone. Then, having raised it to a height, they pile brushwood on it. The cities and the magistrates sacrifice each a cow to Hera and a bull to Zeus, and burn the victims, which are filled with wine and incense, together with the *daedala* on the altar. Rich people sacrifice what they please; persons who are not so well off sacrifice the lesser cattle; but all the victims alike are burned. The fire seizes on the altar as well as the victims, and consumes them all together. I know of no blaze that rises so high, and is seen so far. Just about fifteen stadia down the summit on which they make the altar there is a cave of the nymphs of Cithaeron; it is called Sphragidium, and the story goes that the nymphs gave oracles there in day of old.

272

Pausanias 9.4.1

Πλαταιεῦσι δὲ Ἀθηνᾶς ἐπίκλησιν Ἀρείας ἐστὶν ἱερόν· ᾠκοδομήθη δὲ ἀπὸ λαφύρων ἃ τῆς μάχης σφίσιν Ἀθηναῖοι τῆς Μαραθῶνι ἀπένειμαν. τὸ μὲν δὴ ἄγαλμα ξόανόν ἐστιν ἐπίχρυσον, πρόσωπον δέ οἱ καὶ χεῖρες ἄκραι καὶ πόδες λίθου τοῦ Πεντελησίου εἰσί· μέγεθος μὲν οὐ πολὺ δή τι ἀποδεῖ τῆς ἐν ἀκροπόλει χαλκῆς, ἣν καὶ αὐτὴν Ἀθηναῖοι τοῦ Μαραθῶνι ἀπαρχὴν ἀγῶνος ἀνέθηκαν, Φειδίας δὲ καὶ Πλαταιεῦσιν ἦν ὁ τῆς Ἀθηνᾶς τὸ ἄγαλμα ποιήσας.

The Plataeans have also a *hieron* of Athena surnamed Warlike; it was built from the share which the Athenians assigned them of the booty taken at the battle of Marathon. The *agalma* is a gilded *xoanon*, but the face, hands, and feet are of Pentelic stone. In size it falls a little short of the bronze statue on the Acropolis, which the Athenians also set up as a first offering of the battle of Marathon. It was Pheidias who made the *agalma* of Athena for the Plataeans as well as for the Athenians.

273
Pausanias 9.11.4–5

ἐνταῦθα Ἡρακλεῖόν ἐστιν, ἄγαλμα δὲ τὸ μὲν λίθου λευκοῦ Πρόμαχος καλούμενον, ἔργον δὲ Ξενοκρίτου καὶ Εὐβίου Θηβαίων· τὸ δὲ ξόανον τὸ ἀρχαῖον Θηβαῖοί τε εἶναι Δαιδάλου νενομίκασι καὶ αὐτῷ μοι παρίστατο ἔχειν οὕτω. τοῦτον ἀνέθηκεν αὐτός, ὡς λέγεται, Δαίδαλος ἐκτίνων εὐεργεσίας χάριν. ἡνίκα γὰρ ἔφευγεν ἐκ Κρήτης πλοῖα οὐ μεγάλα αὐτῷ καὶ τῷ παιδὶ Ἰκάρῳ ποιησάμενος, πρὸς δὲ καὶ ταῖς ναυσίν, ὃ μή πω τοῖς τότε ἐξεύρητο, ἱστία ἐπιτεχνησάμενος, ὡς τοῦ Μίνω ναυτικοῦ τὴν εἰρεσίαν φθάνοιεν ἐπιφόρῳ τῷ ἀνέμῳ χρώμενοι, τότε αὐτὸς μὲν σώζεται Δαίδαλος, Ἰκάρῳ δὲ κυβερνῶντι ἀμαθέστερον ἀνατραπῆναι τὴν ναῦν λέγουσιν· ἀποπνιγέντα δὲ ἐξήνεγκεν ὁ κλύδων ἐς τὴν ὑπὲρ Σάμου νῆσον ἔτι οὖσαν ἀνώνυμον. ἐπιτυχὼν δὲ Ἡρακλῆς γνωρίζει τὸν νεκρόν, καὶ ἔθαψεν ἔνθα καὶ νῦν ἔτι αὐτῷ χῶμα οὐ μέγα ἐπὶ ἄκρας ἐστὶν ἀνεχούσης ἐς τὸ Αἰγαῖον. ἀπὸ δὲ τοῦ Ἰκάρου τούτου ὄνομα ἥ τε νῆσος καὶ ἡ περὶ αὐτὴν θάλασσα ἔσχηκε.

(Thebes)
Here there is a Herakleion; the *agalma* is of white stone, and is called Promachos; it is a work of Xenocritus and Eubius, of Thebes; the *archaion xoanon* is believed to be by Daedalus, and that was my impression too. This, it is said, Daedalus himself dedicated in acknowledgement of a benefit received. For when he fled from Crete in a small craft which he had made for himself and his son Icarus, he devised sails for ships (an invention hitherto unknown) in order to take advantage of a fair wind, and so outstrip the fleet of Minos which was propelled by oars. Well, Daedalus himself was saved; but Icarus, they say, steered in a rather unskilled manner and his ship capsized. The drowned man was washed ashore by the billows on an island, then nameless, off the coast of Samos. Heracles found and recognized the corpse, and buried it where there still stands a small mound of Icarus on a headland jutting into the Aegean sea. From Icarus both the island and the surrounding sea derived their names.

274
Pausanias 9.16.3–4

Ἀφροδίτης δὲ Θηβαίοις ξόανά ἐστιν οὕτω δὴ ἀρχαῖα ὥστε καὶ ἀναθήματα Ἁρμονίας εἶναί φασιν [αὐτά], ἐργασθῆναι δὲ αὐτὰ ἀπὸ τῶν ἀκροστολίων, ἃ ταῖς Κάδμου ναυσὶν ἦν ξύλου πεποιημένα. καλοῦσι δὲ Οὐρανίαν, τὴν δὲ αὐτῶν Πάνδημον καὶ Ἀποστροφίαν τὴν τρίτην· ἔθετο δὲ τῇ Ἀφροδίτῃ τὰς ἐπωνυμίας ἡ Ἁρμονία, τὴν μὲν Οὐρανίαν ἐπὶ ἔρωτι καθαρῷ καὶ ἀπηλλαγμένῳ πόθου σωμάτων, Πάνδημον δὲ ἐπὶ ταῖς μίξεσι, τρίτα δὲ Ἀποστροφίαν, ἵνα ἐπιθυμίας τε ἀνόμου καὶ ἔργων ἀνοσίων ἀποστρέφῃ τὸ γένος τῶν ἀνθρώπων· πολλὰ γὰρ τὰ μὲν ἐν βαρβάροις ἠπίστατο ἡ Ἁρμονία, τὰ δὲ καὶ παρ' Ἕλλησιν ἤδη τετολμημένα, ὁποῖα καὶ ὕστερον ἐπὶ τῇ Ἀδώνιδος μητρὶ καὶ ἐς Φαίδραν τε τὴν Μίνω καὶ ἐς τὸν Θρᾷκα Τηρέα ᾄδεται.

There are *xoana* of Aphrodite at Thebes so *archaia* that they say they are *anathemata* of Harmonia, and have been made out of the figureheads, which were made of wood, for the ships of Cadmus. One of them is called Ourania, another Pandemos, and the third Apostrophia. These surnames were given to Aphrodite by Harmonia. She called the goddess Ourania in reference to a love pure and free from all lust; she called her Pandemos in reference to the intercourse of the sexes; and she called her Apostrophia in order that she might turn mankind away from lawless desires and unholy deeds. For Harmonia knew that many a rash deed had been done, both in Greece and in foreign lands, such deeds as common fame afterwards ascribed to the mother of Adonis, to Phaedra, daughter of Minos, and to the Thracian Tereus.

275
Pausanias 9.24.3

θέας δὲ ἄξιον ἐν μὲν Ὄλμωσιν οὐδ' ἐπὶ βραχύτατον παρεῖχον οὐδέν, ἐν Ὑήττῳ δὲ ναός ἐστιν Ἡρακλέους καὶ ἰάματα εὕρασθαι παρὰ τούτου τοῖς κάμνουσιν ἔστιν, ὄντος οὐχὶ ἀγάλματος σὺν τέχνῃ, λίθου δὲ ἀργοῦ κατὰ τὸ ἀρχαῖον.

(Copaic Basin)
At Olmones they had nothing whatever to show that was worth seeing; but at Hyettus there is a *naos* of Heracles, and remedies for the sick are devised by him; he is not an *agalma* with craft, but a rough stone, according to the *archaios* fashion.

276
Pausanias 9.27.1

θεῶν δὲ οἱ Θεσπιεῖς τιμῶσιν Ἔρωτα μάλιστα ἐξ ἀρχῆς, καί σφισιν ἄγαλμα παλαιότατόν ἐστιν ἀργὸς λίθος.

Of the gods, the Thespians honor Eros especially, from the beginning, and their most *palaion agalma* is a rough stone.

277
Pausanias 9.38.1

Ὀρχομενίοις δὲ πεποίηται καὶ Διονύσου, τὸ δὲ ἀρχαιότατον Χαρίτων ἐστὶν ἱερόν. τὰς μὲν δὴ πέτρας σέβουσί τε μάλιστα καὶ τῷ Ἐτεοκλεῖ αὐτὰς πεσεῖν ἐκ τοῦ οὐρανοῦ φασιν. τὰ δὲ ἀγάλματα <τὰ> σὺν κόσμῳ πεποιημένα ἀνετέθη μὲν ἐπ' ἐμοῦ, λίθου δέ ἐστι καὶ ταῦτα.

At Orchomenos there has been made . . . and of Dionysus; but the most *archaion hieron* is of the Graces. They worship the rocks most of all, and [say] that they fell to Eteocles from heaven. The *agalmata* made with form were dedicated in my time, and they too are of stone.

278
Pausanias 9.40.3–4

Δαιδάλου δὲ τῶν ἔργων δύο μὲν ταῦτά ἐστιν ἐν Βοιωτοῖς, Ἡρακλῆς τε ἐν Θήβαις καὶ παρὰ Λεβαδεῦσιν ὁ Τροφώνιος, τοσαῦτα δὲ ἕτερα ξόανα ἐν Κρήτῃ, Βριτόμαρτις ἐν Ὀλοῦντι καὶ Ἀθηνᾶ παρὰ Κνωσσίοις· παρὰ τούτοις δὲ καὶ ὁ τῆς Ἀριάδνης χορός, οὗ καὶ Ὅμηρος ἐν Ἰλιάδι μνήμην ἐποιήσατο, ἐπειργασμένος ἐστὶν ἐπὶ λευκοῦ λίθου. καὶ Δηλίοις Ἀφροδίτης ἐστὶν οὐ μέγα ξόανον, λελυμασμένον τὴν δεξιὰν χεῖρα ὑπὸ τοῦ χρόνου· κάτεισι δὲ ἀντὶ ποδῶν ἐς τετράγωνον σχῆμα. πείθομαι τοῦτο Ἀριάδνην λαβεῖν παρὰ Δαιδάλου, καὶ ἡνίκα ἠκολούθησε τῷ Θησεῖ, τὸ ἄγαλμα ἐπεκομίζετο οἴκοθεν· ἀφαιρεθέντα δὲ αὐτῆς τὸν Θησέα οὕτω φασὶν οἱ Δήλιοι τὸ ξόανον τῆς θεοῦ ἀναθεῖναι τῷ Ἀπόλλωνι τῷ Δηλίῳ, ἵνα μὴ οἴκαδε ἐπαγόμενος ἐς ἀνάμνησίν τε Ἀριάδνης ἐφέλκηται καὶ ἀεὶ νέας ἐπὶ τῷ ἔρωτι εὑρίσκηται τὰς συμφοράς. πέρα δὲ οὐκ οἶδα ὑπόλοιπα ὄντα τῶν Δαιδάλου· τοῖς γὰρ ἀνατεθεῖσιν ὑπὸ Ἀργείων ἐς τὸ Ἡραῖον καὶ ἐς Γέλαν τὴν ἐν Σικελίᾳ κομισθεῖσιν ἐξ Ὀμφάκης, ἀφανισθῆναί σφισιν ὁ χρόνος καθέστηκεν αἴτιος.

Of the works of Daedalus there are these two in Boeotia, Heracles in Thebes and Trophonius at Lebadea; there are two other *xoana* in Crete, Britomartis in Olus and Athena at Knossos; in addition to these there is also Ariadne's Dance, which Homer mentions in the *Iliad*, wrought on white stone. At Delos, too, there is a not large *xoanon* of Aphrodite, damaged on the right hand by time; it goes down into a square *schema* instead of feet. I believe that Ariadne received it from Daedalus, and took the *agalma* with her from home when she followed Theseus; the Delians say that when Theseus was bereft of Ariadne he dedicated the *xoanon* of the goddess to the Delian Apollo, lest by bringing it home with him he should be drawn into remembering Ariadne, and thus find the sorrows of his love forever new. I know no other extant works of Daedalus; for those that were dedicated by the Argives in the sanctuary of Hera, and those which were brought from Omphace to Gela in Sicily, time is responsible for their disappearance.

279
Pausanias 9.40.11–12

θεῶν δὲ μάλιστα Χαιρωνεῖς τιμῶσι τὸ σκῆπτρον ὃ ποιῆσαι Διί φησιν Ὅμηρος Ἥφαιστον, παρὰ δὲ Διὸς λαβόντα Ἑρμῆν δοῦναι Πέλοπι,

Πέλοπα δὲ Ἀτρεῖ καταλιπεῖν, τὸν δὲ Ἀτρέα Θυέστῃ, παρὰ Θυέστου δὲ ἔχειν Ἀγαμέμνονα· τοῦτο οὖν τὸ σκῆπτρον σέβουσι, Δόρυ ὀνομάζοντες. καὶ εἶναι μέν τι θειότερον οὐχ ἥκιστα δηλοῖ τὸ ἐς τοὺς ἀνθρώπους ἐπιφανὲς ἐξ αὐτοῦ· φασὶ δ' ἐπὶ τοῖς ὅροις αὐτῶν καὶ Πανοπέων τῶν ἐν τῇ Φωκίδι εὑρεθῆναι, σὺν δὲ αὐτῷ καὶ χρυσὸν εὕρασθαι τοὺς Φωκεῖς, σφίσι δὲ ἀσμένοις ἀντὶ χρυσοῦ γενέσθαι τὸ σκῆπτρον. κομισθῆναι δὲ αὐτὸ ἐς τὴν Φωκίδα ὑπὸ Ἠλέκτρας τῆς Ἀγαμέμνονος πείθομαι. ναὸς δὲ οὐκ ἔστιν αὐτῷ δημοσίᾳ πεποιημένος, ἀλλὰ κατὰ ἔτος ἕκαστον ὁ ἱερώμενος ἐν οἰκήματι ἔχει τὸ σκῆπτρον· καί οἱ θυσίαι ἀνὰ πᾶσαν ἡμέραν θύονται, καὶ τράπεζα παράκειται παντοδαπῶν κρεῶν καὶ πεμμάτων πλήρης.

Of the gods, the Chaeroneans honor most the scepter which Homer says Hephaestus made for Zeus, and Zeus gave to Hermes, and Hermes to Pelops, and Pelops bequeathed it to Atreus, and Atreus to Thyestes, from whom Agamemnon had it. This scepter they worship, naming it "Spear"; and that there is something divine about it is proved especially by by the distinction it confers on its owner. The Chaeroneans say that it was found on the borders of their territory and of Panopeus in Phocis, and that the Phocians found gold along with it, but that they themselves were glad to get the scepter instead of the gold. I believe that it was brought to Phocis by Electra, daughter of Agamemnon. There is no public *naos* built for it, but the man who acts as priest keeps the scepter in his house for the year; and sacrifices are offered to it daily, and a table is set beside it covered with all sorts of flesh and cakes.

280
Pausanias 10.4.9

Δαυλιεῦσι δὲ Ἀθηνᾶς ἱερὸν καὶ ἄγαλμά ἐστιν ἀρχαῖον· τὸ δὲ ξόανον τὸ ἔτι παλαιότερον λέγουσιν ἐπαγαγέσθαι Πρόκνην ἐξ Ἀθηνῶν.

At Daulis there is a *hieron* of Athena and the *agalma* is *archaion*; they say that Procne brought the still more *palaion xoanon* from Athens.

281
Pausanias 10.19.3

τὸ ἀπὸ τούτου δὲ ἔρχομαι διηγησόμενος λόγον Λέσβιον. ἁλιεῦσιν ἐν Μηθύμνῃ τὰ δίκτυα ἀνείλκυσεν ἐκ θαλάσσης πρόσωπον ἐλαίας ξύλου πεποιημένον· τοῦτο ἰδέαν παρείχετο φέρουσαν μέν [τοι] ἐς τὸ θεῖον, ξένην δὲ καὶ ἐπὶ θεοῖς Ἑλληνικοῖς οὐ καθεστῶσαν. εἴροντο οὖν οἱ Μηθυμναῖοι τὴν Πυθίαν ὅτου θεῶν ἢ καὶ ἡρώων ἐστὶν ἡ εἰκών· ἡ δὲ αὐτοὺς σέβεσθαι Διόνυσον Φαλλῆνα ἐκέλευσεν. ἐπὶ τούτῳ οἱ Μηθυμναῖοι ξόανον μὲν τὸ ἐκ τῆς θαλάσσης παρὰ σφίσιν ἔχοντες καὶ θυσίαις καὶ εὐχαῖς τιμῶσι, χαλκοῦν δὲ ἀποπέμπουσιν ἐς Δελφούς.

I shall now continue with a Lesbian tale. Some fishermen at Methymna brought up out of the sea in their nets a face made of olive wood; it presented an appearance having something of the divine, but foreign, not made up as on Greek gods. So the Methymnians asked the Pythia of which of the gods or heroes it was an *eikon*; and she bade them worship Dionysus Phallen. For this reason the Methymnians kept the *xoanon* out of the sea, and honored it with sacrifices and prayers; but they sent a bronze one to Delphi.

282
Pausanias 10.26.3

Αἴας δὲ ὁ Ὀιλέως ἔχων ἀσπίδα βωμῷ προσέστηκεν, ὀμνύμενος ὑπὲρ τοῦ ἐς Κασσάνδραν τολμήματος· ἡ δὲ κάθηταί τε ἡ Κασσάνδρα χαμαὶ καὶ τὸ ἄγαλμα ἔχει τῆς Ἀθηνᾶς, εἴγε δὴ ἀνέτρεψεν ἐκ βάθρων τὸ ξόανον, ὅτε ἀπὸ τῆς ἱκεσίας αὐτὴν ὁ Αἴας ἀφεῖλκε.

(Chest of Cypselus)
And Ajax, son of Oileus, holding a shield, is standing beside a *bomos*, taking an oath because of the outrage on Cassandra; Cassandra herself is seated on the ground and is holding the *agalma* of Athena, for she overturned the *xoanon* from its pedestal when Ajax dragged her from sanctuary.

283
Periplus Ponti Euxini 66 A.D. VI
Text: K. Müller, ed., *Geographi graeci minores* I (Paris, 1855) 419.66.

Ταύτην την νῆσον λέγεται Θέτις ἀνεῖναι τῷ παιδὶ, καὶ ταύτην οἰκεῖν τὸν Ἀχιλλέα. Καὶ ναός ἐστιν ἐν αὐτῇ τοῦ Ἀχιλλέως, καὶ ξόανον (ἤτοι ἄγαλμα) τῆς πάλαι ἐργασίας.

It is said that Thetis left this island to her son, and that Achilles inhabits it. And on it here is a *naos* of Achilles, and a *xoanon* (or *agalma*) of old workmanship.

Philemon fr. 139 Kock IV–III B.C.
See Athenaeus 13.606 a [**35**].

Philippus IV B.C.
See Aristotle, *De anima* 1.3 [**30**], Themistius *ad loc.* [**363**] and Philoponus *ad loc.* [**153**].

Philo Byblius A.D. I–II
See Eusebius, *Praeparatio evangelica* 1.10.35 d [**102**].

284

Philo Judaeus, *De Abrahamo* 267 I B.C.–A.D. I

Text: L. Cohn, ed., *Philonis Alexandrini opera quae supersunt* IV (Berlin, 1902).

Translation adapted from F.H. Colson, tr., *Philo* VI (LCL, 1935).

ὑγιεινότατά γε μὴν καὶ ὡς ἔνι μάλιστα ἄνοσα πλεῖστα τῶν ἀλόγων ζῴων ἐστίν. ἐν δὲ τῷ περὶ κάλλους ἀγῶνι καὶ τῶν ἀψύχων ἔνιά μοι δοκεῖ νικᾶν δύνασθαι τὰς ἀνδρῶν ὁμοῦ καὶ γυναικῶν εὐμορφίας καὶ ὑπερβάλλειν, ἀγάλματα καὶ ξόανα καὶ ζωγραφήματα καὶ συνόλως ὅσα γραφικῆς ἔργα καὶ πλαστικῆς ἐν ἑκατέρᾳ τέχνῃ κατορθούμενα, περὶ ἃ σπουδάζουσιν Ἕλληνες ὁμοῦ καὶ βάρβαροι πρὸς κόσμον τῶν πόλεων ἐν τοῖς ἐπιφανεστάτοις χωρίοις ἀνατιθέντες.

Indeed, most of the unreasoning animals are exceedingly healthy and especially free from disease. In the competition for beauty, it seems to me that some lifeless objects can beat and surpass the comeliness of men and women alike, *agalmata* and *xoana* and *zographemata* and in general all the works of *graphike* and *plastike* which achieve success in either art, about which both the Greeks and the barbarians alike are enthusiastic, setting them up for the adornment of cities in the most conspicuous places.

285

Philo Judaeus, *De decalogo* 7 I B.C.–A.D. I

Text: L. Cohn, ed., *Philonis Alexandrini opera quae supersunt* IV (Berlin, 1902).

Translation adapted from F.H. Colson, tr., *Philo* VII (LCL, 1937).

ἡ δ' ὀλιγωρία τῶν θείων ἐμφανὴς τοῖς ὀξυδερκέστερον ὁρῶσι· μυρίας γὰρ ὅσας διὰ γραφικῆς καὶ πλαστικῆς μορφώσαντες ἰδέας ἱερὰ καὶ νεὼς αὐταῖς προσπεριεβάλοντο καὶ βωμοὺς κατασκευάσαντες ἀγάλμασι καὶ ξοάνοις καὶ τοιουτοτρόποις ἀφιδρύμασι τιμὰς ἰσολυμπίους καὶ ἰσοθέους ἀπένειμαν, ἅπασιν ἀψύχοις.

This contempt for divine things is clear to those who see more sharply; for, shaping how many myriad forms by *graphike* and *plastike*, men have put *hiera* and *neoi* around them, and having prepared altars, they awarded honors Olympian and divine to *agalmata* and *xoana* and *aphidrumata* of these kinds, all soulless things.

286

Philo Judaeus, *De decalogo* 51 I B.C.–A.D. I

Text: L. Cohn, ed., *Philonis Alexandrini opera quae supersunt* IV (Berlin, 1902).

Translation adapted from F.H. Colson, tr., *Philo* VII (LCL, 1937).

ἡ μὲν οὖν ἀμείνων πεντὰς τοιάδε ἦν· περὶ μοναρχίας, ᾗ μοναρχεῖται ὁ κόσμος· περὶ ξοάνων καὶ ἀγαλμάτων καὶ συνόλως ἀφιδρυμάτων χειροκμήτων· περὶ τοῦ μὴ λαμβάνειν ἐπὶ ματαίῳ θεοῦ πρόσρησιν· περὶ τοῦ τὴν ἱερὰν ἑβδόμην ἄγειν ἱεροπρεπῶς· περὶ γονέων τιμῆς καὶ ἰδίᾳ ἑκατέρου καὶ ἀμφοτέρων κοινῇ. . . .

The superior set of five is concerned with these things: monarchy, by which the universe is ruled; *xoana* and *agalmata* and *aphidrumata* in general, that are made by human hands; not taking the name of God in vain; the observance of the holy seventh day in a properly holy way; the honoring of parents, both each one separately and both together. . . .

287

Philo Judaeus, *De decalogo* 66 — I B.C.–A.D. I

Text: L. Cohn, ed., *Philonis Alexandrini opera quae supersunt* IV (Berlin, 1902).

Translation adapted from F.H. Colson, tr., *Philo* VII (LCL, 1937).

ἀλλ' ὅσοι μὲν ἡλίου καὶ σελήνης καὶ τοῦ σύμπαντος οὐρανοῦ τε καὶ κόσμου καὶ τῶν ἐν αὐτοῖς ὁλοσχερεστάτων μερῶν ὡς θεῶν πρόπολοί τε καὶ θεραπευταί, διαμαρτάνουσι μὲν—πῶς γὰρ οὔ;—τοὺς ὑπηκόους πρὸ τοῦ ἄρχοντος ἀποσεμνύνοντες, ἧττον δὲ τῶν ἄλλων ἀδικοῦσι τῶν ξύλα καὶ λίθους ἄργυρόν τε καὶ χρυσὸν καὶ τὰς παραπλησίους ὕλας μορφωσάντων ὡς φίλον ἑκάστοις, εἶτ' ἀγαλμάτων καὶ ξοάνων καὶ τῶν ἄλλων χειροκμήτων, ὧν πλαστικὴ καὶ ζωγραφία δημιουργοὶ μεγάλα ἔβλαψαν τὸν βίον τὸν ἀνθρώπινον, καταπλησάντων τὴν οἰκουμένην.

But while all who are worshippers and attendants of the sun and moon and the whole heaven and universe, or their chief parts, as gods err—for how not?—by magnifying the subjects above the ruler, their offense is less than that of the others who have given shape to stocks and stones and silver and gold and similar materials, each according to his fancy, and then filled the habitable world with *agalmata* and *xoana* and other things made by hands, the creators of which, *plastike* and *zographia*, have wrought great mischief in the life of mankind.

288

Philo Judaeus, *De decalogo* 76 — I B.C.–A.D. I

Text: L. Cohn, ed., *Philonis Alexandrini opera quae supersunt* IV (Berlin, 1902).

Translation adapted from F.H. Colson, tr., *Philo* VII (LCL, 1937).

μηδεὶς οὖν τῶν ἐχόντων ψυχὴν ἀψύχῳ τινὶ προσκυνείτω· πάνυ γὰρ τῶν ἀτόπων ἐστὶ τὰ φύσεως ἔργα πρὸς θεραπείαν τετράφθαι τῶν χειροκμήτων. Αἰγυπτίοις δ' οὐ μόνον τὸ κοινὸν ἔγκλημα χώρας ἁπάσης, ἀλλὰ καὶ ἕτερον ἐξαίρετον ἐπάγεται δεόντως· πρὸς γὰρ ξοάνοις καὶ ἀγάλμασιν ἔτι καὶ ζῷα ἄλογα παραγηόχασιν εἰς θεῶν τιμάς, ταύρους καὶ κριοὺς καὶ τράγους, ἐφ᾽ ἑκάστῳ μυθικόν τι πλάσμα τετερατευμένοι.

Thus let no one who has a soul worship a soulless thing; for it is exceedingly out of place that the works of nature should be turned to the service of things made by human hands. Against the Egyptians is brought the common charge against every country, but also, as is proper, another charge of their own: for in addition to *xoana* and *agalmata*, they have introduced divine honors for irrational beasts, bulls and rams and goats, telling some fantastic mythic fiction for each one.

289

Philo Judaeus, *De decalogo* 156 I B.C.–A.D. I
Text: L. Cohn, ed., *Philonis Alexandrini opera quae supersunt* IV (Berlin, 1902).
Translation adapted from F.H. Colson, tr., *Philo* VII (LCL, 1937).

ὁ δὲ δεύτερος κεφάλαιόν ἐστι πάντων, ὅσα περὶ χειροκμήτων ἐνομοθετεῖτο, ἀγάλματα καὶ ξόανα καὶ συνόλως ἀφιδρύματα, ὧν γραφικὴ καὶ πλαστικὴ βλαβεραὶ δημιουργοί, κατασκευάζειν οὐκ ἐῶν οὐδ᾽ ὅσα μύθων πλάσματα προσίεσθαι, θεογαμίαν καὶ θεογονίαν καὶ τὰς ἀμφοτέραις ἑπομένας ἀμυθήτους καὶ ἀργαλεωτάτας κῆρας.

The second [*sc.* commandment] sums up all the enactments made concerning the works of men's hands. It forbids the making of *agalmata* and *xoana* and *aphidrumata* in general, of which *graphike* and *plastike* are the harmful creators, and also the acceptance of fabulous legends about the marriages and pedigrees of deities and the numberless and very grave defects associated with both of these.

290

Philo Judaeus, *De ebrietate* 109–110 I B.C.–A.D. I
Text: P. Wendland, ed., *Philonis Alexandrini opera quae supersunt* II (Berlin, 1897).
Translation adapted from F.H. Colson, tr., *Philo* III (LCL, 1930).

παρὸ καὶ θεοπλαστεῖν ἀρξάμενος ἀγαλμάτων καὶ ξοάνων καὶ ἄλλων μυρίων ἀφιδρυμάτων ὕλαις διαφόροις τετεχνιτευμένων κατέπλησε τὴν οἰκουμένην, γραφεῦσι καὶ πλάσταις, οὓς ὑπερορίους ὁ νομοθέτης τῆς κατ᾽ αὐτὸν πολιτείας ἤλασεν, ἆθλά τε μεγάλα καὶ τιμὰς ὑπερβαλλούσας ἰδίᾳ τε καὶ κοινῇ ψηφισάμενος, <καὶ> κατειργάσατο τοὐναντίον οὗ προσεδόκησεν, ἀντὶ ὁσιότητος ἀσέβειαν· τὸ γὰρ πολύθεον ἐν ταῖς τῶν ἀφρόνων ψυχαῖς ἀθεότητα <κατασκευάζει>, καὶ θεοῦ τιμῆς ἀλογοῦσιν οἱ τὰ θνητὰ θειώσαντες· οἷς οὐκ ἐξήρκεσεν ἡλίου καὶ σελήνης, εἰ δὲ ἐβούλοντο, καὶ γῆς ἁπάσης *καὶ παντὸς ὕδατος εἰκόνας διαπλάσασθαι, ἀλλ' ἤδη καὶ ἀλόγοις ζῴοις καὶ φυτοῖς τῆς τῶν ἀφθάρτων τιμῆς μετέδοσαν. ὁ δὴ τούτοις ἐπιτιμῶν τὸν ἐπινίκιον ὕμνον ἐξάρχων ἐδείχθη.*

And wherefore he started to fashion gods, and filled the inhabited world with *agalmata* and *xoana* and countless other *aphidrumata* wrought in various materials, and decreed great prizes and magnificent honors, public and private, to painters and sculptors, whom the lawgiver had banished from the boundaries of his commonwealth. He expected to produce piety; what he accomplished was its opposite, impiety. For polytheism creates atheism in the souls of the foolish, and God's honor is set at naught by those who deify the mortal. For it did not content them to fashion *eikones* of sun and moon, or, if they would have it so, of all the earth and all the water, but they even allowed irrational plants and animals to share the honor which belongs to things imperishable. Such persons did Abraham rebuke and we showed that it was with this thought that he raised his hymn of victory.

291

Philo Judaeus, *Legatio ad Gaium* 98 c. A.D. 40
Text: L. Cohn and S. Reiter, eds., *Philonis Alexandrini opera quae supersunt* VI (Berlin, 1915).
Translation adapted from F.H. Colson, tr., *Philo* X (LCL, 1962).

εἶτα τοῖς ταῦτα ὁρῶσι κατάπληξις ἦν ἐπὶ τῷ παραλόγῳ, καὶ ἐθαύμαζον, πῶς ὁ τἀναντία δρῶν οἷς ἰσότιμος εἶναι προαιρεῖται τὰς μὲν ἀρετὰς αὐτῶν ἐπιτηδεύειν οὐκ ἀξιοῖ, τοῖς δὲ παρασήμοις εἰς ἕκαστον σκευάζεται. καίτοι τὰ περίαπτα ταῦτα καὶ προκοσμήματα ξοάνοις καὶ ἀγάλμασι προσκαθίδρυται, διὰ συμβόλων μηνύοντα τὰς ὠφελείας, ἃς παρέχονται τῷ γένει τῶν ἀνθρώπων οἱ τιμώμενοι.

Then those who saw these things were struck with amazement at the strange contradiction, marvelling how one, whose actions were the opposite of those whose honors he proposed to share as their equal, did not think fit to practice their virtues and yet at the same time invested himself with their insignia each in turn. Yet surely these trappings and ornaments are set as accessories on *xoana* and *agalmata* as symbolically indicating the benefits which those thus honored provide for the race of men.

292

Philo Judaeus, *Legatio ad Gaium* 148 c. A.D. 40
Text: L. Cohn and S. Reiter, eds., *Philonis Alexandrini opera quae supersunt* VI (Berlin, 1915).
Translation adapted from F.H. Colson, tr., *Philo* X (LCL, 1962).

τοῦτον οὖν τὸν τοσοῦτον εὐεργέτην ἐν τρισὶ καὶ τεσσαράκοντα ἐνιαυτοῖς, οὓς ἐπεκράτησεν Αἰγύπτου, παρεκαλύψαντο, μηδὲν ἐν προσευχαῖς ὑπὲρ αὐτοῦ, μὴ ἄγαλμα, μὴ ξόανον, μὴ γραφὴν ἱδρυσάμενοι.

This great benefactor they ignored during the forty-three years in which he was sovereign of Egypt, and set up nothing in our meeting-houses in his behalf, neither *agalma*, nor *xoanon*, nor *graphe*.

293

Philo Judaeus, *Legatio ad Gaium* 292 c. A.D. 40
Text: L. Cohn and S. Reiter, eds., *Philonis Alexandrini opera quae supersunt* VI (Berlin, 1915).
Translation adapted from F.H. Colson, tr., *Philo* X (LCL, 1962).

ὅθεν οὐδείς, οὐχ Ἕλλην, οὐ βάρβαρος, οὐ σατράπης, οὐ βασιλεύς, οὐκ ἐχθρὸς ἄσπονδος, οὐ στάσις, οὐ πόλεμος, οὐχ ἅλωσις, οὐ πόρθησις, οὐκ ἄλλο τι τῶν ὄντων οὐδὲν ἐνεωτέρισέ ποτε οὕτως εἰς τὸν νεών, ὡς ἄγαλμα ἢ ξόανον ἤ τι τῶν χειροκμήτων ἱδρύσασθαι.

Thus no one, no Greek, no barbarian, no satrap, no king, no mortal enemy, no faction, no war, no capture, no sacking, nor any other thing, ever brought about so great a violation of the *neos*, as setting up an *agalma* or *xoanon* or any other hand-made thing.

294

Philo Judaeus, *De specialibus legibus* 1.56 I B.C.–A.D. I
Text: L. Cohn, ed., *Philonis Alexandrini opera quae supersunt* V (Berlin, 1906).
Translation adapted from F.H. Colson, tr., *Philo* VII (LCL, 1937).

ἀναγέγραπταί τις ἐν τοῖς νόμοις τὸ καλὸν τοῦτο τόλμημα τολμήσας. ἐπειδὴ γὰρ ἐθεάσατό τινας ἀλλοφύλοις συνόντας γυναιξὶ καὶ ἕνεκα τῶν πρὸς αὐτὰς φίλτρων ἀλογοῦντας μὲν τῶν πατρίων, τελουμένους δὲ τὰς μυθικὰς τελετάς, ἕνα τὸν ἔξαρχον καὶ ἡγεμόνα τῆς παρανομίας καταθαρροῦντα ἤδη παρεπιδείκνυσθαι δημοσίᾳ τὸ ἀνοσιούργημα καὶ θυσίας ἀγάλμασι καὶ ξοάνοις ἀθύτους φανερῶς ἐπιτελοῦντα παρόντος ἅπαντος τοῦ πλήθους ἐνθουσιῶν, ἀνείρξας τοὺς παρ' ἑκάτερα ἐπὶ τὴν θέαν ἠθροισμένους, οὐδὲν εὐλαβηθεὶς ἀναιρεῖ σὺν τῇ γυναικί, τὸν μὲν ἕνεκα τῆς εὐμαθείας <τῶν> ἃ λυσιτελὲς ἀπομανθάνειν, τὴν δ' ὅτι διδάσκαλος κακῶν ἐγένετο.

There is recorded in the Laws the example of one who acted with this admirable courage. He had seen some persons consorting with foreign women and through the attraction of their love-charms spurning their ancestral customs and seeking admission to the rites of a fabulous religion. One in particular he saw, the chief ringleader of the backsliding, who had the audacity to exhibit his unholy conduct in public and was openly offering sacrifices that were not to be sacrificed, to *agalmata* and *xoana* in the presence of the whole people. So, seized with inspired fury, keeping back the throng of spectators on either side, he slew without a qualm him and her, the man because he listened to the lessons which it were a gain to unlearn, the woman because she had been the instructor in wickedness.

295

Philo Judaeus, *De virtutibus* 221 I B.C.–A.D. I

Text: L. Cohn, ed., *Philonis Alexandrini opera quae supersunt* V (Berlin, 1906).

Translation adapted from F.H. Colson, tr., *Philo* VIII (LCL, 1939).

Θάμαρ ἦν τῶν ἀπὸ τῆς Παλαιστίνης Συρίας γύναιον, ἐν οἰκίᾳ καὶ πόλει τραφὲν πολυθέῳ γεμούσῃ ξοάνων καὶ ἀγαλμάτων καὶ συνόλως ἀφιδρυμάτων.

Tamar was a woman from Palestinian Syria, who had grown up in a house and a city with many gods and full of *xoana* and *agalmata* and *aphidrumata* in general.

296

Philo Judaeus, *De vita contemplativa* 7 I B.C.–A.D. I

Text: L. Cohn and S. Reiter, eds., *Philonis Alexandrini opera quae supersunt* VI (Berlin, 1915).

Translation adapted from F.H. Colson, tr., *Philo* IX (LCL, 1941).

ἀλλὰ τοὺς τὰ ξόανα καὶ ἀγάλματα; ὧν αἱ οὐσίαι λίθοι καὶ ξύλα, τὰ μέχρι πρὸ μικροῦ τελείως ἄμορφα, λιθοτόμων καὶ δρυοτόμων τῆς συμφυΐας αὐτὰ διακοψάντων, ὧν τὰ ἀδελφὰ μέρη καὶ συγγενῆ λουτροφόροι γεγόνασι καὶ ποδόνιπτρα καὶ ἄλλα ἄττα τῶν ἀτιμοτέρων, ἃ πρὸς τὰς ἐν σκότῳ χρείας ὑπηρετεῖ μᾶλλον ἢ τὰς ἐν φωτί.

But [what about] those [who honor] *xoana* and *agalmata*? Of which the true beings are stones and stocks, which, up until a short time ago, were completely formless, with quarrymen and woodcutters cutting them apart from their congenital material; their sibling parts became waterpots and footbaths and some other less honorable receptacles that serve for use in the dark rather than the light.

297

Philo Judaeus, *De vita Mosis* 1.298 I B.C.–A.D. I

Text: L. Cohn, ed., *Philonis Alexandrini opera quae supersunt* IV (Berlin, 1902).

Translation adapted from F.H. Colson, tr., *Philo* VI (LCL, 1935).

πρὸς δὲ τὸν οὕτω διακείμενον ἐραστὴν λεγέτω φρυαττομένη τις τῶν ἐπὶ τὴν θήραν ἀλειφομένων· "οὐ θέμις ὁμιλίας σοι τῆς ἐμῆς ἀπολαῦσαι, πρὶν ἂν ἐκδιαιτηθῇς μὲν τὰ πάτρια, μεταβαλὼν δὲ τιμήσῃς ἅπερ ἐγώ. πίστις δέ μοι τῆς βεβαίου μεταβολῆς γένοιτ' ἂν ἀρίδηλος, ἢν ἐθελήσῃς μετασχεῖν τῶν αὐτῶν σπονδῶν τε καὶ θυσιῶν, ἃς ἀγάλμασι καὶ ξοάνοις καὶ τοῖς λοιποῖς ἀφιδρύμασιν ἐπιτελοῦμεν."

To the lover who is thus disposed, let some haughty one of those who are now in training for the [man-] hunt, say, "It is not permitted for you to take advantage of my company before you turn away from your ancestral customs, and turn to honor the things I do. The proof of the sincerity of your conversion would be clear to me, if you were willing to take part in the libations and sacrifices, which we celebrate for the *agalmata* and *xoana* and the rest of the *aphidrumata*."

298

Philo Judaeus, *De vita Mosis* 2.205 I B.C.–A.D. I
Text: L. Cohn, ed., *Philonis Alexandrini opera quae supersunt* IV (Berlin, 1902).
Translation adapted from F.H. Colson, tr., *Philo* VI (LCL, 1935).

ἀλλ' ὡς ἔοικε "θεοῦ" τὰ νῦν οὐχὶ τοῦ πρώτου καὶ γεννητοῦ τῶν ὅλων ἀλλὰ τῶν ἐν ταῖς πόλεσι μέμνηται· ψευδώνυμοι δ' εἰσὶ γραφέων καὶ πλαστῶν τέχναις δημιουργούμενοι· ξοάνων γὰρ καὶ ἀγαλμάτων καὶ τοιουτοτρόπων ἀφιδρυμάτων ἡ οἰκουμένη μεστὴ γέγονεν, ὧν τῆς βλασφημίας ἀνέχειν ἀναγκαῖον, ἵνα μηδεὶς ἐθίζηται τῶν Μωυσέως *γνωρίμων συνόλως θεοῦ προσρήσεως ἀλογεῖν· ἀξιονικοτάτη γὰρ καὶ ἀξιέραστος ἡ κλῆσις.*

But it seems that he means by "god" now not things relating to the first God and begetter of all, but to the gods in the cities; they are falsely named, having been worked by the arts of painters and modellers; for the inhabited world is full of *xoana* and *agalmata* and such *aphidrumata*, from blasphemy of which it is necessary to refrain, so that no one of Moses' disciples becomes accustomed to pay no regard to the name of God in general; for the name is most worthy of preference and love.

Philochorus IV B.C.
See Sch. Euripides, *Hippolytus* 73 [87].

299

Philostratos, *Vita Apollonii* 6.4 c. A.D. 220
Text: C.L. Kayser, ed., *Flavii Philostrati opera* 1 (Leipzig, 1870).
Translation adapted from C.P. Jones, tr., and G.W. Bowersock, ed., *Philostratus. Life of Apollonius* (Penguin, 1970).

οἱ δ', ἐπειδὴ μακροβιώτατοι ἀνθρώπων εἰσίν, ὀλοφύρονται τὸν Μέμνονα ὡς κομιδῇ νέον καὶ ὅσα ἐπὶ ἀώρῳ κλαίουσι, τὸ δὲ χωρίον, ἐν ᾧ ἵδρυται, φασὶ μὲν προσεοικέναι ἀγορᾷ ἀρχαίᾳ, οἷαι τῶν ἀγορῶν ἐν πόλεσί ποτε οἰκηθείσαις λείπονται στηλῶν παρεχόμεναι τρύφη καὶ τειχῶν ἴχνη καὶ θάκους καὶ φλιὰς ἑρμῶν τε ἀγάλματα, τὰ μὲν ὑπὸ χειρῶν διεφθορότα, τὰ δὲ ὑπὸ χρόνου. τὸ δὲ ἄγαλμα τετράφθαι πρὸς ἀκτῖνα μήπω γενειάσκον, λίθου δὲ εἶναι μέλανος, ξυμβεβηκέναι δὲ τὼ πόδε ἄμφω κατὰ τὴν ἀγαλματοποιίαν τὴν ἐπὶ Δαιδάλου καὶ τὰς χεῖρας ἀπερείδειν ὀρθὰς ἐς τὸν θᾶκον, καθῆσθαι γὰρ ἐν ὁρμῇ τοῦ ὑπανίστασθαι. τὸ δὲ σχῆμα τοῦτο καὶ τὸν τῶν ὀφθαλμῶν νοῦν καὶ ὁπόσα τοῦ στόματος ὡς φθεγξομένου ᾄδουσι, τὸν μὲν ἄλλον χρόνον ἧττον θαυμάσαι φασίν, οὔπω γὰρ ἐνεργὰ φαίνεσθαι, προσβαλούσης δὲ τὸ ἄγαλμα τῆς ἀκτῖνος, τουτὶ δὲ γίγνεσθαι περὶ ἡλίου ἐπιτολάς, μὴ κατασχεῖν τὸ θαῦμα, φθέγξασθαι μὲν γὰρ παραχρῆμα τῆς ἀκτῖνος ἐλθούσης αὐτῷ ἐπὶ στόμα, φαιδροὺς δὲ ἱστάναι τοὺς ὀφθαλμοὺς δόξαι πρὸς τὸ θῶς, οἷα τῶν ἀνθρώπων οἱ εὐήλιοι.

[The Ethiopians] are the longest-lived people on earth; they mourn for Memnon as one who died very young, and they weep over his premature death. The place where [his statue] is set up apparently resembles an ancient market-place, like the deserted market-places in cities inhabited long ago, which have shattered monuments, crumbling walls, seats, doorways, and ornamental herms that have been destroyed either by human agency or by time. The *agalma* faces the morning sun, has no beard, is of black stone, has both feet closed together in the fashion of *agalma*-making in the time of Daedalus, and the hands pressed down on the throne, for it sits in readiness for getting up. This position, the look in its eyes, and the famous expression of its lips, as if it was about to speak, seem not to have impressed the party most of the time, because they still looked lifeless. But when the sun's ray hit the *agalma* at sunrise, they could not withhold their amazement: it made a sound the moment the ray fell on its lips, and its eyes appeared to gaze cheerfully at the light, as the eyes of sunbathers do.

Phlegon of Tralles, *Compilation of Olympic Victors and Chronicles* A.D. II
See Photius, *Bibliotheca* 97 [**301**].

300

Phlegon of Tralles, *De mirabilibus* X A.D. II
Text: F. Jacoby, ed., *Die Fragmente der griechischen Historiker* 257 F 36, p. 1179.22–26; Oracle B, lines 50–70.
Translation of oracle adapted from W. Den Boer, *Private Morality in Greece and Rome. Some Historical Aspects* (Leiden, 1979) 105–106.

Ἐγεννήθη καὶ ἐπὶ Ῥώμης ἀνδρόγονος ἄρχοντος Ἀθήνσιν Ἰάσονος, ὑπατευόντων ἐν Ῥώμῃ Μάρκου Πλα<υ>τίου [καὶ Σέξτου Καρμινίου] Ὑψαίου καὶ Μάρκου Φουλβίου Φλάκκου. δι' ἣν αἰτίαν ἡ σύγκλητος ἐκέλευσεν τοὺς ἱερομνήμονας ἀναγνῶναι τοὺς Σιβύλλης χρησμούς. καὶ ἐξηγήσαντο τοὺς χρησμούς. εἰσὶν δὲ οἱ χρησμοὶ οἵδε·

Νοστήσας δ' ἀπὸ τοῦ βασιλίδα πότνιαν Ἥρην
Ἀργὴν βοῦν θύων πατρίοισι νόμοισι κατ' αἶσαν·
Ὑμνεῖν <δ'> αἵ κε γένει προφερέστεραι ὧσ' ἐνὶ λαοῖς

* * *

Καὶ νήσων ναέται τὴν ἀντιπάλων ὅτ' ἂν αἶαν
Οὐ δόλῳ, ἀλλὰ βίᾳ Κυμαίδα πρόφρονες αὖτε
Νάσσωνται, σεμνῆς βασιληίδος οἵδε τιθέντων
Ἐν πατρίοισι νόμοις Ἥρας ξόανόν τε καὶ οἶκον.
Ἵξει δ', ἂν μύθοισιν ἐμοῖς τάδε πάντα πίθησαι
Σεμνοτάτην βασίλισσαν ἐπελθὼν ἐν θυσίαισιν
Νήφαλα † κεν ῥέξας, ὅσαι ἡμέραι εἴσ' ἐνιαυτοῦ,
Ἐν πολλῷ χρόνῳ αὖ τόδ' ἐφ' ὕστερον, οὐκ ἔτ' ἐπ' αὐτοῖς.
Ὅς κε τάδε ῥέξῃ, κείνου κράτος ἔσσεται αἰεί·
Νηφαλίμων ἀρνῶν τε ταμὼν χθονίοις τάδε ῥέξον.
Ἦμος ἂν ἤδη ἔχῃς μεγάλ' Ἥρης οἰκί' ἀπάντῃ,
Ξεστά θ' ὅτ' ἂν ξόαν' ᾖσι καὶ τἆλλ' ὅσ' ἔλεξα, σάφ' ἴ<σθι>,
Ἐν πετάλοισιν ἐμοῖς (ὑπὸ κερκίδος ἀμφὶ καλύπτραν
Ἱμέρτ' ὅσσ' ἔβαλον γλαυκῆς ἐλάας πολυκάρπου
Ἀγλαὰ φύλλα λαβοῦσα) λύσιν κακοῦ· ἦμος ἂν ἔλθῃ
Ὕμμι χρόνος μάλα κεῖνος, ἐν ᾧ ποτε τἆλλα νεόγν' ᾖ,
Τρὼς δῆτ' ἐκλύσει σε κακῶν, ἅμα δ' Ἑλλάδος ἐκ γῆς.

And there was also born in Rome an androgyne, when Iason was archon in Athens, when Marcus Plautius and Sextus Carminius . . . Hypsaios and Marcus Fulvius Flaccus were consuls in Rome; for this reason the Senate ordered the priests to read the Sibylline oracles, and they interpreted the oracles. These are the oracles:

After returning from him [Apollo Paieon] [the procession must pray] to the queen, mighty Hera, offering a white cow according to the customs of the fathers, as befitting. And they [*sc.* the girls] must sing a song, they who are the most distinguished among the people. [Two lines missing.] Just as the inhabitants of the islands [have done], when they once again occupied the Cumaean land of their opponents, so too must these, with due regard for the ancestral customs, dedicate a *xoanon* and found an *oikos* for the venerable queen Hera. This [disaster] will not come in your own lifetime, but much later, if you have obeyed my words in all these things, after having approached the most venerable queen in sacrificial procession and having made libations without wine every day of the year. The man who does this,

his strength will last forever. Gradually making these sacrifices of drink and rams to chthonic gods, you must do this. If, from now on, you keep *oikia* of Hera that are in every respect great and if the *xoana* are carved, then, on the basis of my leaves through the medium of fate I covered my spell-binding eyes with a veil after I had taken the glittering leaves of the fruit-bearing olive—redemption from disaster. If indeed the time comes for you when all portents take place suddenly, a Trojan will redeem you from all disasters and at the same time from Greece [help will come].

Phoronis ? VI B.C.
See Clement of Alexandria, *Stromateis* 1.164.2 [**47**].

301
Photius, *Bibliotheca* 97 A.D. IX
(= Phlegon of Tralles, *Compilation of Olympic Victors and Chronicles.*)
Text: I. Bekker, ed., *Photii Bibliotheca* I (Berlin, 1824) 84 b 30–33.

καὶ Ἀθηνόδωρος πειρατὴς ἐξανδραποδισάμενος Δηλίους τὰ τῶν λεγομένων θεῶν ξόανα διελυμήνατο· Γάϊος δὲ Τριάριος τὰ λελωβημένα τῆς πόλεως ἐπισκευάσας ἐτείχισε τὴν Δῆλον.

The pirate Athenodorus enslaved the people of Delos and insulted the *xoana* of the so-called gods; but Gaius Triarius having repaired the damaged parts of the city, fortified the island.

302
Photius, *Bibliotheca* 271 A.D. IX
(= Asterius of Amasea, *Sermons.*)
Text: I. Bekker, ed., *Photii Bibliotheca* I (Berlin, 1824) 505 b 5–10.

καταμάθωμεν τῆς ἰαθείσης γυναικὸς τὸ εὐχάριστον. τῆς γὰρ Πενεάδος οὔσα πολιτείας (πολίχνη δὲ αὕτη τῆς Παλαιστίνης) ἀγάλματι χαλκῷ τὸν εὐεργέτην ἐτίμησε, τοῦτο γέρας οὐκ ἀνάξιον οἰηθεῖσα τῆς χάριτος. καὶ χρόνος πολὺς ἐτήρει τὸ ξόανον. . . .

Let us examine the gratitude of the woman who was saved. When Peneades was a polity (it was a small town in Palestine) it honored its benefactor with a bronze *agalma*, having thought this honor not unworthy of the favor. And age pierced the *xoanon*. . . .

303
Photius, *Bibliotheca* 276 A.D. IX
(= Nilus of Ancyra, *On Easter.*)
Text: I. Bekker, ed., *Photii Bibliotheca* I (Berlin, 1824) 514 a 21–24; b 7–9.

ὢ τέχνης ἐξ ὕδατος γλυφούσης ἀγάλματα! καὶ οὐ τοῦτο μόνον παρέχεται τὸ παράδοξον, ὅτι γλύφει τὸ ὕδωρ εἰς ἔμψυχον ξόανον, ἀλλ' ὅτι καὶ κυματουμένην τὴν γονὴν ἔνδον τεκτονεύει.

ὅταν γὰρ ἴδω τεχνίτην ἐξ ὕδατος πηγνύμενον ξόανα, ὀξύτερον αὐτὸν τοὺς ἐκ γῆς ἀναπλάττειν ἀνδριάντας πιστεύω.

O *agalmata* of the craft of carving from water! And is not this alone the marvel, that He carved water into a living *xoanon*, but also that He fashions the seed that it made pregnant within?

For whenever I see the Craftsman forming *xoana* from water, I believe Him to be more dazzling than those who model from earth.

304

Photius, *Bibliotheca* 277 A.D. IX

(= John Chrysostom, *Sermons.*)

Text: I. Bekker, ed., *Photii Bibliotheca* I (Berlin, 1824) 522 a 26–41.

ὅτι φασὶν οἱ ἑλληνισταὶ καὶ τὸ ἰουδαΐζον, τί κομπάζει Παῦλος λέγων, "τὰ ἀρχαῖα παρῆλθεν, ἰδοὺ" γέγονε καινὰ τὰ πάντα· εἴ τις ἐν Χριστῷ, "καινὴ κτίσις." ἐγὼ γάρ, φησί, καινὸν οὐδὲν βλέπω. οὐ γὰρ ἔχεις ὀφθαλμοὺς, ἵνα ἴδῃς ταῦτα. δεῦρο, καὶ ποιήσω σοι ὀφθαλμούς. καὶ ὁρᾷς, καὶ σὺ ποιεῖς ὀφθαλμούς; ναί. καὶ δημιουργὸς εἶ; καὶ πάνυ. σὺ ἀπονενόησαι; οὐχί. οὐκοῦν ποίησον ὀφθαλμοὺς τοῦ σώματος; οὐκ, ἀλλὰ τὸ μεῖζον, τῆς διανοίας. καὶ ποιεῖς μοι ὀφθαλμούς; μάλιστα. οὐ γὰρ ἔχω; οὐχί. σὺ δὲ ἔχεις; ναί. πῶς, εἰπέ μοι; ὅταν ἀπέλθῃς εἰς ναόν, καὶ ἴδῃς ἐκεῖ ξόανον γυμνόν, λίθον ἄφωνον, καὶ εἴπῃς οὗτος ὁ Θεός ἐστιν, ἆρα ὀφθαλμοὺς ἔχεις; μὴ γὰρ ὄφελός τι τῶν ἔξωθεν ὀφθαλμῶν, τῶν ἔνδοθεν πεπηρωμένων; ὁρᾷς ὅτι χρείαν ἔχεις ἵνα ποιήσω σοι ὀφθαλμούς, ὥστε τὸν λίθον σε ἰδεῖν λίθον καὶ τὸ ξύλον ξύλον.

That the Greek-speaking [Jews] say too about being Jewish, what Paul boasts, saying, "The old things have passed away, behold," everything has been born new, if someone [is born] in Christ, "a new foundation."

—For, he says, I see nothing new.

—For you do not have eyes, so that you can see these things. Come, and I shall make eyes for you.

—Do you pray accordingly, and make eyes?

—Yes.

—And you are a craftsman?

—Yes, very much so.

—Have you lost all sense?

—No.

—Well, then, do you make eyes of the body?

—No, but something better, eyes of the mind.
—And you will make eyes for me?
—Surely.
—For I do not have them?
—No.
—But you have [them]?
—Yes.
—Tell me, How?
—When you go into a *naos*, and you see there a naked *xoanon*, a voiceless stone, and you say that this is God, do you then have eyes? For what benefit are external eyes, when the internal eyes are defective? You will see that you have need for me to make eyes for you, in order to see that a stone [is] a stone, and a stock, a stock.

305

Photius, *Lexicon s.v. ξόανον* A.D. IX
Text: S.A. Naber, ed., *Photii Patriarchae Lexicon* I (Leiden, 1864) 455.

ξόανον· ἄγαλμα, εἴδωλον, ζῴδιον, ἀνδριάς.

Xoanon: agalma, eidolon, zoidion, andrias.

306

Photius, *Lexicon s.v. οἱ νομοφύλακες τίνες* A.D. IX
Text: S.A. Naber, ed., *Photii Patriarchae Lexicon* II (Leiden, 1865) 7.

οἱ νομοφύλακες τίνες· ἔδοξέ τισι τοὺς αὐτοὺς εἶναι τοῖς θεσμοθέταις, ἀλλ' οὐκ ἔστιν οὕτως· οἱ μὲν γὰρ θεσμοθέται κατὰ τὰ πάτρια ἐστεφανωμένοι ἐπὶ τὸν Ἄρειον πάγον ἀνέβαινον· οἱ δὲ νομοφύλακες στροφίοις λευκοῖς ἐχρῶντο· καὶ ἐν ταῖς θέαις ἐπὶ θρόνων ἐκάθηντο καταντικρὺ τῶν ἐννέα ἀρχόντων καὶ τῇ Παλλάδι τὴν πομπὴν ἐκόσμουν, ὅτε κομίζοιτο τὸ ξόανον ἐπὶ τὴν θάλασσαν· ἠνάγκαζον δὲ καὶ τὰς ἀρχὰς χρῆσθαι τοῖς νόμοις καὶ ἐν ταῖς ἐκκλησίαις ἐκάθηντο μετὰ τῶν προέδρων κωλύοντες ψηφίζειν, εἴ τι παράνομον αὐτοῖς εἶναι δόξειεν ἢ ἀσύμφορον τῇ πόλει.

Those who are called *nomophylakes*: Some think that these are the same as the *Thesmothetai*, but this is not so; for the *Thesmothetai*, according to the ancestral customs, having been crowned, go up onto the Areopagus; but the *Nomophylakes* used white headbands; and during performances they sat on seats exactly opposite the nine archons and they arranged the procession for Pallas, when the *xoanon* was carried to the sea; and they forced the magistrates to administer the laws and during assemblies they sat behind the *proedria*, preventing a motion from being carried, if something seemed to them to be against the law or inconvenient for the city.

307

Photius, *Lexicon s.v.* οὐδὲν ἱερόν A.D. IX
Text: S.A. Naber, ed., *Photii Patriarchae Lexicon* II (Leiden, 1865) 34.

οὐδὲν ἱερόν· Ἡρακλῆς εἶπεν Ἀδώνιδος ἰδὼν ξόανον· ὡς τῶν εὐεργετησάντων τοὺς ἀνθρώπους μόνων οἰφειλόντων τιμᾶσθαι· ἢ ὅτι οἱ καταφυγόντες εἰς αὐτὸ δοῦλοι ἄδικειν οὐκ εἶχον.

Nothing sacred: Heracles, seeing the *xoanon* of Adonis, said: how only those men are honored who have done beneficial or helpful things; or else, because slaves who took refuge at it did not receive amnesty.

308

Plato, *Euthyphro* 11 B–E IV B.C.
Text: J. Burnet, ed., *Platonis opera* I (Oxford, 1900; repr. 1967).
Translation adapted from H.N. Fowler, tr., *Plato* I (LCL, 1914; repr. 1967).

[ΕΥΘ.] *Ἀλλ', ὦ Σώκρατες, οὐκ ἔχω ἔγωγε ὅπως σοι εἴπω ὃ νοῶ· περιέρχεται γάρ πως ἡμῖν ἀεὶ ὃ ἂν προθώμεθα καὶ οὐκ ἐθέλει μένειν ὅπου ἂν ἱδρυσώμεθα αὐτό.*
[ΣΩ.] *Τοῦ ἡμετέρου προγόνου, ὦ Εὐθύφρων, ἔοικεν εἶναι Δαιδάλου τὰ ὑπὸ σοῦ λεγόμενα. καὶ εἰ μὲν αὐτὰ ἐγὼ ἔλεγον καὶ ἐτιθέμην, ἴσως ἄν με ἐπέσκωπτες ὡς ἄρα καὶ ἐμοὶ κατὰ τὴν ἐκείνου συγγένειαν τὰ ἐν τοῖς λόγοις ἔργα ἀποδιδράσκει καὶ οὐκ ἐθέλει μένειν ὅπου ἄν τις αὐτὰ θῇ· νῦν δὲ σαὶ γὰρ αἱ ὑποθέσεις εἰσίν. ἄλλου δή τινος δεῖ σκώμματος· οὐ γὰρ ἐθέλουσι σοὶ μένειν, ὡς καὶ αὐτῷ σοι δοκεῖ.*
[ΕΥΘ.] *Ἐμοὶ δὲ δοκεῖ σχεδόν τι τοῦ αὐτοῦ σκώμματος, ὦ Σώκρατες, δεῖσθαι τὰ λεγόμενα· τὸ γὰρ περιιέναι αὐτοῖς τοῦτο καὶ μὴ μένειν ἐν τῷ αὐτῷ οὐκ ἐγώ εἰμι ὁ ἐντιθείς, ἀλλὰ σύ μοι δοκεῖς ὁ Δαίδαλος, ἐπεὶ ἐμοῦ γε ἕνεκα ἔμενεν ἂν ταῦτα οὕτως.*
[ΣΩ.] *Κινδυνεύω ἄρα, ὦ ἑταῖρε, ἐκείνου τοῦ ἀνδρὸς δεινότερος γεγονέναι τὴν τέχνην τοσούτῳ, ὅσῳ ὁ μὲν τὰ αὑτοῦ μόνα ἐποίει οὐ μένοντα, ἐγὼ δὲ πρὸς τοῖς ἐμαυτοῦ, ὡς ἔοικε, καὶ τὰ ἀλλότρια. καὶ δῆτα τοῦτό μοι τῆς τέχνης ἐστὶ κομψότατον, ὅτι ἄκων εἰμὶ σοφός· ἐβουλόμην γὰρ ἄν μοι τοὺς λόγους μένειν καὶ ἀκινήτως ἱδρῦσθαι μᾶλλον ἢ πρὸς τῇ Δαιδάλου σοφίᾳ τὰ Ταντάλου χρήματα γενέσθαι. καὶ τούτων μὲν ἅδην· ἐπειδὴ δέ μοι δοκεῖς σὺ τρυφᾶν, αὐτός σοι συμπροθυμήσομαι [δεῖξαι] ὅπως ἄν με διδάξῃς περὶ τοῦ ὁσίου. καὶ μὴ προαποκάμῃς· ἰδὲ γὰρ εἰ οὐκ ἀναγκαῖόν σοι δοκεῖ δίκαιον εἶναι πᾶν τὸ ὅσιον.*

EUTHYPHRO. But, Socrates, I do not know how to say what I mean. For whatever statement we advance, somehow or other it moves about and won't stay where we put it.

SOCRATES. Your statements, Euthyphro, are like works of my ancestor Daedalus, and if I were the one who made or advanced them, you might equally laugh at me and say that on account of my relationship to him my works in words run away and won't stay where anyone puts them. But now—well, the statements are yours; so some other jest is demanded; for they won't stay fixed, as you yourself see.
EUTHYPHRO. I think the jest does very well as it is; for I am not the one who makes these statements move about and not stay in the same place, but you are the Daedalus; for they would have stayed, so far as I am concerned.
SOCRATES. Apparently then, my friend, I am a more clever artist than Daedalus, inasmuch as he made only his own works move, whereas I, as it seems, give motion to the works of others as well as to my own. And the most exquisite thing about my art is that I am clever against my will; for I would rather have my words stay fixed and stable than possess the wisdom of Daedalus and the wealth of Tantalus besides. But enough of this. Since you seem to be indolent, I will aid you myself, so that you may instruct me about holiness. And do not give it up beforehand. Just see whether you do not think that everything that is holy is right.

309
Sch. Plato, *Euthyphro* 11 C (Arethas) A.D. IX
Text: W.C. Greene, ed., *Scholia Platonica* (Haverford, 1938).

Δαιδάλου.
Δαιδάλου, ὡς ἔοικεν, τῶν τῆς γονῆς ὀχετῶν Σωκράτης ἀπόρροια. ταύτῃ μοι δοκῶ κατὰ τὸ συγγενὲς λιθοξοϊκὴν ἀσκεῖσθαι Σωκράτη τέως, εἰ μὴ Ἀρχέλαος ὁ φιλόσοφος ἀπὸ ταύτης ἀναστήσας τῆς τέχνης τὸν ἄνδρα φιλοσοφίᾳ ἠγάγετο· ἐτεκμήρατο γὰρ τὸ τῆς ψυχῆς ἐντρεχὲς καὶ δραστήριον καὶ πρὸς φιλοσοφίαν †ὑπτίως ἔχον, οἷς πρὸς τοὺς ὁμοτέχνους ἀντέλεγεν στερόμενος τῶν μισθῶν. Δαίδαλος δὲ Ἀθηναῖος ἦν τῶν πώποτε ἀνδριαντοποιῶν περιφανέστατος. πρῶτος δὲ καὶ περισκελὲς ἄγαλμα ἐσχημάτισεν, τῶν πρὸ ἐκείνου κατὰ ταὐτὸ συμβεβληκότα τὼ πόδε τὰ βρέτη ἐργαζομένων. ἀφ᾽ οὗ δὴ καὶ ὁ τοῦ περιιέναι καὶ κινεῖσθαι τὰ φιλοτεχνήματα αὐτοῦ ὑπὸ τῶν πολλῶν ἀνάκειται λόγος αὐτῷ, ὃν καὶ νῦν Σωκράτης παίζων Εὐθύφρονα προάγει.

Socrates, as it seems, was the outpouring of the channels of Daedalus' generative organs. By this, I think, [is meant that] Socrates, as if he were his kinsman, for a time practiced stonecutting, except that Archelaus the philosopher made him give up and leave this art, and carried the man off by philosophy; for the readiness of the soul was predestined, and the activity . . . towards philosophy, by which, lacking wages, he spoke out against his fellow-workmen. Daedalus the Athenian was the most celebrated ever of *andrias*-makers. And he was the first to fashion an *agalma* with the feet apart, those before him having made *brete* whose two feet were joined together. And indeed from this the saying about him is offered by many people, that his masterpieces go about and move, which even now Socrates, jokingly, brings up to Euthyphro.

310

Plato, *Meno* 97 C–E IV B.C.
Text: J. Burnet, ed., *Platonis opera* III (Oxford, 1903; repr. 1967).
Translation: W.R.M. Lamb, tr., *Plato* IV (LCL, 1952).

[ΣΩ.] Οὐδὲν ἄρα ἧττον ὠφέλιμόν ἐστιν ὀρθὴ δόξα ἐπιστήμης.
[MEN.] Τοσούτῳ γε, ὦ Σώκρατες, ὅτι ὁ μὲν τὴν ἐπιστήμην ἔχων ἀεὶ ἂν ἐπιτυγχάνοι, ὁ δὲ τὴν ὀρθὴν δόξαν τοτὲ μὲν ἂν τυγχάνοι, τοτὲ δ' οὔ.
[ΣΩ.] Πῶς λέγεις; ὁ ἀεὶ ἔχων ὀρθὴν δόξαν οὐκ ἀεὶ ἂν τυγχάνοι, ἕωσπερ ὀρθὰ δοξάζοι;
[MEN.] Ἀνάγκη μοι φαίνεται· ὥστε θαυμάζω, ὦ Σώκρατες, τούτου οὕτως ἔχοντος, ὅτι δή ποτε πολὺ τιμιωτέρα ἡ ἐπιστήμη τῆς ὀρθῆς δόξης, καὶ δι' ὅτι τὸ μὲν ἕτερον, τὸ δὲ ἕτερόν ἐστιν αὐτῶν.
[ΣΩ.] Οἶσθα οὖν δι' ὅτι θαυμάζεις, ἢ ἐγώ σοι εἴπω;
[MEN.] Πάνυ γ' εἰπέ.
[ΣΩ.] Ὅτι τοῖς Δαιδάλου ἀγάλμασιν οὐ προσέσχηκας τὸν νοῦν· ἴσως δὲ οὐδ' ἔστιν παρ' ὑμῖν.
[MEN.] Πρὸς τί δὲ δὴ τοῦτο λέγεις;
[ΣΩ.] Ὅτι καὶ ταῦτα, ἐὰν μὲν μὴ δεδεμένα ᾖ, ἀποδιδράσκει καὶ δραπετεύει, ἐὰν δὲ δεδεμένα, παραμένει.
[MEN.] Τί οὖν δή;
[ΣΩ.] Τῶν ἐκείνου ποιημάτων λελυμένον μὲν ἐκτῆσθαι οὐ πολλῆς τινος ἄξιόν ἐστι τιμῆς, ὥσπερ δραπέτην ἄνθρωπον—οὐ γὰρ παραμένει—δεδεμένον δὲ πολλοῦ ἄξιον· πάνυ γὰρ καλὰ τὰ ἔργα ἐστίν. πρὸς τί οὖν δὴ λέγω ταῦτα; πρὸς τὰς δόξας τὰς ἀληθεῖς.

SOCRATES. Then right opinion is just as useful as knowledge.
MENO. With this difference, Socrates, that he who has knowledge always hits on the right way, whereas he who has the right opinion will sometimes do so, but sometimes not.
SOCRATES. How do you mean? Will not he who always has right opinion always be right, so long as he opines rightly?
MENO. It appears to me that he must; and therefore I wonder, Socrates, this being the case, that knowledge should ever be prized more than right opinion, and why they should be two distinct and separate things.
SOCRATES. Well, do you know why it is that you wonder, or shall I tell you?

MENO. Please tell me.
SOCRATES. It is because you have not observed with attention the images [*agalmata*] of Daedalus. But perhaps there are none in your country.
MENO. What is the point of your remark?
SOCRATES. That if they are not fastened up they play truant and run away; but, if fastened, they stay where they are.
MENO. Well, what of that?
SOCRATES. To possess one of his works which is let loose does not count for much in value; it will not stay with you any more than a runaway slave; but when fastened up it is worth a great deal, for his productions are very fine things. And to what am I referring in all this? To true opinions.

311
Sch. Plato, *Meno* 97 D
Text: W.C. Greene, ed., *Scholia Platonica* (Haverford, 1938).

δεδεμένα.
τῶν πάλαι δημιουργῶν πλαττόντων τὰ ζῷα συμμεμυκότας ἔχοντα τοὺς ὀφθαλμοὺς καὶ οὐ διεστηκότας τοὺς πόδας, ἀλλ' ἑστῶτα σύμποδα, Δαίδαλος ἄριστος ἀγαλματοποιὸς ἐπιγεγονὼς πρῶτος ἀναπετάννυσί τε τὰ τούτων βλέφαρα, ὡς δόξαι βλέπειν αὐτά, καὶ τοὺς πόδας, ὡς νομίσαι βαδίζειν, διίστησιν· καὶ διὰ τοῦτο δεδέσθαι, ἵνα μὴ φύγοιεν, ὡς δῆθεν ἐμψύχων ἤδη γεγονότων αὐτῶν.

In ancient times craftsmen shaped *zoia* that had closed-up eyes and feet that were not separated, but were set up with their feet together. Daedalus, the finest *agalma*-maker, coming along, was the first who spread apart their eyelids, so that they seemed to see, and set their feet apart, so that they were held to walk; and because of this they were tied, so that they might not flee; since in truth they had now become alive.

312
Pliny, *Historia Naturalis* 35.15–16 A.D. I
Text and translation: K. Jex-Blake and E. Sellers, *The Elder Pliny's Chapters on the History of Art* (London, 1896).

De picturae initiis incerta nec instituti operis quaestio est. Aegyptii sex milibus annorum aput ipsos inventam priusquam in Graeciam transiret adfirmant vana praedicatione, ut palam est, Graeci autem alii Sicyone alii apud Corinthios repertam, omnes umbra hominis lineis circumducta, itaque primam talem, secundam singulis coloribus et monochromaton dictam postquam operosior inventa erat, duratque talis etiam nunc. inventam liniarem a Philocle Aegyptio vel Cleanthe Corinthio primi exercuere Aridices Corinthius et Telephanes Sicyonius, sine ullo etiamnum hi colore, iam tamen spargentes linias intus. ideo et quos pingerent adscribere institutum. primus invenit eas colore testae, ut ferunt, tritae, Ecphantus Corinthius. hunc eodem nomine alium fuisse quam tradit Cornelius Nepos secutum in Italiam Damaratum, Tarquinii Prisci regis Romani patrem fugientem a Corintho tyranni iniurias Cypseli, mox docebimus.

The origin of painting is obscure, and hardly falls within the scope of this work. The claim of the Egyptians to have discovered the art six thousand years before it reached Greece is obviously an idle boast, while among the Greeks some say that it was first discovered at Sikyon, others at Corinth. All, however, agree that painting began with the outlining of a man's shadow; this was the first stage, in the second a single colour was employed, and after the discovery of more elaborate methods this style, which is still in vogue, received the name of monochrome.

The invention of linear drawing is attributed to Philokles of Egypt, or to Kleanthes of Corinth. The first to practise it were Arideikes of Corinth, and Telephanes of Sikyon, who still used no colour, though they had begun to give the inner markings, and from this went on to add the names of the personages they painted. The invention of painting with colour made, it is said, from powdered potsherds, is due to Ekphantos of Corinth. I shall show presently that this Ekphantos is distinct from that namesake of his who, according to Cornelius Nepos, followed Damaratos, the father of Tarquin the Ancient, in his flight to Italy from Corinth to escape the insults of the tyrant Kypselos. . . .

313

Plutarch, *Alexander* 14.8–9 A.D. I–II

Text: K. Ziegler, ed., *Plutarchi vitae parallelae* II.2 (Leipzig, 1968).
Translation adapted from B. Perrin, tr., *Plutarch's Lives* VII (LCL, 1919).

Ἐπεὶ δ' ὥρμησε πρὸς τὴν στρατείαν, ἄλλα τ' ἐδόκει σημεῖα παρὰ τοῦ δαιμονίου γενέσθαι, καὶ τὸ περὶ Λείβηθρα τοῦ Ὀρφέως ξόανον (ἦν δὲ κυπαρίττινον) ἱδρῶτα πολὺν ὑπὸ τὰς ἡμέρας ἐκείνας ἀφῆκε. φοβουμένων δὲ πάντων τὸ σημεῖον, Ἀρίστανδρος ἐκέλευε θαρρεῖν, ὡς ἀοιδίμους καὶ περιβοήτους κατεργασόμενον πράξεις, αἳ πολὺν ἱδρῶτα καὶ πόνον ὑμνοῦσι ποιηταῖς καὶ μουσικοῖς παρέξουσι.

Moreover, when he set out upon his expedition, it appeared that there were many signs from heaven, and among them, the *xoanon* of Orpheus at Leibethra (it was made of cypress-wood) sweated profusely around the time of those days. Although everyone feared the sign, Aristander bade [Alexander] be of good cheer, assured that he was to perform deeds worthy of song and story, which would cost poets and musicians much toil and sweat to celebrate.

314

Plutarch, *Alexander* 24.5–8 A.D. I–II

Text: K. Ziegler, ed., *Plutarchi vitae parallelae* II.2 (Leipzig, 1968).

Translation adapted from B. Perrin, tr., *Plutarch's Lives* VII (LCL, 1919).

Τύρον δὲ πολιορκῶν ἑπτὰ μῆνας χώμασι καὶ μηχαναῖς καὶ τριήρεσι διακοσίαις ἐκ θαλάττης, ὄναρ εἶδε τὸν Ἡρακλέα δεξιούμενον αὐτὸν ἀπὸ τοῦ τείχους καὶ καλοῦντα. τῶν δὲ Τυρίων πολλοῖς κατὰ τοὺς ὕπνους ἔδοξεν ὁ Ἀπόλλων λέγειν, ὡς ἄπεισι πρὸς Ἀλέξανδρον· οὐ γὰρ ἀρέσκειν αὐτῷ τὰ πρασσόμενα κατὰ τὴν πόλιν. ἀλλ᾽ οὗτοι μὲν ὥσπερ ἄνθρωπον αὐτομολοῦντα πρὸς τοὺς πολεμίους ἐπ᾽ αὐτοφώρῳ τὸν θεὸν εἰληφότες, σειράς τε τῷ κολοσσῷ περιέβαλλον αὐτοῦ, καὶ καθήλουν πρὸς τὴν βάσιν, Ἀλεξανδριστὴν καλοῦντες.

But Tyre he besieged for seven months, with moles, and engines of war, and two hundred triremes by sea. During this siege he had a dream in which he saw Heracles stretching out his hand to him from the wall and calling him. And many of the Tyrians dreamed that Apollo told them he was going away to Alexander, since he was displeased at what was going on in the city. Whereupon, as if the god had been a common deserter caught in the act of going over to the enemy, they encircled his *kolossos* with cords and nailed it down to its base, calling him an Alexandrist.

315

Plutarch, *Apophthegmata Laconica* 232 C A.D. I–II

(= *Moralia* 232 C.)

Text: W. Nachstädt, W. Sieveking, and J.B. Titchener, eds., *Plutarchi Moralia* II.1 (Leipzig, 1971).

Translation adapted from F.C. Babbitt, tr., *Plutarch's Moralia* III (LCL, 1931).

Πυνθανομένου δέ τινος διὰ τί πάντα τὰ τῶν θεῶν ξόανα μεθ᾽ ὅπλων ἵδρυται παρ᾽ αὐτοῖς, 'ὅπως' ἔφη 'μήτε τὰ κατὰ τῶν ἀνθρώπων ὀνείδη λεγόμενα διὰ τὴν δειλίαν ἐπὶ τοὺς θεοὺς ἀναφέρωμεν, μήτε οἱ νέοι τοῖς θεοῖς ἀνόπλοι<ς> εὔχωνται.'

When someone inquired why all the *xoana* of the gods erected among them were equipped with weapons, he [Charillus] said, "So that we may not put upon the gods the reproaches which are spoken against men because of their cowardice, and so that the young men not pray to unarmed gods."

316

Plutarch, *Camillus* 6 A.D. I–II

Text: K. Ziegler, ed., *Plutarchi vitae parallelae* I.1 (Leipzig, 1960).

Translation adapted from B. Perrin, tr., *Plutarch's Lives* II (LCL, 1914).

Διαπορθήσας δὲ τὴν πόλιν, ἔγνω τὸ ἄγαλμα τῆς Ἥρας μεταφέρειν εἰς Ῥώμην ὥσπερ εὔξατο. καὶ συνελθόντων ἐπὶ τοῦτο τῶν τεχνιτῶν, ὁ μὲν ἔθυε καὶ προσηύχετο τῇ θεῷ δέχεσθαι τὴν προθυμίαν αὐτῶν καὶ εὐμενῆ γίνεσθαι σύνοικον τοῖς λαχοῦσι τὴν Ῥώμην θεοῖς, τὸ δ' ἄγαλμά φασιν ὑποφθεγξάμενον εἰπεῖν ὅτι καὶ βούλεται καὶ συγκαταινεῖ. Λίουιος δέ φησιν εὔχεσθαι μὲν τὸν Κάμιλλον ἁπτόμενον τῆς θεοῦ καὶ παρακαλεῖν, ἀποκρίνασθαι δέ τινας τῶν παρόντων ὅτι καὶ βούλεται καὶ συνακολουθεῖ προθύμως. οἱ δ' ἰσχυριζόμενοι καὶ τῷ παραδόξῳ βοηθοῦντες μεγίστην μὲν ἔχουσι συνήγορον τὴν τύχην τῆς πόλεως, ἣν ἀπὸ μικρᾶς καὶ καταφρονουμένης ἀρχῆς ἐπὶ τοσοῦτον δόξης καὶ δυνάμεως προελθεῖν δίχα θεοῦ πολλαῖς καὶ μεγάλαις ἐπιφανείαις ἑκάστοτε συμπαρόντος ἀμήχανον. οὐ μὴν ἀλλὰ καὶ συνάγουσιν ὁμοειδῆ τινα, τοῦτο μὲν ἱδρῶτας ἀγαλμάτων πολλάκις ἐκχυθέντας, τοῦτο δὲ στεναγμοὺς ἀκουσθέντας ἀποστροφάς τε δεικνύντες καὶ καταμύσεις ξοάνων, ἃς ἱστορήκασιν οὐκ ὀλίγοι τῶν πρότερον. πολλὰ δὲ καὶ τῶν καθ' ἡμᾶς ἀκηκοότες ἀνθρώπων λέγειν ἔχομεν ἄξια θαύματος, ὧν οὐκ ἄν τις εἰκῇ καταφρονήσειεν. ἀλλὰ τοῖς τοιούτοις καὶ τὸ πιστεύειν σφόδρα καὶ τὸ λίαν ἀπιστεῖν ἐπισφαλές ἐστι διὰ τὴν ἀνθρωπίνην ἀσθένειαν, ὅρον οὐκ ἔχουσαν οὐδὲ κρατοῦσαν αὑτῆς, ἀλλ' ἐκφερομένην ὅπου μὲν εἰς δεισιδαιμονίαν καὶ τῦφον, ὅπου δ' εἰς ὀλιγωρίαν τῶν θείων καὶ περιφρόνησιν· ἡ δ' εὐλάβεια καὶ τὸ μηδὲν ἄγαν ἄριστον.

After he had utterly sacked the city, he determined to transfer the *agalma* of Hera to Rome, in accordance with his vows. The workmen were assembled for this purpose, and Camillus was sacrificing and praying to the goddess to accept of their zeal and to be a kindly co-dweller with the allotted gods of Rome, when the *agalma*, they say, spoke in low tones and said she was ready and willing. But Livy says that Camillus did indeed lay his hand on the goddess and pray and beseech her, but that it was certain of the bystanders who gave answer that she was ready and willing and eager to go along with him.

Those who insist upon and defend the marvel have a most powerful advocate [for their contention] in the fortune of the city, which, from its small and despised beginning, could never have come to such a pinnacle of glory and power against the will of the god who was present with her and made many great manifestations of himself from time to time. And they also bring up similar things, such as the frequent pouring out of sweat of *agalmata*, or *xoana*'s being heard groaning and being seen turning away and closing their eyes, which not a few of the previous writers have told of. And we ourselves might make mention of many astonishing things which we have heard from men of our own time, things not lightly to be despised. But in such matters eager credulity and excessive incredulity are alike dangerous, because of the weakness of our human nature, which sets no limits and has no mastery over itself, but is carried away now into vain superstition, and now into contemptuous neglect of the gods. Caution is best, and to go to no extremes.

317

Plutarch, *Caius Marcius Coriolanus* 37.5–38 A.D. I–II
Text: K. Ziegler, ed., *Plutarchi vitae parallelae* I.2 (Leipzig, 1964).
Translation adapted from B. Perrin, tr., *Plutarch's Lives* IV (LCL, 1916).

ἐπεὶ δ' ἡ βουλὴ τὴν μὲν φιλοτιμίαν ἐπήνεσε, δημοσίαις δὲ δαπάναις ἐποιήσατο τὸν νεὼν καὶ τὸ ἕδος, οὐδὲν ἧττον αὐταὶ χρήματα συνεισενεγκοῦσαι δεύτερον ἄγαλμα κατεσκεύασαν, ὃ δὴ καί φασι Ῥωμαῖοι καθιστάμενον ἐν τῷ ἱερῷ φθέγξασθαί τι τοιοῦτο· "θεοφιλεῖ με θεσμῷ γυναῖκες δεδώκατε."

Ταύτην καὶ δὶς γενέσθαι τὴν φωνὴν μυθολογοῦσιν, ἀγενήτοις ὅμοια καὶ χαλεπὰ πεισθῆναι πείθοντες ἡμᾶς. ἰδίοντα μὲν γὰρ ἀγάλματα φανῆναι καὶ δακρυρροοῦντα καί τινας μεθιέντα νοτίδας αἱματώδεις οὐκ ἀδύνατόν ἐστι· καὶ γὰρ ξύλα καὶ λίθοι πολλάκις μὲν εὐρῶτα συνάγουσι γόνιμον ὑγρότητος, πολλὰς δὲ καὶ χρόας ἀνιᾶσιν ἐξ αὐτῶν, καὶ δέχονται βαφὰς ἐκ τοῦ περιέχοντος, οἷς ἔνια σημαίνειν τὸ δαιμόνιον οὐδὲν ἂν δόξειε κωλύειν. δυνατὸν δὲ καὶ μυγμῷ καὶ στεναγμῷ ψόφον ὅμοιον ἐκβαλεῖν ἄγαλμα κατὰ ῥῆξιν ἢ διάστασιν μορίων βιαιοτέραν ἐν βάθει γενομένην. ἔναρθρον δὲ φωνὴν καὶ διάλεκτον οὕτω σαφῆ καὶ περιττὴν καὶ ἀρτίστομον ἐν ἀψύχῳ γενέσθαι παντάπασιν ἀμήχανον, εἰ μηδὲ τὴν ψυχὴν καὶ τὸν θεὸν ἄνευ σώματος ὀργανικοῦ καὶ διηρμοσμένου μέρεσι λογικοῖς γέγονεν ἠχεῖν καὶ διαλέγεσθαι. ὅπου δ' ἡμᾶς ἡ ἱστορία πολλοῖς ἀποβιάζεται καὶ πιθανοῖς μάρτυσιν, ἀνόμοιον αἰσθήσει πάθος ἐγγινόμενον τῷ φανταστικῷ τῆς ψυχῆς συναναπείθει τὸ δόξαν, ὥσπερ ἐν ὕπνοις ἀκούειν οὐκ ἀκούοντες καὶ βλέπειν οὐ βλέποντες δοκοῦμεν. οὐ μὴν ἀλλὰ τοῖς ὑπ' εὐνοίας καὶ φιλίας πρὸς τὸν θεὸν ἄγαν ἐμπαθῶς ἔχουσι καὶ μηδὲν ἀθετεῖν μηδ' ἀναίνεσθαι τῶν τοιούτων δυναμένοις μέγα πρὸς πίστιν ἐστὶ τὸ θαυμάσιον καὶ μὴ καθ' ἡμᾶς τῆς τοῦ θεοῦ δυνάμεως. οὐδενὶ γὰρ οὐδαμῶς ἀνθρωπίνῳ προσέοικεν οὔτε φύσιν οὔτε κίνησιν οὔτε τέχνην οὔτ' ἰσχύν, οὐδ' εἴ τι ποιεῖ τῶν ἡμῖν ἀποιήτων καὶ μηχανᾶται τῶν ἀμηχάνων, παράλογόν ἐστιν, ἀλλὰ μᾶλλον ἐν πᾶσι διαφέρων πολύ, μάλιστα τοῖς ἔργοις ἀνόμοιός ἐστι καὶ παρηλλαγμένος. ἀλλὰ τῶν μὲν θείων τὰ πολλά, καθ' Ἡράκλειτον, ἀπιστίῃ διαφυγγάνει μὴ γινώσκεσθαι.

The senate commended their public spirit, and erected the *neos* and its *hedos* at the public charge, but they nonetheless contributed money themselves and set up a second *agalma* of the goddess, and this, the Romans say, as it was placed in the *hieron*, uttered some such words as these: "Dear to the gods, O women, is your pious gift of me."

This utterance occurred twice, as they tell the story, which would have us believe what is difficult of belief and probably never happened. For that *agalmata* have appeared to sweat, and shed tears, and exude something like drops of blood, is not impossible; since stocks and stones often contract a mould which is productive of moisture, and cover themselves with many colors, and receive tints from the atmosphere; and there is nothing in the way of believing that the *daimonion* uses these phenomena sometimes as signs and portents. It is possible also that *agalmata* may emit a noise like a moan or a groan, by reason of a fracture or a rupture, which is more violent if it takes place in the interior. But that articulate speech, and language so clear and abundant and precise, should proceed from a soulless thing, is altogether impossible; since not even the soul of man, of the *theos*, without a body duly organized and fitted with vocal parts, has ever spoken or conversed. But where history forces our assent with numerous and credible witnesses, we must conclude that an experience different from that of sensation arises in the imaginative part of the soul, and persuades men to think it sensation; as, for instance, in sleep, when we think we see and hear, although we neither see nor hear. However, those who cherish strong feelings of goodwill and affection toward the *theos*, and are therefore unable to reject or deny anything of this kind, have a strong argument for their faith in the wonderful and transcendent character of the power of the *theos*. For he has no resemblance whatever to man, either in nature, activity, skill, or strength; nor, if he does something that we cannot do, or contrives something that we cannot contrive, is this contrary to reason; but rather, since he differs from us in all points, in his works most of all is he unlike us and far removed from us. But most of the divine powers, as Heraclitus says, "escape our knowledge through incredulity."

Plutarch, *De Daedalis Plateensibus* 6 A.D. I–II
(= *Moralia* fr. 157 Sandbach.)
See Eusebius, *Praeparatio evangelica* 3.1.85 c–86 b [**104**].

Plutarch, *De Daedalis Plateensibus* A.D. I–II
(= *Moralia* fr. 158 Sandbach.)
See Eusebius, *Praeparatio evangelica* 3.7.98 d–8.99 d [**108**].

318
Plutarch, *De fraterno amore* 1 A.D. I–II
(= *Moralia* 478 A–B.)
Text: W.R. Paton, M. Pohlenz, and W. Sieveking, eds., *Plutarchi moralia* III (Leipzig, 1972).

Translation adapted from W.C. Helmbold, tr., *Plutarch's Moralia* VI (LCL, 1939).

Τὰ παλαιὰ τῶν Διοσκόρων ἀφιδρύματα Σπαρτιᾶται 'δόκανα' καλοῦσιν· ἔστι δὲ δύο ξύλα παράλληλα δυσὶ πλαγίοις ἐπεζευγμένα, καὶ δοκεῖ τῷ φιλαδέλφῳ τῶν θεῶν οἰκεῖον εἶναι τοῦ ἀναθήματος τὸ κοινὸν καὶ ἀδιαίρετον.

The Spartans call the *archaia aphidrumata* of the Dioscuri "*dokana*" [beam-figures]; they consist of two parallel stocks joined by two other transverse ones placed across them, and this common and indivisible character of the *anathema* seems entirely suitable to the brotherly love of the gods.

319

Plutarch, *Lucullus* 13.5 A.D. I–II
Text: K. Ziegler, ed., *Plutarchi vitae parallelae* I.1 (Leipzig, 1960).
Translation adapted from B. Perrin, tr., *Plutarch's Lives* II (LCL, 1914).

καὶ τοῦθ' ὑπῆρξεν αὐτῷ τοῦ θεοῦ συναγωνισαμένου· λέγεται γὰρ Ἀρτέμιδος χόλῳ Πριαπηνῆς ὁ χειμὼν ἐμπεσεῖν τοῖς Ποντικοῖς, συλήσασιν αὐτῆς τὸ ἱερὸν καὶ τὸ ξόανον ἀνασπάσασι.

And this success he gained with the assistance of the *theos*. For it is said that it was owing to the wrath of Artemis of Priapus that the tempest fell upon the men of Pontus, who had plundered her *hieron* and uprooted her *xoanon*.

Plutarch, *Moralia* 232 C A.D. I–II
See Plutarch, *Apophthegmata Laconica* 232 C [**315**].

Plutarch, *Moralia* 247 D–E A.D. I–II
See Plutarch, *Mulierum virtutes* 247 D–E [**320**].

Plutarch, *Moralia* 478 A–B A.D. I–II
See Plutarch, *De fraterno amore* 1 [**318**].

Plutarch, *Moralia* fr. 157 Sandbach A.D. I–II
(= *De Daedalis Plataeensibus* 6.)
See Eusebius, *Praeparatio evangelica* 3.1.85 c–86 b [**104**].

Plutarch, *Moralia* fr. 158 Sandbach A.D. I–II
(= *De Daedalis Plataeensibus* .)
See Eusebius, *Praeparatio evangelica* 3.7.98 d–8.99 d [**108**].

320

Plutarch, *Mulierum virtutes* 247 D–E A.D. I–II
(= *Moralia* 247 D–E.)
Text: W. Nachstädt, W. Sieveking, and J.B. Titchener, eds., *Plutarchi Moralia* II.1 (Leipzig, 1971).
Translation adapted from F.C. Babbitt, tr., *Plutarch's Moralia* III (LCL, 1931).

ταῦτ' ἔπραττον οἱ Πελασγοὶ Πόλλιν ἡγεμόνα καὶ Δελφὸν καὶ Κραταΐδαν Λακεδαιμονίους λαβόντες· καὶ μέρος μὲν αὐτῶν ἐν Μήλῳ κατῴκησαν· τοὺς δὲ πλείστους οἱ περὶ Πόλλιν ἔχοντες εἰς Κρήτην ἔπλευσαν, ἀποπειρώμενοι τῶν λογίων. ἐχρήσθη γὰρ αὐτοῖς, ὅταν τὴν θεὸν καὶ τὴν ἄγκυραν ἀπολέσωσι, παύσασθαι πλάνης καὶ πόλιν ἐκεῖ συνοικίζειν. ὁρμισθεῖσιν οὖν πρὸς τῇ λεγομένῃ Χερρονήσῳ θόρυβοι πανικοὶ προσέπεσον νύκτωρ, ὑφ' ὧν διαπτοηθέντες ἐνεπήδησαν εἰς τὰς ναῦς ἀκόσμως, ἀπολιπόντες ἐν τῇ γῇ ξόανον τῆς Ἀρτέμιδος, ὃ πατρῷον ἦν αὐτοῖς εἰς Λῆμνον ἐκ Βραύρωνος κομισθέν, ἐκ δὲ Λήμνου πανταχοῦ συμπεριαγόμενον. ἐπεὶ δὲ τοῦ θορύβου λήξαντος ἐπόθησαν αὐτὸ κατὰ πλοῦν, ἅμα δ' ὁ Πόλλις κατέμαθε τῇ ἀγκύρᾳ τὸν ὄνυχα μὴ προσόντα (βίᾳ γὰρ ἑλκομένης ὡς ἔοικεν ἐν τόποις ὑποπέτροις ἀποσπασθεὶς ἔλαθε), περαίνεσθαι τὰ πυθόχρηστα φήσας ἐσήμαινεν ἀναστρέφειν. . . .

This the Pelasgians did, taking as leaders Pollis and Delphus and Crataïdas, Lacedaemonians. A part of them settled in Melos, but Pollis and his associates, with the great majority, sailed to Crete, testing the truth of the oracles. For an oracle had been given them that whenever they should lose their goddess and their anchor they should cease from their wanderings and found a city in that place. So, when they had come to anchor off that part of Crete which is called the Chersonese, panic confusion fell upon them by night, by which they were so excited that they leaped aboard in utter disorder, leaving behind on land a *xoanon* of Artemis which had been handed down to them from their ancestors, having been brought to Lemnos from Brauron, and from Lemnos had been carried about with them everywhere. But when at sea, as the confusion subsided, they missed this, and at the same time Pollis discovered that the fluke was gone from the anchor (for apparently it had been broken off as the anchor dragged in some rocky places, without anybody's noticing its loss), he declared that the god-given predictions were now fulfilled, and gave the signal to return. . . .

321

Plutarch, *Numa* 8.7–8 A.D. I–II
Text: B. Perrin, tr., *Plutarch's Lives* I (LCL, 1914).
Translation adapted from Perrin.

Ἔστι δὲ καὶ τὰ περὶ τῶν ἀφιδρυμάτων νομοθετήματα παντάπασιν ἀδελφὰ τῶν Πυθαγόρου δογμάτων. οὔτε γὰρ ἐκεῖνος αἰσθητὸν ἢ παθητόν, ἀόρατον δὲ καὶ ἄκτιστον καὶ νοητὸν ὑπελάμβανεν εἶναι τὸ πρῶτον, οὗτός τε διεκώλυσεν ἀνθρωποειδῆ καὶ ζῳόμορφον εἰκόνα θεοῦ Ῥωμαίους νομίζειν. οὐδ' ἦν παρ' αὐτοῖς οὔτε γραπτὸν οὔτε πλαστὸν εἶδος θεοῦ πρότερον, ἀλλ' ἐν ἑκατὸν ἑβδομήκοντα τοῖς πρώτοις ἔτεσι ναοὺς μὲν οἰκοδομούμενοι καὶ καλιάδας ἱερὰς ἱστῶντες, ἄγαλμα δὲ οὐδὲν ἔμμορφον ποιούμενοι διετέλουν, ὡς οὔτε ὅσιον ἀφομοιοῦν τὰ βελτίονα τοῖς χείροσιν οὔτε ἐφάπτεσθαι θεοῦ δυνατὸν ἄλλως ἢ νοήσει. κομιδῇ δὲ καὶ τὰ τῶν θυσιῶν ἔχεται τῆς Πυθαγορικῆς ἁγιστείας· ἀναίμακτοι γὰρ ἦσαν αἵ γε πολλαί, δι' ἀλφίτου καὶ σπονδῆς καὶ τῶν εὐτελεστάτων πεποιημέναι.

Furthermore, his [Numa's] ordinances concerning *aphidrumata* are altogether in harmony with the doctrines of Pythagoras. For the latter maintained that the first principle of being was beyond sense or feeling, was invisible and uncreated, and discernible only by the mind, and the former forbade the Romans to make use of an *anthropoeides* or *zoomorphos eikon* of the *theos*. Nor was there among them any *graptos* or *plastos eidos* of the *theos* in the earlier time, but while for the first one hundred seventy years they were continully building *naoi* and establishing sacred *kaliades* [huts], they continued making no *agalma* in bodily form, convinced that it was impious to liken higher things to lower, and that it was impossible to apprehend the *theos* except by the intellect. Their sacrifices, too, were altogether appropriate to the Pythagorean worship; for most of them involved no bloodshed, but were made with flour, drink-offerings, and the least costly gifts.

322

Pollux, *Onomasticon* I.7 A.D. II

Text: E. Bethe, ed., *Pollucis Onomasticon* (Lexicographi Graeci IX) I (Leipzig, 1900; repr. Stuttgart, 1967).

αὐτὰ δὲ ἃ θεραπεύομεν, ἀγάλματα, ξόανα, ἕδη θεῶν, εἰκάσματα θεῶν, εἰκόνες, μιμήματα, [τυπώματα], εἴδη, ἰδέαι. βρέτας δὲ ἢ δείκηλον οὐκ ἔγωγε προσίεμαι.

These are the things to which we give service: *agalmata*, *xoana*, *hede* of the gods, *eikasmata* of the gods, *eikones*, *mimemata*, [*tupomata*,] *eide*, *ideai*. I myself do not believe that *bretas* is a *deikelon*.

Porphyry, *Adversus Christianos* A.D. III

See Eusebius, *Praeparatio evangelica* 1.10.35 d [**102**].

323

Porphyry, *De abstinentia* 2.18 c. A.D. 271

Text: J. Bouffartigue, ed., tr., *Porphyre. De l'abstinence* II. *Livres II et III* (Paris, 1979).

Διὰ τοῦτο καὶ τοῖς κεραμίοις ἀγγείοις καὶ τοῖς ξυλίνοις καὶ πλεκτοῖς ἐχρῶντο καὶ μᾶλλον πρὸς τὰς δημοτελεῖς ἱεροποιίας, τοιούτοις χαίρειν πεπεισμένοι τὸ θεῖον. Ὅθεν καὶ τὰ παλαιότατα ἕδη κεράμια καὶ ξύλινα ὑπάρχοντα μᾶλλον θεῖα νενόμισται διά τε τὴν ὕλην καὶ τὴν ἀφέλειαν τῆς τέχνης. Τὸν γοῦν Αἰσχύλον φασί, τῶν Δελφῶν ἀξιούντων εἰς τὸν θεὸν γράψαι παιᾶνα, εἰπεῖν ὅτι βέλτιστα Τυννίχῳ πεποίηται· παραβαλλόμενον δὲ τὸν αὑτοῦ πρὸς τὸν ἐκείνου ταὐτὸν πείσεσθαι τοῖς ἀγάλμασι τοῖς καινοῖς πρὸς τὰ ἀρχαῖα· ταῦτα γὰρ καίπερ ἁπλῶς πεποιημένα, θεῖα νομίζεσθαι, τὰ δὲ καινὰ περιέργως εἰργασμένα θαυμάζεσθαι μέν, θεοῦ δὲ δόξαν ἧττον ἔχειν. Καὶ τὸν Ἡσίοδον οὖν εἰκότως τὸν τῶν ἀρχαίων θυσιῶν νόμον ἐπαινοῦντα εἰπεῖν·

Ὥς κε πόλις ῥέζῃσι, νόμος δ'ἀρχαῖος ἄριστος.

On account of this they used vessels of clay and wood and wicker, and especially for public sacrifices, believing that divinity takes pleasure in such things. For this reason, too, the oldest *hede* that are of clay and wood are considered to be more *theia* on account of both the material and the simplicity of their craft. It is said too that Aeschylus, when the Delphians had asked him to write a *paean* in honor of Apollo, said that the best had been done by Tynnichus; if his own work were compared with that man's, the same thing would happen as when new *agalmata* are compared with *archaia* ones; for these, although made simply, are considered *theia*, while the new ones that are elaborately worked, although they are marvelled at, have an inferior notion of god. And thus Hesiod says reasonably, applauding the custom of *archaiai* sacrifices: "When the city makes sacrifices, the *archaios* custom is the best."

324

Porphyry, *De abstinentia* 2.56.6 c. A.D. 271

See also Eusebius, *Praeparatio evangelica* 4.16.156 b [**116**].

Text: J. Bouffartigue, ed., tr., *Porphyre. De l'abstinence* II. *Livres II et III* (Paris, 1979).

Καὶ Δουματηνοὶ δὲ τῆς Ἀραβίας κατ' ἔτος ἕκαστον ἔθυον παῖδα, ὃν ὑπὸ βωμὸν ἔθαπτον, ᾧ χρῶνται ὡς ξοάνῳ.

And the Doumatenes of Arabia each year sacrificed a child, whom they buried under the altar, which they use as a *xoanon*.

Porphyry, *De philosophia ex oraculis haurienda* A.D. III
See Eusebius, *Praeparatio evangelica* 5.11.199 d–13.201 d [**118**].

Porphyry, *Epistula ad Anebonem* ? A.D. 263–268
See Eusebius, *Praeparatio evangelica* 3.4.92 c–d [**106**].

Porphyry, Περὶ ἀγαλμάτων A.D. III
See Eusebius, *Praeparatio evangelica* [**107**, **110**].

325

Proclus, *Chrestomathia* 261–263 Severyns A.D. V
Text: A. Severyns, ed., tr., *Recherches sur la Chrestomathie de Proclus* IV (Paris, 1963).

Κασσάνδραν δὲ Αἴας ὁ Ἰλέως πρὸς βίαν ἀποσπῶν συνεφέλκεται τὸ τῆς Ἀθηνᾶς ξόανον. ἐφ' ᾧ παροξυνθέντες οἱ Ἕλληνες καταλεῦσαι βουλεύονται τὸν Αἴαντα.

Ajax, the son of Ilis, tearing Cassandra away by force, dragged down the *xoanon* of Athena. Being provoked by this, the Greeks resolved to stone Ajax to death.

326

Ptolemaeus Ascalonita *s.v.* ξόανον
Text: G. Heylbut, ed., "Ptolemaeus περὶ διαφορᾶς λέξεων," *Hermes* 22 (1887) 405.23.

ξόανον τὸ ἐξεσμένον λίθινον ἢ ἐλεφάντινον, βρέτας δὲ τὸ βροτῷ ὅμοιον ἤτοι χάλκεον ἢ ἐκ γένους ἐμφεροῦς ὕλης πεποιημένον, ἄγαλμα δὲ τὸ Πάριον ἢ καὶ ἐκ τινος ἑτέρου λίθου κατεσκευασμένον.

A *xoanon* is something carved, either of stone, or wooden; a *bretas*, on the other hand, is like a *brotos* [mortal], either bronze or made out of a similar kind of material; while an *agalma* is made out of Parian or out of some other stone.

327

Rufinus ? A.D. II
(= *Anthologia Palatina* 5.15.)
Text: D. Page, ed., *The Epigrams of Rufinus* (Cambridge, 1978) no. IV.
Translation adapted from W.R. Paton, tr., *The Greek Anthology* I (LCL, 1916).

ποῦ νῦν Πραξιτέλης, ποῦ δ' αἱ χέρες αἱ Πολυκλείτου
αἱ ταῖς πρόσθε τέχναις πνεῦμα χαριζόμεναι;
τίς πλοκάμους Μελίτης εὐώδεας ἢ πυρόεντα
ὄμματα καὶ δειρῆς φέγγος ἀποπλάσεται;
ποῦ πλάσται, ποῦ δ' εἰσὶ λιθοξόοι; ἔπρεπε τοίῃ
μορφῇ νηὸν ἔχειν ὡς μακάρων ξοάνῳ.

Where now is Praxiteles, where are the hands of Polycleitus
that granted breath to the crafts of the past?
Who will mould Melite's scented plaits or fiery eyes
and the splendor of her neck?
Where are the modellers, where are the stone-carvers? For
this form there should be a *neos* as there is for a *xoanon* of the blessed.

328

Rufinus ? A.D. II

(= *Anthologia Palatina* 5.36.)

(= *Anthologia Planudea* 7.142.)

Text: D. Page, ed., *The Epigrams of Rufinus* (Cambridge, 1978) no. XII. Translation adapted from P. Waltz and J. Guillon, eds., *Anthologie Grecque. Première partie. Anthologie Palatine* II (*Livre* V) (Paris, 1928).

ἤρισαν ἀλλήλαις Ῥοδόπη Μελίτη Ῥοδόκλεια,
τῶν τρισσῶν τίς ἔχει κρείσσονα μηριόνην,
καί με κριτὴν εἵλοντο· καὶ ὡς θεαὶ αἱ περίβλεπτοι
ἔστησαν γυμναί, νέκταρι λειβόμεναι.
καὶ Ῥοδόπης μὲν ἔλαμπε μέσος μηρῶν πολύτιμος
< >
< >
οἷα ῥοδὼν †πολιῷ† σχιζόμενος ζεφύρῳ·
τῆς δὲ Ῥοδοκλείης ὑάλῳ ἴσος, ὑγρομέτωπος,
οἷα καὶ ἐν νηῷ πρωτογλυφὲς ξόανον.
ἀλλὰ σαφῶς ἃ πέπονθε Πάρις διὰ τὴν κρίσιν εἰδὼς
τὰς τρεῖς ἀθανάτας εὐθὺ συνεστεφάνουν.

Rhodope, Melite, and Rhodoclea vied with each other for which of the three had the better feminine parts, and they picked me for judge; and like the goddesses who were admired from all sides, they stood naked, dripping with nectar. And the costly . . . between Rhodope's thighs shone like a rose-bed split by hoary Zephyr . . . Rhodoclea's was like glass, with soft, smoothed brow, like a newly-carved *xoanon* in a *neos*. But knowing well what Paris suffered on account of his judgment, I straightway crowned the three immortals all together.

Sanchuniathon
See Philo Byblius *ap*. Eusebius, *Praeparatio evangelica* 1.10.35 d [**102**].

329
[Scylax] p. 39.4 Fabr.
Text: H. Stuart Jones, ed., *Select Passages from Ancient Writers Illustrative of the History of Greek Sculpture* (London, 1895) 6 no. 4.

ἐπὶ δὲ τῷ ἀκροτηρίῳ τῆς ἄκρας ἔπεστι βωμὸς μεγαλοπρεπὴς Ποσειδῶνος. ἐν δὴ τῷ βωμῷ εἰσὶ γεγλυμμένοι ἄνδρες, γυναῖκες, λέοντες, δελφῖνες· Δαίδαλον δὲ φασι ποιῆσαι.

(Soloeis, Sicily)
On the highest point of the cape there is a magnificent *bomos* of Poseidon. On the *bomos* there are carved men, women, lions, and dolphins; they say that Daedalus made [it].

330
Servius *ad* Vergil, *Aeneid* 1.720 A.D. IV
Text: E.K. Rand *et al.*, eds., *Servianorum in Vergilii carmina commentariorum editio Harvardiana* II (Lancaster, Pennsylvania, 1946).

apud Cyprios Venus in modum umbilici vel, ut quidam volunt, metae colitur.

Among the Cypriots Venus is worshipped in the form of a navel, or, as some would have it, a *meta* [conical turning-post].

331
Servius *ad* Vergil, *Aeneid* 2.225 A.D. IV
Text: E.K. Rand *et al.*, eds., *Servianorum in Vergilii carmina commentariorum editio Harvardiana* II (Lancaster, Pennsylvania, 1946).

Masurius Sabinus 'delubrum' effigies, a deliberatione corticis; nam antiqui felicium arborum ramos cortice detracto in effigies deorum formabant, unde Graeci ξόανον dicunt.

Masurius Sabinus says that *delubrum* means an *effigies* made by the peeling of bark; for the ancients formed the branches of auspicious trees, the bark having been peeled off, into images of gods, whence the Greeks say *xoanon*.

332
Servius *ad* Vergil, *Aeneid* 4.56 A.D. IV
Text: A.F. Stocker and A.H. Travis, eds., *Servianorum in Vergilii carmina commentariorum editio Harvardiana* III (Oxford, 1965).

Scholia Danielis: DELUBRA ADEVNT iuxta illud dictum sororis *tu modo posce deos veniam*. 'delubrum' autem dictum aut, ut supra diximus, propter lacum in quo manus abluuntur, vel propter tectum coniunctum, quia una opera abluitur; aut certe simulacrum 'delubrum' dicimus a 'libro', hoc est, raso ligno factum, quod Graece *ξόανον* dicitur.

They approach the shrines. This is close to the sister's saying, "you now ask the gods a favor." The word, however, is *delubrum*, either, as we said above, because of the vessel in which hands are washed; or else on account of the connected roof, which is washed in the same manner; or, undoubtedly, we call a *simulacrum* a *delubrum* from *liber* [wood], that is to say, made from scraped wood, which in Greek is called *xoanon*.

Shorter version: DELUBRA ADEVNT 'delubrum' dictum, ut supra diximus, propter lacum in quo manus abluuntur, vel propter tectum coniunctum, quia una opera abluitur; aut certe ligneum simulacrum 'delubrum' dicimus a 'libro', hoc est, raso ligno factum, quod Graece *ξόανον* dicitur.

They approach the shrines. The word *delubrum*, as we said above, because of the vessel in which hands are washed, or else on account of the connected roof, which is washed in the same manner; or, undoubtedly, we call a wooden simulacrum a *delubrum* from *liber*, that is to say, made from scraped wood, which in Greek is called *xoanon*.

333
Servius *ad* Vergil, *Aeneid* 6.68 A.D. IV
Text: G. Thilo and H. Hagen, eds., *Servii grammatici qui feruntur in Vergilii carmina commentarii* II (Leipzig, 1884).

AGITATAQVE NVMINA TROIAE aut mecum vexata: aut certe *ξόανα* dicit, id est simulacra brevia, quae portabantur in lecticis et ab ipsis mota infundebant vaticinationem: quod fuit apud Aegyptios et Carthaginienses.

Shaken divinities of Troy: either [ones that are] angry with me; or undoubtedly he means *xoana*, that is, small *simulacra*, which were carried in litters and, moved about by themselves, imparted a prophecy; this happened among the Egyptians and the Carthaginians.

Sophocles fr. 238 Radt V B.C.
See Athenaeus 14.637 a [**36**].

Sophocles fr. 452 Radt V B.C.
See Sch. Aeschylus, *Septem contra Thebas* 304 [**5**].

[Sophocles] fr. 1126 Radt
See Clement of Alexandria, *Stromateis* 5.14.717 P.[**48**].

334
Strabo 1.2.8 (C 18–19) I B.C.–A.D. I
Text: A. Meineke, ed., *Strabonis geographica* I (Leipzig, 1866).
Translation adapted from H.L. Jones, tr., *The Geography of Strabo* I (LCL, 1917).

ἐπεὶ δ' οὐ μόνον ἡδὺ ἀλλὰ καὶ φοβερὸν τὸ τερατῶδες, ἀμφοτέρων ἐστὶ τῶν εἰδῶν χρεία πρός τε τοὺς παῖδας καὶ τοὺς ἐν ἡλικίᾳ· τοῖς τε γὰρ παισὶ προσφέρομεν τοὺς ἡδεῖς μύθους εἰς προτροπήν, εἰς ἀποτροπὴν δὲ τοὺς φοβερούς· ἥ τε γὰρ Λάμια μῦθός ἐστι καὶ ἡ Γοργὼ καὶ ὁ 'Εφιάλτης καὶ ἡ Μορμολύκη. οἵ τε πολλοὶ τῶν τὰς πόλεις οἰκούντων εἰς μὲν προτροπὴν ἄγονται τοῖς ἡδέσι τῶν μύθων, ὅταν ἀκούωσι τῶν ποιητῶν ἀνδραγαθήματα μυθώδη διηγουμένων, οἷον 'Ηρακλέους ἄθλους ἢ Θησέως, ἢ τιμὰς παρὰ θεῶν νεμομένας, ἢ νὴ Δία ὁρῶσι γραφὰς ἢ ξόανα ἢ πλάσματα τοιαύτην τινὰ περιπέτειαν ὑποσημαίνοντα μυθώδη. . . .

Now since the portentous is not only pleasing, but fear-inspiring as well, we can employ both kinds of myth for children, and for grown-up people too. In the case of children, we employ the pleasing myths to spur them on, and the fear-inspiring myths to deter them; for instance, Lamia is a myth, and so are the Gorgon, and Ephialtes, and Mormolyce. Most of those who live in the cities are incited to emulation by the myths that are pleasing, when they hear the poets narrate mythical deeds of heroism, such as the *athloi* of Heracles or of Theseus, or hear of honors bestowed by the gods, or indeed, when they see *graphai* or *xoana* or *plasmata* which suggest any similar happy issue of fortune in mythology. . . .

335
Strabo 4.1.4 (C 179) I B.C.–A.D. I
Text: A. Meineke, ed., *Strabonis geographica* I (Leipzig, 1866).
Translation adapted from H.L. Jones, tr., *The Geography of Strabo* II (LCL, 1923).

Κτίσμα δ' ἐστὶ Φωκαιέων ἡ Μασσαλία, κεῖται δ' ἐπὶ χωρίου πετρώδους· ὑποπέπτωκε δ' αὐτῆς ὁ λιμὴν θεατροειδεῖ πέτρᾳ βλεπούσῃ πρὸς νότον. τετείχισται δὲ καὶ αὕτη καλῶς καὶ ἡ πόλις σύμπασα μέγεθος ἔχουσα ἀξιόλογον. ἐν δὲ τῇ ἄκρᾳ τὸ 'Εφέσιον ἵδρυται καὶ τὸ τοῦ Δελφινίου 'Απόλλωνος ἱερόν· τοῦτο μὲν κοινὸν 'Ιώνων ἁπάντων, τὸ δὲ 'Εφέσιον τῆς 'Αρτέμιδός ἐστι νεὼς τῆς 'Εφεσίας. ἀπαίρουσι γὰρ τοῖς Φωκαιεῦσιν ἐκ τῆς οἰκείας λόγιον ἐκπεσεῖν φασιν ἡγεμόνι χρήσασθαι τοῦ πλοῦ παρὰ τῆς 'Εφεσίας 'Αρτέμιδος λαβοῦσι· τοὺς μὲν δὴ προσαχθέντας τῇ 'Εφέσῳ ζητεῖν ὅντινα τρόπον ἐκ τῆς θεοῦ πορίσαιντο τὸ προσταχθέν. 'Αριστάρχῃ δὲ τῶν ἐντίμων σφόδρα γυναικῶν παραστῆναι κατ' ὄναρ τὴν θεὸν καὶ κελεῦσαι συναπαίρειν τοῖς Φωκαιεῦσιν ἀφίδρυμά τι τῶν ἱερῶν λαβούσῃ· γενομένου δὲ τούτου καὶ τῆς ἀποικίας λαβούσης τέλος, τό τε ἱερὸν ἱδρύσασθαι καὶ τὴν Ἀριστάρχην τιμῆσαι διαφερόντως ἱέρειαν ἀποδείξαντας, ἔν τε ταῖς ἀποίκοις πόλεσι πανταχοῦ τιμᾶν ἐν τοῖς πρώτοις ταύτην τὴν θεὸν καὶ τοῦ ξοάνου τὴν διάθεσιν τὴν αὐτὴν καὶ τἆλλα νόμιμα φυλάττειν τὰ αὐτὰ ἅπερ ἐν τῇ μητροπόλει νενόμισται.

Massilia was founded by the Phocaeans, and it is situated on a rocky place. Its harbor lies at the foot of a theater-like rock which faces south. And not only is the rock itself well fortified, but also the city as a whole, though it is of considerable size. It is on the headland, however, that the Ephesium and also the *hieron* of the Delphinian Apollo are situated. The latter is shared in common by all Ionians, whereas the Ephesium is a *neos* dedicated solely to the Ephesian Artemis; for when the Phocaeans were setting sail from their homeland an oracle was delivered to them, it is said, to use for their voyage a guide received from the Ephesian Artemis; accordingly, some of them put in at Ephesus and inquired in what way they might procure from the goddess what had been enjoined upon them. Now the goddess, in a dream, it is said, had stood beside Aristarcha, one of the women held in very high honor, and commanded her to sail away with the Phocaeans, taking with her a certain *aphidruma* from among the holy things; this done and the colony finally settled, they not only established the *hieron*, but also did Aristarcha the exceptional honor of appointing her priestess; further, in the colonial cities the people everywhere do this goddess honors of the first rank, and they preserve the artistic design of the *xoanon* the same, and all the other usages precisely the same as it is customary in the mother city.

336

Strabo 4.1.5 (C 180) I B.C.–A.D. I

Text: A. Meineke, ed., *Strabonis geographica* I (Leipzig, 1866).

Translation adapted from H.L. Jones, tr., *The Geography of Strabo* II (LCL, 1923).

πρότερον μὲν οὖν εὐτύχουν διαφερόντως περί τε τἆλλα καὶ περὶ τὴν πρὸς Ῥωμαίους φιλίαν, ἧς πολλὰ ἄν τις λάβοι σημεῖα· καὶ δὴ καὶ τὸ ξόανον τῆς Ἀρτέμιδος τῆς ἐν τῷ Ἀβεντίνῳ οἱ Ῥωμαῖοι τὴν αὐτὴν διάθεσιν ἔχον τῷ παρὰ τοῖς Μασσαλιώταις ἀνέθεσαν.

In earlier times, then, they were exceptionally fortunate, not only in everything else, but also in their friendship with the Romans, of which one may detect many signs; what is more, the Romans dedicated the *xoanon* of that Artemis who is on the Aventine with the same artistic design as the one the Massiliotes have.

337

Strabo 6.1.14 (C 264) I B.C.–A.D. I

Text: A. Meineke, ed., *Strabonis geographica* I (Leipzig, 1866).

Translation adapted from H.L. Jones, tr., *The Geography of Strabo* III (LCL, 1924).

εἶθ' Ἡράκλεια πόλις μικρὸν ὑπὲρ τῆς θαλάττης, καὶ ποταμοὶ δύο πλωτοὶ Ἄκιρις καὶ Σῖρις, ἐφ' οὗ πόλις ἦν ὁμώνυμος Τρωική· χρόνῳ δὲ τῆς Ἡρακλείας ἐντεῦθεν οἰκισθείσης ὑπὸ Ταραντίνων, ἐπίνειον αὕτη τῶν Ἡρακλεωτῶν ὑπῆρξε. διεῖχε δ' Ἡρακλείας μὲν τέτταρας καὶ εἴκοσι σταδίους, Θουρίων δὲ περὶ τριακοσίους τριάκοντα. τῆς δὲ τῶν Τρώων κατοικίας τεκμήριον ποιοῦνται τὸ τῆς Ἀθηνᾶς τῆς Ἰλιάδος ξόανον ἱδρυμένον αὐτόθι, ὅπερ καταμῦσαι μυθεύουσιν ἀποσπωμένων τῶν ἱκετῶν ὑπὸ Ἰώνων τῶν ἑλόντων τὴν πόλιν· τούτους γὰρ ἐπελθεῖν οἰκήτορας φεύγοντας τὴν Λυδῶν ἀρχήν, καὶ βίᾳ λαβεῖν τὴν πόλιν Χώνων οὖσαν, καλέσαι δὲ αὐτὴν Πολίειον· δείκνυσθαι δὲ καὶ νῦν καταμῦον τὸ ξόανον. ἰταμὸν μὲν οὖν καὶ τὸ οὕτω μυθεύειν, ὥστε μὴ καταμῦσαι ἀναινόμενον, καθάπερ καὶ ἐν Ἰλίῳ ἀποστραφῆναι κατὰ τὸν Κασάνδρας βιασμόν, ἀλλὰ καὶ καταμῦον δείκνυσθαι· πολὺ δὲ ἰταμώτερον τὸ τοσαῦτα ποιεῖν ἐξ Ἰλίου κεκομισμένα ξόανα, ὅσα φασὶν οἱ συγγραφεῖς· καὶ γὰρ ἐν Ῥώμῃ καὶ ἐν Λαουινίῳ καὶ ἐν Λουκερίᾳ καὶ ἐν Σιρίτιδι Ἰλιὰς Ἀθηνᾶ καλεῖται ὡς ἐκεῖθεν κομισθεῖσα. καὶ τὸ τῶν Τρῳάδων δὲ τόλμημα περιφέρεται πολλαχοῦ καὶ ἄπιστον φαίνεται καίπερ δυνατὸν ὄν.

Then comes the city of Heracleia, a short distance above the sea; and two navigable rivers, the Aciris and the Siris. On the Siris there used to be a Trojan city of the same name, but in time, when Heracleia was colonized thence by the Tarantini, it became the port of the Heracleotes. It is twenty-four stadia distant from Heracleia and about three hundred thirty from Thurii. Writers produce as proof of its settlement by the Trojans the *xoanon* of the Trojan Athena which is set up there, the one that closed its eyes, the fable goes, when the suppliants were dragged away by the Ionians who captured the city; for these Ionians came there as colonists when in flight from the dominion of the Lydians, and by force took the city, which belonged to the Chones, and called it Polieium; and the *xoanon* even now can be seen closing its eyes. It is a bold thing, to be sure, to tell such a fable and to say that it not only closed it eyes (just as they say the one in Troy turned away at the time Cassandra was violated) but can also be seen closing its eyes; and yet it is much bolder to represent as brought from Troy all those *xoana* which the historians say were brought from there; for not only in the territory of Siris, but also at Rome, at Lavinium, and at Luceria, Athena is called "Trojan Athena," as though brought from Troy. And further, the daring deed of the Trojan women is current in numerous places, and appears incredible, although it is possible.

338
Strabo 7.4.2 (C 308) I B.C.–A.D. I
Text: A. Meineke, ed., *Strabonis geographica* II (Leipzig, 1866).
Translation adapted from H.L. Jones, tr., *The Geography of Strabo* III (LCL, 1924).

ἐν ᾗ τὸ τῆς Παρθένου ἱερόν, δαίμονός τινος, ἧς ἐπώνυμος καὶ ἡ ἄκρα ἡ πρὸ τῆς πόλεώς ἐστιν ἐν σταδίοις ἑκατόν, καλουμένη Παρθένιον, ἔχον νεὼν τῆς δαίμονος καὶ ξόανον.

(Chersonese)
In this city is the *hieron* of the Parthenos, a certain *daimon*; and the cape which is in front of the city, at a distance of one hundred stadia, is also named after her, for it is called the Parthenium, and it has a *neos* of the *daimon* and a *xoanon*.

339
Strabo 8.3.4 (C 337) I B.C.–A.D. I
Text: A. Meineke, ed., *Strabonis geographica* II (Leipzig, 1866).
Translation adapted from H.L. Jones, tr., *The Geography of Strabo* IV (LCL, 1927).

ἔστι δὲ κώμη μετρία, τὸν Ἀσκληπιὸν ἔχουσα τὸν Κολώτου, θαυμαστὸν ἰδεῖν ξόανον ἐλεφάντινον.

[Cyllene] is a village of moderate size; and it has the Asclepius made by Colotes—an ivory *xoanon* that is wonderful to behold.

340
Strabo 8.3.30 (C 353–354) I B.C.–A.D. I
Text: A. Meineke, ed., *Strabonis geographica* II (Leipzig, 1866).
Translation adapted from H.L. Jones, tr., *The Geography of Strabo* IV (LCL, 1927).

μέγιστον δὲ τούτων ὑπῆρξε τὸ τοῦ Διὸς ξόανον, ὃ ἐποίει Φειδίας Χαρμίδου Ἀθηναῖος ἐλεφάντινον, τηλικοῦτον τὸ μέγεθος ὡς καίπερ μεγίστου ὄντος τοῦ νεὼ δοκεῖν ἀστοχῆσαι τῆς συμμετρίας τὸν τεχνίτην, καθήμενον ποιήσαντα, ἁπτόμενον δὲ σχεδόν τι τῇ κορυφῇ τῆς ὀροφῆς ὥστ' ἔμφασιν ποιεῖν, ἐὰν ὀρθὸς γένηται διαναστάς, ἀποστεγάσειν τὸν νεών. ἀνέγραψαν δέ τινες τὰ μέτρα τοῦ ξοάνου, καὶ Καλλίμαχος ἐν ἰάμβῳ τινὶ ἐξεῖπε. πολλὰ δὲ συνέπραξε τῷ Φειδίᾳ Πάναινος ὁ ζωγράφος, ἀδελφιδοῦς ὢν αὐτοῦ καὶ συνεργολάβος, πρὸς τὴν τοῦ ξοάνου διὰ τῶν χρωμάτων κόσμησιν καὶ μάλιστα τῆς ἐσθῆτος.

But the greatest of these was the *xoanon* of Zeus, which Pheidias the Athenian, son of Charmides, made; it was made of ivory, and it was so large that, although the *neos* was very large, the artist is thought to have missed the proper symmetry, for he showed Zeus seated but almost touching the roof with his head, thus making the impression that if Zeus arose and stood erect he would unroof the *neos*. Certain writers have recorded the measurements of the *xoanon*, and Callimachus has set them forth in an iambic poem. Panaenus the painter, who was the nephew and collaborator of Pheidias, helped him greatly in decorating the *xoanon*, particularly the garments, with colors.

341

Strabo 8.6.10 (C 372) I B.C.–A.D. I

Text: A. Meineke, ed., *Strabonis geographica* II (Leipzig, 1866).

Translation adapted from H.L. Jones, tr., *The Geography of Strabo* IV (LCL, 1927).

καὶ τὸ Ἡραῖον εἶναι κοινὸν ἱερὸν τὸ πρὸς ταῖς Μυκήναις ἀμφοῖν, ἐν ᾧ τὰ Πολυκλείτου ξόανα τῇ μὲν τέχνῃ κάλλιστα τῶν πάντων πολυτελείᾳ δὲ καὶ μεγέθει τῶν Φειδίου λειπόμενα.

. . . and that the Heraeum near Mycenae was a *hieron* common to both [Argos and Mycenae] in which there are *xoana* made by Polycleitus, in execution the most beautiful of all, but in costliness and size inferior to those by Pheidias.

342

Strabo 9.1.17 (C 396) I B.C.–A.D. I

Text: A. Meineke, ed., *Strabonis geographica* II (Leipzig, 1866).

Translation adapted from H.L. Jones, tr., *The Geography of Strabo* IV (LCL, 1927).

Ἔχουσι δὲ κἂν εἰ μὴ πάντες οἵ γε πολλοὶ μυθοποιίας συχνὰς καὶ ἱστορίας· καθάπερ Ἄφιδνα μὲν τὴν τῆς Ἑλένης ἁρπαγὴν ὑπὸ Θησέως καὶ τὴν ὑπὸ τῶν Διοσκούρων ἐκπόρθησιν αὐτῆς καὶ ἀνακομιδὴν τῆς ἀδελφῆς, Μαραθὼν δὲ τὸν Περσικὸν ἀγῶνα, Ῥαμνοῦς δὲ τὸ τῆς Νεμέσεως ξόανον, ὅ τινες μὲν Διοδότου φασὶν ἔργον τινὲς δὲ Ἀγορακρίτου τοῦ Παρίου, καὶ μεγέθει καὶ κάλλει σφόδρα κατωρθωμένον καὶ ἐνάμιλλον τοῖς Φειδίου ἔργοις.

Most of the demes, if not all, have numerous stories of a character both mythical and historical connected with them; for example, Aphidna has the rape of Helen by Theseus, the sacking of the place by the Dioscuri and their recovery of their sister; Marathon has the Persian battle; Rhamnous has the *xoanon* of Nemesis, which some say is the work of Diotus and others, of Agoracritus the Parian, a work which both in grandeur and in beauty is a great success and rivals the works of Pheidias.

343

Strabo 13.1.41 (C 601) I B.C.–A.D. I

Text: A. Meineke, ed., *Strabonis geographica* III (Leipzig, 1877).

Translation adapted from H.L. Jones, tr., *The Geography of Strabo* VI (LCL, 1929).

Οὕτω μὲν δὴ λέγουσιν οἱ Ἰλιεῖς, Ὅμηρος δὲ ῥητῶς τὸν ἀφανισμὸν τῆς πόλεως εἴρηκεν "ἔσσεται ἦμαρ ὅταν ποτ' ὀλώλῃ Ἴλιος ἱρή." "ἦ γὰρ καὶ Πριάμοιο πόλιν διεπέρσαμεν αἰπήν." "πέρθετο δὲ Πριάμοιο πόλις δεκάτῳ ἐνιαυτῷ." καὶ τὰ τοιαῦτα δὲ τοῦ αὐτοῦ τίθενται τεκμήρια, οἷον ὅτι τῆς Ἀθηνᾶς τὸ ξόανον νῦν μὲν ἑστηκὸς ὁρᾶται, Ὅμηρος δὲ καθήμενον ἐμφαίνει· πέπλον γὰρ κελεύει "θεῖναι Ἀθηναίης ἐπὶ γούνασιν." βέλτιον γὰρ οὕτως ἢ ὥς τινὲς δέχονται ἀντὶ τοῦ "παρὰ τοῖς γόνασι θεῖναι" παρατιθέντες τὸ "ἡ δ' ἧσται ἐπ' ἐσχάρῃ ἐν πυρὸς αὐγῇ" ἀντὶ τοῦ "παρ' ἐσχάρῃ." τίς γὰρ ἂν νοηθείη πέπλου ἀνάθεσις παρὰ τοῖς γόνασι; καὶ οἱ τὴν προσῳδίαν δὲ διαστρέφοντες, "γουνάσιν" ὡς θυιάσιν, ὁποτέρως ἂν δέξωνται, ἀπεραντολογοῦσιν. . . .

So the Ilians tell us, but Homer expressly states that the city was wiped out: "The day shall come when sacred Ilios shall perish"; and "surely we have utterly destroyed the steep city of Priam," "by means of counsels and speeches"; and "and in the tenth year the city of Priam was destroyed." And other such evidences of the same thing are set forth; for example that the *xoanon* of Athena now to be seen stands upright, whereas Homer clearly indicates that it was sitting, for orders are given to "put" the peplos "upon Athena's knees" (compare "that never should there sit upon his knees a dear child"). For it is better to interpret it in this way than, as some do, to interpret it as meaning "to put beside her knees," comparing the phrase "and she sits upon the hearth in the light of the fire," which they take to mean "beside" the hearth. For how could one conceive of the dedication of a peplos "beside" the knees? Moreover, others, changing the accent on *γούνασιν*, accenting it *γουνάσιν*, like *θυιάσιν* (in whichever of two ways they interpret it), talk on endlessly. . . .

344

Strabo 13.1.41 (C 601) I B.C.–A.D. I

Text: A. Meineke, ed., *Strabonis geographica* III (Leipzig, 1877).

Translation adapted from H.L. Jones, tr., *The Geography of Strabo* VI (LCL, 1929).

πολλὰ δὲ τῶν ἀρχαίων τῆς Ἀθηνᾶς ξοάνων καθήμενα δείκνυται, καθάπερ ἐν Φωκαίᾳ Μασσαλίᾳ Ῥώμῃ Χίῳ ἄλλαις πλείοσιν. ὁμολογοῦσι δὲ καὶ οἱ νεώτεροι τὸν ἀφανισμὸν τῆς πόλεως, ὧν ἔστι καὶ Λυκοῦργος ὁ ῥήτωρ· μνησθεὶς γὰρ τῆς Ἰλιέων πόλεως φησί "τίς οὐκ ἀκηκοεν, ὡς ἅπαξ ὑπὸ τῶν Ἑλλήνων κατεσκάφθη, ἀοίκητον οὖσαν";

Many of the *archaia xoana* of Athena are shown seated, as, for example, in Phocaea, Massalia, Rome, Chios, and several other places. Also the more recent writers agree that the city was wiped out, among whom is the orator Lycurgus, who, in mentioning the city of the Ilians, says, "Who has not heard that once for all it was razed to the ground by the Greeks, and is uninhabited?"

345

Strabo 13.1.48 (C 604) I B.C.–A.D. I

Text: A. Meineke, ed., *Strabonis geographica* III (Leipzig, 1877). Translation adapted from W. Leaf, ed., tr., *Strabo on the Troad* (Cambridge, 1923).

Ἐν δὲ τῇ Χρύσῃ ταύτῃ καὶ τὸ τοῦ Σμινθέως Ἀπόλλωνός ἐστιν ἱερόν, καὶ τὸ σύμβολον τὸ τὴν ἐτυμότητα τοῦ ὀνόματος σῷζον, ὁ μῦς, ὑπόκειται τῷ ποδὶ τοῦ ξοάνου· Σκόπα δ᾽ ἐστὶν ἔργα τοῦ Παρίου· συνοικειοῦσι δὲ καὶ τὴν ἱστορίαν εἴτε μῦθον τούτῳ τῷ τόπῳ τὴν περὶ τῶν μυῶν. τοῖς γὰρ ἐκ τῆς Κρήτης ἀφιγμένοις Τεύκροις (οὓς πρῶτος παρέδωκε Καλλῖνος ὁ τῆς ἐλεγείας ποιητής, ἠκολούθησαν δὲ πολλοί) χρησμὸς ἦν, αὐτόθι ποιήσασθαι τὴν μονὴν ὅπου ἂν οἱ γηγενεῖς αὐτοῖς ἐπιθῶνται· συμβῆναι δὲ τοῦτ᾽ αὐτοῖς φασι περὶ Ἁμαξιτόν· νύκτωρ γὰρ πολὺ πλῆθος ἀρουραίων μυῶν ἐξανθῆσαν διαφαγεῖν ὅσα σκύτινα τῶν τε ὅπλων καὶ τῶν χρηστηρίων· τοὺς δὲ αὐτόθι μεῖναι· τούτους δὲ καὶ τὴν Ἴδην ἀπὸ τῆς ἐν Κρήτῃ προσονομάσαι. Ἡρακλείδης δ᾽ ὁ Ποντικὸς πληθύοντάς φησι τοὺς μύας περὶ τὸ ἱερὸν νομισθῆναί τε ἱεροὺς καὶ τὸ ξόανον οὕτω κατασκευασθῆναι βεβηκὸς ἐπὶ τῷ μυί.

In this Chryse is also the *hieron* of Sminthian Apollo, and the *symbolon* that preserves the etymology of the name, the mouse, lies under the foot of the *xoanon*. They are the works of Scopas of Paros; and also the history or myth about the mice is associated with this place. This is first recorded by Kallinos the elegiac poet, who has been followed by many others; it relates that the Teukroi, when they arrived from Crete, had an oracle bidding them make their home wherever the Earth-born should attack them. They say this happened for them at Hamaxitus; for at night a great multitude of field-mice swarmed out and ate up all the leather in their arms and equipments. They accordingly remained here, and it was they who gave its name to Ida from the mountain in Crete. Heraclides of Pontus says that the mice which swarm around the *hieron* are regarded as holy, and that this is why the *xoanon* is represented standing on a mouse.

346

Strabo 14.1.20 (C 640) I B.C.–A.D. I

Text: A. Meineke, ed., *Strabonis geographica* III (Leipzig, 1877).

Translation adapted from H.L. Jones, tr., *The Geography of Strabo* VI (LCL, 1929).

ὄντων δ' ἐν τῷ τόπῳ πλειόνων ναῶν, τῶν μὲν ἀρχαίων τῶν δ' ὕστερον γενομένων, ἐν μὲν τοῖς ἀρχαίοις ἀρχαῖά ἐστι ξόανα, ἐν δὲ τοῖς ὕστερον Σκόπα ἔργα. . . .

There are several *naoi* in the place, some *archaioi* and others built in later times; and in the *archaioi* ones there are many *archaia xoana*, but in those of later times there are works of Scopas. . . .

347

Strabo 14.1.37 (C 646) I B.C.–A.D. I

Text: A. Meineke, ed., *Strabonis geographica* III (Leipzig, 1877).

Translation adapted from H.L. Jones, tr., *The Geography of Strabo* VI (LCL, 1929).

ἔστι δὲ καὶ βιβλιοθήκη καὶ τὸ Ὁμήρειον, στοὰ τετράγωνος, ἔχουσα νεὼν Ὁμήρου καὶ ξόανον. . . .

There is also a library and the *Homereion*, a quadrangular stoa having a *neos* of Homer and a *xoanon*. . . .

348

Strabo 14.2.23 (C 659) I B.C.–A.D. I

Text: A. Meineke, ed., *Strabonis geographica* III (Leipzig, 1877).

Translation adapted from H.L. Jones, tr., *The Geography of Strabo* VI (LCL, 1929).

ἔχουσι δ' οἱ Μυλασεῖς ἱερὰ δύο τοῦ Διός, τοῦ τε Ὀσογῶα καλουμένου καὶ Λαβραυνδηνοῦ, τὸ μὲν ἐν τῇ πόλει, τὰ δὲ Λάβραυνδα κώμη ἐστὶν ἐν τῷ ὄρει κατὰ τὴν ὑπέρθεσιν τὴν ἐξ Ἀλαβάνδων εἰς τὰ Μύλασα ἄπωθεν τῆς πόλεως· ἐνταῦθα νεώς ἐστιν ἀρχαῖος καὶ ξόανον Διὸς Στρατίου· τιμᾶται δὲ ὑπὸ τῶν κύκλῳ καὶ ὑπὸ τῶν Μυλασέων, ὁδός τε ἔστρωται σχεδόν τι καὶ ἑξήκοντα σταδίων μέχρι τῆς πόλεως ἱερὰ καλουμένη, δι' ἧς πομποστολεῖται τὰ ἱερά· ἱερῶνται δ' οἱ ἐπιφανέστατοι τῶν πολιτῶν ἀεὶ διὰ βίου. ταῦτα μὲν οὖν ἴδια τῆς πόλεως. τρίτον δ' ἐστὶν ἱερὸν τοῦ Καρίου Διὸς κοινὸν ἁπάντων Καρῶν, οὗ μέτεστι καὶ Λυδοῖς καὶ Μυσοῖς ὡς ἀδελφοῖς.

The Mylasians have two *hiera* of Zeus, Zeus Osogo, as he is called, and Zeus Labraundenus. The former is in the city, whereas Labraunda is a village far from the city, being situated on the mountain near the pass that leads over from Alabanda to Mylasa. Here there is an *archaios neos* and a *xoanon* of Zeus Stratios. It is honored by the people all about and by the Mylasians; and there is a paved road of almost sixty stadia to the city, called Sacred, on which the *hiera* are conducted in procession; the priestly offices are held by the most distinguished of the citizens, always for life. Now these *hiera* belong peculiarly to the city; but there is a third *hieron*, of the Carian Zeus, which is a common possession of all Carians, and in which both Lydians and Mysians have a share as brothers.

349

Strabo 15.1.9 (C 688) I B.C.–A.D. I

Text: A. Meineke, ed., *Strabonis geographica* III (Leipzig, 1877).
Translation adapted from H.L. Jones, tr., *The Geography of Strabo* VII (LCL, 1930).

Ὅτι δ᾽ ἐστὶ πλάσματα ταῦτα τῶν κολακευόντων Ἀλέξανδρον πρῶτον μὲν ἐκ τοῦ μὴ ὁμολογεῖν ἀλλήλοις τοὺς συγγραφέας δῆλον, ἀλλὰ τοὺς μὲν λέγειν τοὺς δὲ μηδ᾽ ἁπλῶς μεμνῆσθαι· οὐ γὰρ εἰκὸς τὰ οὕτως ἔνδοξα καὶ τύφου πλήρη μὴ πεπύσθαι, ἢ πεπύσθαι μὲν μὴ ἄξια δὲ μνήμης ὑπολαβεῖν, καὶ ταῦτα τοὺς πιστοτάτους αὐτῶν· ἔπειτα ἐκ τοῦ μηδὲ τοὺς μεταξύ, δι᾽ ὧν ἐχρῆν τὴν ἐς Ἰνδοὺς ἄφιξιν γενέσθαι τοῖς περὶ τὸν Διόνυσον καὶ τὸν Ἡρακλέα, μηδὲν ἔχειν τεκμήριον δεικνύναι τῆς ἐκείνων ὁδοῦ διὰ τῆς σφετέρας γῆς. καὶ ἡ τοῦ Ἡρακλέους δὲ στολὴ ἡ τοιαύτη πολὺ νεωτέρα τῆς Τρωικῆς μνήμης ἐστί, πλάσμα τῶν τὴν Ἡράκλειαν ποιησάντων, εἴτε Πείσανδρος ἦν εἴτ᾽ ἄλλος τις· τὰ δ᾽ ἀρχαῖα ξόανα οὐχ οὕτω διεσκεύασται.

But that these stories are fabrications of the flatterers of Alexander is obvious; first, not only from the fact that the historians do not agree with one another, and also because, while some relate them, other make no mention whatever of them; for it is unreasonable to believe that exploits so famous and full of romance were unknown to any historian, or, if known, that they were regarded as unworthy of recording, and that too by the most trustworthy of the historians; and, secondly, from the fact that not even the intervening peoples, through whose countries Dionysus and Heracles and their followers would have had to pass in order to reach India, can show any evidence that these made a journey through their country. Further, such accoutrement of Heracles is much later than the records of the Trojan War, being a fabrication of the authors of the *Heracleia*, whether the author was Peisander or someone else; the *archaia xoana* of Heracles are not thus accoutred.

350

Strabo 15.3.15 (C 733) I B.C.–A.D. I

Text: A. Meineke, ed., *Strabonis geographica* III (Leipzig, 1877).

Translation adapted from H.L. Jones, tr., *The Geography of Strabo* VII (LCL, 1930).

Ἐν δὲ τῇ Καππαδοκίᾳ (πολὺ γὰρ ἐκεῖ τὸ τῶν Μάγων φῦλον, οἳ καὶ πύραιθοι καλοῦνται· πολλὰ δὲ καὶ τῶν Περσικῶν θεῶν ἱερά), οὐδὲ μαχαίρᾳ θύουσιν, ἀλλὰ κορμῷ τινι ὡς ἂν ὑπέρῳ τύπτοντες. ἔστι δὲ καὶ πυραιθεῖα, σηκοί τινες ἀξιόλογοι· ἐν δὲ τούτοις μέσοις βωμός, ἐν ᾧ πολλή τε σποδός, καὶ πῦρ ἄσβεστον φυλάττουσιν οἱ Μάγοι· καὶ καθ' ἡμέραν δὲ εἰσιόντες, ἐπᾴδουσιν ὥραν σχεδόν τι πρὸ τοῦ πυρὸς τὴν δέσμην τῶν ῥάβδων ἔχοντες, τιάρας περικείμενοι πιλωτὰς καθεικυίας ἑκατέρωθεν μέχρι τοῦ καλύπτειν τὰ χείλη τὰς παραγναθίδας. ταὐτὰ δ' ἐν τοῖς τῆς Ἀναΐτιδος καὶ τοῦ Ὠμάνου ἱεροῖς νενόμισται· τούτων δὲ καὶ σηκοί εἰσι, καὶ ξόανον τοῦ Ὠμάνου πομπεύει.

In Cappadocia (for there the sect of the Magi, who are also called Pyraethi, is large, and in that country are also many *hiera* of the Persian gods), the people do not sacrifice victims with a sword either, but with a kind of tree-trunk, beating them to death as with a cudgel. They also have Pyraetheia, *sekoi* worthy of note; and in the midst of these there is a *bomos*, on which there is a large quantity of ashes and where the Magi keep the fire ever burning. And there, entering daily, they make incantations for about an hour, holding before the fire their bundle of rods and wearing round their heads high turbans of felt, which reach down over their cheeks far enough to cover their lips. The same customs are observed in the *hiera* of Anaïtis and Omanus; and these also have *sekoi*; and the *xoanon* of Omanus takes part in a procession.

351

Strabo 16.2.35 (C 760–761) I B.C.–A.D. I

Text: A. Meineke, ed., *Strabonis geographica* III (Leipzig, 1877).

Translation adapted from H.L. Jones, tr., *The Geography of Strabo* VII (LCL, 1930).

Μωσῆς γάρ τις τῶν Αἰγυπτίων ἱερέων ἔχων τι μέρος τῆς [κάτω] καλουμένης χώρας, ἀπῆρεν ἐκεῖσε ἐνθένδε δυσχεράνας τὰ καθεστῶτα, καὶ συνεξῆραν αὐτῷ πολλοὶ τιμῶντες τὸ θεῖον. ἔφη γὰρ ἐκεῖνος καὶ ἐδίδασκεν, ὡς οὐκ ὀρθῶς φρονοῖεν οἱ Αἰγύπτιοι θηρίοις εἰκάζοντες καὶ βοσκήμασι τὸ θεῖον, οὐδ' οἱ Λίβυες· οὐκ εὖ δὲ οὐδ' οἱ Ἕλληνες ἀνθρωπομόρφους τυποῦντες· εἴη γὰρ ἓν τοῦτο μόνον θεὸς τὸ περιέχον ἡμᾶς ἅπαντας καὶ γῆν καὶ θάλατταν, ὃ καλοῦμεν οὐρανὸν καὶ κόσμον καὶ τὴν τῶν ὄντων φύσιν. τούτου δὴ τίς ἂν εἰκόνα πλάττειν θαρρήσειε νοῦν ἔχων ὁμοίαν τινὶ τῶν παρ' ἡμῖν; ἀλλ' ἐᾶν δεῖν πᾶσαν ξοανοποιίαν, τέμενος [δ'] ἀφορίσαντας καὶ σηκὸν ἀξιόλογον τιμᾶν ἕδους χωρίς. ἐγκοιμᾶσθαι δὲ καὶ αὐτοὺς ὑπὲρ ἑαυτῶν καὶ ὑπὲρ τῶν ἄλλων ἄλλους τοὺς εὐονείρους· καὶ προσδοκᾶν δεῖν ἀγαθὸν παρὰ τοῦ θεοῦ καὶ δῶρον ἀεί τι καὶ σημεῖον τοὺς σωφρόνως ζῶντας καὶ μετὰ δικαιοσύνης, τοὺς δ' ἄλλους μὴ προσδοκᾶν.

Moses was one of the Egyptian priests, and although he held a part of Lower Egypt, as it is called, he went away from there [to Judaea], since he was displeased with the state of affairs [there], and many people who worshipped the Divine Being accompanied him. For he said, and taught, that the Egyptians were mistaken in representing the Divine Being by the images of beasts and cattle, as were also the Libyans; and that the Greeks were also wrong in modelling anthropomorphic [gods]; for, according to him, God is this one thing alone that encompasses us all and encompasses land and sea—the thing which we call *ouranos* and *kosmos* and the nature of all things that exist. What man, then, if he has sense, could be bold enough to fabricate an *eikon* of God resembling any creature among us? But all making of *xoana* must be abandoned; instead, setting off a *temenos* and a worthy *sekos*, people should worship without a *hedos*; and people who have good dreams should sleep in the sanctuary, not only themselves on their own behalf, but also others for the rest of the people; and those who live self-restrained and righteous lives should always expect some blessing or sign or gift from God, but no other should expect them.

352

Strabo 17.1.28 (C 805) I B.C.–A.D. I
Text: A. Meineke, ed., *Strabonis geographica* III (Leipzig, 1877).
Translation adapted from H.L. Jones, tr., *The Geography of Strabo* VIII (LCL, 1932).

μετὰ δὲ τὰς σφίγγας πρόπυλον μέγα, εἶτ' ἄλλο προελθόντι πρόπυλον, εἶτ' ἄλλο· οὐκ ἔστι δὲ διωρισμένος ἀριθμὸς οὔτε τῶν προπύλων οὔτε τῶν σφιγγῶν· ἄλλα δ' ἐν ἄλλοις ἱεροῖς, ὥσπερ καὶ τὰ μήκη καὶ τὰ πλάτη τῶν δρόμων. μετὰ δὲ τὰ προπύλαια ὁ νεὼς πρόναον ἔχων μέγα καὶ ἀξιόλογον, τὸν δὲ σηκὸν σύμμετρον, ξόανον δ' οὐδέν, ἢ οὐκ ἀνθρωπόμορφον, ἀλλὰ τῶν ἀλόγων ζῴων τινός·

And after the sphinxes one comes to a large *propylon*, and then, as one proceeds, to another, and then another; but there is no prescribed number either of *propyla* or of sphinxes, and they are different in different *hiera*, as are also the lengths and the breadths of the *dromoi*. After the *propylaia* one comes to the *neos*, which has a large and noteworthy *pronaos*, and to a *sekos* of commensurate size, though it has no *xoanon*, or rather no anthropomorphic one, but of some irrational animal.

353

Strabo 17.1.43 (C 814) I B.C.–A.D. I

Text: A. Meineke, ed., *Strabonis geographica* III (Leipzig, 1877).

Translation adapted from H.L. Jones, tr., *The Geography of Strabo* VIII (LCL, 1932).

ὁ γοῦν Καλλισθένης φησὶ τὸν Ἀλέξανδρον φιλοδοξῆσαι μάλιστα ἀνελθεῖν ἐπὶ τὸ χρηστήριον, ἐπειδὴ καὶ Περσέα ἤκουσε πρότερον ἀναβῆναι καὶ Ἡρακλέα· ὁρμήσαντα δ' ἐκ Παραιτονίου καίπερ νότων ἐπιπεσόντων βιάσασθαι, πλανώμενον δ' ὑπὸ τοῦ κονιορτοῦ σωθῆναι γενομένων ὄμβρων καὶ δυεῖν κοράκων ἡγησαμένων τὴν ὁδόν, ἤδη τούτων κολακευτικῶς λεγομένων· τοιαῦτα δὲ καὶ τὰ ἑξῆς· μόνῳ γὰρ δὴ τῷ βασιλεῖ τὸν ἱερέα ἐπιτρέψαι παρελθεῖν εἰς τὸν νεὼ μετὰ τῆς συνήθους στολῆς, τοὺς δ' ἄλλους μετενδῦναι τὴν ἐσθῆτα, ἔξωθέν τε τῆς θεμιστείας ἀκροάσασθαι πάντας πλὴν Ἀλεξάνδρου, τοῦτον δ' ἔνδοθεν. εἶναι δ' οὐχ ὥσπερ ἐν Δελφοῖς καὶ Βραγχίδαις τὰς ἀποθεσπίσεις διὰ λόγων, ἀλλὰ νεύμασι καὶ συμβόλοις τὸ πλέον, ὡς καὶ παρ' Ὁμήρῳ "ἦ καὶ κυανέῃσιν ἐπ' ὀφρύσι νεῦσε Κρονίων," τοῦ προφήτου τὸν Δία ὑποκριναμένου· τοῦτο μέντοι ῥητῶς εἰπεῖν τὸν ἄνθρωπον πρὸς τὸν βασιλέα ὅτι εἴη Διὸς υἱός.

At any rate, Callisthenes says that Alexander conceived a very great ambition to go inland to the oracle, since he had heard that Perseus, as also Heracles, had done so in earlier times; and that he started from Paraetonium, although the south winds had set in, and forced his way; and that when he lost his way because of the thick dust, he was saved by rainfalls and by the guidance of two crows. But this last assertion is flattery and so are the next: that the priest permitted the king alone to pass into the *neos* in his usual dress, but the rest changed their clothes; that all heard the oracles from outside except Alexander, but he inside; that the oracular responses were not, as at Delphi and among the Branchidae, given in words, but mostly by nods and *symboloi*, as in Homer—"The son of Cronos spoke and nodded assent with his dark brows"—the prophet having assumed the role of Zeus; that, however, the fellow expressly told the king that he, Alexander, was son of Zeus.

354

Suda s.v. Δαιδάλου ποιήματα A.D. X

Text: A. Adler, ed., *Suidae Lexicon* (Lexicographi Graeci I) II (Leipzig, 1931) 12.110.

Δαιδάλου ποιήματα: ἐπὶ τῶν ἀκριβούντων τὰς τέχνας. ἐπειδὴ οἱ παλαιοὶ δημιουργοὶ συμμεμυκότας τοὺς ὀφθαλμοὺς ἐποίουν, ὁ δὲ Δαίδαλος ἀνεπέτασεν αὐτοὺς καὶ τοὺς πόδας διέστησε. καὶ Ὅμηρός φησιν· ὃς χερσὶν *ἠπίστατο δαίδαλα πάντα τεύχειν· ἔξοχα γάρ μιν ἐφίλατο Παλλὰς Ἀθήνη· ὃς καὶ Ἀλεξάνδρῳ τεκτήνατο νῆας ἐΐσας.*

Works of Daedalus: with reference to consummate productions of art. Since the ancient craftsmen made the eyes closed up, but Daedalus opened them and separated the feet. And Homer says "who knew how to make all *daedala* with his hands; for Pallas Athena loved him most of all; and who had crafted the even-balanced ships for Alexandros [*Il.* 5.60–62]."

355

Suda s.v. Ξόανον A.D. X

Text: A. Adler, ed., *Suidae Lexicon* (Lexicographi Graeci I) III (Leipzig, 1933) 497.78.

Ξόανον: ἄγαλμα, εἴδωλον, ζῴδιον, ἀνδριάς.

Xoanon: agalma, eidolon, zoidion, andrias.

356

Suda s.v. Οἱ Νομοφύλακες *τίνες* A.D. X

Text: A. Adler, ed., *Suidae Lexicon* (Lexicographi Graeci I) III (Leipzig, 1933).

Οἱ Νομοφύλακες *τίνες· ἔδοξέ τισι αὐτοὺς εἶναι τοῖς θεσμοθέταις· ἀλλ' οὐκ ἔστιν οὕτως· οἱ μὲν γὰρ θεσμοθέται κατὰ τὰ πάτρια ἐστεφανωμένοι ἐπὶ τὸν* Ἄρειον *ἀνέβαινον πάγον, οἱ δὲ νομοφύλακες στροφίοις λευκοῖς ἐχρῶντο καὶ ἐν ταῖς θέαις ἐπὶ θρόνων ἐκάθηντο κατ' ἀντικρὺ τῶν ἐννέα ἀρχόντων· καὶ τῇ* Παλλάδι *τὴν πομπὴν ἐκόσμουν, ὅτε κομίζοιτο τὸ ξόανον ἐπὶ τὴν τὴν θάλασσαν. . . .*

The ones called Nomophylakes: Some think that these are [like] the Thesmothetai; but this is not so; for the Thesmothetai, according to ancestral custom, go crowned up onto the Areopagus, while the Nomophylakes used white headbands and at the performances they sat in chairs exactly opposite the nine archons. And they were in charge of the procession for Pallas, when the *xoanon* would be conducted to the sea. . . .

357

Suda s.v. Οὐδὲν *ἱερόν* A.D. X

Text: A. Adler, ed., *Suidae Lexicon* (Lexicographi Graeci I) III (Leipzig, 1933) 577.798.

Οὐδὲν *ἱερόν:* Ἡρακλῆς *εἶπεν* Ἀδώνιδος *ἰδὼν ξόανον, ὡς τῶν εὐεργετησάντων τοὺς ἀνθρώπους μόνων ὀφειλόντων τιμᾶσθαι· ἢ ὅτι οἱ καταφυγόντες εἰς αὐτὸ δοῦλοι ἄδειαν οὐκ εἶχον.*

Nothing sacred: Heracles, seeing the *xoanon* of Adonis, said how only those men are honored who have done beneficial or helpful things; or else, because slaves who took refuge at it did not receive amnesty.

358

Suda s.v. ῾Ρύσια A.D. X

Text: A. Adler, ed., *Suidae Lexicon* (Lexicographi Graeci I) IV (Leipzig, 1935) 308.308.

῾Ρύσια: ἐνέχυρα. καὶ ῾Ρυσιάζω. φασὶ δὲ τὸν νεανίσκον ἀνελεῖν καὶ τὴν πόλιν ῥυσιάζειν. ἀντὶ τοῦ ἐνέχυρα λαμβάνειν. ᾿Ιωσηπος· πρῶτον μὲν γὰρ ῥύσιον τῶν πολεμίων ἄγων καὶ πολὺ συγκροτήσας ἱππικὸν ἐπαφίησιν αὐτοὺς περὶ Διόσπολιν. ὅπως ἔχοι τὸ ξόανον ῥύσιον ἐν ᾿Ιθάκῃ ὁ ᾿Οδυσσεύς.

Pledges: securities. See also "Seize a pledge." They say that the youth takes and seizes the city as a pledge. Instead of taking securities. Josephus: for, first taking a pledge of the enemy, having trained the cavalry much, he let them loose round about Diospolis. As Odysseus would have a *xoanon* as a pledge in Ithaca.

359

Symeonis Etymologicum s.v. ἄγαλμα A.D. XII

Text: F. Lasserre and N. Livadaras, eds., *Etymologicum Magnum Genuinum. Symeonis Etymologicum una cum magna grammatica Etymologicum Magnum Auctum* I (Rome, 1976) 18. 32/35.

ἄγαλμα· ἀγαλλίαμα, καλλώπισμα, πᾶν ἐφ᾽ ᾧ τις ἀγάλλεται. ἄλλοι δὲ ἄγαλμα εἶπον τὸ ξόανον. τὸ δὲ ἄγαλμα παρὰ τὸ ἀγάλλω, τοῦτο παρὰ τὸ ἀγλαόν, τοῦτο παρὰ τὸ αἴγλη. ἢ παρὰ τὸ ἄγαν καὶ τὸ ἄλλω, τὸ πηδῶ.

Agalma: Transport of joy, ornament, everything in which one glories. Others call an *agalma* a *xoanon*. *Agalma* comes from *agallo* [to glory], this from *aglaon* [splendid], this from *aigle* [light of the sun or moon]. Or else it is derived from *agan* and *allo*, *pedo*.

Synagoge Lexeon Chresimon s.v. Ἄγαλμα

See *Anecdota Bekker* I.334.18 [**11**].

Synagoge Lexeon Chresimon s.v. ξόανον

See *Anecdota Bachmann* I.311.8 [**9**].

360

Tertullian, *Apologeticus* 16.1–11 C. A.D. 197

Text and translation: T.R. Glover, tr., *Tertullian. Apology. De Spectaculis* (LCL, 1931).

Nam et, ut quidam, somniastis caput asininum esse deum nostrum. Hanc Cornelius Tacitus suspicionem eiusmodi *dei* inservit. Is enim, in quinta historiarum suarum bellum Iudaicum exorsus ab origine gentis, etiam de ipsa tam origine quam de nomine et religione gentis quae volit argumentatus Iudaeos refert Aegypto expeditos sive, ut putavit, extorres vastis Arabiae in locis aquarum egentissimis, cum siti macerarentur, onagris, qui forte de pastu potum petituri aestimabantur, indicibus fontis usos ob eam gratiam consimilis bestiae superficiem consecrasse. Atque ita inde praesumptum opinor nos quoque ut Iudaicae religionis propinquos eidem simulacro initiari. At enim idem Cornelius Tacitus, sane ille mendaciorum loquacissimus, in eadem historia refert Gnaeum Pompeium, cum Hierusalem cepisset proptereaque templum adisset speculandis Iudaicae religionis arcanis, nullum illic reperisse simulacrum. Et utique, si id colebatur quod aliqua effigie repraesentabatur, nusquam magis quam in sacrario suo exhiberetur, eo magis, quia nec verebatur extraneos arbitros, quamquam vana cultura. Solis enim sacerdotibus adire licitum; etiam conspectus ceterorum velo oppanso interdicebatur. Vos tamen non negabitis et iumenta omnia et totos cantherios cum sua Epona coli a vobis. Hoc forsitan inprobamur, quod inter cultores omnium pecudum bestiarumque asinarii tantum sumus.

Sed et qui crucis nos religiosos putat, consecraneus erit noster. Cum lignum aliquod propitiatur, viderit habitus, cum materiae qualitas eadem sit, viderit forma, dum id ipsum dei corpus sit. Et tamen quanto distinguitur a crucis stipite Pallas Attica, et Ceres Pharia, quae sine effigie rudi palo et informi ligno prostant? Pars crucis est omne robur quod erecta statione defigitur. Nos, si forte, integrum et totum deum colimus. Diximus originem deorum vestrorum a plastis de cruce induci. Sed et Victorias adoratis, cum in tropaeis cruces intestina sint tropaeorum. Religio Romanorum tota castrensis signa veneratur, signa iurat, signa omnibus deis praeponit. Omnes illi imaginum suggestus in signis monilia crucum sunt; siphara illa vexillorum et cantabrorum stolae crucum sunt. Laudo diligentiam. Noluistis incultas et nudas cruces consecrare.

Alii plane humanius et verisimilius solem credunt deum nostrum. Ad Persas, si forte, deputabimur, licet solem non in linteo depictum adoremus, habentes ipsum ubique in suo clypeo. Denique inde suspicio quod innotuerit nos ad orientis regionem precari. Sed et plerique vestrum adfectatione aliquando et caelestia adorandi ad solis ortum labia vibratis. Aeque si diem solis laetitiae indulgemus, alia longe ratione quam religione solis secundo loco ab eis sumus qui diem Saturni otio et victui decernunt exorbitantes et ipsi a Iudaico more, quem ignorant.

For, in fact, with other people, you have dreamed that our God is an ass's head. This sort of notion Cornelius Tacitus introduced. For in the fifth book of his *Histories* he begins his account of the Jewish War with the origin of the race; and about that origin as about the name and religion of the race he discoursed as he pleased. He tells how the Jews, liberated from Egypt, or, as he thought, exiled, were in the wilderness of Arabia utterly barren of water; and how, dying of thirst, they saw wild asses, which chanced to be returning from their pasture (it was thought) to slake their thirst; how they used them as guides to a fountain, and out of gratitude consecrated a likeness of a beast of that kind. Thence came, I think, the assumption that we too, standing so near Jewish religion, are devoted to worship of the same image. Yet this same Cornelius Tacitus—no, not Tacit, he, but a first class chatterbox when it comes to lies!—in the same History tells how Cnaeus Pompey, on taking Jerusalem, visited the temple to look into the mysteries of Jewish religion, and found no image there. And surely if the object of worship had been represented by any image, nowhere would it have been more likely to be seen than in its own shrine; all the more, because, however trivial the worship, there at least it feared no eyes from outside. For only the priests were allowed to enter; even to look in was made impossible for all others by a veil hung between. *You*, however, will not deny that every kind of baggage cattle and whole donkeys with their goddess Epona are objects of *your* worship. Perhaps this is the real source of our bad name, that, among worshippers of every kind of beast and quadruped, we confine ourselves to the ass!

Yes, and the man who thinks we worship the cross, will prove a fellow worshipper of ours. For when a bit of wood is worshipped—what matters the shape, if the nature of the material is the same? what the form if it is the body of a god? Yet what distinction can you make between the shaft of a cross and the Attic Pallas or Pharian Ceres, each of whom stands there unshaped, a rude pole, a log untrimmed? Every balk of timber, which is set up erect, is part of a cross; we—perhaps—worship a god complete and whole. We have said that in the first instance your gods are moulded by the sculptors on a cross. But you also adore Victories, and in all trophies the cross is the inner structure of the trophy. Roman religion, every bit of it a religion of camps, venerates the standards, swears by the standards, sets the standards before all the gods. All those rows of images on the standards are but ornaments hung upon crosses. I laud your thoughtfulness. You did not want to consecrate crosses naked and unadorned.

Others again (it is really a more refined, a more probable idea) believe the sun to be our god. We shall be reckoned perhaps as Persians, though we do not adore the sun painted on a canvas, seeing we have the sun with us everywhere in his own orb. This suspicion must be due to its becoming known that we turn to the East when we pray. But again a great many of you, in some make-believe of adoring now and then the heavenly bodies among other things, move your lips at sunrise. Equally, if we devote the day of the sun (Sunday) to joy (from a very different cause than sun-worship) we stand next in line to those who devote Saturn's day to resting and eating, wide as they are from Jewish usage of which they know nothing.

361

Tertullian, *De idolatria* 3 A.D. II

Text: J.-P. Migne, ed., *Patrologiae Cursus Completus. Series Latina. Patrologiae Latinae Tomus* I (Paris, 1878). Tertullian, *De Idolatria* 3 cols. 664–665.

Translation adapted from S.C. Greenslade, ed., tr., *The Library of Christian Classics* V. *Early Latin Theology* (Philadelphia, 1956) 85.

Idolum aliquandiu retro non erat. Priusquam hujus monstri artifices ebullissent, sola templa et vacuae aedes erant, sicut in hodiernum quibusdam locius vetustatis vestigia permanent. Tamen idolatria agebatur, non in isto nomine, sed in isto opere. Nam et hodie extra templum et sine idolo agi potest. At ubi artifices statuarum et imaginum, et omnis generis simulacrorum diabolus saeculo intulit, rude illum negotium humanae calamitatis, et nomen de idolis consecutum est, et profectum.

Once, for a time, there were no idols. Before the makers of these monstrosities shot up, the *templa* were solitary and the *aedes* empty, as you may see today in spots where traces of antiquity survive. Of course idolatry was practiced, in fact if not in name. For even today it can be carried on outside a *templum* and without an idol. But when the devil brought into the world the makers of statues and portraits and every kind of image, the practice, untaught as yet but fraught with disaster to mankind, took its name and its development from the idols.

362

Themistius, *Oration* 26.316 a–b A.D. IV

Text: H. Schenkl, G. Downey, and A.F. Norman, eds., *Themistii Orationes quae supersunt* II (Leipzig, 1971).

καὶ πρὸ μὲν Δαιδάλου τετράγωνος ἦν οὐ μόνον ἡ τῶν ʿΕρμῶν ἐργασία, ἀλλὰ καὶ ἡ τῶν λοιπῶν ἀνδριάντων· Δαίδαλος δὲ ἐπειδὴ πρῶτος διήγαγε τὼ πόδε τῶν ἀγαλμάτων, ἔμπνοα δημιουργεῖν ἐνομίσθη.

Before Daedalus, not only were herms worked in rectangular form, but also all the rest of *andriantes*. Daedalus, because he was the first to separate the two feet of *agalmata*, was thought to make living things.

363
Themistius, *ad* Aristotle, *De Anima* 1.3 A.D. IV
See also Eubulus and Philippus [**30**].
Text: L. Spengel, ed., *Themistii Paraphrases Aristotelis librorum quae supersunt* II (Leipzig, 1866) 34.25–29.

οἱ κινουμένην κατὰ τόπον τὴν ψυχὴν κινεῖν τὸ σῶμα ἀποφαινόμενοι παραπλήσιόν τι λέγουσι Φιλίππῳ τῷ κωμῳδοδιδασκάλῳ· φησὶ γὰρ ὁ Δαίδαλος παρ' αὐτῷ κινουμένην ποιῆσαι τὴν ξυλίνην Ἀφροδίτην ἐγχέας ἄργυρον χυτόν.

Those who say that the soul, being moved in its place, moves the body, offer something similar to Philippus the comic poet: for in his work, Daedalus says that he made a wooden Aphrodite move by pouring in silver.

364
[Theocritus], *Epigram* 4
(= *Anthologia Palatina* 9.437.)
Text: A.S.F. Gow, ed., tr., *Theocritus* (Cambridge, 1950) I, 240–241.
Translation adapted from Gow.

Τήναν τὰν λαύραν τόθι ταὶ δρύες, αἰπόλε, κάμψας
σύκινον εὑρήσεις ἀρτιγλυφὲς ξόανον
ἀσκελὲς αὐτόφλοιον ἀνούατον, ἀλλὰ φάλητι
παιδογόνῳ δυνατὸν Κύπριδος ἔργα τελεῖν.
σακὸς δ' εὐίερος περιδέδρομεν, ἀέναον δὲ
ῥεῖθρον ἀπὸ σπιλάδων πάντοσε τηλεθάει
δάφναις καὶ μύρτοισι καὶ εὐώδει κυπαρίσσῳ,
ἔνθα πέριξ κέχυται βοτρυόπαις ἕλικι
ἄμπελος, εἰαρινοὶ δὲ λιγυφθόγγοισιν ἀοιδαῖς
κόσσυφοι ἀχεῦσιν ποικιλότραυλα μέλη.
ξουθαὶ δ' ἀδονίδες μινυρίσμασιν ἀνταχεῦσι
μέλπουσαι στόμασιν τὰν μελίγαρυν ὄπα.
ἕζεο δὴ τηνεὶ καὶ τῷ χαρίεντι Πριήπῳ
εὔχε' ἀποστέρξαι τοὺς Δάφνιδός με πόθους,
κεὐθὺς ἐπιρρέξειν χίμαρον καλόν. ἢν δ' ἀνανεύσῃ,
τοῦδε τυχὼν ἐθέλω τρισσὰ θύη τελέσαι·
ῥέξω γὰρ δαμάλαν, λάσιον τράγον, ἄρνα τὸν ἴσχω
σακίταν. ἀίοι δ' εὐμενέως ὁ θεός.

Follow yonder lane where the oaks are, goatherd, and, having turned [down it], you will find a new-carved *xoanon* of figwood; the bark is still on it, and it has neither legs nor ears, but is equipped with procreant member to do the works of Cypris. A holy enclosure surrounds it, and a spring that flows perennial from the rocks is thick-set about with bays and myrtles and aromatic cypress. Around the spot a vine spreads its tendrils and bears its clusters, and in the springtime blackbirds pour forth their gaily-fluted notes in clear-voiced minstrelsy, and tuneful nightingales raise their honeyed voices and warble in reply. There take thy seat and make petition to gracious Priapus that I may lose my longing for Daphnis, promising him thereon a fair kid for sacrifice. But if he consent not, then, if I win my love, three offerings will I make; for I will slay a heifer, and a shaggy he-goat, and a stall-fed lamb I have. And may the god give gracious ear to thee.

365

Theophilus, *Ad Autolycum* 2.36, 52, 61–67 A.D. II
(= *Oracula Sibyllina* fr. 3.21–31.)
Text: J.-P. Migne, ed., *S.P.N. Justini philosophi et martyris, opera quae exstant omnia, necnon Tatiani, Hermiae, Athenagorae et S. Theophili quae supersunt* (Patrologiae Cursus Completus 6; 1884).
Text of the oracle: J. Geffcken, *Die Oracula Sibyllina* (GCS 8; Leipzig, 1902).
Translation adapted from J.J. Collins, "Sibylline Oracles," in J.H. Charlesworth, ed., *The Old Testament Pseudepigrapha* I (Garden City, 1983) 471.

Σίβυλλα δὲ, ἐν Ἕλλησι, καὶ ἐν τοῖς λοιποῖς ἔθνεσιν γενομένη προφῆτις, ἐν ἀρχῇ τῆς προφητείας αὐτῆς ὀνειδίζει τὸ τῶν ἀνθρώπων γένος λέγουσα·
Καὶ πρὸς τοὺς γενητοὺς λεγομένους ἔφη·
ἄνθρωποι, τί μάτην ὑφούμενοι ἐκριζοῦσθε;
αἰσχύνθητε γαλᾶς καὶ κνώδαλα θειοποιοῦντες.
οὐ μανίη καὶ λύσσα φρενῶν αἴσθησιν ἀφαιρεῖ,
εἰ λοπάδας κλέπτουσι θεοί, συλοῦσι δὲ χύτρας·
ἀντὶ δὲ χρυσήεντα πόλον κατὰ πίονα ναίειν
σητόβρωτα δέδορκε, πυκναῖς δ' ἀράχναις δεδίασται·
προσκυνέοντες ὄφεις κύνας αἰλούρους, ἀνόητοι,
καὶ πετεηνὰ σέβεσθε καὶ ἑρπετὰ θηρία γαίης
καὶ λίθινα ξόανα καὶ ἀγάλματα χειροποίητα,
καὶ παρ' ὁδοῖσι λίθων συγχώσματα· ταῦτα σέβεσθε
ἄλλα τε πολλὰ μάταια, ἃ δὴ καἰσχρὸν ἀγορεύειν. . . .

And the Sibyl, who was a prophetess among the Greeks and the rest of the nations, in the beginning of her prophecy reproaches the race of men saying: . . .
And regarding those [gods] which are said to have been born, she said: . . .

Men, why do you vainly exalt yourselves so that you will be rooted out?
Be ashamed of deifying polecats and brute beasts.
Do not madness and frenzy take away the sense of the mind
if gods steal dishes and plunder pots?
And instead of living in the boundless vault of heaven
they appear moth-eaten and are woven with thick cobwebs.
Mindless ones, adoring snakes, dogs, and cats,
you revere birds and wild serpents of the earth
and stone *xoana* and handmade *agalmata*
and heaps of stones by the roads. These things you revere
and many other vain things which it is disgraceful even to mention.

Theopompus IV B.C.
FGrH 115 F 159
See Ammonius *s.v.* ἱερά [**6**].

366

Johannes Tzetzes, *Chiliades* I.19.536–541 A.D. XII
Text: T. Kiessling, ed., *Ioannis Tzetzae Historiarum Variarum Chiliades* (Leipzig, 1826) 23.

Τὰ δὲ δαιδάλειά φασι κινεῖσθαι τοιοτρόπως·
Τοὺς ἀνδριάντας πρότερον πρὸ χρόνων τῶν Δαιδάλου
Ἐδημιούργουν ἄχειρας, ἄποδας, ἀομμάτους·
Πρῶτος δ' ὁ Δαίδαλος αὐτὸς διεῖλε χεῖρας, πόδας,
Δακτύλους διηρμόσατο καὶ βλέφαρα καὶ τἄλλα.
Ὅθεν ὁ μῦθος πέπτωκε, κινεῖσθαι τὰ Δαιδάλου.

They say that Daedalus' works moved in this way: before the time of Daedalus they produced *andriantes* that were handless, footless, eyeless. Daedalus was the first to separate the hands, feet, fingers, and to arrange the eyelids and other things. Whence grew up the myth, that the works of Daedalus moved.

367

Johannes Tzetzes, *Chiliades* XII, *Historia* 429.590–591 A.D. XII
Text: T. Kiessling, ed., *Ioannis Tzetzae Historiarum Variarum Chiliades* (Leipzig, 1826) 463.

Ἑρμῆς τῆς Μαίας *ὁ υἱός, Ἑρμῆς δὲ καὶ ὁ λόγος·*
Ἑρμῆς καὶ σύμπας ἀνδριὰς καὶ ὁ σωρὸς τῶν λίθων.

Hermes the son of Maia, Hermes also the *logos*;
Hermes both whole *andrias* and heap of stones.

368
Johannes Tzetzes, *Exegesis in Homeri Iliadem* 11 A.D. XII
Text: G. Hermann, ed., *Draconis Stratonicensis Liber de metris poeticis. Ioannis Tzetzae Exegesis in Homeri Iliadem* (Leipzig, 1812) p. 122.12–14.

ἀλλ' οἱ Αἰολεῖς τὸ βραχὺ ο̄ τρέπουσιν εἰς ῡ, οὐ τὸ μακρὸν, ὄνυμα τὸ ὄνομα λέγοντες, καὶ ξύανον τὸ ξόανον, καὶ τὰ ὅμοια.

But the Aeolians turn short “o” into “u”, not the long [o], calling *onoma onUma*, and *xoanon xUanon*, and similar things.

369
Xenophon, *Anabasis* 5.3.12 V–IV B.C.
Text: E.C. Marchant, ed., *Xenophontis opera omnia* III. *Expeditio Cyri* (Oxford, 1904).
Translation adapted from C.L. Brownson, tr., *Xenophon. Anabasis, Books IV–VII* (LCL, 1922, 1961).

ὁ δὲ ναὸς ὡς μικρὸς μεγάλῳ τῷ ἐν Ἐφέσῳ εἴκασται, καὶ τὸ ξόανον ἔοικεν ὡς κυπαρίττινον χρυσῷ ὄντι τῷ ἐν Ἐφέσῳ.

The *naos* is like the one at Ephesus, although small as compared with large, and the *xoanon*, although cypress wood as compared to gold, looks like the one in Ephesus.

370
[Zonaras], *Lexicon s.v.* Ἀγάλματα A.D. XIII
(= *Anecdota Parisiensis* IV.90.1 *s.v.*)
Text: J.A. Cramer, ed., *Anecdota Graeca e codicibus manuscriptis Bibliothecae Regiae Parisiensis* IV. *Excerpta Philologica Pars* II (Oxford, 1841) 90.1.

ἈΓΑΛΜΑΤΑ: *Ξόανα, ἀνδριάντες, παρὰ τὸ ἀγάλλω, τοῦτο παρὰ τὸ ἀγλαὸν, τοῦτο παρὰ τὸ αἴγλη.*

Agalmata: *Xoana, andriantes*, derived from *agallo* [to glory]; this is derived from *aglaon* [splendid]: this is derived from *aigle* [light of the sun or moon].

371
[Zonaras], *Lexicon s.v. ξόανον* A.D. XIII
(= *Anecdota Parisiensis* IV.199.17.)
Text: M. Naoumides, “The Shorter Version of Pseudo-Zonaras, *Lexicon*,” in J.L. Heller, ed., *Serta Turyniana* (Urbana, Chicago, and London, 1974) 476.35.

ξόανον: ἄγαλμα, εἴδωλον· παρὰ τὸ ξέω, ξέανον καὶ ξόανον. οὕτω Φίλων.

Xoanon: *agalma*, *eidolon*; derived from *xeo*, *xeanon* and *xoanon*. Thus Philo.

372

Pap. Leiden, Rijksmuseum van Oudheden J. 384.301–306 A.D. IV
Text: K. Preisendanz, ed., tr., *Papyri graecae magicae* II (Leipzig and Berlin, 1931) 78–79, Col. IX.

ἐπεκαλεσάμην σέ, θεὲ μέγιστε, καὶ διά σου |τὰ πάντα, ὅπως δῷς θείαν καὶ μεγίστην δύναμιν τούτῳ τῷ ξοάνῳ καὶ ποιήσῃς |αὐτὸ δύνασθαι καὶ ἰσχύειν κατὰ πάντων καὶ χωρεῖν ψυχὰς μετατρέπειν, πνεύματα |κινεῖν, ἀντιδίκους ὑποτάσσειν, φιλίας στηρίζειν, πόρους πάντας, περιποιεῖν, ὀνεί||ρους ἐπιφέρειν, χρησμοδοτεῖν, πάθη τε ψυχικὰ καὶ σωματικὰ καὶ ἀσθένειαν ἐμπο|δισμόν τε ποιεῖν, φίλτρα ἐρωτικὰ πάντα ἀποτελεῖν.

I have called on you, greatest god, and through you on the All, that you give divine and greatest power to this *xoanon*, and make it be strong and powerful over all things, and move to bring souls around, to move spirits, to subdue opponents, to secure friendship, to attain all ways and means, to bring dreams, to prophesy, to prevent all suffering, spiritual and bodily, and weakness, to produce every kind of love-charm.

373

Pap. Leiden, Rijksmuseum van Oudheden J. 384.317–321 A.D. IV
Text: K. Preisendanz, ed., tr., *Papyri graecae magicae* II (Leipzig and Berlin, 1931) 79, Col. X.

ὁ δὲ Οὔφωρ |οὗτός ἐστιν, ᾧ Οὔρβικος ἐχρᾶτο. τὸ ἱερὸν Οὔφωρ, τὸ ἀληθές, διὰ πάσης συντο|μίας ἀληθῶς ἀναγέγραπται, δι' οὗ ζωπυρεῖται πάντα πλάσματα καὶ γλυφαὶ |καὶ ξόανα· τοῦτο γὰρ ἐστ[ι]ν τὸ ἀληθές, τὰ δὲ ἄλλα, ὅσα φέρεται διὰ μακρῶν, ἐψευδη|γόρηται μῆκος εἰκαῖον περιέχοντα.

Uphor is the one [*sc.* spell], which Urbicus used. The holy Uphor, the true, is truly written down all in abbreviations, by which all *plasmata* are animated, both *glyphai* and *xoana*; for this is the true one, but the others, those written out fully, were falsely spoken, comprising a pointless length.

374

Pap. Louvre 2391 (Mimaut) 290–304 A.D. IV
Text: K. Preisendanz, ed., tr., *Papyri graecae magicae* I (Leipzig and Berlin, 1928) III, Col. XI.

ἡ δὲ κατασκε[υὴ τῆ]ς ἐνεργείας· |αὔτοπτον θὲς τρίποδα καὶ τράπεζα[ν ἐ]λαΐνου |ἢ ἐκ ξύλου δαφνῶν καὶ [χ]άραξον ἐπὶ τὴ[ν τ]ράπεζαν |κύκλῳ τοὺς χαρακ[τ]ῆρας [τ]ούτους· [signs] *|καὶ σκεπάσα[ς] τὸν τρίποδα σινδόνι καθα||ρᾷ ἐπίθες τῷ τρίπ[ο]δι θυμιατήριον καλόν. ἔστιν ἐπι|θ]εῖναι τῇ τραπέζῃ [ὑπ]ό[κε]νον Ἀπόλλωνα ἐν ξύλω |δ]άφν[ης]· ἐγγράψας ἄ[νὰ λάμναν] χρυσῆν ἢ ἀργυρᾶν ἢ κασσιτ[ερί|νην τοὺς χαρατῆ[ρα]ς τούτους·* [signs] *|καὶ ὑπόθες τὴν λ[άμ]ναν ὑπὸ τὸ θυμιατήριον κα[τὰ ||ξόανον, ὃ ἔκτιστο ἅ[μα το]ῦ θυμιατηρίου, καὶ παράθες π[αρὰ |τὸν τρίποδα δέπασ[τρο]ν ἢ κόγχην ἔχουσαν ὕδωρ κα[θαρὸν |καὶ ἐπιγραψον ἐν τ[ῷ] ἐδ[ά]φει μέσον τοῦ οἴκου περὶ [τὸν |τρίποδα λευκῇ γρα[φ]ίδι τὸν ὑποκείμεν[ο]ν χαρακτῆρα[. |δεῖ προαγνεύειν ἐ[πὶ] ἡμέρας τρεῖς.*

The preparation of the magic operation: place a self-revealed tripod and a table made either of olive-wood or laurel-wood and draw on the table these characters: [signs] and cover the tripod with a clean cloth, put a fine censer. It is necessary to put on the table a hollow Apollo of laurel-wood; write on a [leaf] of gold or silver or tin these characters: [signs] and put the leaf under the censer facing the *xoanon*, which was set up with the censer, and put beside the tripod a goblet or shell with clean water and inscribe on the ground in the middle of the chamber around the tripod with a white stylus the characters below: [signs]. It is necessary to purify three days in advance.

375

Pap. Oxyrhynchus 1117.1–2 (Cairo) c. A.D. 178
Text: A.S. Hunt, ed., tr., *The Oxyrhynchus Papyri* 8 (London, 1911).

Π(αρά) τι(νος) κ(αί) τ(ινος) γενομένων ἐπιμελητῶν χρυσοῦ ξοάνου
Ἀθη[νᾶς τῆς καὶ Θοήριδος
θεᾶς μεγίστης.

From so-and-so and so-and-so, who are the superintendents of the golden *xoanon* of Athena and Thoeris, the great goddess.

376

Pap. Oxyrhynchus 1449.1–20, 40–53 A.D. 213–217
Text: B.P. Grenfell and A.S. Hunt, eds., trs., *The Oxyrhynchus Papyri* 12 (London, 1916).
Translation adapted from Grenfell and Hunt.

Col. i. Frs. 1 and 2

1 *Π[α]ρὰ Αὐρ(ηλίων) Ζωίλ(ου) Ἀπολλωνίου μητ(ρὸς) Αὐρ(ηλίας) Ἀχι[λλίδ(ος) καὶ* 14 letters *μη]τ(ρὸς) Αὐρ(ηλίας) Ταaφύγχ(ιος) ἀμφοτέρων [. . . . .] καὶ τῶν σὺν αὐτ(οῖς) ἱερέων Δ[ιὸς καὶ Ἥρας καὶ Ἀταργάτιδ(ος)*

2 καὶ Κόρης καὶ Διονύσου καὶ Ἀπολλων[ο]ς καὶ Νεωτέρας καὶ τῶν συννάων θε]ῶν καὶ κωμαστῶν προ[τομῶν τοῦ] κυρί[ο]υ Σεβαστοῦ καὶ νίκης [αὐτοῦ προαγούσης καὶ

3 Ἰουλιάς Δόμνας Σεβαστῆς καὶ του θεο[ῦ πατρὸς αὐτοῦ ? Σεουήρου ....]νων αὐτῶν ἱερῶν τῶ[ν ὄντων] ἐν τῇ μητροπόλ(ει) ἐπὶ μὲν το[ῦ Διονύσου ἐπ' ἀμφόδ(ου)

4 Δρόμ(ου) Θοήριδ(ος), τοῦ δὲ ἑτέρου Ἀπόλλωνος .[21 l. θεοῦ μεγ]άλου ἀγαθοῦ δαίμ(ονος) καὶ Νεωτ(έρας) [ἐν τοῖς ἀπ]ὸ νότου τῆς π[ό]λεως ἐπ' ἀ[πη]λ(ιώτην) [μέρεσιν ἐπ' ἀμφόδ(ου) .... ( ),

5 καὶ ἐν τοῖς ἀπὸ νότου ἐπὶ λίβα μέρεσι τῆ[ς πόλ(εως) ἐπ' ἀμφόδ(ου) .... ( ) Νεωτ(έρας)?, καὶ ἐπ' ἀμφόδ(ου)] Πλατ(είας) ἐκ νότ(ου) τοῦ Δημητρ(είου) Διὸς καὶ Ἥ[ρας κ]αὶ Ἀταργάτ[ιδ]ος Βεθεννύν[ιδ(ος)? καὶ Κόρης, καὶ ἐπ' ἀμ-

6 φ[ό]δ(ου) Δρόμ(ου) Γυμνα(σίου) Διὸς καὶ Ἥρας καὶ Ἀταργάτ[ιδ(ος) Βεθεννύνιδ(ος) καὶ Κόρης, καὶ ἐπ' ἀμφόδ(ου) Ἱ]ππώεν Παρεμβολ(ῆς) Πατεμὶτ λα[ύρα]ς [Δι]ὸς καὶ Ἥρας καὶ Ἀταργάτιδ(ος) κ[αὶ Κόρης ?, καὶ ἐν ......

7 τοῦ Κυνοπολ(ίτου) Διὸς καὶ Ἥρας. γρα(φὴ) ἀναθημάτ(ων) [τοῦ κ. (ἔτους) Μάρκου Αὐρηλίου Σεουήρο]υ Ἀντωνίνου Παρθικοῦ Μεγίστου Βρεταννικοῦ Μεγίστου Γερμανικοῦ Μεγίστο[υ Εὐσεβοῦς Σεβαστοῦ.

8 ἔστι δέ· τῶν μὲν ἐν τῷ τῆς Νεωτ(έρας) ἱερ[ῷ, εἰκονείδιον τοῦ κυρίου ἡμῶ]ν Αὐτοκράτορος Μάρκου Αὐρηλί[ο]υ Σεουήρου Ἀντωνίνου Εὐτυχοῦς [Εὐσεβοῦς Σεβαστοῦ

9 καὶ Ἰουλίας Δόμνας τῆς κυρίας Σεβαστῆς [καὶ τοῦ θεοῦ πατρὸς αὐτοῦ Σεουήρου, ἐπι]κειμέ[ν]ων ἐπί τινων ἀναθημάτ(ων) τὰ ὀνάματ(α) τῶν ἀναθ[έντ(ων) 10 l., ἐπὶ

10 γὰρ ἄλλων μὴ γεινώσκειν ἡμεῖν τοὺς [ἀναθέντας διὰ τὸ τὰ ἀναθήματ(α) ἀπὸ ἀρχαί]ων χρόνων ἐν τῷ ἱερῳ εἶναι, ξόανον Δήμητρος θ[εᾶς μεγίστ(ης), οὗ ἡ προτομ(ὴ)

11 Παρίνη, τὰ δὲ ἄλλα μέρη τοῦ σώματ(ος) ξ[ύλινα, 33 l.]ωνιειου .[. .] ω[. .]μ [. .] ἡμεῖν οὐκ ἐπεδείχθ(η). καὶ ἐπὶ [........ τῶν ἐκ τῆς

12 ἄνωθ(εν) συνηθ(είας) κατ' εὐχ(ὴν) καὶ εὐσέβ(ειαν) ἀνιερωθέντ(ων), [26 l. ἀ]νατεθ(ε) ὑπὸ Φρ[α ?]γέν[ο]υς Ὡ[ρί]ωνος, (2nd hand) ξό[α]νον Νεωτ(έρας) χα(λκοῦν) μεικ(ρόν), δακτύλ(ιοι) ε [ἀνατεθ(έντες) ὑπὸ ....

13 Διδύμ(ου), στολὴ καλλαΐνη ἀνατεθ(εῖσα) ὑπὸ τ(ῆς) μητ(ρὸς) Ἀν[26 l. ἀ]νατεθ(ε) ὑπὸ Κάστορος Ἀσκληπ(ιάδου), [βε ?]λένκωτο[ς] μεικ(ρὸς) ἐφ' οὗ ξόανον τῆς Νεωτ(έρας) ἀποθ . [17 l.

14 λιθ(ιν) εὐτόμου λίθ(ου), πηδάλ(ιον) τῆς [Νεωτ(έρας)?, ξόανον 20 l., ο]ὗ ἡ προτομ(ὴ) Π[α]ρίνη, τὰ δὲ περίαπτ[α ἐπί]πλαστ(α), Τυφών τινων μερῶν κα[17 l.

15 κατὰ μέ(σον) κεκολ(λημεν) καὶ τὰ ἐν γλωσσ]οκόμῳ 16 l. λύχνοι χρ(υσοῖ) μεικ(ροὶ) μ]εστ(οὶ) θεῖ[οι] β ἀν[ατε]θ(έντες) ὑπὸ Σαρα[π(ίωνος)] Σαραπ(ίωνος), ἄλ(λος) λ[ύχ(νος)] χρ(υσοῦς) [μ]εικ(ρὸς) μεστ(ὸς) θεῖο(ς) ἀνατεθ(εὶς) ὑπὸ Σαραε(ῦτος) Ἀχ[ιλλ( ), ἄλ(λος) λύχ(νος) χρ(υσοῦς) μεικ(ρὸς) μεστ(ὸς) θεῖο(ς)?

16 ἀνατεθ(εὶς) ὑπὸ Πτολεμαΐδος γυναι[κὸς 26 l., ὧν ὁ στα]θμ(ὸς) δι(ὰ) τῶν κατὰ χρόνο(ν) γρα(φῶν) [δη]λοῦτ(αι), πε[ριδέξι]α παιδικ(ὰ) ι καὶ παιδικ(ὸς) δακτύλ(ιος) α, ἐπὶ [τὸ α(ὐτὸ) χρ(υσοῦ) (τετάρων)?., 10 l.

17 μύστ(ρα) χρ(υσᾶ) β, γρ[α]φε[ῖο(ν)] χρ(υσοῦν) μεικ(ρὸν) α, ορα[33 l. μ]εικ(ρ) α, πάντ(α) ἐπὶ τὸ α[ὐτὸ] χρ(υσοῦ) [(τετάρτων) 9 l.]. χρ(υσ) εὐτο(μο) ἀργυοπ(οιητο?) α (τετάρτων) β, γραφεῖα ἀργ(υρᾶ) [17 l.

18 ψέλιο(ν) ἀργ(υροῦν) παιδι[κ(όν), . .]. . . [34 l. περ]ιδέξ(ια) ἀργ(υρᾶ) β, μηνίσκ(ιον) [. . . . . .ἀ]ρ[γ(υρ), πάντ(α) ὁλκ(ῆς) (δραχμῶν) η (τριωβόλου), στραγγ(αλὶς) ἀργ(υρᾶ) ο[17 l.

19 χ[ρ(υσ)] σὺν πρ(οσ)κυνη[τηρίῳ ? 38 l.] . . [ὁ]λκ(ῆς) (δρ.) δ (τριωβ.), ὄσυπτρον ἀργ(υροῦν) π[αιδικ(όν), ...] ἀργ(υρ) μεικ(ρ) ς, λαμπάδ(ες) ἀργ(υραῖ) καλαὶ Βουβασ[τ 16 l.

20 [παν]τ(α) ἐπὶ τὸ α(ὐτὸ) ὁλ(κῆς) (δραχμῶν?) [40 l. στα]θμὸν [ἔ]χοντα μεστ(ὰ) κη[10 l.] . . ον χυτ(ὸν) λίθ(ινον) ἓν κεκολλημ(ένον), καὶ ἕτερο[ν 16 l.

Col. ii. Fr. 4.

40 τοῦ κυρίου ἡμῶν Αὐτοκράτορος Μάρκου Αὐρηλίου Σεουήρου Ἀν[τωνίνου Εὐτυχοῦς Εὐσεβοῦς Σεβαστοῦ καὶ τοῦ θεοῦ πατρὸς αὐτοῦ

41 Σεουήρου καὶ Ἰουλίας Δόμνας τῆς κυρίας Σεβαστῆς, κλείνη ξ[υλ(ίνη) 57 letters

42 τοῦ Κυνοπ(ολίτου) ἰκονείδιον τοῦ κυρίου ἡμῶν Αὐτοκράτορος Μάρκου [Αὐρηλίου Σεουήρου Ἀντωνίνου Εὐτυχοῦς Εὐσεβοῦς Σεβαστοῦ καὶ τοῦ θεοῦ

43 πατρὸς αὐτοῦ Σεουήρου καὶ Ἰουλίας Δόμνας τῆς κυρίας Σεβαστῆ[ς 59 l.,

44 λαμπ(ὰς) σὺν ζῳδίῳ Κόρης ἀργυρῷ ἀσήμ(ῳ) ὁλκ(ῆς) λί(τρας) α ἔσωθ(εν) ξυλ(ίνη), ἔχου[σα 46 l., ἀνατεθ(εῖσα) ὑπὸ τῆς

45 μητ(ρὸς) Διονυσίας Δείου ἀπ' Ὀξυ(ρύγχων) πόλ(εως) ἀκολούθ(ως) οἷς συνεχωρήθ(η) ὑπὸ Αὐρ[(ηλίου) 59 l.

46 θεου, καὶ Ἰαχχάριον μεικ(ρὸν) ἀπὸ ξενικ(οῦ) λίθ(ου) ἀνατεθ(ὲν) ὑπὸ Ἀνδρομάχ(ου) [60 l.

47 βωμὸς χα(λκοῦς) ἀνατεθ(εὶς) ὑπὸ Ζμαράγδ(ου) ἀπελευθ(έρου) Ἀπολλω(νίου) Σαραπ(ίωνος) ἀκ[ολούθ(ως) οἷς συνεχωρήθη ὑπὸ 39 l.

48 καὶ ὁμοί(ως) πρ(οσ)εγένετ(ο) τῷ α (ἔτει) λαμπ(ας) χρ(υσᾶ) ἔχουσα κατὰ μέσον . [60 l.

49 [ἀ]νατεθ(εὶς) ὕπο Ἡρακλείδου Σαραπίωνος, ἄλ(λος) βωμ(ὸς) ἀργ(υροῦς) λί(τρας) α ὀγκιῶν ε∠[60 l.

50 [θ]εᾶς μεγίστης λι[τρῶν] ιε ἀνατεθ( ) ὑπὸ Αὐρ(ηλίου) Ἰουλίου τῷ α (ἔτει) καὶ ἐν τῷ δ [(ἔτει) 55 l. σεση(μμεν)

51 [ἀ]χρηστ(ο) α, τὰ δὲ ἱμάτια πάντ(α) ἀπὸ τ(οῦ) χρό(νου) σεση(μμένα) ἄρχηστ(α) μηδὲ ἴχνη [60 l.

52 καὶ πρ(οσ)εγέν[ε]το τῷ ϛ (ἔτει) μη(νὶ) Θὼθ ἐν ἱερῷ τῆς Κόρης ξόανο[ν 30 l. ἀνατεθ(ὲν) ὑπὸ 20 l.

53 [γυ]μνα(σιαρχήσαντος), καὶ τῷ διελθόντι μη(νὶ) Φαῶ(φι) κορδικίων ζεῦγος [60 l.

From the Aurelii, Zoilus son of Apollonius and mother Aurelia Achillis, and . . . son of . . . and Aurelia Taaphunchis, both . . . , and their associates, priests of Zeus, Hera, Atargatis, Core, Dionysus, Apollo, Neotera, and the associated gods, and celebrants of the *protomai* of the lord Augustus and his advancing Victory and Julia Domna Augusta and his deified father Severus, at their . . . *hiera* situated in the metropolis, in the case of Dionysus in the quarter of the Square of Thoeris, in the other case, that of Apollo . . . the great god and good genius, and Neotera, in the south-east part of the city in the quarter of . . . , in the south-west part of the city . . . and in the Broad Street quarter to the south of the [shrine of] Demeter [that] of Zeus, Hera, Atargatis Bethennunis, and Core, and in the Gymnasium Square quarter [that] of Zeus, Hera, Atargatis Bethennunis, and Core, and in the Cavalry Camp quarter, Patemit street, that of Zeus, Hera, Atargatis, and Core, and in . . . of the Cynopolite [nome] that of Zeus and Hera. List of *anathemata* [for the 2(.) year of Marcus Aurelius Severus] Antoninus Parthicus Maximus Britannicus Max. Germanicus Max. Pius Augustus. There is: Of objects in the *hieron* of Neotera, *eikoneidion* of our lord the Emperor M. Aurelius Severus Antoninus Felix Pius Augustus and Julia Domna the lady Augusta [and his deified father Severus,] some of the *anathemata* being inscribed with the names of the dedicators, while in other cases we are ignorant of the dedicators, because [the *anathemata* have been] in the *hieron* from ancient times, a *xoanon* of Demeter, most great goddess, of which the *protome* is Parian [marble] and the other parts of the body are wooden, . . . was not disclosed to us. And with regard to other offerings, which were dedicated in accordance with ancient customs for vows or pious reasons, . . . dedicated by Phragenes(?) son of Horion, a small bronze *xoanon* of Neotera, 5 rings dedicated by . . . son of Didymus, a green robe dedicated by the mother of An . . . , . . . dedicated by Castor son of Asclepiades, a small basket(?) . . . , on which is a *xoanon* of Neotera, a stone . . . of well-cut stone, a rudder representing Neotera, a *xoanon* . . . of which the *protome* is Parian marble

and the amulets are of plaster, a Typhon, part of which . . . joined together in the middle, and the . . . in a casket, 2 gold small full sacred lamps dedicated by Sarapion son of Sarapion, another gold small full sacred lamp dedicated by Ptolemais wife of . . . , of which the weight is described in the periodical lists, 10 armlets for a child and 1 ring for a child, making in all . quarters of gold, . . . , 2 gold spoons, 1 small gold pen, . . . 1 small . . . , making in all . quarters of gold, 1 gold . . . well cut and decorated in silver, weighing 2 quarters, . silver pens, . . . a silver bracelet for a child, . . . 2 silver armlets, a . . . silver crescent . . . , in all weighing 8 drachmae 3 obols, a silver pendant . . . a gold . . . with a *proskyne terion* . . . , weighing 4 dr. 3 ob., a silver mirror for a child, 6 small silver . . . fine silver lamps [representing?] Bubastis . . . , in all weighing . . .
(Lines 21–39 continue the list; they are very fragmentary)
40. [a representation] of our lord the Emperor Marcus Aurelius Severus An[toninus] Felix Pius Augustus and his deified father Severus, and Julia Domna the lady Augusta, a [wooden] couch . . . In . . . of the Cynopolite nome an *ikoneidion* of our lord the Emperor Marcus [Aurelius] Severus Antoninus Felix Pius Augustus and his deified father Severus and Julia Domna the lady Augusta, a lamp with a *zoidion* of Core in unstamped silver weighing 1 lb., the interior being wooden, having . . . , dedicated by the mother of Dionysia daughter of Dius, of Oxyrhnchus, in accordance with the agreement of Aurelius . . . and a small shrine of Iacchus of foreign stone, dedicated by Andromachus . . . , a bronze altar dedicated by Smaragdus, freedman of Apollonius son of Sarapion, in accordance with the agreement of . . . Likewise added in the 1st year, a gold lamp having in the middle . . . , [an altar] . . . dedicated by Heraclides son of Sarapion, another altar of silver weighing 1 lb., 5 . *onkioi*, . . . of the greatest goddess weighing 15 lb., dedicated by Aurelius Julius in the 1st year, and in the 4th year . . . , 1 . . . decayed and useless and all the clothing decayed with age and useless, having no traces of . . . Added in the 6th year in the month of Thoth at the *hieron* of Core, a *xoanon* . . . , dedicated by . . . ex-gymnasiarch, and in the past month Phaophi a pair of *kordikia* . . .

377

Pap. Oxyrhynchus 2171 Fr. 2 col. ii A.D. II
(= Callimachus, *Iambus* VI fr. 196.29–31 Pfeiffer.)
Text: R. Pfeiffer, ed., *Callimachus* I (Oxford, 1949) 190, lines 29–31.

.] Λ̣υδιεργὲς δ᾽ ὧ ᾽πι θὤγιον β̣ρ̣[έ]τα̣[ς
. .]άνω κάθηται
. .]ι̣ μὲν τρὶς ἐς τὸ μακρὸ[ν] ιδ̣ [.].[. . .] δέκα

[The throne] on which the holy *bretas* sits is Lydian work . . . in height three times ten. . . .

378

Pap. Oxyrhynchus 2263 Fr. I, ii, 9–30 A.D. II–III
(= *Diegesis* to Callimachus, *Aetia* I fr. 31 B.)
Text: E. Lobel, E.P. Wegener, and C.H. Roberts, eds., *The Oxyrhynchus Papyri* 20 (London, 1952) 127.
Translation adapted from C.A. Trypanis, ed., tr., *Callimachus. Aetia, Iambi, Hecale and other Fragments* (LCL, 1958, 1975) 28–29 *ad Aetia* fr. 31 B.

τῶ]ς μὲν ἔφη τὰς δ' εἶθαρ ἐμὸς πάλιν εἴρετο θυμός τῆς ἐν Λευκαδίαι Ἀρτέμιδος τὸ ξόανον ἐ]πὶ τῆς κεφαλῆς θυ<ε>ίαν ἔχει δι' αἰτίαν ταύτην. Ἠπειρῶται τιν. .η.[.]. .η[.]. . . κατατρέχ[ο]ντες τὴν Λευκάδα ἐσύλων, ἐλθόντες δὲ καὶ εἰς τὸ τῆς Ἀρφτέμιδος ἱερὸν εὗρον τὴν θεὸν ἐστεμμένην χρυσῷ στεφάνῳ. τοῦτον ἐπιχλευάσαντες ἀφεῖλον καὶ τὴν θυ<ε>ίαν ἐν ᾗ σκόρδα τρε{ε}ίψαντες ἔφαγον τῇ θεῷ ἐπέθηκαν. ἐπὶ.ν.[.].. δ' οἱ Λευκάδι[οι] ..θ' ἡμ[έ]ρα[. ἕ]τερον κατεσκεύασαν στέφανον καὶ ἀντὶ τῆς θυ<ε>ία[ς] ἔθηκαν ἀποπεσόντα δ' αὐτὸν προσήλωσαν τῷ ξοάνῳ. πάλιν δὲ μεθ' ἡμέ[ρας] τρεῖς ἐπιτιθεμένου κα̣[ὶ]..με[ί]να[ν]το[ς .] .ης

Thus she spoke; and straightway my heart asked them again. The *xoanon* of Artemis in Leukas has a mortar on its head for the following reason. Inhabitants of Epirus . . . harassing . . . plundered Leukas. When they came to the *hieron* of Artemis they found the goddess crowned with a golden crown. In mockery they removed it, and put on the mortar in which they had pounded garlic which they had eaten. . . . The Leucadians [a day later] made another crown, and put it on [the statue] instead of the mortar, and when it fell off they nailed it to the *xoanon*. Then again three days later the crown which was placed. . . .

379

Adada (Pisidia)
Text: R. Cagnat, ed., *Inscriptiones Graecae ad res Romanas pertinentes* III (Paris, 1906) no. 336.

Θεοῖς Σεβαστοῖς καὶ τῇ πατρίδι Θεόδωρος Νειχομάχου, φιλόπατρις ἀρχιερεὺς [τῶν Σεβαστῶν τὸ β′? κτίστης, υἱὸς πόλεως, πρόβουλος τὸ γ′?] τὸν ναὸν ἐκ [θεμελίων] σὺν τῷ̣ ξοάνῳ̣ καὶ τοῖς ἀγάλμασι ἐκ τῶν ἰδίων ἀνέθηκε καὶ καθιέρωσε.

To the gods Augusti and the fatherland Theodoros son of Neichomachos, friend of the fatherland,
chief priest [of the Augusti the 2 (?), founder, son of the city, delegate the 3? . . .]
the *naos* from the foundations, with the *xoanon* and the *agalmata*, from his private funds dedicated and
set up.

380

Anaphe II B.C.
(= *IG* XII.3, 248.)
Text: F. Sokolowski, *Lois sacrées des cités grecques* (Paris, 1969) no. 129.

[-------------------συντε]-
[λε]σ̣θέντ̣ος̣
δ̣ὲ [τοῦ ναοῦ ἔστω δαμόσ]ιος [κα]-
θ̣ότι καὶ ὁ θεὸς ἔ[χρ]η̣σε[ν· τ]ᾶ̣ς δ᾽ ἐπερωτάσ[ε]-
ως καὶ τοῦ χρησμοῦ ἀντίγραφά ἐστι τάδε·
ἔδοξε τᾶι βουλᾶι καὶ τῶι δάμωι, ἀρχόντων Ξενο-
μνάστου, Ἀριστομάχου, Σωσικλεῦς καὶ βουλᾶς γνώμα·
ὑπὲρ τᾶς ἐφόδου, ἃς ἐποιήσατο Τιμ[ό]θεος Σωσικλεῦς, κατὰ δὲ υἱοθεσίαν Ἰσοπόλιος, ἀξιώσ(ας) αὐτῶι δοθῆ-
μεν ἐν τῶι ἱερῶι τοῦ Ἀπόλλωνος τοῦ Ἀσγελάτα τόπον, ὥσ[τε ναὸ]ν Ἀφροδίτας οἰκοδομῆσαι ὕλαι και λίθοις καὶ χοϊ [χ]ρώμενος ἐκ τοῦ ἱεροῦ ὧν κα χρείαν ἔχηι
ἐν τῶι τόπωι, ἐν τᾶι αἱμασιᾷ̣, ὅπει ἁ ἐλαία ἁ ποτὶ τὸν
Εὐδώρειον οἶκον καὶ τὸν Μειδίλειον· τὸν δὲ τόπον
[ὅ]πει ὁ βωμὸς τοῦ Κτησίου καὶ τὸ ξοάνιον, τὸν τοῖχον
λύσαντα τὰν πάροδον ποιῆσαι ἐς τὸν ναὸν
ταύται, καὶ οἰκοδομηθέντος τοῦ τοίχου τὸν βωμὸν
καὶ τὸ ξοάνιον καταστάσαι πάλιν ἐς τὸν τοῖχον, τὰς δὲ στάλας τὰς οὔσας ἐν τῶι τοίχωι

καὶ τὸν ἀπόρανθρον, ὅσας μέν κα δυνατὸν ἦι,
αὐτεῖ καταστᾶσαι, ὅσαις δέ [κα] μὴ ἦι τόπος, ὅπει κα
δοκῆι χρήσιμον ἦμεν· συντελεσθέντος δὲ
τοῦ ναοῦ ἦμεν δαμόσιον, καθὰ καὶ ὁ θεὸς ἔχρησε,
τᾶς δὲ ἐπερωτάσιος καὶ τοῦ χρησμοῦ ἀντίγροφόν
ἐστιν τὰ ὑπογεγραμμένα.
ἐπερωτᾶι Τιμόθεος [*τὸ*]*ν θεόν, πότερον*
αὐτῶι λῶιον καὶ ἄμειṿόν ἐστιν αἰτήσασθαι
τὰν πόλιν ἐν τῶι ἐπινοεῖ τόπωι ἐν τῶι τοῦ
Ἀπόλλωνος *τοῦ* Ἀσγελάτα, *ὥστε ναὸν τὰς*
Ἀφροδίτας *οἰκοδ*[ο]*μῆσαι, καὶ ἦμεν δαμόσιον,*
ἢ ἐν τῶι ἱερῶι τοῦ Ἀ[σκ]*λαπιοῦ ἐν ὧι ἐπινοεῖ*
τόπωι· ὁ θεὸς ἔχρησε, αἰτήσασθ[α]*ι ἐν τῶι το*[ῦ]
Ἀπόλλωνος, *τελεσθέντος δὲ τοῦ ναοῦ ἀνα-*
γραφῆμεν τό τε ψάφισμα καὶ τὸν χρησμὸν
καὶ τὰν ἔφοδον ἐστάλαν λιθίναν· περὶ δὴ
τούτων δεδόχθαι τᾶι βουλᾶι, δεδόσθαι
αὐτῶι καθάπερ αἰτεῖται, εἴ κα [*δό*]*ξηι*
τᾶι ἐκκλησίαι.

. . . [the *naos*] having been finished, let it be
public property in the way that the god has ordained;
these are copies of the inquiry and of the oracle:
It was resolved by the *boule* and the people, when Xeno-
mnastos and Aristomachos were archons, the motion was Sosikles'
and the *boule*'s:
Concerning the plan, which Timotheos son of Sosikles made,
on the occasion of the adoption of Isopolis, having requested that
a place be given to him
in the *hieron* of Apollo Asgelatas,
so that he could build a *naos* of Aphrodite, using wood
and stones and earth from the *hieron* which could be used
in the place, in the dry-stone wall, where there is the olive tree
which is close to the
house of Eudoreios and that of Meidileios; the place
where there is the altar of Ktesios and the *xoanion*; so that
breaking down the wall he can make an entrance into the *naos*
there, and when the wall was built to put up the altar
and the *xoanion* again at the wall,
and the stelai that are in the wall
and the *aporantrhon* [holy-water vessel], however way it is possible,

to set up again; and for those that it is not [possible to set up],
to be a place wherever it seems serviceable; and when the *naos*
is finished it is to be public property, as the god decreed in
the oracle,
what is written below is the copy
of the inquiry and the oracle.
Timotheos asked the god, whether it is
more desirable, and better for him to ask the city
to build the *naos* of Aphrodite, which is to be public
property, in the proposed place in the [sanctuary] of Apollo
Asgelatas, or in the *hieron* of Asklepios, in the proposed
place; the god responded, [that he should] ask for [the place]
in that
of Apollo, and that when the *naos* was finished,
we should inscribe the resolution and the oracle
and the proposal on a stone stele; the *boule* made a resolution
about these matters, that it be granted to him
just as resolved, if the assembly
resolved.

381

Baglitsa region (Orkistos?) (Phrygia)
Text: W.M. Calder, ed., *Monumenta Asiae Minoris Antiqua* I (London, 1928) 220 no. 417.

ἀγαθῇ [τύχη
Μακεδὼν και Πάμ-
φιλος οἱ Παμφίλου
ἱερασάμενοι τῇ γλυ-
κυτάτῃ πατρίδι τὴν
ἀνάστασιν τοῦ ξοά-
νου παρ' ἑαυτῶν
ἐποιήσαντο

Makedon and Pamphilos, the sons of Pamphilos, having become priests, to the dearest homeland set up the *xoanon* from their own funds.

382

Bargylia (Caria) ? A.D. II
Text: G. Cousin and Ch. Diehl, "Inscriptions de Iasos et de Bargylia," *BCH* 13 (1889) 40 no. 7.

Μαρ. Αὐρ. . . . . . .
σ]αμος, ὁ πρῶτος [τῆς
πόλεως, τῇ γλυκ[υτάτῃ
πατρίδι τὸ ξόα[νον
Ἀπόλλω]νος
σὺν τῷ [παντὶ
κό]σμῳ

Mar. Aur. . . . . . .
s]amos, the *protos* [of the
city, to the dear[est
fatherland the *xoanon*
of Apollo
with [all its
adornment [dedicated].

383

Büyükkadife (Böjük Kadife, Lydia)

Text: J. Keil and A. v. Premerstein, *Bericht über eine dritte Reise in Lydien und den angrenzenden Gebieten Ionien* (Vienna, 1914) 99 no. 148.

Τρόφιμος
Μενκράτους σὺν
καὶ Τροφίμῃ θυγατρὶ τὸν βωμὸν
σὺν τῷ ἐπ' αὐτῷ
ξυάνῳ ἐπικειμένῳ
εκ τῶν ἰδίων καθιέρω-
σεν.

Trophimos, the son of Menekrates, together with Trophime his daughter, dedicated the *bomos* with the *xuanon* placed on it from their own money.

384

Chalcedon I B.C.–A.D. I

Text: F.H. Marshall, ed., *The Collection of Ancient Greek Inscriptions in the British Museum. Part IV–Section II. Supplementary and Miscellaneous Inscriptions* (Oxford, 1916) no. 1012.

Οὔριον ἐκ πρύμνης τις ὁδηγητῆρα καλείτω
Ζῆνα κατὰ προτόνων ἱστίον ἐκπετάσας·
εἴτ' ἐπὶ κυανέας δίνας δρόμος, ἔνθα Ποσειδῶν
καμπύλον εἰλίσσει κῦμα παρὰ ψαμάθοις,
εἴτε κατ' Αἰγαίην πόντου πλάκα νόστον ἐρευναῖ,

νεί(σθω τῶι)δε βαλὼν ψαιστὰ παρὰ ξοάνωι.
ὧδε τὸν εὐάντητον ἀεὶ θεὸν Ἀντιπάτρου παῖς
στῆσε Φίλων, ἀγαθῆς σύμβολον εὐπλοΐης.

Let him who lets his sail down from the halyards call from the stern on Zeus Ourios as guide; whether the way is towards the dark blue eddies, where Poseidon turns the curved waves round by the sandy shores, or to seek homecoming on the flat Aegean sea, let him come, throwing barley cakes before the *xoanon*. Thus Philo the son of Antipater set up the always-gracious god, symbol of good sailing.

385

Cyzicus A.D. 37
(= *SIG*[3] II, 798.)
Text: E.M. Smallwood, *Documents Illustrating the Principates of Gaius, Claudius and Nero* (Cambridge, 1967) no. 401, lines 1, 18–21.

Ἐπὶ Γαΐου Καίσαρος ἱππάρχεωι, μηνὸς Θαργηλιῶνος θ'. . . .

Δεδόχθαι τῶι δήμωι ἐπηνῆσθαι μεν τοὺς βασιλεῖς Ῥοιμητάλκην καὶ Πο|λέμωνα καὶ Κότυν καὶ τὴν μητέρα αὐτῶν Τρύφαιναν, ὑπὸ δὲ τὴν εἴσοδον αὐτῶν τοὺς μὲν ἱερεῖς καὶ τὰς ἱερείας ἀνοί||ξαντας τὰ τεμένη καὶ προσκοσμήσαντας τὰ ξόανα τῶν θεῶν εὔξασθωαι μὲν ὑπὲρ τῆς Γαΐου Καίσαρος αἰωνίου δια|μονῆς καὶ τῆς τούτων σωτηρίας·

In the cavalry command of Gaius Caesar, on the ninth day of the month Thargelion. . . .
It was resolved by the people that the *basileis* Rhoimetalkes and Polemon and Kottus and their mother Tryphaena shall be commended; during their entrance both the priests and the priestesses, having opened the *temene* and added more ornaments to the *xoana* of the gods, shall pray for the continuance of the era of Gaius Caesar and for their salvation. . . .

386

Delos, Inv. A 4202 300–280 B.C.
Text: F. Robert, *Délos* 20. *Trois sanctuaires sur le rivage occidental* (Paris, 1952) 106.

[1][Χ]αῖρε· δίδου δ' ἐρατάν, |[2] Ἀσκλαπιέ, Δαμονόοιο |
[3]παιδὶ χάριν, κεδνᾶς |[4] ὕνεκεν εὐσεβίας, |
[5]Νίκωνι, ξόανον |[6]τόδε τὸ κλυτὸν |[7]ὅς ποτε ὅπασσεν |
[8]καὶ σφετέρας |[9]θῆκεν σᾶμα |[10] ἱεραπολίας.

Hail! Grant beloved favor, Asklepios, to the son of Damonoos for his diligent piety; to Nikon, who once gave this splendid *xoanon* and dedicated a token of your priesthood.

387

Delos, *ID* 1881 (Inv. E 799) c. 113/2 B.C.

Text: A. Plassart, *Délos* 11. *Les sanctuaires et les cultes du Mont Cynthe* (Paris, 1928) 125.

Χαρμικὸς Αἰνησίου
Κικυννεὺς ἱερεὺς γενόμενος
Διὸς Κυνθίου καὶ Ἀθηνᾶς
Κυνθίας ἀνέθηκεν
τὸ ξόανον.

Charmikos, son of Ainesios,
of Kikynna, having become priest
of Zeus Kynthios and of Athena
Kynthia, dedicated
the *xoanon*.

388

Delos, *ID* 2548 I B.C.

Text: F. Robert, "Inscription métrique trouvée au Dioscourion délien," *BCH* 58 (1934) 189.

Τίς τὰ πάλαι πιναρᾶι κεκαλυμμένα θήκατο (λ)άθαι
φαιδρὰ Διοσκούρων ἐν προδόμοις ξόανα;
τίς δ' ἐνὶ μακραίωνι χρόνωι πομποστόλον ἆμαρ
σιγαθὲν πινυταῖς αὖθις ἄγει πραπίσιν;
Ἦ ῥα θυηπολίας ὁ λαχὼν γέρας ὃς δίχα μώμου
ἰθύνει βιοτὰν πᾶσαν Ἀθηνόβιος.
Τοίαδε χρὴ μακάρεσσι τελεῖν γέρα, καὶ τάχα τιμάς·
ἀθανάτων εὐρὼς οὔποτ' ἐπισκιάσει.
Ὧν χάριν εὐσεβίας ὄλβωι βρίθοντι γεγηθώς,
σὺν τέκνοις λιπαροῦ γήραος ἀντιάσαις.

Who made glorious the *xoana* of the Dioskouroi in the *prodomoi*, long covered in mouldy oblivion?
And who, when the day of the procession was long passed over in silence, leads it again with a prudent heart?
He who obtained the honor of priesthood, who steers his whole life straight, apart from blame: Athenobios.
Such are the honors fitting to grant fortunate ones, and soon, decay will never cast shadow on the worship of the gods.
For the sake of these things, rejoicing in happiness, heavy with piety, may you meet with a glorious old age with your children.

389

Elephantine (Louvre.) 196 B.C.
(= *SEG* 8, 784.)
Text: F. Bilabel, ed., *Sammelbuch griechischer Urkunden aus Ägypten* 5 (Heidelberg, 1931, 1934) no. 8232, lines 6–10.
Restored on the basis of British Museum inscription 1065 (the Rosetta Stone), of which it a copy.
See Rosetta [**402**].

στῆσαι δὲ τοῦ αἰωνοβίου βασιλέως Πτολεμαίου θεοῦ Ἐπιφανοῦς Εὐ]χ̣αρίστου εἰκόνα ἐν ἑκάστωι ἱε̣ρ̣ῶι ἐν τῶι ἐπιφαν̣ε̣στάτ̣ωι̣ ||[τόπωι, ἣ προσονομασθήσεται Πτολεμαίου τοῦ ἐπαμύναντος τῆι Αἰγύπτωι, ἧι παρεστήξεται ὁ κυριώτατος θεὸς τοῦ ἱεροῦ, δ]ιδοὺς αὐτῶι ὅπλον ν̣ι̣κητικόν, ἃ ἔ̣σ̣ται κ̣α[τε]σ̣κευα̣[σ]μ̣ένα̣ τ||[ὸν τῶν Αἰγυπτίων τρόπον, καὶ τοὺς ἱερεῖς θεραπεύειν τὰς εἰκόνας τρὶς τῆς ἡμέρας καὶ παρατιθέναι αὐταῖς ἱερὸν κόσμον καὶ τἆλλα τὰ νομιζόμεν]α συντελεῖν καθὰ καὶ [τ]ο̣ῖ̣ς ἄλλο̣ι̣ς̣ θ̣εοῖς ἐν ταῖ̣ς̣ ἑ̣[ορ]τ̣α̣ῖ̣ς̣ κ̣α̣ὶ̣ ||[πανηγύρεσιν· ἱδρύσασθαι δὲ βασιλεῖ Πτολεμαίωι θεῶι Ἐπιφανεῖ Εὐχαρίστωι, τῶι ἐγ βασιλέως Πτολεμαίου καὶ βασιλίσσης Ἀρσινόης θεῶν Φιλοπατόρων, ξόανόν τε] κ̣α̣ὶ̣ ν̣α̣ὸν χρυσοῦν̣ [κ]α̣θ̣' ἕκαστο̣ν ἱερὸν καὶ καθιδρῦσαι ἐν το̣ῖ̣ς ἀδύ||[τοις μετὰ τῶν ἄλλων ναῶν, καὶ ἐν ταῖς μεγάλαις πανηγύρεσιν, ἐν αἷς ἐδοξεῖαι τῶν ναῶν γίνονται, καὶ τὸν τοῦ θεοῦ Ἐπιφανοῦς Εὐ[χαρίστου ναὸν συνε]ξοδεύειν. . . .

390

Ḳal ʿat Kālôtā
Text: W.K. Prentice, *Publications of the Princeton University Archaeological Expeditions to Syria in 1904–1905 and 1909. Division III. Greek and Latin Inscriptions in Syria. Section B. Northern Syria. Part 6. The Djebel Simʿân* (Leiden, 1922) 199 no. 1193.

Σειμίῳ̣(?) και Συμβ] αιτύλῳ̣, θεοῖς πατρῴ̣οις, ...] μ(?) αιος, Ἀφροδισίου, ...] ρας, τῆς γυναικὸς αὐτοῦ, ... ἐκ τῶν ἰ] δίων, μετα τὸ ἀπαρτ[- . . . . τὸν] ναὸν καὶ τὸ χρυσοῦν ξόανον.

To [Seimios (?) and Symb]aitylos, ancestral gods,
. . . . .m(?)aios, son of Aphrodisios, ...
with . . . . . . .ra, his wife, ... at their own
expense, after [completing? the]
naos and the golden *xoanon*.

391

Koptos (Alexandria Museum 70.) August 30, A.D. 103

Text: F. Bilabel, ed., *Sammelbuch griechischer Urkunden aus Ägypten* 5 (Heidelberg, 1931, 1934) no. 8815.

῾Υπὲρ τῆς Αὐτοκράτορος Καίσαρος Νέρουα Τραιανοῦ Σεβαστοῦ |[2]Γερμανικοῦ Δακικοῦ καὶ τοῦ παντὸς οἴκου αὐτοῦ <τύχης> Ἴσιδος |[3]ἐν ἀτρίωι τὸ ξόανον καὶ τὸν ναὸν καὶ τὰ περὶ αὐτοῦ πάντα |[4]ἐπὶ ἡγεμόνος Οὐ[ιβί]ου Μ[αξίμου] καὶ ἐπιστρατήγου Πομπηί|[5]ου Πρόκλου και παραλήμπ[τ]ου καὶ στρατηγοῦ Κλαυδίου |[6]Χρυσέρμου Δίδυμος Θέωνος ῥήτωρ ἀνέθηκεν.| [7]Ἔτους ζ Αὐτοκράτορος Καίσαρος Νέρουα Τραιανοῦ |[8]Σεβαστοῦ Γερμανικοῦ Δακικοῦ, Θὼθ α.

On behalf of the good fortune of Emperor Caesar Nerva Trajan Augustus Germanicus Dacius and of his entire house: Didymos the *rhetor*, son of Theon, dedicated the *xoanon* of Isis in the Atrium, and the *naos* and everything around it, when Vibius Maximus was *princeps* and Pompeius Proclus was Commander-in-Chief and Claudius Chrysermos was Receiver and General. In the 6th year of Emperor Caesar Nerva Trajan Augustus Germanicus Dacius, first day of Thoth.

392

Magnesia on the Maeander ? 197/6 B.C.

Text: F. Sokolowski, *Lois sacrées de l'Asie Mineure* (Paris, 1955) 90 no. 32, lines 41–46.

(= Kern, *Inschriften* no. 98.)

ὁ δὲ στεφανηφόρος ἄγων τὴν πομπὴν φερέτω ξόανα πάντων τῶν δώδεκα θεῶν ἐν ἐσθῆσιν ὡς καλλίσταις καὶ πηγνύτω θόλον ἐν τῆι ἀγορᾶι πρὸς τῶι βωμῶι τῶν δώδεκα θεῶν, στρωνύτω δὲ καὶ στρωμνὰς τρεῖς ὡς καλλίστας, παρεχέτω δὲ καὶ ἀκροάματα, αὐλητήν, συριστήν, κιθαριστήν· . . .

Let the *stephanephoros* leading the procession carry the *xoana* of all the twelve gods in garments as beautiful as possible, and let him build a *tholos* in the *agora* near the *bomos* of the twelve gods; let him spread out three couches, as beautiful as possible, and let him furnish players, a flute-player, a piper, a citharist. . . .

393

Magnesia on the Maeander first half II B.C.

Text: F. Sokolowski, *Lois sacrées de l'Asie Mineure* (Paris, 1955) 92 no. 33, lines 1–10.

(= Kern, *Inschriften* no. 100 a.)

Στεφανηφοροῦντος Πολυκλείδου *τοῦ*
Πυθοδήλου, *μηνὸς* Ἁγνεῶνος,
ὑπὲρ τῆς καθιδρύσεως τοῦ ξοάνου τῆς Ἀρτέμιδος
τῆς Λευκοφρυηνῆς *εἰς τὸν κατεσκευασμένον αὐ-*
τῆι νῦν Παρθενῶνα *καὶ περὶ τοῦ ἐπιτελεῖσθαι αὐτῆι*
καθ' ἕκαστον ἐνιαυτὸν ἐν μηνὶ Ἀρτεμισιῶνι *τῆι*
ἕκτηι ἱσταμένου σπονδὰς καὶ θυσίας, συντε-
λεῖσθαι δὲ καὶ ὑφ' ἑκάστου τῶν κατοικούντων
θυσίας πρὸ τῶν θυρῶν κατ' οἴκου δύναμιν ἐπὶ
τῶν κατασκευασθησομένων ὑπ' αὐτῶν βωμῶν.

Polykleides, son of Pythodelos, was the *stephanephoros*; in the month of Hagneon; Concerning the installation of the *xoanon* of Artemis Leukophryene in the *Parthenon* now prepared for her, and concerning the assessment for her, each and every year in the month of Artemision, on the sixth day, of libations and sacrifices, let there be celebrated by each one of the inhabitants sacrifices before the doors, according to the ability of the house, on the *bomoi* that have been prepared for them.

394

Nicopolis ad Mestum late A.D. I

Text: G. Mihailov, ed., *Inscriptiones Graecae in Bulgaria Repertae* IV (Sophia, 1966) 288 no. 2338.

Ἀγαθῇ *τύχῃ.*
Φλάβιος Διζαλας Εζβενεος *τοῦ* Αματο-
κου στρατηγὸς Ὀλυν[θ]ίας *καὶ* Ροιμηλη-
τικῆς καὶ Δρησαπαϊκῆς *καὶ* Θουκυσιδαν-
τικῆς καὶ ---σηλητικῆς *καὶ* Ζραικῆς *καὶ*
Αθιουτικῆς *καὶ* Βιολητικῆς *τὸν τρ[ίποδα]*
καὶ τὸ ξόανον ἀνέθηκαν αὐτὸς καὶ ἡ σύμβιος
αὐτοῦ Ρεπταρ(ε)ρκος Ἡρακ[λεί]δου *θυγάτη-*
ρ κατ' ἐπιταγὴν τῆς κυρίας Ἀρτέμιδος· *τήν*
τε θυσίαν καὶ [τὸ δεῖπ]νον π(ρ)ῶτος κατέδειξεν
ἱερὰ τῆς κ[υρί]ας Ἀρτέμιδος *τῆς ἐν* Κειρπα-
ροις ὡς [ἡ θεὸς] ἐπέτρεψέν τε καὶ ἐκέλευ-
σεν θυσιάσαι, (ἐπε)ιδὴ η(ὑ)γ(μ)ένος ἦν Φλάβιος
Διζαλας Εζβενεος *καὶ ἡ σύμβιος αὐτοῦ* Ρ[επ-]
ταρ(ε)ρκος Ἡρακλ(εί)δου *θυγάτηρ [ὑπὲρ ἑαυτῶν]*
καὶ ὑπὲρ τῆς θυγατρὸς ἑαυτῶν Αιδεζυ-
ρεος ΟΙΝΕΟΡΚΟΠΗΣΑΝΑ--------
Μ *υἱοὶ καὶ ὁ ἀδελφὸς αὐτοῦ ἱκέτης ὡς*
καὶ ἡ μήτηρ αὐτῶν ΔΙ---ΑΝΜ----

καὶ Εζβενις Τηρου ΑΥ--φιλῆς αὐτῶν
καθὼς οὖν ΔΗΚΡ-----ΥΠΟΥ----
ΜΑ καὶ ἐφετὸν δ' ἔξεστι καὶ πρόβατον καὶ
αἶγα τε---ΚΥ-------------

For good fortune.
Flavius Dizalas, son of Ezbenis, son of Amatokos,
general of Olynthia and Roimeletike
and Dresapaike and Thoukusidantike
and . . . seletike and Zraike and
Athioutike and Bioletike, dedicated the tri[pod]
and the *xoanon*, he himself and his wife
Reptaterkos, daughter of Herakleides,
by the command of the lady Artemis; the
sacrifice and the meal he first introduced
as rites of the lady Artemis in Keirpara
as the goddess commanded and ordered
to be sacrificed, when Flavius Dizalas, son of
Ezbenis had prayed, and his wife Reptaterkos the
daughter of Herakleides, on their own behalf
and on behalf of their daughter Aidezuris
ΟΙΝΕΟΡΚΟΠΗΣΑΝΑ. . . . .
M sons and his brother the suppliant as
also their mother ΔΙ . . . ΑΝΜ . . .
and Ezbenis son of Teros ΑΥ . . . philes their
even as thus ΔΗΚΡ. . . . . .ΥΠΟΥ. . . .
MA and it is allowed and it is possible both a sheep and
a goat . . . KY. . . . .

395

Nicopolis ad Mestum ? A.D. II

Text: G. Mihailov, ed., *Inscriptiones Graecae in Bulgaria Repertae* IV (Sophia, 1966) 294 no. 2341.

Ἀγαθῆι τύχηι.
Τῷ κυριῷ Δὶι Διζαλας Βειθυος τελέ-
σας ἐνιαυτὸν ἁγνῶς τὸν ναὸν καὶ τ[ὰ]
ξόανα κατὰ χρηματισκμόν.

For good fortune.
For lord Zeus, Dizalas son of Beithus having
served as priest for a year in a pure way, [dedicated] the *naos* and the *xoana* in accordance with the oracle.

396
Obruk (Lycaonia)
Text: W.M. Calder, J.M.R. Cormack, *et al.*, eds., *Monumenta Asiae Minoris Antiqua* VIII. *Monuments from Lycaonia, the Pisido-Phrygian Borderland, Aphrodisias* (Manchester, 1962) 49 no. 275.

[X.]M.Γ. |*Πασικράτου κού|ρη πολὺ καλίστη |γλυκυθύμη ἤθαν||*(5)*ε δ'ἐν θαλάμω π|αναώρια ἐργιδυ|γα* (sic) *μνίαν ποιησά|μενος Σαβινεια|νὸς πόσις αὐτῇ||*(10)*ς ἐν δὲ λίθω ξοά|νω γράψας ἐπέ|θηκ' ἐνὴ τύνβ|ω.*

[X.]M.Γ. The daughter of Pasikrates, very beautiful Glykuthyme, died in her bridal-chamber, doomed to an untimely end. Her husband Sabineianos having made this memorial, having written it in polished stone, placed it on the tomb.

397
Oenoanda (Lycia)
Text: *CIG* III, 4380 m.

Ἀγωνοθετοῦντος Ἰουλίου Λουκίου [M]*ει*[*δ*]*ίου Εὐαρέστου,*
Πα[*λαι*] *τυρέως,* [*θ*]*έ*[*μιδος ἀγώνων*] *Εὐα*[*ρ*]*εστ*[*εί*]*ων,*
ἧς συνεστ[*ή*]*σατο ἐξ οἰκ*[*ε*]*ίων χ*[*ρ*]*η*[*μ*]*άτων, Πόπλιος*
Σθένιος Φρόντων Οἰνοανδεύς, υἱὸς [*Πο*]*πλίου Σθενίου*
Λικιννιανοῦ, στεφθεὶς ἀνδρῶν πανκράτιον [*κ*]*οινὸν Λυκίων.*
Παίδων μὲν τὰ πρῶτα πάλ[*η*]*ν ἔστεψε με πάτρη*
   καὶ κύδησε κλυτῇ εἰκονι χαλκελάτῳ
πανκράτιον δ' ἀνδρῶν κοινὸν Λυκίων μετέπειτα
   ἀράμενος πατρῇ θῆκ' ἐρατὸν
   ξόανον.

Julius Lucius Meidios Euarestos from Palaituris presiding at the games, the Euarestian games for which a prize is offered, which he himself arranged from his own funds, Publius Sthenius Fronto, from Oenoanda, the son of Publius Sthenius Licinnianus, being crowned for the pancration open to all Lycian men. Before this, my native town crowned me for boys' wrestling and honored me with a glorious brass image; for the pancration open to all Lycian men, thereafter, having made a vow to my native town, I dedicated a lovely *xoanon*.

398
Oleros (Crete) II–I B.C.
Text: M. Guarducci, *Inscriptiones creticae* III (Rome, 1942) 132–133 no. 1.

Τᾶι Ἀθαναίαι τᾶι Ὠ]*λερίαι ἐπὶ τῶν*
Παμφύλων κοσμόν[*των*-------

τὸν ναὸν καὶ τὰ ξόαν[α------
Ἱμεραίω, Ξενόφιλος--------
Προάγορος Ἀριστοφ̣[--------
Θώρακος, Δίων Καισ[-------
Ἀγαμήδης Αἰδώπω, Ν[------
τος, Δίων Κ[λ]ε̣[οσ]θεσίλ̣[α.

To Athena O[leria when the
Pamphylians made up the body of *kosmoi*[
the *naos* and the *xoan*[*a*
Himeraio, Xenophilos[
Proagoros Aristoph[
Thorakos, Dion Kais[
Agamedes Aidopo, N[
tos, Dion K[l]e[os]thesil[a.

Orkistos
See Baglitsa [**381**].

399
Peiraeus early II B.C.
Text: *IG* II[2], 2948.

τόνδε νεὼ σοι, ἄναξ, Διονύσιος εἵσατο τῆιδε
καὶ τέμενος θυόεν καὶ ξόαν' εἴκελά σοι
καὶ πάντ', οὐ πλοῦτον κρίνας πολυάργυρον αὔξειν
ἐν δόμωι ὡς τὸ σέβειν, Βάκχε, τὰ σοὶ νόμιμα.
[ἀ]νθ' ὧν, ὦ Διόνυσ' ὢν ἵλαος οἶκον ἅμ' αὐτοῦ
[καὶ] γενεὴν σώιζοις πάντα τε σὸν θίασον.

Lord, Dionysios set up this *neos* for you here, and the
fragrant *temenos*, and the *xoana* that are like you,
and everything, having chosen not to increase the plentiful silver wealth
in his house, Bakchos, in order to revere your customs.
O Dionysos, being gracious, preserve his house and
his family and his entire *thiasos*.

400
Portus Ostiae ? A.D. II–III
Text: L. Vidman, ed., *Sylloge inscriptionum religionis Isiacae et Sarapiacae* (RGVV 28; Berlin, 1969) 258 no. 556 a.

Τὸ ξόανον τοῦ |ἁγιοτάτου |θεοῦ Σαράπιδος |[σ]ὺν τῇ Ἴσιδι
[τῇ | |ἐ]ν Μενουθὶ – |--- πωλι ---.

The *xoanon* of the most holy god Sarapis with Isis in Menouthi[s. . . .

401

Qanauat (Canathae) A.D. 218–222

Text: R. Cagnat, ed., *Inscriptiones graecae ad res romanas pertinentes* III (Paris, 1906) 452 no. 1228.

[ʼΥπὲ]ρ σωτηρίας καὶ νεί[κης κυρίου] Αὐτοκρ(άτορος) Καίσ(αρος) M. *[Αὐ-ρ]ηλίου [ʼΑντωνείνου Σ]ε[βαστοῦ Εὐσεβοῦς Εὐτυχοῦς, |καὶ] κυρίας τήθης τοῦ κυρίου [ʼΙουλίας Μαίσης Σεβ(αστῆς) καὶ σύμπαντος |αὐτ]οῦ οἴκου τὸ ξόανον [ἡ πόλις ἀνέθηκεν].*

On behalf of the safety and military success of their lord the Imperator Caesar M. Aurelius Antoninus Augustus Pius Felix and their mistress, his grandmother, Julia Maesa Augusta and his entire house the city has dedicated this *xoanon*.

402

Rosetta (British Museum, Inscription 1065.) March 27, 196 B.C.

Text: F. Bilabel, ed., *Sammelbuch griechischer Urkunden aus Ägypten* 5 (Heidelberg, 1931, 1934) no. 8299, lines 38–43.

Translation adapted from E. Bevan, *A History of Egypt under the Ptolemaic Dynasty* (London, 1927) 267.

στῆσαι δὲ τοῦ αἰωνοβίου βασιλέως Πτο<λε>μαίου, θεοῦ ʼΕπιφανοῦς Εὐχαρίστου, εἰκόνα ἐν ἑκάστωι ἱερῶι ἐν τῶι ἐπιφα[νεστάτωι τόπωι],| [39]*ἣ προσονομασθήσεται Πτολεμαίου τοῦ ἐπαμύναντος τῆι Αἰγύπτωι, ἧι παρεστήξεται ὁ κυριώτατος θεὸς τοῦ ἱεροῦ, διδοὺς αὐτῶι ὅπλον νικητικόν, ἃ ἔσται κατεσκευασμέν|α τὸν τῶν Αἰγυπτίων]|* [40]*τρόπον, καὶ τοὺς ἱερεῖς θεραπεύειν τὰς εἰκόνας τρὶς τῆς ἡμέρας καὶ παρατιθένει αὐταῖς ἱερὸν κόσμον καὶ τἆλλα τὰ νομιζόμενα συντελεῖν καθὰ καὶ τοῖς ἄλλοις θεοῖς ἐν [ταῖς ἑορταῖς καὶ πα]|* [41]*νηγύρεσιν. ἱδρύσασθαι δὲ βασιλεῖ Πτολεμαίωι, θεῶι ʼΕπιφανεῖ Εὐχαρίστωι, τῶι ἐγ βασιλέως Πτολεμαίου καὶ βασιλίσσης ʼΑρσινόης, θεῶν Φιλοπατόρων, ξόανόν τε καὶ ναὸν χρ[υσοῦν καθʼ ἕκαστον τῶν]|* [42]*ἱε<ρ>ῶν καὶ καθιδρῦσαι ἐν τοῖς ἀδύτοις μετὰ τῶν ἄλλων ναῶν, καὶ ἐν ταῖς μεγάλαις πανηγύρεσιν, ἐν αἷς ἐξοδεῖαι τῶν ναῶν γίνονται, καὶ τὸν τοῦ θεοῦ ʼΕπιφανοῦς Εὐ[χαρίστου ναὸν συνε]|* [43]*ξοδεύειν.*

. . . and to set up of the everliving king Ptolemy, the god Epiphanes Eucharistos, an *eikon* in the most prominent place of every *hieron*, which shall be called that of "Ptolemy, the avenger of Egypt," beside which shall stand the principal god of the *hieron*, handing him the emblem of victory, which shall be fashioned [in the Egyptian] fashion; and that the priests shall do service to the *eikones* three times a day, and put upon them the sacred adornment, and perform the other usual honors such as are given to the other gods in the Egyptian festivals; and to establish for king Ptolemy, the God Epiphanes Eucharistos, sprung of king Ptolemy and queen Arsinoe, the gods Philopatores, a *xoanon* and a *naos*, g[olden, in each of] the *hiera*, and to set it up in the *adyta* with the other *naoi*, and in the great festivals, in which there are processions with the *naoi*, the *naos* of the God Epiphanes Eucharistos shall also be carried in procession with them.

403

Sais(?) (Alexandria Museum 1.) A.D. II–III

Text: *ArchPap* 2 (1903) 569 no. 145.

Πρώτως |Πετρώνιος |Κεκροπήιον |ἄστυ Σαϊτῶν |πράξας |Τρειτογενοῦς |ἱδρυσάμην |ξόανον.

I, the *protos* Petronios, having served the Kekropian city of Sais, set up the *xoanon* of Tritogenes.

APPENDIX II
EPIGRAPHICAL CONCORDANCE

AM
14 (1889)
91 no. 11 = Baglitsa [**381**]
ArchPap
2 (1903)
439 no. 42 = Koptos [**391**]
569 no. 145 = Sais? [**403**]
BCH
13 (1889)
40 no. 7 = Bargylia [**382**]
50 (1926)
571 = Delos [**386**]
58 (1934)
184–202 = Delos [**388**]
BMusInscr
IV
1012 = Chalcedon [**384**]
1065 = Rosetta [**402**]
BSAAlex
41 (1956)
57–62: Leontopolis; see *supra* p. 62 n. 146.
E. Breccia, *Iscrizioni greche a latine Nos. 1–568* (Cairo, 1911).
62 = Koptos [**391**]
112 = Sais? [**403**]
BullEpig
1948
172–173 *ap.* no. 120: Nicopolis ad Mestum [**394, 395**]
1953
No. 142 = Delos [**386**]
1965
192–194 *ap.* no. 488 = Portus Ostiae [**400**]
CIG
II
2477 = Anaphe [**380**]
3747 = Chalcedon [**384**]
III
4380 m. = Oenoanda [**397**]
4697 = Rosetta [**402**]

Délos

11. A. Plassart, *Les sanctuaires et les cultes du Mont Cynthe* (Paris, 1928)

124–125 = Delos [**387**]

20. F. Robert, *Trois sanctuaires sur le rivage occidental* (Paris, 1952)

106 = Delos [**386**]

Inscriptiones Creticae

III

132–133 no. 1 = Oleros [**398**]

IG

II^2

2948 = Peiraeus [**399**]

XII.3

248 = Anaphe [**380**]

IGRR

III

336 = Adada [**379**]

1228 = Qanauat [**401**]

IV

145 = Cyzicus [**385**]

J. Keil and A. v. Premerstein, *Bericht über eine dritte Reise in Lydien* (Vienna, 1914)

99 no. 148 = Büyükkadife [**383**]

G. Kaibel, ed., *Epigrammata graeca ex lapidus conlecta* (Berlin, 1878)

779 = Chalcedon [**384**]

944 = Oenoanda [**397**]

O. Kern, *Die Inschriften von Magnesia am Maeander* (Berlin, 1900)

98 = Magnesia on the Maeander [**392**]

100a = Magnesia on the Maeander [**393**]

J. Lebègue, *Recherches sur Délos* (Paris, 1876)

160 no. XIV = Delos [**387**]

MAMA

I

417 = Baglitsa [**381**]

VIII

275 = Obruk [**396**]

R. Merkelbach, ed., *Die Inschriften von Kalchedon* (IgSK 20; Bonn, 1980)

14 = Chalcedon [**384**]

G. Mihailov, ed., *Inscriptiones graecae in Bulgaria repertae*
IV
2338 = Nicopolis ad Mestum [**394**]
2341 = Nicopolis ad Mestum [**395**]
D.L. Page, ed., *Further Greek Epigrams* (Cambridge, 1981)
LXX = Chalcedon [**384**]
W.K. Prentice, *Publications of the Princeton University Archaeological Expeditions to Syria in 1904–1905 and 1909. Division III. Greek and Latin Inscriptions in Syria. Section B. Northern Syria. Part 6. The Djebel Sim 'ân* (Leiden, 1922)
199 no. 1193 = Ḳal 'at Kālōtâ [**390**]
RendAccLinc
1964
197–198 = Portus Ostiae [**400**]
SEG
VIII
784 = Elephantine [**389**]
XVI
855 = Rosetta [**402**]
XVIII
634: Leontopolis; see *supra* p. 62 n. 146
XXIV
626 = Nicopolis ad Mestum [**394**]
XXV
909 = Anaphe [**380**]
SIG^3
II
798 = Cyzicus [**385**]
Sammelbuch griechischer Urkunden aus Ägypten
V
8232 = Elephantine [**389**]
8299 = Rosetta [**402**]
8815 = Koptos [**391**]
E.M. Smallwood, *Documents Illustrating the Principates of Gaius, Claudius and Nero* (Cambridge, 1967)
401 = Cyzicus [**385**]
F. Sokolowski, *Lois sacrées de l'Asie Mineure* (Paris, 1955)
32 = Magnesia on the Maeander [**392**]
33 = Magnesia on the Maeander [**393**]

F. Sokolowski, *Lois sacrées des cités grecques* (Paris, 1969)
129 = Anaphe [**380**]

L. Vidman, ed., *Sylloge inscriptionum religionis Isiacae et Sarapiacae* (RGVV 28; Berlin, 1969)
556a = Portus Ostiae [**400**]

ACKNOWLEDGEMENTS

I thank the following publishers for their kind permission to include the material specified in Appendix I. The testimonia are listed by number. Roman type indicates the Greek or Latin text; italics, translation; and boldface, both.

American Philological Association: 309, 311, 330–332; Société d'édition "Les Belles Lettres": 16–19, 155, 323–324; E.J. Brill: **300**, 305–307, 390; Cambridge University Press: *178–183*, 327–328, *345*, *364*, 385; T. & T. Clark, Ltd.: *47*, *49–55*; Constable Publishers: *159–163*; Walter de Gruyter & Co.: 92, 397, 399–400; Doubleday & Co., Inc.: *48*, *172–177*, *365*; Ecole Française d'Athènes: 382, 388; Edizioni dell'Atheneo: 85, 359; Egypt Exploration Society: **375–376**, 378; Anton Hain KG, Verlag: 76–77; Adolf M. Hakkert: 12, 30; Verlag Otto Harrassowitz: 389, 391, 402; Harvard University Press: *13–15*, *20–21*, **22**, *23–25*, *27*, *32*, *35–37*, **40**, *41–42*, **43–46**, **56**, *57–62*, **63**, *64–72*, *88*, *90–91*, *96–97*, *103*, *139–141*, **154**, *155–156*, *158*, *164–167*, *171*, *284–298*, *308*, *310*, *313–321*, *327*, *334–344*, *346–353*, **360**, *369*, *377–378*; Macmillan Publishers, Ltd.: 29, *187–282*, **312**, 329; Georg Olms Verlag: 3, 9; Oxford University Press: 1, 4, **34**, *38–39*, 83–84, 86–87, **98–102**, **104–125**, 158–166, *170*, 370, 384; Paulist Press: *31*; B.G. Teubner Verlagsgesellschaft: 2, 5, 78–80, 88–91, 93, 363, 372–374; University of Illinois Press: 371; The University Press, University of Manchester: 381, 396; Westminster Press: *361*.

The following texts appear by courtesy of the Thesaurus Linguae Graecae: *6–8*, *13–15*, *20–21*, *23–25*, *27*, *32–33*, *35–39*, *41–42*, *47–49*, *57–62*, *64–75*, *94–95*, *103*, *126–145*, *147*, *149–150*, *152–153*, *156–157*, *167–177*, *184*, *187–299*, *308*, *310*, *313–322*, *325–326*, *334–358*, *362*, *364*, *369*, *377*.

INDEX OF TEXTS

PAPYRUS TEXTS

EPIGRAPHICAL TEXTS

See Appendix II, Epigraphical Concordance

INDEX OF GREEK WORDS

GENERAL INDEX

www.ingramcontent.com/pod-product-compliance
Ingram Content Group UK Ltd.
Pitfield, Milton Keynes, MK11 3LW, UK
UKHW041900190726
13854UKWH00002B/997

9 781555 401542